FEARLESS

FEARLESS

---◆---

A. BARTLETT GIAMATTI
AND THE BATTLE FOR FAIRNESS IN AMERICA

NEIL THOMAS PROTO

AN IMPRINT OF STATE UNIVERSITY OF NEW YORK PRESS

Published by
STATE UNIVERSITY OF NEW YORK PRESS, ALBANY

EXCELSIOR EDITIONS
IS AN IMPRINT OF STATE UNIVERSITY OF NEW YORK PRESS

For information, contact State University of New York Press, Albany, NY
www.sunypress.edu

Library of Congress Cataloging-in-Publication Data

Names: Proto, Neil Thomas, author.
Title: Fearless : A. Bartlett Giamatti and the battle for fairness in America
/ Neil Thomas Proto.
Description: Albany : Excelsior Editions,
an imprint of State University of New York Press, 2020. |
| Includes bibliographical references and index. |
Identifiers: LCCN 2019040336 (print) | LCCN 2019040337 (ebook)
| ISBN 9781438479637 (hardcover) | ISBN 9781438479644 (ebook)
Subjects: LCSH: Giamatti, A. Bartlett. | Yale University—Presidents—Biography.
| Baseball commissioners—United States—Biography. | Italian Americans—Biography.
Classification: LCC LD6330 1978 .P76 2020 (print) | LCC LD6330 1978
(ebook) | DDC 796.357092 [B]—dc23
LC record available at https://lccn.loc.gov/2019040336
LC ebook record available at https://lccn.loc.gov/2019040337

10 9 8 7 6 5 4 3 2 1

CONTENTS

AUTHOR'S NOTE

I met Bart Giamatti for the first time in his small, high-ceilinged office in Woodbridge Hall on the Yale campus. It was December 1979. I recall stacks of aged and ordered books on the surrounding shelves, not mere ornaments to memory or accoutrements to the pretense of power but reflective of an intellectual rather than an academic culture, books read and still relevant to a life in purposeful and vigorous movement. They mattered to Giamatti in some practical yet enduring way as much as the papers and ledgers on his desk. He was handsome, slender, approachable, and friendly. Comfortable with who he was and who he had become, and comfortable with me. He shook my hand and offered me the chair opposite the desk. He moved to a seat closer to me.

I had been asked by Mayor-elect Biagio DiLieto—whose campaign I aided from my return to New Haven in June 1979 through DiLieto's victory in the Democratic primary against the incumbent mayor and through his successful defeat of the Republican candidate in November—to be general chair of the inauguration scheduled for January 1, 1980. In Woolsey Hall on the Yale campus. It was to be the first such mayoral inauguration in the city's history. At the time I appreciated the grand symbolism that Giamatti and DiLieto sought, and I understood, in part, what that meant for my duty as inauguration chair and what it meant for the citizens of New Haven to be in Woolsey Hall for that civic purpose. Giamatti, of course, knew that even better than I did. His own history of family and culture in New Haven, deeply embedded, was closer to the surface in a manner that I did not understand fully until the preparation of *Fearless*. He had been versed sufficiently on who I was by DiLieto. I did not learn until almost six years later, when I introduced my parents to Giamatti during a civic event shortly before his departure from Yale, that my father had known his father in childhood, in the street and in playground games commonplace in their Fair Haven neighborhood. They had lived only a few blocks from each other, two Italian American kids, sons of immigrants. My mother was born in Italy; I was one as well.

Giamatti welcomed my proposal that he sit on stage in a seating arrangement that would include Mayor-elect DiLieto, outgoing Mayor Frank Logue,

A. Bartlett Giamatti at the inauguration of the New Haven mayor, Woolsey Hall, 1980. *NTProto Collection*.

and Governor Ella Grasso. He said he did not want to speak, which was a relief to me. We both, in our discussion—buttressed by a long history he understood with deeper appreciation than I knew at the time—recognized DiLieto's role in vindicating the harm and hard-fought aspirations of generations of New Haven immigrants and migrants from elsewhere in America. Unknown to me at that time, Giamatti had met privately with DiLieto a year or so before his victory in the Democratic primary.

&

To know Bart Giamatti, you needed to know his parents, Valentine and Peggy, and his grandparents on both sides. Especially, you needed to know the history of New Haven and of Yale's relationship to its residents and neighborhoods. Giamatti was acutely knowledgeable of that history. In a manner more revelatory and disquieting than I had anticipated, Yale's roughly exercised parochialism and deeply embedded prejudices and insurmountable eugenics mentality emerged repeatedly. Their effect spread well beyond Yale's halls and New Haven, with a continuity and evolving form that hardly diminished through the moment of Giamatti's selection as president. The Yale corporation's choice in 1977 was more radical and enduringly explosive than perhaps some among them had anticipated at the time, including in the way that, over time, the composition of the student body changed, the selection of subsequent non–Anglo-Saxon presidents was readily accepted, and the university's relationship to New Haven became more candidly understood. Gone was the pretense that former Yale presidents A. Whitney Griswold, Kingman Brewster, and their predecessors had relied upon to New Haven's and the student body's detriment.

&

John Wilkinson, who had been secretary of the university under Giamatti and his classmate (Yale 1960), encouraged me to write the book, a serious look at Giamatti's experience as the first non–Anglo-Saxon president of Yale. My respect for Giamatti and the imperative for thorough documentation were enhanced by frequent and substantively candid meetings with his sister, Elria Giamatti Ewing, and her husband, David; his brother, Dino Walton Giamatti, and Dino's wife, Barbara; and his cousin Helen Ogden and relative by marriage Kim Formica.

Judge and former Yale Law School dean Guido Calabresi was especially forthcoming in his insight about his friend Bart and his own experience, and that of his parents, especially their values and the anti-Fascist imperatives they shared with Bart's parents, as Italian immigrants at Yale and in New Haven. His range of knowledge was broad and deep, predated his friendship with Giamatti, and periodically yielded questions that my research or first-hand knowledge was able to answer. There were painful as well as joyful moments in our effort to recollect and discern facts that, now, inform critical threads in telling *Fearless*.

Guido Calabresi in July 1985, when he was appointed
Dean of the Yale Law School by then-Yale President Giamatti.
T. Charles Erickson/Yale University.

⌐⌐

Giamatti's presidential papers (exclusive of his speeches) and the papers of
those in his administration are not yet available for public examination—a fact
of defining consequence to thorough and accurate research and the foundational
reason that *Fearless* stops where it does. That limitation had two unexpected benefits. First, the powerful relevance of Giamatti's relationship with his parents—
especially his acute knowledge of his grandparents and of his father's experience
in New Haven and at Yale, through the intensity and solidification of Yale's overt
eugenic beliefs and conduct, which transformed into a persistent mentality—
received the thorough research and explication it warranted in understanding

how Giamatti's values were formed. Giamatti's well-known ascendency to the presidency of Yale and his subsequent selection as president of the National Baseball League and Commissioner of Baseball would, I believed, only enhance the reader's focus on the conduct revealed by Yale's and New Haven's archives.

Moreover, and second, certain aspects of Baseball and sports, previously unexplored, and the values underpinning his decision concerning Pete Rose emerged with clarity much earlier in his life and are examined in *Fearless*. Critical early indications of Giamatti's actions and words during his Yale presidency are described and documented in the Epilogue. Observations by others and Giamatti's own words and actions, documented and explored throughout the book, underpin and affirm the essential values that Giamatti intended to and did bring to bear related to fairness at Yale—that is, the end of the eugenics mentality, especially in a university whose liberal intellectual purpose he embraced with his heart and full-throated advocacy and in a city that, as *Fearless* documents, was uniquely central to the formation of Giamatti's values and character.

NEIL THOMAS PROTO
Washington, DC, and New Haven, Connecticut
March 2019

PROLOGUE

THE MEETING: AUGUST 1933

She stood with natural poise, contentment and anticipation on her face; her parents, both pleased and anxious, stood on either side of her. It was a moment of accomplishment and separation. Mary Claybaugh Walton, having begun her junior year at Smith College, was on her way to Italy aboard the liner, the SS *Rex*. The three stood smiling, impeccably dressed in the reserved fashion of the 1930s, for a last photograph before the *Rex*'s departure.

Mary, "Peggy" to her two sisters and her friends and family, majored in Italian studies and Etruscan art. She already had a close-to-perfect grasp of model Italian—the language of Dante and the Florentines adopted at the time of Italy's unification as the nation's official language in government and, with unsettling coercion and long-resisted effect, from one end of the country to the other. She was crossing the Atlantic with a similar, financially well-heeled group of classmates who shared her knowledge of Italy's culture and history and her mischievous commitment to adventure. At Smith, she'd displayed a confident skill at leadership, politics, theater, and music. This visit was a reflection of maturity as well as a valued education.

With the rousing sound of the liner's two-funneled engine and the staccato signal from the dark-suited attendants combing the ship, Peggy's parents—Bartlett and Helen Davidson Walton of old (ancient to some) Anglo-Saxon lineage—took leave to drive back to their spacious, dark-gray-shingled home in countryside Wakefield, Massachusetts.[1]

The SS *Rex* was an Italian-built liner, the fourth-largest liner in the world and among the fastest ships of its class since its maiden voyage in 1931. Unlike its French counterpart built in the Art Deco style typical of the day, the Rex had a classical interior touched with forms of luxury: white sand layered along the outdoor swimming pool and umbrellas of multiple colors sought to create a beach-like effect, and a grand staircase and elegant gold and crystal chandeliers framed the subtly decorated, dark-wooden dining hall where, at the close of the

Bartlett, Peggy, and Helen Walton on the SS *Rex*, 1933.
Elria Giamatti Ewing and David Ewing Collection.

evening, passengers would gather, some in formal dress, for a sumptuous meal and the cordial inquiry necessary to new friendships. It was a fun and exciting setting, Miss Walton's expectation high for camaraderie and practical learning as the ship departed New York, moving gracefully past the city's bold skyline and the iconic Statute of Liberty.[2]

To another passenger, who stood quietly on the careful, tug-assisted transit toward the Atlantic, the Statute of Liberty had special meaning. Valentine John Giamatti—confident, tall, and neatly dressed in tweeds and linen shirt and dark tie—watched in appreciation and an inner sense of history. It was through these waters that his parents (first his father, disappointed by the failed promise of Italian

Valentine John Giamatti, 1933.
Giamatti-Ewing Collection.

unification and the Southern hope for independence and justice, and then his mother and father together) had immigrated to America from their home in San Lorenzello. Angelo and Maria Lavorgna Giammattei (their last name had been mispronounced and misspelled enough times that Valentine settled on Giamatti during high school) now lived in a wood-framed, three-family walkup with their son, three daughters, and a border in the urban, ethnically mixed, working- and artisan-class Fair Haven neighborhood of New Haven, Connecticut.[3]

Valentine had graduated from Yale University in June 1932, a scholar in romance languages and literature and fluent in model Italian. He had entered Yale's graduate program for his doctorate. His education—and the need to help with expenses at home, his own and his family's—had been financed through a Sterling Scholarship, by tutoring of classmates and neighbors in the evenings, in strenuous summer employment, and by teaching college-level Italian and English locally. He also spoke Neapolitan, the dialect of the Naples region where San

Lorenzello was located, one of multiple dialects the newly formed government of Italy could have chosen as a national language but did not. Neapolitan also was the only dialect his parents, relatives, and neighbors understood. Despite the compulsory directive of his public grammar school teachers to speak only the language of America—and the threat of corporal punishment if he violated the prohibition in their presence—he would not unlearn his family's language. His mother, otherwise fully literate, had never learned English.[4]

Preserving the critical thread of language in the family's and his neighborhood's culture, resisting the force to abandon it, was among the simpler duties Valentine insisted on fulfilling. From the moment his parents sought to disembark at Ellis Island, through his entrance into Yale's graduate program, he witnessed and felt the prejudice against southern Italians that northern Italians brought to Yale University and the way that prejudice combined and was amplified publicly and deliberately with the insidious Anglo-Saxon imperative for the purity of its own culture. "It seems quite clear," Yale President James Rowland Angell wrote in 1933, as he surveyed the Italian and Jewish immigrant and African American population that surrounded the university, "that if we could have an Armenian massacre confined to the New Haven District, with occasional incursions into Bridgeport and Hartford, we might protect our Nordic stock almost completely."[5]

Valentine, "Val" to his family and friends and classmates at Yale, was on his way to Italy with others who shared his interest, though, in all likelihood, not precisely. Yale already was convulsed in the dispute that had divided the Italian and Jewish immigrant community and their children from the nation's industrialists, the Catholic Church, and Yale University's corporate officers: opposition to Fascism was vocal and growing among the former; full-throated embrace characterized the latter.

Also, unlike others onboard, Val's passage and expenses were paid through the excellence of his academic accomplishment, his own and family savings, and Yale's newly created but wholly community-funded American–Italian Exchange Fellowship, which provided for prolonged study in Florence and Perugia and a tour of the country's famed artistic heritage. Val also brought with him the confidence to walk the nation's streets and alleyways and speak in local dialects that few, if any, other travelers on his ship had mastered. Investigation and critical observation were at stake.

It was during this trip that Val met Peggy Walton. "I thought he was handsome and polite when we met," Peggy had confided to her children years later. "And I agreed to introduce him to one of my classmates." It was a ruse. A long and mutually embraced courtship had begun, in the custom of the day, and in the hoped-for blending of two distinct cultures and experiences in America, one English, the other, Southern Italian.[6]

Together they would nurture their son, Angelo Bartlett Giamatti, the nine-teenth president of Yale University, the youngest in more than two hundred years, the first Italian American, the first non–Anglo-Saxon, the first president to radically alter the conservative continuity embedded, foremost, in President Angell's definition of morality in New Haven.

❧

What did Val Giamatti witness and learn in New Haven and at Yale—through-out the university's advocacy of Anglo-Saxon purity directed against people and values he cherished? How did he and Peggy convey the principles they thought valuable to their son? What was the culture that endured at Yale and in New Haven when Angelo Bartlett Giamatti entered as a student in 1956—that he witnessed, in its disquieting, enduring reality, through his graduation with a PhD in 1964? And that lingered when he returned from Princeton in 1966 to begin his life as father, husband, and teacher?

❧

On April 15, 1982, A. Bartlett Giamatti, the president of Yale University, walked to the podium, in the chapel at Mount Holyoke College, in South Hadley, Massachusetts. It was the community in which he was raised and the college where his father had been revered as teacher and mentor, the gentle and un-yielding advocate of the Italian language and culture, and, with Peggy Walton Giamatti, the persistent model of civic duty in private life always and only un-dertaken in the gracious, inclusive, and wholehearted manner he defined. Bart had no illusions about what his father had endured in a life well led. There was no mythology, no simple clichés or metaphors of grandeur that should shroud the reality of what his father witnessed or accomplished. Bart had witnessed it as well, the cultural remnants of unfairness, still poignant and intended to pierce, that with the guidance of family and neighborhood, had helped form the pow-erful principles about fairness in his father's and now his own life. Bart's sister, Elria, and his brother, Dino, knew Bart would capture in his eulogy, with the el-egance of words and the skill of the orator he had commanded since childhood, the depth of love that characterized their feelings and the principles in life their father had lived by daily and, with care and certainty, had taught each of them.[7]

Peggy Giamatti knew it as well, watching, waiting for her son to speak, remembering, perhaps, the moment in the fall of 1956 when she and Val had waved goodbye to him at Phelps Gate, the formal entrance to Yale University, so he could begin his freshman year. Or maybe the moment when she and Val had first met or, perhaps, the long history in culture, in England and in Italy, that had tempered both their lives and, with serendipity, had brought them together and to this moment as their son, who had melded those cultures into one, began to speak.

PART I

AMERICA:

THE WALTONS AND GIAMMATTEIS

Because of [my father's] openness, an openness that hated shadows and caviling and prejudice and stereotyping of individuals in any form—he had suffered from that himself—he was open above all to ideas.

—A. Bartlett Giamatti,
Eulogy for Valentine John Giamatti, April 15, 1982

From England to America

Who can set a limit to . . . the influence of a life that is thoughtful and earnest and idealistic, a life that finds its circumference not in the contracted circle of its own selfish interests but in the welfare of humanity.

—Mary Emma Woolley, President, Mount Holyoke College

The Formation of Family Values: The Waltons and Davidsons

Peggy Walton understood a central thread in America's formation: the insidious force and harm of Anglo-Saxon prejudice.

King Henry III of England was nine years old when he assumed the throne in October 1216. He was Catholic. When, following civil and European wars, Henry was ready to govern without formal guidance from others, he promised to enforce the terms of the Magna Carta, which had been negotiated by his father, King John, in 1215. Though that enforcement flowed unevenly, well beyond Henry's reign, the principle of constraining the monarchy's—the government's—arbitrary rule was set in time, if not yet in stone. It became one hard-earned, critical antecedent to how men and women who immigrated to America thought about the values underpinning the form that government should take. Henry III's Catholicism did not survive. England and other parts of growing Great Britain became Protestant, the product of Henry VIII's pique with the Catholic Church over divorce and the intellectual and spiritual revolt against the Church led by Martin Luther and John Calvin.[1]

One other outcome of Henry III's reign—through his marriage with Eleanor of Provence—was five children, and varied descendants. Two of those descendants, Thomas Rogers and his son Joseph, were passengers on the *Mayflower* when it arrived in Plymouth, Massachusetts (so named), in 1620, the moment of disembarkation that provided the essential factual predicate in the later, quintessential Protestant, Anglo-Saxon claim for being "the white man par excellence" in America. Joseph Rogers survived the first winter and married. Rogers and his wife finally settled in Maine's first community, Berwick. Rogers was an ancestor of Mary ("Peggy") Claybaugh Walton, Bart Giamatti's mother.[2]

In 1634, Richard Bartlett, a shoemaker from West Sussex, and in 1635, the Reverend William Walton of Devon and his wife, Elizabeth, arrived. Walton's grandfather served as private secretary to Sir Francis Walsingham, who was secretary of state and chief of intelligence during the reign of Elizabeth I—the era of William Shakespeare and Edmund Spenser. With the settlement of Bartlett and Walton, the enduring geographic base of family life for Peggy Walton was largely settled: Maine and Massachusetts.[3]

⁂

In the English settlement of America's northeast coast, Protestantism took various forms, none more dogmatic in its proscriptions for acceptable conduct and self-centered in its belief for exploiting others than Calvinism. It was the form embraced largely by the English colonists in Boston Bay settlements. Jonathan Edwards (Yale 1720) refined it with two critical tenets: God, Edwards believed, had specially elected individuals to determine the cultural and social rules—and the law—of those people who needed to be governed, that is, the doctrine of the elect, predestination, theological determinism, what cultural historian Vernon Parrington described as "the theological complement of the class prejudices of the times." The Calvinists "were . . . rigidly aristocratic," the ministry brutally hierarchical in its exercise of control. Everyone else was "born to sin and heirs to damnation." Also implicit in the same tenets, until it became explicit, was that "God means us to be ambitious. . . . The Protestant religion encourages success in capitalist endeavor. . . . Business was virtuous, and success was blessed." The consequence was easily predictable: support for slavery, suppression of Native Americans, justification for slavery after it was outlawed in Massachusetts, missionary zeal beyond the pale, and, in time, the cultural foundation for the "Great Race" and the "science" of eugenics.[4] Parrington put it plainly: "That the immigrant Puritans brought in their intellectual luggage the system of Calvin . . . must be reckoned a misfortune, out of which flowed many of the bickering and much of the intolerance that left a stain on . . . New England history."[5]

Those Calvinist tenets were challenged elsewhere, including by Peggy Walton's ancestors in one evolving Protestant variation in which community control and consensus—a form of democracy—were paramount: Congregationalism. Thomas Hooker, an intellectually gifted minister, became an ardent foe of Boston Bay's Calvinism. He emphasized "the voice of the individual subject" and sought "to remove the veil [of Calvinist sanctimony] from the faces of the common people . . . thereby proving his right to be remembered among the early stewards of our American democracy."[6] That community control and consensus and "voice of the individual" happened in South Berwick, Maine (as Berwick grew and incorporated into North and South), where, by 1825, in the First Parish Congregational Church, Peggy Walton's more immediate ancestors—the ones she would have observed or heard about directly and who tempered her fate—came to worship.[7]

⁓

In a family to which history mattered, there was irreverence for custom that formed the family's values and Peggy's in a way that mattered in her son's life.

Two of Peggy's ancestors were members of the Society of Friends—Quakers—in abhorrently conservative, Calvinist Salem, Massachusetts, in the early years following the landing at Plymouth. Banished by the governor under pain of death for not being Calvinists, they took refuge on Shelter Island in Long Island Sound, where both died of privation and exposure. Neither would renounce their religious beliefs. Their children, Daniel and Provided, were separated from them yet refused, also under threat of banishment, to abide by the governor's directive. With the confirmation of the local court, the governor directed that both children be sold as slaves. It was only the failure to find anyone who would take them that led to their freedom. Within the Walton family lore, the conduct of the Calvinists was understood as "gut-wrenching" and flat-out "persecution." The lesson for the Walton ethic was plain: religious tolerance mattered. Quakerism remained in the lineage and was embraced in the family culture. And Boston Bay, the symbol of Calvinist intolerance and how it was inherited or praised by successive generations of Anglo-Saxons resonated in abhorrence as well. A further cleavage in values had occurred.[8]

Edward Burleigh Davidson—Peggy's uncle (her mother's brother)—married Leah Friend of Ellsworth, Maine. Her father, an artisan tailor from Prussia, came to Maine in the 1850s, and there he met her mother, also from Prussia. The family was Jewish. Leah went to Wellesley College and became a teacher. Edward went to the University of Maine, where they met. The Friends retained their religious beliefs. Edward and, now, Leah Friend Davidson were embraced within Peggy's family culture. Certainly, everyone who entered the Davidson family was well educated. Good judgment in making marriage choices was at play. At a time of emerging anti-Semitism, especially among Anglo-Saxons, embracing the differences in religious beliefs and cultures was considered good judgment.[9]

To add clarity to those values was another family characteristic. In a succession of large homes, the last built in 1890, Matilda Burleigh, Peggy's maternal great-grandmother, and her grandmother, Elizabeth Burleigh Davidson (when she became head of the same household), regularly housed family members in need of support—after the loss of a spouse, the advent of ill health, the need for more space for children. The home was where Peggy's mother was raised and lived for a period with her new husband, Bartlett, before moving to Mayfield, Massachusetts. The house was built atop a gently sloping grass hill, spring yellow with white trim, three stories high, with a wrap-around porch and grand views that included the nearby Berwick Academy. Inside was a large piano room and library with large windows that looked out toward trees and rows of flowers and shrubbery. Following the wedding of Peggy's parents in 1910, the reception was held on the porch and inside. Peggy lived there periodically during planned visits with her grandmother. Holidays were hosted there, well into Peggy's adulthood and marriage. The house was a lesson in stability, continuity, and the value of certainty of welcome.[10]

CIVIC DUTY

Both sides of Peggy's family had business acumen, with resulting financial comfort, and participated in political and civic life in their community. Both characteristics defined the opportunities and purpose for education, women included.

The context is important. New England had waterpower for electricity and access for ships and ferries. The cities had intellectual and financial wealth and, from the 1850s on, burgeoning railway networks and immigrant arrivals with artisan skills—tailors, artists, fine shoe craftsmen, printers, sculptures, masons, and tool and machinery makers. The immigrants were English, Scottish, Irish, Eastern European Jewish, Southern Italian, and others. These forces were occurring—roughly, unevenly, and relentlessly—within a growing nation moving and settling west; among frequent, sometimes meanly contested labor–management disputes from women and men who would not be exploited; and, in time, through two major conflagrations for which resource mobilization mattered for leadership and victory—the Civil War and World War I. The Waltons and the Davidson–Burleighs helped define that mixture. Their businesses: textiles (clothing and blankets), shoes (boys and girls), and community banking.

William Burleigh, a lawyer, was the first to seek elective office. In 1823, just three years after Maine was admitted to the Union, William was elected a member of Congress. He was described as a "John Quincy Adams Democrat." His son, John, was a ship captain. Once married, John took his wife, Matilda, on a rugged voyage in 1850 "down the coast of North and South America, through the passageway of Cape Horn, and north, into San Francisco harbor."[11] They continued to Hawaii, Japan, India, and around the Cape of Good Hope, up the African coast, and back across the Atlantic, a journey of nineteen months. Matilda Burleigh, Peggy's maternal great-grandmother, who died just before Peggy's birth, had traversed the world. Her tone and manner defined what was possible and expected.[12]

John and Matilda purchased existing woolen mills in South Berwick. The business prospered. John was elected to the state legislature as a Republican in 1862, when the party of Abraham Lincoln was severely challenged in other states that had remained in the Union. In 1864, John was chosen a delegate to attend the national Republican convention held in Baltimore that nominated Lincoln for a second term. From 1873 to 1877, John served in Congress. Matilda also set a standard for civic duty. She was active in the First Parish Congregational Church and in the political life of Washington, DC, and Maine. Their home, the yellow and white house on the hill, became "the center of hospitality" for the South Berwick community.[13]

Matilda's three children (Peggy's great-uncle and great-aunts) went to private school and then to Berwick Academy. When Matilda's son, John, went on to Exeter Academy in New Hampshire, the two daughters, Elizabeth and Ann, went to Washington, DC, to live with their parents. John graduated from Williams College in 1878 and then from Harvard Law School. Elizabeth (Peggy's maternal grandmother, who attended Peggy's wedding in 1937) and Ann went to private school in Portsmouth, New Hampshire, and learned to play the piano, quilt, speak French, recite poetry, and attend theater. Matilda also took Elizabeth and her other two children to Europe for four months. This travel was a preparation for civic duty as well as an education. In 1893, Matilda and others petitioned the state legislature to establish the Children's Aid Society of Maine. She became a board member. When Matilda's husband died, she took over the presidency of the family-owned mill company.[14]

Elizabeth, Matilda's daughter, married James Davidson from Indiana. They lived in Lafayette, Indiana, where James engaged in a successful law practice. They had three children, including Helen, who would become Peggy's mother. Their summers were spent with Elizabeth's family in York, Maine, in modest, family-owned cottages along the coastline. In 1889, James, Elizabeth, and Helen moved east, into York, and James entered into the practice of law there. When the York National Bank of Maine was formed, its board asked James to be president. Elizabeth, who "moved with grace and poise," was well informed and "most gracious to everyone." When James died, Elizabeth became president of the York National Bank of Maine.[15]

Helen Davidson was raised within the cultural milieu of her grandmother, Elizabeth, and her great-grandmother, Matilda. She attended Smith College in Northampton and graduated in the Class of 1908. She also was, early on and for the remainder of her life, a steadfast, informed fan of the Boston Red Sox—witness to players like Tris Speaker and Smoky Joe Wood, to the last of the World Series victories in 1918, and to the seemingly endless plague of doom that flowed from the sale of Babe Ruth to the New York Yankees in 1919. As a baseball fan, she observed the stunning scandal of gambling, the Chicago White Sox descent into infamy in 1919, and the rise of Kenesaw Mountain Landis as the Commissioner of Baseball who preserved the game's integrity by explicit rule, his own fist-held temperament, and his rapier slice through wrongdoers. She read and cheered the awesome skill of the young, instantly popular Ted Williams. Without prompt, she was prepared to engage in commentary, dialogue, or good old-fashioned argument. At base, she was the relentless force that made Valentine Giamatti, and his son, Bart, Boston Red Sox fans.[16]

Enter the descendants of William Walton.

New England

Creating the Setting

Wakefield, Massachusetts, was incorporated in 1644. Wakefield's citizens were civic minded and staunchly for independence from England. In a public gathering, as the war approached, they voted unanimously to "adhere to [the] sentiments and stand by [the Declaration of Independence] to the last." Many of the town's men joined the Revolutionary War army, slogged through mud, endured the numbing frost and snow of winters, and fought for a nation still in formation. The town's earliest settlers included the Waltons, descendants of those who landed in 1635.[1] Arthur Gould (A. G.) Walton, Peggy's grandfather, was born in 1855; attended public schools, including Wakefield High School; and, in 1882, married Mary Ellen Bartlett. Within two years, their son Bartlett Walton, who would become Peggy's father, was born. The Waltons attended the local congregational church.[2]

The same forces that created entrepreneurial opportunities for the Burleighs and Davidsons created them for Arthur Walton. In 1899, at age forty-six, he partnered with two others to form the Walton & Logan Company to manufacture children shoes in a factory in Lynn, Massachusetts, and later expanded to Chelsea, Lawrence, and other locations in New England. Arthur acquired complete ownership in 1909. At the height of its productivity, A. G. Walton produced thirty-five thousand pairs of shoes a day, with three thousand employees.[3]

Throughout this business success, the Waltons made civic contributions: the creation of the Mary E. Walton public grammar school and the Mayfield High School athletic field (Walton Field) among them. Mary chaired the Mayfield Liberty Loan drive to raise funds for World War I, and the Walton factories organized and cooperated with employees to support troops, at home in training and abroad in combat. Arthur Walton was among Massachusetts' most notable business leaders; his financial and geographic reach was national.[4] He lived to witness Peggy Walton's birth in 1914 and her marriage to Valentine Giamatti in 1937.

☙

A. G. Walton & Co.'s fate and productivity were deeply entwined with the immigrant artisan operators who made shoes, printed catalogs, and refined leather products. Strikes occurred, some uneventful and resolved easily. Other strikes were more prolonged and contentious. Walton Shoes worked successfully with the American Federation of Labor–affiliated Boot and Shoe Workers' Union in the company's factory in Lawrence, but in late 1915 through early 1917, A. G. Walton confronted much rougher treatment and violent confrontations in Chelsea by strikers from the United Shoe Workers, whom he refused to recognize. As was evident elsewhere in the nation, New England was in transition; a new or different set of values was introduced into commerce and industry–worker relationships. The fight had a long, contentious, at times murderous history throughout the country, but at base it was often the Southern and Eastern Europeans, including Southern Italian artisans and laborers, who, committed to being American on their own terms even when faced with loss of life and livelihood, insisted on dignity and fairness. Their insistence was still in its early stages; much more was to come, including resentment and anger methodically channeled against them by those in control of the nation's laws and wealth.[5] A. G. Walton adjusted. The Chelsea plant never shut down completely, including during the Great Depression.[6]

Yet one nonlabor episode is worth recounting, not for its insight into the Waltons' character but for the tenor of the culture that surrounded it. In late November 1921, four gunmen robbed the Walton Shoe Company in a daring daytime attack. Shots were fired, a cash payroll of $28,000 was taken, and the men escaped readily in automobiles. No one was injured. The robbery was reported widely. One reason for its notoriety, emphasized in the *New York Times* as well as in the local papers: "The hold up and escape, barring its lack of fatality, in many respects duplicated the Sacco-Vanzetti payroll robbery at South Braintree."[7] Only a few months earlier, Bartolomeo Vanzetti and Nicola Sacco—in an unreservedly and boldly displayed unfair trial teeming with ethnic and political prejudice—were convicted of murder and robbery in a nationally, then globally, covered trial in Dedham, Massachusetts. The prejudice was welcomed in an ethic of Anglo-Saxon justice, in which polite violence reigned, including through the apparatus of law and the acceptable ease of corrupt conflicts of purpose.[8] The process and the outcome were yet another affirmation of Parrington's judgment about the prejudices that haunted New England—the way that the authority to intimidate was exercised, and the nature of the Anglo-Saxon exercise of power as pervasive and politely violent, that is, that masqueraded in the pretense of poise, righteous rhetoric, and self-serving rules of law. Neither prudential nor civil thinking or fairness prevailed against Boston's emanating dark aura and the evolving depth of eugenics.[9]

All four robbers in the A. G. Walton robbery were caught. None was Italian or Italian American.

⌘

Bartlett Walton, A. G.'s son, attended Phillips Academy (Class of 1900, honors graduate) and Harvard (Class of 1904; Franklin Roosevelt was his classmate). After graduation from Harvard, Bartlett joined the firm, informing his classmates that he was "making shoes." His sister, Alice, attended Smith College. It was through her that he met Helen Davidson.[10]

In 1910, they married in South Berwick's First Parish Congregationalist Church, where Helen's parents, James Davidson and Elizabeth Burleigh, had been married in 1883. They moved into the Davidson-Burleigh home for a period of time. Their three children—Elizabeth ("Betty"); then Mary ("Peggy"), born in 1914; and Kathryn—were born in Wakefield. The depth and tone of influence and character in Peggy's life came primarily through her mother and from the Davidson-Burleigh thread of the family.

By 1919, Bartlett was the vice president of A. G. Walton & Co.[11] The family's new two-story home in Wakefield featured dark-gray shingles; dormer windows on the second floor; porches, both open and enclosed; rooms ample in size for children, guests, and large holiday gatherings of relatives; and an interior painted in warm New England colors, with a piano (Bartlett was an accomplished pianist), library, and large fireplace. Spacious lawns, flowers, and leafy trees, and curved and gracefully sloping streets surrounded the house, as if this section of the town had been planned in the landscaped wonder of Frederick Law Olmsted.[12]

In the early 1920s, the Waltons purchased a weathered, multiroom dark-brown-shingled cottage on the beach along the rugged shoreline of Bustins Island, in Maine's Casco Bay, a long ferry ride from South Freeport. No electricity, no paved roads. The experience was central to Peggy's youth—rowboats; bird watching; shell collecting; cookouts; swimming; reading; long talks with parents, cousins, and grandparents; and imaginative forms of self-entertainment and family games. Her personal photograph album is filled with snapshots of group swimming, game playing—tennis, volleyball, and basketball—beach walking, and boat riding. Photographs of Peggy show her jumping, strutting, arms embraced in friendship, laughter in the play, and then quiet, pensive moments alone, her dark hair tussled, contentment on her round face, a confidence from stability in her look. Bustins Island was distant, rustic, casual, without pretentiousness in its time and context, intended for family fun, privacy, and rejuvenation. Put differently, it was not Newport, Hyannis, or Kennebunkport. The cottage remained in the Walton family well into the 1970s. It is where Peggy vacationed with her parents and, later in life, with her own family, including her son Bart.[13]

One other family characteristic was the Walton and Davidson-Burleigh knowledge of the culture of New England and of those with wealth and power, old and new—how it was exercised and by whom. The family had separated itself from the arrogance of Boston and the proscriptive bigotry of the Calvinists and their successors, yet it recognized when that arrogance masqueraded in subtle forms of condescension in other locations and institutions, though often not much masquerading was deemed necessary. For this family of South Berwick, Maine, and Wakefield, Massachusetts, knowing and using the cultural rules, spoken and implied, to ensure that no one in their family was denied access or treated differently was understood as a practical asset to be learned and exercised when necessary. Peggy Walton understood that asset and how to use it.

PEGGY WALTON, ITALIAN BY CHOICE

Peggy Walton attended public schools in South Berwick and Wakefield, including Wakefield High, which her grandfather had attended. She was an excellent student. She declined the offer to attend a private school of her choosing. Surprising both parents and some acquaintances, she mischievously opted for the excitement of the dangled alternative: a convertible roadster. Her friends welcomed it. For college, her choice was preordained: Smith. In addition to her father's sister, Alice, and her mother, Helen, seven other relatives preceded her,[14] and her two sisters were there at about the same time.[15] Peggy's choice of study, however, was a departure: Italy, its history, culture, geography, art, and language.

When, between 1868 and 1872, Sophia Smith set forth in her wills the intention to found a women's college, it was both revolutionary in its purpose and precise in its form. The male intellectual lights at the all-men colleges in New England expressed skepticism. Sophia persisted. She wanted her college to "furnish for my own sex means and facilities for education equal to those which are afforded now in our colleges to young men," which would ensure that "reforming the evils in society will be greatly increased [and the] power for good will be incalculably enlarged." The college would be located in Northampton. She also wanted the living arrangements to encourage camaraderie. Residences would be small houses and cottages, with mixed classes. Smith opened formally in 1875. In the 1890s, with its fate assured financially, the campus was planned and planted by famed landscape architect Frederick Law Olmsted.[16] Admission was nonsectarian. The curriculum was decidedly liberal arts in scope and depth.[17]

Wesley House, just off Elm Street, was where Peggy resided on entering Smith in 1931; she then lived in Haven House nearby for the remainder of her education. Both houses were within easy view of Chapin Lawn and Paradise Pond, two elements in President William Allan Neilson's insightful retention of Olmsted to give botanical splendor to the Smith campus. Peggy was elected to the student government association, then called the House of Representatives; was a member of the sophomore and junior choir; and took courses in music history. She already had skill at the piano, her father's talent. A majority of her courses and time, however, were devoted to the study of Italy.[18]

The Italian language was first taught at Smith in 1899; by 1901, Italian became an independent department. Within less than a decade, the department "developed into one of the most flourishing in the country."[19] In 1931, Smith selected its first group of juniors to spend a year in Italy. The program was well designed: departure in August, the month of September in Perugia "devoted chiefly to work in the language offered by the University for Foreigners," followed by prolonged stays in Florence and Rome and travel south into Sicily and north to Venice and the Alps.[20] By 1931, however, the nature of Italian politics and government had changed. The rise of Fascism and the well-entrenched leadership of Benito Mussolini had yielded dissent and oppression in Italy, and tumult and political line drawing in the United States.

When Peggy entered Smith in the fall of 1931, the Department of Italian had among its faculty Michele Cantarella, a leader of anti-Fascist Italian exiles. He had joined the faculty in 1929 as professor of Italian literature. Cantarella was born in Southern Italy, in Giarre, Sicily, where Giuseppe Garibaldi's war for independence combined with Sicilian uprisings that insisted on freedom from the Spanish Bourbon family monarchy. Cantarella's indigenous ancestors had experienced the Spanish and, later, the Northern Italian oppression firsthand. With his wife, Cantarella formed a center for translating literary works that expressed opposition to Fascism to combat Mussolini's industrial, financial, and religious supporters in America.[21] Later, in 1931, the Italian Department, "in common with the rest of the college, [also] received a notable stimulus from the appointment of Professor G. Antonio Borgese," who remained on the faculty throughout Peggy's time at Smith. "His wide scholarship, his eloquence, and his enthusiasm were felt throughout the institution."[22] So was his vehement anti-Fascism. Later, after Peggy's graduation, both Cantarella and Borgese supported the formation of the anti-Fascist Mazzini Society in America, organized in Smith's hometown by their mutual friend, Gaetano Salvemini. The society's purpose was to expose Fascist agents and influence in America, especially the financial and moral support provided by American banking interests—J. P. Morgan and Rockefeller only the most notorious—and the Irish-dominated Catholic Church. The society was named after Giuseppe Mazzini, the liberal advocate for Italian democratic institutions who most inspired Garibaldi's imperative to take up arms in the South.[23]

Peggy Walton's introduction to the realities of Italian politics and anti-Fascism began in earnest. She experienced the teachings of both men. She had studied the history and form of Etruscan art. Her proficiency in the Italian language was excellent, a prerequisite for selection for her junior year abroad. She was a member of the International Relations Club. She was elected president of the Italian Group, students who embraced with her the opportunity to experience Italy firsthand. In 1932, her sister Betty, a year ahead of her at Smith, returned from Europe; on a brief journey through Italy, she had taken special note of Fascism's symbols and effects, and in "seeing . . . brown shirts."[24] When, in August 1933, Peggy walked onto the ocean liner SS *Rex*, waved goodbye to her parents, and prepared for departure to Italy, she brought with her a sophisticated knowledge of what, during her stay, warranted quiet attention. She also had an informed temperament about the kind of man who might engage her intellect and share her commitments.[25]

From Southern Italy to America

The myth of the brigands ["resistance fighters," in the Neapolitan vernacular] is close to their hearts and a part of their lives, the only poetry in their existence. . . . The brigands unreasonably and hopelessly stood up for the life and liberty of the peasants against the encroachment of the State.

—Carlo Levi, *Christ Stopped at Eboli*

The Giammatteis and Lavorgnas: The Challenge of the Northern Problem

Angelo Giammattei, Bart Giamatti's namesake and grandfather, and Bart's grandmother, Maria, understood the meaning of fairness. They had witnessed and their family had experienced and withstood its cruelly executed denial in Italy and, again, in New Haven.

᪣

Genoa. On May 5, 1860, at nine-thirty in the evening, Giuseppe Garibaldi left the villa of his friend, Augusto Vecchi, "walked through the grounds of the Palazzo Spinola towards the sea, accompanied by a number of his officers. He was wearing his red shirt and baggy grey trousers with a silk handkerchief round his neck. He carried his poncho, 'made of thick Sardinian cloth, in bandolier fashion. He wore his saber, his knife in his belt, his revolver slung on his back, and his Colt's repeater carbine on his shoulder.' Under the trees at the edge of Palazzo's ground and on the rocks by the sea, the volunteers were waiting." To band together under Garibaldi's leadership, many among the volunteers had traveled at considerable risk from throughout the peninsula, defying the deadly exercise of authority by the ruling government, which they'd be certain to confront on the journey south. More than a thousand men made the voyage from Genoa that night, five hundred nautical miles by sea to Sicily.[1]

The Sicilian people had begun their uprising against the oppressive rule of the Spanish Bourbon family. It was not the first time. The Sicilians and the people of the South—the *Mezzogiorno*—wanted independence and the liberty of choice in a democratic order. Garibaldi intended to give it to them. His military obstacle was the massive Bourbon Army. His political and more cunning obstacle was in the North, King Victor Emmanuel, and the king's prime minister, Count Camillo Cavour. Neither was willing to contribute fighters or money to the democratic independence revolt against the Bourbons occurring in the South or to withdraw the government's protection, also supported by the French, of the Papal States in Rome, whose vast land holdings and exploitation made them, to Garibaldi, mere foreign "strangers" that warranted removal.[2]

Between Rome and Sicily was Naples, where the solidly ensconced Bourbon king, Francis II, inflicted his harm mercilessly like a dull, steady, dispiriting disease. Naples had enormous wealth in gold, universities, and global commerce. Its capture was essential to the South's future. Within Francis's direct sphere of arbitrary power, to Naples' northeast, was the town of San Lorenzello, the home for generations of the Giammattei and Lavorgna families, the ancestors of Angelo Bartlett Giamatti.

⤮

"*Garibaldisimo* as a well-determined political movement" had practical conflicts among three personalities, and one human force.[3] Giuseppe Mazzini, a grand thinker who advocated democratic principles and Italian unification, lived mostly in exile from his birthplace in Genoa. His writings were admired in America and understood among insurgents in the South. Cavour was an aristocrat in the Piedmont, more comfortable with the financially elite of any nation than with his own people. He was especially fond of the French, whose language he preferred to that of what he viewed as the detestable men and women now risking their lives aboard Garibaldi's ships.[4]

Cavour considered the South the epitome of lowlife. The South was "Africa," said with every racial diminutive available. His parochialism was one thread of his prejudice: he'd never traveled as far south as Rome. Historian David Gilmour wrote, insightfully, "Cavour was a great Piedmontese, he was not a great Italian." Democratic principles were not among his imperatives. Cavour had authority; he was the reason Mazzini remained in exile. Cavour feared Garibaldi because of the latter's unwavering commitment to equality—voting should be universal, and women should vote—and his unparalleled appeal to anyone in legitimate revolt against oppression. Cavour's most discomforting fear: Garibaldi was incorruptible and could lead men in battle.[5]

There was a fourth personality. It was not the king, Victor Emmanuel, who had little skill other than how to exploit others. Deeply entwined in Cavour's calculations, Mazzini's idealism, and Garibaldi's strategy—without which independence, democracy, and unification had neither prospect nor voice in the place it mattered—was the fourth personality, the human force: the people living in the peninsula's South.[6]

Garibaldi landed in Marsala on August 14. The Sicilian uprising was then five weeks old. The Bourbon military was debilitated. He took Palermo. His success yielded confidence in freedom and in the opportunity for education, commercial development, and relief from arbitrary imprisonment and crushing taxation. Lives were further dedicated to battle with those expectations. They were expectations also based on Sicily's place within Roman and Greek history.[7]

Garibaldi crossed the Strait of Messina into Calabria on August 18 and, with growing numbers of volunteers, humiliated the Bourbon contingents. In the North, apprehension pervaded Cavour's mentality. His fear was a resurgent South more intent on independence than on unity, on the insurmountable exercise of liberty under Garibaldi's protection. The Northerners were right to be fearful, not of Garibaldi but of the people of the South.[8]

Just as he reached the town of Cosenza on August 31, almost two hundred miles from Naples, Garibaldi was joined by volunteers from towns in Campania. "The Legions of Garibaldi" included "the San Lorenzello Brigade"—intellectuals, artisans, farmers, women, and dissident priests—organized by the town's leading families and liberal activists who had spread Garibaldi's writings and poetry and news of his presence. Family life and survival were at stake. Included were the Lavorgnas, among the town's founders, and the Giammatteis, their fate and the town's tied to the fate and principles of their community's decision. Equivocation was neither embraced nor would it later be available.[9]

Garibaldi moved methodically toward Naples. It was among the largest and most architecturally sophisticated cities in Europe, its university renowned, its port facility larger and more financially successful than Genoa's in the North. The Bourbons spoke the Neapolitan dialect. "Before 1860, with Naples at its base, the Kingdom of the Two Sicilies was the richest part of the entire peninsula"; the Bank of Naples gold reserve was 443 million lire, twice the combined reserves of the rest of the peninsula. In a democratic order, with Naples' economic engine joined into the other industries and artisan crafts that existed throughout the South and into Sicily's Palermo and Messina, the South would have the foundation for growth. Southerners knew, as well, what British historians, journalists, and travelers had long described: Southerners "were humanely tolerant of all kinds of people" and "able to look at things as they are in the classical daylight, without mist and introspection." As later observed, "The people of the South are somehow immune to the neuroses of the North. . . . This alternative way of seeing draws attention to the permeable boundaries of the Adriatic Coast to trade and immigration, and contributes to a re-conceptualization of Southern Italy as being at the center of the Mediterranean, rather than at the periphery of Europe." Anticipation of giving life to governance must have thrilled every volunteer who took up arms and every family that awaited its fate. Cavour dispatched his army to join with the French to protect the Papal States.[10]

With more than twenty thousand volunteers and the aid of novelist Alexandre Dumas, Garibaldi reached the massive Bourbon Army of Naples. By September 4, the Bourbon king withdrew north and repositioned himself with forty thousand troops near Gaeta and Capua, north of the Volturno River. With the aid of French and Northern Italian passivity, Garibaldi would make his stand. The welcome that Garibaldi received in Naples was "riotous" with joy.[11]

Garibaldi's insurrectionist volunteers, the San Lorenzello Brigade among them, stood poised along the Volturno River. They were exhausted, their effort long in duration, their equipment primitive, many among them wounded and without medical supplies. Garibaldi could not risk losing Naples back to the Bourbon Army. Cavour's army as well as the French also confronted him. King Victor Emmanuel interceded, arrived in Naples, and assured Garibaldi that unification and liberty were foremost in his mind. Garibaldi, always and only the warrior, agreed. He left the South's fate to Cavour. He returned home. Unification was agreed to in a quick, uneasily coerced referendum, the king's and Garibaldi's assurances critical to the South's thinking.[12]

The reality was quite different. One historian observed: "The duel between Cavour and Garibaldi was not only the duel between conservative Italy and radical Italy, between monarchy and revolution. . . . It also was a duel between reality and dreams, between the real Italy and idealist Italy." The "duel" was aptly described, if you were a Northerner. For Southerners, it was a duel between elitist, parochial privilege to govern by dictate and the independence and democracy the South believed it had earned. Cavour never intended to give honor to the purposes for which Southerners had died.[13]

༄

Unification had been achieved, a nation created with a horrible, enduring cost and the emergence of a permanent stain in the Southern Italian mind. In the grand fanfare that spread globally, especially in the United States and England and perpetuated by educated and political *strata* in Piedmont who controlled the power to define their own reality, Cavour and Emmanuel had led unification, Garibaldi was their instrument, and Mazzini was the wayward intellectual with the grand idea. All were from the North. Statues, memorials, street and plaza names, testimonials, and proclamations were imposed on towns throughout Italy. Revision of fact was in the making. That the insurrection and war was fought in the South, that first Sicilians without Garibaldi, and then Neapolitan and Calabrian citizens in the thousands with Garibaldi, challenged and defeated the Bourbon Army with no practical help from the North was torn asunder and replaced by a mythology that served neither truth nor ethics nor the practical needs of those who sought and expected fairness. The stain was readily embodied rhetorically among Southern Italians: "The Northern Problem."[14]

THE EDUCATION OF MARTIAL LAW

More than one hundred thousand members of the Piedmont army—half its total force—occupied the South. The stage was set for repression. Historical revisionism was embraced further as a critical tool to justify the repression. England and America were willing receptacles for deception: England because it wanted the French out, and America because it was enthralled in its own fight for "unification," as if all nations were formed the same. The Piedmontese troops, it was said and written, moved south to repress "brigands"—understood in the Western world as analogous to criminals—and to promote "unification." Neither was accurate.[15]

The Northern Italian Army destroyed entire villages and towns. Oxford historian Denis Mack Smith described the beginning: "When the Piedmontese entered Neapolitan territory in October 1860, one of [their] first actions was to shoot every peasant found carrying arms. This was *a declaration of war* on people who needed arms to defend their property." The killing continued unconstrained. Smith's colleague, Christopher Duggan, described the horror visited on the Campania towns of Pontelandolfo and Casalduni in August 1861: hundreds murdered indiscriminately, the villages burned while people slept until it was too late to run, valuables stolen, women raped, the total killed between four hundred and what was in time estimated to be closer to three thousand, the few survivors left homeless with the memory of families lost forever.[16]

The burning, sacking, and slaughter became method. Some villages were surrounded, their water sources stopped until thirst and starvation led to death or easy imprisonment. Duggan recognized that, "How many died in the first years of unification is unclear." Italian and other historians from the twentieth and twenty-first centuries have given light to a set of facts previously muted by fear or muzzled by the North. Records of towns destroyed and people killed apparently were kept and publicly chronicled—as if in a manner of pride and accomplishment, not unlike what America witnessed daily when David Halberstam's aptly described "Best and the Brightest" in the Pentagon and White House reported what Americans saw each night on television about North Vietnamese or Vietcong killed. The Body Count. Victory in sight, according to Robert McNamara (Harvard MBA 1939), McGeorge Bundy (Yale 1940), William Bundy (Yale 1939), and Walter Rostow (Yale 1936). The North did the same, tolling the casualties in the army's assault against towns of "brigands": Guaricia, 1,322 dead; Campochiaro, 979 dead; Casalduni, 3,032 dead; Pontelandolfo, 3,917 dead; Viesti, 5,417 dead; and more towns and villages throughout the South. The estimate of Southern Italians killed is between "tens of thousands," which Duggan found easily credible, to one hundred fifty thousand, which he found "not impossible." Others historians have higher estimates. "Killings of this kind," Duggan concluded with palpable lament, "do not make the official records."[17]

Duggan and Professor Richard Gambino estimated that more than eighty thousand took up arms against the Northerners. They included women—tough, angry women who defended their families with rifles and shotguns, characteristic of a cultural value and imperative little understood in America when, a generation later (including in New Haven), Italian women emerged as labor leaders insistent on fairness. Some of those captured were sent to concentration camps, tortured, or left languishing in stillness until dead. Others were executed when they refused to take an oath to the invading army. The method got worse in 1863, when the parliament enacted Law 1409, which allowed the summary execution of relatives of those suspected of resistance. The 1863 enactment was the imposition of martial law on the entire South.[18]

Exploitive taxation was imposed, more onerous and unfair than the Bourbons had extracted. Liberty was pummeled. Initially, much of the revolt and repression were centered in Basilicata and Campania, in or near San Lorenzello, home of the Giammatteis and Lavorgnas.[19] Naples was dismembered. The 443 million lire in gold reserve were flat-out confiscated by Piedmont. The Naples port facilities were dismantled to stop competition with Genoa's shipping industrialists. Roads and schools were neglected. Jobs were lost, investment discouraged. And the centrality of the Neapolitan language to commerce, education, and governance was ended. One local dignitary protested to the new "Italian" parliament: "This is invasion, not annexation, not union. We are being plundered like an occupied territory." A critical source for economic and cultural improvement was gone.[20]

In 1866, the final manifestation of resistance occurred. Forty thousand men and women insurgents took control of Sicily. "Many among them . . . six years earlier had poured down from the hills in support of Garibaldi." It was a brutal and ugly outcome. Palermo was bombarded. Men and women were summarily executed. Excuses were fabricated—the "brigand," once again politically defined—to justify the North's conduct.[21] Decades—actually generations—later, the memories of the horror imposed by the North and the gallantry of defiance and irreverence for arbitrary order held solidly in the Southern mind.[22]

꙳

In America there was little appreciation for the underlying political and human imperative that drove the gut-wrenching conversations within Southern families about departure.[23] Historians and commentators in the United States adhered closely to the simple and appealing Emmanuel-Cavour-Garibaldi-Mazzini hagiography. It fed a growing prejudice founded in the racist remnants of the Civil War, the resurgence of the Klan in the Northeast as well as in the South, and the growing embrace of eugenics. In 1896, Harvard historian and later president A. Lawrence Lowell wrote, "Victor Emmanuel is the model constitutional king."[24]

The outcome Garibaldi sought had not materialized. He couldn't change the Piedmontese or the American mentality. *He* wrote "scornfully: 'It was a very different Italy which I spent my life dreaming of, not the impoverished and humiliated country which we now see ruled by the dregs of the nation.'" He also wrote to a close friend that, "The outrages suffered by the southern populations are beyond comparison."[25] In Italy, educational programs were nationalized to make the revisionist history truth.[26] The people of the Italian South knew better. African American intellectual Booker T. Washington saw through the Northern pretense as well. After visiting the sulfur mines and farms of Sicily in 1910, he wrote, "The Negro is not the man farthest down." The harsh reality of a disquieting future had to be confronted: When and where to go? It would happen shortly within the Giammattei and Lavorgna families.[27]

ॐ

Italian historians, intellectuals, and Southern Italians have recognized the North's actions and the "Great Brigandage" in similar ways: "Class warfare carried on by the dispossessed masses and brutally criminalized and repressed by the new Italian state," and the "mostly hidden racial prejudices by Northern soldiers and civil servants against the southerners." What did occur, especially with the imposition of martial law, was "clearly the character of a civil war. . . . The exploited poor [in the South] answered the North with 'our time has come.'" It was an "armed peasant revolt against . . . the Italian government and by those landowners who supported it." Under this definition and imperative for freedom, the American analogue to Southern Italian "Brigandage" was the Revolution's Francis Marion, the "Swamp Fox," or the Civil War's John Brown, the abolitionist. What Southern Italian men and women endured was the frontal imposition of the "Northern Problem" writ large, the North's utter failure of principle, the denigration of any obligation for lives sacrificed, families uprooted, and the full meaning of freedom and unity sought by Garibaldi, Mazzini, and Southern families. In the mid–twentieth century, the North's actions between 1861 and 1866 likely would have been challenged formally as genocide.[28]

4

THE CHOICE

PRESERVING IDENTITY

Those men and women who departed San Lorenzello said goodbye to a town that sat on the slopes of Mount Erbano near a narrow gorge between Mount Monaco di Gioia and the Titerno River, a tributary of the Volturno, where the town's volunteers had stood with Garibaldi. The town's origins trace into the third and sixth centuries; its Roman fortifications and Greek and Etruscan cultural influences suggest even earlier civilizations. The location, in the Valley of the Samnites, produced fierce people who resisted forcefully the imposition of rule from the Romans and the Papal States. The "Cave of the Brigands"—where the resistance fighters hid or were protected—was only a town away. The Lavorgnas were among San Lorenzello's founders and contributors to the civic good.[1]

Each family engaged in the same conversation about departure. Added to their anxiety were other variables, unsavory and unavoidable. The families knew of the Italian government's harsh repression of thousands of women organizers who had insisted on fair wages and working conditions in a fledgling union movement in Sicily, Basilicata, and Campania. Smith Professor Jennifer Guglielmo described it this way: "The Italian government responded swiftly." In 1894, a state of siege was declared and forty thousand troops once again occupied the South. "Movement leaders and participants were arrested, beaten, and gunned down in the street or executed in prison." Despite the similar wholesale killings they had witnessed less than a generation earlier, Southern Italians refused to stay silent and forgo their insistence on fair treatment.[2]

Reprisals against Italian immigrants in America added to the apprehension. Several immigrants were lynched in West Virginia, others in Colorado, more still in Mississippi. The highest danger loomed in the American South, where the Jim Crow laws and, worse, the mentality that justified them spread beyond the widespread cruelty imposed daily on African Americans. In Hahnville, then Tallulah, Louisiana, the homes of Italian immigrants were breached. Five were lynched, their bodies riddled with bullets. "Their offense?" as Professor Richard

Gambino described it: "They had permitted Negroes equal status with whites in their shops"—conduct that Southern Italians had engaged in for generations with peoples from Africa, Arabia, and Greece.[3] In Tallulah, "a rationale behind the lynching was the argument made by white citizens . . . that 'to insure white supremacy no other course was possible than the course pursued.'"[4]

Keen awareness rang loudest, however, with news from New Orleans: the horrendous killing of eleven Italian Americans, the single largest lynching in America's history. March 14, 1891. No one was charged with this act of mass vigilantism. The town's leaders—the government—rejoiced in self-commendation. The Italian government intervened and, then, in a manner readily understood by Southern Italians, largely backed away. Far more frightening was the reaction to the lynching in the northeast United States, where the Lavorgnas and Giammatteis hoped to settle. Theodore Roosevelt, then a U.S. Civil Service commissioner, said he believed the lynching was "a rather good thing"; the *New York Times* editorialized that the Italians were actually "descendants of bandits and assassins" (a reflection of the Northern Italian rationale for its brutal repression in Southern Italy); and Massachusetts Senator Henry Cabot Lodge, referring to the Italians, said that this "great Republic should no longer be left unguarded from them." The *New Haven Register* parroted Lodge's assumption and mentality. The lynching, it wrote, had been carried out, not by a "wild mob" but by the "best elements in town, including professionals and merchants," against "murderers." It was the Anglo-Saxon form of polite violence. No participants in New Orleans sought to hide their identity. The "law" did it for them. More of the same rough and rhetorical attacks against Italian immigrants followed (an estimated forty-seven were lynched into the next century).[5] One optimistic note for the Giammatteis and Lavorgnas: the Italian immigrant community in New Haven expressed outrage, and the families believed they could still expect an America built on fairness and the supremacy of law, not on stereotypes.[6]

Coupled with uncertainty about circumstances in America were concerns about the base conditions travelers were to face on the ships that offered transport there. Filth, lack of sanitation facilities, food poisoning, and contagious diseases spread in the stifling crowdedness of "steerage" below the water line. The horrendous conditions "exceeded only by the older African slavers" were permitted by the government in the North for decades until, perhaps embarrassed by criticism, officials required changes. The changes were marginal. As one passenger from San Lorenzello described his thirty-five-day trip from Naples to New York, "[we] were all in the bottom of the boat there, and who was getting sick and who was crying." There was no respite. The "welcome" into America rarely improved the tone.[7] Observed by Bartolomeo Vanzetti: "I saw the steerage passengers handled by the officials like so many animals. Not a word of kindness . . . to lighten the burden of fears that rests heavily upon the newly arrived on American shores. Hope . . . withers under the touch of harsh officials. Little children who should be alert with expectancy, cling instead to their mothers' skirts, weeping with fright."[8]

Of more enduring importance, an intentional stigma accompanied their journey across the Atlantic: racism. Gambino described it this way: "The Northerners, together with the Italian Government, convinced American officials that there were two distinct groups of Italians, or in the words used in official American documents of the time, two different 'races.'" American immigration officials categorized Southerners separately.[9]

❧

Francesco and Maria Giammattei—the grandparents of Angelo and Francesco, and their sister Concetta—were age forty and thirty-five during the earliest, vengeful manifestation of the Northern repression. Angelo, Francesco, and Concetta's parents, Ambrosio and Rafaella, were adolescents when tempered by the ugly conflagration at nearby Pontelandolfo and Casalduni. As a family, no doubt with care and trepidation, they decided that their younger son, Angelo, born September 3, 1882, would go first.[10]

In 1896, when Angelo left San Lorenzello at age thirteen—apparently with family friends—he played a typical role in the careful methodology employed by many Southern Italian families. He served as the explorer, the scout, the gatherer of intelligence. He journeyed to New Haven and joined others from his own and nearby valley towns. He lived on James Street, in the heart of the Fair Haven neighborhood east of downtown, and found work and camaraderie among those from his village and among other Italians. By 1900, if not before, he wrote, read, and spoke English.[11] In 1900, the Giammatteis decided that Francesco, their older son, then twenty-four, would join his brother. The brothers shared a room, first at 266 Hamilton Street on the eastern edge of New Haven's Wooster Square neighborhood closer to downtown. They then moved to 150 St. John Street, nearer the Italian immigrant community's newly ordained refuge, St. Michael's Church, an Italian Catholic haven in a city dominated by the more dogmatic Irish.[12]

Those who departed the sounds and aromas of home and the comfort of parents and siblings never to be seen again (Angelo left behind his parents and two sisters) brought with them memories of those moments of hard choices and courage. The careful exercise of native wit they developed and exercised in a foreign and often inhospitable culture remained deeply embedded in the history of each family for generations to come. Bart Giamatti, by all accounts, was among those who knew precisely what his paternal grandparents had endured in Italy, on the voyage to the United States, and in New Haven.[13]

Thus, in political and cultural terms, began the Southern Italian *Diaspora*. Between 1890 and 1924, more than four million men, women, and children left their homes in Southern Italy—the Great Migration, as it is called—without any objection or discouragement from their government. Some were artisans—tailors, teachers, wood craftsmen, labor organizers, midwives, artists, machinists, seamstresses, and printers—with valued skills awaiting the opportunity to bring them to bear. They and others brought expectations about community self-help and the duty of fair treatment. They brought ideals about how to preserve the health and destiny of family members and others in need of charity; knowledge of the soil and how to grow fruits and vegetables and raise livestock with little land; and a canny sense of tools, seasons, weather, and nurturing. Above all, they brought an unyielding commitment to, as Bart Giamatti recognized it two generations later, "the inevitability of hard work," physical and mental. Not "hard work" as the Protestant ethic defined it—efficient, self-made (or the pretense of it) monetary gain justified by God's will—but, as Richard Gambino explained it, "Work . . . as moral training for the young. And among adults, it is regarded as a matter of pride. To work is to show evidence that one has become a man or a woman, a full member of the family. So strong is the ethic that it governs behavior quite apart from considerations of monetary gain. . . . It is a moral wrong not to be productively occupied [in] . . . something done by oneself and for one's family."[14]

These immigrants knew, instinctively and empirically, where their interests lay. They understood repression and when and how to fight against it or, as they had done against the North, how to survive without losing their integrity and identity. Foremost, government, the wealthy, and the Church hierarchy were not to be relied upon unless proved, unequivocally, to be trustworthy. Communal and family relationships were central to trustworthiness, stability, hard work, nurturing, duty of care, and risk taking. It was not accidental that when, a generation later, the famed urban thinker and observer Jane Jacobs began her work to shatter "urban renewal" propaganda, she examined as a model to be emulated the commitment to community organization and care of others that pervaded Boston's North End Italian immigrant community. All of those values would be tested in America.[15]

The choices to leave were deliberately made, not just to seek gainful employment elsewhere—as is often and simply portrayed—but to seek a new paradigm in life, to embrace more choices in geographic location, employment, culture, education, and the liberties denied them by the Northern government. Many among the Southern Italians were political émigrés, not just emigrants.

REDEFINING THE RULES

By 1902, Angelo was working at the New Haven Clock Company on Hamilton Street, among the nation's largest manufacturers of clocks and watches. He was perfecting the artisan craft of watchmaking, a skill that would ensure financial stability for the family he intended to raise in New Haven. He also was developing a solid grasp of the local manner of acquiring and renting property. His community sensitivity and sterling reputation were evident to others. In March 1904, his professional prospects solid, he returned to New York and made the arduous ocean journey to Naples, and then to San Lorenzello. On April 14, 1904, he married Maria Grazia Luigia Lavorgna.[16]

Maria Grazia (Mary Grace), then twenty years old, had three sisters and four brothers. Two years earlier, in 1902, her brother Antonio (Anthony) had immigrated to America. He settled in New Haven. Maria's grandparents, Martino and Maria Lavorgna and Nicola and Maria Sagnella, were in their forties when Giuseppe Garibaldi brought his volunteers to the Volturno River. Maria Grazia's parents, Luigi and Maria Giovanna Lavorgna, had been, like Angelo's parents, in their early teens when they were forced to live under martial law. Now fifty-four and fifty-five years old, they'd imparted to Maria Grazia confidence in risk taking, skill at managing family and household and in preserving family dignity, and a practical and intuitive knowledge of property. Her parents also knew that her older brother provided further buffer to the risk of emigration.[17]

Angelo's sister Concetta, then eighteen years old, joined Maria and Angelo. Within days of the marriage, the three of them made their journey to New Haven aboard the liner, SS *Perugia*. On May 5, 1904, they sailed past the iconic Statue of Liberty, which Maria and Concetta witnessed for the first time, undoubtedly with their high hopes reassured by Angelo. When they had prepared to embark, the ship manifest submitted to the United States Immigration Service categorized each of them as "Nationality: *Italian* Race: *South*."[18]

Within one year, Concetta was married. She lived in Fair Haven and had nine children. Angelo's brother, Francesco, married, had seven children, and also lived in Fair Haven. Maria Grazia's brother Antonio married and had four children. Their sister Raffaela, still in Italy, married Angelo Santello from nearby San Salvatore. After he immigrated to New Haven and settled in Fair Haven, Raffaela joined him with their son. They eventually had six children. Other Lavorgnas and Giammatteis from San Lorenzello and nearby Telese followed their cousins into New Haven.[19]

In late 1904, Angelo and Maria moved to Main Street, near Angelo's sister Concetta. In May 1905, they had their first child, Rafaela, followed by Adelina and Ambrosio (who died within a month). With a growing family, Angelo and Maria moved to Market Street, also in Fair Haven. The Santello family moved next door. Valentine John Giammattei (Giamatti) was born in 1911, followed by his brother, Americo, in 1912 and his sisters, Florence, in 1915, and Helen, in 1920. Valentine's sister Rafaela married John Festa in 1925, Florence married Louis Ruggieri in 1941, and Helen married George Urquhart in 1940. All had children, who, as they grew and married, lived in the same two- or three-family homes as their parents did or elsewhere in Fair Haven. Valentine's extended family—dozens of aunts, uncles, and cousins—were all, largely, within walking distance. Their presence in New Haven would later influence Val and Peggy Giamatti's decision to seek Bart's admission to Yale.

⁓

Bart Giamatti's paternal grandparents and extended family confronted immediately two forces they hadn't expected in New Haven: the ugliness of eugenics and racism (they already were labeled racially) and the pernicious insecurity and jealousy of the Northern Italians transplanted to America. New Haven's Puritan origins and temperament had melded with Yale's solid cultural, and later formal institutional, embrace of eugenics. The Northerners and the "Northern Problem" had found a receptive home.

PART II

VALENTINE GIAMATTI

THE NEW HAVEN THEY ENTERED

In a loving household, in an extended family, in a neighborhood made up almost exclusively of Italian immigrants and second-generation Italian Americans, my values and preparation began to take shape. In addition to the extraordinary love and dignity that my parents provided is the concept of people caring about and taking care of others. We had lots of people looking out for us. I could extend this principle of caring for others. But from my upbringing, I had a nagging feeling I wasn't doing enough.

—Dr. Anthony Fauci, Sons of Italy Foundation, 2016

DEFINING NEIGHBORHOOD AND CITIZENSHIP

Valentine Giamatti had aspirations and duties. Attaining them—"doing enough"—required the discipline of intellect and body, the hard-headed guidance of family, the experience of neighborhood, and the intuitive sense of choices, and when and how to make them. At stake was the challenge of defining citizenship.

⁓

The entirety of New Haven is only nineteen square miles in size; Brooklyn, New York, is ninety-six square miles in size.

Italian immigrants dispersed, generally, into three neighborhoods: Wooster Square, Fair Haven, and Hill/Oak Street/Legion Avenue. Each neighborhood varied in the range of ethnicities—Italian, Jewish (mostly Eastern European and Russian), Polish, Irish, Lithuanian, Greek, African American (descendants of New Haven's Anglo-Saxon–owned slaves and migrants from the southern United States), and "American," working-class Anglo-Saxon. The geographic origin of Italian immigrants also varied, from northern Lombardy and central Marche to southern Sicily, though most were from villages in Calabria and Campania. Differences abounded in food, clothing, religious beliefs, language, education, and occupations. By choice or necessity, those differences were learned and integrated into daily life. "Most of the families who lived [in the Hill/Oak Street/Legion Avenue neighborhood] were Italian or Jewish, but Oak Street—which included . . . the commercial stretch known as Legion Avenue . . . [was] where new arrivals scrambling for a foothold usually wound up. Jews, Italians, African Americans, Poles, Russians, Ukrainians, Irish, Greeks, and others lived cheek by jowl in long rows of dark, timeworn tenements and cold-water flats." As one resident described Legion Avenue, "It was alive, it was exciting, it was always uplifting, and we all felt that it belonged to us. It was our neighborhood. Sunday mornings on Legion Avenue were unbelievable: the hustle, the bustle, people came from all over to shop, to eat, to socialize." Each of the neighborhoods served the same integrative purpose.[1]

By 1910, approximately thirteen thousand Italian immigrants lived in New Haven; by 1930, it was more than twenty-six thousand. That number grew, in part, because the Italians remained committed to the preservation of neighborhood life—even when others were drawn by the lure of suburbia or, later, were forced to leave by the ill-conceived rupture of urban renewal. The Italian Americans' bonds to their neighborhoods would endure for generations, with their numbers reaching as high as one-third of New Haven's population in the 1950s and beyond, when it mattered in the life of Bart Giamatti, who entered Yale in 1956. Italian Americans, many by choice, remained urbanists.[2]

The land use pattern in all three neighborhoods was mixed use: homes were on the second floor, workplaces—butcher and pastry shops, shoemakers, tailors, and restaurants—were at street level. Three-, four-, sometimes seven-unit cold-water residential walkups were clustered in tree-lined neighborhoods, people visible and paying attention, always protective of "playable" streets—what urban naturalist Jane Jacobs later characterized as the safety derived from "eyes upon the street." Market Street, where the Giammatteis lived, and the streets off Ferry Street, where they later lived, were precisely that way. Throughout the neighborhoods were public schools, churches, synagogues, and community halls.[3] Farmers markets were held weekly in all three neighborhoods. The Giammattei homes had side and back yards. Vegetable gardens were common.[4]

These neighborhoods—and downtown New Haven, adjacent to Wooster Square and Hill/Oak Street/Legion Avenue—also reflected fluid urbanity in terms of where people worked (industry such as Sargent's, L. Candee Rubber, New Haven Clock, National Folding Box, A. C. Gilbert), worshipped, enjoyed recreation (Waterside Park in Wooster Square had baseball fields, fishing piers, dance pavilions, and boat launches), fished (Mill, Quinnipiac, and West Rivers, and the Long Island Sound shoreline), and moved to accommodate growing families, widowhood, or bohemian life.

"Neighborhood" shops were rarely "local." Quality and imported clothing, fabric, and foods attracted citywide attention. The neighborhoods were traversed frequently through the common, easily understood, rectilinear street grid and by a streetcar system that was extensive, inexpensive, and nondiscriminatory.[5]

Fair Haven housed the studio of muralist Francis Corio, who painted the grand ceilings of New Haven's Saint Francis and Saint Michael's churches and stage sets for New York's Metropolitan Opera House, including the production of Giuseppe Verdi's *Aida*. Admired, too, were portraits painted by the budding artist Rose Gherardi, whose father, a stonemason, inspired her with stories about Raphael and Michelangelo. Nearby was Joseph Simone, renowned for painting the ceilings in New Haven's new Polish church, Saint Stanislaus, and in Saint Mary's Church.[6] Italian opera singers made guest appearances at neighborhood festivals to sold-out audiences. The radio added opera from New York, heard on Saturday afternoon, often accompanied by the radio owner's words and gestures shared with neighbors and welcomed. And the Shubert Theatre, often on short notice, sought local extras to sing in the chorus or play walk-on parts. My uncle and father, as young boys from Fair Haven, were among them. Immigrant audiences filled Fair Haven's school auditoriums to see Italian- and English-language plays, from Shakespeare to local creations, performed by ad hoc neighborhood troupes.[7]

෴

Valentine John Giammattei (Giamatti) was born on February 9, 1911, and raised in this setting of practical skills, cultural influences, and ethnic and racial diversity. He was originally named Ambrosio Valentine when registered with the Catholic diocese. "Ambrosio" was his paternal grandfather's name, and the name given to Angelo and Maria's first son, who died shortly after birth. For reasons now unknown, the name was changed when Angelo and Maria registered his birth officially in New Haven. "Valentine" was not an uncommon name, but it also was not a family name. Departure had occurred in the Italian immigrant culture. The family was now in America. They named their next son Americo. Val was born at home at 18 Market Street, with the aid of a midwife, and baptized at St. Michael's Church.[8]

The family moved to 264 Ferry Street, a three-story house.[9] Val attended Strong School on Grand Avenue, a sturdy brick structure in the Collegiate Tudor style—high ceilings, wide corridors, steeped in architectural traditions reflective of scholarship. Val did not speak English when he entered. Corporal punishment and ridicule by teachers and classmates followed. It was at Strong School, or maybe in the schoolyard or walking home with his brother or sisters, that the attack or fight and rock throwing that permanently scarred his face occurred. As his son, Dino, said succinctly: "It was the Irish kids." At stake for Val was not resentment but the practical meaning of fairness. That experience and likely other slights and injuries inflicted on friends and family were the subtle beginning of a principled thread in life.[10]

Instructors were obliged to teach not only English, but also the Anglo-Saxon version of American history, form of government, and principles of equality as if they were faithfully practiced in New Haven. It was probably Val's first introduction to the hypocrisy of Anglo-Saxon values, the formal imposition of the unsubtle directive: "citizenship means be just like us"; actually, be just like we tell you to be.[11]

Val would not give up the Neapolitan dialect. His later penchant for speaking and reading multiple languages was encouraged by the culture and grammar of Neapolitan, multiple other Italian dialects and languages used by neighbors and friends, and English from early in childhood—what each word meant to the user as well as to the listener and reader. Model Italian had been introduced as a course in New Haven's high school. Val was exposed to it (and found it was never purely distinct from the dialects, less so as it was freshened by literature and usage) and to Neapolitan in operas, stage shows, radio, and what he later acknowledged was his "favorite hobby: Reading." Through his cousin, Joseph DiCerbo, he likely also was introduced to Latin. He was becoming a historian of language in a practical way related to life. He also was coming to appreciate the allegory: looking for the hidden meaning, searching for the underlying truth, motive, or goal. The allegory is a central intellectual, instructional, and advocacy imperative in Catholicism, which in varying forms was everywhere around him, including in his home.[12]

&

Through Val's college years, more than eighty Italian immigrant self-help community groups existed in New Haven, with formal membership of ten thousand, informal family membership making the total closer to thirty thousand. They provided burial funds; unemployment aid; fresh food; sickness stipends; courses in Italian history, English, drawing, and sewing; and the ubiquitous "outing." Added to the practical collegiality of these settings were the Industrial Sports Leagues, the Church Leagues, the Society Leagues, softball, baseball, basketball, football, and bowling—each game regularly attended, engaged in by men and women, reported on daily in the newspapers and followed closely.[13]

The Circolo di San Carlino, close to the Giammatteis' home, held benefit performances in the Society's five-hundred-seat theater to raise funds for the construction of St. Michael's Church and to provide the opportunity for community members to perform dramatic, dance, operatic, and musical skills—the mandolin, the piano, the violin—that were supported by an encouraging audience, actually another form of "hard work" that would ensure confidence, poise, and an appreciation of possibilities in life. The early life of operatic performer Rosa Ponselle (Ponzillo) is one such example. Guided by operatic lessons and her parents, encouraged by New Haven entrepreneur and New England vaudeville impresario Sylvester Poli, and financially aided by her friends—including nationally famed and locally beloved surgeon Dr. William Verdi—Ponselle performed regularly at the Café Mellone on Center Street in New Haven and in the San Carlino Society's theater until she was able to say "that I, Rosa Ponselle from New Haven, was what the Metropolitan needed for *La forza del destino*, which [Enrico] Caruso was crazy to sing." They did it together, in 1918, at the Metropolitan Opera House. In 1921, she sang at the dedication of the Tomb of the Unknown Soldier in Arlington, Virginia. Her success wasn't seen as merely individual accomplishment but as the valued possibility of community encouragement. Dr. Verdi and Sylvester Poli would later play a similar role in the life of Valentine Giamatti.[14]

Within these societies, the dialogue was about generational transition into a new, at times hostile culture in which the experience of others mattered. Angelo and Maria were among those models. Val would have witnessed the basis for his parents' reputation and would have participated in their friendships.[15] These community societies also reflected the deep-seated distrust of government's willingness to, with fairness, help others acculturate into America—the "Northern problem" transferred to another, now American iteration. The societies were critical to combating the uncertainty of fate. Southern Italians and other immigrants and newly arrived migrants recognized that the democratic values they had fought for were at stake, as were the family and neighbors they banded together to help. Alexis de Tocqueville, with his appreciation of "public associations in civil life," would have immediately recognized this ethic and applauded the reality of its practice. He also appreciated that such conduct was not derivative of England's values or so "constantly or adroitly used in that country."[16]

৵

Acculturation was challenged daily. Responsibility for managing the transition fell primarily on women—mothers and daughters. The duty to exercise that responsibility carefully was Maria Giammattei's. It centered on managing money, dealing with ethnic slurs and discriminatory conduct—experienced by her son, Val, and typically directed against Italians seeking employment—and ensuring proper conduct outside the home.[17]

In July 1910, Sylvester Poli—who supported the discontent among Italian workers over their wages and conditions of employment and the efforts on their behalf by his neighbor, Augusta Lewis Troup—challenged the manner in which *only* "Italian" ethnicity was selected for print in the *New Haven Evening Register* (owned by John Day Jackson, Yale 1890) each time someone was arrested. "In reading the daily newspapers during the past fifteen years [when Jackson's father took control] . . . ," Poli wrote in a letter to the editor, "how rarely do we read the newspaper description of a crime committed by John Jones, an American, James Blank, an Englishman, or Paul Dash, a Frenchman. . . . Why then this insidious distinction against the Italian?" This discrimination, Poli wrote, "is an unfair reflection of a people, the great overwhelming majority of whom are . . . law abiding." It is "a fact . . . that the constant repetition . . . does tend to degrade

Angelo Giammattei and his grandson, George Urquhart (Bart's cousin).
Giamatti-Ewing Collection and Giammattei-Lavorgna Family Collection.

[Italians] in the eyes of their fellow-citizens." Poli's letter had little effect. The Neapolitan heritage also had proverbs, guidance in practical ways to deal with slurs and reflect proper conduct. "The most often heard of these proverbs," wrote Anthony Riccio, "was '*Fa Buon'e scurda, fa male e pensa.*' Do good [actions] and forget, do bad and think about it. . . . Wrongful actions eventually bring their own punishment." And to avoid bringing shame to the family name within the neighborhood and the institutions of America, '*Cammina con una faccia pulita,*' Always walk with a clean face."[18] Adherence was required daily.[19]

Managing money was the most transformative imperative in establishing their family's definition of citizenship. "It was the women who saved the money," Riccio said. "They had the toughness to manage." Maria witnessed it in her family and village. In America, the regularity of industrial wages ensured a predictable weekly sum. Angelo was on solid ground historically at New Haven Clock.[20] Savings came from managing expenses: walking to work, mending clothes (knowing how to "turn" Angelo's dress shirt collars), and repairing shoes.

The sacrifices were not shared evenly. Women carried a heavier burden, though the expectation to contribute to each other's well-being, regardless of gender, was taught daily. Val's relationship with his sisters and his appreciation for both the decisive role of strong-willed women and the contribution they made to his life never left him and was conveyed especially to his son Bart. An errant, improperly dressed, or underfed child was recognized—at school and in the neighborhood. Maria Giammattei ensured that never happened.[21]

YALE'S LABORATORY FOR EXPERIMENTS

In June 1907, the mayor of New Haven, John P. Studley—a Republican (Yale 1875)—appointed a committee that would "employ experts to prepare a plan for the improvement of New Haven." The committee was composed almost exclusively of Yale graduates. The members included industrialists—among the wealthiest men in Connecticut—who contributed a modest $100 each to its operation. Five months after the committee was named, in response to public complaints that it excluded women and Italians, the committee added "Mr. Poli . . . in order that our Italo-American citizens might be represented." It's unclear what role, if any, Poli actually played.[22]

The committee retained two men of renown to undertake the study and prepare the plan, both capable of bold vision yet precisely the kind of intimate detail essential for neighborhood and architectural preservation: Cass Gilbert, who already was commissioned to design the New Haven Public Library and the needed railroad station, and the landscape architect Frederick Law Olmsted Jr., who with his father had designed and helped give practical life to parks, roadways, and new communities throughout the nation. By 1910, the City Beautiful Movement, which both men defined, had melded into variations of urban subtlety, which architectural historian Alan Plattus correctly described in his later review of the 1910 Plan. City Beautiful advocates had learned from their experiences, beginning with the Chicago Columbian Exposition in 1893 (built on a massive swamp) led by Daniel Burnham and Olmstead Sr. (with Jr.'s participation) and the post-Exposition plan for densely urban Chicago. The planners discovered how to blend design refinements, how to persist in advancing practical schemes that would serve *all* a city's residents, and how to attract private sector enthusiasm and financing. That was precisely the methodology Gilbert and Olmsted Jr. knew was critical to the success of New Haven's plan.[23]

Unheeded or unwelcomed by the committee's members was the admonition that Gilbert and Olmsted Jr. shared in light of the demographic studies they commissioned. The Olmsted family also had lived in Connecticut and knew the condescending temperament of the committee's "New England stock" and the insular protectiveness of the Yale culture. New Haven, the two men wrote and Plattus noted, "is being transformed from the pleasant little New England college town of the middle nineteenth century, with a population of relatively independent, individualistic and self-sufficing householders [that is, 'the New England stock'], into the widespread metropolis of the twentieth century, the citizens of which will be wholly dependent upon joint action for a very large portion of the good things of civic life." And, "The matter of first importance is the population"—that the changes should ensure both widespread benefits and the *full sharing* of the required physical alterations.[24] "People of the old New England stock," Gilbert and Olmsted Jr. wrote "still *to a large extent control the city,* and if they want New Haven to be a fit and worthy place for their descendants it behooves them to establish conditions about the lives of *all* [emphasis in the original] the people that will make the best fellow-citizens of them and their children. . . . [A] *laissez faire* policy applicable to New England Yankees is not going to suffice for them." That is, step up, share in the physical alterations, and raise private funds.[25] Gilbert and Olmsted Jr.'s second admonition also was borne of both men's experience: fear that the architect would act alone and determine the form or control the fate of the plan. Plattus described it this way: "That tension, which has provided one of the central themes in the history of American architecture and urbanism . . . is certainly lurking behind one of the main premises of the 1910 Plan: the need for collective responsibility and action to temper the worst effects of individualism." This second admonition had deeper meaning than Gilbert or Olmsted Jr. may have appreciated.[26]

෴

The plan's merits, recognized then and later, derived from its smartly conceived grand vision—an expansive tree-lined parkway that connected the New Haven Green (and new library) via a public square to the new railway station, with the essential preservation of neighborhoods through the deliberate adjustment of street setbacks, lot reconfigurations, and enhanced and new parks. The plan also envisioned a new transit line, civic monuments, and street widening *in the Yale neighborhood and near the university proper.* Olmsted Jr. added particularly his respect for the existing street grid, which signaled his respect for the neighborhoods, and with prescience he adhered to the principles Jane Jacobs later embraced. Mayor Frank Rice's proposal to ensure municipal financing for new and repaired sidewalks and related streetscapes was a Jacobsian affirmation of critical practicality. In 1913, the mayor and elected legislators also created the City Plan Commission, led by committee member George Dudley Seymour, and in time established a new zoning ordinance and public aspects of the plan. The mayor did what he said he would do.[27]

Olmsted Jr. and Gilbert were worried, though not about the mayor. To arouse meaningful private financial support, they needed to speak for the plan not in the neighborhoods but at Yale and address the skeptics in and affiliated with the university. They held multiple talks at Yale's School of Fine Arts. Their unease was justified. The failure of the largely Yale-affiliated establishment (and Yale as an institution) to provide financing through a variety of techniques used imaginatively elsewhere—Chicago, especially from 1901 with its largely privately financed 1907 Chicago Plan, was the national model—ensured that the 1910 Plan, in its most important visual and practical respect, did not take hold.[28] The "old Yankee stock" remained tight fisted and lacked vision, and Yale's embedded parochialism would not allow it to embrace changes to its own geographic sphere of existence regardless of the benefit to New Haven.[29]

The 1910 Plan remained a "top-down," Yale/New England stock–generated plan, with New Haven as the immovable site for experimentation. It was a disquieting precedent. The institutionalization of eugenics at Yale would shortly transform New Haven's neighborhoods into "laboratories." Within less than a generation, Yale, accompanied by the insecure New Haven mayor, Richard C. Lee, would declare war on the 1910 Plan through conduct, public money, and a perspective that neither respected New Haven history and democratic experience nor had any regard for the integrative value of urban neighborhoods. Unlike the 1910 Plan, none of the Yale/Lee "urban renewal" experimentation occurred within the areas considered "Yale," and little if any money came from New Haven's industrial, business, Yale, and "New England stock" leaders. Valentine Giamatti would be in the middle of Yale's eugenics assault. His son Bart would witness the same mentality in Yale's wholesale distain for New Haven's neighborhoods.

THE CHALLENGE TO CITIZENSHIP

While Val attended grammar school, in November 1919 and again in January 1920 A. Mitchell Palmer, the attorney general of the United States, incited the nation with his infamous raids, aided by local and state officials and supported by industrialists and Protestant religious leaders. Though a broad range of nationalities were suppressed, Italians "bore the brunt of the outrage."[30] Most Italians in New Haven believed at first that the raids did not risk exposing *legitimate* radical activists (certainly not for the Giammatteis when Angelo had dutifully registered for the draft in 1918 as required by law), but that they risked applying broadbrush stereotyping of the group of which they were part. Also demonstrated with clarity was that "law," in the hands of the attorney general of the United States, could be—and was—implemented in a malleable, malicious way by those who controlled it. In Connecticut, most raids and arrests were made without warrants or adjudicated without actual trials. Men and women were placed into prison cells without sanitation, amid numbing cold and demeaning filth. The raids were directed against alien immigrants, especially Russian and Eastern European Jews and Italians, though others, including those born in America, were arrested for having spoken critically of capitalism. Labor union activists were the central focus; membership was presumptive evidence of disloyalty. Justice Department agents lied in affidavits.[31]

Seventeen Connecticut cities, including New Haven, were subjected to unpredictable intrusions into homes and union halls. Italian immigrants already had organized strikes and complained of poor working conditions in New Haven's industries. They had a reputation for insisting on a definition of fairness that few industrialists shared. They remained vulnerable and visible. It did not matter that more than three hundred thousand Italian Americans served in the Armed Services. The *New Haven Evening Register* sent a forceful, insidious signal to teachers, employers, government officials, political leaders, academics, and classmates, and to Italians like Angelo and Maria, about who warranted watching: "There are citizens of the United States . . . born under other flags . . . who have poured the poison of disloyalty into the very arteries of our national life," warned President Woodrow Wilson.[32] During the second raid in January, more New Haven workers were arrested for distributing pamphlets that advocated the formation of labor unions. The *Register* denounced them as "undesirables."[33]

Criticism directed against Palmer did not change his underlying imperative. The law was intended to preserve an Anglo-Saxon–dominated capitalist system. Within a year, two new arrests were made related to a bank robbery in South Braintree, Massachusetts: Bartolomeo Vanzetti and Nicola Sacco. In Italy, Benito Mussolini soon emerged as the nation's leader, with the aid of black-shirted thugs and an ideology supported by American industrialists, bankers, the Catholic Church, and the president of Yale. Mussolini's rise would further place Italian immigrants and their children into a caldron of infamy not of their making. Many immigrants, including the Giammatteis, learned a lesson about identity—that theirs had become the subject of unfettered public and private scrutiny. In raising children born in America, these immigrants learned that yet more care and discipline were required; that is, more skill would be needed to negotiate a place where aspirations and stability could be met in a manner reflective of their own values.[34]

THE YORK SQUARE CAMPUS

When Val Giamatti entered New Haven High School in 1924, he was placed in the Classical Program for college-bound students. His primary sustenance, the stability and principles of conduct in his life, came from two sources: his family and his Fair Haven neighborhood.

New Haven High School, when first constructed on York Square in 1893 and 1894, was composed of two grand buildings designed in the Collegiate

Gothic style on a unique six-acre campus of walkways, trees, benches, shrubbery, and lighting. It was located on Yale's northern periphery. The campus was readily accessible by walking and trolley—including through Yale's public streets—from all of the city's neighborhoods.

Hillhouse High School (named for James Hillhouse, Yale 1773) had an academic curriculum that covered the liberal arts and classical studies, including Latin and Greek. Its faculty included Hillhouse's own graduates (the school was originally founded in 1859 in the center of New Haven), many of whom had received degrees from Yale and the French-inspired New Haven Normal School. The leading administrators lived throughout the city. From its first graduate to enter Yale in 1861, Hillhouse described its intention plainly: "The majority of High School boys in college preparatory courses prepare for Yale; the girls prepare for various colleges for women," including "Mount Holyoke, Smith, Vassar, and Wellesley." Hillhouse was a feeder school to Yale. It was compared in quality to Boston Latin.[35]

Boardman Manual Training School (referred to as Boardman Trade) was constructed first. It offered educational programs in practical trades to those residents wanting their children to learn carpentry, plumbing, electrical wiring, printing, woodworking, metal work, fashion design, and business accounting, all taught by men and women who were masters in the trade. Hillhouse and Boardman Trade were connected by an exterior walkway on three levels, which allowed students to choose classes in both settings.[36]

The third school—Commercial High School, later renamed for Wilbur Cross (Yale 1885, PhD 1889, graduate school dean, and former governor)—was built in 1920 in a similar architectural style. Dr. William Verdi, Education Board president, supported the expanded opportunity for high school diplomas and college education sought by immigrant communities, trade unions, and business interests. Collectively, the campus served three thousand to thirty-five hundred students daily. The three schools were considered "perhaps the finest, the most notable, the most progressive, and largest in size and numbers in New England." By the second decade of the twentieth century, the urban campus educated first- and second-generation Jewish, Italian, Polish, African American, Irish, and Catholic students.[37]

⁂

Val Giamatti was tall, rapier thin, and sinewy, his hair full, brown, and neatly combed; he was strikingly handsome and agile in his gait. Fashionable suits, tweed jackets, white shirt, tie, and starched collar marks every photograph taken of him during his four years of high school. So, too, does a warm, yet reserved temperament. He was studious, not easily distracted but easily approachable. Val's class included John Foster Furcolo, Eugene Rostow, and Salvatore Joseph Castiglione. Furcolo, later Massachusetts' first Italian American governor, and

Castiglione, whose parents also emigrated from Southern Italy, remained close friends throughout Val's life. The four were walking the path once traversed by Thomas Bergin (Hillhouse 1921, Yale 1925, PhD 1929) and would leave a slightly more worn one for Vincent Scully (Hillhouse 1936, Yale 1940, MA 1947, PhD 1949). Bergin and Scully were faculty members at Yale during Bart Giamatti's presidency.[38]

᷄ঌ

Yale's new president, James Rowland Angell, appointed in 1921, enhanced the university's physical stature (with the aid of John Sterling's large bequest), brought the school closer to the York Square campus, and also strengthened Yale's academic vitality (including the reintroduction of Model Italian). Because the university "wished to encourage able undergraduates to consider teaching as a career. . . . It seemed of prime importance that those students who were to be teachers of the next college generation should acquire finesse and poise of character." A highly regarded program of graduate study in education administration and teaching was introduced that would remain vital and praised until eliminated, amid local disappointment and frustration, by President A. Whitney Griswold in the 1950s.[39]

In an enduring way, however, Angell's ascendancy only further detached Yale from the city, especially from its Italian immigrant and Italian American citizens. Yale had begun the formal institutionalization of eugenics. President Angell, generously supported financially by the Carnegie and Rockefeller foundations, the Laura Spelman Rockefeller Memorial Fund, and the Yale Corporation, was one of eugenics' most powerful national advocates. His advocacy was not an "episode" or confined to the actions of a few "malicious" personalities. Eugenics continued in various forms long thereafter, from what historian Christine Rosen described as the "non-institutional roots Eugenics planted in the U.S. culture." Its insidious harm, eventually with fatal effect to the York Square campus and the city's neighborhoods, intensified at the time Valentine Giamatti entered Hillhouse High School in the fall of 1924.[40]

THE DARKEST AURA AND ITS REACH

THE EMBEDDED CULTURE OF YALE'S EUGENICS

The irregular area of land that made up Yale University comprised individuals (its student body and much of its faculty) who were largely white, Anglo-Saxon, and Protestant—that is, self-proclaimed "American." Along with the blocks that housed Yale faculty (and the older Anglo-Saxon neighborhoods nearby), "Yale" was segregated.[1] Three exceptions primarily occurred only during the daytime: the entrance of maids, maintenance workers, and clerical personnel, most of whom lived in New Haven; full-time students who were "day students"—that is, those students who lived at home and commuted daily to class, which may have been one-quarter or more of the student body; and the students of New Haven High School located on the York Square campus.[2]

To Yale's south and southwest was the Hill/Oak Street/Legion Avenue neighborhood. To its north was the Dixwell Avenue/Newhallville neighborhood, which was evolving from a largely Jewish, Irish, Italian, and indigenous African American neighborhood to a commercially vibrant, socially committed community—Baptist, Congregationalist, and Catholic churches, and, in short order, the Dixwell Community House—of migrating African Americans.[3]

To Yale's east and southeast was downtown New Haven, originally planned in nine squares, which followed, as described by Vince Scully, the New Haven–born Yale architectural historian, a model derivative of "the Spanish monk Juan Bautista Villalpando."[4] The plan's northern boundary served as a cultural entranceway or, as Yale sought architecturally and almost as an implicit form of preserving cultural purity, more like the outer edge of a moat. The massive "double frontage" construction on Elm Street, and along Chapel and College streets began in the 1870s without consulting the citizens of New Haven. The construction evoked "alarm" and disquiet deeply rooted, and, in short order, the first of many long, hard-fought legal and civic challenges by New Haven into the 1890s as to which among Yale's buildings were, in fact and law, publicly funded by Connecticut taxpayers, aided financially by New Haven residents, or legitimately tax exempt. The "alarm" was for good reason. There was a history, even by the turn of the century and not unrelated to the physical, financial, and cultural harm still to come, that was worthy of a reckoning—fought, lurking still, and then fought again. There was no hiding behind the moat.[5] "It cannot be stressed too much that the college has never been wholly a private institution," Yale historian Kelley wrote. "At first it was the beneficiary of aid from the colony and the people of Connecticut. Throughout the eighteenth century Connecticut's contribution [the euphemism for taxpayer-funded appropriations] amounted to more than one half the total gifts to the college. . . . [and] since 1745 it has been indirectly subsidized, to one degree or another, by city, state, and nation through its exemption from taxation."[6]

Beyond architecture, there were the roughly intrusive, felonious, at times riotous temper of Yale students themselves and the complacency or unwillingness of its administrators to quell their conduct throughout the nineteenth and into the twentieth century. The students' view of civic responsibility was detached from their place in New Haven as a community. It was unclear who should be held accountable for their behavior.[7]

∞

The university founders' Calvinist superiority, though sometimes cloaked in Congregationalist garb, was rarely restrained. When, in 1726, Yale chose Elisha Williams (thirty-two years old, the youngest man ever to lead Yale), they did so knowing he "was firmly attached to Calvinism. . . . 'It was the grim God of unalterable law he preached, not the God of love of the older ministers and of his fathers.' Nothing could have been more pleasing to the trustees. . . ."[8] The thread of that Calvinist mentality, the Jonathan Edwards "elect," what Vernon Parrington believed was a "misfortune" in the depth of its "intolerance," found a more pervasive, permanently embedded iteration that governed Yale and was felt in New Haven and throughout the nation through the twentieth century. Yale graduate Madison Grant (Class of 1887) confirmed the legitimacy of what was to come in his book, *The Passing of the Great Race*, published in 1916. "It has taken us fifty years [since the end of the Civil War]," Grant wrote, "to learn that speaking English, wearing good clothes, and going to school and to church, does not transform a negro into a white man. . . . [and America faces] the Polish Jew, whose dwarf stature, peculiar mentality, and ruthless concentration of self-interest are being grafted upon the [Anglo-Saxon] stock of the nation." Grant's denigration of Southern Italians was well known: "A group not homogeneous with the old native American population is the Italian. It began arriving after 1870 then it soon became a flood. . . . Northern Italy has furnished some fine types of immigrants. . . . Southern Italy, . . . which formed the great mass of Italian immigration . . . was of extremely inferior type. . . . Of quite a different racial stock from those of the more northerly provinces." "In America," Grant continued, "we have nearly succeeded in destroying the privilege of birth; that is the intellectual and moral advantage a man of good stock brings into the world with him. We are now engaged in destroying the privilege of wealth."[9]

Grant's view—and that of others—flowed easily into the receptive pores of the "elect" mentality that tempered Yale from the outset. So, too, did Owen Johnson's (Yale 1900) *Stover at Yale*, published in 1912, the less-than-fictional "unique and unforgettable college hero. One of the 'chosen.'" Kingman Brewster's biographer wrote that, "Brewster and most other freshmen . . . had already been indoctrinated in the Yale spirit by Owen Johnson's great college novel. . . . On football Saturdays, most undergraduates rode out to the Yale Bowl in old-fashioned yellow streetcars that ran along Chapel Street, pitching pennies to local children who ran alongside the cars." "We knew we were the elite of the country," one of Brewster's classmates put it. For Johnson, and Stover, the people of New Haven often reflected (in a characterization that lingered for author Lewis Lapham, Yale 1956) "the stench of the town." After a raucous time at "[Sylvester] Poli's Daring-Dazzling-Delightful Vaudeville" theater, one of Stover's classmates said: "Let's get out of here. . . . There's nothing but xylophones and coons left." Later, Stover's classmates captured a longhaired dog, and, with delight, "they beheld an Italian barber lolling in the doorway of his shop." The barber—portrayed with broken English and a simple mind—offered to cut the dog's hair. When he asked to get paid, they informed him the dog was not theirs:

> "Shall we run for it?" said Waters, as they went hurriedly up the
> block.
>
> "Wait until Garibaldi gives chase—we must be dignified," said
> McNab, with an eye to the rear.
>
> "Dagos have no sense of humor. Here he comes with a razor—scud
> for it!"[10]

That racially tinged rhetoric and the university's fairly consistent, condescending attitude toward New Haven and its neighborhoods also were boldly embraced among the university's administration and, as deeply if not as blatantly, among its most prominent faculty.[11]

THE YALE SOLUTION

The "science" of eugenics emerged with visible notoriety in 1883, when the Englishman Francis Galton, a cousin of Charles Darwin, claimed to prove that humans evolved through hereditary genes unaffected by the environment or learning. We were all largely fixed in place, certainly by the late nineteenth century, the theory concluded. Galton's "science" was *measurement*: body type—eyes, skin, and hair color, height, posture, and especially the human brain, its size and shape. Being among the Anglo-Saxon elite (Galton's model) had nothing to do with education, group or individual experience, or luck. John Calvin would have added that God ensured their elevated place. Later eugenicists did, including from the pulpit. The "solution," as it evolved, foremost in the United States, was stated unequivocally: select and segregate the "feeble-minded" and "unfit" (defined through changing, often arbitrary variables) into institutionalized "colonies" with little more than basic custodial care, compile lists of people and families unworthy of procreation or marriage, and perform sterilization, or worse, without consent.[12]

Eugenics was discredited quickly and criticized forcefully by the Catholic Church. "Science," however, was hardly the force in play. In England, Galton's solutions, though not his presumptions, largely lapsed. In Germany, eugenics already had advocates with enduring yet still limited appeal. In America, eugenics took on virulent vitality, especially, in Jerome Karabel's words, from the "iconic institutions, exerting a broad influence on the national culture": Princeton, Harvard, and Yale.[13]

⚬⚬

Yale's Madison Grant, a politically connected New York patrician born into wealth and colonial heritage and the founder of the New York Zoological Society; Theodore Lothrop Stoddard (Harvard 1905), a member of a wealthy Protestant family; and Henry Fairfield Osborn (Princeton 1877), president of the Museum of Natural History, were among eugenics' most vocal proponents. Stoddard's writings were "standard reading at the Army War College"; his book elevating Anglo-Saxons, *The Rising Tide of Color against White World-Supremacy*, was praised publicly—in the South—by President Warren G. Harding.[14] Ministers took to the pulpit. Christine Rosen summarized the religious doctrine: "The Kingdom of God required eugenically fit believers."[15]

Four practical forces elevated the Grant-Stoddard-Osborn "solution": fear that Southern Italian immigrants (who were also Catholic) and Russian and Eastern European Jews would infect the nation's gene pool; deep racial and financial fear by industrialists that continued advocacy for African American Reconstruction–era rights (voting and education particularly) would ensure a recurrence of civil war; the loss in the Civil War of the upper strata of white Southern youths and the need to replenish their loss by constricting the propagation of others (to do otherwise, Theodore Roosevelt declared publicly, was "Race Suicide"); and, among the universities that claimed to educate white Anglo-Saxon leaders (Yale, Harvard, and Princeton), the deep apprehension that the children of Jewish immigrants, particularly, would displace Anglo-Saxons if intellectual merit alone determined admission. "When different races intermarry," Stoddard wrote, "the offspring is a mongrel—a walking chaos so consumed by his jarring heredities that he is quite worthless." Grant, with the patina of scientific precision, called interracial marriage "disharmonic combinations."[16]

YALE'S REACH NATIONALLY AND IN WASHINGTON, DC

In 1910, the Carnegie Institute of Washington, DC, established the Eugenics Record Office in Cold Spring Harbor, New York, which operated for the next twenty-five years. It was visible, aggressive, and predatory. States submitted lists of people who should be institutionalized. The office compiled its own list.[17] Indiana took the lead in enacting sterilization laws. Connecticut followed. Lawsuits stopped them and others, and more legal action was likely.[18] The leading advocate and crafter of a new legal approach was the Eugenic Record Office's Harry Laughlin (Princeton 1917, DSc), who had become an "expert" on eugenics. Following the Second International Conference on Eugenics in 1921, the Eugenics Committee of the U.S.A. was formed; in 1925 it was renamed the American Eugenics Society. The AES's founders included Harvard-educated Robert Yerkes, Princeton-educated Laughlin, professors Irving Fisher and Ellsworth Huntington of Yale, and Yale Medical School Dean Milton C. Winternitz. The AES was funded primarily by the Carnegie Foundation. Carnegie's president, albeit briefly but when it mattered, was James Rowland Angell.[19]

Congress enacted immigration restrictions in 1910, began to fund eugenics studies in 1911 at the rigorous prompting of Yale's Fisher, and enacted more restrictions in 1917 based, in part, on Senator Henry Cabot Lodge's model for restricting Italian immigrant voting in Massachusetts. Fisher found welcomed affirmation from the nationally circulated *Good Housekeeping* and the *Saturday Evening Post* and from Vice President–elect Calvin Coolidge ("Whose Country Is This?"). In an effort directed primarily against Southern Italian and Jewish immigration, which was most feared, Congress enacted the 1924 Immigration Act (and the related National Origins Act) that, with other racial exclusions but no subtlety, allocated future immigration to the percentage of the racial stock that existed in America at the time of the 1890 census. Connecticut Senator Frank Brandegee (Yale 1885) voted for it.[20]

The law's restriction had numerous effects. Southern Italian and Eastern European Jewish immigration was severely curtailed. Those already here were singled out for opprobrium, the legal imposition of the negative stereotype. Northern European immigration expanded. Before the 1924 act was in place, the movie *Black Stork* (1917), which portrayed the value of deliberately allowing a "disabled" infant to die, was distributed publicly. By 1915, twenty-seven states had enacted statutes authorizing sterilization, followed soon thereafter by the formation of colonies of "unfit" persons and the enactment, primarily in the South, of statutes that barred interracial marriage or marriage of the "unfit" altogether.[21]

The definition of who was subject to the law of the "unfit" was broad and arbitrarily derived, and it fluctuated not merely from state to state but from "doctor" to "doctor." More than sixty thousand *recorded* sterilizations occurred in the United States. It is not known how many sterilizations occurred under the cloak of other operations, how many individuals were institutionalized and sterilized for "political" offenses, and how many bloodlines were flat out stopped among people not given the voice to understand, let alone oppose, the surgery. The effects are unknown on the people subjected to "study," indefinite in duration and psychologically or physically humiliating. Put differently, America had become, in yet a new iteration, a hard, scary, unpredictable place to raise children if they might fit someone's definition of "unfit."[22]

YALE'S REACH IN CONNECTICUT AND AT HOME

Connecticut followed Indiana's simple statutory model, initially with the strong advocacy of, among others, Yale botanist Edmund Sinnott, and George Henry Knight (Yale 1902, Honorary MA), superintendent of the Connecticut School for Imbeciles in Litchfield County. "The sturdy emigrant," Knight said, "who comes to this land of promise full of hope, brings his misfortunes with him. . . . The hard life of the women in the fields, perhaps the inheritance of generations of poverty and oppression,—all these make themselves felt in the number of defective children found among our foreign population." Five hundred and fifty-seven people were sterilized in Connecticut while the law was in effect. Women had oophorectomies (surgical removal of the ovaries) or salpingectomies (cauterizing of the fallopian tubes), and men had vasectomies. Approximately two hundred recorded operations were executed by 1924, primarily on women. What followed after congressional affirmation and federal endorsement was full-bore implementation and expansion of eugenics' solutions. Unsettled, and the subject of strategic discussion among eugenics' supporters, was the prospect of renewed judicial challenge to impede the effort. In the interim, the "solution's" imperative took predictable, strengthened form.[23]

Southern political and financial interests, especially the anti-immigrant, anti–Catholic, anti–African American Ku Klux Klan, prospered in their legitimacy aside the intellectual and cultural imprimatur from Princeton, Harvard, Yale, Carnegie, and Rockefeller, and the welcomed embrace of the Democratic and Republican parties. The Northeast had experienced it before. "Cotton thread holds the Union together," Ralph Waldo Emerson wrote in 1846, "united John C. Calhoun [the South Carolina senator, Yale 1804] and Abbott Lawrence [the leading New England textile manufacturer]. Patriotism for holidays and summer evenings, with music and rockets, but cotton thread is the Union." In his bid for mayor of New York City in 1835, Samuel F. B. Morse (Yale 1810), already a well-known inventor, advocated anti-immigrant and anti-Catholic restrictions; later he denigrated the democratic premise of the Declaration of Independence, and defended slavery's Christian virtue: "Slavery or the [broader] servile relation, is proved to be one of the indispensable regulators of the social system, divinely ordained. . . ." To oppose slavery, Morse contended, is a sin "worthy of excommunication." It was New Haven and Yale's *modus operandi* as well, including when Newport, Rhode Island, served as the second-largest port for the importation of slaves into the United States and certain of Yale's founders owned slaves or advocated slavery's virtue as based on God's imprimatur.[24]

༚

James Rowland Angell's intent to institutionalize eugenics into Yale's curriculum and building program took form quickly. The AES national office was moved to New Haven, at 185 Church Street, and chaired by Yale Professor Irving Fisher;

Yale President James Rowland Angell.
Library of Congress.

the office moved later to 4 Hillhouse Avenue, easy walking distance to President Angell's office. The national headquarters would remain in New Haven for the next eighteen years, until 1939. Yale faculty members held the AES presidency twice: Fisher, from 1922 to 1926, and Huntington, from 1934 to 1938. In the interim, the presidency—the exercise of its powers included visits to New Haven and Yale—was held by, among others, Harry Laughlin (1927–1929).[25]

In short order, Angell brought to Yale two prominent eugenicists—Harvard's Yerkes and Clark Wissler, a "racial psychologist" and curator at the Museum of

Natural History.[26] By 1924, with funding from the Laura Spelman Rockefeller Memorial Fund and research funding commitments from Carnegie, Angell transformed the psychology discipline located in the Philosophy Department into a new Institute of Psychology. Its collective purpose was to enhance the depth of study (and advocacy) in, essentially, two areas: human migration and reproduction. The Institute of Psychology offered "a concrete example of institutionalized eugenic thinking at Yale." In 1925, Yale offered a course titled "Coercive Restrictive Eugenics"—described in the leading textbook of the era, *Applied Eugenics: You Are the Society*, as the relative merits of execution, castration, and sterilization.[27]

Angell's grander purpose, which slowly took interdisciplinary form involving virtually every department and school (especially the School of Medicine), was the Institute of Human Relations. With a "generous gift from the Rockefeller Boards," the Institute would be centrally located within the new Sterling Hall on Cedar Street, proximate to the Hill/Oak Street/Legion Avenue neighborhood, amid the immigrants that eugenics' advocates believed were unfit for admission into America. When a question arose about how to describe the Institute's purpose, Angell wrote privately to Princeton-educated Henry Osborn (with carbon copies to Provost Seymour, Professor Wilbur Cross, and Dean Winternitz) that, "Personally, I quite concur with you in your belief that in the long run better human breeding is far and away the most important single consideration in the improvement of human life."[28] Going forward, the integrative academic purpose Angell envisioned, like the spindling of a broad spider web no doubt nourished by the availability of funding and prestige, came to fruition. Angell and others on the faculty ensured that the "concrete example of . . . eugenics thinking" was now institutionalized throughout the university.[29]

There was one additional thread to the eugenicist definition of who constituted a "Nordic" or "Teutonic" that loomed above New Haven like a smarmy, circling apparition ready to materialize and pounce on its prey. Better still, ready to show that it belonged among the "fit." From the outset of Madison Grant's *The Passing of the Great Race*, "Nordic" included Northern Italy. The apparition, when ready to descend, would find its earthly nest in Yale's Institute of Human Relations.[30]

Forming the Intellectual Life

This hunger for personal liberty and yearning for freedom from exploitation. The very perception of a world unchanging in its harshness or hostility bred into its strength, including its strength to resist all outsiders, and bred into individual Italians, particularly the poor, as well a reticence and an instinct for independence.

—A. Bartlett Giamatti, "Commentary" in *The Italian Americans*, 1987

Hillhouse and Religion

Valentine Giamatti thrived culturally and intellectually at Hillhouse High School. The school's motto was modest and filled with expectation and promise: "We Finish to Begin." His class included thirty-five different nationalities (slightly less than half the class was female), a diversity he thrived in. He was a member of the French Club and the Debating Society, became vice president of the Italian Club, and was a member of the track team.[1]

It was likely at Hillhouse that Val had his first serious intellectual and in-depth experience with Jewish students, as friends and as thinkers. Throughout his life, he spoke to his children with deep respect and admiration for their accomplishments and diligent persistence, recalled with distinct clarity by his son Dino and daughter, Elria. "My father loved the Jews," she said. "The best students he had." No doubt his admiration stemmed from the candor with which his Jewish friends spoke and wrote about their family experience, encouraged by the Hillhouse faculty and known through parents, grandparents, and relatives in Eastern Europe and Russia. In the Hillhouse *Gleam*, one of the school's three literary publications, Anna Lev (Hillhouse 1927) wrote "The Pogrom." "The gloomy and dismal aspect of everything [in the village of Goudoff]," she began, "seemed to foretell that something evil was to happen. My grandmother knew that all this mystery meant a pogrom, or, in other words, a massacre of the Jews." Perhaps Val had heard the stories, passed on in the oral tradition typical of the Neapolitan culture, of how villages near his family's had been burned and people killed with crass wantonness. He'd likely heard and read about the lynching and

The Italian Club, 1928, in the Hillhouse High School yearbook.
Valentine Giamatti is in the first row, third from the right.
New Haven Historical Society.

malicious forms of discrimination that had occurred in America directed against
Italians and African Americans, an ugliness he'd been spared that, in all likelihood, only increased his appreciation for what Anna Lev had described with
such immediate poignancy. Neither suspected that her story foretold what lay
ahead. In important respects, the rationale for an eventual nation-sponsored methodical pogrom was being explored and aided right across the street.[2]

⁊

Though it's probable that Val was introduced to aspects of Dante's work at Strong
School, the meticulous, comprehensive introduction to the Italian Renaissance
occurred at Hillhouse. The analytical depth and form of his engagement that
would last a lifetime and affect his son related, in part, to his Catholicism and to
how his breach of faith occurred during this period.

   The Southern Italian immigrant experience with the Catholic Church can
best be characterized as gradations of irreverence. Southern Italians had experienced the clergy and hierarchy in Italy and the intolerance of the Irish priests in

New Haven enough to disconnect their belief in God, which most held, from the sometimes-liturgical superficiality and disrespectful conduct of the clergy. The clergy were entitled to cordiality, not deference. "Church" as an institution was as much a social place as it was a place of worship. There also was the practical role of the saints, called upon to provide guidance, protect family members in travel or illness, ensure good fishing and crops, or calm the weather. Saints were held accountable almost as people if they failed. Historian Anthony Riccio put it succinctly: "The church was smart enough to incorporate [Greek and Roman gods] into their [teachings and] organization. Look at Saint Michael for example—he's wearing a Roman legion outfit," the knight-warrior. Their depiction in statutes, paintings, and books fluctuated with the artist's studied vision, certainly made legitimate since Michelangelo fashioned the Sistine Chapel drawing largely on his own. Evil always took graphic form: Eden's apple, the horns and tail of the devil, the black ravages of disease, the slithering serpent. Purgatory took practical form: an actual place where final judgment was still uncertain, where you could languish in punishment of a kind conjured up arbitrarily by the priest or the Pope. And there was the Church's intolerance of dissent, condemning people and ideas (mostly from Italians) in forceful denunciations from Galileo or Giordano Bruno to the swift slash of the nun's ruler for saying "thank you" in Neapolitan.[3] All of these practices, filled with allegory, multiple meanings, interpretations, and leaps of faith and fate derived from Pagan myths and practices, were in Val's cultural milieu and were later understood by his son Bart.[4]

While Val was a student at Hillhouse, he took a prolonged summer camping trip north into Connecticut's forests and lakes—lush, green, and still primitive— his camping gear in tow, his neighbor and cousin Dolph Santello and two friends accompanying him. The trip to Lake Quassapaug was filled with fishing, hiking, good talks, and horsing around. On the way back, they stopped at a church. Val apparently wanted, if possible, to get some fresh water to share with his cousin or to make a phone call home. After a brief period, he walked out, angry and disappointed. The priest had refused his request. Val did not repeat what was said. One effect, over time, was estrangement, then departure. Though he may have continued to adhere to some rituals—his parents remained Catholic—he didn't bring the formal practice of Catholicism into his marriage, only the cultural heritage that imbued the Italian immigrant experience that he'd come to know.[5]

His departure loosened Val to explore the writings of Dante and others who treated Christianity as related to life, choices, and values explored without the constraint of faith, with the Church and clergy as symbols, icons, representative of something more than the Church defined. He was freed to seek truth or, certainly, reason and the application of imagination—allegory. There also was the quintessential virtue of departure, closely connected to the values he had witnessed that became central to his life and, later, to his son's: fairness in dealing with people, openness in dealing with ideas.

HILLHOUSE AND MODERN LANGUAGES

In the spring of 1925 and in December 1926, the Connecticut chapter of the New England Modern Language Association held its annual public meeting on the New Haven High School campus at Hillhouse. The meeting brought together, in formal (symposiums) and informal (teas, smokers) public discussion, well-known university and private and public high school linguists devoted to the form and manner of teaching romance languages. It was an exciting time historically. Many academic settings were introducing new methods (fast learning, emersion in various ways, experiences drawn from training linguists during World War I) of teaching romance languages (French, Italian, and Spanish) and their history, literature, and culture. Relevant to Val's (and later, Bart's) vocational direction and friendships, it was roughly during this time that Middlebury College began its highly regarded summer language program, and shortly thereafter, its program in English at nearby Bread Loaf, Vermont.

Yale's newly appointed associate professor of Italian, Angelo Lipari, was among the participants in the Hillhouse-based meetings. The discussions mixed erudite Italian, French, and Spanish pronunciation with funny asides and deep insights expressed in the dialect heard from family members in ways the convention of language could not capture. Reverence for the profession of teaching was entwined with the headiness of breaking new ground. It was here that Val met Lipari and that Val's interest in teaching acquired the knowledge of practical, engaging possibility.[6]

THE REALITY OF LAW WITHOUT FAIRNESS

As Val Giamatti prepared to enter his senior year, the immigrant and migrant families of New Haven were struck with two successive and, for some, decisive dictates about what America's elected and judicial officials meant by "law."

On May 2, 1927, the United States Supreme Court decided *Buck v. Bell*, which affirmed the legality of the state-imposed sterilization of Miss Carrie Buck. Connecticut's existing law was affirmed implicitly. President Angell's decision to elevate and institutionalize eugenics at Yale was affirmed as well. So, too, was the attitude of its graduates and those in New Haven who held tightly to the same mentality of prejudice.

The decision was brief, without nuance, and it barely mentioned Carrie Buck or questioned the "science" that warranted her institutionalization and surgery. Oliver Wendell Holmes elevated his Boston Brahmin ancestry (his father had favored eugenics' principles, as he did himself) and unconstrained parochialism into nationally acceptable ideology. "It is better for all the world," he wrote, "if instead of waiting to execute degenerate offspring for their crime, or to let

2065   High School. New Haven, Conn.

James Hillhouse High School, at the time that Val Giamatti attended it.
Joseph Taylor Collection.

them starve for their imbecility, society can prevent those who are manifestly unfit from continuing their kind. The principle that sustains compulsory vaccination is broad enough to cover cutting the Fallopian tubes. . . . Three generations of imbeciles are enough."[7] It did not matter that Carrie Buck had conceived not because she was "unfit" or "promiscuous," but because she had been raped. The decision was 8–1. Only Justice Pierce Butler dissented. No legislature or governor or president could have accomplished it: sterilization and the underlying rationale of eugenics became the law of the land.[8]

Connecticut's legal apparatus continued unabated with yet more confidence. In Virginia, Carrie Buck's fallopian tubes were "cauterized using carbolic acid followed by alcohol." The long-sought strategic outcome had been attained. More states followed with new statutes. More doctors were assured they were justified in performing sterilization.[9]

෴

The second hammer of fate fell quickly from the same court. The trial and the jury determination of guilt of Sacco and Vanzetti in 1921 never left the news, certainly not in the daily Italian-language papers, the *Jewish Daily Forward*, the labor and national press, and the homes and communal societies of Italian immigrants. The controversy was, as Bart Giamatti recognized five decades later, "painful [and] redolent with injustice and suspicion." Within the immigrant community in New Haven, the apprehension was palpable and frightening. Much was at stake.[10]

As the appeals moved toward the scheduled execution in August 1927, attention to the controversy flared brightly. Demonstrations in support of both men occurred throughout the United States and eventually throughout the world to cities in the Far East, Europe, South America, Africa, Russia, Canada, and Australia. Respected newsmen, lawyers, and civil liberties advocates spoke and wrote about the judge's biased evidentiary rulings and statements. The *New Haven Evening Register* published its own and Associated Press stories daily, often on the front page.[11]

At Yale, in April and May 1927, the case drew serious attention, primarily because of Harvard Professor Felix Frankfurter's support of both men. His book, *The Case of Sacco and Vanzetti*, preceded by an article in the *Atlantic Monthly* magazine, and the analytic outspokenness of the Yale Law School faculty spotlighted the case. Yale College Dean Percy T. Walden, however, reflecting his own and, in all likelihood, President Angell's position, had a different take: "The Sacco-Vanzetti case is in the hands of the properly constituted authorities. I have confidence that it will be justly and legally executed."[12] Dozens of universities throughout the nation, through faculty resolution or petition, supported a new, impartial review of the prejudicial conduct that had permeated the trial. Among those doing so were President Mary Emma Woolley and sixty-one faculty members of Mount Holyoke College and 127 faculty members of Smith College.[13]

In the summer, under complaints from Italian societies in America, Mussolini sent an envoy to Massachusetts Governor Alvan Fuller but refused to say anything publicly in support of men who advocated political views antithetical to his rule. Both Sacco and Vanzetti were anti-Fascists. Mussolini only further separated himself from Italian Americans. Congressman Fiorello LaGuardia also interceded with Fuller. It didn't matter. After investigations by lawyers and journalists, one of the crime's actual perpetrators confessed. It didn't matter. Vanzetti's sister, Luigia, "slight, weighing less than 100 pounds" made the arduous journey from Villafalletto to see her brother and seek the intercession of the Catholic Church in Boston. It didn't matter. The legal team was then composed of Boston's most distinguished lawyers, joined by a young Pittsburgh lawyer, Michael Angelo Musmanno, who originally went to Boston at his own expense with his father's blessing. He carried a clemency petition from the Sons of Italy in America. The petition described the growing apprehension: "If these two men are placed upon the electric chair, a pall of gloom will settle over all Italians in this country. And the millions of law-abiding sons of Italy, from New York to California, now claiming the stars and stripes as their own, will wonder how, under the ample folds of liberty and equality of that beloved flag, the cause of true Americanization has been advanced. They will wonder if, after all, they are not outcasts. . . ."[14]

Luigia Vanzetti and Rosina Sacco, 1927.
Fotostock/NTProto Collection.

The legal team, following affirmation of the court's decision by the Lowell Committee, petitioned the United States Supreme Court to review the Massachusetts decision and asked individual Justices to stay the execution. Holmes denied it three times.[15] All of this conduct was covered in the *New Haven Evening Register* daily.[16]

At this juncture, the correlation of "law" to the exercise of unfairness was, to many immigrants, too plain to be worthy of any further expectation.

Ringing persistently into the soul of parents of Italian American children were Vanzetti's closing words in court: "I have suffered because I was an Italian, and indeed, I am an Italian." Resounding permanently in the still moments in Italian American households was the last plea, made by Rosina Sacco (wife of Nicola Sacco) and Luigia Vanzetti to Governor Fuller in his chambers, in the Boston State House, only hours before the scheduled execution. Musmanno was with them. "'In Italy we look upon America as a land of . . . mercy,'" Musmanno later recounted Luigia Vanzetti telling the governor. "'And you have the power of mercy. And will you not extend that mercy for these two tortured men, who have already suffered seven long years? Imagine how my heart was cut to pieces when after nineteen years, I saw my Barto so weak. . . . Has this great, good government of America not tortured him enough already? On my knees, oh, Governor!' and she knelt on the floor before him. 'I implore you, do not let America become known as the land of cruelty. I beg of you for mercy! Mercy! Mercy!' With rosary beads in her uplifted hands as tears flowed to the carpet under her knees, Miss Vanzetti prayed to [Fuller] for pity." It didn't matter. Musmanno recited the closing moment. "Mrs. Sacco, quivering, lent a trembling hand. I took Miss Vanzetti's other arm, and the three of us stumbled from the room."[17]

Front-page headlines in the *New Haven Evening Register* captured the controversy's closing moments: "Hope Wanes for Sacco and Vanzetti." New Haven's Rose Sansone, then thirteen years old, recalled their death vividly decades later: "Sacco and Vanzetti. They were innocent, you know. It was not right." She hesitated, searching. "There was a song. I heard it. It was about them. It was not right." On the night of August 22, 1927, her father walked with her to the street corner near their home in Fair Haven, only a few blocks from the Giammattei home, where they joined other neighbors, who waited quietly, one in restrained tears, perhaps still hoping as young Rose did that something would stop the execution. When it didn't, her father—my grandfather—took her hand and they walked back. Although she shared her views later in life with her children and me, she'd been admonished that night not to speak about it again in public. It was an imperative widely shared: how, for the time being, to avoid harm in overt and insidious forms.[18]

❦

To Bart Giamatti, writing in 1989, Virgil's *Aeneid*—the "poem about those who would become the Italic people"—was about "the making of a new city [and] *fato profugus*, [people] driven by fate." In his grandparents and then his father, Giamatti saw with clarity "faces for whom nothing is unfamiliar [and life is] without illusions." Aspirations for fairness or justice remained unyielding to all the forces in play.[19] Defining the principles of citizenship warranted yet more discipline, yet harder work, and the skill at negotiation to ensure their attainment. They certainly did for Valentine Giamatti.

THE STERLING SCHOLARSHIP

Val Giamatti's excellent academic accomplishment warranted, in the faculty's estimation, admission to Yale. With their recommendation and his success on the admissions test, he received a John Sterling (Yale 1864) Scholarship that would cover all four years of his tuition. It was a stroke of good fortune, not only because he could not otherwise afford to attend Yale. Sterling and those setting up the scholarship program insisted that a definite number be awarded to graduates of New Haven High School, selected jointly by the high school and the university.[20] Sterling ensured that New Haven residents (and others from Bridgeport, Stratford, the Naugatuck Valley, and Hartford) with the requisite merit and without connection by class, ancestry, financial contribution, or the legacy of a family graduate would be able to attend Yale.[21] For Val Giamatti, retaining the scholarship also meant he needed to maintain a high average for all four years and demonstrate earned income throughout the year. With his family's financial help and support, he would become a day student. That, too, was good fortune. The preservation of values, the ethic that formed citizenship, would remain solidly grounded. The expression of his intellect and the depth of his intent to "teach" was the central channel through which he could devote his energy. He also would confront another reality. "In the Yale College Class of 1927 . . . there were four students of Italian descent; three of their fathers had been born in Italy." When Val Giamatti anticipated his first class at Yale University in the fall of 1928, he knew he would be a pioneer—visible, watched, and specially judged.[22]

༄

On Friday, June 15, 1928, Valentine Giamatti graduated from New Haven High School's Classical Program with "honors for all four years." The graduation ceremony was held in Yale's Woolsey Hall in the sweltering heat. Seven hundred and ninety students sat attentively. On stage to hand out the diplomas was Mayor Thomas Tully.[23] The Giammattei family took their seats along with hundreds of other families and friends, neatly attired, waiting for a moment of historical importance.

Following the ceremonial pattern of welcome and experience-laden admonitions about the future, the New Haven High School Quartet walked solemnly to center stage. Prepared for them, in musical rendition, was the poem "Invictus"—Latin for "Unconquered"—written by William Ernest Henley. The audience turned from respectful to silent. For many of the graduates, Henley's individual persistence was read as their duty going forward to reflect the values derived from their family and neighborhood.

> Out of the night that covers me,
> Black as the pit from pole to pole,
> I thank whatever gods may be
> For my unconquerable soul.

In the fell clutch of circumstance
I have not winced nor cried aloud.
Under the bludgeoning of chance
My head is bloody, but unbowed.

Beyond this place of wrath and tears
Looms but the Horror of the shade,
And yet the menace of the years
Finds, and shall find me, unafraid.

It matters not how straight the gate,
How charged with punishments the scroll,
I am the master of my fate:
I am the captain of my soul.[24]

Diplomas were awarded that evening amid the cheers and relief of family, friends, school administrators, and teachers. The Woolsey Hall setting was grand, and the Giammatteis were, no doubt, joyous to have their son complete high school in America. They knew, too, that the family burden of helping him would continue for four more years, and that he could become the first to graduate from an American college in the city they called home. As he accepted his Honors diploma, handed to him by Mayor Tully, and he glanced briefly at the audience before him, perhaps he saw not only his own graduation four years to come but also the duty to ensure he'd not be the last in his family to do so.

❧

The six-acre York Square campus was the pivotal geographic place of interaction—and, through its daily attendance, a form of mutual educational and cultural exposure—between Yale and New Haven. Thirty-five hundred students daily walked or rode the trolley through the neighborhoods of New Haven, some worked part time close to school, and all became familiar with the center of New Haven as well as with each other. Memories made and aspirations shared in this urban and tightly knit intellectual and social setting brought students and faculty together, and the campus enhanced the architectural and long-term cultural purpose of the city. It was not until the mid-1930s, with the completed construction of Payne Whitney Gymnasium across the street and the construction nearby of the Hall of Graduate Studies, that Yale buildings appeared on the edge of the York Square campus. Both buildings were designed in an architectural style that melded with the three schools. At the time, the Board of Education and the administrations of both institutions considered the proximity an asset. Within less than a generation, the cultural value these schools provided for citizenship in New Haven would be torn asunder.[25]

8

The Yale He Entered

Negotiating Citizenship

Admission criteria for entering Yale College has been the decision-making juncture in which discrimination—racial, ethnic, and religious—has been the most easily and frequently exercised, often hidden beneath euphemisms like "character" and selecting "leaders." With respect to Hillhouse High School graduates, many of whom met the criteria for discriminatory exclusion in this era, their unquestioned intellect, the selection skill of the Hillhouse faculty, and, in an important way, the insight of John Sterling preempted or lessened the exercise of any such conduct by Yale officials. It was in this same era that President Angell, with a foresight even he could not have imagined would occur in practical effect under President A. Whitney Griswold, made the observation: "It seems quite clear that if we could have an Armenian massacre confined to the New Haven District, with occasional incursions into Bridgeport and Hartford, we might protect our Nordic stock almost completely."[1] Day students, Val particularly, had in their favor the *optional imperative*, thoughtfully exercised, that regular students did not: study, not away from other students but away from the cultural distraction and expectation embedded in the presumptuous meaning of "character" and "leaders."[2]

☙

By the turn of the century, once regular students were admitted, remaining at Yale had stopped being an intellectual task subject to a decisive level of expectation. Put differently, "deteriorating academic standards were a subject of intense internal discussion." The admission criteria premised on something other than committed intellect had yielded frustration among the faculty.[3] In *Stover at Yale*, for example, it's not until well into the story that any of the main characters actually study or even that others are respected for doing so.[4]

The "deteriorating academic standards" reached bottom in 1902. A committee chaired by Professor Irving Fisher, the avid eugenicist, concluded that, "in fact, hard study has become *unfashionable* at Yale." Threads to this problem had become icons of *acceptance* in admission and into the Yale culture: the value of "belonging," that of competing in sports or of entrance to social societies as an obligation to Yale (Brooks Mather Kelley attributed this value to preparation for the rough and tumble of the corporate free market), and something more subtle but pervasive—the notion of "Brave Mother Yale," in the words of a university song introduced in 1900, deliberately intended to elevate the enduring preservation of the institution among all other imperatives ("Fairer than Love of Woman, / Stronger than Pride of Gold.").[5] The athlete had become far more important in student life—and in forming the university's reputation—than the scholar. The anti-intellectual problem, with other serious consequences related to students' immaturity as citizens, had not left Yale's admission process well into the twentieth century.[6]

What appeared constant *among students*, particularly beneficial to day students and implicit in the principle rejected in *Stover at Yale*, was "Yale democracy" as practiced in that era with respect to each other, albeit only while they were students. Thomas Bergin, who became a friend of Val Giamatti's while they were both in Yale's graduate school, confirmed this dichotomy in his own recitation of what it was like being a day student, who, because of the need to have gainful employment, "could not [like 'the average Yalie'] afford to waste time." "My undergraduate Yale," Bergin explained, ". . . had been for many years, a school for the elite . . . where they could be assured of four years of joyous competition . . . and irresponsible activity—with collateral deference to scholarship. . . . I was not [one of the elite]. . . . Up to graduation time, most of my classmates and practically all of the prominent citizens passed me on campus with no sign of recognition. . . . I confess I was not happy about my status, . . . I had read all the books I could get my hands on dealing with Yale life. *Stover at Yale* I not only read but practically memorized."[7] Yet Bergin gave grateful vent to the meaning of "democracy" among classmates in matters of academics. "I must recognize in all fairness," he wrote, "that the Doric Yale of those days recognized talent readily enough in areas where it could display itself. . . . Phi Beta Kappa [the national honor society] offered a clean competition. . . ." Although "my classmates didn't have anything against scholarship, they thought of it as relatively unimportant in the scheme of things." Bergin understood fully the opportunities Yale provided and later acknowledged that he'd stuck to the "grind."[8]

Val Giamatti, by all accounts then and throughout his life, never sought the Stover ethic. He chose, fully exploited, and enjoyed the disciplined path borne of intellect and the preservation of good character where enduring friendships emerged from those attributes rather than from being "chosen" or from relegating the excellent faculty to being only builders of "leadership." It was part of negotiating citizenship, the thoughtfully channeled use of his commitment, including to his family's place in America.[9]

LEARNING DANTE AND THE ACADEMIC LIFE

Angelo Lipari joined the Yale Romance Languages Department faculty in 1924 as an associate professor. It was probably plain to him shortly after his arrival that Yale had neither Catholic nor Jewish professors by design; it would not have them until, between 1945 and 1946, Dean William Clyde DeVane promoted one of each.[10] Lipari's "tenure" was secure; so, too, was the limit to his academic promotions despite the fact that his knowledge of French and Spanish literature, the Renaissance, Dante Alighieri, and *La Divina Commedia* was substantial.[11]

The manner in which Dante and his work was embraced in America (and taught by Lipari) enhanced its attraction to Valentine Giamatti and, later, to his son Bart. John Chipman Gray provided the historical context for his reading of Dante in his review of *The Divine Comedy* in 1819. Although neither the French literati nor some among the English appreciated Dante's literary power, Gray wrote that that failure stemmed from the most central and enduring character-istic of Dante's work: the allegory. What did the words mean? Answering that question required a unique knowledge of literary, religious, and Italian history. Even though rarely accomplished, success opened into an appreciation for virtu-ally all the literature that followed. "[Dante] formed by his Divine Comedy a language . . . for flexibility and harmony," including in the works of Shakespeare, Milton, and subsequent Italian poets such as Ariosto, later a favorite of Bart Giamatti's, and Edmund Spenser, whom Bart knew could only be appreciated by understanding Dante.[12]

To Gray, the heart of the *La Divina Commedia*'s enduring mystery was understood by Italian scholars: the story was accessible—not unlike the sev-enteenth century's Christian allegory *Pilgrim's Progress* by the Englishman Paul Bunyan was to "the delight of children, in the humblest classes of society." And to lead the reader and Dante (who put "himself" into the poem, another liter-ary precedent and allegorical enticement) through "all the regions far beyond the sphere of all earthy objects and feeling," Dante chose "his adored" Italian poet Virgil. Through Virgil, Dante asks "questions in natural philosophy," "meets with all the saints of the new and old Testaments, and with many of the most distinguished worthies of the early ages," and explores the teachings of "Pagan and Christian theology." He also explores the importance of Virgil's "Elysian Fields." "Dante," Gray concluded, "is the poet of our hours of sober contempla-tion." Put differently, to appreciate, teach, and write about Dante's *Commedia*, to appreciate its relevance to numerous other settings in life, you needed to know a lot and foremost to have a solid grasp of the responsibility of exercising your own imagination. The *Divine Comedy* as allegory was the way Dante was taught at Yale and by teachers of all grades in America, and certainly in Italy. It was the way Valentine Giamatti learned it. That approach would be challenged later (in both Giamattis' view, unpersuasively) when Bart entered his first post-Yale teaching position at Princeton.[13]

Lipari also established the Yale Italian Society, which sponsored lectures throughout the city as well as within the university. Through the Society, Lipari organized highly regarded plays performed in Italian by the society's student members in the Little (Lincoln Street) Theatre, off campus. He also brought another imperative to bear on the lives of his Italian American students, readily understood from the discriminatory mentality he'd witnessed at Yale: be careful of your personal conduct, the way you make sexual and moral choices, all of which are being judged with a jaundiced eye and subject to gross stereotyping inside and outside the university. Lipari's admonition would have fallen on informed ears: many among his students had heard the same admonition from their mothers. "*Cammina con una faccia pulita.*" Always walk with a clean face.[14]

⁓

Val's academic focus was in the Romance Languages Department.[15] He was a member of the Italian Society and retained his excellent academic performance as he entered his junior year.[16] In the spring of 1931 his skill in Model Italian reached such a high level of erudition that he was asked by Professor Lipari to recreate one of the main characters in Luigi Chiarelli's three-act comedy *La Maschera e Il Volta*, "The Mask and the Face." Val was among the few members of the cast or crew who were Italian American.[17] The play was a success, including, for Val, as a means of teaching.[18]

Val also was obligated, by the conditions of his Sterling Scholarship and his financial circumstance, to work throughout the year. In the summer, he worked at A.C. Gilbert, a large factory well known nationally for its erector set, model trains, chemistry sets, and enamel-protected electric wiring. Val's job included moving materials in and out of vast ovens, where the enamel would bake. Years later he would complain that his work was a contributor to the heart and lung problems he suffered. It's unclear when Val also began to smoke cigarettes, which he continued to do well into his life. What is clear is that the *Yale Daily News*, in almost every edition during this era (and for decades to come), included quarter- and half-page advertisements for cigarettes intended for the elegantly dressed, dog-hunting, automobile roadster–owning students. One advertisement assured readers, "What's there to be afraid of? *Everybody inhales!*"[19]

Val continued to tutor other students in Italian, "coached plays" at New Haven's International Institute for Foreign Women, and taught Italian and French in the New Haven Evening High School. It also was during this time that Val's sixteen-year-old brother, Americo, died unexpectedly from an epileptic seizure. That loss lingered inside him throughout his life.[20] He also completed thirty credit hours in education training at Connecticut State Normal School located on Howe Street, a few blocks north of Yale, next to the home of Sylvester Poli (which the Normal School occupied as office space after Poli's death). In support of Val's teaching skills, Associate Professor Lipari said of Val: "He is potentially the best Italo-American student I have ever had in class. I have the greatest faith in him."[21]

THE NORTHERN PROBLEM DESCENDS

By the 1930–1931 school year, at the time Val was focused on his academic specialty, Lipari recruited Italian-born (1906, in Florence) Uguccione ("Hugh") Ranieri di Sorbello onto the faculty as an instructor. Di Sorbello distained Mussolini and Fascism, and when war was declared later by the United States, he joined the Allied Intelligence Service. At this juncture, however, he and others were confronted with the reality that President Angell embraced Mussolini and Fascism. The near unanimity against Fascism that existed, for example, at Smith College and Mount Holyoke did not exist at Yale. The administration's embrace of Fascism and eugenics melded into Yale's embrace of the Northern Italian intent to ensure its privileged place among the Nordic race.[22]

✦

At the end of the nineteenth century, Dr. Cesare Lombroso of Verona, Italy, developed the "scientific" conclusion that by taking measurements of the human skull and using other genetic indicators he could determine that a person is a "*born* criminal." Lombroso claimed that Southern Italians were inclined to this inherited fate. Lombroso's "School of Positivist Criminology" was challenged in Italy as unscientific and incorrect in terms of the intellect of Southern Italians. Lombroso's "science" was adopted in the United States as gospel with respect to the eugenic manner of characterizing the inherited gene that caused permanent criminality in men and women. To add credence to Lombroso's work, Madison Grant had made clear that Northern Italians were "Nordic." Among those boastful of Lombroso's influence on his research, writing, and thinking was Italian-born Dr. Vittorio Racca. In early 1930, Racca, who had worked for the Rockefeller Foundation as a criminology consultant, had been welcomed into Yale's Institute of Human Relations. He claimed to have "a thorough understanding of the background of the Italian immigrants." Angell confirmed Racca's credentials and proper disposition with his friend, Raymond Fosdick, who was on the board of Rockefeller. The institute, its executive secretary, Mark May, explained, "wanted to make New Haven and the surrounding territory its major laboratory."[23]

Racca's research occurred in the Wooster Square neighborhood. The result of his study was an Institute Preliminary Report—titled "Crime Among Italian Immigrants: Immigrant Adaptation to America and Criminality"—done in cooperation with other faculty affiliated with the institute, and labeled "strictly confidential." President Angell held his copy among his "personal" papers. As Racca reported to Angell: "When [Italian immigrants] come to this country they bring . . . no culture, no moral principles, no religious beliefs." In the Italian American homes he visited, "I have never seen a man or a woman, boy or girl, read; only rarely have I seen newspapers." "Must we wonder," Racca queried, "if the second generation of immigrants, the one which is supposed to be bred under ideal American conditions, presents a higher and worse form of criminality than that of the first generation, to [sic] often a criminal generation."[24]

ை

On May 9, 1931, the Institute of Human Relations was dedicated at Yale in a grand ceremony broadcast on the NBC network and celebrated on the front and interior pages of the Yale Daily News. Angell, by then a globally known eugenicist, led the preliminary introduction of invited speakers.[25] Governor Wilbur Cross, former dean of the graduate school, was there as the master of ceremony.

It was Cross, as will be described later, who played an essential role in the evolution of Yale's soon-to-be-completed embrace of South Carolina Senator John Caldwell Calhoun, in whose honor the university would name one of its residential colleges. And it was Cross who, in 1925 (while graduate school dean), crafted his lecture at Brown University, where, in describing the changes in science that marked the twentieth century he elevated those "who have pursued their investigations honestly. . . . They are the obscure devotees of Truth." He included among them men who had shown that, "By selecting the parents, not only may morons be eliminated, but . . . women may be relieved of the burden of children." And that, "Some men and women . . . are dangerous to the state and must be toned down a bit," including by "injections" to their "sex glands." Cross then concluded that these "biological inventions" (as he called them) "would probably meet with considerable opposition owing to the prejudices of the people. But we have a strong government. . . . The number of our Cabinet Officers has already more than doubled since Washington's time. A Secretary of Eugenics would mean only one more." Cross, though bold and candid about embracing the subject and forms of eugenics in his words, characterized those ideas as "too sanguine *just now.*" As he stood before the new institute's audience in May 1931, those ideas had finally been transformed into a legitimized, public reality at his alma mater and by the laws of Connecticut he now enforced.[26]

Cross also would have had confidence in the eugenics advocacy of the next speaker, President Herbert Hoover's secretary of the interior, Ray Lyman Wilbur, an advocate for eugenics, and in the supportive comments of the Medical School dean, Dr. Milton Winternitz. The *Daily News* especially captured Winternitz's perspective: "Point of View of the Institute Has Profoundly Affected Medical Teaching at Yale School." Eugenics, Winternitz declared, tempered the instruction of Yale-educated doctors. And the *Daily News* described another example of the institute's work in progress: "A survey of a selected district in New Haven, comprised largely of foreign-born parents and their children (mostly Italians) . . . being made by Dr. Vittorio Racca."[27]

THE RETURN: GRADUATION

On June 21, 1932, Valentine Giamatti and his classmates, black gowns flowing and mortarboards in place, entered Woolsey Hall from the Hewitt Quadrangle. Parents, faculty, and friends cheered in wonder and relief before they rushed in to take their seats. It was mid-morning, the day filled with clarity and promise.[28]

Val had gained admittance to Yale's graduate school in Romance Languages. Having achieved the "highest attainment" as an undergraduate, he was awarded the Bidwell-Foote Fellowship to continue his studies.[29] His friend Salvatore Castiglione accompanied him into the graduate program. Val also had been elected into Phi Beta Kappa, the highest-ranked and most prestigious society of accomplished scholars in American academics.[30] Maynard Mack, headed for Yale's graduate school in English, also walked that day with Val into Woolsey Hall. The Yale chapter of Phi Beta Kappa had elected Mack as its president. The society's motto: "Love of learning is the guide of life." It captured the imagination and conviction of each of them. Likely sitting in the audience was another friend Val had made, Professor Roswell Ham, who taught courses in English and English literature; like Val, Ham was a proponent of theater as a teaching methodology. Ham also was, by training, a professional actor. Their paths and shared values would cross again in a time and manner of instructive meaning in the life and choices of Bart Giamatti.

On this day in June, the Giammatteis could take comfort in their collective accomplishment. The son of Italian immigrants—Southern Italian immigrants—born and raised in the Fair Haven neighborhood of New Haven, had done it. So, too, had his family.

9

FASCISM AND RACE AT YALE

The ideals of civic unity, liberty of individual choice and freedom from foreign oppression were, from Dante on, constantly articulated, and the core of these values . . . would be carried at various levels of consciousness by . . . immigrants to the New World.

—A. Bartlett Giamatti (Yale 1960, PhD 1964), "Commentary" in *The Italian Americans*, 1987

PRELUDE: METHODS

Although Hebrew was taught at Yale as early as the 1730s, apparently to understand the Old Testament and "ecclesiastical history," neither it nor the method of learning it was ever connected to the culture and practice of the Jews of Poland, Russia, and elsewhere who came to New Haven. Yale's anti-Semitism was bold, explicit, and pervasive. Jews were a different race and could not be as "intellectually gifted" as wealthy Protestant boys.[1] President Angell, with the aid of his dean of admission, Robert Corwin, manifested contempt for Jews, especially "Hebrews" of "local origin" with unequivocal certainty. That mentality, shared candidly with other northeastern universities and the Yale Corporation, remained Yale policy, with only subtle variations, for decades to come. That policy also was understood by prospective students.[2]

With respect to Italian Americans, Dean Winternitz confirmed the Angell-Corwin approach at the Medical School. "Never admit more than five Jews, take only two Italian Catholics, and take no blacks at all," he was reported to have told his own admission committee. Yale also would not make Angelo Lipari a full professor, and, as was probably quite apparent to both Salvatore Castiglione and Valentine Giamatti—and perhaps, too, to Thomas Bergin (who taught Italian while in graduate school)—no Catholic was going to make full professor. Though only eight students of the 1932 graduating class were of Italian descent (six born in or near New Haven), that was enough of an increase over the four who had existed in the entire college the year before Val entered to warrant heightened apprehension. That apprehension likely increased—and tempered admissions—when Italian Americans of "local origin" excelled academically to a historically consequential degree.[3]

The admissions application and all regular reporting forms filled out by current students required disclosure about parents, country of birth, mother's maiden name, and the student's membership in local religious institutions. Corwin thought the answers would "rarely leave us no doubt as to the [student's] ethnological classification." Val Giamatti's questionnaire, filled out in each of his years at Yale, included precisely these questions, though he didn't answer most of them. Protestant boys whose relatives had graduated from Yale were excluded from taking any I.Q. tests, which only provoked the search for the right euphemism to ensure inclusion and perpetuation of the Anglo-Saxon race—"leaders," "legacy," or "poise"—that is, the "Yale Man." Still a decade off, though its origins likely emerged during this unvarnished eugenics era: the nude photograph, taken against measurement devices. The classic eugenics tool.[4]

It was precisely at this time that Hitler formally transformed eugenics into law in the broad sterilization mandate of "The Law for the Prevention of Hereditary Diseased Offspring" (enacted in July 1933) and in, among others laws, "The Restoration of the Professional Civil Service" (enacted in April 1933). Hitler had embraced his intent to purify the Nordic race in *Mein Kampf* and praised the manner in which it was practiced in the United States, especially by its state governments, including Wilbur Cross's Connecticut, where sterilization had become a model of implementation. The Rockefeller Foundation—whose actions were known to Angell, Winternitz, and Cross—had provided eugenics research funding to German scientists as early as 1929 (and would continue to do so through 1940), as well as financial support for Mussolini.[5] In New Haven, the fate of Jews in Europe especially was well known. "The Pogrom" that Anna Lev described in her 1927 article in the *Hillhouse Gleam*—part of Valentine Giamatti's understanding of the meaning of being Jewish—took on a practical significance that he and others no longer had to imagine.[6]

෴

A colloquy about principles, rough and ugly in tone and duration, was taking place in New Haven. Sides were drawn. In the fall of 1921, "a threatening crowd of anti-Fascists so unnerved [Fascist Italian Deputy Giuseppe] Bottai, that he spoke for only ten minutes before leaving the theater under police escort." He'd come to New Haven, at Mussolini's request, to argue against Italian immigrant support for anti-Fascist efforts in the United States and Italy. It didn't work. "About 30 local radicals," led by Italians from New Haven and the region, "clashed with sympathizers of the Fascisti." Riot police were called. The Fascisti were characterized as "a sort of Ku Klux Klan, suppressing all radical movements and meting out summary punishment to those deemed unpatriotic." The Fascist vice counsel, Pasquale DeCicco, who maintained a cordial relationship with Angell, remained in New Haven to ensure no replication of the Bottai experience occurred. He failed. "In the mid-1930s, [the local chapter of the Ladies' Garment Workers' Union] sponsored one of Italy's leading Italian socialists, Giuseppe Emanuele Modigliani, to speak against Fascism at a huge rally at Fraternal Hall on Elm Street in New Haven." New Haven's Italian Americans never embraced Mussolini's anti-democratic ideology. Once Mussolini invaded Ethiopia in 1935, Italian Americans in the three neighborhoods remained indifferent, mostly hostile, to his entreaty for support.[7]

In April 1933, in New Haven's Wooster Square neighborhood, Italian Americans continued their insistence on fairness in a manner neither Yale eugenicists nor others in industry welcomed. Members of the establishment hoped, perhaps, that the suppression demonstrated in the Palmer Raids, in the anti-immigrant fervor of the 1924 Immigration Act, and in the execution of Sacco and Vanzetti had brought protests to an end. They didn't. Jennie Aiello, in her late teens, led the movement in a manner born of the ethic that tempered her immigrant parents and neighbors, and the African Americans, Poles, Jews, and Italians who worked in the garment trade with her. Women were paid $4.50 a week for fifty-four hours of work in unsanitary, unventilated, and unheated sweatshops, precisely the kind of conditions, writ large, that led to the horrendous loss of life in 1911 at the Triangle Shirtwaist Company in New York City. Picketing occurred amid "police brutality and . . . freezing rain." When the school and park districts wouldn't allow the strikers space to meet, the Italian social clubs nearby opened their doors for warmth and camaraderie. The strike, led by women, was successful.[8]

Although Mussolini's anti-Semitic laws were not enacted until 1938, anti-Semitic harassment in Italy began much earlier. In 1925, when Gaetano Salvemini, who later made his home in Northampton, Massachusetts, and Carlo Rosselli, the famed anti-Fascist who was later assassinated by Mussolini's Blackshirts, needed help in the highly risky distribution of anti-Fascist pamphlets, Rosselli's wife, Marion, engaged others in defying Fascists who sought to stop them. Historian Stanislao G. Pugliese described how a twist of fate and commitment to principle brought a famed anti-Fascist to the steps of New Haven and to the not easily opened door of Yale. Pugliese writes that Renata Calabresi, who was born in Ferrara and received her doctorate from the University of Florence, helped "to distribute copies of [the pamphlets] along with her brother, Dr. Massimo Calabresi. For [their] actions, [they] were briefly imprisoned, [beaten], and eventually fled into exile." They arrived in the United States in 1939. Massimo, married to Bianca Finzi-Contini, obtained a research fellowship at Yale provided with financial support from others to fully underwrite Yale's expenses. Yale would not pay. The couple settled in New Haven with their two sons, Paul and Guido. Massimo continued his defiance.[9]

COMMUNITY SELF-HELP AND
THE ITALIAN FELLOWSHIP EXCHANGE PROGRAM

In March 1929, Stephen Duggan, president of the New York–based Institute of International Education (IIE), met with Yale President Angell with the intent of initiating a fellowship exchange program proposed by the Italian government. Duggan, an active, progressive former City College of New York professor, believed that educational interaction among people ensured dialogue and informed opposition to repressive governments. Among his close friends were Edward R. Murrow and his wife, Janet Huntington Brewster Murrow, a graduate of Mount Holyoke. Edward Murrow would soon become Duggan's assistant. Among the beneficiaries of Duggan and Murrow's initiative was Valentine Giamatti.[10]

On "our own side," Angell wrote internally, "I am wondering whether our Italian constituency might not be interested to get together a fund . . . during which time we could try out such a venture." Angell suggested that then-Dean Wilbur Cross "might sound [Professor] Charles Bakewell as to the further possibility that Dr. [William] Verdi or the local Italian colony would interest themselves in such an undertaking." Yale would not spend a penny.[11] Conditions were agreed upon, foremost that the selection of the Yale student would be the province of Professor Angelo Lipari, who knew Verdi.[12] Verdi and his friend Sylvester Poli contributed the financing. What mattered to both of them was that an Italian American boy or girl could go to Italy to study, gain a credential, and see firsthand what was occurring to its people—and that Lipari made the selection.[13] By 1933, when Val was chosen for departure in August, Poli and Verdi had served the purpose they had sought.[14] Without their help, Valentine Giamatti would not have traveled to Italy. "Fate," Bart Giamatti wrote, in ways he knew personally and poignantly with respect to his father, "is the constant companion."[15]

YALE'S PERMANENT EMBRACE OF RACE

In the fall of 1933, shortly after Val boarded the ocean liner SS *Rex* on his journey to Italy, Yale's new residential colleges opened. Their construction signified an intention to ensure closer relationships and school spirit (the practical implications of "Mother Yale") among students. The colleges given proper names honored men who, with a minor exception, had been slaveholders or advocates of slavery (an ethic that would continue through the Griswold-Brewster period). None resonated more deliberately and proudly in the Yale culture than the designation granted to John Caldwell Calhoun.

Yale's historical relationship with the Confederate states, before and after the Civil War, came to light when the university announced that one of its new residential colleges would be named after Calhoun (Yale 1804), perhaps the most notable advocate—intellectual, political, practical, and always economic—for the virtue of African human bondage. The Yale Corporation's knowledge of those facts was not a deterrent; far more likely, given Angell's embrace of eugenics and its institutional presence at Yale, holding Africans in bondage may have been considered an attribute worthy of subtle, insightful praise. Angell made the announcement, as he did other things related to race and discrimination, with a superficially benign public delicacy. The appeal to Yale's alumni in the former Confederate states and Yale's deliberate efforts to solicit—in part by being solicitous of their culture—the former Confederacy's loyalty and donations underpinned the deeply embedded religious and racial treads in the university's institutional values.

Yale solicited students from the South early in its history. In 1815, Professor Benjamin Silliman—himself a slaveholder—traveled to Charleston, South Carolina, to meet with Yale graduates, including "members of the Gadsden, Grimké, and Legare families." All three families included prominent political and national "leaders," including James Gadsden (Yale 1806) and Thomas Grimké (Yale 1807, Honorary Degree 1830), and all three had a history as prominent slaveholders.[16] Among the Yale students in the same era was Calhoun, who was a student of Silliman's. Yale historian Brooks Mather Kelley suggests that Silliman's conservatism may have affected Calhoun's later views. In 1832, when Yale officials returned south to solicit funds, Calhoun declined to contribute, but slaveholder Thomas Grimké did.[17]

In the presidential election of 1876, when it appeared that Democrat Samuel Tilden would be elected president of the United States, the Republican candidate, Rutherford B. Hayes, and the leadership in his party cut a deal of momentous consequence. The still-unreported Southern states would ensure that their electoral votes were cast for Hayes if he agreed to withdraw federal troops from Louisiana and South Carolina, thus ending the singular protection the former slaves had in the South. Hayes was elected. In short order, the Democrats largely joined in, as white Southerners took complete control of political and economic power. Ugliness in its most horrific form followed, not only in the Jim Crow laws but also in the actions of those who—through assumed moral superiority and assured cockiness toward anyone who was dark-skinned or Catholic or (like the Italian immigrants) both—lynched or shot anyone recognized as having befriended or engaged in commerce with African Americans. Frederick Douglass grasped the meaning of the 1876 deal in a speech he gave in 1883: "Whatever else I may forget," he said, "I shall never forget the difference between those who fought for liberty and those who fought for slavery."[18]

In 1901, as part of its bicentennial celebration, Yale dedicated Woolsey Hall (also known as Memorial Hall) on the corner of Grove and College streets. Yale's plan, in part and in time, was to recognize Yale graduates who died in service to the Confederate Army. The university's officials connected that plan to the former Confederate states' alumni, especially in South Carolina, long before the plaques containing those names were dedicated in 1915. South Carolina alumni—comforted by Yale's homage to Calhoun—already had been "prominent in their liberality. They sent a special contribution."[19]

In 1913, following a plan hatched in 1910 on the Yale campus and at the Taft Hotel, alumni from South Carolina and elsewhere gathered for a privately financed train ride south, led by Professor of English Wilbur Cross. They observed "the one-mule-power negro plus the 100,000 horse-power hydro-electric plant," which was "making a new South Carolina," and listened to "Madame Bleckley [host of a barbeque dinner], who gave with inimitable humor a monologue of an old-time negro mammy." Once reaching the University of South Carolina, Professor Cross gave his speech on "Yale and South Carolina." In it, as reported back to *all* Yale alumni, he "spoke in glowing phrases of that greatest of Yale's sons and the greatest of the sons of Carolina, John Caldwell Calhoun." He also described Yale's plan with respect to naming Confederate soldiers in Woolsey Hall, as reported the next day in the *Columbia State* in this way: "The proposed memorial to Yale men who died in service in the War Between the Sections that should carry conviction to Southern doubters . . . of the exact justice of the Yale disposition toward the people of this section of the United States." The Woolsey Hall memorial "does not discriminate by implication or otherwise against either side of the War. . . . That their names are not grouped according to their respective allegiances [and] will not even by indirection to a possible inference that her sons and their respective countries . . . are not to be held in equal respect." Those traveling with Professor Cross and their South Carolina host were from throughout the Northeast, each respected and consequential in their professions, all returning from their journey with "individual good word for . . . South Carolina . . . attested in formal resolutions vociferously adopted [during] an all day love-feast." Calhoun and the former Confederacy had been anointed unabashedly into the Yale culture, in and outside the university campus.[20] In April 1913, the celebration of success "in linking the University with the South" was noted, including support for the formation of "the Southern Federation of Yale Clubs."[21]

Angell's announcement yielded no notable disquiet on the Yale campus. What is plainly evident is that the selection of Calhoun, contrary to Angell's pretense that he was chosen by the Yale Corporation after a year of study because he was the university's finest reflection of "the Civil State," represented the personification of a cultural and financial imperative of long standing in search of an opportunity to be irrevocably embedded. Angell and the Corporation found it in the naming of the residential college.

FASCISTS: YALE EMBEDS ITS DEMONS

In the spring of 1934, after Val had departed for Italy, the Fascist government decided to send a contingent of 350 students to tour the United States, especially the northeastern locations with large Italian American populations. Fifty of the students were prominent athletes, including two Olympic runners. Harvard (Cambridge and Boston) and Yale (New Haven) were included on the tour. The Olympiad was scheduled to open in Berlin in 1936. The students were expected to arrive in New Haven on October 6 after a brief stop at Harvard. Gustavus T. Kirby, a member of the United States Olympic Committee who chaired the joint Italy-America reception committee, informed President Angell of the details of the Yale visit.[22]

Vittorio Racca, still retained by the Institute of Human Relations, informed Angell he'd welcome the opportunity to act as guide and interpreter. Angell accepted the offer.[23] The plan was to welcome the students in a grand ceremony on the Hewitt Quadrangle, hold a luncheon in the University Dining Hall, offer a celebratory welcome at the Yale–Columbia football game (enabling the Italian students to "march in their college uniforms into and around the stadium giving one or two of their songs and salutes"), and honor the guests at a major dinner hosted by Governor Wilbur Cross. Planning for the arrival and events went relatively smoothly and quietly through September, including when President Angell agreed, as he wrote it, to "appear in the Hewitt Quadrangle at 11:45 on Saturday, October 6, to salute the young Fascisti."[24]

On October 3, the plan was disrupted. The Harvard Corporation and Harvard's new president, James Bryant Conant, refused to accept a large scholarship endowment from a Harvard graduate, Dr. Ernst Hanfstaengl, because of Hanfstaengl's close affiliation with Hitler and the Nazi-instigated harm imposed within German universities. Also in the background was the widely criticized acceptance of an honorary degree from a German university by Roscoe Pound, dean of the Harvard Law School. In the forefront was the October 3 letter from Louis Jacob Kaye, a Yale student, who wrote to Angell in protest on behalf of the Yale chapter of the National Student League.[25] In response to the league's letter, Angell directed that his assistant inquire into Kaye's background. The reply began, "A New Haven Jew"—precisely the place Angell would have expected dissent and cultural irreverence to originate.[26]

On October 6, the Italian students paraded into the Hewitt Quadrangle. The weather was damp and chilly, and rain fell throughout the brief ceremony. Local and university reporters were there; the *New Haven Evening Register* covered the event pictorially. Italian vice-counsel DeCicco held the umbrella over President Angell as he addressed the assembled students, who also included the chairman of the organizing committee, Gustavus Kirby. When Angell finished his remarks, the Italian students cheered and, it was reported, the "Fascist salute followed and a very loud *L'viva Mussolini*."[27] As the ceremony ended, two dozen or more students standing nearby on Wall Street began to chant, "*A Bas Il Fascismo*" ("Down with Fascism"). Some students were from the National Student League, but most were not. Within moments, the three hundred or more Fascisti coalesced and shouted back. As the *Register* described it, a Nordic-type "tall Italian" student, "Shoulder[ed] his way into the compact group of agitators. Fist swung, there was the thudding sound of hard blows of flesh on flesh, and the fighting began. . . . A rush of Fascisti then swept" the demonstrators down Wall Street to the lawn between Berkeley and Sprague Hall, then toward College Street. Two women demonstrators were beaten. One man was kicked when he went down. The police intervened to ensure that what the *Yale Daily News* had characterized as a "Thrilling Attack" came to an end.[28]

That afternoon, promptly at 1:30, the Italians dressed in various regalia and carrying the Fascist emblem marched into and around Yale Bowl. At halftime, the Yale band played a "tumultuous rendition of the Fascist national anthem 'Giovinezza.'" The Italian athletes joined in. That evening, at the large gathering held in West Haven, Governor Wilbur Cross, it was reported the next day, embraced Fascist Italy and the Italian students. "You young men," he said, "are representative of the mind and spirit of the new Italy, built by Mussolini upon the foundations of ancient Rome. As you proceed on your way, I ask you to carry home with you over the seas, the good wishes of the Governor of the state of Connecticut for careers happy and prosperous."[29]

It rained through most of the game. Yale lost to Columbia. The following day, the "young Fascisti" made their way to Columbia University. The National Student League kept up its opposition to changes witnessed in Europe. In setting out "the tragic plight of Hitler's Germany," the league also chided "the contentions of gullible freshmen writing in the *News*," who sympathized with the Nazi mentality, prognosticating, perhaps unwittingly yet insightfully, what in time would be the Yale-based formation of "America First" and its welcome onto the Yale campus of Charles A. Lindbergh, a fervent admirer of the Nazi government and, long before then, an avowed eugenicist.[30]

Part III

FAMILY

ROMANCE OF THE HEART AND THE LIBERAL MIND

VALENTINE GIAMATTI AND PEGGY WALTON

In August 1933, Val Giamatti departed for Italy. He was entering, in real terms, the Fascist temperament that he'd begun to assess in New Haven and at Yale and, with caution, he now could assess in the streets and neighborhoods of Italy's countryside and urban neighborhoods.

He must have sensed freedom in the SS *Rex*'s movement, though he stood erect and stationary. Perspective that comes suddenly with distance, from being alone, intent on emerging even amid the thrill of the ocean liner's thunderous entrance into the expansive green-gray tumult and impervious soot-gray fog of the Atlantic. There was clarity for certain about the depth of his educational accomplishment, not merely as a credential but as a way of thinking and living, and an awareness of the fullness of his persistence, no doubt felt as duty, to expand his knowledge and his skill at analyzing it. He had resisted the Anglo-Saxon values he'd been exposed to and every effort to denigrate the culture that he admired, that had given him the confidence to get to this juncture. Physical costs no doubt had been paid. As he mentally waved goodbye, for now, to the poignant words of Emma Lazarus, he recognized he was returning to Italy as an Italian American whose parents believed in Liberty's entreaty and ensured he did as well.

On board, within hours of departure, as his daughter, Elria, and son, Dino, tell it, Val saw Peggy Walton from a distance. Her letters home indicate she recognized his presence and the warmth of his smile and interest immediately. The opening moments of a courtship had begun. Unbeknownst to both of them, Dante and the range of Italian history, culture, and language he embodied and the insight into life he taught actually would be a central thread that would weave ceaselessly throughout their life together and into the lives of their children.

⁓

The Atlantic crossing of the SS *Rex* was not Peggy's maiden voyage on an ocean liner. During the spring holiday of 1933, she had traveled to Bermuda aboard the *Monarch* with six classmates. There is a tone in her photographs—with friends, on the beach, in town—and in the recollections she later shared with her children of fun, a continued embrace of irreverence and life. The photographs suggest maturity in stylish dress, in the casual suit, high waist with mid-calf skirt, the slightly boxed shoulders, the slouch hat, and in the proper manner when it was called for, as if in a second sense, a confidence in her persona, still evolving yet steady and thoughtful inside. What emerged as well was an underlying seriousness of purpose: she brought it especially to her intent to explore her talents—music, piano, theater, and a congenial social skill, each in her family model of experience—and in her embrace of Italy, particularly the Etruscan culture and its remaining artifacts.

Etrusci—as the Romans referred to the geographic center of the Etruscan civilization (modern Tuscany)—reached as far south as Campania (the region that includes San Lorenzello and the villages from which many of New Haven's immigrants departed) and was highly cultured in written language, artistry, and trade that expanded north into present-day Europe and south into Greece and Asia. Commerce and skills moved and intermixed frequently and easily. Of special relevance to Peggy's interest, Etrusci was the home of Publius Vergilius Maro, Virgil in English, who was born near the town of Mantua, Lombardy, in 70 BC. Mantua was described in Virgil's famed and (by Dante Alighieri) cherished and respected epic of the founding of Rome, the *Aeneid*.[1] The power of Virgil's influence on Dante was reflected in Dante's decision to make Virgil his guide, from the onset of the *Commedia* through Dante's journey into Hell, then upward to Purgatory and his glimpse of Paradise.[2]

Peggy brought her knowledge into her relationships and, in time, into her own family. On her first visit to Italy, she expected to see what the Roman Empire and modern-day Italy deliberately, or by inadvertence, preserved. That is, which threads of knowledge and artifacts might ultimately prevail through the menace of Fascism.

&

By the time the SS *Rex* sailed through the Straits of Gibraltar into the Mediterranean, Peggy and Val had met. Her album includes his photograph on board. They had each other's attention.[3]

The ship's passengers disembarked in Naples. Val visited his family in San Lorenzello and Telese, probably with arrangements made through correspondence from his parents and, quite likely, with the companionship of a new friend, Norman Burns (a Yale graduate studying for the foreign service), who later became the best man in his wedding to Peggy. What occurred in either village was not recounted in the family lore, though elements of the warm welcome are easily imagined.[4]

Val rejoined the group in Naples, at the Hotel Britannique, on the Corso Vittorio Emanuel, which had a fulsome view of the Bay of Naples, the port where his parents and thousands of others departed from Italy. Every moment, felt in stillness only on the outside, must have been filled with the joy and unease of imagining and appreciating what preceded that departure, and the unsettled hopes and physical demands of the voyage that followed. He had seen their home. As best he could, he would absorb those memories for reflection later, knowing they would reemerge at will, on their own. Within a few days, Val, Peggy, their friends and mentors were on the train north to Perugia, where the Italian University for Foreigners was located and where language instruction would be commingled with walking excursions into the city and countryside.[5]

For Val, three variables in conduct emerged with permanence. First, he often walked off the well-defined path, engaged in conversation, and sought to learn more of what, no doubt, he'd witnessed in San Lorenzello and Telese. Doing so separated Fascism's undemocratic principles and the adoration of Mussolini, now commanded by power, from the values of shopkeepers, workers, and farmers. Second, in few photographs did he not have a cigarette in his hand or reach for an offer of one. And, third, his dress was impeccable, with three-piece suits, tweed jackets, fashionable long collars, and subtle ties. American and distinctive, his slender body and full head of hair formed a look that, as his later photographs embodied, combined a Cary Grant style, Tyrone Power ruggedness, and William Holden attractiveness.

With a keener grasp of the language and a diploma of Italian-language proficiency, the group traveled to Assisi, the birthplace of Saint Francis. They knew of Saint Francis's influence on Dante—the practical meaning of wandering, making a pilgrimage, writing and speaking about life, and confirming the unchallengeable value of the "lived' experience" in doing so.[6] In play for Val was affirmation of his own means for judging life and, later, in guiding his children by word, example, and experience.

They traveled northeast to San Marino, then south to Rome, later still to Sicily, then north again across the Straits of Messina, a passageway made famous, in part, by Garibaldi.[7] Then they reached Florence, Dante's place of birth, life, civic contribution, and cherished memory. The women stayed in apartments on the via Borgo Pinti, in the oldest district in the city, a narrow fieldstone walkway located near the Basilica di Santa Croce, the burial place of Michelangelo, Machiavelli, and Galileo. It was no small matter that among these universally recognized artists of words and science and the human form stands only an empty tomb, a grandly designed cenotaph, dedicated to Dante Alighieri as if Florence longed for his return home, from his stop in Ravenna—along the road of exile dictated by Florence's governing family—where he was dutifully buried. The allegorical meaning of the written tribute, "Honor the most exalted poet," was related but surpassed by the endless meanings of Dante's journey—perhaps incomplete, perhaps still lingering in the historical conscience of Florence, no doubt of special significance to one of his enduring admirers in the practicalities of life, Valentine Giamatti. For similar reasons, Florence and New Haven would form Bart Giamatti's understanding of "the City."[8]

ॐ

In early spring, Peggy learned that her parents had attended her father's Harvard reunion, Class of 1904. It was held on the White House lawn, the celebration hosted by Bartlett Walton's classmate, Franklin D. Roosevelt.[9] In late July and into August 1934, Peggy, Val, and the group of students traveled to Venice, the last place of their formal journey. It was in Venice that Val, and perhaps his friend Norman Burns, separated from the group and headed to France, then filled with cultural and political tumult from Spain, Germany, and Italy.[10] During Val's travels in France, he met descendants of the family of Louis Antoine Jean Baptiste, Chevalier de Cambray-Digny, who was born in Florence of French parents in 1751. Chevalier (a title reflective of nobility and chivalry) de Cambray-Digny entered the French Royal Artillery as both soldier and engineer. His correspondence and records of meetings—which Val received—with Benjamin Franklin during Franklin's tenure as ambassador in Paris and later with Thomas Jefferson preceded Digny's arrival in the fledgling United States and, following meetings with George Washington and members of Congress, his formal order of attachment to the Continental Army. The letters and notes involved three languages and cultures—French, Italian, and English—and forms of documented bravery and principles of leadership in support of democracy that led to a rarely given congressional commendation and a portrait by Charles Willson Peale, painted in 1784, just before Digny departed for home. Val was excited. These were precious, unique documents, an untold story worthy of serious research and introduction into the American academy at a time when foreign cultures, including those of Italy and France, were understood, welcomed, and emulated. He returned to New Haven intent on respecting his pledge to Digny's family to give life to this story and, in doing so, expand his education in the romance languages and the history of America. The life of Digny would form his PhD dissertation.[11]

It was in Venice as well that Helen Walton joined Peggy. As they traveled together to Lake Lucerne and Lake Como and into the Swiss Alps, ending Peggy's sojourn when they sailed to England, it's likely Peggy confided in her mother that she'd met Valentine Giamatti of Yale and New Haven. As Elria Giamatti Ewing recalled it, Helen Walton was at first skeptical. Indeed, another departure in their family culture was in the making. But, as Helen certainly knew, her daughter had precisely the temperament and skill to evoke "departure" and ensure her happiness in doing it. Completing her degree at Smith was never a question. Courtship, however, was now sanctioned. For Val, the likelihood was that Angelo and Maria—their daughter Helen had married a non-Italian—would insist on only two conditions: finish your degree at Yale and get a position teaching that reflects your accomplishments and dreams. And they would expect Peggy to come to New Haven. His parents also would have had one admonition: don't forget who you are and how you got that way.

COURTSHIP, VERMONT, AND MARRIAGE

Val completed his coursework at Yale and continued teaching at New Haven Community College, while still living at home. In April 1935, he visited Peggy at Smith, likely staying at the Hotel Northampton on King Street long enough so that, with others, they could rehearse their roles in the Smith College production of *Come le Foglie* by Giuseppe Giacosa, April 30, at the Student's Building. Val took the lead role, Massimo Rosani, and Peggy played Signora Irene.[12] Though it would be a few years before Federal Theatre Project Director Hallie Flanagan would leave her position at Vassar to join the Smith faculty and further elevate its theater program, Val and Peggy recognized a practical purpose in theater that connected it to life, a medium for romance, and liberal values about education. The play was a success.[13]

In June, Peggy graduated *cum laude* from Smith. Continuity emerged readily on the smile and subtle exuberance of Helen Walton's face and composure. She'd done it again: two daughters had graduated from Smith College. Helen and Bartlett had arranged for Peggy to spend a year in New York helping one of her father's business associates, as she honed some of the skills she had not perfected at Smith: typing, bookkeeping, scheduling, public relations, and the business culture. The Waltons also invited Val to their home in Wakefield. No awkward moments arose; the cultural adjustment was easily managed. His attributes of polite manner and sociability worked. Peggy's character worked magic in New Haven as well, when she spent a few nights with the Giammatteis, including with Val's sister Helen and her husband, George. The contentment on Val's face in the photograph that Peggy took during that visit on the Yale Campus and held in her album until she died reflected certainty about the choice they would soon agree to.

Two other events, however, occurred in such entwined conjunction as to be the product of pure serendipity. Yale rejected Val's proposed PhD topic on the life and contribution of Cambray-Digny (no explanation is extant, though he'd done considerable research and a fulsome outline of his intent by then and had visited the Library of Congress in Washington, DC). Also, likely through Val's continued teaching relationships at New Haven Community College or New Haven Teachers College, came the offer to teach Italian and other languages in the fall of 1936 at the newly established Vermont Junior College in Montpelier, Vermont, nestled in the Green Mountains and next to ethnicity-rich Barre. The national introduction of junior colleges into the educational system had blended perfectly and timely with the growing interest in romance languages. The setting for marriage was created. Bartlett and Helen Walton of Wakefield, Massachusetts, announced the betrothal and wedding of their daughter, Mary Claybaugh Walton, to Valentine John Giamatti of New Haven, Connecticut, to be held in South Berwick, Maine, in July 1937.[14]

Val headed for Montpelier. He would help define a new chapter in American higher education and lay the groundwork for marriage. In his way, he was the pioneer, what his parents would have understood as an American name for the subtle confidence of the immigrant.

11

MELDING THE PAST INTO THE FUTURE

He could not be closed. He gave all the time, without stint, without calculation, without assuming a treaty for reciprocity. Even when he gave you what in this chapel I can only refer to as *Inferno*, you loved him all the more because he did you the endless and essential human favor of caring about you and saying so. He always told you how much he cared—for my Mother always first and forever, for his children and grandchildren, for his sisters, friends, students, books, Mount Holyoke, out across the world.

—A. Bartlett Giamatti,
Eulogy for Valentine John Giamatti, April 15, 1982

VAL AND PEGGY: DEFINING STABILITY AND IDENTITY

Val Giamatti was setting precedent; the expectation for excellence was high. The demand for post–high school education in America, especially in rural settings, had increased the dialogue among educators and state and nonprofit institutions to ensure its availability.[1] In fall 1936, when Val took up residence in Montpelier, the new junior college blended the historical imperative for education of the Northern Methodist Church with the independent strain of New England educators. Church services (the "Chapel Programs") were intended to be more ethical and humanitarian in nature, reflections on life, with students encouraged to seek their own formal religious services in or outside the college. The trustees selected Dr. Arthur W. Hewitt as president. Twenty-five students were selected for the first class. Their advisor was Professor of Romance Languages Valentine Giamatti.[2]

Val taught Spanish, French, Italian, and the history of Western Europe. He thrived in the collegiality and the expectation for active faculty participation in enhancing student life through clubs, counseling, field work, and practical discussions on professional and educational choices. Vermont, like Connecticut, had the dark specter of eugenics in its culture. The University of Vermont, with the support of the American Eugenics Society, had sponsored various studies on "bad heredity" among sixty Vermont families as the basis for institutionalization and sterilization. State laws enacted primarily in 1931 were bolstered by the Supreme Court's decision in *Buck v. Bell*. Unlike in Connecticut, the movement was largely discredited after an ignoble start directed against French Canadians, Native Americans, Southern and Eastern European immigrants, rural Anglo-Saxons, and religious minorities. There is no indication Val was ever overtly subjected to racial or ethnic prejudice while in Vermont, conduct he would have recognized immediately if directed against him or anyone he mentored or taught. The proximity to Barre (where some students lived) and his experience in New Haven made him especially conscious of seeking out anyone being treated unfairly and to right the wrong, a now deeply settled belief found of experience, not from reading or from the *noblesse oblige* of privilege.[3]

In his own Chapel Program talk to students, Val provided a "tour through Italy accompanied by a vivid delineation of the Italian and his life," separating the people he'd met in Italy and those he knew in New Haven from Mussolini—a prelude, maybe a prescient foundation, to how he'd attack Fascism when the war came. He also accomplished, by staying unflinchingly focused on Italy, the Italian language, and Italian Americans, as much immersion as he could encourage in the subject he was in Montpelier to teach and exemplify. During his first year, he introduced the "Italian Supper," during which, under his guidance, students prepared Southern Italian cuisine, listened to Italian-language songs, and participated in acting skits. His skill and comfort as an educator, with the thoughtful touch of empathy, with storytelling, and with an appreciation for the impediments confronted by the families of each student he encountered, had emerged solidly. His experience at Yale and in New Haven taught him that he could and wanted to define the meaning of Italian American in accordance with values he held and his own meaning of citizenship. The class asked him to remain as their advisor as they moved into their second year.[4]

༄

On July 3, 1937, Val and Peggy were married in First Parish Church of South Berwick, Maine, where her parents and maternal grandparents had married. Relatives from both sides of the family were present. The president of Vermont Junior College, the Reverend Arthur Hewitt, performed the ceremony. The best man was Norman Burns, then living in Washington, DC.[5]

The reception was held at the Davidson home, the yellow home on the hill, decorated with blue larkspur and yellow snapdragons. The newlyweds exchanged books as a wedding gift; the title of his book to her has been lost in family memory; her gift to him, however, was a seventeenth-century Italian-language edition of Dante's *Divine Comedy*. After cutting the cake, the bride changed into a green linen skirt, a natural colored coat of linen, and a green scarf and sports hat. They left immediately for a farm north of Montpelier that they'd rented for a honeymoon. It would be a brief stay. Val had to prepare for classes. Peggy had already been to Montpelier, decorated, and moved furniture into their new home—a house with an attached barn on East State Street, adjacent to the campus. On the back of one photograph in her album she exclaimed: "Our home!" In modified form, the house still stands.[6]

THE PERSISTENCE OF EUGENICS: YALE AND CONNECTICUT

Following President Angell's departure from Yale in 1937 and the publicized, vicious application of eugenics in Germany and the institutionalization of anti-Semitism in Italy—more a political embarrassment to the eugenics community in the United States than a deterrent—members of the Yale faculty who, it appears, had never advocated eugenics' validity were able to assert only marginal control over the content of the Institute of Human Relation's distinct studies of the Italians in New Haven, the lingering stereotypes, the harmful clichés, the generalization that tempered how they were viewed in and outside of Yale, or the adulation still directed at Vittorio Racca.[7] Sterilization in Connecticut also continued.[8]

Between 1935 and 1938, while Wilbur Cross was in his second term as governor, the legislature established, with his approval, a commission to "study the laws and facilities of Connecticut pertaining to the prevention, treatment and care of mental defects and disease and allied problems." Given the broad definition of "mental defects" devised by eugenicists (which Cross, with his history, understood fully) and the well-known meaning of "prevention" already defined in Connecticut to include sterilization and enforced by Cross while governor, the commission's mandate was broad and consequential. The commission's chairman, former Senator Frederic Walcott (Yale 1891), then Cross's commissioner of welfare, was an avowed eugenicist. The Carnegie Institution, the Eugenics Record Office, and its director, Harry Laughlin, were retained to undertake the study. Laughlin, shortly honored in Germany for his work on "racial cleansing," was well known to Cross.[9] Cross "duly instructed" the commission to undertake "a thorough survey of the human resources—good and bad—of the State of Connecticut [especially] the racial, moral, and economic cost of those human inadequates . . . ," including those who were antisocial, inebriate, blind, deaf, and crippled or deformed. The goal, as understood by Carnegie and Laughlin from Cross's directive and reiterated in the final report, was to ensure that Connecticut "conserved"—a term of art and presumable science—its most socially and culturally acceptable breed of citizen.[10]

The Carnegie-Laughlin study and analysis indicated that one in 145 citizens of Connecticut were "feebleminded." Approximately seventeen thousand residents would need "card-indexing . . . by name," including "pedigree notes on the quality of family stock," compiled in each town. The bias, demonstrably

Yale Dean and Connecticut Governor Wilbur L. Cross, circa 1933.
Connecticut State Library, State Archives.

in conflict with the study's own factual findings, was directed against "the more recent immigrant races." Of the people who were sterilized in Connecticut up to that point owing to one of the acceptable criteria—namely, "proven hereditary degeneracy" that "might pass on to their offspring"—408 were women and 25 were men.[11] Laughlin also made clear that as a matter of law, the state's prospective conduct, like its conduct to date, was protected by two Connecticut attorney general opinions and the decision in *Buck v. Bell*. What remained was who in the Connecticut government or medical community would, after reviewing all the indexed families and individuals, make the choice of who should be sterilized on a scope beyond the widespread, arbitrarily imposed existing practice.[12]

The report, *The Survey of the Human Resources of Connecticut: 1937*, with attendant field studies and exhibits (embossed with the official State of Connecticut seal), was submitted to the commission and made available to the public for review. The five volumes of the report and its "findings was [*sic*] accepted by the Commission on November 2nd [1937] in a meeting held at the Hartford Club." The commission, by resolution (November 10, 1938), and the governor, by letter (November 14, 1938, which enclosed the resolution), both acknowledged their respective review of the report's contents. The commission expressed its gratitude to the Carnegie Institution and Laughlin for "this scientific study," and stated that, "We feel that this compilation of data forms an important initial step in a comprehensive scientific study of the essential facts concerning racial and family roots, upon which the success of a long-time practical policy of human conservation must depend." The commission also recommended that Laughlin and Carnegie undertake additional study. In his letter to Laughlin, following his own review of the report, Governor Cross wrote, "As Governor of the State I wish to add my high appreciation of the comprehensive report which was conducted under the direction of the Carnegie Institution. I wish to express my gratitude in full measure."[13]

The report also was distributed publicly and reviewed in the *Hartford Courant* on November 27, 1938. The report, the *Courant* reviewer wrote, "does not make pleasant reading. . . . [The report's solution] is a reduction in the reproduction rate of defective family stocks, [which] carries terrifying implications." The reviewer was dubious: "The laws of human nature are not as simple as those that govern, for instance, the color of sweet peas."[14]

Wilbur Cross lost the general election for a third term in November 1938. He had failed to transform eugenics *any further* into the laws of Connecticut. The institutionalization and sterilization laws remained in place. So, too, did the mentality that justified both, at Yale and in New Haven, where Val's family, their neighbors and friends, and Val's childhood memories held strong, if not defiant, to values he, too, abhorred.

VAL AND PEGGY: DEFINING VALUES

Peggy's knowledge of Italian, Etruscan art, and the New England region became a complement to Val's duties and the college's expectations about creating a family atmosphere for student learning. Val also was named an assistant dean while preserving his full teaching duties, including a course in civics, the duties of citizenship. The couple attended numerous college social events together, and Val judged a highly prized Vermont poetry competition. His popularity grew; so did their collective skill in entertaining and demonstrating that they understood and cared about enhancing the community intellectually and culturally. It was a trait that lasted a lifetime, one central to the context in which Val and Peggy raised their children.[15]

In 1937, Val and Peggy purchased property in East Dover, Vermont, south of Montpelier. In time, they built a modest chalet—rustic, simple, large enough for family visits—and called it "Sugar Hollow." They'd settled in New England. They would also later buy a small cottage on Martha's Vineyard—unassuming, basic in accoutrements, not on the water—both places reflective of the settings Peggy had experienced as a child, enjoyed in the same private, family-oriented manner. With the purchase of the East Dover property especially, in a way familiar in his heritage, Val Giamatti became a simple, seasonal grower of fruits and vegetables.[16]

Val remained in frequent correspondence with his family in New Haven—particularly his sister Helen—his success and marriage shared regularly with neighbors and friends. As he likely learned, the fate of New Haven, its residents, and neighborhoods was on a different, deeply disquieting path.

THE PERSISTENCE OF EUGENICS: YALE AND NEW HAVEN

In June 1938 and January 1939, following very public criticism of eugenics and Germany, Dr. Vannevar Bush, the newly appointed president of the Carnegie Institution, stopped funding the Eugenics Records Office and dismissed Laughlin. Perhaps with an irony and suggestive of a method of perpetual punishment Dante might have inflicted, Harry Laughlin suffered from epilepsy, which, as historian and lawyer Paul A. Lombardo wrote, "under his Model Law would have marked him for sterilization."[17]

In 1939, however, the American Eugenics Society still advocated the need "to cut off the supply of weaklings who are potential burdens to themselves and society." The prospect of war also provided a cloaked rationale for new forms of experimentation.[18] Dean Winternitz remained at the Medical School until 1950. Eugenic "science" continued to be published and taught. One of the nation's most prominent personalities, who brought together as effectively as any other advocate not in government the strains of anti-Semitism, anti-immigrant sentiment, eugenics, and conduct that endorsed Nazi thinking and German militarism, was Charles A. Lindbergh. He shortly emerged on the stage in Yale's Woolsey Hall.[19]

&

In November 1939, Lindbergh made the intersection of his racial and eugenics views with the conduct of American foreign policy unabashedly clear in the nation's most widely circulated magazine, *Reader's Digest*. His goal, a well-understood genuflection to Hitler as much as the advocacy of neutrality in the European war, was to keep America distant from the brutal display of German aggression. In "Aviation, Geography, and Race," Lindbergh posited that "[aviation] is a tool specially shaped for Western hands, . . . another barrier between the teeming millions of Asia and the Grecian inheritance of Europe—one of those priceless possessions which permit the White race to live at all in a pressing sea of Yellow, Black, and Brown." It was time, he admonished America, to create a "Western wall of race and arms. . . . We can have peace and security only so long as we band together to preserve that most priceless possession, our inheritance of European blood, only so long as we guard ourselves against attack by foreign armies and dilution by foreign races." When Lindbergh was embraced and invited to Yale, his eugenics belief and anti-Semitism were no mystery.[20]

&

Eugenics cast an attitude in every setting possible that affirmed discrimination and the permanent, invasive means for enforcing it in law and practice as a worthy, permanent societal *modus operandi*. A generation of "leaders" had been educated in it, had witnessed it, and had been tempered by its correctness. Angell, Lindbergh, Winternitz, and Cross confirmed its legitimacy. It endured with resilience in form and mentality. Many people were harmed and experienced the effects, even if they didn't know the cause. Families needed a way around it, maybe through it. There was no singular route, no agreed-upon path. Attaining dreams and preserving values in New Haven, as it had been for Val Giamatti and others who wanted to do both, still warranted persistence and skill at negotiation.

Yale historian Brooks Mather Kelley referred to the Angell presidency as "the Triumph of the University." Indeed. Not surprisingly, one word does not appear in the text of Kelley's history: eugenics. Still embedded in stone and with its own distinct, wrought-iron arched entranceway, as if it's alive in more than spirit, is Yale's Institute of Human Relations, a memorial to a sadistic morality, embedded along with Yale's other institutional names, surrounded by chilling cries from the neighborhoods of New Haven and beyond, still lingering in the memory of families, still demons lingering in Yale's culture.[21]

&

In Montpelier, by early spring 1938, if not sooner, word was out. Peggy was pregnant. In the *Phoenix*, a periodical written by Vermont Junior College students, the publisher prognosticated: "Can You Imagine Prof. Giamatti wheeling a baby carriage?"[22]

PART IV

ANGELO BARTLETT GIAMATTI

Finding Home

The Stable Dynamic of Transition

The New England Baptist Hospital in Boston—"The Baptist," as it was called—had its religious origins in the Baptist Congregationalist movement of Roger Williams, who was banned by Puritan dogmatists "into the wilderness," as it then existed (actually he founded the colony of Rhode Island). The Baptist, established in 1893 and located on Parker Hill, was distant from the sounds and bustle of Boston, with stunning views of Boston Harbor.[1]

Peggy returned to Wakefield, Massachusetts, to rest under her mother's guidance. It was early spring. As the due date approached, and in a manner reflective of the time, she moved into Baptist. Val traveled back and forth as frequently as he could, while maintaining his teaching schedule. On April 4, 1938, Peggy gave birth to a healthy son, whom they named Angelo Bartlett, after both their fathers. From the outset, he was called Bart to distinguish him (in the family manner) from Peggy's father, who remained a central part of Bart's upbringing. Although "Angelo" was used periodically, in school registries and on his first passport, Bart's childhood friends in South Hadley and adult friends throughout his life referred to him as Bart. Proper respect had been given to Val's father, and Val—having himself been a departure from the cultural tradition—was comfortable with "Bartlett" and "Bart," knowing, as he and Peggy agreed, that the Italian American cultural tradition and his family experience would, in time, still be an integral part of his son's upbringing, knowledge, and life. At Vermont Junior College, the Class of 1939, the first graduating class, declared in the *Phoenix*: "To Angelo Bartlett Giamatti we bequeath the official title 'Class Mascot of the Graduating Class of 1939.'"[2]

Though the school calendar was filled with welcomed intensity unabated by Bart's birth—enrollment doubled, new courses were offered, Val and Peggy joined the reception for new students in September, and Val chaired the annual Christmas Party—two events of consequence occurred that provided new direction. Peggy, Val, and Bart spent their first holiday with Peggy's parents and family in Wakefield. That family framework, expected, proximate, and embraced by both parents, remained constant throughout Bart's childhood and into the lives of his children. And Val and Peggy made the necessary inquiries at Harvard about the possibility of Val completing his PhD there. Once accepted, Val announced their departure from Montpelier to Cambridge, to the chagrin, yet warm wishes, of faculty and students.[3]

CAMBRIDGE:

THE HARVARD EMBRACE AND THE MOUNT HOLYOKE OPPORTUNITY

Val sought a PhD from the Graduate School of Arts and Sciences. Harvard placed him on a track to receive a Doctor of Philology (the study of language through its history and culture) by the June commencement of 1940. He immediately sought information on housing for married students.[4] Shaler Lane, lined with a row of unique, attached brick townhouse duplexes, built in 1920, is like an idyllic village enclave in Cambridge. For young Bart and his parents, the setting was perfect for daytime strolls, picnics, intimate entertainment, and easy proximity to the graduate school, retail, and the occasional dinner out.[5]

Harvard welcomed Val's proposed dissertation topic. Looking through the Department of Romance Languages and Literature archives from this period, one can clearly see that the dean and others sought, from existing faculty and PhD candidates, detailed biographical and linguistic studies of Europeans who effectively crossed borders to influence the political and literary life of another nation.[6] A study of the political conduct of Chevalier de Cambray-Digny in the American Revolution, properly developed, fit readily within Harvard's framework.

In the midst of completing his research and writing, Val learned that his younger sister, Adelina, had died from a heart ailment. Within months, his mother, Maria, died from a "cerebrovascular accident, cardiovascular disease, [and weakening from] three previous attacks." She was sixty-four years old. Val quickly made two brief visits to New Haven for the wake and funeral, both held in the Hill/Oak Street/Legion Avenue neighborhood. The deaths from heart disease were a harbinger, an indelible inheritance. He had been close to his mother and his sisters; retained a deep relationship (as his son would later) with his older sister, Helen; shared with each of them the duty to help pay family expenses; and though she'd declined, he'd offered to pay for Helen's college education. His part-time teaching positions involved women students, whom he'd also mentored. Those female relationships, now complemented with the highly educated women in Peggy's family, ensured that at Vermont Junior College he understood the dreams of women from rural, working-class families of varied religious and ethnic backgrounds and that he knew how to intercede to ensure that they were treated fairly and equally. This experience in valued temperament and training mattered when, in the late spring of 1940, he received a phone call from Mount Holyoke College—likely at the direction of its president, Roswell Ham—seeking his interest in teaching at this famed, woman-founded, all-women student body college in South Hadley, Massachusetts.[7]

The serendipity, the unexpected virtue embedded in Yale's rejection of his topic, had yielded a pathway to marriage and successful teaching in Vermont. That rejection yielded another gift that stood solidly in a life now better understood: a Harvard degree, the fulfillment of his commitment to the Cambray-Digny family, and, equally compelling, proof of his persistence—a tribute to his mother and a signal forward, with subtle, deep, immigrant-like striving, at this moment for his son to witness and later, as Bart came to understand it, to emulate. Val Giamatti was still moving toward the life he and Peggy envisioned, as they planned their family relocation to South Hadley.

Val was awarded his PhD from Harvard at a grand ceremony on the Sever Quadrangle, held on June 20, 1940. The president of Harvard: James Bryant Conant. Among the graduates: John Fitzgerald Kennedy. In the audience: Helen Walton and Bart Giamatti. In the Boston Baptist Hospital: Peggy Giamatti and their six-day-old daughter, Elena Maria.[8]

⌘

Val continued to fill out the Yale alumni form necessary to keep an active, current relationship with his 1932 graduating class. When their daughter was born, he noted on the alumni form that his son, Bart, had transformed her name into "Elria." With an affection that still holds, the name was embraced by all within the family, including by Bart's younger brother, Dino. Val, who religiously attended his class reunions and embraced old friends with joy and comfort, never lingered at Yale events. And though he consistently paid his class dues, he declined to contribute to the university's annual fundraising drive. He'd seen and experienced its underlying culture and, in the end, had graduated with the highest academic rank possible, values intact. He had no illusions.[9]

YALE AND NEW HAVEN:
THE VIRTUE OF NOT BEING THERE

In the late 1930s and into the early 1940s, Yale's largely white Anglo-Saxon tone and manner solidified and detached it further from the American culture. When Kingman Brewster—who became Griswold's provost and Bart's predecessor as president—arrived in the fall of 1937, Yale students, "'as a whole, [we]re rich. Their families . . . represent[ed] the economic royalists of America'. . . . Three-quarters of Yale's students had attended preparatory schools, where a year's

Elria and Bart Giamatti.
Giamatti-Ewing Collection.

tuition exceeded the country's average annual income." Brewster had attended the boys' preparatory Belmont Hill School, just outside Cambridge. In private grammar school—the time period within which he developed his accent—"he was usually driven by his grandfather's chauffeurs." It was a cultural tone readily understood among his peers.[10] *Stover at Yale* was their guide. Charles Seymour, Yale's new president, "declared his responsibility to be 'the preservation at Yale of spiritual values that have come down from long generations of Yale men.'" That spiritual underpinning melded into another presumption central to university and student attitude about education: "Those who became leaders at Yale would someday lead the nation."[11]

The exceptions to this orientation—apart from day students, whose numbers dwindled with the advent of residence halls, and those involved in Christian organizations, who congregated in Yale's progressive-oriented Dwight Hall—were limited.[12] Brewster's attention and sense of obligation, for example, were directed elsewhere; always "a little full of himself: he arrived at his *Daily News* office each day in a three-piece suit with a gold watch fob across his vest."[13] "Ever since they were undergraduates, of course, [Kingman] Brewster and his friends . . . were also elitists. . . . They thought that the best men should make the decisions. . . . They resisted the idea that elite authority should, in any substantive way, be devolved or dissipated."[14] His view on the posture he sought, through most of his life and certainly at Yale in 1940, "suggested the original definition of aristocracy."[15] New Haven was merely a "shabby industrial city" on which, by architectural design and inbred cultural selection, Yale, as Brewster biographer Geoffrey Kabaservice acknowledged, had "turned [its] back."[16]

ॐ

Under Seymour's guidance, the deliberateness of anti-Semitism (Jews were called "Brooklyn Boys") and of excluding "Mediterranean individuals" in admission decisions continued unabated, despite the efforts of Connecticut's legislature.[17] Convinced that Protestant boys were superior, "Yale's administrators and admissions staff thought they knew what embryonic leaders looked like, but they wanted to measure that."[18] It may never be clear what purpose the photographs served observant Yale administrators—young men, sixteen, seventeen, eighteen years old, in the nude, standing against measuring rods, full frontals and side photographs taken—except to preserve and scientifically rationalize cultural purity and keep an eye on "exceptional" students. Joseph Soares summarized the practice in *The Power of Privilege*, drawing, in part, from the revelatory work of Ron Rosenbaum for the *New York Times Magazine*, published in 1995. Social and cultural critic Dick Cavett (Yale 1958) also described the ritual—"stark lighting (and the stark nakedness) and . . . a whiff of . . . the concentration camp"—and the presumption (the relationship between "body types and destiny"). Most troublesome, Cavett concluded, was that "nobody objected."[19] The practice continued during the Griswold and Brewster era and then during the Brewster presidency with a character so deeply embedded as the acceptable norm that, even then, no one questioned it.[20]

With respect to the School of Medicine, Dr. Milton Winternitz, then professor of pathology, affirmed with rejuvenated assertiveness "the importance of investigation in the field of medicine" during wartime. "It is obvious," he said, "what this growth of the Yale School of Medicine means to the National Defense." Experimentation sponsored and conducted by Yale had special application, once again, to the people of New Haven's neighborhoods. The "feebleminded," "increasingly . . . viewed as that intermediate step in the research process between mice and 'normal humans,'" included those men, women, and children residing within mental institutions and prisons (already stigmatized by Connecticut's eugenics laws and sterilization surgery) and New Haven's orphanages. In *Against Their Will*, drawing from the Medical School's formal reports on its experimentation, the authors described Yale's conduct with respect to one such experiment: "One of 'the most important findings,' of the experiments of hepatitis," the authors wrote, "for example, was that 'the disease can be produced by feeding feces from a case of infectious hepatitis.' To do so required 'human volunteers.' . . . The key players in this drama, which 'inoculated' dozens of subjects, included the Yale University School of Medicine, the Middletown [Connecticut] and Norwich [Connecticut] State Hospitals, and the federal Correctional Institution of Danbury, Connecticut. In their effort to demonstrate that 'gamma globulin will protect injected individuals against infectious hepatitis,' 'a girls school in Providence, R.I., and a Catholic Institution for children in New Haven' were the subjects of study." The formal report suggests that the New Haven institution was the Saint Francis Orphan Asylum, a then-Dickensian construct, dark, dank, where the nuns administered corporal punishment daily. Reported patient recollections indicate that the orphans were primarily Irish and Italian Catholic boys and girls from impoverished families in New Haven.[21]

⸎

By the late 1930s, Yale's labor force comprised among the lowest-paid employees in New Haven, subject to rough, often arbitrary, conditions of employment. President Angell's massive construction program and the introduction of the residential college system had increased the need for maintenance workers, maids, and clerical (so-called white-collar) personnel in a manner that only elevated the visible, harmful effect on workers' lives and families. The first attempt to unionize in 1937 failed, but lessons were learned. Yale was a visible public institution with a state charter. Further, Labor's fate had a complex dynamic to it, with multiple participants, on and off the Yale campus, who were affected by and could affect the content and direction of contracts.

The Reverend George Butler of Summerfield Methodist Church, located near Yale in the Dixwell/Newhallville neighborhood, brought the seriousness of the problem to public attention in his 1938 article in *Nation* magazine. Other unions joined in the fight. On campus, interest and support came from the Christian imperatives of students and ministers at Dwight Hall.[22] Within New Haven, it was the Yale maids and supportive women who mattered. Moreover, Yale's ill-purposed effect on New Haven had become a permanent reality in the public dialogue.[23]

In May 1941, Local 142, United Construction Workers, Congress of Industrial Organizations, was formed by a vote of the Yale employees. Impasse emerged quickly in negotiations over the terms of a new contract: Yale refused to accept a "union shop"—a contract provision in which the employer agrees to hire only union members or those people who agree to join the union. The strike began on November 10, 1941. Mediators for the state of Connecticut arrived on campus. Four hundred strikers encircled portions of Yale and walked peacefully down Elm Street. Maids and janitors were the largest number among them. The strike lasted a day. An agreement was reached. Some workers now had a recognized union; other benefits also were included in the contract. The union shop was not among them. Not yet.[24]

The contentiousness between Yale and Labor had begun. Angell and Seymour set the tone. Griswold would choose the cold pathway of condescension. Brewster would turn contentiousness and his embedded condescension toward employees into a compelled "civil rights struggle" for workers' rights.[25] In time, Yale workers included Val Giamatti's sister Helen and two of his cousins when his son Bart, as president, sought to depart from the temperament and assumptions that long governed Yale's disquieting treatment of its employees.

HOME

South Hadley, Massachusetts, was settled in 1721 and formally organized into a town in 1775. Its total area is approximately eighteen square miles (about the size of New Haven), its form of government, an elective representative council. The town's character has historical roots in the American Revolution, and its residents specially mark "The Loyalty and Patriotism of Our Citizen Soldiers Who Fought for Liberty and The Union in the Great Rebellion of 1861–1865" through a granite obelisk—Gaylord Civil War Monument—that stands in a neatly configured green space adjacent to small shop retail, modest residential offerings, church, and a post office (a depiction of "South Hadley" was painted inside during the Franklin D. Roosevelt years), together referred to as the Village Commons. The Commons was in the northern section of the town at the intersection of College, Hadley, and Woodbridge streets when the Giamattis arrived. The town was further defined by industrial growth, especially along the Connecticut River in the southern section of town, referred to as South Hadley Falls. The Falls and its industrial life—especially its attraction for Irish, French Canadian, and Southern and Eastern European immigrants (Polish, Lithuanian, and Italian in particular)—were still bustling and productive in 1940.[26]

Mount Holyoke College, founded in 1837 by educator Mary Lyon, was designed and landscaped by Frederick Law Olmsted and his sons between 1896 and 1922. Mount Holyoke is the oldest continuing institution of higher education exclusively for women in the United States, its campus situated in the northern section of the town and proximate to the "Great Rebellion" monument and the

Village Commons. High-achieving graduates from South Hadley High School were admitted with financial support from the college.[27]

The town is surrounded by Holyoke, another industrial city adjacent to the Connecticut River, and Chicopee, the home of Westover Air Force Base, established in 1940. Many of Westover's off-base personnel and families lived in South Hadley, and their children attended the public schools. A sizable Jewish community was active in Holyoke and in regional commerce; many families lived in South Hadley, and their children attended the public schools. The modestly rugged Mount Holyoke Range State Park was nearby, available for hiking and skiing. And within the periphery of the town was agricultural land, with working farms, especially dairy. Once World War II began, some English and German refugees arrived, each family with children in need of friendship, a public school education, and the transition into America. Also nearby was the rapidly growing city of Springfield, where Val's former Yale classmate Foster Furcolo would enter elective politics successfully as a liberal Democratic member of Congress, altering a view that western Massachusetts was a Republican stronghold and that the Democratic Party depended on Boston for its strength. Boston was a two-and-a-half-hour drive from South Hadley.

For Peggy, the town was a setting that required sensible insight, grace, and the exercise of informed skill to give fullness to her family's aspirations and her own. She had confidence in those skills. She and Val would also be close to her parents, sisters, and cousins, for holiday visits especially, and to their vacation property in Vermont. For Val, there was the prospect of intellectual and educational growth for himself and the community. His experience in Montpelier, within the college and among the diversity of the student body; his PhD dissertation, which blended European heroism and intellect into the cause of American freedom; and the presence within the region of Italian Americans and other ethnic families with a broad range of skills, backgrounds, and aspirations all provided a base for high expectations. The family moved immediately. They settled temporarily in Mount Holyoke–supplied housing on College Street as Peggy, especially, looked for a home close to the campus and near the Center School, one of the town's four grammar schools that Bart and Elria could attend. They purchased a spacious two-story colonial crafted house, with an attic, basement, and garage, and with large front and back yards, at 29 Silver Street, within sight of Mount Holyoke and walking distance to the Center School. Both children could walk home for lunch, past the "Great Rebellion" tribute and the college that would add definition to their lives and, within a few years, the life of their brother, Dino.[28]

13

WITNESS IN WAR

He often said he was shy, he was naïve, he was retiring, and he believed it—though of course no one else did or could. He was simply too central, too much the source, the origin of too much, to be believable in those moments when he would reveal how reticent he was. . . . He may have felt himself in check but for none of the rest of us did he ever appear to be anything but running at full tide.

—A. Bartlett Giamatti,
Eulogy for Valentine John Giamatti, April 15, 1982

THE COLLEGE THEY ENTERED

At Mount Holyoke College, and in South Hadley, the Giamattis, especially their son Bart, gave vent to a family definition of the public duty of the private life, borne foremost in experience and values, now nurtured and encouraged by the historical culture created by the college's founder.

⁓

Mary Lyon, a famed educator, intent on physical and cultural risk taking in pursuit of her purpose, was born in western Massachusetts in 1797, not far from the site she selected for Mount Holyoke. Her purpose was clear: make higher education—not including domestic skills, but based on a rigorous academic curriculum—available to women of all economic means. The culture of that insistence endowed the college as well, and never left it. When it opened in November 1837, Lyon defined Mount Holyoke's goal: public service, teaching, a duty to society's people in need wherever required, and an academic and practical excellence that would ensure both. "Go where no one else will go," she admonished students. "Do what no one else will do."[1]

In 1893, students were given an institutionalized voice in the college's governance. Among the new subjects introduced during this era was Italian, first taught, still unpredictably, by an adjunct lecturer and then occasional professor.[2] In 1900, Mount Holyoke embarked on a profoundly liberal tone. In Mary Emma Woolley, the college selected a model worthy of emulation or available for just a good talk about guidance in life. Woolley chose a faculty that ensured her goals were reached. Education was as much about citizenship, preparation for the life fully led, and the intellectual capacity to make any choice a woman wanted. On January 1, 1901, at the age of thirty-eight, she was inaugurated president.

Woolley appointed her partner, Jeannette Augustus Marks, as an instructor in English. Marks had been an accomplished student at Wellesley, and the two women formed what has been characterized as a lifelong partnership until Woolley's death. Mount Holyoke embraced a relationship of unusual character in its era. The relationship did not affect Woolley's tenure, the acceptance of her policies, or the timing of her departure. At play, in time and over a long period of time, was, among many, an education in understanding, tolerance, and an appreciation that the goal of Mount Holyoke was to provide an excellent education. Marks added to that in ways well known, especially to any prospective faculty member, including Valentine Giamatti and, later in life and during Bart's presidency of Yale, Val's son. Woolley, in addition to expanding the college physically and in its academic offerings, was a determined, globally recognized, forceful advocate for women's education and suffrage, and civil liberties and political rights.[3]

When Woolley announced her retirement in 1936, at age seventy-four, she expected, as did the Board of Trustees, that her successor would be a woman. After a number of women declined the position, the trustees interviewed male candidates, including Roswell Gray Ham, then on the Yale faculty. When Ham was appointed, anger, disappointment, and opposition were voiced by Woolley, national organizations, and alumnae, but the tumult in Europe, already felt on the college's campus, and Ham's liberal attitude in speech and practice came to displace the uproar over his selection.[4] He took office in September 1937. He was tall, solidly built, and gregarious by nature. Early on, he received a note of welcome from Robert Frost, albeit tongue in cheek: "Meanwhile as from one Native Son to another my best wishes for a long and prosperous term in office." Both men were born in California.[5]

❧

Mount Holyoke's American Student Union chapter supported Franklin D. Roosevelt's New Deal. The chapter's forceful president was Ella Tambussi of Windsor Locks, Connecticut, who entered during Woolley's tenure, thrived under Ham's, and foretold, with accurate criticism, the early iteration of the McCarthy-era attack on "Communists" that, in time, was directed against Mount Holyoke. For Ella Tambussi, there was nothing detached or purely academic about a Mount Holyoke education.[6]

With the earliest stirrings of war in Spain and elsewhere in Europe, students were encouraged by faculty to speak and write about the radical alteration of ideological and military forces emerging in Europe, and the rising militarism in the United States. Generally, Mount Holyoke's student body opposed America's entrance into war, though many among them, as well as Ham and the faculty, made the transition to support England and war's preparation as nations fell to Nazi and Fascist military superiority.[7]

As the likelihood of war engrossed the campus, Val opened his temporary home on College Street for student classes, a practice the college encouraged. During one class, Peggy was hanging clothes to dry and caring for the two children in the next room, when young Bart walked in "with dark hair and wearing a suit" and disrupted the class. The move to Silver Street was welcomed. Ella Tambussi, who "took on 'babysitting chores' to earn money," was entrusted with Bart and Elria.[8] Life, however, was in quick transition. Val formed the Mount Holyoke Dante Club, composed of students but open to others, which met regularly in offices on campus and in his home. Plain that the war would be against Italy, Val intended the Club as the vehicle for the sponsorship of college and community events centered on Dante, his era, and his writing and—on and off the campus and in cooperation with other groups—the elevation of the Italian and Italian American culture. It was a critical moment: Italian Americans already were enlisting in huge numbers to fight Fascism especially. In establishing a base to meld his intentions, Val joined the Massachusetts Chapter of the Sons of Italy in America in order to expand the cultural opportunities for his students and his own social contacts. Val also joined the American Anti-Fascist Committee.[9]

YALE: LATE TO THE NATIONAL STUDENT DEBATE

As in Mount Holyoke, in universities throughout the nation students formed groups in response to the growing tension in Europe as early as 1934, and with greater intensity by 1938. They included the American Student Union and its offshoot, Youth Committee Against War, directed by student activist Fay Bennett.[10] Student opposition coalesced around the meaning of democracy in the United States, concern about people not included within its benefits and principles—sharecroppers, slum dwellers, immigrants, African Americans, laborers, and the poor. Looming as well was the wartime draft. Who'd be exempt, and who'd be the first to go into harm's way, was well known by poor and working-class young men.[11]

Republicans, troubled by Roosevelt's popularity and commitment to seek a third term, coalesced around any movement that would ensure his defeat. Others were overtly pro-Hitler, anti-Semitic, or vehemently anti-Roosevelt in sentiment (like Kingman Brewster's father). Some with deep pockets financed opposition under a range of banners, some unseemly. In May 1940, in a national radio address, Charles Lindbergh added further clarity to his adulation of Hitler's conduct, and his declared eugenics beliefs. "A week after Germany's . . . invasion of the Low Countries, . . . Lindbergh told a national radio audience that 'the only reason we are in danger of becoming involved in this war is because there are powerful elements in America who desire us to take part. . . . [A] small minority . . . [who] control much of the machinery of influence and propaganda.'" "Listeners," historian Marc Wortman explained, "realized he was speaking primarily about Jews."[12]

Progressive Senator George Norris of Nebraska, who had opposed American entrance into World War I, strongly supported American preparation and entrance into the war being waged in Europe.[13] He was not alone, especially among Yale's international affairs faculty.[14]

⚬

The national debate did not materially alter the relatively passive student culture at Yale until the late spring of 1940. The broad cultural influence of eugenics and its presumptions were part of the reason. So, too, was the smallness of the world many Yale students lived in, the relative comfort and confidence about the choices available that many among them enjoyed and expected without apprehension of change. The transformative moment, according to Wortman, began in June 1940 with former Secretary of State (under Herbert Hoover) Henry Stimson's radio address from New Haven, followed by Yale Professor Arnold Whitridge's "Where Do You Stand?, an Open Letter to American Undergraduates," published in the *Atlantic* in August, and Yale President Seymour's "War's Impact on the Campus," published in the *New York Times Magazine* in September. Each man warned about the danger of American isolation. Whitridge and Seymour especially lamented the absence of voices that understood the peril extant in Europe among the select young men who mattered to them.[15]

Discussion at Yale about organizing began informally. Kingman Brewster, a junior and head of the *Yale Daily News*, joined the existing debate among a small group of law students led by Robert Stuart Jr. The consensus was to express skepticism about the underlying value of America's entrance into the war. The group's primary rationale was Lindbergh's: America could be defended by air power regardless of the outcome in Europe. Lindbergh expected the victor to be Germany. Brewster and the others, albeit peering through a gilded historically clouded looking glass,[16] joined the ongoing substantive debate. Their fate in the world they expected to move in was at stake, though they remained unsettled about precisely which values, historically and properly formed, mattered to them generationally. They were "often at a loss when asked to describe what they believed in."[17] By late June, just after Stimson's radio address, "The Emergency Committee for Defense of America First" was formed.[18] Within days, Stuart and Brewster orchestrated the Committee's embrace of Lindbergh; its almost immediate trajectory *away* from students; and, by choice, its melding into the full political breath and fate of evolving and sophisticated adult agendas, money, skill, and identity.[19]

Conservative Republican Party leaders, especially Robert Taft, were the first to be asked by Brewster to join. Taft accepted, followed by substantial corporate money and a radical transformation into a national organization headquartered in Chicago.

Lindbergh, at the request of Brewster and Stuart, came to Yale in October 1940, was entertained, and then was introduced to the audience by Brewster and Assistant Professor Richard Bissell at Woolsey Hall, and the new identity of "America First" was solidified. Lindbergh became the national spokesperson, and membership in "America First" included the full range of prejudices that existed in America. Brewster was no longer entering the debate purely or independently as a student. He had knowledgeably brought that purity, and freedom, to an end, including for others.[20]

Yale students were overwhelmingly for Wendell Willkie, as were many people in and around the university.[21] Roosevelt had supporters among the faculty and students for and against aiding England.[22] To the recently arrived political émigrés from Fascist Italy, the Calabresi family, as their son Guido recounts it, Yale supporters of "America First" were "naïve" about the danger. Roosevelt easily won the popular and electoral vote, and thanks to the heavy turnout for him in the Italian, Irish, and Jewish neighborhoods, he trounced Willkie in New Haven.[23] Dean William DeVane immediately sought to preserve the liberal atmosphere that had prevailed throughout the debate. Under the banner headline, "Faculty, Students Unite in Urging Renouncement of Party Differences," DeVane wrote: "I sincerely hope Americans, especially disappointed voters, will pull together for the good of the country." At Yale, that meant a large majority of students and their parents.[24]

☙

Debate over American intervention came to a visible head in the form of the proposed Lend-Lease Act (making war materials and other assets available to England under favorable terms). United States Senate hearings were scheduled. The setting was grand: the cavernous Caucus Room. The *Titanic* hearings were held there. Newspaper coverage was national, wire service even broader. Dozens of witnesses sat and awaited the call. It was February 7, 1941. Two individuals were chosen to represent "youth's generation": Kingman Brewster (invited by Senator Hiram Johnson, R-California), and Fay Bennett (invited by Senator Gerald Nye, R-North Dakota). When called, each would sit, alone, around a table, only a few feet away from the Committee's members who chose to be there, and present their views.[25]

Brewster's full testimony, read into the record,[26] was grandly parsed, imprecise and incorrect in knowledge of government, and uninterrupted by custom (though it took Senator Johnson four questions at the outset to get Brewster to acknowledge he was there as "chairman of the Yale Chapter of the America

First Committee"). To supporters of President Roosevelt (already reelected), Brewster included an *ad hominem* attack on him and those people who supported American aid to England (they'd engaged in "deceit and subterfuge"), while he praised Lindbergh's "courage and straightforwardness."[27] The subsequent questions put to Brewster tied him to the national organization (and by implication, its followers, financers, leaders, and prejudices);[28] pierced as incorrect his assertion that enactment of the proposed bill would give the president unprecedented authority to risk American entrance into the war;[29] and probed his harsh form of criticism of those with whom he disagreed, in a manner likely intended to demonstrate, as Senator Alben Barkley (D-Kentucky) conveyed in his questioning, Brewster's ill-informed factual predicates and his intolerance of "the exercise of freedom of speech" by others.[30]

Fay Bennett represented the "Youth Committee Against War," composed of "hundreds of thousands of American young people who are firmly dedicated to the ideals of democracy." Her testimony, though it included deference to those experts (she did not mention Lindbergh) who believed the United States could deter an invasion, was premised on the need for the nation to concentrate, foremost, on perfecting "the ideals of democracy." Unlike "America First," and absent from Brewster's testimony and cultural milieu, Bennett spoke about the "Unsolved problems at home. The thousands of young people who await their future in the long lines outside the employment office . . . the farm boys chained to a land which has no room for them, the Okies who ride hungry on California's wide macadam roads, the faceless boys and girls on the street corners of New York." "What," she asked, "are we doing for democracy here in America?"[31]

༄

Yale students and recent graduates did not embrace the Yale Chapter of America First (or its student or national leadership) as the organizational vehicle for expressing their opposition to war or the proposed Lend-Lease bill.[32] The bill became law on March 31, 1941. In April, Brewster declined to continue his participation in America First, though he continued to walk in Lindbergh's shadow, his "childhood adulation," as Kabaservice explained it, preserved throughout the remainder of his life.[33]

Yale students (including Brewster) and, later, Lindbergh, as well as millions of other Americans, including thousands of men from New Haven's neighborhoods, enlisted or were drafted into the United States' military effort to defeat Japan, Germany, and Italy.[34] Women in New Haven joined the nursing corps; others among them led in the transformation of New Haven's industrial power into munitions, logistical, and clothing supplies essential to the nation's global commitment. Medal of Honor recipient Marine Corps Gunnery Sergeant John Basilone drove through New Haven's streets, with respectfully displayed civic and military honors, to raucous admiration. He appeared before a filled house of awestruck citizens at the New Haven Arena to encourage the sale of war bonds, before returning to participate in the landing at Iwo Jima, where he was killed.[35] Yale undergraduates and graduates killed in action, honored in their hometowns, later would have their names added to the foyer inside Memorial Hall. For those still alive, and for subsequent Yale students who'd experienced the meaning of the Great War and World War II, Memorial Hall and the Hewitt Quadrangle became something in the nature of hallowed ground. In New Haven's neighborhoods, heavy costs were paid within families, bravery in combat often recognized, sometimes not, and burials and the joyful return of a loved one deeply and quietly embedded in memory.[36]

GIAMATTI AND HAM: CITIZENSHIP IN WAR

To Val, the theme of his position was derived from what he had experienced in Italy and in New Haven: separating the Italian people, here and abroad, and their commitment to democratic values and fairness from the indefensible conduct of government officials or irresponsible leaders. One photograph of Val's father, Angelo, taken around 1941 or 1942, is with his grandson George on his shoulder, walking through the neighborhood, an Italian immigrant leading the responsible private life. In August 1943, Angelo Giammattei died at age sixty-one. The cause was a heart attack, another indication, perhaps not yet absorbed fully by his son, of a genetically weak heart. Val and Peggy, likely with their son, Bart, then five, would have traveled to New Haven, where Angelo was buried alongside his wife, Maria. The generational baton in America had unequivocally passed. Angelo had done what he set out to do since age thirteen: settle and raise a family in New Haven and leave them as secure and stable as he and Maria Grazia possibly could do. For Val, the generational duty was his to continue. He did, as his son witnessed.[37]

As an anti-Fascist, Val addressed audiences throughout the South Hadley region during the war, especially at the Holyoke Jewish Center and, during weekends or semester breaks, in Waterbury, Connecticut, and Albany, New York.[38] In September 1943, Val Giamatti—"born in America and of Italian extraction," the *Holyoke Transcript-Telegram (Holyoke Telegram)* wrote, a description he'd now carry with the pride of his mother and father still vivid in his mind—spoke to a capacity audience in Holyoke as a member of the American Anti-Fascist Committee. Calling on his experience in Italy of combing the streets and shops and what he knew from the Italian immigrant and Italian American communities in New Haven and now Massachusetts, he criticized the Allies for encouraging the Italian people to oppose Mussolini, yet ridiculing Italians as cowards—a short-sighted attitude, with no regard for the Italian men and women aiding the rescue of captured Allied soldiers or protecting Jews from capture by occupying German troops. "A long succession of foreign tyrants and broken promises [thinking, in part, of the disappointment from Italian Unification, and previous rulers among the French, Spanish, and Catholic Church] makes the Italian of today cynical and uncertain as to which way he should turn." He had learned firsthand, he said, that the people of Italy welcomed Americans and people of other nations who did not intend harm. The Allied invasion had, in fact, just begun. Apprehension among the Italian people, he concluded, was high.[39]

It was a theme in thought and experience articulated in New Haven by Italian refugee and anti-Fascist Dr. Massimo Calabresi.[40] The Calabresis and the Giamattis did not know each other yet, though there was, already, a meeting of minds. Roswell Ham, subjected to FBI investigations and attacks on his patriotism and the college's integrity, never wavered in his support of Val's conduct.[41] Within the Giamatti family, the news coverage of Val's outspoken views was preserved in the family's archives and was the subject of discussion and education through the remainder of their lives.[42]

❧

The men from South Hadley who fought and died in the cause of preserving freedom were buried in the town's cemeteries, some, perhaps, in Arlington National Cemetery and others abroad. Their heroism was entombed and recognized in the Gaylord Civil War Monument in the Village Center. A solemn tribute to them, nurses, and all the others who fought was paid in a townwide commemoration held yearly, where, in one moment of that tribute, a student of the highest oratorical skill recited Lincoln's Gettysburg Address. In time, it would be Angelo Bartlett Giamatti.

14

FAMILY LIFE IN SOUTH HADLEY

CITIZENSHIP AND RESPONSIBILITY

Valentine and Peggy Giamatti settled into a community with precisely the liberal, practiced values they wanted for their children: education, knowledge, and respectful, welcomed treatment of others. They began to entertain immediately. As Val learned about South Hadley, friendships developed throughout the community, especially in the Falls, and the range of people invited to Silver Street from the outset was as varied as the town's culture.

Roswell Ham and Val Giamatti had known each other since Yale. They had developed a warm, engaged, and productive relationship that benefited both of them as well as their families through frequent visits and discussions. Their students, too, were welcomed into the Giamatti home in a close-knit world where educational excellence and mentoring were expected and appreciated. Rose Criscitiello Longo, one of Val's first students, described it: "At a party that Val had at his house, President Ham was there. And he was out in the kitchen washing dishes."[1] It's in this context, though only in a complex thread of influences still to come, that Bart Giamatti later spoke warmly about his father: "I think I learned all my real lessons from my father. . . . He really was the person who taught me about teaching, and by watching him, about scholarship. I saw him teach all the time, not just in the classroom. . . . He was the first person to introduce me to literature and he gave me to understand that the academic world, while it's never a perfect world. . . . is one where there are real aspiration and ideals."[2] When Bart, asked his view of his predecessors as presidents of Yale, said that he knew them "as persons, and perhaps that's why they aren't public figures to me," he described what his parents also gave him: the sense to judge character not based on title or power or presumptions unearned but on values, especially those he'd come to cherish by witnessing them in his parents and those who entered their, and his, life daily. In this influence was a form of irreverence.[3]

❧

Val turned his attention to teaching and, with Peggy, to their manner of family and civic duty. In promotional literature issued by the college, Val stands tall, book in hand, as if in the midst of a lecture. He was chair of the newly formed Italian Department. He taught three, at times four classes: Italian, in progressive stages; Dante in Italian; Dante in English, one of the most popular courses on campus; and, occasionally, Portuguese. The Dante Club membership grew, "with President Roswell Gray Ham as prime enthusiast." The club produced plays in Italian; in his second year, Val directed the play *La Pelliccia*, a one-act farcical comedy about the corruptive effect of greed.[4] He organized bus trips into Boston for students and parents to museums, libraries, and theatrical productions dealing with Italian works, scholars, and historic locations in Italy and America. He deliberately invited Bart's friend Frank White to come. Bart and Elria joined as well. Club meetings were hosted at the Giamatti home and at President Ham's, with "informal discussions led by such Dante scholars as Prof. Angelo Lipari of Yale."[5]

Val brought practicality to the challenge of appreciating Italian, Dante, and the *Commedia*. Peggy organized a language laboratory; her superior skill in Italian grammar aided students in pronunciation and sentence structure. Val wrote a textbook, *Minimum of Italian Grammar*, when few such books existed.[6] Since at least the time of Galileo, Dante scholars also had sought ways of conceptualizing Dante's journey. Artists imagined moments, locations, often in grand, horrific depictions, sometimes in tiers of gradual terror or punishment. What remained was the need for a diagram, a teaching tool, one that conveyed enough detail of the journey into the *Inferno* and out of it to make it easier for readers to follow, to give more life to how Dante saw and thought about each tier and the variations of degradation directed to whom. In the 1580s, Galileo had returned to Florence after studying mathematics and medicine at the University of Pisa and gave public lectures "to the Florentine Academy on the conic configuration of Dante's Inferno." Not satisfied with what he found, Val blended some earlier and some new drawings and his own annotations into *Panoramic Views of Dante's Inferno, Purgatory, and Paradise*, which illustrated all three places in Dante's journey. It was published and used by students and other faculty members in teaching subjects in which Dante or the Renaissance mattered.[7]

Val continued to give talks throughout New England about the war's effects and the people of Italy. He had insight into aspects of American foreign policy and how it was perceived. In a region growing with Italian Americans and with the need to understand risks and changes abroad, Val's credentials substantiated his credibility as a welcomed, lucid intellect and doer on matters of importance to many in the audience.[8]

∽

Val and Peggy's activities, in a community where the college's faculty often brought exotic travel, substantive speakers, and published writings into public view, were covered by the press and enjoyed by townsfolk with a wondrous relish. Those activities were embraced as part of the town's definition of itself. When Bart entered Center School (Elria followed shortly), Val became president of the Center School Parent Teacher Association, and Peggy became head of the transportation committee. The PTA's activities were covered frequently in the Holyoke newspaper. Meetings were held at the Giamatti home. No matter the issue the PTA addressed or the activity he encouraged, Val and Peggy did the actual work, shared easily the value of the contribution made by others, and knew how to connect that value to the college's and community's well-being.[9] The Giamattis had become citizens of South Hadley.

PUBLIC SCHOOL, FRIENDSHIPS, AND THE ETHIC OF FAIRNESS

Bart's parents developed close friendships with neighbors on and near Silver Street; their reputation centered on openness, their home easily accessible for their children's friends, their temperament welcoming and no doubt discerning about how their children learned about life and from whom.[10] Shared birthday celebrations and lunch with whomever they were playing were commonplace and reciprocated by other parents. Val applied the same mentoring skill he embraced as a teacher to Bart's friends, making sure they were encouraged to learn and were included on day trips. In the view of Bart's friend Frank White, Val made each of them feel "special." It didn't matter what their parents did professionally. Val's experience had shown him that supportive parents and neighbors were what mattered. Peggy Giamatti always was gracious, neatly dressed, "astute, [and] absolutely beautiful" as her hair turned prematurely gray and she kept it that way. Jean MacLeod Keatley, who lived nearby, described her father's recollection of laughter from his early visit to the Giamatti home after Bart began walking: "Dad was talking to Valentine, and Bart came into the room as a little toddler and he said he wanted some beer juice," which was what both men were drinking. "A very fun family."[11] Val was called "Babbo" by his children, a deeply affectionate Italian word for "father" and a comforting name that Bart's friends used also.[12]

Shortly after moving in, the Giamattis built a tennis court in the backyard, which later Bart and his friends were expected to repair whenever it was used, as part of a family obligation. "Babbo was a rigid taskmaster," when it came to obligations, Bart's friend Bill Mazeine said. Peggy knew how to play tennis; Val, undeterred by the smoking that he and others believed was unrelated to health, taught himself to play, and both parents taught Bart. Neighbors, including the parents of Bart's closest friends—the Mazeines and Vitalis—played there regularly. Bart's skill, developed with the applied seriousness he'd bring to many of his commitments in life, eventually startled Bill, who was one year older but was defeated by Bart in a hard-fought battle that won the younger boy the Marienfeld Summer Camp singles tournament as they both reached adolescence.[13]

Bart swam in the summer in College Pond (and in the college's pool in the winter, opened for the public schools' use) and would sled-ride down the hills that defined the Mount Holyoke campus. With Bill and Jean, he bicycled along campus walkways and internal roadways, through the nearby golf course, and in and around neighborhoods too distant to be revealed to parents on his return. With his friends Bill, Andy Vitali, and Frank White, he joined the Cub Scouts long enough to earn some badges and meet new friends. Val and Peggy often provided rides and hosted meetings in their home. Scouting provided Bart with a classic introduction—as it did Guido Calabresi, who'd joined the Boy Scouts in New Haven—to diverse friendships in a broad geographic area, to enjoyment of the outdoors central to his parents' experience, and to a form of Americana. Bart's parents also opened their Vermont cottage to Frank, Bill, and Andy and their families. The visits were informal, roughhousing allowed, Elria and Dino joining in, with, as Bill recalls, laughs and downhill skiing.[14]

Bart also enjoyed and excelled in the intensity of playing touch football. He was the quarterback, the play caller, the strategist, the passer, the team leader. The context mattered. It wasn't just that you could play with only four players, in a yard or on the street. Once Bart reached fifth and sixth grade at Center School, he played regularly on the adjacent field, at lunchtime, during exercise class, on Saturdays. More importantly, by seventh and eighth grade, he played in the citywide grammar school league that required regular interaction with the sometimes bigger, no-nonsense tough boys from the factory-worker families who lived in South Hadley Falls, boys he'd meet again in high school.

Center School had its own tough kids. One photograph came quickly to the mind of his friends Andy, Bill, and Jean, as if it were iconic: on the Center School field, the huddle, everyone bent over or crouched down, heads close together and peering inward, backs and rears only visible to the chronicler, the team ready for direction. And among them, the boy standing tall, surveying the field before calling the play, the quarterback, Bart Giamatti. His friends made clear that from the outset Bart was neither intimidated nor discomfited by playing against tough boys, or befriending them. He'd watched his father do it regularly in life. They agreed on the rules of the game and stuck to them. Order meant fairness. For as skinny a kid as he was, on the field neither size nor the seemingly unintentional block that sent him sprawling deterred his persistence or disrupted his focus. He was fearless.[15]

❧

In grammar school, two of Bart's friends and classmates, Sally Benson and Jean MacLeod Keatley, recalled his fledgling skill at oratory, the stand-alone speech, often memorized, and the debating skill that exceeded everyone else's, finding its origins and still evolving. Bart also learned to play the clarinet in sixth and seventh grade, not a talent he preserved but a thread in the weave of theater and, in time,

The Quarterback. Bart Giamatti, right, looks downfield. Friends include Bill Mazeine, who has his back to the camera, and Andy Vitali, in the rear, who also looks downfield. *William Mazeine Collection.*

his knowledge of the unreconstructed subculture around him. His contribution with clarinet of a distinctive sound melded carefully into a harmonious melody when performed, properly, as an ensemble. In the *Girl's Newspaper*, published by the female students at Center School, under the banner "Female-Fables," Martha

Johnson reported on the Variety Show held in the auditorium, which included poetry readings, songs, a "little skit" by Jean MacLeod (Keatley), a tap dance, and a performance in which "Billy Mazeine, Bart Giamatti, and David Hamilton played a clarinet trio called The Ambassador."

The "Female-Fables" also reported on another performance: the "Seventh grade put on a show similar to the Big Show. Janice Holmes took the part of Tallulah Bankhead. Bart Giamatti was Jimmy Durante. . . ." It's not clear how he played Durante, an Italian American born to immigrant parents from Salerno. In that era, Durante was well known as a "strong driving" jazz pianist who'd coupled successfully with renowned African American singers, as well as being a singer and comedian—talents that would later define him. It was not the first time Bart impersonated or mimed characters; he often did it at home or with friends in school, usually in a skit. But, as his friend Andy Vitali explained, always with purpose in mind, to make a point, to laugh at himself through a means that educated those around him, to focus on irony, or to challenge belief or expectation. Mimes would often include slapstick, the gesture, the prop, or the incongruous article of clothing. At play were lightness and insight about life, ir-reverence in the nature of allegory, the impersonation or gesture as another way of conveying attitude. It was as much a skill as a trait. It lasted a lifetime and included, as Andy described it, an interest in movies, in Hollywood, in whether for the fun of it the two of them couldn't write or direct or make movies as well as anyone. Other students also took to the stage that day at Center School. They played the Andrews Sisters, Ginger Rogers, Fred Astaire, and Marlene Dietrich. Frank White played Spike Jones. Bing Crosby and Bob Hope, and the bandleader Meredith Wilson, played by Andy Vitali, also made an appearance.[16]

Bart had a broad range of interests; with parental encouragement, he pursued each. He'd decline an invitation to play in order to read; the western cowboy and pioneer fables of Zane Grey were his favorite. Drawn from Grey's travels and ex-perience, they spoke to the journey, adventure, values about goodness, right think-ing, and unsuspected mysterious twist in nature that confronted the pioneer, the American immigrant still moving. *The Heritage of the Desert* (1910), *Knights of the Range* (1936), *The Last of the Plainsmen* (1908), and *Riders of the Purple Sage* (1912) were among them. Bart's father enjoyed them as well. Years later, when Bart and Andy went off to France and Italy aboard a steamer out of Canada, Val, Peggy, and Dino drove west, through the land of Grey's adventures, into California to visit friends. When they returned, there were long evenings of adventures shared, knowledge acquired and integrated into life—for Val something more to bring into the classroom, for Bart something thematic to mold into life.[17]

෨

Throughout Bart's childhood, holidays, family birthdays, and celebratory mo-ments like graduations among his mother's parents, sisters, and their children involved frequent visits to their homes or to Bart's grandparent's home or to the Burleigh-Davidson's yellow and white home on the hill. Bart, Elria, and Dino had close relationships with their mother's extended family, which lasted through Bart's life. He actually postponed the date of his inauguration as president of Yale because of the planned birthday celebration for his grandmother, Helen Walton.

There was caring and encouragement and a recognition of responsibility for sensible conduct and the full expression of love in return. It was a framework that was consistent. The larger family photograph—Bartlett and Helen Walton, their children, husbands, and grandchildren—reflected how many people dressed (suits, ties, Bart and his father in bow ties, women in dresses) for a Thanksgiving or Christmas celebration in the 1940s and 1950s. Inside, both Bartlett Walton and Peggy would have played the piano, and it's likely the children would have added recitations. There is a decent prospect that Val would have read excerpts

Thanksgiving 1950. Rear (left to right): Herbert Moss, Valentine Giamatti, Lane Fuller. Middle back row (left to right): Bartlett Walton, Betty Walton Moss, Peggy Walton Giamatti, Kathryn Walton Fuller, Helen Walton. Middle front row (left to right): Bart Giamatti, Elria Giamatti, Lennie Moss. Front (left to right): Dave Moss, Dino Giamatti, Vickie Moss, Win Fuller, Ware Fuller. *Giamatti-Ewing Collection.*

from Charles Dickens's *A Christmas Carol*, which in form and characters was influenced by Dante Alighieri.[18]

At one Thanksgiving gathering, as the children complained of hunger the eve before the big dinner, Uncle Val—"Babbo" by then—proposed something only his children had experienced. Cousin Lennie Ogden described it: "None of us had tasted 'pizza' before," she said (Val likely said "apizza" or "ah-beetz").[19] Val, Lennie said, knew somehow just where to go. Off he went, he told the children, to visit a friend's restaurant in town. He returned with a still-bubbling pizza in hand. It was a holiday introduction of an enduring kind.[20]

❧

In May 1947, at Val's instigation, the trustees at Mount Holyoke, with President Ham's encouragement, committed to provide a suitable place in the college for meetings of Italian organizations throughout Massachusetts, Italian-language laboratories, and meetings with Italian clubs of other colleges. "It has always been my dream," Val said, "to have a *Sala Italiana* on the campus of Mount Holyoke"—a "large Italian room to be the center of Italian activities." Ham "declared that any funds raised 'would have many times their actual value in strengthening Italian upon the Mount Holyoke campus and giving it the high position it deserves.'" Val already had raised donations from Sons of Italy organizations and individuals. "Besides money gifts, Mr. Giamatti has been given several pieces of authentic Italian furniture including an inlaid Florentine table." With an insight that many Italian Americans shared, Val created a reserve fund "to finance Italian movies, lectures and the purchase of books and records which would help spread a better understanding and appreciation of Italy and Italian culture." And, to perfect the department's offerings, Val also hired Luciana Ribet, an anti-Fascist from Italy, to aid in the laboratory work for the growing number of students.[21]

In these actions and civic and family involvement, something much deeper was in play: defining the meaning of Italian American, certainly in western Massachusetts, in their own community, and everywhere Val, Peggy, and their children traveled. Val would tolerate no discrimination in words or conduct, no matter who the source or the object. Rose Criscitiello Longo recalled that within Mount Holyoke, "I felt no discrimination because of my Italian heritage." Andy Vitali expressed the same sentiment with respect to his childhood in South Hadley. Val and Peggy's values were shared and embraced in the settings they could affect. They set the standard, the principle that Bart, Dino, and Elria witnessed, expected, and emulated. It was, indeed, an experience far different from Val's life in New Haven and the culture of Yale.[22]

15

MATURITY FROM EXPERIENCE

Val Giamatti was not saintly—he distrusted saints, as any sensible person
should—but he was idealistic. He really thought one should think well
of others, and act on those beliefs. . . . When some person or event
failed to meet his working assumptions about the best in people, he
reacted with characteristic generosity of spirit. . . . He never reacted with
meanness to meanness; he was incapable of bitterness and completely
devoid of cynicism.

—A. Bartlett Giamatti,
Eulogy for Valentine John Giamatti, April 15, 1982

THE FIRST SABBATICAL: BART'S INTRODUCTION TO ITALY

There is a photograph, published in the *Holyoke Transcript-Telegram*, of the Giamatti
family meeting with Pope Pius XII in Rome, at the Vatican. It's April 1948. Elria
is facing the camera, standing only a few inches from Pius, whose profile view is
facing young Bart, then ten years old. His parents are focused on the Pope, Peggy
in the background, Val, smiling broadly, nearest his son, seeming to want to hear
the Pontiff's words in Italian. "Pope Pius imparts his blessing," the caption pro-
claims, and the Pontiff's index finger is reaching toward Bart. It's a unique moment in anyone's life, made more so by the fact, subsequently verified, that the
Pope sought to raise his ring finger first, as Popes are wont to do, knowing that
protocol required the expected response. Bart, however, declined to kneel and
kiss it. It wasn't that he was impolite, though to curtail his irreverence required
more than protocol. Likely it was that he understood precisely why they were
there. It wasn't because they were exemplary or good Catholics—or for that
matter even Catholic. The Pope was to be respected, not revered. It was Bart's
father who had performed the good deed because of principled, not religious,
beliefs. The context mattered.[1]

   Mount Holyoke encouraged a yearlong sabbatical after seven years of teaching. Going to Italy, ultimately to Rome via Florence, made sense because not only
was it a place of special meaning to Val and Peggy, but also they could immerse

At the Vatican, Pope Pius XII meets with, from left,
Elria, Val, Bart, and Peggy Giamatti, 1948.
Giamatti-Ewing Collection.

their children in the Italian culture they loved. Since the early years of the war, as Val spoke in support of the anti-Fascist cause, he learned about the fate of children in Italy orphaned by the death or displacement of parents. The Pestalozzi Children's Village Foundation had created a home in neutral Switzerland to care for orphans from France, Italy, Germany, and the United Kingdom. Along with the Sons of Italy chapter in Massachusetts, Val raised money among friends and other Italian Americans and would continue to do so as the foundation and the Catholic Church created similar villages near Rome. The founders arranged the audience with Pius XII so that he could thank Val. For the Giamatti family, especially Bart, it was a unique and revealing moment, and an affirmation of his parents' values. The photograph captured in the *Holyoke Telegram* endured, a kind of folklore in South Hadley, especially among Bart's friends. Bart's irreverence, real and reflective of his confidence, was considered sensible.

⬥

Val had remained in contact with faculty at the University of Florence whom he'd met during his first visit in 1934 and corresponded with various Italian and American archivists to increase his knowledge of Chevalier de Cambray-Digny. He entered the university's doctoral program and began to incorporate new documentation into his PhD dissertation, which he'd begun to translate into Italian. Once in Florence, he completed the necessary program requirements, and on June 25, 1948, he received his doctor of letters degree from the University of Florence, family in attendance. He and Peggy returned to Florence and the university for every subsequent sabbatical. The family continued down to Rome.

The children enrolled in the Overseas School of Rome, then in its infancy and located a brief transit ride or thirty-minute walk from the small Hotel Eliseo, where the Giamattis stayed. The Overseas School was granted use of a villa by the British Royal Air Force that was once used by Benito Mussolini's son, Bruno. The school opened with a sophisticated curriculum, skilled teachers, and American (and other nations') academic accreditation. The building, like the others on the estate, was constructed in the grand neoclassical architectural style. At the time the Giamatti children entered, the Overseas School was described this way by Joseph Harrison, Mediterranean news chief of the *Christian Science Monitor*: "The only activity on the Torlonia estate—and that activity is plenty—is supplied by the goings-on . . . [of] the Anglo American Overseas School of Rome, where some 90 howling youngsters, my 7 1/2-year-old daughter among them," play baseball, football, eat their lunches, and learn. "On the school's roster are American, British, French, Chinese, Philippine, South African, Russian, and a handful of Italian children." Though Harrison was certain that, to the children, "Mussolini is merely a vague and unimportant name," to Val Giamatti the transformation of this estate from the residence of the Fascist dictator he distained to an Allied headquarters to an American and British School that educated multiple nationalities must have been deeply gratifying, an educational experience he made certain his children understood. His children made friends and, in ways still subtle, came to understand the meaning of Italy in their parents' lives and their own.[2]

The Giamattis found portions of Italian towns in rubble, people in need of food, clothing, and shelter, the police sometimes replaced by Allied soldiers, and the risk high for vandalism when walking the streets at night. The new government was trying to conduct elections in the free society Italians wanted. The Communist Party was aggressive in courting voters, seeking to establish itself as the practical imperative for Italy's future. The debate was intense in Rome. Elria Giamatti recalled times when her father would leave the hotel, sometimes with his son Bart, to walk the streets and converse with shopkeepers or avowed Communists to argue about Italy's future using his thorough knowledge of dialects, acting the advocate for democratic parties and positions. His conduct caused apprehension, and Peggy corralled him. But he wrote home to his friends in the Sons of Italy, who released his letter to the local press: "The political situation at the present moment is very tense," he began. "For the first time there is a real war scare. The elections loom very large. The one desire on the part of

most is to have them over and done with. . . . The Communists are very well organized and financed. The other parties are doing their utmost. . . . The hope of
all of us is that they will be defeated, and civil war in Italy, if not a third war, will
be averted."[3] When they returned to South Hadley, Val was invited to describe
his views on conditions in Europe, and in Italy especially.[4]

Bart heard what his father said, read what he'd written, and witnessed both
in the war-torn neighborhoods of Italy, as well in South Hadley and at home.
Knowledge had been acquired, tested by experience, and then spoken publicly.

MIDDLEBURY: PERFECTING KNOWLEDGE

In the spring of 1951, Val was invited to join the faculty at the Middlebury
College Summer Language School by its director—and Val's former Yale classmate—Dr. Salvatore Castiglione. Val and Peggy took up quarters at Middlebury
for the duration of the summer. Their children, with the exception of planned
visits onto the Middlebury campus, spent the summer at the Marienfeld Summer
School Camp in Chesham, New Hampshire.

The language program had its origins in 1914. Lilian Stroebe, professor of
languages at Vassar College, was searching, literally, for a new location to continue her interest in the intensive, wholly immersive teaching of German during
the summer months. Middlebury College—remote, softly settled in the Green
Mountains of Vermont, liberal in its educational philosophy, founded privately
in 1800 and made coeducational late in the same century—readily embraced
Stroebe's entreaty. In the summer of 1915, the program began. The summer
school's purpose was at the forefront of precisely the movement in America that
recognized the value of foreign language teaching, made more so by World War
II, then the conflict in Korea, the elevation of the United Nations in the public
dialogue, and the global role and duty of the United States. Val would be teaching "Intermediate Grammar and Composition" and "Italian Literature of the
Renaissance" daily from late June to mid-August.[5]

Already on the faculty when the Giamattis arrived was Dr. Bianca Finzi-
Contini Calabresi, who'd been teaching there since 1947. Her responsibilities
included courses on the "General View of Italian Culture" and "Oral Stylistics—
The Difference between What Is Merely Correct and What Is Italian." Peggy
Giamatti, though having a more informed grasp of the grammar than anyone
else in her family then or later, took the class, seeking a better feel for precisely
the "difference" Dr. Calabresi knew critical to speaking and teaching. A friendship was formed, in part because Peggy's experience at and since Smith and
Val's outspokenness as an anti-Fascist joined in empathy and practicality with
the deeply personal and family experience of the Calabresis. And although Val
understood acutely the crassly drawn distinction made between Northern and

Southern Italians in Italy, in America, and at Yale, he likely knew that aspects of that difference would be irrelevant as the Calabresis defined their place in New Haven and at Yale.[6]

YALE'S ANTI-CATHOLICISM

"Buckley Slams Atheism, Collectivism at Yale," proclaimed the *Yale Daily News* on October 15, 1951. The book: *God and Man at Yale* by William F. Buckley Jr. (Yale 1950). The "slams" were Buckley's dissection of why Yale failed to teach free market capitalism in its Economics Department and, related to that failure, what Buckley believed were the appropriate Christian values of individualism and belief in God that underpin the free market. That is, Yale had become a proponent of "atheism" and "collectivism," the code words in that era for Communism. His solution: the Yale alumni should use their financial power to direct the Yale Corporation to order the faculty to correct this mistaken approach or face dismissal.[7]

&

Buckley was a military veteran in an era of men who "were serious [and] had purpose." He was, as one of his classmates attested, "someone to be reckoned with immediately. He was taking initiatives as soon as he got to Yale. He arrived in full stride. . . . with a mission." That drive continued during his senior year, when he began the book, drew personal observations, and assessed documentation, and then it emerged full bore after graduation with the book's publication. Buckley exercised precisely the form of "leadership" Yale had promoted since its inception, except that it was directed at Yale.[8]

Buckley's conceptual framework—to call upon the wealth of the old WASP alumni, whose latent power as contributors gave them a role they did not have before, that is, to become "leaders"—was potentially masterful. So, too, was his timing. The university's distinctive place in the narrow world that mattered on the advent of its 250th anniversary—an English-derived educational culture that, in America, included comparison only to Harvard and Princeton—was in play, especially to Yale's newly selected president, A. Whitney Griswold. At the anniversary's formal pageant, in the midst of adulation of the university's special identity, Yale affirmed that Buckley's critique had touched two connected nerves: first, the cultural, "Mother Yale" imperative of largely unquestioned alumni giving and, second, that the imperative was at that time more vulnerable and more critical than ever because of Yale's underlying faulty financial and property decisions.[9]

&

God and Man at Yale was neither well written nor substantively persuasive, yet it recognized directly and implicitly the known and acknowledged intellectual inadequacy in Yale's departments of Economics and Religion. The initial Yale and student response was properly moderated in tone and educationally instruc-tive. The *New Haven Evening Register* treated the book like an internal, albeit stress-filled Yale matter. The *Springfield* (Massachusetts) *Republican* merely noted its publication.[10] The few book reviews that *God and Man* provoked might not have been written—or might have been written differently—had Yale responded as a confident educational institution. It couldn't, largely because it wasn't. To the Corporation and Griswold, the book was danger.[11]

In 1951, Yale was grappling with the serious effects of financial misjudg-ment on its endowment and operating budget. The problem was exacerbated by the imprudent sale of university property that might have been available for potential income or Griswold's hoped-for expansion, especially in New Haven. The fact that such property was "sorely missed" brought to the fore Yale's deeper display of its cultural character toward the neighborhoods that surrounded it.[12] "Christianity" in the elitist iteration remained part of Yale's culture and its nur-tured, professed distinctiveness. Its anti-Semitism was well known, and its eu-genics leadership was instilled in its memory and conduct. It had been so for generations—that is, among generations of graduates that now composed the alumni.[13] Instead of a subtle response, Yale, at the explicit direction of Griswold and the Corporation, engaged in a fulsome, bigoted attack.

Yale graduate McGeorge Bundy's public rebuke of *God and Man* in the *Atlantic* on November 1—at times meandering, affected by "unfeigned anger," and tempered by contradiction—gave emphasis to what Buckley did not acknowledge and what Bundy contended was critical to his argument and, presumably, why Yale had to rise to the grand defense of its integrity: Buckley Jr. was a "Roman Catholic." He had engaged in a "savage attack" on Yale motivated by his religious belief.[14] Buckley later claimed, accurately, that Yale President Griswold endorsed or originated as an essential theme the characterization of Buckley's approach as that of the "militant Catholic."[15]

Once the "Catholic" argument was articulated, the epithets blossomed, and so did the historical and cultural hypocrisy: Buckley was a "fascist"; his ideo-logical position was as plain as "the nose on Joe Stalin's face"; and according to Yale Corporation member Frank Ashburn, Buckley was an adherent to the pur-poses of the Ku Klux Klan.[16] The more vindictive, darker anti-Catholic response came from another Corporation member, the Reverend Henry Sloane Coffin: "Mr. Buckley's book is really a misrepresentation and distorted by his Roman Catholic point of view. Yale is a Puritan and Protestant institution by its heritage and [Buckley] should have attended Fordham or some similar institution." It was the argument Dean Winternitz of the medical school and President Angell of the university had used in every way they could. Buckley, seeing the opening, embraced fully the notoriety and the epithets.[17]

Others at Yale showed that Buckley's Catholicism was unrelated to the argument he'd made.[18] The "Catholic" argument by the decidedly nonegalitarian-driven Bundy, was wholly antithetical to a "liberal" or even legitimate public position in mid-twentieth-century America.[19] In New Haven, largely Catholic in culture, the Yale response was another reflection of its prejudice and detachment from the city. The irony was that Buckley was barely likable and was no democrat; his authoritarian solution contradicted the social duty exercised by Italian immigrants, Italian Americans, and others in New Haven in forming societies to ensure the protection of rights and the encouragement of family and neighbors, wholly independent of Catholicism or the Catholic Church.[20] Buckley was as elitist in his perspective, tone, and life as Bundy, Griswold, and Coffin. The "debate" became an ugly spat between like-minded men and their form and degree of prejudice.

Val Giamatti likely shook his head in bewilderment. At its highest level, the university didn't want to shed its underlying eugenics culture even though, despite its best efforts, the composition of its student body and its faculty was changing. The Giamattis of South Hadley were not Catholic, but Val abhorred prejudice every day of his life and taught that to his children. And the Giammatteis and Lavorgnas in New Haven—his sisters, their families, and his cousins, and Bart's aunts, uncles, and cousins—were Catholic.

MARIENFELD: FUN, AND PERFECTING SKILLS

The Marienfeld Summer School Camp was established in 1896 exclusively for boys. By the time the Giamatti children began attending, it had expanded to include distinct, nearby facilities for girls. Elria was there. And Bart was joined by his friend Bill Mazeine and Bart's future brother-in-law, David Ewing.[21]

Bart played softball and tennis (here he defeated Bill Mazeine in the tennis singles tournament) and got his first serious introduction to square dancing. In a photograph taken during a boy-girl mixer, his posture and facial expression reflect something cerebral, watching and learning; then, in the next image, he's out on the floor, joining his friends. This was the beginning of his dancing experience. When he returned home, his mother, and Bill's and Andy's, arranged for dance lessons at Margaret O'Brian's Dance School in nearby Holyoke. For almost two years, the lessons taught the boys the waltz, fox trot, and other formal dances. It's unclear how good Bart was at them, but performance and the value of experience was something he embraced. Jean Keatley added context: The rock-and-roll craze was just emerging but was not what they were doing. "We had dances, and I have plenty of memories of those. I went with him to a dance.

I have a picture of us at a table, and I have some little flower thing on my wrist. This was 1951, '52. It was fun." The photograph captured eight students dressed in gowns or white dinner jackets, smiling, learning, enjoying the moment. Yet on Bart's face is something more: purpose and awareness.[22]

At Marienfeld, Bart assumed the responsibility of managing editor and contributing writer to the *Marienfeld Monitor*, the camp newspaper. His articles exhibited humor and parody. Baseball and softball dominated the news. "Midget Softballers Beat Wa-Klo 24-7," and "The Jr.-Sr. Softball Team Takes Wa-Klo," where, it was reported, "Bart Giamatti . . . got four hits for six times to the plate." In the lead article in one edition, Managing Editor Giamatti described the game between Marienfeld and a team from the town of Harrisville. "All through the fray," young Giamatti wrote, "the battery, the whole battery, and nothing but the battery for our team was Bob Fear catching and Tom Foster pitching." After identifying the rest of the lineup, Giamatti described the winning combination of hits in the first inning that led to two runs: "This may not seem to be enough for two runs, but there were three walks, two hit batsmen in succession, and a two base error—which Van Horn still says was a hit! I happen to know he practically felled the scorekeeper with a bat when he heard it wasn't a hit. (I know because I was the scorekeeper.)"[23]

Bart returned to Marienfeld a few times. He also, however, expected change of consequence to come. The parents of some of his friends were assessing the value of private preparatory schools for their children. For the Giamattis, it was a discussion about college, including Yale. When the family reunited in South Hadley and Val returned to teaching, war that had broken out on the Korean Peninsula in June 1950 had reached the Mount Holyoke campus in an unexpected yet predictable way.

16

The Duty of Citizenship:
Mount Holyoke as Prism

The Korean War and the Roaming Specter of Accusation

The FBI's investigation of Roswell Ham for "un-American" activities in 1943 yielded alleged conduct that remained in its files. The Senate, led by Senator Patrick McCarran of Nevada, soon joined the House Un-American Activities Committee. By early 1951, investigation of state universities and colleges had occurred. In *Naming Names*, Victor Navasky draws on recorded testimony to identify the effect described by California faculty members and librarians: "We lived with the constant sense of being hunted." Private schools would be next. A. Whitney Griswold was praised within Yale when he spoke in support of academic freedom and the exercise of free speech. Unlike Ham, however, neither Griswold nor Yale was the subject of scrutiny. The university's influence in Washington, DC, protected them. Ham, always defiant and principled, had three obligations: preserve the integrity of Mount Holyoke from unfair accusations, assure the faculty it must continue to teach citizenship in the classroom and act as models, and encourage the college's graduates to use their liberal education without fear.[1]

With the Korean War in progress, Ham looked to the 247 young women graduating from Mount Holyoke in June 1951 to assume a special duty. "In the words of George Bernard Shaw, 'Liberty means responsibility,'" he said. "'That is why most men dread it.'" Ham expected the graduates seated before him, who'd "been encouraged to develop" not "pure intellect [which] . . . is an incomplete human being" but the fullness of a liberal education. "Within our pattern of freedom and order," liberal education gave each graduate the duty not "to surrender your liberty and accept the higher instruction of some omniscient despotism." The threat to civil liberties, Ham recognized from his entire career, was imminent in the abusive exercise of political power. "Men," Ham concluded, "are sometimes masters of their fate, ladies largely so. In a precarious world it may well be that your generation of women may have to be the chief conservators of our values."[2]

cᴠ

In eighth grade, as Sally Benson recalled with preciseness, Bart succeeded in making the best recitation of Lincoln's Gettysburg Address among his classmates. The
recitation was part of a larger schoolwide tradition, encouraged by civic groups and
adopted by the town as a way of elevating the role played by those who'd given
their lives in the cause of other people's freedom. Every grammar school student,
beginning in fifth and sixth grade, had to learn it and recite it at a meeting of classes in the auditorium. Bart, standing on stage, led the recitation at Center School.
The best orator in the grammar schools "would then stand at the Gaylord Civil
War statue on the Village Green and recite it to the town—following a Memorial
Day parade and before going to the Evergreen Cemetery" and the other town
cemeteries to pay tribute to the veterans buried there, accompanied by taps and
military honor guard. The parade was solemn in tone, led by veterans and nurses,
some in wheelchairs, others on crutches, the crowd reverential as they clapped and
as parents conveyed the parade's meaning to their children. Girl Scout and Boy
Scout troops followed. In 1952, the selected orator was Bart Giamatti. Dressed in a
dark suit, white shirt, and tie, he portrayed Abraham Lincoln on the Village Green.
His erudition and hand gestures had been perfected. Preparation in school and at
home had ensured it.[3]

The solemnity of this special moment was heightened for Bart and his family, as it was among the other citizens in attendance. Ominous realities within
South Hadley and Mount Holyoke tempered the words that Lincoln, through
Bart Giamatti, recited that day: young men from town had enlisted in the military
and congressional committees, the FBI, and the Commonwealth of Massachusetts
were investigating "un-American activities" in private colleges. The duty for
South Hadley families: fully exercise civic liberty daily and without fear.[4]

cᴠ

In the fall of 1952, Val and Peggy Giamatti, registered Democrats, supported
Adlai Stevenson (D-Illinois) for president of the United States. Bart, then fourteen, his sister, Elria, recalled, helped her and Dino organize and deliver posters
and literature throughout the neighborhood. Students on campus were encouraged to express political positions—and did. Eisenhower and Richard Nixon
won in Massachusetts. At a time when visibility and clarity of intent mattered,
the Giamatti family was on public display for students, friends, and neighbors. Val
also agreed to moderate widely publicized forums and debates for local candidates in the nonpartisan election for the Board of Selectman and for the School
Committee and Planning Board. He was trusted and admired.[5]

In November 1952, the United States Senate Committee on Internal
Security announced it would undertake investigations into Communist influence on faculties at fourteen schools. Mount Holyoke was not among them. A
week later, however, in an internal memorandum to J. Edgar Hoover's assistant,

Clyde Tolson, an FBI agent focused on the conduct of Roswell Ham. Ham got wind of the FBI investigation and the existence of a broader investigation into Mount Holyoke. He "requested information from the bureau as to the alleged Communist infiltration in the school." The request reached the FBI's Washington, DC, headquarters. The Bureau's "Boston office [had] orally acknowledged receipt of Ham's letter and advised him that information in the Bureau's file is of a confidential nature." The FBI files also indicated that "It was further recommended that [BLACKENED] be interviewed by the New York Office to determine the identity of Bureau Agents who advised her concerning Communism at Mount Holyoke." The director noted on the above recommendations: "O.K. H[oover]." By early 1953, Mount Holyoke had made the list. Ham, undeterred, protected the college.[6]

In a fateful election, in 1954, the Giamattis worked with special diligence to support Val's former classmate, New Haven–born Congressman John Foster Furcolo for the United States Senate.[7] In 1948, with the support of war veterans, labor unions, a growing Italian American population, and a personal appearance by President Harry Truman, Furcolo had defeated the incumbent congressman handily. Unlike the Irish- and Kennedy family–controlled Boston, Furcolo was not beholden to the Catholic Church or willing to demonstrate the fidelity shown by Joseph and John F. Kennedy to Senator Joseph McCarthy. He was close, however, personally and politically, to Speaker of the House and Boston Congressman John McCormack, who, mythology aside, was Canadian, not Irish.[8] Furcolo was elected, and to the consternation of the more conservative John Kennedy, he was the first freshman Truman invited to the White House. McCormack appointed him to important legislative committees. His visibility rose.[9]

Furcolo was reelected in 1950. His career was admired in New Haven. Ted DeLauro, a resident of the Wooster Square neighborhood, was among a cadre of hometown supporters who followed Furcolo closely, his daughter, Congresswoman Rosa DeLauro, later recalled.[10] In early 1952, Furcolo made a canny political move. He resigned from Congress to accept appointment as Massachusetts state treasurer by Governor Paul Dever, who was concerned about the growing conservative Irish strength in the Democratic Party. When in November Governor Dever lost reelection, Furcolo won in a statewide race as treasurer. His political framework had changed. John F. Kennedy was able to defeat Henry Cabot Lodge in 1952 in Massachusetts, with Furcolo's support on the statewide ticket. In 1954, Furcolo was prepared to challenge the old Yankee establishment, Republican Senator Leverett Saltonstall. It was classic, historical, and expected. Every labor union in the state endorsed Furcolo. Kennedy secretly aided Saltonstall.[11]

The Giamattis organized in South Hadley, children at the forefront. As the election grew near, Kennedy had not yet delivered on his commitment to individually endorse each member of the Democratic slate of candidates. When Kennedy made a television appearance to do so, with Furcolo sitting with him, he endorsed by name only the gubernatorial candidate, Robert Murphy. The outrage was immediate, considered an effort to thwart the rise of Italian Americans in the party and Furcolo's liberalism and growing notoriety in Washington, DC, and an effort to satisfy Kennedy's need to be embraced by the Boston Brahmins. Furcolo barely lost.[12] The underlying historical tension between the Irish and the Italians manifested itself in political life. It was not the first or last time.

After Furcolo was elected governor in 1956, the first Italian American to do so (he won handily in South Hadley), he appointed Valentine Giamatti to "the special commission on the Civil War Centennial." The appointment was important to South Hadley residents and their deliberate reverence for the "Citizen Soldiers Who Fought for Liberty and the Union" and the importance of active citizenship. The appointment also further enhanced the respect, love, and understanding of principles in life and how they were formed between father and son.[13]

A. WHITNEY GRISWOLD AND DICK LEE: THE ROVING SPECTER OF URBAN RENEWAL

Although A. Whitney Griswold and his wife, Mary, lived on Hillhouse Avenue, neither was a product of New Haven or had an upbringing outside their own cultural milieu. In selecting him for the presidency, the Corporation was aware fully of "his gift of mimicry [in a "thick Italian American accent"], fierce intolerance of the shoddy and second rate," and "hot-tempered" (one observer called him a "sudden man"), "opinionated" manner.[14] Griswold's view of Yale's place in the world as it entered its 250th year: a greater focus on Yale College and the de-emphasis of graduate-level programs or anything that seemed parochial. That temperament and agenda further diminished New Haven's relevance to Yale, except for its expansion.

During the time of the Buckley-Yale debate, the director of Yale's News Bureau, Dick Lee, was the Democratic candidate for mayor of New Haven, his second attempt. He'd never gone to college but donned the Yale image, in tweeds, bow tie, and membership at Mory's eating club, home of the a cappella singing group Whiffenpoofs. His education would be a source of insecurity and deference throughout his political life. To Griswold, he'd write, "My heart is always in the right place as far as Yale is concerned and you know it, and I'm sure you know of my loyalty to you."[15]

ॐ

Lee, although actually Scottish, English, and Irish, emphasized his Irish heritage in New Haven political life. His quintessential skill was in public relations, which he'd done for decades.[16] It was during the failed 1951 mayoral campaign that

Lee—an alderman (elected city council member), mayoral candidate in 1949, and lifetime resident of New Haven—claimed he first became aware of the housing conditions in portions of the Hill/Oak Street/Legion Avenue neighborhood, though this neighborhood was filled with Democratic voters and he'd campaigned there previously. Allegedly, he said to himself then or perhaps only seven or eight years later, or perhaps not at all, that, when he "came out of those homes on Oak Street, and I sat on the curb and I was just sick as a puppy. Why the smell of the building; it had no electricity, it had no gas, it had kerosene lamps. . . . It was just awful." This experience, described in these words, became the *post hoc* moral rationale for urban renewal, though they were not uttered until 1958 or 1959 to Yale author Robert Dahl, when the *real* destructive effects in the neighborhoods throughout the city were, by then, well known to thousands of New Haven residents. At stake wasn't just Dahl's naïveté or knowing complicity in falsehood but, from the impending 1953 campaign onward, the disparity between Lee's rhetorical and political skill—guided, in critical moments, by Yale—and the harm being done to New Haven.[17]

During the post–1951 election period, Lee was introduced by members of Yale's faculty to the contours of the Federal Housing Act of 1949, which made available federal grants for the elimination of "slums." Yale already focused on the act's application in neighborhoods that mattered to it. That the ethnic and racially discriminatory underpinnings, history, and purpose of this law and other nationally promoted efforts to change urban zoning or support suburban housing might have warranted cautionary embrace didn't matter to Lee or, given Yale's eugenics' culture, to those who explained it to him. And when, in 1941, Maurice Rotival, a roadway-driven visionary of regional living who'd come to New Haven at Yale's invitation to teach, proposed a plan to city officials, they largely ignored it. The reason for that neglect, which emerged in the 1953 campaign, likely was beyond Lee's inquisitiveness to understand, though Rotival understood the reason perfectly. Dick Lee was until then a substantively vacuous candidate ready to be filled. In time, Griswold did it.[18]

☙

Lee's strategy for 1953 was to get the old Yankee Republicans and the Yale-dominated wards to turn out strongly in his favor.[19] He had two related prospects for accomplishing that goal. Two Italian American Democrats had won citywide office in 1951 when Lee had lost. Mark Barbarito and Arthur Barbieri both outpolled Lee *and* Mayor William Celentano.[20] Celentano was liked but plainly not revered among Italian Americans. The 1951 election was the first solid sign of permanent transformation in New Haven's political party alignment.[21] That could help Lee next time. The second prospect for victory: old Yankee-driven and Yale Italian American–driven prejudice against Celentano. It was a tactic Lee was familiar with, used successfully before to defeat Celentano in 1939 in what

Judge Guido Calabresi recalled as the "most racist campaign going."[22] In 1951, the normally conservative Republican wards had supported a socialist rather than "Irish" Catholic Lee or Italian American Celentano. Lee and Griswold understood how to ensure that didn't happen again.

In November 1951, the *Yale Daily News* covered the annual Wilbur Cross–Hillhouse High School football game, a thirty-year, celebrated local rivalry of the two schools located on the York Square campus. The game, held at the Yale Bowl before more than twenty-five thousand people, was broadcast live. The *Daily News* coverage declared, in unsubtle terms, that little had changed in Yale's understanding of the city and Italian Americans since Owen Johnson penned *Stover at Yale*—except for gradations of willful ignorance and the comfort to publicize it.

The game was played around the seasonal theme of Harvest Festival. Joint school and citizen rallies were held at York Square, a grand parade, the election of a king and queen, and—with local business support—the awarding of special trophies to both teams at the culminating event, the Harvest Festival Ball. The three-day news coverage brought special awareness to something both schools and citizens knew: the participants on and off the field were African American, Italian, Irish, Polish, and Jewish. "In a thrilling climax to a breathtaking Harvest Festival Pageant," the *New Haven Evening Register*'s Frank Birmingham reported the next day, "Hillhouse Nips Wilbur Cross 14–13."[23]

In "Town and Frown," *Yale Daily News* reporter Norman Roy Grutman stoked, unabashedly, the embedded prejudice with something in the nature of gutter-based ethnic ridicule that, by 1951, should have run its course. The Cross-Hillhouse game, Grutman began, was the "annual playing of the Pizza Bowl. Vying for the kudos of the crowd were the Muzzarellas [*sic*] of Hillhouse and the anchovies of Wilbur Cross." On the reviewing stand, "garbed in his ceremonial toga, [was] William C. Celantano [*sic*] . . . the mob's choice." Celentano "could afford to smile for he had made good his sneer at Lee, 'You'll win—over *my* dead bodies.'" Grutman continued: Yale students who wanted to occupy the best seats for the game, he wrote, were subject to a "nefarious proletarian Mafia job, [that] was largely responsible for toppling the Patricians from the best seats." The Yale students would have to wait. "Last Saturday belonged to the new Romans who ate onion bread and garlic while the Muzzarellas [*sic*] knocked the stuffings [*sic*] out of the anchovies. The margin of victory being one pizza after touchdown."[24] The *Daily News*, under criticism, responded with another form of calculated ridicule. Although Grutman, the *News* wrote, "was merely spoofing legitimately," the *Daily News* did not intend "to insult all Italians." Bart Giamatti would later lament the acceptability of this form of prejudice: "when it became taboo in 'polite' or 'liberal' society or 'educated' discourse and circles to tell racist stories or jokes or Anti-Semitic stories or jokes or to make clearly racist or bigoted remarks about Blacks or Jews, the so-called Italian (or Polish) joke has filled the void." Giamatti also put the writer's (Yale's Grutman included) grammatical mistakes into proper context when he added, with polite restraint, "The ambiguity remaining in [one supposedly lucid writer's prose] may make my point about the difficulty of mastering English as he asserts his."[25]

Lee had the foundation for a political strategy: fear of Italian American dominance in the party most likely to win. At a time of fiscal unease at Yale, especially over property for expansion, Lee was Yale's man, and he believed Yale, defined in votes cast, prejudice, and the cultural adulation he sought, was his.

THE RESURGENCE OF YALE'S CIVIC IRRESPONSIBILITY

Yale could not shed its inability or unwillingness to manage its own culture: the student riots and university-tolerated misdeeds of the nineteenth century returned. On May 13, 1952—as Lee was preparing for his third campaign—a dispute arose on one of the public streets that cross through Yale. Two ice cream vendors were arguing over who had rights to be where. Yale students took sides; yelling and shoving began. Police officers arrived and thought they had calmed the parties, until water balloons and firecrackers were thrown from residence hall windows. Assistant Dean Lewis Wiggin ordered students to return to their residence. He was ignored. Empty beer cans were hurled, more firecrackers exploded, rubbish was emptied onto the street, a fire was lit, a bus was caught in the commotion, fisticuffs ensued. A motorist caught in stalled traffic had his car windows broken. Eighty police in full fighting mode arrived, and firemen were called. Once the fire was out, the hoses were turned on students. Police sought to force them inside the gated campus grounds. Water balloons were tossed at the police, and a brick was thrown. Policemen brandished nightsticks and used them. Students were injured. At least three officers drew their guns.

The student rioters rose to fifteen hundred. A group walked into the local United States Army and Air Force recruiting station, took the "recruitment flag, and paraded through the streets with it raised on high." Some New Haven High School students, walking home or out for lunch, were caught in the melee. Yale students rushed toward the Taft Hotel, a few blocks from the university. Its owner locked the front doors, sought police protection, and got it. The police chief, Howard Young, said, "This is a mob and we're treating them as such. . . . Several skulls were cracked." Police forced the students back onto the campus. Four were arrested and charged with inciting a riot, breach of peace, or interfering with the police. The university bailed them out. Griswold apologized the same day to the community and ordered an investigation.[26]

To some students, and likely their parents, it was a mere "spring frolic," an "amusing demonstration," a "'good-humored' riot." Neither the mayor nor the

city employee union leader saw it that way. Such glib rationales were about protecting privilege and reflected embedded parental and university values. Mayor
Celentano was direct: the student conduct was a "full fledged display of disrespect and disregard for law and order and left our New Haven community
uneasy."[27] Before the day was up, Mayor Celentano and Police Chief Young had
met with Griswold in his office. Officials from the two ice cream vendors were
prosecuted. Chief Young agreed that the "gun play . . . was entirely uncalled for."
Griswold focused on student conduct that "set back the relations of mutual respect and confidence between the University and the City."[28]

The story was covered nationally.[29] It was not the image Griswold wanted
projected—certainly not one that he expected from future White Anglo-Saxon
"leaders" or that reflected well on his own strict, Protestant moral rectitude. As
president of Yale, Griswold also took guidance from the President's Committee
on Manners and Morals, chaired by Dean William DeVane. A subcommittee of
the full committee suggested one possible solution worthy enough to include
in their formal minutes: Yale should be coeducational. That guidance, it appears,
settled snuggly in Griswold's mind.[30]

No disciplinary action was taken against any students. To many citizens in
the city, the student conduct was engaged in with impunity and based on the
detached world where Griswold, the personification of Yale, drew and dispensed
his values.[31] Both New Haven police and Yale officials also learned lessons about
riot control, none more important than the need to contain students within the
university's grounds when violence arose or, from Yale's perspective, to ensure
violence didn't spread outside the Yale campus. Otherwise, Yale students would
evoke a police—and a political—response about public safety.[32]

Griswold, no doubt, was troubled personally for an additional reason. He and
the Yale Corporation had a plan for expansion but neither the land nor the resources to accomplish it. And, the mayor of New Haven, William Celentano, did
not hold Yale in high regard, certainly not with the reverence held by Dick Lee.

෴

For Val Giamatti, the Kennedy-Furcolo episode had the racial, ethnic, and eugenics tinge of insecurity he'd experienced and witnessed in New Haven and at
Yale. The episode didn't evoke a rule or code, just a readily understood warning,
applied uniformly: to be watchful for the emergence of prejudice, for the way
that others are treated, for favoritism when it's not warranted or that underpins
unfairness to others. It was the duty of citizenship.

PART V

PRINCIPLES

THE CONNECTIONS FORM

He was a great teacher for two reasons, I think: first, because of his passion for connecting ideas to the way we live our lives; and second, because he found, as he inevitably would, the right, the appropriate, the precisely fitting poet to think about and to cherish and to talk to every day—Dante.

—A. Bartlett Giamatti,
Eulogy for Valentine John Giamatti, April 15, 1982

ORATORY AND DEBATE: THE INTELLECT AND PURPOSE

Bart rode the bus daily to South Hadley High School. He, Bill, and Andy would gather in front of Frank White's house for the daily ride, but a soda in Holyoke or a touch football game with the local Falls kids periodically disrupted the bus trip home. And there was the forbidden act—Bart and Andy would hitch a ride home. Almost invariably, the driver was someone they knew, going near Silver Street—just distant enough for the boys to conjure up an explanation for their worried mothers.

Like other college-bound students, Bart took at least two languages: Latin and French. It was the beginning, not of language study (he already had a solid knowledge of Italian and its dialects, and likely aspects of other languages), but of the culture of words—derivation, sound, and purpose—often used to teach language. Latin especially opened an enormous range of foreign cultures and literature. Greek, Hebrew, and Arabic texts had been translated into Latin, including the Bible and writings of Jesus's disciples. Southern Italian scholars from Salerno, Naples, and Sicily made many of these translations, a fact that affirmed Val's appreciation—and eventually Bart's knowledge—that the influence of Italian scholarship, pre- and post-Dante, was based on an entire peninsula's contribution. It also was from these writings that English translations were made, critical to the early education of American literary and political figures. The breadth of knowledge, and its integration, reflected in Bart's later teaching and writing as English professor, Renaissance scholar, and president of Yale, began during this period of his life.[1]

Bart's debating and oratorical skills improved. On the debate team with him were Frank White, Andy Vitali, Bill Mazeine, and Jean McLeod Keatley. "We used to have speech contests in high school," Jean said, "and he would always participate in the Extemporaneous Speaking contest, which was this scary thing where you would just stand up there and pull something out of a hat and just start talking, and I thought, 'Wow, I could never do this.' [Bart] was fabulous and he was funny and he could talk about anything, absolutely anything, and of course he won. And he was great at debating. I would have to struggle with it and would have to debate the other side and stay up all night working on it, and he would just go 'bub, bub, bub.' He was just so wonderful with the language." His quick mind was developing, challenged by ideas and the use of words, the right ones, crafted together in order to persuade. Body movements necessary to reflect conviction and purpose were entwined in a way he exercised with growing confidence. He'd begun to develop his own voice and manner of expression, his own analytical skills about content.[2]

Bart's skill was known: the subjects that moved him, when he did his best, were Americana. In February 1954, he won the annual American Legion Oratorical contest for South Hadley High School students, presented at an assembly of the full student body and town residents in the South Hadley Town Hall. He chose as his subject "The Constitution and Your Responsibilities." And, again, in May, he rose to speak at the Town Hall and won the M. J. Moriarty Prize for his recitation of "A Constitutional Bill of Rights." Second place went to his friend Jean.[3] A seriousness of purpose and the melding together of knowledge about America, its structure and rights, and the responsibilities of its citizens was in play. He witnessed the responsibility of citizenship at home, and it was a thread in his heritage. And something more: "There are some people who just have a presence, even as a young child," Sally Benson recalled, "because there is something about them, some presence. Bart was a small, skinny kid. But there was something about his personality that was memorable. . . . We all remember him."[4]

His parents' temperament was engrained in Bart's attitude about himself and his treatment of others. His intellect was solid. He was, Bill Mazeine said, "well-rounded," an "intellectual" but not "nerdish." To Jean MacLeod Keatley, "Bart was very funny, and he was very smart . . . smarter than everybody else. He was very popular. We all thought very highly of him. . . . He excelled at everything."[5]

BASEBALL AS SPORT AND CHARACTER

Although Bart and his friends would sometimes listen to Yankee games on the radio at the local gas station, once he got a small radio to put in the attic, it was all Red Sox, for himself and his friends. Like many young fans, he knew the batting averages, league standings, and personal history of the players. The culture, the feel, the connection to those playing the game in distant Boston, imagined vividly, blended into the words heard on the sometimes static-interrupted, real-time play-by-play. The gritty knowledge that mattered, however, came from the sandlot and school yard, the learned batting stance, the base stolen, the squeeze bunt, the leaping one-handed catch as you slide on the green grass of the outfield. Baseball was a game he played. Imagination had foundation in experience. He was "a decent player," Bill said, and, as his friend and later brother-in-law David Ewing confirmed, Bart was quick to organize a game whenever enough players were available. The glove had been passed from Helen Walton to Valentine Giamatti to Bart.[6]

∽

With fathers in tow, Bart and his friends went on drives to county fairs, antique auctions, and most memorably, to Boston, to Fenway Park, to watch the Red Sox play. In one especially poignant interview, just prior to his death, Bart described, with the value-laden recollection that tempered how he formed judgments, one moment in memory of his favorite player, Bobby Doerr. David Halberstam captured it—and more—in *Summer of '49*:

> Doerr was as comfortable with himself as [Ted] Williams was not. . . . Williams would tell Doerr, "You could be a three-hundred hitter—it's all there for you." "Ted, damn it," Doerr would reply, "I love to hit as much as you do, but I'm a middle-infielder, and I'm in the game on every pitch, and it drains you terribly. . . ."
>
> [Bart Giamatti] had chosen Doerr carefully. . . . Bart liked to play second base, which was the shortest throw in the field. That was Bobby Doerr's position. . . . Bart knew that [Doerr] was extremely popular with his teammates and not a carouser. Everyone on the team was said to look up to him. That made him a perfect role model, especially for a professor's son.[7]

In these two paragraphs, Halberstam identified two values that, no doubt, would have emerged had Halberstam later written about Giamatti at Yale. "I'm in the game on every pitch." Doerr's words reflected not only Giamatti's embrace of Doerr as a "perfect role model" or a second baseman, but as the participant, the player constantly in action yet deeply observant of what's evolving on the field, his speed and agility to either side critical to the play, his knowledge and intuition of what's going to happen next, his demeanor and voice known to the batter, to the other players, to the pitcher. Each skill properly melded or distinctly used was essential to his teammates. Doerr was, as Ted Williams said, and likely Bart Giamatti safely assumed, the team's "Silent Captain."[8]

Doerr's moral character would have mattered not only because Bart was a "professor's son." Those moral values added to Doerr's skill, elevated it, and for Bart that would have mattered because of the values that emanated from his parents and his grandmother. Halberstam slid nicely into this implication as he described something else central to the young Giamatti and baseball, hardly unique among boys, but important to what Bart was learning in other contexts as well: "He was not sure whether baseball had more meaning for him because he was the son of immigrants [he actually was not, though close enough to be a fair premise]—the sport could have been a shortcut to the center of American culture." It was in important respects and, as Giamatti's later writings about baseball pitcher Tom Seaver or boxer and poet Muhammad Ali or his own experience in baseball affirmed and continued to allow, he found a window for witnessing the natural and daily meaning of "the game" in kitchens, back yards, bars, factories, and just in holding a glove, and he walked through it, including when, as he later must, he also looked at the cultural and linguistic origins of baseball in "athletics" and in "the City." That would be years off, but it was here, in South Hadley and with baseball, that Bart's form of inquisitiveness and manner of learning was an early iteration—as playing Jimmy Durante was—of being "On the Road," of looking beneath the icons and data into, as Halberstam put it correctly, "the center of American culture." And, in a foundational, related way, there was Bart as the son of an Italian American father, from New Haven, Connecticut, himself the son of immigrants, the meaning of which Bart would come to learn intimately, especially when he entered Yale. As Halberstam engaged Giamatti in dialogue, Bart also offered that he had formed his "own all Italian all-star team: catcher, [Lawrence 'Yogi'] Berra; first base, [Dolph] Camilli, second base, [Anthony] Lazzeri; shortstop, [Philip] Rizzuto; third base, [Frank] Crosetti; outfielders, Dom DiMaggio, Joe DiMaggio, [Sabath 'Sam'] Mele, [Allan Lee 'Zeke'] Zarilla, and [Carl] Furillo; pitcher, [Vic] Raschi and [Sal] Maglie." Halberstam insightfully pointed out, "That he was starting as many as six Yankees did not bother him. There are loyalties, and there are loyalties; sometimes they intersect, sometimes they do not."[9]

On the Red Sox team, he also admired Dom DiMaggio, Joe's brother. His skill warranted inclusion on Bart's all-Italian team, as it did on numerous American League All-Star teams. It may have mattered to Bart that Dom was only five feet, nine inches tall and wore glasses; what also would matter, as he came to appreciate the fullness of the Italian American experience, was that Dom's mother and father, during the same era as their sons' contribution to the definition of Americana, were precluded from traveling to the restaurant they owned near San Francisco's Fisherman's Wharf and stigmatized as being a threat to America. Bart's father would have known this World War II story. It underpins the moment when Val and Peggy, for a period of time, cautioned their children not to speak Italian in public.[10]

❧

Bart talked later about this time in his life, but not like it was distant—he'd kept close to his friends, his parents lived in the same home until his father's death, his brother and sister lived near them. His reflections on the meaning of baseball, although deeply personal and definitely as a Red Sox fan, captured his own and other people's factual and aesthetic foundation for the imaginative impulse in a life still evolving. His recollection of the earliest Red Sox game he attended mattered, forty-four years later, because of the way he remembered it. "I guess my first memory of Fenway Park," he said, "about 1945 or '46. I think it was Boo Ferriss pitching. I had never seen anything like that. I was probably 7 or 8 years old. I mean, that is really the ground level memory. All the rest comes out of that. I was just astonished at the whole environment. You listen to the radio when you are a little kid. It seemed huge. And it seems more than you can absorb. Just trying to take it all in. I remember feeling as if I were gaping. I went with my father and my uncle. And I just remember sitting there, feeling, 'I am overwhelmed by this.'"[11]

He attended more games at Fenway with his father and his friends, Andy, Bill, and Frank, including against the Yankees. Even the seemingly unconnected moments—"sitting in Frankie White's father's Chevrolet in the garage listening to the World Series between the Red Sox and the Cardinals. . . . Why were we in the car . . . doubtless running down the battery, is still one of those mysteries I've never quite understood"—contained connections to friendship, shared values, the love of parents, the "game" as the filament that interrelated them all and made the memory permanent, and just joy. He had, in his way, as he said, "hoped not so much to be the best who ever played the game as simply to stay in the game," the Bobby Doerr second baseman, to retain the evolving feel of that "first memory." Bart's words were more than a commentary on baseball.[12]

☙

Bart's skill as a player, barely adequate as competition got stiffer and as his intellectual imperatives came more to the fore, was tempered, though not lessened, by a skiing accident. His friend Frank White remembered it keenly. They were skiing on nearby Mount Holyoke, not high, but requiring a rope lift to get to the top. Bart's ski caught in snow-covered rocks and a mogul, his hand unable to retain its grip on the rope, and with a rough fall he broke an anklebone. For weeks he was in a plaster cast and relied on crutches, yet he retained his daily, off-season knowledge of who was being traded for whom in an era when that rarely happened but was enormously consequential when it did.[13]

Frank, who went on to play baseball at South Hadley High School, doesn't recall Bart's having a deep desire to make the team, and says that the ankle injury alone had diminished Bart's ability to play but wouldn't have been a deterrent to anyone who truly wanted to play. Andy Vitali, who was in Bart's class, described his interest in wanting to travel with the team, to see other towns, and—as continued to be the case later when Bart entered Phillips Academy in Andover—to enjoy the diversity, the ethnic and cultural diversity, and the way that athletic skills came together in teamwork, strategy, and camaraderie. Bart's brother, Dino, confirmed precisely that underlying imperative and the comfort Bart derived from it.[14]

The South Hadley coach, Tom Landers, tried Bart out for second base. The competition was strong and, probably of no surprise to him, Bart didn't make the team, yet the experience, the knowledge of how it was done, what was involved, was worth the effort. He became the team's manager for the season. His parents welcomed it; he got to travel. Few observations by others revealed more about his temperament than this one by Landers: "He hung around with everyone and mixed with everyone. I never heard anyone say anything bad about him." He may not have played in Fenway (never a dream but perhaps having his words displayed in his honor was, which did happen), but he had learned close up the skills required to play each position, the techniques for sliding and pitching and how they were taught, the forms of injury, the purpose of equipment, the role of umpires beyond the obvious, the manager's choices, the scorekeeper's methodology for determining talent, and the meaning of talent. He also could then, and for the remainder of her life, talk authoritatively about baseball with his grandmother, Helen Walton.[15]

Those four men—Bart, Frank, Bill, and Andy—remained friends for Bart's lifetime.

BART'S TRANSFORMATION AND THE YALE PRELUDE

The Dante Fair was held each spring, beginning in 1949 and again in 1950, 1951, 1952, and 1953. Its purpose was to raise funds to purchase clothing and other necessities for the various "Boys' Town" orphanages located in Italy, and for the Holyoke College Foreign Student Scholarship Fund. The fair, its theme based on Dante and the Renaissance, was staged on "the lawn of Associate Prof. Valentine Giamatti's home, preceded by a [townwide] costume parade." The Giamatti children all helped prepare the yard and ensured everyone enjoyed the festival. They each understood that beneath it was a serious purpose, and that the town had made that purpose a civic one.[16] These also were grand events in South Hadley history, enjoyed widely and recalled easily. Norma Stiles Monat, who still lives in South Hadley across from the old Center School, recalled that, "I was a child of maybe six years and I was thrilled to be part of it. . . . It was pretty remarkable that one family in town had so many people that they knew that they could actually throw a fair in their back yard."[17]

In March 1953, Val took the train from Springfield to New York City to attend a luncheon for his friend and former Yale faculty member Uguccione Ranieri di Sorbello. Di Sorbello, recognized for heroism in aiding the rescue of Allied soldiers during the war, had been appointed the Italian cultural attaché by the democratically elected government in Italy. The reunion was gratifying for both of them. The following day, Val met with Monsignor Carroll-Abbing, who had come in from Italy. Together they purchased winter and summer clothing for the Boys' Town residents from the proceeds the Dante Fair had raised the previous spring.[18]

⬩⬩⬩

Val's reputation as Dante scholar and skilled lecturer was recognized in 1954 by the Association of American Colleges. "Under an endowed plan," the AAC selected him as "an outstanding lecturer" to travel throughout the nation to colleges and universities that would not easily have access to men and women of such knowledge. He would speak on "Present Day Italy," "Dante and Contemporary Living," and "subjects related to Romance languages and the Renaissance." For Val, these were subjects, academic and practical, that he'd made immediately relevant in and out of the classroom, including in his own life and code. The first lecture was scheduled shortly at "West Virginia Wesleyan College and several other Southern Colleges." He departed immediately. For his children, there were letters, stories on return, lessons in geography, and cultures and people explored. For Bart, another thread in "On the Road."[19]

⬩⬩⬩

"When we were discussing colleges we'd like to go to, Bart knew it was going to be Yale," his friend Andy Vitali recalled. The decision by Val and Peggy that Bart should attend Phillips Academy in Andover, Massachusetts, likely was made before they left for Italy, in the summer of 1954, on Val's second sabbatical. They would not return until the summer of 1955. Bart needed to be certain of his admission for the fall of 1955. In the cloistered world that defined Phillips, it was possible to meet with the headmaster, with the proper introduction and credentials, and be admitted at the last minute. Transferring from a public high school was a high cultural hurdle to overcome, even with Bart's excellent accomplishments.[20]

Val and Peggy were aware of the power of Phillips Academy as a "feeder school" to Yale, a place where the headmaster's list submitted to the dean of admission was a guarantee of admission. Grades, though relevant, were hardly critical if even discussed with a student in an "interview." Although a day student at Yale and the graduate of public high school, Val would have had numerous classes with Phillips Academy students. He also knew that public school students with Italian American surnames, although among Yale's most accomplished academically, had little prospect of admission on their own merit. The assumptions that were embodied in the feeder school's reputation of who *it* admitted combined readily with the fact that, at Yale, excellent academic credentials were not the criteria for admission. Not surprisingly, the effort to solidify the relationship between Yale and the boys' preparatory schools began under President James Rowland Angell. Boys who attended such schools also could pay board and tuition—that is, be "'paying guests' with the right cultural attributes." Phillips provided the largest number of admissions.[21]

Val's challenge was to accept that Yale was the place for Bart. It had one major factor going for it: Yale was in New Haven and close to family members. The challenge was to ensure, as best Peggy and he could, that Bart would thrive on the intellectual stimulation and the broad cultural offerings; that is, given Val's experience, he knew his son was smarter than most everyone he would encounter at Yale. The prospect of intellectual or academic discrimination, once Bart was admitted, was lessened by Val's knowledge that, with persistence, he never was constrained in attaining excellence at Yale—the Thomas Bergin formulation. And, once again, family members were nearby to ensure that Bart preserved perspective and had a place of family-oriented refuge. Unlike through most of Bart's childhood, Val's family would become more essential to Bart's fate. There also were some of Val's friends on the faculty: Maynard Mack and Thomas Bergin among them. There would be no special privilege associated with that, but Bart, once admitted, would be watched and encouraged and, when appropriate, know he had a place for guidance and candid discussion. In 1947, when Dean William DeVane had expressed his concern (echoing previous Yale faculty) that among Yale's undergraduates he wished to see "greater concern for intellectual things," Val would have agreed and considered DeVane precisely the person to fashion an education milieu for Bart. In the end, Val and Peggy had confidence in Bart's wit and his skill at preserving his identity and values within a culture whose influence would be more pervasive, more of a challenge, than it had been for a day student. Getting Bart into Phillips Academy required the application of Peggy's knowledge of how this elitist school's New England culture operated and how to ensure her son was admitted not to the culture but to Phillips Academy.[22]

Peggy had the knowledge of the persuasive meaning of "legacy" at Phillips and of how to use her family's reputation to satisfy it: graduates of Smith, her father's graduation from Phillips Academy and Harvard, Val's Yale and Harvard degrees, and the presumptions and relationships that flowed from those credentials in New England. It was not a hurdle of the intellect for Bart to be admitted, but a challenge of culture. The Overseas School of Rome also had a solid reputation in America. Many children of the American Foreign Service (itself elitist in its Ivy League composition, as if it was their private domain) attended the Overseas School. The certainty that Bart would attend the school for a full year would mean Phillips was not accepting a public school graduate. Two other factors likely also came into play or, more accurately, were an unspoken benefit: the Giamattis, in a setting where religious affiliation mattered, were not Catholic, and the Giamattis, in a setting where wealth's appearance mattered, would pay the full board and tuition.[23]

Though the precise timing and sequence of events is unclear, Bart was admitted, at least tentatively, or knew that admission was likely, before the family departed for Val's second sabbatical.

THE FATEFUL VISIT

Val, Peggy, and Bart drove to New Haven to visit Val's sister Helen and her family before the Giamattis departed to Italy.[1] During the visit, the Giamattis likely also learned the known agenda of the newly elected mayor, Dick Lee. Although not the highest vote getter in the 1953 election—a tribute that continued to go to Mark Barbarito—Lee had finally succeeded in defeating William Celentano. The margin of victory, though partially derived from increased Democratic turnout and crossover voters in wards that had previously favored the Republican Party, came primarily from larger victories in the Yale-, Yankee-, and Irish-concentrated wards than in 1949 and 1951.[2] Lee's strategy had worked. Following his victory, Lee did not resign from his position at Yale. He sought a leave of absence.[3]

❧

During the campaign, Lee paid heed to the Yale-based advice he had received about the 1949 Housing Act and, with veiled and misleading public articulation, to the plan put forth by Maurice Rotival in 1941.[4] In fact, Mayors Murphy and Celentano had set aside the Rotival Plan as a basis for action, except in narrowly selected ways they wanted to pursue.[5] It wasn't just that the Rotival Plan was too grand and expensive for both of them; it was that its primary focus was not New Haven. The plan's purpose was to bond New Haven to the primacy of the suburbs, to redesign it as an economic vehicle for what Rotival identified as the "Quinnipiac Valley Region," a geographic and political fiction with no boundary and, necessarily, no purpose.[6] At the geographic core of the fiction, Rotival placed the historic downtown center of New Haven and the adjacent area, the Hill/Oak Street/Legion Avenue neighborhood. (Rotival rarely referred to this or other historically recognized places in New Haven as a "neighborhood.")[7] Rotival was unequivocal about what needed to be done: "The problem does not lie in the suburbs . . . but, in the very center of the organism." New Haven must "attack the disease . . . in the very center of the city . . . where the disease lies, that is also where the surgeon should put the knife. . . . and, by rapid succession of surgical operations, restore it to its logical functions."[8]

The fate of thousands of existing residents and families, largely Italian, Jewish, and African American, many working class, including owners of family-operated small businesses of long standing—as well as religious and community service institutions, structurally sound residential and office buildings, and the well-known existing street grid—were of no importance to ensuring the plan's fictional underpinning. All must be demolished. "The most serious failure [in the approach taken by Mayor Celentano]," Rotival wrote in 1954, "is the complete absence of a plan for relocation[,] which is not a plan for building new houses." This area, according to Rotival, was "for middle and upper income families." It was "necessary to relocate low income families displaced from slums." Rotival made no accommodation for their fate, other than to build more "public housing" elsewhere, an obligation he left to others to handle. That families might move to the suburbs was of no consequence to Rotival.[9]

A second condition in Rotival's plan was applicable in all the neighborhoods it affected (Dixwell/Newhallville, Wooster Square, Fair Haven, and Hill/Oak Street/Legion Avenue): strictly enforce the purposefully suburban-based values embedded in the Herbert Hoover–era "model zoning code" of 1923 and 1924. The model code, which prohibited "mixed-use" (the presence of commercial, business, or retail operations on any floor of a house) in residential settings, had a disquieting history in racial and ethnic discrimination. By design, its advocates sought to keep African American and European immigrants out of their neighborhoods through a zoning scheme that would not allow uses—apartments, multifamily houses, small commercial and retail shops—that typified the living and employment needs of both groups. People associated with such uses were placed in the same category as a "public nuisance"—rodent infestation, sewage, or crime.[10] In an urban setting, the model code was intended to discourage the then-conventionally walkable or racially and ethnically integrated urban neighborhood, and to ensure that suburban values, especially the consolidated, single-purpose retail location, dominated New Haven's neighborhoods. The model code was another form of ethnic and racial cleansing.[11]

To accomplish these goals, Rotival proposed a third pillar in his plan: the creation of citizens groups to support his role as *the* planner. His intent was direct, and he'd used it before: displace existing governmental plan structures and public accountability and provide an independent means for funding his activity.[12]

Once the future was premised on serving the Quinnipiac Valley Region—a "rapid succession of surgical operations," the enforcement of a discriminatory zoning scheme, and the "relocation" of "poor" people the essential imperatives—New Haven's boundaries, its municipal history, and neighborhood culture in every neighborhood except the Yale wards, broadly defined, became marginal, if not irrelevant to the plan's fate. The plan was intended to unmoor New Haven from its past.

YALE SOLIDIFIED: THE DECEPTION ELEVATED

Mayor Celentano understood Rotival's regional, ethnic, and racial intent; the Yale influence; and the 1949 Housing Act. His response to the 1941 plan, and to the conditions extant in some of the Oak Street neighborhood's housing, was to create a modestly empowered Urban Redevelopment Agency, as required by the 1949 act. Drawing from his 1952 City Report, he focused first on fifteen acres—roughly the equivalent of six to seven city blocks in the Hill/Oak Street/ Legion Avenue neighborhood—for the rehabilitation of residential structures or, if beyond structural repair, to demolish and rebuild them. He also proposed to improve the neighborhood roadway system. During the campaign, he treated these changes as elementary aspects of sound city administration. It was precisely this New Haven–centric neighborhood preservation approach, with little or only temporary relocation, that Rotival disliked.[13]

Lee prided himself on his knowledge and skill in public relations, in how to sell. During the election campaign, he advocated "The New Haven Plan," along with a city-based "Citizen Action Committee." In his "Six Part Plan," he analogized his intention to effectuate "slum clearance" with what, in 1953, was considered the model for cities to follow: "The Baltimore Plan," a largely neighborhood-centric preservation plan initiated by citizen groups and guided by Baltimore Mayor Thomas D'Alesandro Jr. It was, in effect, what the people of Boston's North End and many of the working-class residents of New Haven already were doing. From the outset, however, Lee put a deceptive public gloss on how he intended to undertake "slum clearance," and never left it. He also left the discussion of "regionalism" largely to Yale surrogates, none of whom dis-cussed—actually ever mentioned—the centrality of the fictional "Quinnipiac Valley Region." Lee's *public* thrust was simple: regional cooperation meant merely sharing the cost of "sewage disposal" and "the building of through-highways [exit and entrance ramps of an interstate]." All intended, he said, without meaningful explanation, to be "one significant source of new revenue for cities like New Haven," as if New Haven's geographic integrity remained central in the plan.[14]

⌘

Rotival was one of the first people to congratulate Lee on his victory. Meetings and correspondence ensued among Lee, Edward Logue (Lee's assistant, and shortly executive director of the Redevelopment Agency, then development administra-tor), and Rotival in December 1953.[15] Rotival reiterated the scope and purpose of his plan, which had two interrelated roadway components: a major road-way around New Haven's central core (the "Ring Road"), which included the Dixwell Avenue/Newhallville neighborhood, and a massive "connector" from the proposed state interstate highway into and through the Hill/Oak Street/Legion Avenue neighborhood, both roadways designed with varying, often massive rights-of-way, as if built in the suburbs. The newly designated "redevelopment" area was expanded to forty-five acres (compared to Celentano's fifteen acres), *exclusive* of the connector's massive entrance and exit from the interstate in multiple directions (Hartford, New London, and New York), through the Fair Haven neighborhood, indiscriminate in its destructive effect and no longer, except in public relations pretense, centered on "slums." In Rotival's plan, with the new redevelopment area and the connector, hundreds more families would be displaced, and hundreds of shops, churches, stores, and community-laden street corners, stickball locations, and small parks were intended for demolition. Waterside Park, which had once served the Hill/Oak Street/Legion Avenue, Wooster Square, and Fair Haven neighborhoods, was sold to the state to ensure the construction of the highway and connector, and so was the proximity, culture, and history of the people's daily access to Long Island Sound and the social, commercial, and recreational life it encouraged.[16]

Unaffected by the redevelopment area designation or the proposed connector were the Yale Medical School, affiliated hospital, and the Institute of Human Relations. Included in the plan, following a meeting with Yale officials, were new residential facilities for Yale faculty and students. "In this way [and others] Yale's institutional concern shaped the selection of the Oak Street neighborhood for redevelopment."[17]

తు

Contract negotiations began, and Rotival, on the safe assumption his terms would be accepted, continued his planning through 1954 under interim agreements. Rotival opened an office in New Haven and turned immediately to his friends at the Yale departments of Architecture and Planning, and the Law School faculty, particularly Nicholas deB. Katzenbach. The Planning Department shared and supported Rotival's—now formally Lee and Logue's—plan based on the undefined "region," suburban values, and the place of modern architecture and the anti-historical mentality within it.[18] In September, Lee established his Citizens Action Commission. Privately, Lee informed its new chairman that the commission's real purpose was "to stimulate and win public support for a comprehensive program of redevelopment for New Haven," for which the commission would be the cheerleader. Yale President A. Whitney Griswold was appointed vice chairman. Rotival, as if managing the script, was appointed the commission's consultant. As Lee later informed Griswold, "This is public relations—nothing more, nothing less."[19]

Griswold already had decided he'd bring modern architecture to Yale. He had admired Eero Saarinen from the outset and wanted him not only to join the faculty but also to serve as the university's architect and planner. It's unlikely anyone, outside of Yale, much cared what Yale did to its campus, however visible its buildings might be along public thoroughfares. Griswold, with Lee's endorsement for reasons that defied any pretense that his history as a ward alderman mattered to understanding or preserving the elements of the neighborhood, received Lee's assurance that urban renewal plans would be shared in their earliest stage of thinking with Saarinen, and later with Paul Rudolph (whom Griswold appointed dean of the Department of Architecture), Douglas Orr (another modern architect who had worked with Rotival on his 1940s plans), and Yale's real estate agents. All three architects, Griswold, and the real estate agents became planners, intimately involved with Rotival, Lee, and especially Logue. The lesson from the 1910 plan experience was learned by Mayors Murphy and Celentano but discarded by Lee and Yale. Lee and Yale were at war with New Haven's past. Yale had the city government as a largely compliant partner. And, once again, unwittingly, the city's residents were subjected to, as Rotival called it, "The New Haven Experiment."[20]

On January 1, 1955, Rotival and Richard C. Lee entered a formal contract that explicitly included the "Quinnipiac Valley Region" as its planning foundation and all of Rotival's conditions and plans. Lee and Logue had accepted the Rotival Plan politically and contractually. It would be six years before Rotival would even attempt a definition of the "Quinnipiac Valley Region."[21]

ᖍ

The broader context mattered and would matter, in time, in New Haven. Rotival was part of the "modernism" movement that had its origins in post–World War I Europe and that Griswold embraced unreservedly, prominently, and as criteria for judging Lee. Yale's Saarinen, Rudolph, and Orr helped form its mentality and iterations. Modernism's most visible introduction in the United States was during the 1939 World's Fair in Flushing Meadows–Corona Park, New York. The theme: "The World of Tomorrow." Virtually all the fair's architecture, and especially the General Motors Pavilion—Futurama—reflected it: highways, glass, steel, reinforced concrete, and the rectangle (the tombstone, as others called it), which were actually singular monuments to the architect, Norman Bel Geddes. Rotival's entire approach was the glamorously presented yet dangerous mixture of the architect and planner—precisely the danger Frederick Law Olmsted Jr. and Cass Gilbert admonished New Haven city and civic leaders to avoid in 1910. That admonition now had a more momentous, actually ominous meaning. Gilbert and Olmsted were focused on New Haven. Rotival, with Yale's imprimatur in numerous practical forms, was focused on the illusive "Quinnipiac Valley Region."[22]

In the late 1930s, Jane Jacobs began to write about cities—short observational articles about the dynamic meaning of seemingly small actions such as adding sidewalks and lighting, and then the post–World War II attention to the growth of abandoned houses and commercial structures in need of repair or reuse in urban neighborhoods. She joined *Architectural Forum* magazine and wrote about the efforts undertaken in northeastern cities to revitalize portions of each with mixed results. By 1956, she confronted the modernist mentality—the wholesale demolition and the broad, anti-historical approach to neighborhood culture—first at a widely attended conference at Harvard and, in 1956, in print. She was not the only critic (they later emerged in the New Haven business and political community as the Rotival-Yale-Lee-Logue Plan unfolded), and the debate—really, the choice—for civic and government officials was on. In the 1950s, however, when it mattered, no voices of opposition or displays of concern about neighborhoods, or their residents, or the businesses and culture that defined them, from preservationists or from Yale, in any department or quarter, were heard.[23]

❧

To the general public, including the Giammatteis, Lavorgnas, and Val and his family, New Haven simply had a new mayor. Few people knew, fewer yet understood, precisely what Rotival, his colleagues at Yale, Lee, and Logue had planned and how it would affect neighbors, neighborhoods, and New Haven's fate and identity. In eighteen months, Bart Giamatti would begin his formal relationship with Yale and become a citizen of New Haven, the place his father once called home. He would bear witness.

19

THE CITY

The father, who gives us life, teaches us to live together. And in revealing this civilizing impulse through the father . . . to impose civilization within and without himself, his desire and need to earn citizenship in a city of man. . . . So the father tells the son in . . . that deep, dark place in the self where the roots of the self begin, so the son learns to be the father, to his people, to his city, to himself.

—A. Bartlett Giamatti, *Play of Double Senses: Spenser's* Faerie Queene

DANTE AND FLORENCE: ALLEGORY AND CIVIC DUTY

The Giamattis departed for Rome aboard the SS *Italia* in July. It was the beginning of Val's second sabbatical and a transformational phase in Bart's life, at age sixteen. In a family in which education, instruction, and sharing were an essential imperative of daily life, and the expectation to learn was paramount, he experienced his second transoceanic venture, then train travel in Western Europe, its museums, street vendors, ruins and new construction, ancient churches and synagogues, and famed libraries and educational institutions. The family traveled from La Havre to Paris, where Val engaged in more original research on the life of Cambray-Digny that he believed would someday be of value to other scholars. Then to Holland, Belgium, and Rome, still recovering from the physical devastation of war, as democratic institutions sought stability proximate to deadly challenge. The Soviet Union had occupied much of Eastern Europe, a special place of origin for many of the families who had immigrated into New Haven, into South Hadley and Holyoke, and who were now friends and colleagues of the Giamattis.

When the Giamattis traveled through Florence on their way to Rome, it was their second visit as a family, yet likely the first when, for Bart especially, Florence's history had practical, certainly more comprehensible, meaning. This was the place where Dante actually lived, where his famed Beatrice, whom he elevated to the high reaches of Paradise in the *Commedia*, lived, walked, married, and died. It was the place where he crafted his sonnets to her loss and "brought them together in the work called *Vita Nuova* ["New Life"], an extraordinary composite of poetry and narrative" that identified the places where he'd conducted his unrequited love. "Dante," Yale professor R. W. B. Lewis wrote, "associated himself with his native city to a degree almost incomprehensible in modern times. Florence was not merely his birthplace; it was the context of his being." How he conducted his life in this city warranted, and in Italy received, special attention related and in addition to his work.[1]

⁓

Dante Alighieri's *Commedia* was taught in the United States as allegory; his journey and the words he chose were intended to convey concepts, feelings, character, moral imperatives—selfishness, deceit, envy, avarice, love, justice, goodness, evil, beauty, and others—each filled (or not) with multiple meanings or with discernible purpose, some only facially apparent, though most words received new interpretation before the old ones evaporated in disrepute or lingered and awaited rediscovery. From the outset of Dante's embrace by writers, poets, painters, and playwrights—some of grand renown in their time and later—and by teachers from high school into the academy, the *Commedia* was read that way. That meant its meaning constantly awaited discernment. Val Giamatti learned it that way at Yale. He taught it that way at Mount Holyoke. What his son experienced in the daily manner Val discussed at home or that Bart overheard in his lectures was how allegory had application to life, to lessons about acceptable conduct, to a way of evaluating literature or literary figures or political leaders—their pronouncements, their conduct, the graciousness or villainy they brought to bear into the lives of others—and, most critically, to the reader's own conduct and choices. That manner of teaching was the way the Italians knew it and taught it from long before the United States existed.

Bart's introduction to Dante, foremost through his father, also would have involved at least three other threads of enduring moral and intellectual strength. First, the *Commedia*'s canticles (episodes) were to be memorized so that they could be repeated easily. Knowledgeable sequence of the words, once settled, increased focus on Dante's grammar, correct pronunciation, and cadence; his integration of various dialects; and the meaning—that is, the allegorical meaning beneath and within the words. Although memorization could take on almost superhuman dimension—as, for example, the remarkable skill of the accused heretic Giordano Bruno in memorizing hours of lectures and readings—for Bart, memorization became a commonplace skill he acquired early and retained his whole lifetime. Poetry, he learned, also was the way men and women wrote. It was used in normal correspondence among friends, including by Dante, in communicating subtleness or conveying insight, where elegance in skill conveyed respect for the subject and recipient. Or not. Second, Dante had established a new language. His purpose was both literary and civic. He hoped he "might unify a people beyond the limits of" the multiple dialects. And in the new language Dante created was the challenge of translation. "Love" is one such word—its meaning not confined to the emotional feeling between a man and woman, here Dante's longing for Beatrice, but in one interpretation, as a source of liberation from constraints and the beginning of creativity. It was not merely a matter of understanding the methodology of the new language Dante used, but how those words (like "love") would be understood and translated by numerous scholars into their local language for public consumption. The potential for widespread use through local languages was great; actual use became biblical in dimension. Third, whatever Dante's poetic methodology or purpose, in the *Commedia* he wrote in a manner that displaced God. He chose—in words he hoped would endure—who made it to purgatory and who was stuck in hell for eternity and who was in or likely to be admitted into paradise. He judged the conduct that justified their place and punishment. There was not merely a brilliant form of order and new language in the *Commedia*, but also a form of bold irreverence, explained, respected by Dante and his readers, yet profound and inescapable. Bart learned that as well.[2]

Two elements of broader influence and more local context also were central to the subtleties contained in knowing this period as a starting point, as both Giamattis did: Dante's influence going forward as well as its derivation, and Dante's civic conduct in Florence. Historian William Manchester captured the first of these elements in *A World Lit Only by Fire: The Medieval Mind and the Renaissance—Portrait of an Age*. After the early precursors of the Renaissance era and the fulsome introduction of Virgil and the Greek and Latin poets and mathematicians, through their elevation in new language and context by Dante, through the slow emergence of the "printing press," and through the persistent public critiques of scholars, theologians, and teachers, came the period called the Renaissance. "The reawakening—the establishment of new ties with the gems of antiquities . . . [was] one of the great triumphs of the Renaissance." This "reawakening" was, Manchester concluded, "the rarest of cultural phenomena, an intellectual movement which alters the course of both learning and civilization." Much of this phenomenon originated and was nurtured in Italy and by regional scholars with access to writings, art, and those men engaged in both, and in England and its related nations, Scotland and Ireland, where the influence of Rome and, largely through it, Greece had permanent effect and melded with original thinking. Many of these scholars moved from the world of "floppy brims hooding their ears, bowed over manuscripts desks . . . poring over manuscripts and proofs in several languages" into public life—scholars such as Thomas More and Edmund Spenser of Britain and, more central to the Giamattis, Dante Alighieri.[3]

Each of these scholars increased his influence, and his own knowledge, through the conduct of civic duty. Dante Alighieri was intimately involved in the life of Florence, and even in exile he paid heed, took initiative, and was called upon to improve his city's political fate in the evolving peninsula of Italy, filled with city-states and the constant rivalry of European dynasties and worldly popes bent on expanded power. Florence may be walled, but its excellence in literature, art, music, parks, planned urban-architecture, theater, commerce, and the meaning of civic duty, even among the wealthy, made it a prize to be held—and a prize to be protected. To ensure both of those, Dante served as soldier, strategist, and diplomat during threats of invasion and conflict; he served as one of six priors—councilmen—in the city government, "became notable for putting the welfare of the commune above all other considerations," and believed "it was the duty of highly educated persons to speak out concerning urgent political challenges." He held as model citizens those men and women who created programs for those in need of education and proper housing and who imposed taxes on the nobility to do so. To Dante, "Florence was the ideal city-state, which is to say, the ideal human habitat." He was convinced Paradise was a "City," that even the gods were "united in a sort of civic society"—one explanation for his elevation of Virgil from Rome: "in the opening lines of *Aeneid*, the poem Dante most revered, Virgil promised that his poem will tell of 'a man who suffered in war until he could found a city.'"[4]

*

Valentine Giamatti came from New Haven, a very politically and civically engaged city. He'd witnessed and participated in the fate of his neighborhood and the way his own family and those families around him created a civic and cultural environment to improve the quality of their lives and the lives of their children and neighbors. It was private conduct with public purpose and effect. He'd learned, too, about how, at Yale and in New Haven, the effects of discrimination, the power to impose it, were stultifying on those affected and ugly in intent. It's clear, as his son would later learn, that Angelo and Maria Giammattei were at the heart of that learning and, no doubt, as Val found mentors and friends in Fair Haven, the Hill, Wooster Square, or Newhallville, in high school and at Yale, and later in South Hadley and Mount Holyoke, his own intuitive and learned skill as teacher could be exercised in the neighborhood of his choice and its voluntarily created institutions. Dante's life—and Bart would later add to it an informed knowledge of the life of Edmund Spenser—mattered, even as an affirmation of the learned importance of civic duty and responsible citizenship, already a comforting and worthy model in his life.

Knowing the breadth of Dante's writing, more importantly how the works of subsequent eras called upon and were influenced by it in and outside of Italy— certainly including Edmund Spenser and William Shakespeare, and writers, poets, and artists well into the twentieth century in America—effected an appreciation for the enduring, if not paramount, meaning of having such knowledge as the base for thinking about life and making judgments. It did for Valentine Giamatti, and, in his exploration and knowledge of the meaning of civic duty, it did for his son, as Bart's own life later unfolded in New Haven, at Yale, and in baseball.

⌘

In immediate terms, Florence took on a renewed and deeper meaning as the Giamattis entered—as a city, as Dante's home, as historical drama, as one critical origin of the Renaissance's meaning, and as a place where Bart's father had walked the streets, argued about Italy's democratic virtues, and been awarded its university's highest diploma.

VIRGIL'S ROME: FATE AND CHANGE

Rome was different, but only in kind. Rome was where Horace, Tibullus, and Ovid wrote, in Latin, their prose and poetry translated and spread throughout the world. Most important, it's where Virgil had made his mark, his place of lucid writing, where his life and work made him Dante's mentor and guide. Virgil, like Dante, understood civic life, politics, and the crafting of history through poetic storytelling. When he left the neighborhood of his Etruscan village and culture and traveled to Milan, Rome, and Naples to complete his education, he met and befriended Octavian, who became Caesar Augustus. Virgil recognized there was a powerful story to be told. Octavian encouraged it. To learn the *Aeneid*, as Dante and many others did, as the Giamattis did, was to learn what was cherished universally as enduring allegory. Beneath it also was practical meaning and real-life application. Virgil was no academic. Indeed, in the academy and among historians, he was Italian.[5]

⌘

Bart, Elria, and Dino enrolled in the Overseas School of Rome, now relocated to a new campus on the Via Cassia, a daily bus ride from the Hotel Eliseo, where the family, again, took residence. The Overseas School had expanded its educational opportunities, and its enrollment had increased as more nations assigned foreign service officers to Rome's embassies and consulates, American military and business leaders came to Italy to work, journals and newspapers established outlets, the United Nations established a presence, and, as archives opened, academics came to study, paint, and learn music. Bart made friends quickly, a few of whom he later called upon when he and Andy Vitali crossed the Atlantic in a steamer after his freshman year at Yale.

Bart also wrote for the *Overseas Herald*, the school newspaper. He described his observations in the "First Day of School," with the light touch of irreverence and parody:

It is *always* the opening day, and second, it is always hectic. The first quality mentioned was figured out by an involved process of logic known only by a few, most of whom are dead. The second statement, however, that it is hectic, is supported by a number of facts which follow: buses are late—in no order; classes are started—in wrong order; and teachers are always—in disorder.

After a few additional observations about the meaning of "home" room compared with our "room at home," he turned to "our first class. It was Italian. Fine, We were in Italy, where Italian happened to be the fashion of the day. . . . Besides we had once heard a saying, 'When in Rome, do as the Romans do.' So we did. However, French, our next class, presents a problem. We weren't in France and [it] had never coined a 'When on the left bank. . . .'"[6]

The Rome of 1954 and 1955 was quite different physically from what the family had experienced immediately after the war. Theater abounded and fed into Val, Peggy, and Bart's interests. The new realism in movie production, stories shot in the streets, sometimes without full scripts, the works of Luchino Visconti, Vittorio De Sica, and Roberto Rossellini (*Rome, Open City*), well known and discussed, were slowly tempered by the early work of Federico Fellini, but equally important, by the discovery of Rome by American filmmakers. Just before the Giamattis arrived, *Roman Holiday*, starring Gregory Peck and Audrey Hepburn, was shot in areas near where they resided and showed Rome clean with modest traffic, with male tourists in jackets and ties, women in dresses. The Tiber River flowed rapidly, and its shores were discernible. A readily discussed continuity, however, was the attraction of Rome to literary figures, where freedom of thought could be unleashed, among them Edgar Allan Poe, Herman Melville, Henry James, Percy Bysshe Shelley, Nathaniel Hawthorne, Émile Zola, James Fenimore Cooper, Miguel de Cervantes, and the German writer Johann Wolfgang von Goethe, whose work, a decade later, Bart would teach at Princeton.[7]

The family visited Boys' Town and other locations where Italy was coming to grips with the effects of Mussolini's reign and Hitler's occupation. Val located a 1491 illustrated edition of Dante's *Commedia*, and Peggy located some special examples of Etruscan pottery, both of which would be shared in Val's teaching.[8] And Val continued to send reports back on the new developments in Italy's cultural life, including that it had moved forward with a new "medical psychological center for emotionally disturbed children and a hospice for vagrant boys recently released from prison. . . . And the establishment of a new Girls Town" in Rome. As for his family, he said that his children, "were very happy in Rome "and that "the names of their friends sound like a roll call of the United Nations." His observations, and the fate of his work and his family's life, continued to be welcomed by the local South Hadley community.[9]

One of Bart's reflections on this time in his life, this increasingly deeper exposure to the Italian experience in America at its origin, written thirty-two years later—after he'd been a highly praised teacher, writer, president of Yale, and dutiful son, brother, parent, and mentor—was that he had begun to meld two imperatives together: the American sense of the possible and "Italian fatalism, a sense of history and the fragility of institutions."[10] He was reflecting on the practical meaning of fate and its unpredictability, the larger forces at play and the imperative, which he would capture in his first publication, *The Earthly Paradise and the Renaissance Epic*, about the insightfully examined yet intense embrace of daily life blended with mutability, the constancy of change. He wrote about it again, in only seemingly simpler terms, in "The Green Fields of the Mind," saying that just "when you need [baseball] most, it stops." By then, in 1977, Giamatti had attained, and held, his allegorical best. He'd return to the merging of fate and change once more, in 1987, when he looked to Virgil and the hopeful Italian immigrant experience in a new land and wrote that they knew, intuitively, that "fate is the constant companion." In play was continuity, from grandparents, to parents, to his own life.[11]

POIGNANT MOMENT

When they returned to South Hadley toward the end of summer 1955, Val began to speak more frequently about his hopeful view of Italy's future. He was particularly welcomed on his return to the Holyoke Jewish Community Center, where he described the impressiveness of social and physical reconstruction in postwar Italy. And the entire family was portrayed in a large photograph in the *Holyoke Telegram*. Val sat to the left, holding his recently acquired addition to an increasingly known and valued collection of Dante's *Commedia*. Peggy sat in the center, smiling, the essential and culturally informed guardian of the family, reflecting the contentment of parent, wife, and citizen who'd nourished each of their lives. Dino and Elria sat on either side of Peggy, each holding a piece of Etruscan pottery. Bart stood in the rear, leaning in, something in the nature of anxiety and adventure on his face, only a few days away from leaving home and entering a world where, indeed, his intellect and wit, his skill and manner of managing expectations and cultural differences would be tested. These things he knew: his parents would be lovingly and practically supportive, his values had been solidly conveyed though perhaps not yet tested in depth, and his father had set an example and traveled the same cultural distance even without leaving his hometown.[12]

An Education

Phillips at Andover: The Introduction

At first, he told his brother, Dino, "I hated it." He was away from home, among only boys, with one African American in his class and two Asians. Of the approximately 220 seniors, only five had Italian American surnames. However, the most widely known person on campus—to whom the graduating class dedicated its yearbook—was Stephen Sorota, "who came . . . in 1936 [and] . . . never lost to Exeter." Sorota was the football and track coach, who "was not only admired by the boys he train[ed], but [was] a coach's coach." Sorota was a Fordham graduate and a starter on the football team, a senior when Vince Lombardi was about to enter. In short order, Bart adjusted, not by altering his behavior in any way but in recognizing that his temperament (especially his manner of making fun out of life), his skill as the insightful mimic, and his ability to help others channel their intellect and interests were assets that were respected and welcomed. Self-motivation mattered in a school located in a rural setting with boys who still struggled with self-identification and the meaning of wealth and who definitely had a need for entertainment as fun, as mischief, or as a way of learning. Bart's Italian American heritage and surname had meaning mostly, it appears, as a form of distinctiveness in a setting where it mattered to his carefully exercised freedom—and seriousness of purpose—that many others had not been raised within or encouraged to pursue.[1]

అ

Samuel Phillips Jr. founded Phillips Academy in 1778. Phillips is the nation's oldest incorporated school (few states in the nation at the time allowed for incorporation), exclusively for boys, grades nine through twelve. Its mottos: "The end depends on the beginning," *Finis Origine Pendet*, and "Not for self," *Non Sibi*. Nearby, in New Hampshire, was Phillips Exeter. Founded by Samuel's uncle, John Phillips, in 1781, its education was governed by Calvinist religious rules. Its motto added a third imperative: "By the Grace of God," Χάριτι Θεοῦ.[2]

The Phillips Andover architecture was of the nineteenth century, close to the English boarding school in tone, amid splendidly grand vistas, New England greenery, and—during the long, usually bitterly cold winters—snow-capped walkways, shrubbery, wrought-iron lampposts, and wooden benches. Near Phillips, "P.A." as it was referenced by students and neighbors, was the highly regarded Abbot Academy for girls (incorporated in 1829), its setting equally as attractive, its intellectual opportunities and support for the availability of professional choices for women revolutionary from its inception, and its rules of conduct strict—especially about nonfraternization with the nearby Phillips boys, except pursuant to stringently guided rules. This manner of constrained interaction between young men and women only enhanced the value placed on the normal, real-life experience Bart had had in South Hadley. He would witness more effects on male maturity, or the lack of it, when he reached Yale.[3]

Bart already had experienced the campus setting in the American School in Rome, albeit he did not live in it. Virtually every activity in life occurred on the Phillips campus. To the extent there was modest diversity among students (primarily from New England, New York, New Jersey, and Pennsylvania), it came not in the introduction of broad geography (he'd been with classmates and family friends from all those places and others in South Hadley and at summer camp, and from multiple countries at the American School), but from the more concentrated manner and attitude of wealth, the range and comfort of choices it ensured, or the delay in making choices and how that manner and attitude played out academically and socially. In an important sense, his world was getting smaller. In the "Senior Editorial," though its writers were grateful for their experience at Phillips and recognized their classmates were headed for Ivy League schools, they wrote primarily about "lost opportunities." "We had no purpose of ambitions for afterwards; and therefore we did not train for anything. . . . In this way many simply accepted Andover instead of 'hoarding each minute as a miser hoards his gold.'"[4] That was not Bart. There were exceptions among his classmates, those like him with both a clear sense of direction and a fuller appreciation for the intellectual and related avenues for pursuing interests that existed at Phillips. He explored, exploited, and recrafted the opportunities. In a way he came to appreciate, Phillips was an introduction to the culture of Yale.[5]

৵

The headmaster was John Mason Kemper. The faculty had pedigrees and credentials. Intellectual opportunity loomed. Bart was housed in Foxcroft Hall, with a clear view of the towering Samuel Phillips Hall. Foxcroft housed only seniors, so the school allowed them more freedom than others, presumably to study, and more time for entertainment. His roommate, William ("Kip") Schmidt III, was from Falls Church, Virginia. They bonded nicely. "Like me, [Bart] was not very athletic! His wit endeared him to his teachers and his classmates. I marveled at the deft way he did anything."[6]

Freedom and choices aside, the day was structured. Chapel or assembly was held daily at 7:45 am, followed by classes, lunch held by class, more classes, dinner, and study from 8 pm to 11 pm. Proper dress was required, shirts, ties, and jackets during the day. Sunday Morning Chapel, in "liberal Protestant faith and system of values," was mandatory.[7] Structure took another form: rules of discipline. Academic cheating, failure to attend Sunday Chapel, owning a car, possessing or drinking alcohol, possessing or using firearms, "or conduct unbecoming a gentleman" were among the violations. A violation ensured "demerits," the prospect of various extra responsibilities, and, if serious enough, expulsion. Students also were assigned work duties within the school, regularly scheduled, supervised, and mandatory. One form of conduct was allowed: "Boys in the upper two classes only may smoke at certain specified times and places." Permission was required, and Bart received it from his parents. Headmaster Kemper smoked as well. The school catalog carried this half-page advertisement: "Man, that's Pleasure!" Next to a young man sharing a cigarette with a young woman was the admonition, "When classes are through, And your girl's close to you, Here's a good thing to do—Have a CAMEL!"[8]

Athletics were mandatory; swimming had to be mastered. Bart already knew how. He was a regular attendee at the football and baseball games and knew both coaches. His classmate and friend Tom ("Rags") Bagnoli starred on the baseball team. The baseball coach, Fred ("Ted") Harrison, was the English instructor, whom Bart admired for his wit, his knowledge of the classics, and because he— like Bart and Tom—liked baseball. Implicit in Bart's admiration and his continued attraction to the game was diversity. It was as much about who played as about how they played.[9]

DISRUPTION

Bart joined the French and Spanish clubs for the camaraderie and to further perfect his knowledge of each culture. The clubs also played an annual football game against each other, in the snow in the early winter of 1955. He sought the position of Class of 1956 secretary and kept it for years after graduation. He was an active member of the Student Congress, which revised its own Constitution to ensure more definitive student obligations in the Academy's life—a photograph of him appears in the *Phillipian*, the school newspaper, in dialogue with other members about the changes. Central to his place in the class culture, however, was participation in what students called "Philo"—the Philomathean Society, founded in 1825, as a "forum for the discussion of local, national, and international issues. From time to time there are debates against visiting teams . . . [and] a prize debating contest." It was a club of great expectations that had fallen on disinterest in a campus culture that elevated not the intellects but the athletes. Bart and his friends changed that. They created "The New Philo."[10]

They immediately began "pick-up" debates, deciding on the spot what the topic to resolve should be, a practice Bart had experienced at South Hadley High School. The approach ensured much wider participation and experience. He became a teacher as well as debater. Two hundred students joined. Philo sponsored a Jazz Festival in the fall, which was "a tremendous success," and a few "'spectaculars' or special features" around planned debate topics. "Should Hawaii be a state?" was one. In November 1955, "the masses thronged to the faculty room to see the ever-powerful team of Mrs. Blensley, Hallowell, and Harding [faculty wives] do battle against the potentially potent school contingent of Al Blanchard, Dick Parks, and Bart Giamatti. The students won the audience, and the wives won the debate." The "Winter term featured three more 'different' debates. A Philo discussion of what decides genius was broadcast to the greater Lawrence listeners by Station WCCM. Giamatti [nicknamed 'Bart' and 'Matts'], Rozencrantz, Crosby ['Cros'], Sterling, Karle ['Jaybird'], and Blanchard gave a discussion, which made the mistress of the airwaves glow with pride and admiration. Later in the term McCall ['Call'], Giamatti, Forrest, and Knipe ['Nipes'] defeated a Roxbury Latin team on the topic of government aid to students. This was the first time in many years that a P.A. group had defeated the rather acid speeches of any Roxbury group." The victory over Roxbury highlighted the *Phillipian*'s next edition: "Philo's Forrest, Knipe, McCall, Giamatti Drop Roxbury Latin." By the spring, Philo confidently challenged the Harvard freshmen, though it's unclear the contest ever occurred. Bart and his friends Langley ("Kaize") Keyes, and Andrew Charles ("Andy") Forrest were pictured in the yearbook, *Pot Pourri*, properly postured for the next debate: "FACES . . . Keyes tries the explanatory method, Forrest the wide-eyed wonder technique, while Giamatti sneers at the audience." Philo had altered the school culture; Bart and his friends had disrupted the status quo.[11]

Throughout the school year, Bart, like others among his classmates, continued to find ways of entertaining each other, though few antics seem to surpass the skit or mimicry. There was little competition, however, over the seniors' favorite movie: James Dean, Natalie Wood, and Sal Mineo in *Rebel Without a Cause*. For Giamatti, the trench coat, the dangling cigarette, the slicked-back hair, and the black leather jacket captured the look, the base for the monologue, and, in time, the challenge to get those listening to see and learn something else—an insight delivered from an unexpected source, not the erudite teacher, but the rough street kid, maybe Brando in *On the Waterfront* (1954) or, later, from his favorite reading genre, the detective story, Giamatti as the Bogart character, Dashiell Hammett's Sam Spade. Seeping through the mimic was theater, the way writers used characters of unorthodox or sometimes just troubled or even conventional dimension to express profound, enduring insights or truths. At base was excellent writing; around it was the means of delivery. It was an offshoot of the debate technique he'd mastered, and the same means of education, in variation, that popular comedians—Jackie Gleason as Ralph Kramden, the bus driver; Ernie Kovacs as Percy Dovetonsils, the poet; Imogene Coco and Sid Caesar in multiple roles—used as much for satire about life as for the laughs.[12]

In February, students filled the audience seats for the annual—actually the ninetieth—"Draper Speaking Competition," won by Andrew Charles Stewart Forrest, "this year's English Exchange Student." "Forrest, Hegeman, and Giamatti Victors in Ninetieth Draper Speaking Competition" read the *Phillipian* the following Wednesday. In an effort that ranked third among seven entrants, Bart reprised and reexamined a subject of special interest—Abraham Lincoln—and a new technique to do so. The *Phillipian* reviewer wrote, "This contestant . . . was very serious and composed. His text, The Perfect Tribute by Mary Raymond Shipman Andrews, was concerned with the events before, during, and after, Lincoln's momentous Gettysburg Address." Bart preceded the speech with a "small commentary . . . in much the same style as the popular television show, *You are There.*" He stopped at the rostrum "and donned a pair of glasses," changed his manner and appearance "as though the old and famous president were actually on the stage."[13]

In April, the famed "Means Essay" competition brought five experienced orators to the stage. The competition, an almost hundred-year tradition, required "an original essay" and its recitation. Although Bart was awarded second place by the judges, the reporter disagreed. "Contrary to the judicial findings, I thought that Bart's 'Sic Transit Gloria,' was the best essay. Unlike the five others, Giamatti's essay *moves*: eats in, gouges around a little and then slides out. With coinage like 'the country is plagued by ultimate inner rot and is being socially emasculated,' Giamatti urgently calls his listeners to go out" and change it. Although the oration was not recorded, the reporter's description suggested the emergence of a writing style to complement the manner of his oratory skill—his ability to capture you, move you, and not let you go until he finished. Bart's observations about society, the recognition of "inner rot," what was occurring below the surface, was a reflection of insight and his intent, still evolving, to describe in words reflective of being "On the Road" perhaps, the motives underlying conduct not easily noticed by others.[14]

Bart had helped channel the skills of others in a way that shared the accomplishment and caused enjoyment and education among classmates. It was the form of leadership he liked, being the mentor, the example, like his parents' example, the more subtle display of merit earned, not presumed. One photograph in the Phillips yearbook readily strikes attention, not of Bart speaking, yet far more complimentary. Three students, laughing and clapping, the photograph's caption: "Reaction to Giamatti's Speech." "Until Bart came along," Tom Bagnoli wrote some years later, "non-jocks were invisible members of the senior class. His wit galvanized the student body." At the end of the year, his classmates considered him "original" and "cynical" and ranked him third in "Entertainment," behind "making your bed."[15]

❧

Far more formal in manner than he'd experienced before was the matter of meeting girls. Abbot and Phillips had worked that out in a way both fun and farcical. Meeting someone informally was impossible, actually a violation of Abbot's code and probably considered "unbecoming a gentleman" at Phillips. Though no rumor of youthful "Splendor in the Grass" circulated (or was even possible), Bart had one advantage and comparative comfort: those early dancing lessons at Mrs. O'Brian's Dance School, square dancing at summer camp, and the experience of the formal "date" with Jean MacLeod put him in good stead. It's unclear whether he learned the jitterbug, the jive, or the Lindy hop, though with his temperament for the value of culture and theater, they likely struck his imagination.[16]

❧

The June 10 commencement ceremony at Phillips was simple and, by tradition, the same each year. It began outdoors, parents and families standing and sitting, the Giamattis among them, as the graduates walked in modest solemnity down through the Great Quadrangle into the Chapel in Samuel Phillips Hall. Headmaster Kemper received each graduate individually, accompanied by his parents. He also gave the formal address, "Four Years at Andover."

Bart was not overtly political in conventional terms, though he understood the subtleness of group dynamics and the place of merit within it. His parents' community and civic and charitable actions, including their involvement and his own in the campaigns of Stevenson and Furcolo, were personal, principled, and value driven, fundamentally about fairness (discrimination), ensuring opportunity, and, in the 1940s and 1950s, about freedom from interference, which meant McCarthyism and all its manifestations as it seeped down into communities, business, and, of special consequence, Mount Holyoke. A citizen's civic duty in daily life, in the manner his parents exercised it, was to act responsibly, to preserve order in conduct as the means to preserve freedom for others, and to protect against discrimination and unfairness. Bart always was comfortable with his values and their evolution, the manner in which he treated others, and the manner in which he expected to be treated. If anything, he seemed leery of politics as a constraint, filled with posturing and the pretense of "leadership" that, when exercised, did little more than constrain and channel rather than encourage the individual choices and conduct of others—especially, he came to believe, the choices and conduct of students. It was a view in evolution, open to nuance and learning, and he would witness conduct and thinking at Yale that further defined it. In more immediate terms, he learned at Phillips Academy, close up and daily, that the knowledge and skills he'd acquired at home, in public school, and through his own reading, observation, and experience were easily comparable to those of any privately educated classmate.

Of the 220 graduates in the Andover Class of 1956, 215 were admitted to thirty-five colleges. Fifty-two would be headed to Yale University. Yale's dean of admission or his surrogate would have visited the school and interviewed—more likely simple met—the Phillips seniors, and the cultural arrangement struck, once again. This time, the arrangement included Angelo Bartlett Giamatti.[17]

21

YALE

The Renaissance epics often . . . force us back toward life, civic and active; they urge us to learn, by reading, how to live—not how to substitute books for the world.

—A. Bartlett Giamatti,
Play of Double Senses: Spenser's Faerie Queene, 1975

THE CHOICES

The physical contours of the Yale campus, his father's experience there, and the university's culture, historic and in its relationship to New Haven, were generally familiar to Bart when he walked through Phelps Gate, parents nearby and belongings in tow, in the fall of 1956. Even though Yale now had a residential college system, as was customary he first moved into Vanderbilt Hall on the Old Campus, part of the walled exterior viewed from Chapel Street, where he'd live for his freshman year along with 170 others. Many of the residents near him also were from Phillips Academy. Unlike them and many others (including upperclassmen, faculty, and administrators), he had family in New Haven and a dual form of cultural sensitivity: he was acutely aware of the pointed, hurtful, and practical effects of discrimination that his grandparents and father were subjected to and had witnessed against others. So far, in his own life, he had not felt discrimination's effects in the same manner or heard it directed explicitly against him in South Hadley or at Phillips Academy.[1] He had every reason to expect it would happen at Yale.

John Wilkinson, from Oil City, Pennsylvania, entered Phelps Gate at the same time and the Yale campus for the first time. Decidedly Catholic, Irish, liberal in the manner defined by Pope Leo XIII in his 1891 encyclical on social teaching and Dorothy Day in her daily life, Wilkinson was spotted by the local nuns, who recognized his intellect, excellent grades, and moral compass and convinced the regional Yale Club that he was worthy of recommendation for admission. He'd already been accepted at other Ivy League schools and at Notre Dame, with full scholarships or close to it. The club ensured he'd have full

Angelo Bartlett Giamatti.
Giamatti-Ewing Collection.

scholarship support at Yale, for which he'd have to perform part-time employment duties throughout his four years. He accepted. John moved into a different
section of Vanderbilt Hall, with a different entranceway than Bart's and disconnected by hallways. Unlike most of his classmates, he planned to deliberately
explore New Haven's vibrant Dixwell/Newhallville neighborhood in search of a
Catholic church to attend and to determine if, time allowing, he could make a
useful, voluntary contribution to the community.

These two young men, Giamatti and Wilkinson, though eventually aware of
each other (John recalled seeing Bart in his "Bogart trench coat"), did not meet
until years later, after both their lives had acquired definition at Yale and outside
of it. In ways neither of them anticipated at eighteen years old, they had entered
a garden, green and inviting—its history disquieting, its purpose suspect and
disreputable to many of those who lived around it—for which, in twenty-one
years, Bart would be held accountable and John, with others, would help him
define his duty.

When Val and Peggy waved goodbye, they knew they'd conveyed to their
son the principles of responsible conduct, and the depth of encouragement and

John Arthur Wilkinson.
With the permission of John Wilkinson.

support, to hold him steady in confidence and ensure that his imagination and intellect flourished. Likely still lingering for Val was his knowledge, acute and permanent, that unfairness was deeply engrained in the Yale culture. It was not likely that he expected, and in less time than anyone might predict, that his son would witness and confront precisely the unfairness he had witnessed, derivative of Yale's embedded eugenics mentality.

ENGLISH: THE FIRST CHOICE

Giamatti early on made a choice at Yale: for all the knowledge and relative comfort he had in languages and their derivation—Italian and its dialects, Latin, French, and a modest grasp of German, ancient Greek, and Spanish—he viewed an academic career in Italian or languages as confining, that is, too "logical" an outgrowth of his heritage and, within Yale's broader environment, not respected among others in academic or community circles. He also was familiar with the fate of Professors Angelo Lipari and Salvatore Castiglione, both excellent teachers.[2] Valentine Giamatti's success at Mount Holyoke had been enhanced by his timing (the broad influence of foreign language and Italian study in the 1930s) as well as by excellent teaching skills and the dedicated enthusiasm of Roswell Ham. At Yale, however, something historically comparable was occurring. Bart entered Yale at precisely the time that the English and Comparative Literature departments were engaged in a robust intellectual and practical debate with national implications about how "English Literature" should be defined and how it should be taught.

On the Yale faculty were literature scholars Bart later identified as important to his knowledge and success. Foremost was Maynard Mack, his father's classmate and friend, who became a full professor in 1948 and, later, chair of the English Department at a time that mattered in Bart's fledging, already credentialed career as a teacher. Mack, who recognized Bart's demonstrated depth of intellect, took a personal interest in guiding him. Other members of the faculty included Professor René Wellek and Thomas Greene, who taught English and comparative literature; Professor Thomas Bergin, who though not in the English Department had a remarkable grasp of languages and Renaissance writers (one of Giamatti's already evident strengths); Professor Lowry Nelson, who taught comparative literature and later directed Bart's PhD dissertation; and Professor Richard Young, who taught English from 1952 through Giamatti's admission into the doctoral program and whom Giamatti credited in the most endearing way possible: "My father and Richard Young first taught me to love the literatures of Italy and England."[3]

In his "History of the Department," Professor Paul Fry introduced this era at Yale with Chauncey Brewster Tinker. Though Tinker had departed Yale by the time Bart arrived, he was legendary as a teacher as well as a scholar. He also was an opponent of "The New Criticism"—the discipline, popular in the late 1940s and 1950s, that viewed poetry especially with "objectivity," not with a focus on the historical period within which it was written or necessarily the background of the poet, but on the words and rhyme and resulting point of view or theme. Proponent Alvin Kernan, then a young faculty member, described it succinctly as "concentration on the idealized and isolated artifact itself." In a manner that also elevated the practice of debate and made the department tradition all the more exciting to know and enter, Tinker "waged pitched battles with the young Maynard Mack (never a wholehearted New Critic . . .) on the floor of the Davenport Senior Common Room." Held with the same if not greater reverence than Tinker was English Professor William Clyde DeVane, who had left the department in 1938 to become dean of Yale College (during the anti–World War II debate) and remained so throughout Giamatti's undergraduate and most of his PhD program. He was, to Giamatti, the iconic example of courage and leadership in the face of prejudice in a position that, later, Giamatti would have been content to attain in academic life.[4]

This 1950s era of debate, and the teachers involved in it, readily engaged Bart and never let go. In important respects that engagement was broad as well as deep. It melded into and encouraged his embrace of the cultural perfection of languages and words that were not, by others' standards, "academic"—his broad range of oratory skills; his caricature of Dean, Mineo, and Bogart and the underlying purpose of mimicry; his earlier start as Jimmy Durante at a time when Durante's insights into human nature, in a form that would make any English teacher cringe, were accurate, widely appreciated, funny, and challenging to capture properly as education. The elevation of words and how they were expressed were all around him, in new literary magazines, television, and his favorite vehicle, radio. For all the attention paid to the exodus to suburbia, it also was an exhilarating time of challenges to identity and language in a subculture Giamatti heeded, when Jack Kerouac took to the road, when Route 66—movie director John Ford's "Road of Flight" in John Steinbeck's poignantly crafted *The Grapes of Wrath*—meant exploration for identity in America as well as hope for a new life. When Dean and Mineo struggled with the hidden, urban power of awkwardly parsed words and displaced feelings in the ranch-house culture of *Rebel Without a Cause* (1955); when Glenn Ford and Sidney Poitier spoke to the power of teaching in the urban roughness of *Blackboard Jungle*; when Allen Ginsberg's words in a poem ("Howl") provoked a publicly sensational court battle in 1957; when Bob [Zimmerman] Dylan came from Minnesota to Greenwich Village, New York, to be with people like himself; when, as Rachel Donadio put it in the *New York Review of Books*, "American critics worried about the collapsing distinction among highbrow, middlebrow and lowbrow" literary culture, Bart was not among those critics.[5]

Within New Haven, Giamatti felt not merely comfort but growth and education through conversations with family members he'd visit on Sundays for dinner or with friends of his father and those who remembered his grandparents—or with local tradesmen or university workers, whom he easily spoke with about what they were doing and what was occurring in New Haven. The neighborhoods were familiar to him, and what he didn't remember he now walked. His grandmother's wake was held in the Oak Street/Hill/Legion Avenue neighborhood; Dixwell/Newhallville was where his grandparents and father once lived and where he visited his Aunt Helen. Within a few years, he'd develop a close and enduring friendship with Ella Scantlebury, one of the Dixwell Avenue neighborhood's most prominent civic and political leaders. At Hillhouse High School, heady students seeking admission to Yale and other colleges or learning how to fix cars or become tailors listened intently to the Five Satins singing Fred Parris's "In the Still of the Night" at the Dixwell Avenue Community House or, for a select few, witnessed the song's recording in the basement of Saint Bernadette's Church School in Morris Cove on the other side of the city.

Or they heard Patricia Hurley and the Ballads from the Oak Street/Hill/Legion Avenue neighborhood, who sang "Before You Fall in Love" in neighborhood concerts in and around New Haven, amplified in Alan Freed's sometimes riotous concerts that in May 1958 were banned in New Haven by Mayor Dick Lee.[6]

In Wooster Square, there was St. Michael's Church, where Bart's father was baptized; the various societies formed by men and women who created self-help institutions, civic in purpose, and places of camaraderie for others who came from towns in Italy that Bart had heard about or seen; and the famed pizzeria on Wooster Street, "Frank Pepe's," whose owner knew Angelo and his son Val. Now the next generation of owners and managers welcomed Bart. His walks there, and his ease in introducing classmates much farther, if not deeper, into New Haven than they'd venture for reasons other than the "apizza," were more than a pleasant diversion. A cultural and family colloquy was in play.[7]

⁓

Bart was excited about being at Yale. His father's admonition about intellectual rigor without distraction always in mind, his own confident insistence ensured the full exploration of what and who existed within Yale's corners and heights, its history as written, and its culture unspoken. Within a few months, his friend and future brother-in-law, David Ewing, came to visit with their mutual friend George Nash, both ready to submit applications for admission to Yale and Harvard. Bart gave them the tour, pointed out places of historic note, described members of the Corporation, and touted with enthusiasm the quality of the faculty and facilities. In the end, he convinced his friends that Yale, not Harvard, was the place to be. They both agreed.

What happened inside a classroom at Yale in the English Department and what occurred outside of it didn't necessarily blend easily, but they did in time, in Bart Giamatti's awareness and imagination, and in the excitement of cutting-edge cultural and literary tension in both places that he saw as one.

"THE NEW HAVEN EXPERIMENT": UNIMAGINED INTENT AND HARM

A contradictory and unsettling murmur on the street, outside the campus among Bart's relatives and family friends, and inside President A. Whitney Griswold's office, slowly slithered to the surface. Yale and New Haven's newly elected mayor were planning the radical alteration of the New Haven that Angelo and Maria Giammattei had entered and made home. Bart's renewed generational colloquy with family and history in New Haven occurred just at the time radical change was about to be imposed in its neighborhoods. The horrendous tumult and the permanent politicization of attitude among residents in all of the neighborhoods would exceed anything that had occurred since the city's founding or would occur for the remainder of its municipal life. The effects would be physical,

cultural, and roughly personal to families in lives shattered, ways of living denigrated, businesses and jobs lost, and the value of permanence and raising a family
generationally disrupted. The discussion, for Giamatti and for an increasingly informed citizenry, was literary as well; less polite in language than Dante's, its full
meaning among residents not quite clear as matters unfolded in the Oak Street/
Hill/Legion Avenue neighborhood and were witnessed in Wooster Square, Fair
Haven, and Dixwell, but the intention of those residents Bart would have heard
was uttered plainly enough: Where in Purgatory, more likely the Inferno, would
Dante have placed Mayor Dick Lee, Yale University, and A. Whitney Griswold?

Bart Giamatti, unwittingly, would witness the "New Haven Experiment"
with far more familiarity than most of his classmates. The Yale he would preside
over in 1978 would be substantially more expansive than the one he entered in
1956. The university was the primary beneficiary, physically and monetarily, of
the radical alterations it and Mayor Lee brought about. Those alterations began
publicly with a deception about the terms under which New Haven was selling
its three high schools—Wilbur Cross, Hillhouse, and Boardman Trade on their
unique six-acre York Square campus—to Yale University.

The Loss of Civic Duty

Yale: The Experiment Unfolds

Once elected, Lee acted immediately. So did Yale, particularly Griswold. Yale, long aware of the Rotival Plan, understood precisely what the Oak Street Connector and wholesale removal of residential and commercial buildings would mean. They were "in line with long term interests of the University. . . . Forty and fifty years hence this land will be available for educational uses. . . ." For this goal to be reached, the Oak Street Connector, with all its radical effects, had to be built. Though of no interest to Yale per se, it would clear the land of virtually everything and lessen the value of the private property that remained. Yale had only to be mindful that "there be no covenant entered into . . . that . . . blocks land for educational purposes on a tax free basis."[1] With exceptions minor in consequence, Yale's architects, real estate agents, and Griswold were involved and at times defined every action that could aid Yale, especially in the Oak Street and later Dixwell Avenue neighborhoods, where Yale wanted plans to serve its interest and influence the community's character in the Saarinen/Rudolph/Orr/Rotival image.[2] They and other modern architects became city-employed architects as well. Yale was taking no financial risk, and its "leadership" mentality in its historic form and parochial purpose defined the "public purpose."[3]

It might appear that Lee had the advantage. Yale had made poor financial and property decisions, and Lee had the momentum of victory and power of government. But it was never a game of chess; the relationship was closer to Follow the Leader, or even Simon Says. Lee placed Ed Logue in charge of urban renewal and, in time, in control of most of city government to accomplish it. Logue was the product of Yale, with the embedded mentality of self-centeredness about race, ethnicity, and class that defined its dominant cultural thread. He once took a course from Rotival. Logue hired the "most arrogant people who had ever served in the management of so modest an American city." None of the men hired were born in New Haven. They were from "elite schools," Yale included, and unable and unwilling to interact with city employees and Democratic Party officials. Many shoveled into positions and then out to other cities in order to move up in their careers. Logue "often communicated with subordinates by humiliating them." Lee (with his own disquieting imperatives and displaced identity), Griswold, Logue, and about everyone they hired shared one certainty of mind: "Oak Street . . . was all too obviously not WASP or suburban or middle class, it was not [by Yale] recognized as a community."[4] That it was "one of the few integrated enclaves in New Haven . . . home to Jews, African Americans, Italians, and even some White Russians" mattered in its dissolution. Under Rotival's "Quinnipiac Valley Region" mentality, his artificially premised vision was their practical duty to implement, even though it would be almost three years before Logue had any concrete certainty of what Rotival meant by the "QVR," and he never did have certainty that it had any definite geographic meaning in law, nor that it was recognized, even informally, by any towns, half-towns, elected officials, or business interests. It's likely Lee never asked; he certainly never talked about it publicly. As late as 1961, Norris Andrews, the city planner, still wanted Rotival to explain what "region" New Haven was included in.[5]

From the outset, Yale had the initiative, the long-term perspective, the power to ensure fulfillment of its purpose, and the ability to manage Dick Lee.

༄

In March 1955, Lee, in a private meeting with Griswold, proposed to sell the three high schools and the York Square campus to Yale. The building of one new public high school had been proposed during the Celentano administration, and the recommendation to eventually build two new high schools—in the western and northeastern parts of the city—had even earlier antecedents, though they did not require the sale of the three existing school buildings and the York Square campus.[6] Lee ignored the original policy decisions governing new school construction. His offer also came in a context in which, by choice, Yale already had begun to separate itself from educating residents of the community in and near New Haven. In early 1954, Griswold announced his intention to shut down the university's graduate-level Department of Education, which was largely centered on teacher training. New Haven teachers, administrators, and principals had availed themselves of the Yale programs; for many years, New Haven State Teachers College, located near Yale, had engaged in joint programs. Valentine Giamatti gained teaching experience there. The Connecticut commissioner of education, Finis Engleman, who was a Yale graduate, former president of the Teachers College, and Yale faculty member (and keenly aware that Yale was state chartered and a beneficiary, historically, of state taxpayer funds), responded to Griswold's announcement with dismay. The laudatory outcomes of the program that Engleman recounted didn't matter to Griswold. Lee voiced no objection. Yale's Department of Education shut down. Resentment lingered. Detachment increased.[7]

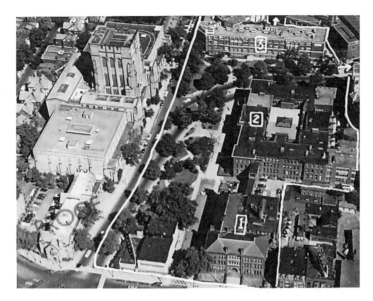

The York Square Campus, circa 1954. From south to north: 1. Boardman Trade, 2. James Hillhouse, and 3. Wilbur Cross schools. The campus had direct access to Ashmun Street (north of Wilbur Cross school) and York Street (east of Hillhouse school). Yale's Payne Whitney Gymnasium is to the west. *New Haven Historical Society.*

Lee was informed internally by his city planner, Norris Andrews, that the market value of the York Square campus land and buildings was well in excess of the amount calculated by the city's (Yale-recommended) external appraiser in a valuation determined for "insurance purposes."[8] Andrews was aware of New Haven's leverage over Yale and the fact that none of Yale's residential colleges had required the amount of land contained in the York Square campus. If a sale had to occur, Wilbur Cross and its land could be preserved easily for future city use. Within Yale, Lee's proposal was considered something akin to a miracle. "The Corporation and administration agree that this land is of tremendous importance to the University. . . There is really no land owned by the University which would be suitable for a college or colleges. If the high school property is permitted to go into commercial hands . . . the problem of securing other suitable land in the immediate vicinity of the center of the University could not help but be excessively expensive if not impossible."[9] Lee's proposal was the classic insider's "sweetheart" deal.

The detailed terms were contained in a "confidential memorandum" to Griswold, signed by Lee. Yale would pay $3 million, well below the market value.[10] In early July, the offer by Yale to buy the land, postured as a good

neighbor gesture to help the city meet its educational goals, was made public
as if it were a mere bid; it was understood that way by the *New Haven Evening
Register*, unaware of the confidential memorandum.[11] Though public contentiousness continued through the 1955 mayoral election,[12] and the Board of Park
Commissioners refused to allow use of the park sites Lee sought for the new
schools, the Board of Aldermen approved the Yale "bid" and, contrary to any
previous education study, the two new schools were set for construction close
to each other, substantially removed from downtown, and scheduled to open
by September 1958.[13] The taint of the sale, easily recognized by New Haven's
intuitively sophisticated electorate, meant the loss to thousands of alumni of the
memory embedded in the schools and York Square campus, loss to Yale (and
New Haven) of its daily connection to the city's young people and their families,
and loss forever of the centrality of New Haven's urbanity to those who would
have been educated within it.[14]

THE COMPULSORY DIASPORA

To build the Oak Street Connector, never sought by Connecticut officials, the
entire interstate, I-95 and I-91, had to weave deeply inward and then outward
through neighborhoods and for a purpose not contemplated by an interstate
highway's purpose. Federal funding came through the effort of Yale Corporation
member Senator Prescott Bush (R-Connecticut), who was intimately aware of
the connector's value to Yale's long-term intention. On the basis of Lee, Rotival,
and Bush's full-throated directive about highway location, Connecticut officials
began to notify families and businesses of "the taking of [their] private property."
The effect was almost immediately cataclysmic.[15]

   "[Hill/Oak Street/Legion Avenue] was really a neighborhood," Teresa
Gabucci said. "Legion Avenue was mostly all two and three family homes. You
didn't lock your doors, if you were sick your neighbors ran over. No one ever
moved away. . . . The Jews and Italians really struggled to get ahead because
they were all just working people. [Now] it's all barren. . . . My father died
six months after they moved. And, we always say, 'They missed it, all their lives
just revolved around that little neighborhood' . . . you walked to everything."[16]
Warren Kimbro, an African American, "was born and raised on Spruce Street, a
one-block street just off Oak that no longer exists."[17] He described it this way:
"You had blacks, you had whites, there was one Cuban family, we had an Indian
family from India, there were Greeks, Italians, Russians, Polish, Jewish, French,
English, German, Cape Verdean, West Indian—and all this on just a one-block
street! On the corner of Oak and Spruce streets you had a public bathhouse. On
another corner, there was a package store. There was also a moving-and-storage
company, two scrap-metal businesses, and Mr. Mentes across the street had his
little popcorn cart and his goat; he sold popcorn down on the Green." The

neighborhood, he added, did have rats and cockroaches, "but it was also filled with working families tied to churches, synagogues, schools, and each other."[18]

Kimbro experienced what people in other neighborhoods, only blocks away and within walking distance, did as well. "People say to me now, 'You know so much about this culture or that religion!' Well, how do you not, in that neighborhood? When Passover comes you have to understand why there's Passover. Or why on Easter the Italians are doing this or the blacks are doing that. . . . Did they need to tear down some buildings? Yeah," he mused. "But the row of houses from 29 to 17 Spruce [Street], they were like brownstones and had indoor plumbing—you could have probably rehabbed those." He also made clear what everyone in Oak Street/Hill/Legion Avenue neighborhood was told: "They said they were going to build buildings for low- and moderate-income people to live in there. So everyone said, 'That'll be good! We'll have our neighborhood, but we'll have these new buildings.'"[19] City officials lied to the residents. Yale, in all its iterations and with its insider knowledge, remained silently acquiescent.

The forced relocation especially pierced the dignity of older people and shifted an unexpected form of responsibility onto their adult children. "I think that's what killed them. . . . When they took away their house on Legion Avenue," Louis and Rose Marie Guarino lamented.[20] "He ruined the Polish neighborhood; . . . He ruined the Hill section," Theresa Argento said, knowing how accessible and inviting those neighborhoods were for older residents. "Whether you like it or not, you have to move. That changes your whole perspective, you don't like it. . . . It's not a free country—you're dictating to me. . . . Was that fair to my mother . . . to be despondent and unhappy? . . . All the old people had to go to the suburbs . . . most of them moved to East Haven. . . . And they took away a lot of history."[21]

There was redlining; people were relocated into places to concentrate them, away from others, African Americans especially. Seventy-five percent of those relocated went into public housing, including those designed in unlivable modules and concrete slabs by Rudolph and other modernists, creating, in one setting, "more of a ghetto than a vibrant neighborhood fabric."[22] Others displaced were showed rentals or houses only on street blocks that were poor and exclusively Italian American or Jewish. The expansiveness of the highways' right-of-way, three hundred feet, took the elegant home of Sylvester Poli, along with those of his working-class neighbors. For residents who had to move, many sought to move together, into the suburbs, to West Haven, East Haven, North Haven, Woodbridge, or to remain in New Haven, in the Newhallville neighborhood, or to move to New Haven's periphery in Westville or the Annex or the unaffected parts of Fair Haven or Wooster Square. "They still wanted to be together."[23] Retaining residents in New Haven was never Rotival's or Lee's goal.

❧

Almost thirty thousand individuals and ten thousand families were displaced by urban renewal. To the normally staid *New Haven Evening Register*, they were considered "refugees," their individual stories painful to report, sadder and generationally disruptive for each to endure. Those refugees were 20 percent of the city's population, not distributed widely or evenly or fairly but directed deliberately against its immigrant, African American, working-class, and poor residents. The deceit and apprehension spread quickly. Many people lived in homes and apartments in need of repair, not demolition; the definition of "slum," they'd come to learn, was skewed to include anyone of a certain kind, regardless of their living conditions. Many of those families who remained would be forced, by necessity or circumstance, to contemplate isolation, the familiarity of friends, neighborhoods and the purpose they served about to be torn from the continuity of memory.[24]

Added to the demolition, first implemented in the Oak Street/Hill/Legion Avenue neighborhood and then elsewhere, were religious, community, and office buildings the *Register* would later catalog, none with reported structural problems. In all, 184 buildings were razed in the Oak Street neighborhood, assessed at $6,000,000. None among them had reported physical or safety deficiencies. All those buildings were in productive, daily use, some by nationally known companies (including "Film City"). Others, locally owned, were solidly established, neighborhood based, and used citywide. The few religious institutions and society halls not demolished were permanently separated from their parishioners and members, lingering, surrounded by rubble and deadness, many certain of demolition from neglect or disrepair or the patience of the purchaser with deep pockets and the long view—Yale among them. Nothing was committed for construction that would replace the full tax value of what was destroyed, largely because Rotival's plan, and Yale's imperative, never required it.[25]

☙

By early June 1955, the effects and fear entered the Wooster Square neighborhood and continued unabated for most of Bart's time at Yale. He knew the neighborhood. The *Register* headline captured the haunting ugliness of "urban renewal surgery": "Home-Loving Wooster Square Refugees Want to Know: Where Do We Go Now?" In a family-created garden, built meticulously by her husband and neighbors over a seven-year period, stood Mrs. Josephine Ferrigno. Nearby were Mrs. Louis Gallina and Mrs. Margaret Vece. The fences that once separated homes around them had been taken down, the trust among these Italian American families unequivocal, their stability in raising children in the modest, shared multistoried residences they cleaned and cherished critical to their identity in America.[26] "The redevelopment wasn't targeted to places that needed bathtubs or had shared bathrooms," Tom Consiglio said. It was wholesale, including brownstone houses.[27] Dr. Ralph Marcarelli, whose family had lived in Wooster Square since their arrival in New Haven, knew the neighborhood's life and New Haven's history: "We had a thriving city, pretty much self contained. Perfection? No, of course not. . . . There were poor neighborhoods but they were not slums. . . . And even those poorer neighborhoods were very colorful, very human, a beehive of activity."[28] "It was a disaster when they threw down Wooster Street," said Luisa DeLauro, a seamstress, active in labor organizing among women in the needle trade, her family the owner of a pastry shop in the neighborhood. "They cried, they didn't want to leave Wooster Street because everything was there." For hundreds of residents in the Oak Street/Hill/Legion Avenue and Wooster Square neighborhoods, easy, walkable access to Long Island Sound—parks, recreation, fishing, and civic events—was lost to the demolition and landfill necessary to the Lee/Rotival scheme. New Haven no longer had a waterfront that, from the city's founding, had been a critical physical and cultural definition of its urban identity.[29]

These residents were under no illusions. "It was a political highway," said Eugene and Frances Calzetta, in two respects.[30] "They made the curve, even the engineer made the remark, 'This was the worst planning ever. . . . All the homes on Wooster Street, Hamilton Street, Franklin Street. . . [Lee] never won in that ward." He was "diabolically proud" with "huge draconian ambitions," declared Marcarelli, who also spoke the Italian language and all its dialects with perfect mastery, a Yale PhD who had known the Giamatti family since Bart's childhood. "[Lee] found something to launch himself into the national spotlight and he did that largely in conjunction with Yale University."[31]

❧

Political organizing would take time, easily close to a generation—the Diaspora had its debilitating effects, and Lee and Yale had money for jobs and contractors—but not the underlying recognition that organizing was a necessity, what grandparents and parents and neighbors would discuss, learn, and advocate. To many people forced to move, the distain for Yale, for the self-professed "liberals"—a label embraced illogically and filled with demonstrable prejudice, condescension, and without a discernible humane sense of fairness—grew deeper. It was from the neighborhoods that concern for labor—particularly women in the needle trades or factory workers in dangerous trades—found its sustenance, leadership, and full-fledged organization, not found in the conservative, exploitive mentality of Yale and its presidents. The politicalization would spread to other neighborhoods in time, as urban renewal spread and the moral and practical hypocrisy of its advocates was laid bare. No one within or affected by the Diaspora was able or willing to help. Not yet. Civic life, as they had practiced it within their neighborhoods, wasn't enough to protect them. They would become what, in fact, they'd chosen to be no matter their form of arrival or new, forced relocation in New Haven: deeply rooted urbanists who refused to leave New Haven or its identity to Dick Lee and Yale University. They'd have to redefine civic duty in a city that Yale and its mayor sought to destroy.[32]

❧

In two strokes that reflected distain for urban education, and through the urban renewal planned and evolving in the Oak Street/Hill/Legion Avenue, Fair Haven, and Dixwell Avenue neighborhoods, Griswold and Lee had begun to accomplish in fact and formally in law what President James Rowland Angell could only express privately in the prejudice of eugenics: "An Armenian massacre confined to the New Haven District. . . ."[33]

By the time the cataclysm had its insidious effect in the Wooster Square and Fair Haven neighborhoods, the debate about where Dante would place Dick Lee, Yale University, and A. Whitney Griswold had ended. Urban renewal, however, would take on another unexpected horror, centered in the Wooster Square neighborhood yet felt deeply in each of the neighborhoods already under threat: the Franklin Street Fire.

FATE

January 24, 1957. Nearly 3 pm. Wooster Square. Nearly zero degrees outdoors. Ice crusted the sidewalks and windowpanes. Within moments the fire's smoke and flames reached the third and fourth floors of 62 Franklin Street, in which nearly a hundred garment workers labored, almost all women. They came from the Oak Street/Hill/Legion Avenue neighborhood, Wooster Square, Fair Haven, Dixwell, Newhallville, and the Annex. "The screams of the trapped, the hysterical and those lucky enough to get out filled the neighborhood," as the *Journal Courier* described it, as neighbors and school children described it, and as nearby workmen and small business owners described it, many of whom called the fire department and rushed to the aid of those trying to escape. Four alarms brought seven companies of firefighters within minutes.[34]

Inside were women as young as seventeen, such as Sophie Christodoulides, in her first job in America, others in their thirties and forties, and Matilda DiRuccio in her sixties, skilled, practicing a craft generations old, each trying to earn money for her family. Some among them had been threatened by urban renewal's forced relocation. All were now threatened by the shameless lack of even elementary building safeguards. Within minutes they were "engulfed in a nightmarish holocaust." It was forty-six years since the Triangle Shirtwaist Factory Fire in New York. Only sixteen years since an almost identical fire had occurred in the same neighborhood on the same street. Ten died then. No one—not the owner, the insurer, the mayor, or housing inspector, not the fire inspector or anyone else in government, state or local, labor, or politics—had acted. Not the bravest or most courageous of firefighters—present immediately, conduct exemplary, moral and emotional imperative tested because they knew these women as friends and neighbors—would have been able to save them. Thousands rushed to the scene and stood in the cold along Chapel Street, praying aloud, helping to deliver coffee and food to the firefighters from the local restaurants, helping to throw sand over the ice, watching as ambulance after ambulance drove in to take

The Franklin Street fire, 1957. The Associated Press wrote that "High on
the escape may be seen the huddled bodies of hapless factory workers . . . ."
Joseph Taylor Collection.

a burn victim away, others to take away bodies charred or women dead from
smoke inhalation, or injured while jumping three or four floors, or just crushed
on the inoperable fire escape.[35]

In double-sized headlines that evening, the *New Haven Evening Register* reported: "Fatal Factory Blaze Shocks City, Death Toll of Nine Now Probable." It
continued that way daily. The number of dead rose quickly, ten, twelve, thirteen,
and then slowed; the other women endured constant pain, their bodies 60 percent, 80 percent, 90 percent covered in burns, their lungs filled with fluid, each
struggling to live, their children nearby holding their hands until the end came,
until all the dead, fifteen in total, were identified in the *Register.* Three men, each
trying to save others, died in the fire. It would be two more weeks before the
last women died, Matilda DiRuccio.[36]

The ward's alderman and the International Ladies Garment Workers
Union joined together and called for a citywide commission to undertake an

investigation. It never happened. Ed Logue came to a community prayer meeting called primarily as a tribute to the fire's victims and their families. With detached condescension, atop Lee's crassly manipulative public relations gambit, Logue declared the importance of more demolition and said to expect more "slum pockets" to be removed and families relocated. The new highway's location (the inward sway necessary for the Oak Street Connector) would divide the community in half, though, he reminded everyone, it was still subject to his power to change the route, along with the fate of dozens of families. The new school, he announced—yet another modern concrete block that, once built, bore no relationship to the neighborhood's architecture—will have "a piazza to enhance the Italian-American appearance of the Wooster Square area." Neighborhood retail shops would be moved, he said, into a "shopping center to the south"— the suburban model likely no one in the audience believed had anything to do with the neighborhood culture they had thrived in. The existing culture wasn't worthy, and the future did not include concern for safety conditions in any of the existing factories.[37]

The exoneration of everyone from wrongdoing left the victims' families with little compensation to help with even expenses. The insurance companies balked, the state provided only the prescribed workmen's compensation, and New Haven did nothing. The memory endured, in families, in the neighborhoods affected, in the Wooster Square neighborhood especially, and among Bart Giamatti's family in New Haven.[38]

༄

Perhaps the fire's horror was another indicium of "fate"—at least that was the way some older immigrants saw it. Bewildered, perplexed, uncertain if they were seen as people. Perhaps, at the time, "fate" was the way Bart Giamatti witnessed it, in the unexpected political force imposed by others on the life conscientiously led. Urban renewal and the enduring sting of the Franklin Street Fire certainly were the beginning of his practical understanding of politics and the meaning of "The City," which was now his residence.

Yet something decidedly more consequential emerged in the unexpected work needed to preserve family culture. It would take different forms in different neighborhoods, but the intuitive skill that foresaw the selfish pretense about public good that Lee and Yale embraced in the 1950s would take on political character, still evolving in discernible resistance and successes: First in the 1961 mayoral election and, predictably, in outright civil disorder in the neglected racially and ethnically mixed cradle of urban renewal—the Oak Street/Hill/Legion Avenue neighborhood. Later in the earned, politically astute resistance to urban renewal's last, dangerous vestige—the Lee/Kingman Brewster/Mary [Mrs. A. Whitney] Griswold effort to impose the Rotival-Lee "Ring Road" through the Dixwell Avenue and Dwight neighborhoods in order to protect Yale. And later still, in the mayoral election of 1977 near the time of Giamatti's selection as president, when candidate Biagio DiLieto emerged and barely lost in a Democratic primary and, again in 1979, when he won.

To Giamatti, the meaning of this evolving conduct was personal as well as communal—that perhaps Yale's culture, the place for him and others to thrive intellectually like few other places in the nation, had begun to resemble some irreducible reality not much changed since his father's carefully managed matriculation. For Bart, in the legitimate awe of his father's accomplishments that were still unfolding, and in the growing confidence in his own skill, was the meaning of resilience and persistence, the timely challenge to fate.

ON THE ROAD: THE STEAMER TO ITALY

The Giamatti family separated during the summer months of July and August. Val, Peggy, and Dino traveled west in the family station wagon, an almost six-week-long automobile tour.[39] "Diversity of the country side, the hospitality of the people in the Western States and a delicious buffalo steak dinner stand out," Val reported back to the *Holyoke Telegram*. Dino also remembered that his father complained frequently. He'd decided to stop smoking and had to work at resisting the temptation to start again.[40]

Bart and Andy Vitali had planned their Atlantic voyage with only one essential detail: the TSS *Neptunia* (twin screw steamer, one funnel) out of Montreal, a stop in Quebec, across the Atlantic to Southampton, England, and then the ship's final destination, Le Havre, France. Tourist class: twin beds and a portal. A week in duration. Minimal baggage, only what they could carry. The objective was Rome. Val drove the two of them to portside and waited for the embarkation. It was July. They'd be gone for a month. Val headed back home; preparation was still required for the family road trip across America.

Andy had been to Italy with his father right after World War II to visit family, and like Val's experience during his first sabbatical, the Communist Party was active and visible. This was Bart's third trip; he'd do the talking. And because of his experience in the American School, he knew people; their phone numbers and addresses were readied for use.

Tourist class was clean, the passengers memorable and sociable, the food basic, the tables communal. They ate and talked with sturdy-built European laborers with important technical skills, gregarious, talkative in their own language and, occasionally, recognizable English. They'd been working on hydroelectric dam projects in Canada and New England for Con Edison. Bart tried his penchant for languages by winging a few Eastern European dialects that, it seemed, actually worked. The boys ate heartily, their new friends more so. Andy and Bart explored the ship daily, including a few places "restricted" by signage, and mischief abounded. The *Neptunia* held steady until a few miles out, then began swaying and bobbing so that handrails and agility in grabbing them became essential. There also were girls on board, from oil-rich Texas headed to Paris to shop, play, and shop some more. They were friendly, easy in conversation, and into the shared high jinks. The weather became stormy, the sea rough, the swales high and strong. As they steamed north, Andy and Bart saw icebergs, bigger than either of them imagined—dangerous, awesome, and seemingly indestructible.

Once they landed, Bart called friends, who came to meet them in Le Havre. Exhaustion didn't overwhelm their enthusiasm. They crashed a black-tie social in Paris; Andy dressed as and acted the chauffeur. The next day they boarded a train, changed trains in a few stations along the countryside, and settled in Rome. They spent the first few nights in the *Pensione Manfredi*, near the Spanish Steps, accomplished with a little financial help from their parents. Bart made more phone calls. Invitations to dinners and a party followed. With Rome as a base, they followed old Roman Empire routes Bart had set out, through villages and hill towns, walking, taking trains, and hitching rides, talking with shopkeepers, farmers, other visitors from Europe, from America, and from other provinces in Italy. Then, like two explorers, they maneuvered to Naples, Capri, Vesuvius, and, Andy recalls, made a visit to see San Lorenzello and Telese. Bart handled the languages, one for Rome and multiple others for the regions. *Pensioni* were chosen, prices worked out, sleep rarely prolonged. When they stopped in Venice on the return north, the streets were flooded. They went to Harry's Bar, acted older and had a drink, maybe Harry's famous "Bellini." Sitting across the room might have been Maria Callas, the spirit of Ernest Hemingway, the magic of Charlie Chaplin, and, in 1957, actually Orson Welles. No sightings that night, but there were photos of the famous on the wall, and maybe a new character mimic in formation.

On August 20, the two young men made Le Havre in time to board the *Neptunia*. A new group of workers joined them, headed to Canada for more Con Edison hydroelectric work. A few of the Texas girls were returning as well. Fun was had, and no icebergs spotted. By August 28, with a few stops in between, the steamer arrived in Quebec. Andy Vitali's father was there to pick them up.[41]

Andy was about to enter Babson Institute in Massachusetts to pursue a business degree and interests that had brought success and comfort to his own family and his father's work at Mount Holyoke. Bart was ready for shared discussion with his parents and Dino about their adventure west, Zane Grey come to life, and what he experienced in Europe—maybe not yet all of what he learned and was still absorbing from being on the road. Within a few weeks, he was back in New Haven and settled into his permanent residence for the next three years: Saybrook College. The tumult around him continued.

UNDERSTANDING YALE

From the first . . . to the last . . . he was a man of powerful will, capable of the most ferocious self discipline. . . . This lifelong story of unrelaxed discipline.

—J. B. Priestly, 1947

SAYBROOK: IN HISTORY

Saybrook College was named after a geographic location, with English antecedents important to the university's history: Old Saybrook, Connecticut. William Fiennes (1582–1662) was of English nobility, the First Viscount Saye and Sele. He was politically active and a righteous Puritan. Together with the Second Baron Brooke (Lord Brooke), and reflective of the religion's entrepreneurial fervor, he formed the Puritan Company that founded the town of Old Saybrook, located to the east of New Haven, on the entrance to the Connecticut River. In 1701, the Collegiate School was established in Old Saybrook, though it's unclear the Viscount and Baron had much to do with it. The school was removed to New Haven seventeen years later to form what became Yale College. In 1957, when Bart entered Saybrook, the Fellows in the college—full-time teachers or others of prominence who lived there or devoted considerable time to its residents under the same umbrella—established the "Fellow's Prize." It was intended, as the college described it, as an "award . . . to seniors for distinguished intellectual achievement above and beyond the call of academic duty." It was in Saybrook that Bart formed new friendships and, in a way that emerged quickly, a base (in a form he likely grasped easily) for activities inside it and within the broader university and New Haven community.[1]

Saybrook's history, English and American, not unlike other threads and locations of historic note and memorials and statutes in and around the campus, held credence for Giamatti. His mother's family history likely was part of that comfort; his interest in English literature and in the history of its institutions and peoples—including in the likes of Yale's Nathan Hale, whose statute and engraved words, expressed in defiance of authority, he walked by daily as a freshman—were as well. His "place" within it, as his family experience and subsequent life make clear, had a more precise meaning. His emphasis on that history, which he embraced fully and often and later articulated authoritatively, related to the university's founding academic and intellectual purpose, its continued improvement in excellence and expectation of students, and what he and others made of the opportunity Yale provided. His embrace understood but deliberately excluded the alleged virtue of the Anglo-Saxon culture and certainly at least two of the implications in conduct and perspective that others drew from it: condescension directed against others, however rationalized or manifested, and correlation of that history, in its nature, to the presumption of "leadership." Giamatti's form of embrace would, in time, especially when he became president, rankle and discomfort the earnest believers who needed to ensure their distinctiveness and bolster their identity. His form challenged the conventional credence central to A. Whitney Griswold's and Kingman Brewster's proscription of the Yale identity that both men embraced tightly. He would, in time, crack their conservative mold. He began, however unwittingly, by continuing to give definition to his emphasis on civic duty for his own contentment and aspirations, and for others to see.

TEACHING: THE SECOND CHOICE

"I think I learned all my real lessons from my father," Giamatti once said, in prelude to describing the most influential factor in his thinking about the values that underpinned his choice to pursue teaching. "He really was the person who taught me about teaching, and by watching him, about scholarship. I saw him teach all the time, not just in the classroom. . . . He was the first person to introduce me to literature and he gave me to understand that the academic world, while it's never a perfect world . . . , is one where there are real aspirations and ideals. . . . I decided to be an academic. I don't know when or quite even why." The demanding, respected academic path for Bart—not merely as a discipline but as a way of life—was English and all its related disciplines in England, America, other English-speaking countries, and those writers whose work was translated into English or relevant to the comparative study of non-English writers and texts. "Respected" because of the quality, national reputation, and demanding expectations of Yale's English faculty and department and the discipline required to attain that way of life.[2]

In the fall of 1954, the English Department had hired ten new teaching assistants, each of whom wanted to join the tenured faculty. Alvin Kernan was among them. During Bart's fulsome immersion into the substance, cultural breadth, and temperament of the English faculty, DeVane and Mack also appointed Marie Borroff, "the first woman ever to receive a tenured appointment in the department," and R. W. B. Lewis, who brought literary skill and deep knowledge of American literature, from Emerson to Saul Bellow; "a seminal book, *The American Adam: Innocence, Tragedy, and Tradition in the Nineteenth Century*"; and the "definitive biography of Edith Wharton."[3] Also among the faculty during Giamatti's matriculation was another leading advocate of "the New Criticism," poet and novelist Robert Penn Warren, author of *All the King's Men* (1946), and Harold Bloom, whose range of thought was so deep and broad, integrated, and imaginative that he retained only a brief tenure in the English Department (he was appointed professor of humanities and retained a long, personal relationship with Giamatti that lasted through his presidency). Important to Giamatti as well was the Jewish presence on the faculty, and those professors' appreciation for education and teaching: Bloom, Geoffrey Hartman, Charles Feidelson, Don Hirsch, and Harry Berger. They all joined and were eventually led by Maynard Mack, who, as Paul Fry described him, "was a colossus in the department for many decades, and is best known for his *King Lear in Our Time* and his magisterial biography of Pope."[4]

Bart's leg up toward an academic career would be languages, their derivative place in English works, his knowledge of grammar, his still evolving writing and oratory skill, and his existing knowledge of Dante and the Italian Renaissance writers who had influenced subsequent English, European, Middle Eastern, and American writers. His practical feel and aggressive openness to the American culture, for how neighborhood values and daily life, including in the now-permanent thread of athletics and civic duty he'd witnessed and experienced, mattered to what "English" meant and how it could be learned, observed, and, with imagination, taught. English and comparative literature and teaching were perfectly suited to the heartfelt base of his imagination and his awareness of its origins.[5] The English major also had foreign language and other requirements he could meet—in fact, would welcome: a reading knowledge of Latin, Greek, French or German, and variants of Old English that would take him back to every Walton ancestor about whom he and his mother would welcome knowing.[6]

❧

In the fall of 1957, Val visited his son in his new digs at Saybrook College. He and Peggy had successfully entertained a delegation of Mount Holyoke trustees who were studying the effective way Val had set up the college's modern language program. Among the trustees was Janet Brewster Murrow (Mount Holyoke 1933), the wife of Edward R. Murrow (and from the same lineage as future Yale president Kingman Brewster). She befriended Peggy, with whom she shared a similar background, including marriage to a determined albeit more volatile husband. Val's personality and the depth of his skill had ensured a solid and appreciative evaluation from the trustees. He had accepted a visiting professorship at Trinity

College in Hartford, teaching a course on *The Divine Comedy*. He came to New Haven to give two lectures and accepted an invitation to display thirty volumes of his renowned, multilanguage collection of editions of Dante's work at Yale, including a 1555 edition "famous for being the first to use the word 'Divina' in 'La Divina Commedia.'"[7] The books remained on display for a year.[8]

When Val visited Bart, he found his son, in demeanor and analysis, already appreciative of Saybrook College and the "residential college system"; the value of the attentive, engaged Master; and the friendships he was making. In *Bart Giamatti: A Profile*, Robert Moncreiff, following a discussion with Bart's friend Dan Catlin, captured one indicative element of what had emerged much earlier in Bart's life and was affirmed at Yale: "Catlin particularly admired Giamatti's strong independent streak. He went his own way and developed friends across a broad spectrum of campus constituencies far beyond his Andover classmates—athletes, theater people, serious students. . . . Unlike most of his classmates . . . Giamatti [also] had strong opinions about the content of his courses," a penchant formed long before he arrived at Yale and from a master of teaching that, later, also would form the basis of dissent and his expectation of faculty and teaching at Princeton. Val also would have found his son still smoking—common among his classmates, permitted in classrooms, and as widely advertised in the *Yale Daily News* as it had been when Val was there. One cartoon strip read: "Inside an observatory attached to a leading university," as an older man nods toward a telescope pointed into space. The professor says to a student: the "spectroscope acts like a filter," like "the filter on a cigarette is important, too. That's why I smoke Viceroys."[9]

ON THE ROAD: DEFINING HIMSELF

Over one thousand freshman entered Yale in 1956. Among them were only a dozen or so young men with Italian American surnames.

During Bart's four years at Yale, there was depth in political debate—the Soviet Union invaded Hungary (and Hungarian refugees made their way into New Haven's neighborhoods and public high schools); Vice President Richard Nixon gave a talk, as did the Reverend Billy Graham. Governor Orval Faubus of Arkansas spoke, and former President Harry Truman spent a few days as a Chubb Fellow at Timothy Dwight College. Locally, "Mayor Lee predicted that New Haven would be the first slumless city in the country." Bart knew what that meant.[10]

Symposia were organized around grand topics. William F. Buckley and Norman Thomas debated at Woolsey Hall on the forms of international control that should govern the atom and atomic weapons, Ayn Rand arrived and spoke on her own form of individualism, and "American Democracy was the topic for a three-day convention," during which Pete Seeger and Odetta [Holmes] sang and "Voices rose and fell; [and] students poured in from other colleges."[11] *All the King's Men*, the movie made from Robert Penn Warren's book, was shown at Linsly-Chittenden Hall, the home of the English Department.[12] Generally at Yale, the recognized internal tension that pervaded the student body was centered on something more fundamental and disquieting than the flow of issues and forces affecting the nation or the world or New Haven. Giamatti would speak to it when he'd give the Class Oratory in 1960, as his classmates were about to enter the real world. Though the challenge of the "atomic age" was plainly acknowledged, and its horrendous terror as unpredictable change loomed in a manner without precedent, a "cloud of unconcern more deadly (some would say) than [radioactive] fallout, hung on the intellectual horizon." At "Yale the apathy remained," though for some, it was an attitude more superficial than real—there endured, at base, an uncertainty in values or in how to think about how to proceed, that the predictable niche in life wasn't so certain. Though students were required to wear jackets and ties to dinner and during classes, "there were beards. . . . The winds that blew were not winds of doctrine," but for some, Giamatti included, winds of the cultural undercurrent, the forces unhinged and churning that even the Class of 1960 would have to reckon with in the real world, that he was open to reckoning with now. He was hardly a beatnik (though he later grew a beard), but he knew how to walk the streets and listen, to pay attention to apprehension, unease, motive for conduct, and what wasn't said. In Bart's junior year, Allen Ginsberg and fellow "beat" poet Gregory Corso came to Yale. Ginsberg, who read from Corso's and Kerouac's works, attracted such an unexpectedly large audience of undergraduates that the event was moved to a larger venue moments after it began.[13]

The issues, forces, and topics heard were grand. So, too, was the tumult in, around, above, and below the student body. It would get more intense and unyielding in time, when A. Whitney Griswold hired the Reverend William Sloane Coffin as chaplain.

⊷

Giamatti was elected to the Freshman Prom Committee (where something in the nature of normal coeducation was involved); later to the fraternity Delta Kappa Epsilon (a home for athletes); the Pundits, "ten undergraduates supposed to be Yale's greatest wits, who met regularly for lunch and sparkling conversation," where Giamatti would have welcomed other forms of humor and insight; the Elizabethan Club, "that singular Yale institution possessed of a tidy white house on College Street that holds a priceless collection of rare books, including a Shakespeare First Folio and several quartos" that affirmed, in daily conversation, Bart's academic interest; and the Undergraduate Affairs Committee, a governing council of students with limited authority yet often robust debate. He also was elected to the Aurelian Honor Society, about to enter its fiftieth year since formation. The society's purpose was to emulate the principles of social duty exemplified by the most intellectual of the Roman Emperors, Marcus Aurelius—principles found especially in his famed work, *Meditations*. Only two years before, the society—which had included Henry Chauncey Jr., who had joined the Griswold administration after graduation—recognized and issued a report critical of the anti-intellectual fervor among students in the university that faculty committees had raised frequently throughout the nineteenth and twentieth centuries and, in the visible form of untethered student riots, had and would continue to haunt Griswold's thinking about, among other things, admissions.[14] The society also engaged in charitable works and met with faculty for defined discussion of an era and language Bart sought to perfect.[15]

∂~

The three activities that mattered to him the most, in terms of his time, relationships, and long-term and deeper moral and education imperatives, were his three-time election to the Annual Charities Drive, his selection to the senior society Scroll and Key, and his efforts and education in the Dramatic Association ("the Dramat").

The Annual Charities Drive, the Yale College undergraduate commitment to raise funds from students for charities, included groups and institutions in New Haven. It was a commitment that took Bart throughout the university (four thousand students made donations in 1958–1959) and into the New Haven community to decide, along with other members, where the funds raised should be distributed (sixteen organizations received funds in 1958–1959). As "a sophomore, he was in charge of [that] year's Law School Drive, which surpassed its goal by a substantial margin." His civic imperative and skill were widely known and appreciated among his classmates. In his junior year, he became coordinator of the graduate school drive.[16] In December 1958, Bart was "elected chairman of the Yale Charities Drive" for his senior year. His photograph appeared on the upper fold of the *Yale Daily News*. "In accepting his new office, Giamatti stated, 'We're all thankful for the opportunity to carry on charity within the Yale community. We have received many new ideas from the student body.'"[17] In this charitable commitment, which he would be called upon to exercise in a citywide effort during his presidency of Yale, Giamatti reflected the meaning of civic duty and how to execute it that he'd continue to think and talk about. He had witnessed charitable conduct in his parents, not as an impulse but as a concentrated duty, and he knew that its social value could only be shared and perhaps emulated by others through the real example in which he and his classmates were engaged.

The Dramatic Association at Yale had a long, though recently challenged history when Giamatti joined. It was founded in 1842, "devoted to producing good theatre." To accomplish that purpose in 1957 and 1958, something in the nature of a *coup d'etat* occurred. Giamatti's role is unclear, but redefining institutions to ensure more robust participation and wider stretches of imaginative action were already in his recorded experience. "Dominated by an elite," one student reported, "the Association had fallen apart. . . . It seemed that the so-called 'Dramat spirit' was a relic of the past." That all changed sometime in Bart's junior year. "The desire for a more responsible Association inspired a revision in the constitution." Board meetings were opened, each member was required to work weekly, each play involved shared responsibilities and broad knowledge of each task, and actors and technicians were no longer treated differently. Funds were raised, and new productions organized and performed. The Dramat also took its production of *Julius Caesar* on the road. "At a special performance for high school students in the New Haven area, a large audience . . . sat absorbed in the play for two and one-half hours."[18]

Bart auditioned and got roles in, among others, the highly acclaimed *The Inspector General* (as Osip, the valet to one of the leading characters) and *The Façade* (he played a prep school bully; a reviewer thought he was "miscast but he handles the part with great sensitivity and this makes his motivation credible").[19] Theater was a thread in his life—his parents on stage together, his father as actor, director, and teacher, an ongoing colloquy with both of them about theater, the confidence of imagination necessary in the classroom, in oratory, in debate, theater's purposeful meaning and use in education, his admired skill of the writer, his understanding of the mimic as actor with purpose—and somewhere in his embrace of theater was the undistilled adolescent conversations with his friend Andy Vitali about Hollywood and making movies. It also was at Yale, and in theater, that Bart met Toni Smith.[20]

Toni graduated from Syracuse University in 1958 (with a major in English and experience in theater). She was admitted to the Yale School of Drama, intent on exploring her skill in acting and expanding her own penchant for interpreting language. (Although Yale College was still exclusively male, Yale had admitted women to its graduate programs since 1892.) She had a simple, lovely face, blond hair, and a swimmer's slender body. Toni's father, Abram Smith, was the highly regarded director of athletics and head football coach at Plainfield High School in New Jersey from 1943 to 1968, with a well-known local reputation as a portrait painter and as an insistent academic guide for athletes. Her mother, Kathryn Brown Smith, won the silver medal in national swim competitions in 1927 and 1929 in the ten-meter platform high-dive event; Kathryn's father, Captain Alfred Brown, was a skilled long-distance swimmer. Toni inherited and learned the endurance (you could not touch bottom), grace, and artistry necessary to perform successfully in the AAU (Amateur Athletic Union) synchronized swimming competition. She was a national finalist in 1954.[21] Informed risk, public ventures, and education as a vocation tempered her family history. Plainfield, far more dense than South Hadley, had the feel of a New Haven neighborhood before urban renewal. Toni met Bart Giamatti in *Cyrano*, the Dramat's student adaptation of French dramatist Edmond Rostand's play *Cyrano de Bergerac*. It was spring of 1958. She had a complex, starring role, opposite Dick Cavett; Bart had a minor speaking part. A courtship began.[22]

Toni was cast in other plays, minor and major roles, which tested her reason for exploring her skill on stage, learning the meaning of memory and the psychology of audience.[23] What she took from her Yale experience was that her knowledge of English and the stage, and her presentation skills, could be effectively valued in a classroom. She entered Columbia University's teaching program and graduated with a degree in English. She integrated into it her knowledge of theater as performer, the meaning of audience in anticipating and engaging reaction, and the value of a school drama program as student education rather than merely as a forum for showcasing outsiders. She later brought that knowledge of theater and language into the classroom when she began teaching. Whether Bart appreciated it fully at the time is unclear; those skills and perspective would add marital character, become practical useful assets for critiquing his speeches before and during his presidency of Yale, and add to the family's antecedents in acting available to their children.

✧

Yale's societies continued to hold a special place in the Yale culture. Each society had known purposes expressed in their founding charters or constitutions, fairly discernible preferences for membership (scholars, athletes), and a demonstrated commitment to defining and expecting high principles of intellectual respect and social conduct among its members. Each society had its own meeting hall or room, most considered private property albeit maintained and served (dining, house cleaning, external furbishing) through an arrangement with the university. Students were "tapped" in the junior year by graduating seniors. There is, within this society tradition, a thread of "Mother Yale"—the value of contributing, through participation, in defining Yale, not merely yourself or your organization, through the purposeful act of "belonging," a value called upon periodically to ensure the university's preservation and, related but distinct in form, garner contributions from alumni. Within the Yale culture, society membership was, for *some* members, a means of evaluating each other later in life, a "distinction" (Skull and Bones), within a "distinction" (Timothy Dwight College), within a "distinction" (Yale). Those distinctions mattered even within Yale's daily life.[24]

From the outset of his entrance to Yale, Bart was encouraged by Maynard Mack to seek membership in Scroll and Key. Mack's role is one of the reasons the society retained value for Bart long after graduation. In 1942, Mack had written its history. Although only six copies were printed for publication, Giamatti and others no doubt read it (Bart would collaborate later with Mack and others to update the history through 1977). In *The Society as an Ideal: The Pains of Vigilance, 1871–1942*, Mack described an early moment in Scroll and Key's formation: "This meeting, too, was the occasion of the first literary exercise—a conversation, for there were yet conversations in those days—on Charles Dickens." For Giamatti, a second factor in his interest was that the membership included athletes, men who brought diversity in interests and perspective into gatherings and conversation, maybe some ethnicity as well, the same form of diversity and for the same reason he'd sought all of those traits at Andover.[25]

Perhaps the most endearing reason the society retained its meaning to Bart throughout his adulthood was Ella Maria Brown Scantlebury. She was about sixty years old when they met. She was born in London to West Indian and Irish parents. Her husband, Burt Scantlebury, was a chef and steward at Scroll and Key, where she frequently helped him. Burt had been a soldier in the British Army. In 1957, around the time of Giamatti's selection, Burt Scantlebury died, and Ella was offered the responsibility to manage all the society's dining and related food service. She accepted. She had been deeply involved in the Dixwell Avenue neighborhood's political activities and, by then, had been elected co-chair of the Democratic Party Ward Committee. She immediately took on the responsibility of registering more African Americans and ensured the ward never voted Republican again. She also knew the Dixwell Avenue/Newhallville neighborhood before "urban renewal," including the centrality of the Dixwell Community House in neighborhood youth and elderly programs; and, as an active Catholic in St. Martin de Porres Church, she'd directed and supported numerous community activities. Once Bart became a member of Scroll and Key, she said, "He would come into the kitchen and chat with me about politics in the city and how things were going. . . . We got very close." It was a friendship he treasured and learned from until he died. "When he was named president of the University," she recalled fondly, "I was his honored guest at the table when he was installed into office. He was like a son to me." In early 1961, when Bart entered "alumni" status at Scroll and Key, Ella was named to fill the office of city treasurer and, that same year, won in her own right in a transformative mayoral and neighborhood election. Her exchange of knowledge with Bart, in and outside of the kitchen and dining room, took on a deeper, more instructive form; for him, a better-informed basis when, as president of Yale he sought to craft his own relationship to a different but historically minded New Haven, deeply affected by discrimination and neighborhood tumult yet resiliently filled with aspiration.[26]

LEARNING GRISWOLD AND BREWSTER

STRIKE THREE: THE HIGH SCHOOLS

In May 1958, A. Whitney Griswold severed New Haven's high school students from their historical relationship to the Sterling Scholarship. The high schools were almost out of Yale's physical sight, only weeks away from the bulldozer. On May 6, Griswold "inform[ed]" Lee by letter "that at its last meeting the Corporation voted to bring the award of our New Haven Scholarships" and the process of selection by local high school faculty and others to an end. The New Haven program, he wrote, was unfair to Yale alumni elsewhere in the nation. Lee replied with palpable anger, probably from repressed disappointment and expected political embarrassment. Neither he nor the program was important enough to warrant consultation. Yale's decision, he wrote, was nothing more than a "fait accompli."[1]

The pool of aspiring New Haven high school students for such scholarships (and increasingly, members of the high schools' faculty that would help choose them) was largely Italian American, African American, Irish, and Jewish. Ending the program atop the sale of the three schools and the loss of Yale's teacher education program further undermined Lee's insistence, hollower than he recognized, that the town-gown relationship had serious purpose and value. Perhaps, at some level, he recognized that he had contributed to Griswold's confidence in making a unilateral decision. In his letter, Lee also reflected on the Sterling Scholarship's history and challenged Griswold's rationale for abandoning it: "This whole New Haven scholarship program," he wrote, "was set up forty years ago. . . . Comparison with Long Island or Chicago is ridiculous." "I want nothing to do with this program now," he concluded. "I want no responsibility for telling anyone about the changes in it. That is Yale's job, not mine." Griswold sought to mollify him in his reply letter by playing to Lee's ego and peculiar insecurity, reminding him he was, after all, a Fellow "of one of our colleges," nominated personally by Griswold, and he noted how restrained the university had been when New Haven's superintendent of schools expressed dismay that

Yale had done away with its graduate program in education. The ameliorative worked—that is, for Lee and Griswold.

Architectural historian Professor Vincent Scully, who lived through this era and had deep personal connections to Hillhouse High School (as did Bart, then living only a block away from it), never lost the clarity of attitude that was widely shared in New Haven at the time, and for decades to come: "The fact that one of the New Haven Scholarships created out of Sterling funds might well send one of their children to Yale . . . was lucky enough. . . . The unfortunate part . . . is that Hillhouse and [Wilbur Cross] and Boardman Trade had all been demolished to make way for Yale buildings . . . and the high schools had been banished to less central, less significant, locations. . . . For this and other reasons most young New Haveners could never hope to go to Yale, and resented it. And in just those years Yale chose to abolish its New Haven Scholarships, reinstating them only in 1979, during the Giamatti presidency."[2] In that same Scully framework, Wilbur Cross closed its doors in June 1958 in splendid glory. Its basketball team, coached by Salvatore "Red" Verderame, ended the year undefeated, winning the District League, the Connecticut Interscholastic Athletic Association Tournament, and the New England High School Basketball Tournament. Cross began that season on its home court, the Winchester School in the Dixwell Avenue neighborhood, with an unexpected, perhaps allegorical, win against its older, more experienced across-the-street rival: Wilbur Cross 42, Yale Freshman 40.[3]

THE RECURRING NIGHTMARE: RIOTS

In early February 1958, the student temperament that Griswold abhorred but couldn't seem to manage exploded on the Yale campus. "Seventeen Freshmen Reported to the Dean for Riot Activity," reported the *Yale Daily News*.[4] It was as if the 1952 riot—there had been a larger one (twenty-five hundred students involved) in 1953—though fresh in Griswold's mind, was probably unknown by Yale's Class of 1962, or it was merely a precedent to challenge.[5]

At nighttime, in the courtyard of the Old Campus, students threw "refuse, burning papers, and fire crackers" out the residence hall windows and engaged in "disturbing the peace." Yale police interceded immediately to regain quiet. Room numbers were taken. No one was punished beyond a reprimand. *In loco parentis* (in the place of a parent)—Yale and its president were like parents to their children albeit in a physical setting that extended beyond the campus and with less delegated authority to discipline—was the presumption and resulting temperament of freedom to act that Griswold could not dampen. Another ripple of disturbance occurred on April 9 that Yale police could not confine. Forty undergraduates were arrested by New Haven police.[6]

Commemorating St. Patrick's Day, March 17, had deep antecedents in New Haven. Catholicism (and the Irish American special form of adherence to its dictates) was central as an organizing principle, followed by the importance of projecting, for themselves as well as others, Irish American accomplishment in civic and political life. The evolution from the black-tie Hibernian Ball during the Celentano administration back to a once-heralded grand parade took hold in 1956. Dick Lee was mayor, and the Irish thread in his ancestry ensured cooperation, support, and his own prominent role. Forty-five hundred people marched, and forty-five thousand spectators lined the route. The parade began north of the Yale campus, at St. Mary's Church, home to the founding of the Knights of Columbus, went west, then south, east past City Hall, and then north, up Elm Street through the Yale campus (past Saybrook College) and back to St. Mary's. No incidents of note occurred. Until March 1959.[7]

The weather was cold, the wind still but with occasional bluster, the street and sidewalks cleared of recently fallen snow, and the marchers and crowds as large and enthusiastic as ever. The parade made its way up Elm. Between College and York streets, as a police contingent of uniformed officers in parade dress walked smartly toward Saybrook, "200 Yale students started throwing snowballs." Female marchers, in their high school uniforms, short skirts fluttering, scrambled in the unexpected onslaught. Top hats became targets. Imperfect pitching caused onlookers to scatter. Several police were hit. "Fifty members of the city force, under orders, charged the students. . . . During an attempt by city and Campus police to clear the streets, two or three snowballs from high in Calhoun [Hall, also on Elm,] fell on the assembled group" of police, students, and bystanders. Nightsticks emerged, fire trucks showed up, and water hoses were trained and unleashed "on the Calhoun facade." Snowballs were thrown at passing motorists. Students broke windows on Yale property. Hundreds more students joined in the melee. The total exceeded fifteen hundred. Police chased students inside Battell Chapel, unwilling to draw a line that students expected. Students, the *Daily News* reported, "waved swastikas and swore at police." Students were arrested. President Griswold "arrived on the scene. . . . [with] Campus police stationed at various points on Elm Street and city police keeping guard." Four students were suspended, though not expelled. Arrests and turbulence continued over a three-day period. Twenty-five students were arrested immediately, eventually forty-one. One broke a patrol wagon window. Seven students were from Saybrook College, where Giamatti lived. Griswold ordered students to stay off the street for two days. "Childishness is too weak an excuse," Griswold said. "Boorishness is the better word." Dean Harold B. Whiteman "read the President's remarks to freshmen" and commented that "this is a black mark on the University."[8]

Griswold recognized that lurking among the "electric currents generated by the Irish . . . , the Italians and the Jews," was whether anti-Catholic ridicule underpinned the students' conduct. Though he likely didn't recognize it, Yale's public anti-Catholic attack on William F. Buckley and its own historic demeanor concerning Catholicism were well known by New Haven's residents. Internally,

Griswold would not accept any excuse, though his reasoning was reflexively condescending. "In assessing the guilt," he wrote, "I have it constantly in mind that the brighter and better educated you are and the more advantages you have, the greater your responsibility to avoid giving offense to your fellow men—especially to those whose education and advantages have been inferior to their own."[9] The *New Haven Evening Register* editorial view also focused on student judgment: "The "difference between . . . youthful bravado . . . and ultimate resistance on a public street which no policeman can possibly ignore or tolerate" was not a line students and parents were willing to accept.[10] The *Yale Daily News* expressed a different perspective: "We support President Griswold completely," but police misconduct exacerbated the riot, certainly through an enforced expectation that students likely hadn't experienced. The "riot," as the *Daily News* called it, received unfavorable national attention. Whatever other ethnic, racial, and religious constraints Yale imposed in its admissions decisions, Griswold couldn't seem to discern a method that constrained "undergraduates [it did admit] . . . to live up to their responsibilities as members of the Community" and not bring "disgrace upon all of us." For the second (perhaps the third or fourth) time in his tenure, Yale students had embarrassed him.[11]

Lee, also embarrassed, appointed a three-man commission "to investigate the causes of 'friction and disturbances involving Yale students, New Haven police and citizens during recent years.'" Two were Yale graduates. Griswold embraced the proposal. He added, however, a revealing, pragmatic correlation about what also was uniquely at stake for Yale that also placated Lee: "By giving this commission the full cooperation it deserves, I believe that this community, both New Haven and Yale, may be able to set as good an example . . . as the city of New Haven, under Mayor Lee's leadership, has already set in [urban] redevelopment."[12]

The commission found shared responsibility. To Yale's dismay, the commission, after extensive inquiry at Harvard, also found that Cambridge police had "little trouble" with students, and that Harvard, to improve its relationship with the local community, made annual payments in lieu of taxes and paid twenty years of full taxes on newly declared tax-exempt property. The Harvard/Cambridge experience was ignored by Lee and Griswold.[13] The commission also actually suggested that to enhance town-gown relations, "Yale offer prizes for the best essays written by local high schools' pupils on such subjects as the 'The Importance of Yale and New Haven to each other.'"[14]

Charges against forty-one students and one professor arrested were, essentially, dropped, "in the best interest of all concerned," and in anticipation of the commission's report, which the city attorney said "will . . . contribute greatly to bring about the desired results."[15] What did come out of the commission's work, however (and Griswold's internally prepared analysis to "end once and for all . . . incidents that are no longer tolerable,"), was not a change in temperament among students admitted to Yale (more "riots" were to come). It was the gradual evolution in the way Yale and New Haven, institutionally and mutually, developed strategy and methodology to deal with student and public disturbances.[16]

ADMISSIONS: THE FOUNDATION FOR CHANGE

The continued effort to find euphemisms for admission requirements to cover racial and ethnic discrimination—"leadership," "manliness," "character," "sound body," "promise," and the touting of the number of national "leaders" Yale graduated—deluded no one about precisely what the alumni committees and admission staff in New Haven were doing. In 1951, as Griswold took the helm, *Time* magazine captured the Yale mentality: "Consciously or unconsciously, Yale had traditionally waited for others to lead. . . .Yale had stood from its earliest beginnings for conservatism triumphant."[17]

An evolution in thinking and concrete action toward diversity, however, including the admission of women, began in the waning yet still vibrant days of Griswold's control of the presidency. In what Yale Law Professor Alexander Bickel appropriately called a "colloquy," when, as here, an issue engaged people who mattered in the Yale culture, Griswold saw the need and then laid the irrepressible foundation for change.[18] The strongest imperative for doing so does not appear to be some kind of epiphany about merit or the result of a visitation to Paradise or an embrace of fairness with respect to race or class or gender. Griswold was too practical and deeply embedded in the white Anglo-Saxon culture for that. It was the riots and the anti-intellectualism that pervaded the conduct of those undergraduates admitted in accordance with "requirements" that ensured both. The riots and immaturity had gone on long enough that there was no reasonable basis to believe that a modest tweak in the admission process would change it. Griswold, with help, focused his emphasis on Yale as an institution, not Yale as only the repository for alumni children and those who looked like them. He already had encouraged—actually unleashed—change in likely *applicants* for admission with indirection: the appointment of Jews to the faculty, particularly at the Law School. Those appointments also included Italian and Catholic Guido Calabresi. Dean DeVane, with more and earlier prescience, had done the same in the Department of English, including the appointment of a woman as professor.[19]

The persistent effort of Jewish graduates, rabbinical leaders on campus, and faculty concerned with enhancing intellectual quality intensified toward the end of Griswold's tenure. The anti-Semitic discrimination, especially, was too obvious to ignore. Griswold insisted on documentation not only of the numbers of Jewish applicants and admitted students but also of the manner in which discrimination was exercised at Yale and through alumni committees. In 1962, he also approved a policy "effective for the class that would enter in that fall," which called for "the removal of 'economic, social, and religious or racial barriers to the fulfillment of . . . the democratic ideal of equal opportunity."[20] When one of Yale's most prominent Jewish graduates, William Horowitz (a classmate of Griswold's), who remained in Connecticut and eventually New Haven, took the lead, the impediments to change had their most vociferous and skillful advocate toward final destruction. On his second attempt, Horowitz was elected by the alumni as the first Jewish member of the Yale Corporation. The foundation for discrimination had been cracked, albeit only discernibly. The remnants of the *ancien régime*'s personnel and the presumptions and euphemisms of elitism, including his own, remained Griswold's next task to manage.[21]

Griswold also elevated the discussion about admitting women as undergraduates; intellect and responsible civic conduct were his imperatives.[22] He negotiated discretely with the presidents of Smith and Vassar until their new program was announced in the *New York Times* in March 1958, when Bart Giamatti was a sophomore: "Yale College to Admit Co-eds from Smith and Vassar in Fall."[23] Yale established a two-year master of arts degree program that included student teaching in the greater New Haven area. Women would be admitted in their senior year, receive their bachelor degree from their own school, and live in Yale's graduate women's hall. The program, disconnected from providing educational opportunities for local men and women, likely made negative impressions in New Haven, especially among educators. Nationally, and in the emerging Bickel form of colloquy, the announcement took a different form.

The *Yale Daily News* contended that the Smith-Vassar program had been "misinterpreted." Female students were not being admitted to Yale. Though asserting that the women would not be enrolled in the undergraduate college, the *Daily News* also acknowledged that the women would take "a special undergraduate senior honors seminar" with undergraduate men. The university's clarification, sought by the *Daily News*, added to the colloquy: "This [program] did not mean an *imminent* change of policy to admit [female] undergraduates."[24]

There was, no doubt, a small universe of people who awaited Yale's attainment of normality, certainly Giamatti, who understood and had experienced the value of co-education. Harvard had integrated undergraduate connections with Radcliffe (other Ivy League schools had something comparable to Harvard's stilted albeit relative normality), and numerous other private and public universities, by law, were co-educational.[25] The *Harvard Crimson* also examined precisely what Griswold and faculty long had recognized: virtually no studying occurred on weekends, when women were entertained and alcohol consumption flourished. The consequence, the *Crimson* suggested, was considered "catastrophic . . . for the continued good health of undergraduate education at Yale." And, as Griswold also recognized, some high-level undergraduate talent was selecting Harvard. In

November, the *Crimson* followed up with a stunning quote from an anonymous "Yale administrator": "The only reason Yale would consider taking women is that private education has an obligation to educate all young people." Some male students welcomed it. Nine female students entered the program, most or all with bachelor's degrees. The program, which changed in format and was short lived, included among its early graduates John Wilkinson, Bart's future university secretary (MA, Yale 1963) and Virginia Tansey (Wellesley 1961; MA, Yale 1962). A courtship began. John and Virginia married, but the program was ended under Kingman Brewster.[26]

The *Yale Daily News* lent credence to the unnatural effect on the undergraduate riot mentality from the absence of women within months of Griswold's death. The subcommittee of Yale's "Manners and Morals" Committee reached a similar conclusion concerning undergraduate "health" after the 1952 riot. The colloquy was on. Maturity was the primary objective. It appeared to come incrementally closer when Griswold initiated, Dean of Admissions Arthur Howe led and completed, and the Corporation unanimously approved (at the time of Griswold's death) the recommended policy that Yale should have "needs blind" admissions: students could be admitted regardless of whether they could pay, though in practice, beneath its rhetorical impression, the policy still involved the increasingly awkward preservation of elite preferences, which shortly Kingman Brewster, Griswold's successor, unequivocally affirmed. Change, however, was irreversible.[27]

☙

Kingman Brewster, who preceded Giamatti as president, lacked Griswold's confidently exercised skill at persuasive colloquy or his precise form of recognized institutional commitment to Yale.[28] When he took charge, he immediately returned to the rhetoric of yesteryear, the euphemism of the *ancien régime*: admission to Yale and the Yale degree were correlated to creating "leaders" and "leadership." "Yale is one of those institutions," Brewster wrote in the widely disseminated special edition of the *Yale Alumni Magazine*, "which claims to be truly an asset to the survival of Western Civilization," harkening back, certainly not out of ignorance, to the unsubtle echo of eugenicist Madison Grant (Yale 1887) and a thread in Yale's history—the nude photographs were still being taken—well known to many of the alumni and the faculty, who were educated, benefited from, and were living in or near it. "Leadership," "Training for Leadership," "Yale's Role in the Education of American Leaders"—the subjects of Brewster-approved seminars and pamphlets—were central to Brewster's mentality and a pervasive mantra throughout his presidency. They were euphemisms imbued with the history of exclusion, a term that rang loudly with the elite presumption that you needed to be trained by us, to be like us, to be one of us.[29] The Griswold expectation had become clouded, its momentum temporarily stifled in Brewster's return to yesteryear. As Brewster would come to realize, the colloquy was so strong in the American culture and solidly based in reason to be an unstoppable force that, with yet further awkwardness, he would have to manage to a concrete semblance of completion.

Bart Giamatti witnessed this painful, at times bumbling, transition to attaining mere normality.

Neither Griswold nor Brewster

Yale is not in business for profit. It expends for its employees and its students every available dollar.

—A. Whitney Griswold, 1953

Yale is one of those institutions which claims to be truly an asset to the survival of Western Civilization.

—Kingman Brewster, 1966

Workers: The Moment of Choice

The most decisive historical moment in Yale's relationship with its employees occurred during Griswold's administration. What began as an investigative report during the presidency of Charles Seymour, and came to decision by 1953, involved a strategic approach to Labor that, if adopted, might have altered the university's history. The remnants of eugenics mentality ensured it would not.

In 1938, Seymour, subjected to public criticism concerning Yale's treatment of its employees, created a faculty committee chaired by Emerson Tuttle, master of Davenport College, "to probe the labor problem." The committee "recommended that the university shorten work hours, raise janitors' salaries, and centralize personnel responsibilities in an office of employee relations." The strategic premise of these recommendations contained the choice, in an early iteration: "The University should take the lead in setting standards, [and] making a greater attention to humane considerations than those in competitive business or industry." The Corporation, especially the Reverend Henry Sloane Coffin and Yale's assistant treasurer and comptroller, Thomas Farnham, believed there was "no place for organized labor in philanthropic institutions."[1]

In 1939, Seymour hired Yale's first director of personnel, R. Carter Nyman. Nyman was thwarted immediately; he could not integrate his ideas on labor relations into the university's approach. In 1941, a union formed among some blue-collar workers, and a strike occurred, but the union lacked power in numbers and therefore effect in order to get much of what it sought—especially a "union shop" (the requirement that employees, once hired, must join the union and pay dues) or meaningful improvements in wages or working conditions. In 1950, when Griswold took office, Nyman (who knew Griswold) wrote to him a "Preliminary Summary" concerning present and future personnel needs.[2] Nyman's strategic premise for labor relations added definition and intent to the premise of the 1938 Tuttle Report: "Size, complexity of institution and research functions require supplementary administrative, professional and technical services." Yale, he contended, must recognize that nonfaculty employee support for ensuring the success of the university's mission is interrelated in value and purpose with that of faculty, not separate from it. With this as a premise, Nyman argued that, in the absence of professional employee management experts, Yale cannot "develop a well-rounded, long range personnel program" or understand that "ambivalence in our administrative attitude of mind toward such matters" results in "employment conditions [that] are not as good as we feel they should be and employees are influenced to be ambivalent in their attitude of mind toward Yale; which is unsatisfactory." In the accompanying narrative, Nyman called for, among other things, improved working conditions; cultural, health, and educational programs (access to Yale for employees and their children to improve skills, improve physical and family well-being, sports teams, tours of the university); and wages and benefits "more favorable with the rates of local business and better paying eastern universities."[3]

Griswold rejected Nyman's premise and narrative. He accepted instead, in a disingenuously simple formulation, a derivative of the Coffin and Farnham premise. When contract negotiations began in late March 1953, and the strike began on May 7, Griswold—although not the lead negotiator—defined the framework publicly and privately.[4] In his May 7 statement, at the outset of what became a fourteen-day labor strike to get a ten-cent-an-hour raise and a union shop, Griswold wrote to the university at large: "Yale is not in business for profit. It expends for its employees and its students every available dollar. There is no question of retaining anything for private benefit or corporate gain. . . . The demands now submitted to us by the Union could be met only at the expense of students, faculty, and other employees. . . . With all these fairly in mind I do not see how the Union's demands can be met." Yale, of course, had "profits" in the form of dividends, interest, and restricted and unrestricted contributions, all of which were wholly within its control to invest or spend in pursuit of its mission.[5]

Gaddis Smith (Yale 1954, PhD 1961), chairman of the *Yale Daily News*, and the *Daily News* itself could not have echoed Griswold with more exactitude.[6] On May 7, in a letter directed to the *Daily News* in the conventional manner ("To the Chairman of the News"), Martin Fenton Jr. (Yale 1956) wrote that the "Union has presented a strong case for its demands. I wonder . . . what the University has to say on its behalf." The next day Smith, not the university, replied.

"University in the Right," the editorial declared. "In his remarkably clear-headed statement President Griswold emphasizes the one salient point that the union seems to have overlooked. . . . Yale," said the president, "'is not in business for profit. It expends for its employees and its students every available dollar. There is no question of retaining anything for private benefit or corporate gain.'" Smith opposed the ten-cents-an-hour raise and the union shop and supported the use of students to replace workers.[7] He also subsequently and gratuitously ridiculed the union's position on "strike breakers."[8]

The Griswold and Smith position was challenged. One law student accused Griswold of using students as strikebreakers. Students and faculty at the Law School and the Divinity School and among the Christian organizations at Dwight Hall supported the employees.[9] Philosophy Professor Paul Weiss wrote directly to Griswold. His challenge went right to the choice Nyman sought and Griswold and the Corporation rejected. The amount of the wage increase was so small, Weiss began, that, "wisdom would dictate yielding at once. To yield later is to build up *ill will in the entire city*, to spoil relations for quite a while, and to gain little else." To Weiss, "the open shop [which Smith advocated] is about as dated as child labor," and the "employees are entitled to wages comparable to that paid to their neighbors. Our poverty is no excuse nor salve for them." Griswold, "distressed" by Weiss's letter, reiterated that "we are a charitable institution . . . we have no profits," and, in effect, everything else he included in his public statement. Weiss, in reply, expressed his willingness to circulate Griswold's position. Weiss added, however, that "on the whole the administration has not handled the strike well." Then, in a way that affirmed Nyman's premise, Weiss added, "I think we do not give special scholarships to the children of our workmen; . . . we do not hold adult education classes for our employees. Our firemen and cooks are firemen and cooks and nothing more. . . . It is not a direct concern of theirs that we have such a splendid scholarship system, that our buildings need to be repaired, or that our faculty is inadequately paid. We have not allowed it to be their affair." Weiss believed, as he wrote to Griswold, that "Yale might have to make reductions in scholarship amounts, in faculty raises or hiring, or ask faculty to eat less. . . . So far as the administration argues its case as if it was the duty of the workers to help us carry on this work, it seems to me it is an error."[10]

The immediate outcome of the strike was a five-cent pay increase and no union shop. Griswold's and the Corporation's decision was more enduring. It solidified Yale's framework for labor relations. Four matters of importance emerged for both sides to learn. First, students, faculty, the Union, and university staff (white-collar employees) raised questions about the absence of publicly shared and accurate financial information, which was controlled by the university.[11] The Griswold and Smith claim about "no profits" wasn't accepted on its face.[12] Second, both sides recognized the importance of the student role. In a largely undemocratic setting and conservative culture, the greater though not exclusive burden to persuade the group most affected daily of the merit of its position rested on the Union.[13] Third, and a lesson learned of necessity yet with more astuteness by the Union (and Professor Weiss), was the role played by the citizens of New Haven. Fourth, there persisted, throughout the Griswold era, something in the nature of physical civility between Yale and its employees.[14] Tension continued between the Union and the police (private property and public safety were at risk), but neither Union members nor the police engaged in conduct comparable to the student conduct or police response demonstrated in the repeated student riots. That civility on both sides ended under Brewster.

The union's ability to gain the leverage necessary to succeed in its purpose required more members—that is, more classifications of workers had to join the union. In May 1955, with Griswold's choice to reject the Nyman premise, the dining hall employees voted to join the Union (later renamed Local 35), which now represented all the hourly wageworkers on the Yale campus.[15]

⌀

In April 1958, Giamatti experienced his first and only strike as an undergraduate by the citywide Carpenters Union against general contractors throughout New Haven, including Yale. Picketing began on April 10. Though the strike caused only a minor disruption to student life, he'd witness cooperation among all the unions in the city to aid the workers' goals, including not crossing the picket line.[16] Also, debate mounted that reflected a growing unease—maybe for the first time—that the world of economic, corporate, or parental certainty within which many students entered Yale was changing. In "The Growing Threat of Unionism," the mentality that Gaddis Smith had embraced as *Daily News* chairman was reiterated by a comparison: unions had the kind of unfettered influence once exercised by the robber barons of the nineteenth century. In "On the Right to Work," senior Frederick Cowles challenged the same Smith embrace of Yale's official position against the closed shop, when he expressed the closed shop's merit in ensuring the stability and worth of labor unions to protect employees.[17] Giamatti would have welcomed informed debate, as he always had. He had friends in South Hadley whose parents were in labor unions, his own parents befriended union members, he knew union employees at Yale, his Aunt Helen and other relatives were in or worked with union members, and he was aware fully that within New Haven, men and women had fought to form unions. In his family history, his mother's parents and grandparents had earned financial comfort in business, though, as he was aware, labor unions were an essential part of that history. His family's comfort was not fortune; it would not endure beyond the generation his mother represented (all those business interests had been sold), and nothing in his parents' values or civic and political activity drew cultural or economic lines in forming friendships.

In May 1962—when Giamatti was a graduate student, husband, and father and living in a Branford, Connecticut, apartment—Yale and its employees
entered into an agreement without a strike. In addition to a wage increase, the
Union (Local 35) also gained the closed shop. In acquiring this right, the Union
had overcome the Griswold-Smith argument. Strength in size, persistence, and
technique mattered and grew in hard-fought sophistication within the disquieting mentality Yale's president and Corporation had chosen.[18]

☙

Griswold, in the insular nature of his vision, had treated blue-collar employees as
if they were easily malleable, vulnerable financially, and culturally never part of
his neighborhood. At Yale, in 1953, the university's social scientists were studying
the psycho-physical effects of the "drinking habits of Jews," to be followed by
the effect of alcoholic beverages on Americans of Italian descent. Yale's freshman
class planned to produce a show in blackface. These were studies and degrading
characterizations of much of Yale's employee workforce.[19] Griswold also retained
the insular mentality of President Seymour, who, when confronted with Yale
employees picketing on Elm Street, wrote, "If everyone would personally mind
his or her own business . . . we would be going along very happily." Griswold
had ensured through his own actions that Labor was the last and potentially
strongest connection between Yale and the New Haven community. Put differently, Labor remained almost the singular funnel through which the community
at large could channel its own historical knowledge of Yale directly into the
university. Griswold helped form a latent whirlwind that would be enhanced in
informed potency by Brewster's rough and condescending disregard for Labor's
"civil rights" and the Union's earned knowledge of the skill and temperament
essential and acceptable to accomplish what it sought from Yale.[20]

What remained solidly embedded—which Giamatti witnessed and which
still existed when he was selected president—was the structured framework in
labor relations, fixed perspective, and problematic history that Griswold, Brewster,
the Corporation, and the Union had established.

YALE'S URBAN BLESSING: CRACKED

Lee and Logue, with Yale's insistence and Senator Prescott Bush's financial help,
began, by 1959 and 1960, the geographically largest phase of urban renewal:
the almost wholesale destruction of the city's retail establishments, large and
small, family and corporate, owned in downtown New Haven. Yale positioned
itself as the financial guarantor for the largest proposed project, a suburban-style
mall, boxy in the modernist style, largely windowless, oddly arranged so that its
large retail core faced not downtown New Haven, as the previous large retail-
ers had, but toward the new connector and the suburban traffic that Rotival

claimed privately and contractually would drive in from throughout the fictional Quinnipiac Valley Region into the mall's sleek new concrete parking structure, designed by Yale's Paul Rudolph. If the project failed, Yale would get the land. It bore little or no financial risk.[21]

The criticism of the merits and risks of urban renewal, albeit only relatively known, were now directed to Griswold. He wore three hats, distinguishable only by title: president of Yale, vice chairman of the Citizens Action Commission, and self-interested developer. Ethical conflicts abounded. The Central Civic Association of New Haven ("We are the storekeepers in the center of New Haven") complained to him about the discriminatory effects of the downtown urban renewal plan on smaller, long-time city merchants.[22] A lawsuit was filed to stop the project's inequity. Lee, Logue, and Griswold were not interested in dialogue. In the purpose of the Rotival Plan and in Yale's narrowly focused investment interest, the fate of the small businesses downtown was of ancillary concern, if even that.[23]

The mythology of eliminating "slums" wholesale had, by 1960, found additional power in its national, more than local, public relations appeal. Lee had well-known ambitions: the United States Senate seat and his own need for public adulation. The mythology, however, was based in large part on modern architecture and on the iconic, Griswold-cultivated image of the modern architect, the equally mythological and more damaging notion that unleashing the "architect" and elevating his personal rummaging about in roughly hued concrete was the equivalent of good, worse still "liberal" planning and public policy when imposed on immigrants, working-class, and poor people. Modern architects wanted forums, showcases, and employment. The national media embraced New Haven's "Model City," and Lee, Logue, Griswold, Saarinen, and Rudolph became urban models.

In 1954, the Eisenhower administration, with support from the Ford Foundation, sponsored the American Council to Improve Our Neighborhoods (ACTION). The council and Ford's purpose was to promote the value of urban renewal, more so to counter criticism of its obvious effect: the destruction of immigrant-rich and African American neighborhoods. Lee was their vehicle. "There were soon stories in *Time*, *Life*, and the *Saturday Evening Post* as well as *Harper's Magazine*, about the daring and wonderful work that Mayor Lee and his aides were doing there." Even fear of Communism was relied upon as a justification.[24]

❧

The national publicity had two effects: no one in the neighborhoods believed it, and Dick Lee, the Citizens Action Commission, and Yale's president thrived on every word of it. Robert Dahl's *Who Governs? Democracy and Power in an American City,* published in 1961, added, out of ignorance or inadequate scholarship or insecurity, to the false mystique about Lee and urban renewal.[25]

Jane Jacobs, on the basis of her earlier writing, growing observations through-out the country, and real experience in New York City, challenged the Eisenhower and the Ford Foundation ACTION mentality in 1961 with *The Death and Life of Great American Cities*. Ed Logue had entered the debate, with "Urban Ruin—or Urban Renewal?," his own Lee-Rotival–parsed rationale for the wholesale de-struction of any urban setting that resembled a neighborhood. With a tragic irony that he seemed never to grasp, Logue argued that the fate of urban civilization could be determined only by replicating the clean, uninhabited form used in New Haven and imaged in "Urban Ruin" for all to see: the Oak Street Connector. In providing his savior-like rationale for the harm already done, Logue conveyed to others his own personal ambitions to spread the grand Rotival mentality and the Dick Lee condescension toward the working class and the poor into a liberal-coated form of forced dispersion or essential concentration for whoever needed to be relocated.[26] It was that mentality and disquieting condescension that gave rise to Jacobs's observation that, "Ed Logue always horrified me. . . . But I learned from him," and that began the steady rise of her legitimacy as a critic who would endure, though not quickly enough, certainly not for New Haven.[27]

The ultimate harm, felt daily in the lives and dislocation of families, was that other, much larger cities (Detroit, Newark, St. Louis, Los Angeles, Pittsburgh) sought to emulate or outdo New Haven—destroying ethnic and racially mixed and African American neighborhoods through demolition, highways, and mas-sive relocation and building so-called housing in uncaring form, the aptly named "tombstone" especially. In this mythology and obsequiousness was a disquieting strain of White Anglo-Saxon eugenics, modified and camouflaged in the late twentieth century in the pretense of urban renewal. Fault lines from reasoned anger steadily ruptured the surface in New Haven.

❧

In the stunning grandiosity of the downtown urban renewal plan, Lee also had included the death of the structural base of the city's memory and iden-tity: James Gamble Rogers's classical-temple federal courthouse and post office, Henry Austin's High Victorian Gothic City Hall, and, likely, the destruction of William Allen and Richard Williams's Greco-Roman county courthouse and Cass Gilbert's New Haven Public Library, all situated around the New Haven Green. He'd replace them with the modernist re-creation of individual person-alities in the further ripping in two of New Haven's past from its future. Though too late and perhaps too culturally detached to preserve New Haven's neighbor-hoods and families—and at first directed to protect historic structures on Yale's campus destined for demolition and replacement by yet another Orr-Saarinen-Rudolph tribute—the New Haven Preservation Trust was formed in 1961. Its primary, albeit narrow, and important focus was the New Haven Green and the preservation of these buildings and their historical purpose.[28]

As the trust's members surveyed New Haven, they also located buildings in Wooster Square that warranted preservation. Local residents welcomed help in the loneliness of their increasingly organized resistance to preserve the remainder of their neighborhood and way of life. Within a year or so, the trust recruited Yale Professor Vincent Scully. The chief judge of Connecticut's federal judiciary proclaimed opposition to the courthouse's demolition. Though Griswold; his successor, Brewster; and Lee persisted with raw legal power, they could no longer avoid the colloquy over the propriety of their vision in what physically remained in New Haven. The 1961 mayoral election would begin, in unexpected ways, the erosion of that power.[29]

26

THE PURPOSEFUL MAN

YALE: THE DEGREE THAT MATTERED

Bart's moment at Yale, the singularity in the culture of receiving the baccalaureate degree, Class of 1960, was near at hand. Receiving it carries the indelible
credence of being a Yalie, an Eli, a True Blue. First, however, other matters required his attention.

Bart had proposed to Toni in September, she accepted, and the announcement was carried in the *New York Times*. Ahead were wedding preparations, ensuring the comfort of family and friends in Plainfield, the logistics of arranging
their post-marriage residence, and Toni's graduation from Columbia University.
Bart served as toastmaster for the last dinner meeting of the Aurelian Society, its
Fiftieth-Year celebration, and, during a likely cheerful, nostalgic celebration for
many about to leave Saybrook College, the Fellows granted their 1960 Fellows'
Prize to A. Bartlett Giamatti, for his exceptional contribution to the college and
university. Finally, Class Day—a moment of commemoration among graduating
seniors and few adults, except for the Yale employees who set up chairs, perfected
the acoustics, and prepared and served the food. Some among them Bart welcomed as adults who had contributed to his education in life.[1]

CLASS DAY ORATORY: PROPOSING A PATH

Rain poured mercilessly. Umbrellas or tents wouldn't matter. The Class Day
ceremony, normally scheduled for the ancient aura of the Old Campus, was
moved inside the bold modernity of the newly constructed Ingalls Hockey
Rink. Saarinen and Griswold's signature emblem of the new world was by then
already known as "The Whale." Bart had been selected by classmates and faculty
judges in a competitive process to give the Class Oration on a subject of his own
choice. Though the remarks have no title, twenty-two-year-old Giamatti spoke
to a theme, still evolving in his mind, directed as much toward guiding himself
as his classmates.

He premised his oration on the recognition that "Ours is the Anxious Age and we are indifferent, beat, silent . . . and, we are told, . . . we are apathetic. . . . Yet, I think these labels indicate only symptoms, not the real disease, and that to find the disease we must look deeper still." He reminded his classmates of the past, some elementary principles of forming a future that evolved from ancient thinking that, though instructive, were not, alone, sufficient to explain this moment. "What we lack," he said, "is . . . a unified and unifying body of belief. Here is, I think, the disease, of which apathy and the rest are merely symptoms." He described the modern artist, perhaps the modern architect as well, as disregarding the past, which, he could see, had provided the antithesis of a "unifying theme," professing instead to seek a "new religion" in modernity. But, he said, the "final outcome . . . is not profound." It was, he continued, merely another symptom, "unable to fill the void." Griswold and Saarinen might have shuddered in discomfort. Bart was, after all, in "The Whale" on land newly tax exempt, once in the Dixwell Avenue neighborhood.

Bart also discounted what he called the "unabashed self-centeredness" of the "Busy reaction"—"to be involved in involvement" to the exclusion of all else, to focus on "the troubles of America too fast. . . . With passionate intensity [such men] are making a frantic effort to *Be* something, and they are in danger of leaving very little room for becoming anything else. The gates for growth, for change, for maturing love, are closed. . . . For just as they closed the door to the process of any spiritual development, they have—at the same time—also excluded the possibility of ever being wrong." Such an approach is "no less guilty of dodging the real issue at stake—overcoming the void." He proposed an approach through this moment, in case "any one [in the audience] has been asleep."[2]

"What I have said is that there is a difference between Apathy and Contemplation, and between the man who shouts aloud that he is going to shoulder all the responsibilities of the race, and the man who has faced himself, has found himself to be strong, and who will then proceed to act. . . . It is to be creative and humane men in society that we have come to Yale, and I hope it is with this goal that we leave. Let us not always seek a sedative, in one form or another, for what ails us, but let us seek a cure. . . . I have cited the past . . . with an eye to re-evaluating yesterday so that we will be able to fashion a creed, a myth, for the uncertain tomorrow. This does not mean a ten-point program. . . . Rather it means the gradual development of a noble and creative way of life, the way of loving concern that St. Paul indicated to the Corinthians when he said: 'Though I have the gift of prophecy . . . and all knowledge . . . , and have not charity, I am nothing.'"[3] Giamatti was, in practical, functional terms, encouraging concentration on the creed of gaining stability as "humane men"—not on presuming to be a leader—to prepare for tumult, so-called modernity, and uncertainty, and the civic duty in the responsibly led private life.

"BEAT"

Being "beat," as Giamatti (or Kerouac, Ginsberg, or Corso) used that term was not the same as inattentive. For all the adulation that emanated from A. Whitney Griswold, members of the faculty, and the *Yale Daily News* for Dick Lee, 1960 Class Historian Albert S. Pergam saw and wrote the reality with tongue-in-cheek clarity. "The history of civilization is influenced by its environment," young Pergam wrote in the yearbook. "The University and the city are indivisibly linked. We know this well . . . the mayor, whose earnest endeavors to reduce every building in downtown New Haven to a parking lot have gained acclaim from automobile manufacturers throughout the world. The university has steadily purchased every inch of land about itself in anticipation of a future moat. The New Haven high schools have vanished. . . ."[4] Griswold had almost succeeded in ensuring that the university's tax-exempt expansion and deliberately constructed urban moat was near completion to be filled, in time, in his "modernist" image. None of this escaped Bart's attention and, as Citizen Pergam made clear, he was not alone.

The class poet, who like Bart was selected through competition, read his work to the Class Day audience in Latin.[5] In the special "Feature" to the yearbook, Associate Professor Vincent Scully wondered aloud about the meaning of Yale's (really Griswold's) embrace of "Modern Architecture at Yale." His observations reflected a theme he may have shared with Giamatti. He carefully posited modern architecture's singularly shared characteristic: "Their variety [in design] . . . derives more partially from the difference between the architects who designed them." Though grateful that more harm wasn't done by their work ("mutilation" performed at the Art Gallery, which he hoped was temporary) and that Saarinen's and Orr's proposals for Hillhouse Avenue were not adopted, he needed to move from one place to another place to gain a sight line from which a complementary observation of Yale's new architecture was possible. And as for Saarinen's description of his intent for the two new colleges (the look of Tuscan villages) that would replace Hillhouse and Boardman Trade (he never intended to use the Wilbur Cross property and did not), Scully dug pointedly beneath Saarinen's rhetoric and decided to withhold judgment: "It remains to be seen whether Saarinen can solve the problems of structure, scale and lighting to the point where the buildings as such may become integrated wholes and impress us thereby with the reality rather than the make-believe of the special world which he professes to create."[6]

☙

In April 1959, Griswold named the two new colleges after Ezra Stiles, a former slaveholder and president of Yale, and Samuel F. B. Morse (Yale 1810), well known for inventing the telegraph and the famous "Morse Code," and notorious among civil rights historians, or any historian of American history at Yale in 1958 and 1959, as arch-racist, anti-Catholic, and anti-immigrant. Both men were eugenicists in twentieth-century terms.[7] The decision-making process occurred largely in private, while race and integration were of deep public concern, certainly from the United States Supreme Court decision in *Brown v. Board of Education* in 1954, through Governor Orval Faubus's resistance to school integration in Little Rock, Arkansas, in 1957, and the almost daily attention they received in the *Daily News*. Griswold and those around him were aware of Yale's decision to honor John C. Calhoun and the solicitous effort to secure Southern money and students that occurred through the efforts of Wilbur Cross.[8] In the internal debate over the naming, none of this mattered as a factor to be weighed—certainly not a decisive one. Some imperatives were just too embedded in the Yale culture.[9] The decision was announced shortly after Martin Luther King Jr. spoke in Yale's Woolsey Hall.[10] And Morse and Stiles College would be, for the residents of New Haven for as long as there was memory, the New Haven High School campus Dick Lee gave to Yale University.[11]

GRADUATION: WOOLSEY HALL, JUNE 12, 1960

Griswold—"Whit," as he was called, not as an abbreviation for "Whitney" but for his sharpness of mind and biting wit—was, in his nature, not easily accessible to students. He was fair skinned, slender by conditioning, with the 1950s look—the fitted suit, thin tie, and white shirt. Griswold abandoned the large office held previously by the president for a smaller, inner office with high ceiling, high bookshelves, a small desk of ancient vintage, and accoutrements of lighting and artistry that ensured the concentration of mind. Giamatti, two decades later, embraced it for the same reason. Griswold rarely held or attended meetings (in a simpler era, not because he delegated) and took regular holidays and summer in Cape Cod and into the small world—New York, New England, and Chicago—where, in the 1950s, much of Yale's alumni wealth was located, especially among a few families who had the shared duty to preserve Yale's unique place in America. That wealth was central to the construction of twenty-six buildings during Griswold's presidency, especially in the sciences, and to the acquisition of property in the Oak Street/Hill/Legion Avenue and Dixwell/Newhallville neighborhoods and the three high schools in York Square. Griswold was white Anglo-Saxon Protestant and acted it, including with all its presumptions about race, religion, ethnicity, and intellect. His principles, strongly held, were formed in that context. He also conveyed them in his expectations about Yale as an elite place and its graduates as leaders. He had high standards for conduct. His primary focus, in his vision for Yale, was Yale College and undergraduate liberal arts education. His letters were direct about his intention and rarely referred to telephone conversations. Much of his time was devoted to writing. He had been, throughout Giamatti's four years, an informed speaker, though his themes were simply put and more in the nature of directives rather than ways of thinking or reflective of the complexity of life or choice.[12]

Griswold's inaugural address as president emphasized the importance of liberal education in pointed, succinct ways. The nation, at that time, was deeply affected by Senator Joseph McCarthy. Both "liberal education" and "Communist" had connotations that were suspect, in some settings considered a danger, if not handled properly. Griswold—though, in time, he would assure everyone that Yale had no Communists on its faculty—challenged the obligation of scholars to take "test oaths" (the loyalty oath), precisely what the federal government had come to require for certain forms of federal assistance for universities and students. Few among his peers had done so. And at Yale, McCarthy had supporters, including on the *Daily News*.[13]

Throughout his undergraduate years, Bart heard Griswold return to this theme, something akin to protecting the university from virtually any form of outside threat to its freedom to think, to express and engage in debate, and to teach. Griswold described the context within which this freedom to express would occur, using the word "order." He stated: "A free society depends more than any other, upon a moral order and rule of law, for only those can give it the cohesion for which other societies rely mainly on force. . . . The moral order and the rule of law are the vital business and the fundamental responsibility of all of us, scientists, humanists, students, teachers, and university presidents." Griswold's comparison was to the authoritarian regimes that existed, preeminently in numerous Communist nations. Giamatti would not have disagreed with that use in its context, though he knew that "order" in the wrong hands, including those of the attorney general of the United States and Yale presidents, was abused and discriminatory. In the late 1970s and into the 1980s, however, and using a different set of cultural principles, Giamatti wanted "order" to be the means of ensuring fairness, the constraint on prejudice, that it ensured the fullness of debate was available, in fact, to everyone.[14]

Griswold's definition of a liberal education (keeping the Anglo-Saxon presumptions in mind) was that, "We have conceived a broader purpose for higher education . . . which regards all education as a preparation for life . . . available to all who have the capacity to partake of it. . . . We must not allow that preparation to be limited by anything other than the individual's innate ability to benefit by it." Of course, Yale did impose limits, in its admission process and in ugly, widespread ways outside of Yale, but the notion of "education as a preparation for life," was one reality Giamatti already believed and had witnessed through his father. In time, he would articulate with fullness its more complex elements and form practical guidance to students as to what it meant at Yale, and in life.[15]

When he stepped to the rostrum on June 12 in Woolsey Hall, Griswold struck similar themes. He called upon his own Protestant background, and Yale's, to set out Jonathan Edwards's dark view of the unavoidable power of the devil's evil mischief, his potentially disabling effect in sowing doubt on young men's choices. Griswold turned to the "sermon" given to the Class of 1860 to find a warning to those in attendance one hundred years later. "The responsibility for distinguishing between good and evil and making the right choice between them rests as heavily upon us as it did upon our ancestors. In truth it rests more heavily." There was nothing new for young Giamatti, except to understand the basis in Griswold's experience that evil's creation of "fear" could "stupefy" these graduates into the more harmful failure to make *any* choice at all so as to "deaden our sense of responsibility for the way we lead our own lives, [which could] so greatly impair the standards and prospects of our civilization that its survival might become a matter of indifference even to its members." Griswold called upon the graduates: "The more an individual makes of himself . . . the more he can do for others." Griswold was concerned about the fate of the nation; Yale men must use this "power of a kind" as leaders to ensure the country "shall be stronger and stronger." To Giamatti, the value that ranked the highest was his father's determination to be enhanced in his civic duty by his heritage and experience in life; his degree and intellect were a means for doing that, not a license to lead.[16]

Honorary degrees were given that day to thirteen "Distinguished Men," including Professor of English Robert Penn Warren and, in a private "special commencement" (a practice Bart engaged in when it was his right to do so), the Doctor of Humane Letters was bestowed on the recuperating Cole Porter (Yale 1913), who, in addition to his popular Broadway musicals also "as an undergraduate . . . won acclaim for writing the words and music of two of Yale's perennial football songs," "Bulldog, Bulldog" and "Bingo."[17]

Bart graduated *magna cum laude*. He'd been selected into Yale's Graduate School of English, a candidate for the doctor of philosophy in comparative literature limited to students "based not only on the character and scope of the applicant's academic record, but also upon his ability to meet at the time of admission the requirements in Latin and the modern languages." Once in the program, he'd have to acquire and demonstrate essential skill in Gothic, Old English, Old Norse, Old Irish, and the "English language during the Renaissance." He'd also have to ensure the faculty that he'd performed "work of distinction in which the student displays powers of original scholarship"—the dissertation. He applied for and received, through Yale, a Woodrow Wilson Fellow scholarship for all four years of the program.[18]

As parents and family watched, A. Whitney Griswold conferred upon A. Bartlett Giamatti and his classmates Yale's *imprimatur*, Class of 1960. For

Valentine and Peggy Giamatti, their commitment to ensure a Yale education for their son had succeeded. For Valentine Giamatti, the moment had special, complex poignancy, shared by and with his son. In that similar moment of pride and hard-earned accomplishment, as Maria and Angelo had watched their son graduate from Hillhouse High School in 1928, then Yale in 1932, the dream of continuity, however far-fetched even if only hard work was required, had occurred in life.

27

REFINEMENT, EXPANSION, AND PERSPECTIVE

[The City is] always the norm by which all is judged. The City is always
the ultimate center of action, the true source of value."

—A. Bartlett Giamatti,
The Earthly Paradise and the Renaissance Epic, 1966

FAMILY: MATURITY OF CHOICE

On June 18, 1960, Bart and Toni were married in the Crescent Avenue
Presbyterian Church, its steeple tall and visible from any approach through
Plainfield's active retail center or sedate residential streets. The ceremony's notoriety, gentle style, and large entourage of maids and ushers were easily observed
from the plaza in front of City Hall, completed in 1919 and dedicated to Civil
War and Great War combatants, or from just across the street in a small circular
park centered by the American flag. Bart's brother, Dino, was his best man. In
attendance were friends from Saybrook and Bart's childhood, now adults, Frank
White, Bill Mazeine, and Andy Vitali.[1]

The couple returned to Connecticut. They'd rented an apartment in Branford,
just east of New Haven. Bart labored at his graduate course work, which included preparing for a rigorous oral examination on comparative literature and
thinking about the subject of his PhD dissertation. Toni began teaching English at
the private girls school, Day Prospect Hill, not far from Yale. She remained there
for the remainder of her life, in part-time and full-time positions, through the
school's merger with Hopkins Grammar in 1972. Students immediately embraced
her original teaching approach and enthusiasm, which blended her acting skills
and her encouragement to students to explore their imagination.[2] In early August,
Valentine and Peggy Giamatti visited Branford to spend the weekend. They were
planning to take Val's next sabbatical in Italy, this time at the request of Middlebury
College to establish its first language program in Florence. Bart, too, would later
be invited to join Middlebury's Bread Loaf English Program.[3] In early 1961, Toni
announced she was pregnant. On October 3, 1961, Marcus Bartlett Giamatti was
born in New Haven, Connecticut.

Smith-Giamatti Wedding, 1960. Toni's sister, Sandy (to Bart's left), was maid of honor. Best Man Dino Giamatti is on Toni's right. Elria Giamatti is in front of Sandy Smith. Members of the wedding party also included Frank White, Bill Mazeine, Haj Ross, and Peter Knipe.
Giamatti-Ewing Collection.

BART: GAINING PERSPECTIVE ON GRISWOLD AND BREWSTER

Yale could not have been more involved in a local election than it was in 1961. Yale's long-term intention, still materializing through land acquisition in the demolished Oak Street neighborhood and acceptance of land offers from New Haven to protect Yale's flank in the Dixwell Avenue neighborhood, melded with Dick Lee's political aspirations and one clear element in the Oak Street neighborhood that Yale had encouraged. The only housing built there would be two high-rise, upscale "University Towers," apartment buildings touted in the new lexicon Lee had fostered: "The location is completely central, the atmosphere is suburban." To Lee, as he told the Citizens Action Commission, "We have to make the City livable for all people—the poor as well as the rich."[4]

In 1962, Connecticut Democrats had to select a candidate to run against Yale Corporation member Senator Prescott Bush. Lee hoped that a major victory in New Haven in 1961 would catapult him into contention for the nomination, though he would have a formidable opponent, Secretary of Heath, Education, and Welfare and former Governor Abraham Ribicoff. Lee predicted an eleven-thousand-vote margin of victory in New Haven. Bush had no intention of ensuring Lee's success in even getting the senatorial nomination. He'd stop Lee in New Haven. And he did.[5]

Republican nominee Henry Townshend, a Yale graduate, was an attractive and accomplished speaker who sought to reexamine redevelopment. His appeal took three forms: first, downtown businessmen who, unlike many members of Lee's Citizen Action Committee, could actually vote in New Haven, rallied to his cause; second, the urbanists, families forcibly relocated but still remaining in New Haven, many of whom were Italian American and Jewish, bucked the Democratic Party locally; and third, Prescott Bush provided his support.[6]

For the Democratic town chairman, Arthur Barbieri, it was a matter of working especially closely with the African American, Irish, Jewish, and Italian leaders in the Dixwell Avenue/Newhallville neighborhood, including Ella Scantlebury and others, to register new voters and get them to the polls. African American voters had demonstrated in front of City Hall and in their neighborhoods over the lack of housing. They saw through Lee's charade in the Oak Street neighborhood and beyond. They wanted housing, not luxury apartments. Political power was massing on Yale's flank.[7]

Bush campaigned hard for Townshend. "New Haven's urban renewal program appears to be in trouble," Bush contended. Lee, he said, "was overly-ambitious."[8] Lee won by only four thousand votes. He received fewer votes than almost all the other Democratic candidates for citywide office. The *New Haven Journal Courier* concluded that five thousand Lee supporters in 1959 deserted him in 1961. His disappointment was palpable; his political ambition ended, except in his mind. In the Dixwell/Newhallville neighborhood, however, those elected included Alderman John Daniels Jr. (later state senator and mayor) and Bruce Morris (later a highly regarded and politically powerful state representative), and the new citywide treasurer, Bart Giamatti's friend Ella Scantlebury. They expected patronage from the mayor. "It's not what we demand, it is what we rightly deserve," Daniels said. They'd ensured Lee's victory. One Democratic alderman who survived Lee's downdraft because he'd essentially run as an independent was Bart Guida (a foe of Lee's projects), who also later was elected mayor.[9]

The future, many residents realized, lay in the Democratic Party; they'd have to organize to redefine it. Through the election of 1961, every neighborhood in New Haven had acquired acute, informed political sensibility. When Bart Giamatti was selected president of Yale in 1977, the human and financial cost of the university's physical expansion and its role in various New Haven "experiments" were well known among the urbanists. Dick Lee, though no longer mayor, and many of his cohorts, including at Yale, who shared in his glamour and underlying condescension, also were still alive. The roughness of the cultural and political dynamic had not ceased.

⁓

Griswold, who'd recovered from cancer surgery in 1961, suffered a fatal relapse and died on April 19, 1963. He was fifty-six years old.[10] He had been president for virtually the entirety of Bart's time as a student. His successor, Kingman Brewster (selected as provost in 1960), was president for the last year of Bart's doctoral program and when Bart returned to teach in the fall of 1966. They were the two most obvious "models" he knew, and he had followed them closely. He held Griswold in much higher regard, but only in a comparison of the relative disregard of principle.

Griswold's failure was not only in the specifics of what he did or how he did it, but in the form he used to keep a personal relationship with New Haven's mayor. Indeed, near the end, in June 1961, he granted the honorary degree that Lee hungered for and insisted on, bestowed as much as a thank-you for Yale's grand acquisition of now tax-exempt property as it was as a nod to the closing moment of Yale's need for Lee's loyalty. The specifics mattered: Griswold, in his Anglo-Saxon ethos and in the remnants of the eugenics mentality, was personally detached from the city's history and social and cultural forces, and so were many administrators and faculty. He had been unfair in urban renewal; ended the serious connection to the city in education, including the Sterling Scholarships; and reflected the inability or unwillingness to *act* daily in the exercise of his civic duty as Giamatti came to define and exercise its principles long before he became president. Giamatti's dislike of Lee, the harm he'd done and his continued solicitation for recognition, likely also began while he was a student and solidified during Brewster's—and definitely his own—presidency.

Giamatti admired Griswold's emphasis on the value of liberal education, what Griswold described as the university's duty "to awaken and develop the intellectual and spiritual powers in the individual before he enters upon his chosen career." That meant an emphasis on Yale College and on the arts and sciences. Griswold's concern about the "anti-intellectualism" that had haunted Yale for generations—reaffirmed in his Freshman Report issued in the spring of 1962 and widely praised though not implemented because of his death—was equally unacceptable conduct to Giamatti. He embraced Griswold's resolve concerning the duty of students to adhere to the most rigorous expectation of academic excellence.[11]

The correlation among "anti-intellectualism," the "riots," and the admissions process had been exposed during Griswold's presidency. Giamatti, who'd attended public schools and welcomed, as normal, women as friends and colleagues in debate, oratory, fun, and conversation, also favored the full opening of the undergraduate college (it already existed in the graduate, law, and medical schools) to more racial, ethnic, and definitely gender diversity. He had thrived at Phillips and at Yale, but he knew—and later would feel personally—the university's deep

Bart Giamatti, while a Yale PhD student, gives a lecture.
Giamatti-Ewing Collection.

institutional embrace of the eugenics ethic in a lingering if not a new formulation. The eugenics ethos in any form, and no matter how applied, needed to end.

Bart knew he would bring every means to bear, every skill and value he had, in and outside the classroom, to teach in a way that made learning a joy, an education, and a basis for liberal inquiry that could last a lifetime. That would be his duty. His additional obligation, foremost as teacher—still his aspiration—was to ensure that students had the freedom from the kind of inhibiting, ideologically presumptuous outside influence that he'd witnessed Roswell Ham protect against at Mount Holyoke and that, though as a less direct but no less insidious threat, Griswold spoke against at Yale. His father never sought to impose his own political or ideological views on his students, except to preempt any conduct that smacked of unfairness, to elevate the value of knowledge acquired, and, in his own life, to make civic choices that embraced and exemplified both fairness and knowledge. That model remained central to Bart's identity.

ↄ∂

The memorial service for Griswold reflected the sorrow felt throughout the campus. For the people of New Haven, his passing was likely of little consequence. Yale would continue to act with selfishness. The overt disrespect for Griswold's principled concern about student conduct came, however, and with no surprise to New Haveners, from within the Yale campus.[12]

Just days after Griswold's burial, Yale students, once again, engaged in a rough, riotous outburst that exceeded the 1959 and perhaps the 1952 riot. In this episode especially, which occurred while Bart was in his PhD program and no longer on campus, student conduct was decidedly more traumatic and physically harmful than what Yale and New Haven had or would again experience.[13] The Lee Commission's findings and recommendations, even with Griswold's participation, didn't matter. Their failure laid bare another reality: students have a short-term perspective, four years at most. Griswold's moral rectitude was gone. Brewster, now acting president, was in charge.

May 9, 1963. The *Daily News* described it: "The disturbance began shortly before midnight, when cherry bombs and shouts rained the Old Campus. Campus police effectively discouraged the budding freshman uprising by locking the Old Campus." The Old Campus remained quiet for an hour until "upperclassmen emerged from the colleges in further effort to spark a riot." They had no luck. "They milled aimlessly around Elm Street." The New Haven Police arrived and encouraged them to get off the street. "Suddenly, at about 12:30, the freshmen began pouring . . . into the street." Upperclassmen joined. They totaled fifteen hundred students. "And a huge throng was bearing down on the Taft Hotel. The Taft incident marked the turning point of the riot." According to Yale students later interviewed, "400 students came charging across the New Haven Green toward the Taft, six police squad cars came screeching up and men with clubs charged the students and dispersed them." The Taft Hotel, a destination in 1952 as well, was once again targeted because, it was speculated, the Taft was "where visiting girlfriends bed down for the night." Apparently, four hundred of them.[14] Some students were arrested there. Others filed back to Elm Street, "where the real violence began." First, several students lifted a Volkswagen into the middle of the street. Water bombs, bottles, and cherry bombs were thrown from residence hall windows into the assembled crowd. Police began swinging with more accuracy. One policeman drew his gun; another officer fell and was beaten. "The tide of the riot swept through the entire campus."[15]

Yale's Dean Powell stated, "In my opinion, the New Haven police were very patient for about an hour, trying to herd the students back into the colleges. However, when the students began to approach the Taft Hotel, which is private property, the policemen felt they had to make a stand. . . . Then, however, the men were hit by bottles, water bombs, and cherry bombs from the windows, and some of them were infuriated. . . . I won't say that all the police action was justified." Some students disagreed. "Never before have I seen a municipal authority blatantly . . . attack a restless crowd of students," one student wrote. Kingman Brewster weighed in, with balance or ambiguity. His "indictment of student irresponsibility" was noted by the *Daily News* as a "forewarning" not to do it again. "Some members of the New Haven Police Department abandoned their self control," Brewster added. To the *Daily News*, Yale was engaged in "one-sided pursuit of town-gown relations" and "with great fairness . . . the University [as Brewster explained] will only take 'appropriate disciplinary action whenever we have evidence of irresponsible and dangerous conduct.'" Brewster made plain, however, that "the only reliable path to responsible police behavior is responsible student behavior."[16]

The rioting had no political purpose, no underlying social cause or objective. The "unhealthy" diagnosis suggested by Harvard, and recognized by Griswold, still plagued Yale. Forces were in play, however and finally, that Griswold had instigated—he had hired the Reverend William Sloane Coffin as chaplain; altered, at least in written policy, the admissions process; and introduced changes in the ethnic composition and societal perspective of the faculty, especially at the law school. Societal forces (civil rights, nationally) were crystallizing slowly, then cataclysmically in a way Brewster, still not appointed president, struggled to recognize and handle. None of these changes, or Brewster's uncertainty, would have surprised Giamatti. He'd witnessed the harm of the *ancien régime* and likely hoped Griswold's changes, properly managed, might lead in short order to the demise of the underlying eugenics ethos. They didn't.[17]

As if in a separate world trying, futilely, to reconcile it into one, the *Daily News*'s editor described "An Isolated Riot?" The *Daily News* expressed concern that with respect to ugly racial and voting rights repression in Birmingham,

Alabama, by then unassailably clear, there had been "inactivity and apathy . . . by a majority of Yale students," some of whom had engaged in the New Haven riot for reasons "not attempting to alter their social environment."[18] The *Daily News* also reported the occurrence of another public demonstration, which it referred to as a "race riot." In the Dixwell Avenue neighborhood, a peaceful march turned into a confrontational one, as local residents, and one Yale student, protested Mayor Dick Lee's failure to provide good housing and "a breakdown in negotiations between CORE [Congress of Racial Equality] and the New Haven Redevelopment Authority."[19] The residents of Dixwell had been demonstrating since at least 1960, when they staged sit-ins at City Hall. They'd witnessed what, in fact, Lee and Yale had done in the Oak Street/Hill/Legion Avenue neighborhood: demolish working-class housing and neighborhoods and build only a limited number of moderate- and upper-income apartments.[20] Yale, many of its students, and its president were, indeed, in a separate world.

Coffin: Directed and Purposeful Energy

In the spring, summer, and fall of 1963, the formation of a "creed, a myth . . . a noble way of life" that Giamatti hoped might happen took form at Yale. Its definition and "energy"—as Bart later said directly to their central force—came from the moral and intellectual imperatives of William Sloane Coffin.[21] Coffin took the lead—disciplined, methodical, his actions highly risky physically and always visible—to integrate African Americans in the South into institutions and the voting booths from which they'd been excluded for a century, with only a brief interruption during the post–Civil War era of Reconstruction. In his weekly sermons, he insisted on a reasoned historical and intellectual underpinning to his purpose. The nation also saw a resurgence of Catholic Social Teaching, the creed and practical action once embraced by the Reverend John Ryan, now embraced by Father James Groppi of Milwaukee and, shortly, Cardinal Joseph Bernardin of Chicago.[22] To anyone taking the long view, backward and forward, Coffin's imperative for civil rights reflected the gallant knight challenging the eugenics attitude Yale knowingly justified, fostered, and paid tribute, run amok in the South with terror and law to support it. Coffin was among the original "Freedom Riders," in a group that made its way from New Haven in May 1961 through Atlanta, and into Montgomery, Alabama, and the kingdom of Governor George Wallace.[23]

Along with Coffin's efforts, members of the Yale Law School faculty also joined the existing fray and lonely battles of others in court and elsewhere. On the Fourth of July, 1963, in Baltimore, Maryland, Coffin was arrested and jailed (again) for supporting the integration of the Gwynn Oak Amusement Park. Also jailed that day were four others, including the future secretary of the university under Giamatti, John Wilkinson. Coffin traveled to Mississippi with thirty-three Yale students to organize African American voter registration. As a practical matter, Yale was in a long transformation. Brewster, however, was an informed bystander; the transformation that began to redefine elements of Yale internally in the late 1950s and into the 1960s was not of his making. His awkwardness showed quickly, having its base in his tentativeness about the meaning of the First Amendment, evident since his testimony before Congress when he denigrated opponents of "America First," and in his general ignorance of the New Haven community where he was living.[24]

∾

Governor George Wallace accepted the September 14, 1963, invitation by the Yale Political Union (founded by Griswold as a student) to speak on November 4, during the period Wallace had planned a tour through the Northeast. On September 15, an explosion in the 16th Street Baptist Church in Montgomery, Alabama, killed four young African American girls. Wallace's response was cold in tone and purpose. Mayor Dick Lee, knowing of the Yale invitation, contacted Brewster directly and made his position public. Wallace, he said, was "unwelcome" in New Haven. He wanted the invitation "rescinded." At the time, Lee was engaged in a reelection campaign against two opponents—Henry Townshend, who'd come close to defeating him in 1961, and Raymond Paige, an African American with an uncertain drawing power within the discontented Dixwell Avenue/Newhallville neighborhood.[25] The election was the day after the scheduled Wallace speech. Lee claimed, and Brewster accepted as true, that a Wallace speech would "damage" the "feelings of the New Haven Negro population." Lee's assertion also was understood to mean that Yale should not expect the New Haven Police to arrest African Americans in the event of an outbreak of violence. Brewster had neither the experience nor knowledge to independently evaluate Lee's fear and political agenda. He had his own fear. Griswold's "moat" around the university was not complete.[26]

At stake at Yale were the First Amendment and the meaning of freedom of expression within one of the nation's most visible universities. Once again, Yale and Brewster supported Dick Lee, with no regard or even rhetorical emphasis on the principle of free speech. Brewster personally advised the Political Union's board to disinvite or, as later claimed, though *not* by Brewster, to postpone Wallace's scheduled speaking engagement. The Political Union agreed. The board's members, with no greater knowledge than Brewster's, assumed the legitimacy of Brewster's fear and the accuracy of the Dick Lee threat. The next day, September 20, the *Daily News* headline read: "Political Union Withdraws Speaking Invitation to Alabama Segregationist Governor Wallace at Request of Provost Kingman Brewster." Brewster's public statement of September 20 and a second one issued on September 27 (an official statement) made plain he sought to have the November 4 invitation "rescinded."[27] The *Daily News* editorial drove right to the heart of the First Amendment principle, and Brewster's rationale for failure to adhere to it: "We are shocked by the Provost's statement . . . by the attitude expressed in Mayor Lee's telegram, and by the final action of the Political Union." The *Daily News* challenged Brewster in every respect, including his assertion about the African American community: the *Daily News* had "faith in the Negro community," that following the peaceful, mass demonstration in Washington, DC, there was no reason to think New Haveners would act any differently. The African American leaders in the Dixwell Avenue neighborhood concurred. "We think the issue is one of the right to speak; all voices have the right in an academic community," the *Daily News* editorial declared. Pointing to Coffin's advocacy in the South, the *Daily News* stated that Wallace had the same right in the North, including being "confronted by the Yale and New Haven community, both white and black." The *Daily News* also believed Brewster threatened to "refuse the Political Union use of a University auditorium if it decided to maintain the Wallace invitation."[28]

Students picketed City Hall.[29] Harvard, Radcliffe, Brown, and Princeton scheduled Wallace and others for debates and forums. The *New York Herald Tribune* criticized Brewster's action as being "highly unfortunate" and representing a "gloomy reflection on the relationship between town and gown." The right to speech, it concluded, "deserves strong deference." To the *Daily News*, Yale had once been, "A champion of free thought and open mindedness. In large measure, this is the result of President Griswold's role as the national spokesman for liberal education and academic freedom."[30] Students and groups within the law school invited Wallace. He declined. The Yale radio station organized a panel to question Wallace during his time at Harvard. He agreed. The panel was composed of, among others, two leaders of the New Haven African American community, precisely the leaders Lee and Brewster expected to lead the violence. One of them, the Reverend Edmund Edwards, had said he wanted Wallace to speak at Yale because of the "right of an individual to speak."[31]

Brewster's handling of the Wallace episode, and others that followed, had consequences. In 1974, he was forced by faculty resolution to convene a committee chaired by historian C. Vann Woodward to examine his record of failure with respect to freedom of expression at Yale. Brewster's conduct, and the Woodward Report, would have effects well into Giamatti's time as a faculty member and during his presidency, now only fourteen years away.[32] "Freedom of speech," Giamatti's provost, William Brainard, said, was a fundamental principle present in every discussion of how to deal with student protest or demonstration.[33]

FATE

FAMILY: THE COURAGE IN INSPIRATION

In the summer of 1963, Valentine Giamatti suffered a heart attack at fifty-two years old. He had been a smoker, certainly a principal cause of the attack. He had stopped smoking, but the benefit was marginal. Both his parents had had heart-related disease. So, the inhaled tar and nicotine likely seeped deeply into vulnerable lung passages already permanently susceptible to harm. The subsequent manifestation of the Charcot-Marie-Tooth inherited nerve and muscle disorder was in his extremities, in his feet and legs, and was gradually noticeable in his appearance. Those effects were managed carefully with a cane, eventually two, and braces. There was no cure.[1]

He rose from bed, situated temporarily in a makeshift room on the first floor of his house, to attend his daughter, Elria's, August wedding to David Ewing at the Mount Holyoke College Chapel.[2] In time, he began swimming frequently, benefited by his son Dino's success as the owner and manager of elegant family resorts in Martha's Vineyard, later along the Maine coast, and in Dino's second home in Bonita Springs, Florida, along the Gulf of Mexico. The swimming helped Val's mobility and, because the exercise was family centered, his constant embrace of living joyfully actually expanded, his imperatives undiminished. It was a life earned, tempered, he knew and said frequently, by good fortune and nothing, certainly not discomfort, would be allowed to suppress its daily embrace.[3]

In 1963, Bart was married, working on his PhD dissertation, and with Toni, raising their son, Marcus. As he moved ahead in his own life, when he looked to his father he could see, foremost, his father's insistence on living longer, not slowing in his pursuit of excellence as a teacher, or in travel with his family, or in entertaining friends and students, or in ensuring the enhancement of what, by globally accepted standards, was a remarkable compilation and thoughtful organization of a diverse and valuable collection of editions of Dante's *Divine Comedy*.

Uncertain that he had inherited the same traits, but certain that he should expect it, Bart clearly formed an approach to the remainder of his life that, for him, involved two threads: first, his own family, being a conscientious parent and husband, and second, his discipline and seriousness about how to meld that family obligation with his intellect and related professional imperatives. What gave both of these threads definition was that at no time did his father's life, as he had lived it before Bart was born or continued to live it in South Hadley, in any way remain anything except a model, both an aspiration and an inspiration. Bart's own conduct would be a reflection on the intent to continue to solidify the Giamatti place in America, to ensure continuity from his grandparents' dedication in betrothal in San Lorenzello through the establishment of citizenship in New Haven as Angelo and Maria wanted to define it, and, in time, the foundation for his children's lives. It was a generational imperative, derivative of the Italian immigrant family experience, understood genetically and embraced intensely, as if Bart had mastered a compass in two directions. When he wrote, only a few years later, "So the father tells the son in . . . that deep, dark place in the self where the roots of the self begin, and so the son learns to be a father, to his people, to his city, to himself," he was describing an unfettered belief.[4] There was sublime courage involved, not subtle in thought—a full-bodied embrace of life that knowledgeably looked forward and was exercised with a keen mind.[5]

COMPARATIVE LITERATURE AND EDMUND SPENSER: THE THIRD CHOICE

Bart Giamatti was introduced to excerpts and the historic context of the first six books (twelve had been anticipated) of Edmund Spenser's *The Faerie Queene* in South Hadley High School's English Literature course. The precise context likely was England, the reign of Elizabeth I (1558–1603), and Geoffrey Chaucer's *Canterbury Tales* as the primary antecedent. Bart's parents, his father particularly, helped him make the connection to the Italian writers and the Renaissance influences that Spenser acknowledged had provided part of his poetic vision in forming *The Faerie Queene*. As Bart later described, that parental introduction included a "confluence" into his mother's English cultural lineage.[6] The depth of his interest and his own means of examining and expressing it blossomed in clarity at Yale.

౼

The Faerie Queene (the first three books were published in 1590, the second three in 1596) is a story of various knights, men and one woman, of noble lineage, beginning with the Redcrosse Knight, each of whom undertook a special quest primarily at the behest of the Faerie Queene (Gloriana), Queen Elizabeth. The quests were filled with obstacles. Executing each one required choices that involved daring, intrigue, failure, and success, each "canto"—story—intended to tell a moral tale. *The Faerie Queene* is one of the longest poems in the English language. Spenser devised his own form of poetry for it, which came to be known as the Spenserian stanza, itself part of the challenge in reading and understanding it.

In political and religious terms (which mattered to Giamatti), the England that Spenser wrote in was Protestant, largely a conservatively driven blend of Puritanism and Calvinism, which, among other things, required writers to have a moral or religious purpose in their works. Writing had to teach; the reader must come away with a moral lesson to contemplate. That also meant the writing must be "allegorical"—the story, however drawn from history, must tell a fictional tale that involved, for example, holiness, temperance, justice, courtesy, good, evil, truth, deceit, and the ultimate triumph of virtue. The era was described in the monarch's name, Queen Elizabeth I, who professed to be a virgin, thus adding a personal virtue (chastity) to the acceptable ones that made their way into *The Faerie Queene*. In a broader context, this also is the period of England's grand acquisitions of foreign lands, war (especially against Catholics), and explorations, including in America (Elizabeth was referred to as, among other titles, the Queen of Virginia; Roanoke was founded and settled, albeit briefly, in 1585). Among England's renowned soldiers and explorers—also a writer, political figure, and spy—was Sir Walter Raleigh. He helped quell a rebellion in Ireland, was awarded several estates for his success, and was embraced by the Queen, at least figuratively. Many of these historic and political themes—a celebration of her reign, not unlike the way Virgil's *Aeneid* celebrated Augustus Caesar—are represented in *The Faerie Queene*; Spenser's intention in doing so was purposeful, including in his use of the Queen's relationship with Walter Raleigh.

In a manner similar to Dante, and reflective of Chaucer,[7] Spenser was active in governance. He was a civil servant in Ireland at a time when English repression was rough and life filled with danger.[8] In writing *The Faerie Queene*, Spenser sought to ingratiate himself with Elizabeth, to exercise his poetic skills—already known—to seek favor at court, financial comfort, and prestige among his literary peers. Much of his poetry, including *The Faerie Queene*, was written in Ireland. In acquiring an estate there granted to him by the English government, Spenser became Walter Raleigh's neighbor.[9] Once completing the first three books, Spenser turned to Raleigh to help him gain the Queen's attention, her *imprimatur*. In his "Letter to Raleigh," a kind of preface to the poem, Spencer pleaded his respect for Queen Elizabeth and, in describing the poem's content, demonstrated its aesthetic power and the role Raleigh could play in elevating it. It was a political maneuver, not at all unusual in the era. It worked. Raleigh read portions of the poem to Elizabeth, who agreed to award Spenser monetarily for life through a process, apparently, of historic note.[10]

In classical literary terms, Elizabethan England fully embraced the Italian Renaissance. That William Shakespeare (whose plays were performed during this era) drew from, among other people and locations, characters and settings in Italy reflected that embrace. Greek and Latin epics, Virgil, Dante, and the Italian writers, such as Petrarch, Ariosto, Ambrogini (Poliziano), and Tasso, and the Catholic Church provided the foundation for how to think about writing grand and lengthy stories. Giamatti's knowledge of this tradition was close to genetic: "The epic alone had the size and scope to encompass what poets felt about life," he wrote. "The great epics of the Renaissance are tales of journeys, crusades, wandering, pilgrimages, explorations—all leave-takings in search of a home, or something permanent, final, and fixed."[11]

The written form of such grand epics was invariably poetry, the format changed (which word and line rhymed with which word and line) to accommodate the purpose and, though the story was a journey, a quest, the obligation for moral teaching was uniquely English. In a way that joined moral imperatives with overtly religious ones, the place to be attained, or a central location for good, evil, deceptive enticement to evil, or pure leisure and joy, was "the garden"—an earthly paradise (atop the mountain, in the distant sea) or in a preternatural location (Heaven, Hell, Eden, or, in Virgil's *Aeneid*, Elysium, "the luminous fields where the true and faithful gather")—but rarely a garden that was not in constant change, evolving, in what the poets, especially Spenser, referred to as "mutability."[12]

Giamatti was, from the outset of his writings, especially taken by this notion of change, the uncertainty of it. Later in life, when reflecting on disappointment in an unexpected turn in baseball, he dug deep into this reality of change and the imperative, based on the recognition that uncertainties loom, to live life fully: "The Old Poet Spenser said: 'Nothing is sure that grows on earthly ground.' He had seen the flux of matters mortal, and he knew the only constant is corrosive change. He made of that knowledge a goddess, Dame Mutabilitie [in *The Faerie Queene*], and gave her sway over all things below the moon. . . . He thought he knew it all. He did not." In a related setting, Giamatti would write later, "For the poets of the Renaissance, nothing was ever quite done with, nothing was truly final—in art as well as life."[13]

The "garden" and "mutability"—though the primary focus of Giamatti's PhD dissertation and first book (and, later, a central metaphor that he used to reintroduce baseball to America through his own temperament; it helped that baseball was first played on Elysium Field in Hoboken, New Jersey)—was not, however, ultimately the central geographic "place" to Renaissance writers that was worthy of attainment, and certainly not to Giamatti as teacher, writer, and president of Yale. That centrality, to which all else evolved, belonged to "the City."

৵

The Earthly Paradise and the Renaissance Epic was a sweeping study of "Paradise"—the endless argument "about the location and nature of man's lost state of bliss. Where was it now? Who was there? What was it like and what did it mean?"

To answer these and related questions concerning the demise of interest in even the questions, Giamatti revisited, with insightful care, virtually the length of the Renaissance, Dante through Spenser, and further back to the Greek belief that Paradise was North in Arktikos (though not cold), through the biblical setting and unsettling conduct in Eden (the fall from grace), and forward to Columbus, who "thought he had found the blessed land across the wide waters, and he was certainly not the last man to search."[14]

"In the epics of the Renaissance," Giamatti wrote, "the garden was dealt with at length for perhaps the last time in western literature. We would be mistaken, however, if we concluded that man ceased to search for the lost state of bliss and innocence. Indeed, the hope of finding it seemed to increase enormously with the discovery of the New World, and American literature itself is constantly read as a record of the quest for happiness and innocence in the great unspoiled garden. And though we no longer have any hope of finding Elysium or Eden in the outer world, the search still goes on. . . . [for this] oasis of harmony. . . . Man's need to find the place has in no way diminished; though the more he turns in, the more his hope for arriving there has waned." That is, "every affirmation [of what appeared] demanded a question, and reaffirmed man's sense of conflict, elusiveness, division. [The search] could be exhilarating but also exhausting, and depressing, this sense of limitless [choices] and endless possibility whose darker side was fearful flux and mutability." To combat the "elusiveness, exhausting, and depressing" journey, a life must not "lack intelligence," it must, as Virgil said to Dante in the *Divine Comedy*, retain "the good of the intellect."[15] You must always keep your intellectual wits about you.

In *The Earthly Paradise*, Giamatti explored the meaning of landscape and place, and how, for Dante, Spenser, and other poets, they were used to describe symbols, but, in time and in Bart's life, also places with practical meaning. "Although their exact meaning has long been debated," Giamatti wrote, "what is interesting to us is that the castle of Limbo [in *The Faerie Queene*] is the first of so many walled and buttressed edifices, the first of so many symbols, whether dedicated to good or evil, of the City." This setting, he noted, "was similar to scenes in [Virgil's] *Aeneid* and [Homer's] *Odyssey*"—taking himself and the reader through Virgil and back to the Greek view of the City. "Here Dante gives the pagan poets a dwelling place which approximates the best they portrayed in their poems. They live in an Elysium [yet] this benign landscape blends, for the first time, the twin notions of City and Garden . . . luminously integrated in the rose of the City of God." There is "the necessity for passage through the Garden as a prelude for acceptance in the Heavenly City," until Beatrice, as Dante's new guide, promises him, "the pilgrim[,] citizenship in the City of God." He now has "fully become part of the garden and therefore he is ready for the ascent to the City." She described it this way, as Giamatti characterized it: "The City is now revealed . . . as an amphitheater with tiers. . . . Then immediately Beatrice exclaims: 'See how large our city sweepeth!' It is almost as if the poet were consciously alternating images of the Garden and the City. Finally, the City includes all"; it is "always the norm by which all is judged. The City is always the ultimate center of action, the true source of value." And, within the City, Dante—as Giamatti explored throughout his life—"emphasizes the responsibility of man, in his essential uniqueness, to conduct himself. . . ." It is with that "responsibility," that "duty," that man exercises his "freedom within order"—freedom without arbitrariness toward others, what, in the civility inherent to the City, is the duty of fairness.[16]

These were more than academic themes. Dante's civic life, the Florence he helped define, Spenser's—and the Renaissance poets'—understanding of the moral strength in the meaning and attainment of the garden, and the centrality and preservation of the City in defining civic duty were slowly fusing into an integrated core of historical knowledge. His knowledge of New Haven, tracking the lives of his relatives and friends, witnessing Griswold and now Brewster, gave his thinking emotional and moral underpinning and sharper cadence in moving through life as the excellent teacher and responsible citizen he wanted to be. His parents' life, in various forms, took on more useful guidance. His family—his wife, Toni; his son, Marcus Bartlett; and his daughter, Elena, born in March 1964—ensured both the immediacy of love and the meaning of continuity from his grandparents. Bart was forming a practical view of the world, actually principles for living, and his place and duty in it. His writing, the process of thinking and forming words to express himself, was one means for forming, testing, and affirming his principles in daily living.

࿇

While completing his dissertation, Giamatti collaborated with Yale colleague T. K. Seung in preparing a pamphlet for modest distribution, close to an exercise in admiration and an expression of the love of learning—"Master Pieces: From the Files of T. G. B.," Thomas Goddard Bergin. It included works selected and edited by Seung (who also studied under Bergin) and Giamatti. The effort reflected Bart's depth of inquiry, the value of capturing the past, here a man's character, in the preservative manner of the written word.[17] Bart also co-edited with two fellow graduate students a more challenging work published in 1962: *The Songs of Bernart de Ventadorn*. Ventadorn was a troubadour (a balladeer, a minstrel), a poet and musician who wrote the poetry of "courtly love" to music. The work contains a forward by Professor Bergin. "The young scholars who have prepared this edition," he wrote, "have labored with the enthusiasm of youth itself and the dedication of true scholarship to prepare a work which will be of value to their fellows for years to come. . . . I have been pleased and honored to be associated with their enterprise." For Giamatti, it was not about preparing the definitive work but about preserving the linguistically oblique yet valuable past of an imaginative maker and scholar of culture to ensure that he, and his work, had a future. His father reflected the same humanist value in exploring and documenting the life of Cambray-Digny.[18]

THE WELCOME TRYOUT: PRINCETON

Not unlike Major League Baseball, there is within the higher education world, certainly then among the Ivy League schools, something in the nature of scouts and, though the term likely was not frequently uttered, a farm system. Princeton had the former, and Yale provided rookie players that others could entice and sign. Princeton sought Giamatti. He had twice taught Italian during Yale's summer school program and had given lectures and provided mentoring to undergraduates. Princeton's scouts thought he was "gangbusters."[19]

The PhD dissertation, accepted in fulfillment of the department's requirements, was a credential for entrance into the Yale Department of English or of Comparative Literature. A position was not available, not yet. The offer he received from Princeton conveyed he was accepted into the narrow academic circle that mattered at Yale. He, and certainly Maynard Mack, would have viewed Princeton as an opportunity for growth as a teacher, for the likely publication of the first book based on the *Earthly Paradise*, and for a credentialed transition back to the place—home in more than one way—that he preferred. The risk was that Princeton would recognize Bart's excellence as teacher, mentor, academician, colleague, and future dean (or more) and do what was necessary to keep him.

In June 1964, A. Bartlett Giamatti graduated from Yale with a PhD in comparative literature. By the fall, he had entered the classroom at Princeton University as a lecturer in languages and comparative literature.[20]

29

Fearless

We cannot escape epic's long view: that rest will come by never resting, that peace will come only by war, that all your future will be devoted, despite yourself and at your best, to finding a memory from the past.

—A. Bartlett Giamatti,
Exile and Change in Renaissance Literature, 1971

Princeton

Giamatti would teach Italian to freshmen and serve as a preceptor—a tutor—in a large freshman course on European literature. The family moved into an apartment for junior faculty aside Lake Carnegie, created and financed by Andrew Carnegie to aid the Princeton crew team during Woodrow Wilson's presidency of the university.[1]

Bart sought a career with the prospect of a broader spectrum for teaching, writing, and thinking about life than Princeton offered him. From the outset, New Haven, in ways integral yet distinctive from Yale, also tugged at his sense of roots and in its comparative civic sophistication and diversity. The more challenging change in career and life was for Toni. She was committed to teaching, had already demonstrated a respected skill in the classroom and empathy with students in New Haven, and both place and vocation were largely put aside to raise her two children in Princeton, New Jersey, a small town of little distinction dominated by a university largely detached from life's realities, especially those reflective of what she and Bart believed. Princeton University's cultural embrace and advocacy of racism and eugenics were well known.[2] Within that history was the deliberate, albeit unsuccessful, exercise of wealth and condescension to exclude the "working-class" University of Washington crew team, who had defeated the Ivy League–dominated Pennsylvania team on Lake Carnegie, from going to the 1936 Olympics for lack of funds.[3]

Toni also had her own form of persistence and family-driven history at stake. Not only did her pedagogical skill hold steady and grow when they returned to New Haven, but she, too, would establish a precedent, a break from an Anglo-Saxon expectation that never held sway for her: she'd become the first wife of a Yale president to retain, with rigorous intent and success, an independent professional life. Her husband, when it was his time to say it, affirmed the centrality of her choice to their marriage.[4] From the moment Toni settled into Princeton, New Haven could not have been far from her own heart. Princeton, however, was Bart's first moment of truth, in career, outside of Yale, in life, and with respect to what he believed and how that might be tested.

ROBERT HOLLANDER: GOOD FORTUNE DISCOVERED AND MADE

When Giamatti met Professor Robert Hollander, they immediately developed a close friendship. "We were like brothers," Hollander said, with gratitude for an unexpected, joyful passage in life. Hollander taught comparative literature— French, German, and Italian—and a one-semester course on Dante's *The Divine Comedy*. The two lunched regularly at Andy's Diner on Nassau Street, attended Yankees–Red Sox games in New York, discussed family matters, and most importantly, shared, often in intense debate, the meaning of Dante's *Comedy*. The debate was hardly academic, certainly not to Giamatti.[5]

"Bart really cared about the truth," Hollander said. He had a powerful self-confidence. He was "quick and not afraid," but never at the cost of seeking and acknowledging truth about literature and life, even on a matter close to his heart—Dante's underlying intent and the use of allegory. The evolving divide among *Dantisti*—scholars and students who live, with devoted singularity, within the poems' continuously expanding revelations—had reached Princeton. It sparked debate among famed Italian scholars, old and new; the teachers at Yale with whom Giamatti studied; and his father, whose deeply held perspective Bart knowledgeably shared, versus Professor Charles Singleton of Johns Hopkins University and his young, well-versed Princeton protégé, Bob Hollander.

Hollander came to Dante much later in life than Giamatti did, but with no less personal endearment, and, in time, he was acclaimed for his unique Dante scholarship. At first, he saw his friend Bart as "Italian, native Italian"—that is, a scholar with something in the nature of genetic knowledge. He accepted— and challenged—Bart's form of proprietorship over Dante's work. The debate Professor Charles Singleton provoked, with Hollander as his learned advocate, was, in broad terms, simple and radical. Did Dante intend and write *The Divine Comedy* as allegory (the Giamatti view), the characters, settings, and language reflecting something larger, not obvious, enduring, and even elusive—love, deceit, evil, including the poem's characters (Virgil as representing "Human Reason" or Dante, the poem's Pilgrim, as representing Adam or "mankind")? Or did Dante write the epic as largely *history* (the Singleton-Hollander view), choosing real people (himself and Virgil) with known personal history whom Dante encountered along his journey to God. In elementary terms, Singleton declared, "The fiction of the *Comedy* is that it is not fiction."[6]

The debates at Andy's Diner were illuminating for both men. Only with rigorous and persuasive argument did Giamatti acknowledge that Singleton had a perspective, though he did not embrace it. Giamatti, who chaired the department's Italian Lecture Committee, was enjoined by Hollander to invite Singleton to speak. He did, introduced him with grace and respect, and, to Hollander's delight, sat him next to Hollander over dinner.[7]

A departure in thinking did not occur. What certainly happened is that Giamatti nurtured what was becoming a permanent natural instinct—digging deeper into historical and political context, understanding memory, cultural and societal as well as personal, and the power and certainty they can provide in thinking about future choices. As Giamatti interpreted John Milton's guidance in exploring Dante's work and life: "For only by the past can the future be told; only by earth can Heaven be imagined; only by what we had can what we shall, be revealed." Different from the lawyer's constant search for antecedents, if not precedents, in arguing for change in the law, Giamatti's purpose was more akin to the practical comfort in knowing history and the method for critical research required to battle, in words and conduct, practical chaos when the duty is yours to do it.[8]

As Hollander also explained and Giamatti's subsequent history affirmed, Dante and the other Italian poets, such as Giovanni Boccaccio, Ludovico Ariosto, and Francesco Petrarch, were not Giamatti's central study. He already knew Dante and *The Comedy*. Collectively, these Renaissance poets were all part of a "necessary passage" to the other poets Giamatti admired, especially England's Sir Edmund Spenser and the era that surrounded him, including the Renaissance poets' influence on theater and William Shakespeare. The debates with Hollander, fundamental, respectful, a grand welcome to Princeton and friendship, enhanced the navigational certainty of the passage.[9]

❧

Hollander deeply liked Giamatti, their pathway to this moment of friendship not dissimilar. Hollander was German-Jewish through his father, a Wall Street banker, and Irish Catholic through his mother, a believer in Catholic social teaching. It was an educated upbringing, yet different from Giamatti's. Hollander was raised in New York City, among tough kids capable of provoking a fight, with bat in hand. He had learned survival skills—the intuitive expectation of danger, an urban geographer's constant sense of surroundings, and anticipating, deflecting, or confronting the anti-Semitic slur. Yet their approach in the face of threat or unfairness was quite similar—if anything, Giamatti's was fresher, combative no matter the risk of harm, intent when necessary on reasoned argument so there was no misunderstanding about acquiescence. Hollander captured that mentality in a way others later experienced. It was during a Yankee–Red Sox game in the Bronx. The two were seated next to two men of imposing physical stature, both Yankee fans. In the face of tension that Giamatti, once verbally confronted, wittingly escalated, Hollander recognized the risk of fisticuffs that might ensue, which he feared would harm Giamatti and him both. Giamatti would not give an inch to vocalizing his opposition to the Yankees or, apparently, to the limited space on the armrest that separated him from the more formidably sized of the two men. Hollander's urban instincts told him to leave. Giamatti, closer to the harm, wouldn't budge. He had no fear. Eventually, at Hollander's insistence, they moved.[10]

There was, however, more in play. Hollander had gone to private schools, a feeder school, and then entered Princeton as an undergraduate. He had, he believed, resolved any inner unsettledness of religious and ethnic identity that might otherwise evolve from the anti-Semitic discrimination endemic in the Anglo-Saxon settings he'd been educated in. He didn't believe that Bart had—that being Italian American at Phillips Academy was likely a lonely experience. Hollander also recalled that less than a handful of students with Italian American surnames existed at his own preparatory school. Mechanisms had to be developed to deal with it, none more powerful and effective than intellectual accomplishment—Hollander's and Giamatti's (and Bart's father's) intuitive and correctly applied mechanism—and, for Bart, seeking ethnic and cultural diversity in the athletes and their coaches to enhance the prospect of normality, continuity, and reality in his daily life. Even the seeming tomfoolery, the mimicry to laugh about life and to have Bogart, Mineo, and Dean be, at times, both the means for widening who and what was relevant to life and learning, but *also*, with indirection, to ridicule life's more staid adherents to the status quo or unearned presumptions about the source of wisdom. It was at Phillips that those already existing traits of learning, communication, fun, and, foremost, intellectual rigor certainly served as mechanisms worthy of matured application. It also was at Phillips that he was credited with having radically altered the definition of the popular and successful student.

What both men had come to appreciate, in Princeton's and Yale's culture, was how to deal with the white Anglo-Saxon means of causing disabling harm without the bat and quite distant from the rough neighborhood—the power to promote, the condescending, often withering slight, the subtlety of absolute discrimination through the country club, eating club, or board room, and the various insidious means of exclusion—the admissions requirements and advocacy of eugenics—to preserve purity, that is, through polite violence and in select forms of judgment, or the deliberate absence of it.

Even at Princeton, Hollander believed that Bart seemed to anticipate the disabling slur, the dismissal of his view not on intellectual merit but on ethnicity—"the Dago"—as if he'd experienced it before and could recognize its budding formation in conversation or what was unsaid in the exaggerated, often incorrect, hand gesture. "Self-confidence in a very young man" rankled some, Hollander noted. As Bart's sister, Elria, his brother, Dino, and others also noted, Bart would have defied *any* form of denigrating or discriminating words or conduct, been angered by it, seen it as an unfair box no matter whom it was directed against, read it correctly as an insult to his parents and his family and anyone who looked different. The cultural integration of his parents' heritage in values and culture had formed solidly, and he would not suppress either thread in it. To Giamatti, wrongdoing was wrongdoing. What had formed was a liberalism, not merely of spirit but ingrained in life, about the subtlest forms of discrimination, no matter whom they were directed against, that he retained throughout his life.[11]

REVISITING *EARTHLY PARADISE*: THE JOURNEY AS MORAL SCALE

In 1966, Princeton University Press published Giamatti's Yale PhD dissertation, *The Earthly Paradise and the Renaissance Epic*. He and Toni celebrated. Publication was a judgment about the quality and contributory value of his first serious work. In the academic world he'd chosen, it was a sign of credibility, temporary celebrity, and future promise.[12]

In *Earthly Paradise*, as he refined the dissertation for publication, Giamatti also was forming thoughts in writing, principles for the practical life. It was a process of thinking and writing that matured in meaning up through moments before his death twenty-three years later. No principle was more important that this one: the *journey* matters. The ethical and moral judgments one makes in the journey are of practical meaning to the success and emotional warmth of attainment, that wherever "Paradise" may be located—and Giamatti described location almost exclusively in geographic terms—the journey refers to "a way of life" in getting there. That "way of life" requires that those seeking paradise try to "do true justice"; attainment is "a reward for virtue" and comes with "adherence to a moral scale of values"—guidance crafted into words and tested daily in life—antithetical in fundamental and daily practice to the unearned life, the Calvinist proscription of the "elect," the Anglo-Saxon presumption of "leadership," the despicable conduct and still vibrant mentality of eugenics.[13]

Making the journey disclosed human imperfections. The search, sometimes the battle, at risk of life, limb, or reputation, was to discern what those principles were. Giamatti, in the seriousness of his research and impeccable erudition, sought those principles in his own life, for his own life, and in the lives of those around him, certainly those for whom he had a duty: students, his children, parents, and himself, believing, as Giamatti said and did, according to his friend

Bob Hollander, that he was required to undertake the search. As he wrote only a few years later: "We cannot escape epic's long view: that rest will come by never resting, that peace will come only by war, that all your future will be devoted, despite yourself and at your best, to finding a memory from the past."[14] At Princeton, Giamatti was roughly between ages twenty-three and twenty-eight. He was forming his guideposts about living in earnest and truth and the imperfections of trying. Those guideposts were more grounded and open to change because they were challenged, at Princeton, for the first time in real life by his own past, and by his duty as parent in a lineage in which conduct reflected backward as well as forward. And in the debate over lunch or coffee with Bob Hollander, the fault lines were acknowledged, the rhetoric insightful and civilized, the absence of deference beyond cordiality not permitted.

Giamatti identified this duty of engagement—that rest will come by never resting—as a humanist with an extraordinarily informed knowledge of Judeo-Christian writings and culture. His life and conduct suggested he, more so or in ways different from or perhaps earlier in life than his father before him, entered the moral, ethical, and practical fray deliberately, to constantly ensure and test his duty of engagement to himself and to others. These were exacting criteria for engaging life; certainly it was an intellectual and physical weight, to be mulled and enjoyed daily as the embrace of the singular life on earth. And inescapable if not foremost in his mind was that Dante was Italian, that Italian poets from throughout the nation who preceded and succeeded Dante were embraced by English and American poets and literary figures, that his Anglo-Saxon mother had embraced Italy, the Italian language, culture, and history, and, most importantly, she had embraced his father, an Italian American from New Haven, Connecticut.

REVISITING *EARTHLY PARADISE*: GEOGRAPHY

Giamatti posited two schools of thought about Paradise at the outset, one that "considered the earthly paradise a symbol of the celestial home of the souls"; the other school "thought of the earthly paradise as a truly 'terrestrial' place, 'in some normally inaccessible part of the earth, which might become the goal of man's search and, in [a] literal as well as metaphorical way, the object of his dreams.'" The Renaissance poets gave life to the second school. So did Giamatti.[15]

In *Earthly Paradise*, Giamatti goes backward in history first, to, among others, Homer's *Odyssey* (roughly 1000 BCE), where, in important respects, the notion of paradise—the Garden—finds its popular if not poetic origins. "The description of the Elysian Fields which are promised" to those worthy of paradise is described in *Odyssey* (Giamatti, quoting from the poem) as "the gods intend you for Elysion with golden Rhadamanthos at the world's end, where all existence is a dream of ease." Virgil reintroduced Elysium in his epic poetry (roughly 29–19 BCE), as a location "inhabited by those who are blessed . . . and those (most of the rest) who drink at Lethe and assume new bodies."[16] More importantly, Virgil introduced the notion that Elysium is not merely a location in the present, but a place of the past and the future. Dante (roughly 1308–1320 CE) modified this terrestrial place in a significant way that is both "delightful and dangerous."[17]

Here is how Giamatti melded Homer, Virgil, and Dante into his own characterization of the relationship between a "way of life" and geography: "That a landscape or garden has been traditionally used to image the ideals, or condition, of a soul is an assertion substantiated by many of our observations. If this statement were true of no other work, it could be amply demonstrated with reference to the greatest poem chronicling the soul—the *Divina Commedia*. For again and again, Dante gives us a landscape . . . whose physical characteristics provide an index for the spiritual or moral level of life. *Setting constantly implies significance.*"[18] Geography, infused with values, perhaps only attainable through the elevation and practical application of virtue in the journey, mattered. Put differently, there is peril, expectation, and decisive judgment in geography—Purgatory welcomes errant behavior; Eden and God welcome "a dream of ease." Remaining, still, is "The City."

∽

"The City" is often overlooked or relegated in meaning in the later embrace of Giamatti as "Renaissance Scholar," especially when, as commissioner of baseball he often referenced the imagery of the "garden" in the context of the baseball field. "The City," however, goes to his rootedness—historical, family-driven, and practical—in South Hadley, in New Haven, and at a Yale crossed by public thoroughfares and a source of harm and tension to New Haven's urbanity and urban structure, and powerfully elevated in importance as he reflected on the critical choice of where to truly call home.

In *Earthly Paradise*, "the City" is found in Giamatti's discussion of Dante's (the pilgrim's) journey when, near the end of the epic, he meets Beatrice, who is about to lead him to God. She "says to the pilgrim: 'Here shalt thou be short . . . and with me everlastingly shalt be a citizen of that Rome whereof Christ is a Roman.' Here," Giamatti writes, "in the midst of the spectacle, Beatrice is promising the pilgrim *citizenship in the City of God* as a consequence of his self-cultivation in the Garden. This tercet [three-line stanza] . . . emphasizes again that Eden is not an end, but a most important way station on the journey to a greater end. . . . the City in the garden." Once properly prepared by Beatrice, "the pilgrim has fully become part of the garden and therefore he is ready for *the ascent to the City.*"[19] He notes, "Here, where will and desire are one, where perfect stillness creates motion, the twin images of Garden and City are married in the final, luminous vision."[20]

At the end of *Earthly Paradise*, Giamatti laments the passing in literature and culture of reliance on paradise as being geographically discernible, yet it has not disappeared—it's been moved to perhaps where it belonged all along. "Here, for the first time, we notice how things are beginning to turn inward; how the earthly paradise, no longer securely anchored by faith and a rigid literary tradition to a place in the 'real' world, will become increasingly a general symbol in the mind of man for the soul of man. We can note, in short, the origins of that process whereby Milton's traditional Eden will become finally 'A paradise within thee, happier far.' "[21] The transformation of paradise from "earthly" into "the mind of man for the soul of man" lingered in Giamatti's life and found a welcomed and eloquent counterpoise to challenges of ethics and truth "for the soul of man" in baseball, and a controversial, practical, and threatening battle with the *ancien régime*'s lingering prejudice at Yale. At base, Giamatti was in preparation; he knew precisely what was at stake, and where. He did not seek a safe haven.

REVISITING *EARTHLY PARADISE*: FREEDOM WITH ORDER

It is in this context of "the City" that Giamatti turned to two additional threads of thinking of later consequence in his life, still evolving in words and conduct: the meaning of freedom and the correlation among freedom, order, and the public duty of responsible citizenship. Giamatti introduced these threads through his interpretation of Dante. "The pivotal landscape of the [*Comedy*] remains . . . the terrestrial paradise. In this garden of *freedom with order*, the innocent life of man *before the Fall* and the blessed life of the soul in Heaven are both imagined. The past and future of the race are concentrated and symbolized in the garden. And, although no two men ever have the same soul and therefore the same journey, the garden of Eden is the locus . . . for the personal redemption of Dante the pilgrim. And, it is *in entering this . . . City* and the garden . . . that Dante . . . emphasizes the *responsibility of a man*, in his essential uniqueness, to conduct himself."[22]

The words "freedom with order" are used here to describe the terrestrial paradise "before the Fall," before Adam and Eve succumbed to Satan's entreaty and God banished them from Eden, when Paradise was lost and the power of evil was acknowledged by humanity. Toward the end of *Earthly Paradise*, Giamatti turns to Milton's *Paradise Lost* to define the reality of what precisely was lost. "For only in the perspective of time do we see that in *losing paradise* '*true Liberty Is lost*, which always with *right Reason dwells Twinn'd* . . .' " In losing Paradise, "man's future is linked to Chaos by Sin and Death, and his garden has become 'The haunt of Seals and Orcs, and Sea-mews' [Seagulls'] clang.' " The metaphors aside, threats to liberty and freedom now loom, caused by government *or* by those who'd seek to define or replace "order" with their own self-serving clang of Sea-mews. "Freedom within order," Giamatti concluded, "that most precious of all the balances . . . is gone. Where ideal government within and without was the norm, now man is 'estrang'd in look and alter'd style.'"[23]

The challenge posed by the threat to freedom "after the Fall," rests, as Giamatti posited, on the exercise of "responsible citizenship" to contest the insidious power of evil and its harm in order to ensure that liberty is preserved.[24] Moreover, as Giamatti understood, the responsibility for preserving liberty is premised on the preparation and insight necessary to recognize the reality of complex change in the harm caused by evil and *its* meaning of order. "Thus . . . the garden . . . must reflect *all* that is within [the imperfections of Adam and Eve]; it must also include that potential for change, change for the better or change for the worse" and "the struggle between warring elements within a man's soul."[25] Also, one of the most profound realities of *The Comedy*, worthy of reiteration here and understood by Giamatti, is Dante's *irreverence* toward *imposed* order—Dante, not God or the clergy, chose *who* suffered *which* often interminable shame and punishment. For all the reverence Dante presumably shows toward ultimately attaining God's order, he does it by engaging in his own exercise of liberty as the responsible citizen. And, as Giamatti understood and wrote, the entire nature of allegory is mutability—change in interpretation, challenges to it, and an unsettledness that warrants constant vigilance to anticipate change and seek purpose and fairness.

This view of "freedom with order" espouses a liberal principle in historical terms about how freedom to express and act with fairness are at risk of loss when order is imbalanced and the imbalance (evil) takes hold. The historical examples of this imbalance are numerous, and Giamatti had witnessed them challenged—Giamatti's father spoke forcefully, in Italy and the United States, against the imbalance in Italy under Fascism and its threat in America, raised money in Mount Holyoke for the orphaned children of Italy to correct the imbalance caused by Mussolini's terror, and added an anti-Fascist to the Mount Holyoke faculty to be sure the point about freedom was made. Giamatti witnessed imbalance and its effects in New Haven, through his grandparents' experience and his father's with the insidious force of eugenics and, later, urban renewal. Giamatti's earliest written notions about freedom were about how to ensure—that is, the responsibility of man to ensure—that "order" remained balanced so that freedom can thrive. Balance ensured fairness to others. It was a constant battle. Others, later, gave the term "order" as Giamatti used it as having a conservative "political" meaning that Giamatti neither intended nor acted or taught. He detested discrimination in any form, canvassed for Adlai Stevenson and Foster Furcolo, never in any form lent credence to anti-Semitism or those who sympathized with Fascism, and was a vehement advocate for the First Amendment. At Yale, after his return, he voted against President Kingman Brewster's effort to throttle vocalized and dramatized student opposition to Yale's institutionalized racism, which he knew about in its earlier iterations. And, Giamatti, unlike his immediate predecessors at Yale as president, was not a registered Republican.[26]

In *Collision at Home Plate*, James Reston Jr. simplified, then distorted, Giamatti's thoughts about "order" to artificially posture him as the emerging foil from a structured life to Pete Rose's life of "disorder."[27] Foremost, Giamatti confronted directly Pete Rose types from childhood on, including, by then, Yale types, only without the uniform. Rose lied publicly, privately, and in a court of law from the outset. Cocky kids who believed the rules applied to everyone else except them knew neither fairness nor its meaning in the discrimination directed against those who believed, lived, and played by reliance, if not insistence, on fairness, for some as the only way to be in the game, including in playgrounds, school yards, and universities. When it came to fairness, no special exemption existed for anyone.[28]

Giamatti was, if anything, suspicious and irreverent with respect to "calls for order" by established authority that relieved personal duty, constrained liberty, or was the pretext for unfairness. The Rose decision was not the first time he expressed or lived by that principled expectation.

CHOICES AFFIRMED

At Princeton, Giamatti began to perfect his teaching skills and their value in his life and career. His evaluations reflected his success: "A first rate Instructor in Italian," an "excellent preceptor. Highly regarded by . . . the head of the course," "a first-rate teacher, warm, dedicated, and stimulating." Department Chairman Edward Sullivan concluded that Giamatti was "A very promising young man." "Well grounded in his subject, alert and vigorous, he is at the beginning of what will surely be a very fine career." After only one year of a three-year appointment as an instructor, Sullivan recommended Giamatti be promoted to assistant professor in the upcoming academic year, 1965–1966. The appointment was approved.[29] In the next academic year, Giamatti added to his teaching duties: preceptor (again), advisor to candidates for bachelor's degrees, and guest lecturer in a course given by Hollander on Dante, Cervantes, and Goethe. Out of these experiences, and his own reflections, he developed an academic model that fused the *Aeneid* and the *Iliad* into comparative literature that, once perfected, would define one of his immediate and enduring contributions to teaching at Yale. Here, too, was the early test: the classroom, developing a style that integrated substance, that yielded the gratification of accomplishment—reaching, churning, provoking young minds to learn critically. The duty as preceptor and advisor took him outside the classroom, where instruction was more personal, where the relationship warranted providing insight and guidance, and encouraging the student to think about "a way of life" that involved the mind. There was for Giamatti—a work still in progress—accomplishment early, recognized formally in the faculty promotion and the excellence of his evaluations. At Princeton University. He was moving swiftly, and with stunning intellectual alacrity.[30]

It also was at Princeton that the responsibility of family took on force and began to form into the meaning of love he'd known as a child from his own parents. "The fall was clouded by the near-fatal illness with meningitis of their three-year-old son Marcus. . . . My *moule* (little one)," as Bart described Marcus daily at the more frequent meetings he'd have with Hollander after he visited the hospital. "The boy . . . made a full recovery, but Giamatti was uneasy about the absence of a sophisticated teaching hospital. . . . He already thought of himself as an 'exile' from his true home at Yale, and the experience with Marcus intensified that feeling."[31]

Other family realities emerged, not unrelated to geography. Although they maintained the requisite faculty social interaction, the Giamattis did not entertain, an academic expectation they both seemed to defy.[32] Perhaps it was Toni's responsibility for two children, or their modestly sized apartment overlooking Lake Carnegie, or the absence of neighborhood alternatives like those that existed in New Haven, or Toni's knowledge that her husband wouldn't be at Princeton long enough to warrant entertaining. Or perhaps, as Bart acknowledged, his "spare" time was valuable in research, writing, and combing libraries, all of which were critical to ensuring he was an excellent teacher, his singular aspiration. Toni, and perhaps Bart, also brought skepticism about the genuineness of those around both of them. Although Giamatti was "immensely popular with his peers[, h]e was noticed by his elders, but not always favorably. . . . Bart, they thought, was too much of a regular guy to be a real scholar."[33] Narrowness in the insular competitive life of Princeton and in the culture's definition of "scholar" was in play, especially when thinking about a true home for work and family. Giamatti knew that (and Toni would have as well) and was, in all likelihood, testing it.

Toni also grasped how to aid her husband's career in the rough jousting of academia at this elevated level and within his insistence on merit. In *Earthly Paradise*, Giamatti introduced the transcendent significance of the Renaissance poets in England in a way that provides insight into how Bart and Toni may have managed the character of the Princeton environment and their place in it: "The literature of the Renaissance turned man's sense of life's ambiguities back upon life itself. It studied the difference between illusion and reality. The obvious example is Elizabethan drama, constantly concerned with disguises, madness as an illusion or new reality, false identities, incantations and magic—with the implications of the metaphor that the world is a stage, that life is a setting for illusion."[34] Theater was, for Bart and Toni, an element in teaching, in the lecture as art form to encourage and enlighten individual students, and an element in the way Bart, often with Toni's studied critique as his public persona expanded, expressed his wit and irreverence, or sometimes his reverence for life to a broader audience. In the acknowledgments to *Earthly Paradise*, Bart wrote, "My wife, in spite of her disclaimers, is owed the greatest debt of all."[35]

☙

Maynard Mack, by then chairman of the Yale English Department, "had sounded [Bart] out in his first year at Princeton about returning to Yale, but Giamatti, newly promoted to assistant professor, thought it would be unseemly to leave so soon and under those circumstances."[36] Forces at play made the offer immediately enticing. Bart, as his sister explained, never had a solid grasp of the nuances of model Italian and lacked enthusiasm for teaching it.[37] To meet his deeper intellectual and academic imperative, formally being in the English Department mattered. He knew and understood Yale as a place of excellence in teaching, certainly as Maynard Mack would prescribe it, within which he could thrive. And New Haven had neighborhoods, family members, and more ethnic, religious, and racial diversity than he'd found at Princeton. Toni would have welcomed the move. Her professional life would regain its meaning, and together they could decide on schools they both knew, and be close to excellent medical facilities. It's likely Mack and Giamatti reached a *modus vivendi* about how and when to proceed.

Moncreiff authoritatively captured the sequence in *Bart Giamatti, A Profile*: "But when Mack called again on a fall Friday in 1965 with the offer of an assistant professorship commencing in the 1966–67 academic year, Giamatti decided that the time had come. Mack knew that Princeton would fight back, and he told Giamatti he wanted an answer by the following Monday. Over the weekend, Chairman Sullivan moved heaven and earth to produce a proposal that Hollander says was the best deal ever offered to an assistant professor . . . immediate promotion to associate professor with tenure, in the Italian Department, [and] the promise of a full professorship after the briefest interval that academic decencies would permit. But Giamatti had made up his mind. . . . '[In] spite of all our efforts Bart Giamatti had decided to accept the post of Assistant Professor at Yale. . . . It was clear practically from the beginning that nothing could keep him here at this time.'"[38] But Chairman Sullivan was not deterred. Princeton was not finished. "We may well be making efforts to bring him back here," he informed the president. And they did, with a stunning offer, including in the English Department, only a few years later.[39]

☙

I read to Bob Hollander a story he told Robert Montcreiff, that after leaving Bart on his last night in Princeton, "there were tears in his eyes. . . ."[40] They saw each other again, but only irregularly: Princeton–Yale football games in New Haven, a lecture on Dante that Hollander gave at Mount Holyoke in honor of

Valentine Giamatti, and the unplanned encounter on the road during Giamatti's presidency when quiet, personal asides among old friends could be exchanged with discretion.

Giamatti had and would continue to have deep friendships of special, intense character, cultural and intellectual in nature, but also including those who struck memory. He nurtured them. The thoughtfulness in the wave or gesture, the glib yet insightful one-liner, or the question about family was the way he approached life daily and learned from it. His experience, especially through both his parents' embrace of people in their own community and his own interest in people who contributed to community, had deepened his appreciation for what others in Ivy League settings might—and often would—consider plebeian, pedestrian, a waste of time. Time was valuable to Giamatti, but many of these moments—with struggling students in a course or in the midst of choice, the barber, the car mechanic, the maintenance workers, people who knew his father or grandfather, his children's friends, the working-class parent who sought his counsel about the university's culture—blended into his humanism intellectually and emotionally. It was an embedded value to take all such moments seriously. He was profoundly a listener: he paid attention; the conversation was never idle.

These skills and character would be welcomed and enjoyed by many colleagues and friends when he returned to New Haven, and to Yale. The English Department provided the widest and most fulsome embrace, and had the most rigorous of expectations. Bart's place there must have been a source of anticipated joy. He also had no illusions. His skills and character would be tested severely, including his preparation for the ethnic slur and the reality of a Yale still haunted by an Anglo-Saxon and eugenics mentality—especially the roughness of envy when he reached the presidency,[41] his heritage alone a practical threat to the status quo within which many around him were nurtured and judged, and had prospered. Yale had a disquietingly mixed genealogy that "continu[ed] to resonate."[42]

Epilogue: Yale — In Epic Battle

I never did have a big plan. I just wanted to be a professor of English—at Yale, I hoped—and when I accomplished that, it was almost immediately taken away from me.

—A. Bartlett Giamatti, April 1989

Giamatti's aspiration when he returned to Yale was, as he said, to be an English professor. It was, as well, to be not ordinary, to give active life to all the values and manners he possessed and intended to explore further as he sought, foremost, to gain tenure. That professional aspiration, as it played out and was affirmed in daily conduct and thoughts shared, molded into a grander, albeit fluid one founded in the model of Maynard Mack's intellect and Dean William DeVane's integrity. He would welcome being the chair of the English Department or the dean of Yale College. In the continuity of the duty derived from the immigrant experience, as he knew and understood it, and from the affirmation of his mother's values, attaining such an aspiration, in New Haven as well as at Yale, would blend together his own iteration of the Renaissance manner as he defined it with the authority to engage others civically, preeminently in matters of fairness. Tempered, always, by the reality of change and, what he knew would never leave him, the unsettling force of fate.

⁓

Professor Robert J. Clements, who had developed the first doctoral program in Italian at New York University, established a similar program in comparative literature in 1965. Perhaps in the hope of eventually enticing Giamatti to the Greenwich Village campus, Clements invited him to teach in the summer school program offered for graduate students. Clements was a Renaissance scholar who'd written extensively on Michelangelo and, in 1961, had crafted an insightful commentary on the Sacco and Vanzetti controversy.[1] Clements and Valentine Giamatti were both members of the Dante Society.

Bart taught the "Pastoral Tradition in European Literature," commuting every Tuesday and Thursday from late June to late July, while Toni, Marcus, and

Elena (son Paul was born in 1967) settled into New Haven and the Yale community. It's likely Bart considered the NYU opportunity valuable, for the teaching experience in a different setting, new relationships in the subject he preferred, and yet another credential that would increase his validation at Yale and reflect precisely the kind of course he wanted to teach.[2]

⟊

At Yale, Linsly and Chittenden Halls were two distinct buildings, each constructed in the Romanesque and Gothic style between 1888 and 1890 to serve as the university's library. Once the library was relocated into the new Sterling Memorial Library, the two buildings were joined in the 1930s into classrooms, lecture rooms, and faculty offices. The re-formed Linsly-Chittenden Hall has two entranceways: one on High Street, near Chapel, the second inside the Old Campus, proximate to Vanderbilt Hall, where Bart Giamatti lived as a freshman. Within LC, as it is commonly called, are the departments of English and Comparative Literature.

The interior of LC is oak paneled, with quarry tile floors, subtle colors, and the atmosphere of purpose conducive to encouraging the serious intellect intent on learning. Within its hallways and stairwells were displayed two specially regarded stained-glass works: *Education*, a large allegorical piece commissioned by Simeon Baldwin Chittenden from the Louis Comfort Tiffany Glass Company, which was installed in 1890 in the original library, and twelve smaller stained-glass depictions collectively called the George Park Fisher Memorial Windows, now lost or mislaid. *Education* remains, installed in LC's high-ceilinged cathedral-like lecture hall just off the High Street entrance and referred to as 102 LC Hall. In this building, Bart Giamatti received the depth of his classroom education in English and comparative literature, successfully completed his coursework for his PhD, and argued—sometimes in Latin or Italian or French—the virtues, judgments, and future of literary works central to education in the humanities and all of its derivatives. He now entered LC almost daily as a member of the faculty.[3]

He intended to write and lecture, with an imagination solidly and purposefully based, on education, on Spenser, on the Renaissance writers,[4] on writers and chroniclers in English, especially from America, including those who contributed to athletics—Bart connected these writers to their toughness in the culture they helped define. He introduced a course of study that melded Virgil and Homer into comparative literature and was exciting to his colleagues, popular among students, and enduring within the department. "Homer to Brecht," as Sterling Professor and Giamatti protégé David Quint explained it, required the full reading of the original translations of *The Aeneid*, *The Odyssey*, and *The Divine Comedy*. Giamatti's skill as lecturer, his ability to bring dramatic life to a person and setting, to hold students in awe, then in contemplation, was recognized early. So were his scholarship and its practical contribution to teaching. His promotions were without precedent.[5]

As the Renaissance historian and thinker, he knew literature, its derivatives, and their value. As Guido Calabresi witnessed during a university-wide committee meeting, Bart chastised one well-known faculty member who disparaged early Renaissance writers and, once he established that the faculty member had never read them, Bart challenged the mediocrity of "these nineteenth-century second-rate English writers we all are forced to read."[6] When Charles T. Davis, professor of English and chair of the African American Studies Department, sought to devote the "last seven months of his life to writing," Giamatti, as Professor Henry Louis Gates Jr. described it with special gratitude, conferred on Davis the John Musser Chair of American Literature to ensure he could finish his work on African American literature and culture. Giamatti also wrote the foreword to the effort's culmination, *Black Is the Color of the Cosmos*, edited by Professor Gates. In it Bart dwelt not only on the depth and poignancy of Davis's scholarship, but on something of essential importance in life as he and Davis embraced it: "His urbanity went deep, to the root of the word and the man. . . . He built cities, human commonwealths, wherever he was. . . . No good idea was beyond his reach or his embrace. Charles knew what was right and he had the courage and the confidence to say so. . . . And because of his courage and confidence, it is a more just world."[7]

Mineo, Bogart, Dean, and others were never far from Giamatti's mind or skill as teacher, nor was having fun with life in forms that spoke to his irreverence and his breadth of what's relevant in teaching, content as well as method.[8] In continued play was more than scholarship, though Giamatti's intellectual depth and skill at explaining complexity and his precise, moving erudition, already formidable, would exceed any of his predecessors as president. Learning, teaching, defending, advocating, and continuing to expose the American culture, its subcultures, those still "On the Road," and those still seeking recognized identity for living daily[9]—particularly, during his presidency, gay students, always an object of eugenics denigration and its lingering mentality at Yale[10]— were in his sight and mind and warranted his advocacy. He provided it publicly, departing from the Corporation's antiquated ambivalence about fairness in sexual orientation, and privately, at the highest level of government.[11] In the depth of his inquisitiveness, and of his innate and learned sociability, also was another enduring characteristic, when, in unique fashion, he gave meaning to the Renaissance integrated use of knowledge. His way of speaking, the now-instinctively exercised cadence of oratory and insightfulness in debate, mattered in his aspiration and was captured by his classmate, friend, and later secretary of the university, John Wilkinson. "If he were sitting here," Wilkinson said, "you'd be mesmerized."[12]

⌖

Giamatti also was at the mere beginning of what cultural historian Sean Wilentz observed well after Giamatti's death at age fifty-one: "Bart Giamatti was a phenomenon who lived the lives of several men even though his own ended tragically early."[13] In play was a daring imperative. Giamatti wrote it plainly and repeated it in variations: "That rest will come by never resting." It was a view of history, the primary principle, among others, for guiding his life that would hold its own in the face of change and fate—and, in a form that was essential to that imperative, which he intended to leave as legacy, if only to his children: "For all the knowledge that we will never succeed in the work of our lives, we must continue to choose to continue. For all the frustrations and fears that each of us has and will have in our short time, we must choose to pursue to the end of choosing the best we know for ourselves and for each other, and in that choosing, long and late, we will connect with each other."[14]

‹›

When he returned to Yale in 1966, what lingered and had been affirmed through the Brewster presidency was the eugenics mentality, the unworthy presumption of "leadership," the nude photographs, the unprincipled disregard of the First Amendment, the condescension toward Labor,[15] and the awkward, demeaning approach to the admission of women.[16] Giamatti's personal relationship with Brewster was always congenial, but he'd witnessed and always disdained the pretense and implication of "leadership" as the fundamental principle for guiding students. He knew it was only the outward manifestation of an underlying, decaying core of elitism, discrimination, and coercion.[17]

In settings within the university, among some faculty and students, the embedded eugenics mentality appeared only to weaken in the willful failure to acknowledge it, though it surrounded them in tributes to slaveholders and slavery advocates, in the grand monument to the Institute of Human Relations, in the memory and values of those who'd been educated within its aura, and in the luster of new buildings constructed atop a once vibrant neighborhood at lasting, still repetitive, human cost. Dick Lee was still mayor in 1966, and Giamatti would witness the fragile pretense of urban renewal and Yale's pervasive role and hypocrisy in crafting it crack loudly and split irrevocably, immeasurable harm permanently done, as it was in cities that formed and followed the same path throughout the nation. Giamatti disliked Dick Lee's actions and manner from the outset of his return to New Haven, even more so when he became the president. That irrevocable death was led foremost in the Oak Street/Hill/Legion Avenue neighborhood by African American urbanists, who no longer lived in a neighborhood that once served as the respected means for integrating into the cultural and vocational life of their choice. Their leaders did all they could to improve lives and deter violence, but African American and older immigrant families were still being forced out, moving to distant cities as Lee continued to build and widen roadways at the cost of neighborhood, population, and family stability.[18]

Yale was, at the base, the powerful cause and the plainly evident beneficiary of the neighborhood's geographic constraint and the community erosion and neglect by official and unofficial design of the government and the university. Brewster and his administration did everything they could not to acknowledge Yale's role, partially out of the need to shift the blame elsewhere and partially from the reality that, in the end, Yale now had property interests there and in the Dixwell Avenue/Newhallville neighborhood that it needed to preserve and expand, which required, as under Griswold, only patience and rhetorical soothing. Internally, one Yale administrator wrote to Brewster, "The problem is exacerbated by the tendency of Negroes to concentrate around University areas. The Medical School is surrounded by a rapidly growing Negro ghetto . . . , which [is] raw material for violence to persons and property. . . . It will not be long before Yale and [the] Whitney Avenue residential area will be a white island in a black sea. Urban renewal projects move much too slow to counteract the effects of these rapid population shifts."[19] Externally, Brewster also deflected requests for modest forms of serious assistance to Oak Street/Hill/Legion Avenue organizations for the same reasons and the subtle exercise of his own power as landowner. "I made a solid promise that any expansion by Yale," he replied to one request, "which involved withdrawal of housing [would be met] by the creation of substitute housing in at least the equivalent amount. [However]," Brewster continued, "I can't speak for the Hospital." More "relocation" was in play—the Diaspora of African Americans—and resentment directed against Yale was informed and precise.[20] And understanding had effects, for good reason and short duration, among a new generation of less compliant students in the School of Art and Architecture who had recognized the harm that Rudolph and their alumni had done in the Hill and elsewhere. Brewster squelched their effort and intent mercilessly.[21]

Externally and internally, Brewster and State Representative Mary Griswold led publicly and privately Dick Lee's insistently displayed proposal to build the massive "Ring Road,"—a completion of the Rotival/Yale/Lee Plan—that would have surrounded Yale, blocked it off from the Dixwell Avenue/Newhallville neighborhood, split and disconnected it from the Dwight neighborhood, and, with a direct connection to the Oak Street Connector, enclosed the Yale Medical School against further encroachment by the increasingly African American and Puerto Rican population in the Oak Street/Hill/Legion Avenue neighborhood. The four- to six-lane roadway (underground only through Yale's neighborhood) required the relocation of a thousand families, some for the third time, and forty-five small businesses in three neighborhoods, a circumstance that history had shown often meant the likelihood of commercial failure. Griswold introduced the bill for funding in the Connecticut General Assembly in early 1967, after Brewster and Lee met privately with Governor John Dempsey to affirm their commitment. Yale's architects, still playing the planner role, said the new road "could be the greatest boon to the Yale campus." Internally, Brewster also saw it as a way for Yale to close off public streets to serve its purpose.[22] Opposition arose immediately from the racially and ethnically mixed Dwight neighborhood, expressed poignantly before the sympathetic Board of Aldermen. Its members from the Fair Haven and Wooster Square neighborhoods had experienced enough of Yale, Lee, and highway construction that had denigrated neighborhoods, with Yale acquiring more property in the devastation, and from the African American leadership in Dixwell/Newhallville—especially State Representative Bruce Morris, who had come of age in the 1961 election and was highly respected in the state legislature.[23] They heard the anger and fear of their people, which echoed the words of coerced Italian, Polish, Jewish, and African American residents whose lives had been shattered, their anguish of loss expressed without effect.[24] Within Yale, Vince Sully, who'd come from the same Dixwell/Newhallville neighborhood as Dick Lee, confronted Lee directly with detailed reasons for opposition.[25] Brewster, Lee, and Griswold persisted. The condescension and unfairness of the eugenics mentality held sway. The moat needed completion. Collectively, the three wrote and testified for the project.[26] African American and other community leaders who'd witnessed the deliberate demise of neighborhood structures warned Lee and Yale in reports and meetings that violence could occur in New Haven if jobs, good housing, and the ability to start or acquire small businesses—all once the common hallmark of the Oak Street/Hill/Legion Avenue neighborhood especially—were not created. Signals abounded. They mattered only on the margin.[27]

In the withering August heat of 1967, the "civil disturbance" on Yale's periphery came to the fore, hard, angry, and historically expected. It began in the remnants of the Oak Street/Hill/Legion Avenue neighborhood and spread to areas where other urbanists, children of immigrants displaced by urban renewal, also lived in the Fair Haven and the Dixwell/Newhallville neighborhoods. Discontent was widespread, and urban renewal's political education came more and more to the fore.[28] Hill families and community leaders, especially Fred Harris of the Hill Parents Association, knowledgably fearful of harm to elderly parents, women, and children from the stray bullet, tear gas, fires, looting, or the aggressive or inexperienced policeman, sought and received refuge in homes and churches throughout New Haven and into North Haven and Hamden, except for one place where, twice, NAACP and Hill leaders were turned down: Yale. Brewster said it personally. No. Not here.[29]

The national repercussions were broad, grand, and embarrassing, especially to the erstwhile news sources, including the *New York Times*, which had elevated Lee's effort like public relations sycophants and were now forced to acknowledge his failure.[30] The cataclysmic event ended Dick Lee's career. He was publicly forced by aldermanic leaders, especially Alderman Bart Guida and others during the 1967 campaign, to recognize that New Haven, beginning with the sale of the York Square campus and Yale's acquisition of more and more property transformed into tax-exempt holdings in the Hill, Dixwell, and elsewhere, had, to no one's surprise, rendered the city unable to finance its own programs. Brewster's insular mentality and definition of duty, and his knowledge of Lee's seeming conflict of interest with the Ford Foundation and interest in a professorship at Yale, played Lee's insecurity and its result: Lee's leverage had waned.[31] Brewster and the Yale Corporation said no to taxes and the "Guida Amendment."[32] Lee was reelected by a disinterested, turned-off electorate, but would not run again. In 1968, State Representative Bruce Morris and others ensured the death of the "Ring Road."[33] Lee's appearance at the 1969 Democratic Town Convention was met with derision and open hostility, led by African Americans and other urbanists. They knew what every mayor since Dick Lee would learn: it would take a generation or more to undo or find a new path away from the harm—insidious and in some ways not yet recognized—that Yale and Lee had done to the history and lives of those people who had chosen New Haven as their home. Proposed mayoral candidates among delegates included John Daniels, who'd come to maturity in the 1961 campaign, and Henry Parker, the chair of the Black Coalition.[34]

The new Democratic candidate, Italian American Bart Guida, who disliked Lee and urban renewal (his own neighborhood had been devastated by the inward sway necessary for the Oak Street Connector), had authored the "Guida Amendment" and was aware of Yale's role historically. When he sought a second term as mayor, Guida was met with overtly racist commentary by the *Yale Daily News*, still locked in the eugenics mentality in its varying rhetorical, now self-determined and disingenuous "liberal" iteration, which looked everywhere but in the mirror for scapegoats. Since the *Daily News* had ridiculed and stereotyped Mayor William Celentano and the Wilbur Cross–Hillhouse Harvest Festival football teams and coaches in 1951, that mentality of condescension had become deeply comfortable and accepted. "Look at Guida, for example. . . . Worse, he's Italian. We all know, or should that a mere trace of mazzorella [*sic*] on a politician's breath suffices to make card-carrying liberals retch. Guida fairly reeks of the stuff." The Republican candidate, Paul Capra, was acceptable, the writer, Hank Levine, concluded, because, though also Italian he'd been "decreased" and worked in Yale's admissions office. He was like us. Capra, the *Daily News* proclaimed as endorsement, was the heir to Dick Lee, though Capra criticized Guida as being "the candidate of orthodox, spendthrift liberalism in this election." Guida won the Democratic primary in 1969 and 1971, and the general election. In both elections, he won the African American wards. Predictably, the Yale wards voted Republican. The *Daily News* commentary, deliberately copied and circulated among selected Democratic voters, ensured Guida's victory.[35]

Giamatti, likely with the Griswold experience in mind and especially as witness to Brewster's history and plainly detached mentality, told Bread Loaf graduates at Middlebury College what he'd learned in New Haven: "Educational institutions were trying to justify themselves in terms of a system they were legally exempt from and often intellectually opposed to. They were using the language of the City to deny any responsibility to the city. And many students and much of the world at large . . . were not quite prepared for this combination of condescension and fastidious indifference. 'Entire affection hateth nicer hands,' said the old poet, [Edmund Spenser]; if you truly love, as you say, you must touch."[36]

❧

In the willful neglect of memory within Yale—or perhaps, more accurately, timidity or acquiescence in the "Mother Yale" culture and in its persistent vitality among some alumni—the eugenics mentality's strength became pointed, more "sudden" in its manifestation, more intended to hurt, the creed of a withering culture exercised with more virulent and defensive fervor. A. Bartlett Giamatti, once he'd risen visibly as the likely, then selected president, blended elements of his heritage, real-life humanistic principles, and irreverence for actions that smacked of timidity or willful neglect, traits that the eugenics mentality abhorred and always had. "Bart saw and knew every bit of this," his friend, then–Professor of Law Guido Calabresi, recalled vividly. "And it was one of the reasons that we were friends. And it was one of the reasons why before he became president, when that was in the works, we walked all day talking about it and what he would be and whether he could do it and so on." Giamatti was, to some, a threat. He knew it.[37]

One of the earliest reactions to Giamatti's ascendancy as president was from Mary Griswold. "At least he's not Catholic," she said, with enough directness and in a setting certain to ricochet quickly in a cloistered world. It did. Giamatti was offended and angered. Her comment went to the heart of the intolerance he abhorred. More worrisome, an acceptable tone of critique was defined, with deep origins in the Yale culture, certainly evident in her husband's reign.[38] During the evening celebration of his formal induction as president, a conversational exchange made in uninhibited comfort was overheard by Giamatti, his parents nearby. He described it: "The wife of one of the trustees was asked by another patron who the new president was, and she replied, 'Oh, I don't know, some little wop.'"[39] The rules of engagement were set. Merit alone would be judged on two levels: one properly assessed and spoken, the second decidedly more insidious and, no doubt, masqueraded.

The challenge to Giamatti's intellect and political skills, the need to manage and outmaneuver the rough, ugly dynamic in Yale's culture, emerged immediately, as he knew it must. It came atop the harsh practical challenge from

Angelo Bartlett Giamatti, Yale president-designate,
greets a student on the Yale campus, 1978.
United Press International Corporation / NTProto Collection.

the university's severe financial and physical fragility, aggravated by Brewster's mismanagement.[40] The Corporation, and Acting President Hanna Holborn Gray, made clear that Brewster had created an "urgency" that threatened Yale's "academic strength." What Mary Griswold and others just didn't reckon with was Bart's principled intellect and rhetorical skill; his fearless commitment to challenge prejudice—recognized since childhood, at Princeton, and by the president of Notre Dame, the Reverend Theodore Hesburgh;[41] his spirited persistence in protecting Yale's liberal purpose against conservative, presumptuous intrusion;[42] his insistence on fairness; and his keen knowledge and outspokenness about Yale's discriminatory history. "Individuals were excluded from Yale," he told students, "because of quotas, absolutely unacceptable rules based on race or religion. Those days are gone and must never return."[43] He knew it firsthand. He retained and relied on the self-confidence, solidly based in childhood and parental love and model; a deep commitment to "the City" in its civic purpose, especially to its high school students;[44] the civic duty of education "to lead us to some sense of citizenship";[45] and a love for Yale in its finest attributes when, in the fall of 1966, at age twenty-eight, he walked, once again, through Phelps Gate.

His character was not free of flaws and imperfections. Foremost was his own ceaseless failure to overcome threats to his health, self-imposed and reinforced in part by the culture of his era, and a failure to recognize the depth of those threats, two of which were inherited. In a way ironic, by ignoring this threat he displayed a unique and persistent courage of time and place, a Rooseveltian courage that, on reflection, he attributed warmly and accurately to his father. There also were flaws in his judgment, though not in his values, and he intended to use those values foremost to discredit fatally the eugenics mentality, that it "must never return," when the responsibility was his to exercise as a teacher, writer, and mentor and, in eleven years, when he was elected president of Yale at age thirty-nine. He was, as he always had been—through the strength of his father's persistence and his parents' moral and civic guidance, and as the adolescent quarterback looking downfield in the playing fields of South Hadley or as the second baseman in the Bobby Doerr–model—intent to be "in the game," ready to do epic battle, however defined and no matter the adversary.

Acknowledgments and Reflections

I considered writing a book about Bart Giamatti in 2006 and 2007. I retained historian and New Haven journalist Allan Appel, on the advice of a friend—the author, historian, and linguist Anthony Riccio—to do some preliminary research on Bart and his father's family in New Haven, and on his father's experience in the public schools and at Yale. I then spoke with John Wilkinson, who'd been secretary of the university under Giamatti and a friend of mine during the time I remained in New Haven. He encouraged me to write the book, a thorough examination of Giamatti as the first non–Anglo-Saxon president of Yale. I learned shortly after that, also from John, that Robert Moncrieff, a Yale graduate and friend of English Professor Maynard Mack, was writing a book on Giamatti and had received the imprimatur of the Yale Press for its publication. I expected that it would be a full biographical study and that Moncrieff would have ready access to essential information that would ensure a thorough study, even if not to the extent or in the nature that Wilkinson believed warranted. I decided, instead, to pursue another subject dear to me and reflective of my work in the law, my own family history, and new research previously unexamined: Hawaii's last constitutional monarch, Queen Liliuokalani, and her purposeful time living in the United States following our Navy's force-driven overthrow of Hawaii's elected assembly and the denigration of the Hawaiian culture (including by missionaries and through the Calvinist condescension that emanated from Yale). I did not return to the idea of a Giamatti book until early 2014, following my reading of Moncrieff's insightful but limited book and other works. I sat, once again, with Wilkinson to explore his thinking with more care and exactitude. He has been helpful ever since, though the factual content of *Fearless* and the manner of its presentation are wholly my responsibility.

&

As I stated in my "Author's Note" at the beginning of the book, my respect for Giamatti was enhanced by meeting his sister, Elria Giamatti Ewing, and her husband, David; his brother, Dino Walton Giamatti, and Dino's wife, Barbara; and his cousin Helen Ogden and relative by marriage Kim Formica. They were generous with their time and direct in their candor. Helen and Kim shared their own genealogical research into both sides of his family. Elria and David also shared family photo albums, including a special one from Bart's mother. My respect for Giamatti also evoked the full rigor of my training as historian and appellate lawyer and required a persistent inquisitiveness and thoroughness about facts. I was able to give full and complete vent to that obligation by retaining two exquisitely trained archivists and historians: Dr. Joan Cavanagh of New Haven and Dr. Peggy Ann Brown of Virginia. Dr. Cavanagh toiled in New Haven, including at the Ethnic Heritage Center at Southern Connecticut State University, employed her expertise in labor history in New Haven and at Yale, and waded with me through literally tens of thousands of pages of Yale's archives. Dr. Brown searched in the National Archives and in libraries and often obscure sources throughout the nation, with a solid grasp of racial and ethnic documentation she'd once demonstrated in a civil rights case we'd worked on together in northern Virginia. Both historians used their own relentless persistence and probing skill to uncover documents we had been seeking, oftentimes locating them with yet more unexpected, relevant, and revealing additions that warranted further probing to gain the necessary understanding of the earlier ones. I'm grateful for the professionalism they both demonstrated, though the burden of the ultimate product is mine alone.

As I also explained in my "Author's Note," Giamatti's presidential papers, exclusive of his speeches, and the papers of those in his administration are not yet available for public examination. In addition, a serious analysis of those papers; the Yale Corporation; and former faculty, students, city residents, or national leaders who praised him and others who did not, as well as a proper analysis of the setting, would warrant a research and writing task comparable in duration, effort, documentation, and thoroughness to what was undertaken here. That limitation had two unexpected benefits, which I also described at the outset: First, the powerful relevance of Giamatti's relationship with his parents and his family history and of Yale's persistent history of imposed privilege and prejudice would receive thorough attention in the research and writing of this book. Second, once the presidential and related personal papers of Giamatti become available, any thorough effort to examine his presidency will now have the full benefit of the historical context and the documented conduct of his predecessors at Yale and in New Haven.

꿍

I am grateful to Yale University's chief archivist, Judith Schiff, whose knowledge of the university's archives and skill as historian and chronicler helped me understand how to examine the correspondence of others who had exchanged notes with Giamatti, in light of the fact that his presidential papers were not open for review. Schiff's guidance also was helpful when I looked through archival material at Princeton University, Harvard University, Mount Holyoke College,

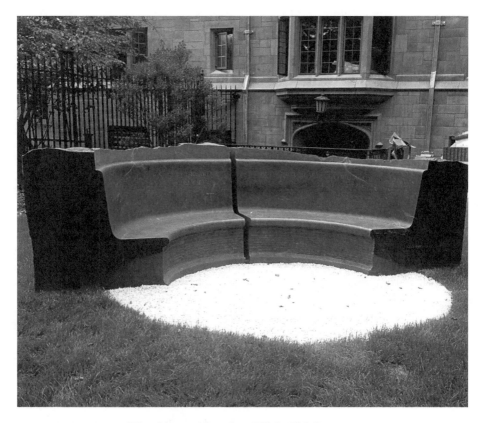

The Giamatti bench at Yale's Old Campus.
Mark Aronson.

Middlebury College, and Phillips Andover Academy, where there were no such constraints.

The archivists in each of those institutions, particularly at Mount Holyoke, which houses Valentine Giamatti's papers and Dante book collection, were thoroughly professional, gracious, efficient, and welcoming. At Mount Holyoke particularly, and in other locations in South Hadley and among Bart's childhood and adult friends, the memory of the Giamatti family is a wonderful, permanent, and respected thread in the life of the community. It was at the college that I saw "Babbo's Bench," a tribute to Valentine Giamatti presented by his family while he was still alive, now housed on the campus grounds. It added poignancy to another bench, placed by Bart's classmates in tribute to his temperament and presidency, that rests serenely within sight of Phelps Gate and is often occupied by students within Yale's old campus.

෨

I devoted considerable time to researching available aspects of Giamatti's presidency, especially his relationship with Mayor DiLieto and the only limited documents within the city's archives. Karyn Gilvarg, who directed city planning during DiLieto's tenure, was crucially helpful, as was DiLieto's chief of staff, Joseph Carbone, and DiLieto's economic development administrator, John Sawyer. Historian Anthony Riccio and longtime New Haven resident and cultural factotum Rosemarie Foglia Lemley added timely insight and correction when needed, as did Giamatti's friend and Yale professor John Merriman; Giamatti's friend and Princeton colleague Professor Robert Hollander; Giamatti's friend and provost William Brainard; former Speaker of the Connecticut House of Representatives Ernest Abate, who, at Giamatti's request, met with Giamatti privately over luncheon to discuss firsthand the university's interests and their respective lives; and Bart's special administrative assistant and friend Regina Starolis. My goal was to understand as best I could what had occurred during that time to enhance my insight and depth of inquiry into what had preceded it.

I also engaged in the same form of research, albeit with less intensity and for the same purpose, into Giamatti's time as president of the National League and Commissioner of Baseball. The archivist and her staff at Cooperstown were supportive and patient with my inquiries and accommodated me thoughtfully during my visit to the "A. Bartlett Giamatti Research Center."

෨

My two editors, Marcy Gessel and Linda Stringer of Publications Professionals LLC, were diligent, persistent in the constancy of their reviews, and probing to ensure accuracy and consistency throughout the manuscript. The State University of New York Press warrants special praise. It embraced *Fearless*, subjected the manuscript to careful scrutiny, and provided the support necessary to give life to what I sought to capture in the subtitle: "The Battle for Fairness in America." I also had the benefit of candid readers who probed unreservedly and posed questions and observations of considerable value: Clifford and Pat Chieffo, Thomas Bolle and Anne Stubbs, Dr. Philip Piccigallo, and Anthony Riccio. I additionally benefited from a discussion about the content and anticipated response to *Fearless* with David Maraniss, whom I befriended during the theatrical production of *Lombardi*, inspired by his book *When Pride Still Mattered*. He was generous with his time and guidance. And then there was The Study at Yale, my "home" in New Haven, where I always felt welcomed and comfortable and where, for long periods of time, I was able to reflect on old and new research and form thoughts in moments of quietude.

In the end it was, as it always has been when matters of values and ethics are in play and judgment and responsibility are required, the love and guidance of my parents, Matthew and Celeste Proto, that came to the fore daily in researching and writing this book. They, like Bart Giamatti and the immigrants and migrants who entered New Haven, now seem larger to me in their courage and their intent to ensure, through civic duty and fairness, that their neighborhood and city were better than when they had entered and that their children and neighbors were educated formally and in life with values they had defined, not those others had insisted on. Though the responsibility for *Fearless* is mine, I'm grateful to them for giving me the persistence to ensure its completion.

NEIL THOMAS PROTO
Washington, DC, and New Haven, Connecticut
March 2019

NOTES

PROLOGUE

1. See photograph of Bartlett, Helen, and Peggy Walton on board the SS *Rex*; interviews with Elria Giamatti Ewing and David Ewing; author's review of Peggy Walton's photo album ("Property of M. C. Walton" in script, and "Junior Year, Italy, Met Babbo, Rex-ship"). The album begins in 1924 and ends in 1937. "Babbo" is an affectionate, model Italian name for "father"—Peggy was chronicling her life and her family's as wife, mother, and historian. Personal visit by author to Wakefield home in 2015.

2. The description of the SS *Rex* is derived from the "Blue Riband," the recognition award given to liners crossing the Atlantic according to speed, and a YouTube film of the SS *Rex*.

3. According to different ship manifests, New Haven Census forms in 1910, 1920, and 1930, various New Haven street and telephone directories, and public grammar school records, the name is listed as "Giammati," "Giamatto," "Giammatte" (1917–1918 Draft Registration Card), "Giammattei," and "Giamatti." When Valentine's parents died, their last name was listed as "Giammattei," which was their correct name when, after marriage, they departed Italy for America. See *New Haven Register*, April 29, 1940, death of "Maria Grazia Lavorgna Giammattei, wife of Angelo Giammattei." The family gravestone in St. Lawrence Cemetery in West Haven, Connecticut, reads, "Giamatti."

4. Anthony Riccio, "Going to School," in *The Italian American Experience in New Haven* (Albany: State University of New York Press, 2006), 42–51. Review of attendance records, Strong School (Fair Haven); interview with Celeste Proto (1990).

5. Letter, James Angell to Robert N. Corwin, January 6, 1933, Yale University Archives; see also Jerome Karabel, *The Chosen: The Hidden History of Admission and Exclusion at Harvard, Yale, and Princeton* (Boston: Houghton Mifflin, 2005), 119; Joseph A. Soares, *The Power of Privilege: Yale and America's Elite Colleges* (Stanford, CA: Stanford University Press, 2007), 26.

6. Interviews with Elria Giamatti Ewing and David Ewing.

7. Eulogy for Valentine John Giamatti, April 15, 1982.

CHAPTER 1

FROM ENGLAND TO AMERICA

The epigraph is from Mary Emma Woolley's speech, "The Relation of Educated Women to the Peace Movement," Carnegie Hall, New York (April 1907).

1. What also began to emerge in concrete form toward the end of Henry's reign in 1272 was the elementary formation of parliamentary government and the actual representation of other people's interests, yet another constraint on the conduct of government. It melded with other French, Italian, Scottish, and Native American experiences that tempered the formation of constitutional government. See, for example, Rousseau, Montesquieu (France), and Hume (Scotland) in Vernon Louis Parrington, *The Colonial Mind, 1620–1800*, vol. 1, *Main Currents in American Thought* (New York: Harcourt Brace Jovanovich, 1927), 236, 271, 273–356; John F. Kennedy, *A Nation of Immigrants* (London: Hamish Hamilton, 1964), 13–14; U.S. Congress Joint Resolution 175 (August 5, 1994); "Iroquois Constitution: A Forerunner to Colonists' Democratic Principles," *New York Times* (June 28, 1987); Gary Boyd Roberts, "Notable Kin: Yale, Its Presidents, and Kings, Part Three," *New England Ancestors* (Winter 2001): 40–41; Winston Churchill, *A History of the English-Speaking Peoples*, vol. 1 (New York: Dodd, Mead, 1956), 242–84.

2. Interview, ancestral charts, notes, and email exchanges with Helen ("Lennie") Moss Ogden (great-granddaughter of A. G. Walton), daughter of Elizabeth Walton (the older sister of Mary Walton Giamatti), and A. Bartlett Giamatti's cousin. The "white man par excellence" is from Madison Grant, *The Passing of the Great Race: Or, The Racial Basis of European History* (New York: Charles Scribner's Sons, 1916); see in particular "The Nordic Race," 75, and "The European Races in the Colonies," 80.

3. Ogden interview, ancestral charts, notes, and email exchanges.

4. Parrington, *Colonial Mind*, 14. See also Merle Curti, *The Growth of American Thought*, 3rd ed. (New York: Harper & Row, 1964), 29, 46, 107; Wilbert R. Shenk, "Introduction," in *North American Foreign Missions, 1810–1914: Theology, Theory, and Policy*, ed. Wilbert R. Shenk (Grand Rapids, MI: William B. Eerdmans, 2004), 3 (and related footnotes); David W. Kling, "The New Divinity and the Origins of the American Board of Commissioners for Foreign Missions," *Church History* 72, no. 4 (2003): 791–819; Neil Thomas Proto, *The Rights of My People: Liliuokalani's Enduring Battle with the United States, 1893–1917* (New York: Algora, 2009), 13–15 (and related endnotes), 15–21; Chris Lehmann, *The Money Cult: Capitalism, Christianity, and the Unmaking of the American Dream* (Brooklyn, NY: Melville House, 2016), 3–69; Christopher Lasch, *The True and Only Heaven* (New York: W. W. Norton, 1991), 52–63; Parrington, *Colonial Mind*, 122; Curti, *The Growth of American Thought*, 44. For a period of time (1925–1931), Curti taught at Smith, which still awards a prize in his honor. See also Wendy Warren, *New England Bound: Slavery and Colonization in Early America* (New York: Liveright, 2016) (African, Caribbean, and Indian slavery); Christopher Brown, "Puritan Guilt," *New York Times Sunday Book Review*, July 3, 2016, 18.

5. Parrington, *Colonial Mind*, 11.

6. It was, in part, out of this theological view that the notion of individual rights made its way, and not without argument from others, into the American dialogue and,

in time, the Bill of Rights, the first Amendments to the United States Constitution. Parrington, *Colonial Mind*, 60–62.

7. Anglo-Saxon naming patterns and the way heritage was recognized affected Peggy's own family. Ellen Maria Higgins married Nathaniel Jabez Bartlett. Their daughter, Mary Ellen Bartlett, married Arthur Gould Walton. Their son, Bartlett Walton, was born in 1884 in Wakefield, Massachusetts. Robert Parks Davidson married Jane Sarah Claybaugh, who had a son, James Davidson. John Holmes Burleigh married Matilda Buffum. Their daughter, Elizabeth Burleigh, married James Davidson. Together, they had a daughter, Helen Buffum Davidson, born in 1885 in South Berwick, Maine. The Anglo-Saxon manner allowed for last names to be easily interchangeable with first and middle names—making nicknames essential.

8. Ogden interview.

9. Ogden interview. A third "exception of consequence" existed: geographic. For a time—shortly after the American Revolution—New England was considered something in the nature of the center of the universe, civilized and cosmopolitan, especially by those who lived in its towns and cities. Coming from Kentucky or Ohio or Indiana carried little cachet, or confidence that character and heritage would be known. When James Davidson of the Ohio and Kentucky Davidsons proposed to marry Elizabeth Burleigh of South Berwick, the culture of geography was accommodated on the basis of James's merit and love of his wife. Education probably also mattered. James graduated from Bowdoin College in 1878. He likely met Elizabeth through her brother, Walter, also at Bowdoin. As explained, James and Elizabeth are Helen's parents and Peggy's grandparents.

10. Ogden interview with the author, as well as a detailed essay, "From Sea to the South," prepared by Rebecca H. Fernald (1973) as part of a Winter Study Project, Williams College, provided by Ogden for the author's use, and the author's personal visit to the Burleigh-Davidson home (now part of Berwick Academy).

11. Fernald, "From Sea to the South," 2.

12. During the voyage, when "the ship's officers abandoned the journey in order to prospect for gold, Matilda took on the cooking, and directed the crew until others could be hired." Fernald, "From Sea to the South," 4–5. Quincy Adams was ambassador to Russia and secretary of state to Presidents Madison and Monroe, respectively, who were "Democratic-Republican." William Burleigh, like Adams, was committed to a strong national government; a nation founded by individuals, not states; opposition to slavery; and opposition to states' claim to nationally owned lands.

13. Fernald, "From Sea to the South," 6–9.

14. Matilda and her children traveled from Glasgow, Scotland, through England and Western Europe, and back across the Atlantic. Fernald, "From Sea to the South," 17–18; "Report on the Formation of Children's Aid Society," Maine Senate, 67th Legislature, No. 110 (1893).

15. Fernald, "From Sea to the South," 18, 26. Elizabeth Davidson became president in 1903. See Old Berwick Historical Society (September 18, 2010); Fernald, "From Sea to the South," 26. See also "The Only Woman Bank President in New England," in *Brooklyn Daily Eagle*, May 19, 1907; *Richmond Planet* (Virginia), April 19, 1906; *Cumberland News* (British Columbia), July 4, 1906; and *Independent* (New Hampshire), February 11, 1903.

16. Interviews with David Ewing and Elria Giamatti Ewing.

CHAPTER 2
NEW ENGLAND

1. Most of Wakefield's land was purchased from the nearby Saugus Indians in a reportedly friendly transaction. The town was located ten miles north of Boston. It was Calvinist, then Congregationalist, in religion and proximate to the "Great Lake," Lake Quannapowitt, a source of recreation, aesthetic wonder, and fish. See "Wakefield, Massachusetts," Wakefield Historical Society (1994).

2. See "First Parish Church, Congregationalist Church, History since 1644," www.fpccwakefield.com.

3. Interview with Helen ("Lennie") Moss Ogden, who is A. G. Walton's great-granddaughter and Elizabeth Walton's daughter. See also Public Documents of Massachusetts, vol. 10 (1912). Wakefield's rural character and culture had changed dramatically in 1845 with the arrival of the Boston and Maine Railroad and the establishment—by Cyrus Wakefield—of large foundry and rattan (wicker) factories. In 1907, Walton's firm moved to the waterfront in Chelsea, on the edge of Boston, closer to water and rail traffic, and to the immigrant artisans and laborers who could now walk to work daily. From the outset, A. G. Walton & Co. employed one thousand to eighteen hundred operators and each day produced twelve thousand pairs of shoes, which were sold to retail outlets nationally through the efforts of sixty sales representatives. By 1911, the company printed its own catalogues, generated its own power and light, maintained its own machine repair shop, and established a second plant in Derry, New Hampshire, and subsidiary operations in Lawrence, Massachusetts; Bridgton, Maine; and Barnstead, New Hampshire.

4. In 1907, the Waltons purchased their grand home for comfortable family and community entertainment, a three-story Victorian house that overlooked Lake Quannapowitt. Arthur continued to purchase property throughout Wakefield, mindful, perhaps, of its enduring value commercially and as long-term security for his family. See Concetta Lake, "Chelsea under Fire: Urban Industrial Life, Crisis, and the Trajectory of Jewish and Latino Chelsea" (honors thesis, Boston College, 2011); *The Goodrich, A Monthly Magazine* (B.F. Goodrich, Akron, OH), vol. IV, no. 8 (April 1915), 21; Mark Sardella, "The Walton Family of Wakefield, Massachusetts," August 29, 2013, www.marksardella.wordpress.com.

5. They included mostly Russian and Eastern European Jews; Polish, Lithuanian, and recent Irish immigrants who lived in Chelsea; and Southern Italians, who came in from Boston's North End. See, for example, *Annual Report of the State Board of Conciliation and Arbitration for the Commonwealth of Massachusetts* (1912, vol. 10, 48, and 1917, 117–30); Chaim Rosenberg, *The Great Workshop: Boston's Victorian Age* (Portsmouth, NH: Arcadia, 2004), 152; Margaret Herman Clarke, *Chelsea in the 20th Century*, (Portsmouth, NH: Arcadia, 2004).

6. Strikes were often resolved by mutual concession and the mandatory intercession of the Massachusetts Arbitration and Mediation Board. See previous endnote and *Annual Report, State Board of Conciliation and Arbitration* (year ending December 31, 1916), Pub. Doc. 40, 122; *Chelsea Record* (August 18, 19, 21, 24, 25, and 29, 1916; September 8, 15, 21, 22, 23, 24, 25, 26, 27, 28, and 30, 1916; and October 3, 5, 17, 18, and 23, 1916). A. G. Walton & Co. had avoided any entanglements emerging from the strikes in 1908 and 1912 in Lawrence, and there is no indication it incurred the wrath and the sophisticated intellect of Carlo Tresca or the oratorical and organization skills of Elizabeth Gurley

Flynn in any of its labor relations. On many occasions, Walton granted concessions; on all occasions, the worker-operators seem to have won all or much of what they sought in terms of pay increases and equitable treatment, as those terms were then defined, including among those men and women who sought union affiliation or went out on strike.

7. "Four Highwaymen Get a Payroll of $28,444," *New York Times*, November 27, 1921. See also Sardella, "The Walton Family of Wakefield, Massachusetts."

8. The judge was Webster Thayer, the quintessential Boston Brahmin. His publicly prejudicial utterances, in and outside of the trial, should have disqualified him by any standard of judicial ethics. Within a few years, as the appeals, still tainted with the most overt bigotry, played out in vain in the courtroom and in the region's newspapers, Massachusetts Governor Alvan Fuller, a Republican, appointed a culturally and ideologically narrow Anglo-Saxon commission headed by Harvard President A. Lawrence Lowell to review the evidence and the judiciary's conduct. It was an exercise in malice, the kind of ill intent that would have placed Fuller somewhere between The Evil Counselors and The Sowers of Political Discord deep in Dante's *Inferno*. The outcome was both predictable and, as subsequent evidence showed, corrupt. A. Lawrence Lowell was the archetypal Calvinist in temperament; his anti-immigrant and anti-Semitic views were well known—his business connections and the imperative for quelling the aspirations of Italian and other immigrant artisans and the formation of labor unions, less so. His prejudgments independent of the evidence were recently uncovered as if they were revelation. See Stacy Jolna et al., "Harvard Documents on Sacco-Vanzetti Case May Fuel Controversy on Fairness Issue," *Washington Post* (February 1, 1978). Lowell was a widely recognized eugenicist and vice president of the Immigration Restriction League.

9. In a well-known reenactment of the Sacco and Vanzetti trial by the American Bar Association in 1996, with adherence to the elementary rules of evidence and proper prosecutorial and judicial conduct, it was the unanimous opinion of those involved—including the first Italian American U.S. attorney general, Benjamin Civiletti—that neither man should have been brought to trial. For a summary of the trial, see *American Bar Association Journal* (ABA) (October 1996): 120. Civiletti represented the defense. The video of the mock trial is in the author's possession. See also Richard Gambino, *Blood of My Blood, The Dilemma of the Italian-Americans* (Garden City, NY: Anchor Books/Doubleday, 1974), 119–23; Neil Thomas Proto, "Sacco and Vanzetti: An Unfinished American Injustice," *Italian America* (September 1996): 10–14; Proto, "Only Silence Is Shame: The 70th Anniversary of the Execution of Sacco and Vanzetti," *Italian America* (April 1997): 11–13; Proto, "Sacco and Vanzetti and the Italian Experience in America," Graduate Club, New Haven, Connecticut, February 19, 1999, reproduced along with other commentary and photographs in "The Enduring Meaning of Bartolomeo Vanzetti and Nicola Sacco within the Italian American Experience," www.saccovanzettiexperience .com. And see, generally, Theodore Grippo, *With Malice Aforethought: The Execution of Nicola Sacco and Bartolomeo Vanzetti* (Bloomington, IN: iUniverse, 2011). In the end, the commission and Fuller were a lesson in excess, feigned justice that, in time, was more an embarrassment than the calming placebo Fuller had hoped, undertaken as if naïveté reigned in *all* of Boston's neighborhoods, let alone globally where the commission was denounced. The entire trial and appeals, and the execution of both men in 1927, had a horrifying effect among Italian immigrants and Italian Americans: an enduring recognition of how fairness was defined and injustice determined in America and by whom. The

problem of prejudice directed against Italian immigrants actually was broader and deeper than many among them appreciated, at play here and elsewhere in the nation in the guise of eugenics. Its intellectual home in New England, the preeminent font for its legitimacy in law, education, culture, and commerce, was at Harvard and Yale.

10. During preparatory school and college, he traveled globally. He retained an active relationship with Harvard and his college friends. Harvard College, Class of 1904, *Secretary's Second Report* (1910); *Harvard Catalogue* (1904, 1908); Ogden interview.

11. Bartlett struggled periodically with medical issues throughout his life. Ogden interview.

12. *Shoe and Leather Reporter Directory*, annual (1919), 658.

13. Helen had spent summers as a child with her parents and mother's family (the Burleigh-Davidsons). Peggy and her sisters also enjoyed summer visits to Wianno Bay in Osterville, on the southern shore of Cape Cod, and to Camp Tahoma for Girls in Piermont, New Hampshire. Ogden interview; personal visit by author to York and review of family photographs. Bartlett Walton had a gracious personality and organizational acumen. He prospered from the family business and contributed to its growth and the quality of its commercial reputation. His father retained the helm, certainly in ownership control until, in gradual stages, his interests were sold off, along with much of his vast holdings of real property, to ensure considerable financial comfort for his son and others in the family. The Waltons readily endured the Great Depression.

14. Helen's three sisters, Elizabeth (Class of 1910), Marion (Class of 1912), and Mary (Class of 1916); their cousin, Dorothy Davidson (Class of 1919); and their Burleigh cousins, Clara (Class of 1904), Louise (Class of 1908), and Anita (Class of 1910). Ogden interview. The story of the "roadster/private school" choice came from Elria Giamatti Ewing.

15. Elizabeth (Betty) (Class of 1934) and Kathryn (Class of 1939). In addition were cousin Elizabeth (Class of 1939); cousin Deborah (Class of 1948); Alice's daughter, Jean (Class of 1936); Jean's daughter, Ann (Class of 1961); and Betty's daughter, Lennie (Class of 1963). Ogden interview.

16. William Allan Neilson, *Smith College: The First Seventy Years* (unpublished manuscript), ca. 1946 (with Harry Norman Gardiner, Professor of Philosophy at Smith). Neilson was Smith's second president, from 1917 to 1939. See also, Witold Rybczynski, *A Clearing in the Distance: Frederick Law Olmsted and North America in the Nineteenth Century* (New York: Scribner, 1999).

17. "Higher culture in the English language and literature, ancient and modern languages, mathematical and physical sciences, useful and fine arts . . . intellectual, moral, and aesthetic philosophy" were prescribed in Sophia Smith's will. She made her intention plain: "I would have the education suited to the mental and physical wants of women. It is not my design to render my sex any less feminine, but to develop as fully as may be the powers of womanhood, and furnish women with the means of usefulness, happiness, and honor now withheld from them." Though the school's emphasis was Christian, admission was "without giving any preference to any sect." Neilson, *Smith College*, 18–19. See also Art. III of Smith's will.

18. Dr. Peggy Ann Brown email to the author (from archivist, Smith College), June 30, 2015.

19. Neilson, *Smith College*, 58.

20. "In October, to Florence to continue linguistic preparation, followed by courses in language, literature, history, and art. . . . Using week ends for excursions to places of historic and artistic interest. From Perugia . . . Assisi, Orvieto, Todi, and other Umbrian towns, from Florence, Siena, Pisa, Arezzo, Revanna [sic], Venice, and San Marino. In the Christmas vacation . . . to the Dolomites for winter sports, and at Easter to Rome and Sicily." Neilson, *Smith College*, 58–59.

21. "Michele Cantrarella, Anti-Fascist Leader, 88," *New York Times* (January 23, 1988).

22. Neilson, *Smith College*, 59.

23. Borgese was born in Sicily in 1882. His cultural and political heritage also entwined with the Southern Italian embrace of Garibaldi's principles. Borgese taught at universities in Turin, Rome, and Milan. His journalism, politically based novels, and pedagogical skills were renowned. So, too, was his open challenge to the Mussolini regime. R. J. B. Bosworth, *Mussolini's Italy: Life under the Fascist Dictatorship, 1915–1945* (New York: Penguin Books, 2006), 25–27 (Salvemini). See also the introduction to Gaetano Salvemini, *Italian Fascist Activities in the United States* (New York: Center for Immigration Studies, 1977).

24. Ogden interview and notes.

25. Gaetana Marrone, ed., *Encyclopedia of Italian Literary Studies*, vol. I (New York: Routledge, 2007), 295–98. Borgese became an active member of the Mazzini Society, which was formed in 1939 by Gaetano Salvemini, in Northampton. Salvemini was born in Molfetta, in Southern Italy. Ogden interview and notes (2015 and May 4, 2016); Salvemini, *Italian Fascist Activities in the United States*, "Introduction."

CHAPTER 3
FROM SOUTHERN ITALY TO AMERICA

Epigraph is from Carlo Levi, *Christ Stopped at Eboli*, trans. Frances Frenaye (New York: Farrar, Straus, 1963), 139–40.

1. Christopher Hibbert, *Garibaldi and His Enemies: The Clash of Arms and Personalities in the Making of Italy* (Boston: Little Brown, 1966), 199–200, quoting from Alexandre Dumas, *On Board the "Emma": Adventures with Garibaldi's "Thousand" in Sicily*, trans. R. S. Garnett (London: D. Appleton, 1929), 39. Garibaldi had arrived in Genoa weeks earlier from his home on the island of Caprera, situated on the northeastern edge of Sardinia, governed by the Piedmontese Kingdom of Sardinia from its capital in Turin. Garibaldi received intelligence daily. The timing of departure from Genoa was critical.

2. Hibbert, *Garibaldi and His Enemies*, 193; Christopher Duggan, *The Force of Destiny: A History of Italy since 1796* (London: Allen Lane, 2007), 82–84, 169–70.

3. Hibbert, *Garibaldi and His Enemies*, 199.

4. "Neither pope nor king," Mazzini wrote, would free Italy. "Only God and the people will open the way of the future to us." Mazzini's admirers included abolitionist William Lloyd Garrison. In short order, Garibaldi's skill and usefulness would be discussed by Lincoln in light of the impending Civil War in the United States. Hibbert, *Garibaldi and His Enemies*, 199–200. See also Denis Mack Smith, *Modern Italy: A Political History*, University of Michigan Press: Ann Arbor (1997), 69–70.

5. David Gilmour, *The Pursuit of Italy: A History of a Land, Its Regions, and Their People*, Farrar, Straus and Giroux: New York (2011), chap. 8.

6. Duggan, *The Force of Destiny*, 244 (Garibaldi and Lincoln).

7. British and American ships nearby were sympathetic to the uprising and reported Garibaldi's movements. He was known and admired in the English-speaking world. His daring, as a strategist and relentless leader and fighter, was only confirmed in the Sicilian campaign. Gambino, *Blood of My Blood*, 52. Southern vitality dated to the intellectual and architectural flourishing during its governing relationships with Greece and the unity of the Roman Empire. Thomas Aquinas, from the village of Roccasecca, thrived in this milieu. People recalled eating, working, and living in harmony with others without fear.

8. "The [Southern] population are frantic in their demonstrations of joy," an English observer wrote. "All the men appear to be armed, and are joining." Six thousand farmers "with shot-guns, axes, and scythes" quickly augmented Garibaldi's force. Hibbert, *Garibaldi and His Enemies*, 266–67.

9. "The History of the San Lorenzello Legion," www.brigantaggio.net/Brigantaggio/Storia/Local/SLorenzello1.htm, translated into English by the linguist and cultural historian Anthony Riccio, New Haven, Connecticut (June 9, 2016).

10. Sharon Ouditt, "Introduction, The End of Europe," in *Impressions of Southern Italy: British Travel Writing from Henry Swinburne to Norman Douglas* (New York: Routledge, 2014), 5nn12–13 (online edition). See also note 19 in that chapter.

11. "Naples," Garibaldi said, "is in danger. We must go there today, at once, this minute." Garibaldi was cautioned not to enter Naples without thousands of his volunteers. He had no such apprehension. The Neapolitan troops remained cowed by the unusual presence and strength of the people's commitment to Garibaldi, to freedom, and, in all likelihood, to preservation of the city that would provide an essential thread to the future. Unexpectedly, Mazzini arrived in Naples. In Turin, alarm reigned. Cavour plotted Mazzini's capture and removal. Mazzini escaped, but not until his presence was well known and its purpose and his message applauded. Hibbert, *Garibaldi and His Enemies*, 277–80, 287, 297–301.

12. Garibaldi was at that time fifty-three years old and arthritic yet still "heedless of danger and miraculously impervious to it." When the first confrontation arose, he led the charge, bayonet fixed, unfazed by risk, intent on victory. Yet the Bourbon troops held firm, capable of a decisive thrust south if Garibaldi faltered. The principles of Mazzini and Garibaldi were deeply embedded in the people's confidence. The narrowness of the choices—Garibaldi contemplated and rejected a representative assembly to decide, and voting occurred in the presence of Garibaldi's troops—and the euphoria over seeming victory that would protect their families and villages took hold. Hibbert, *Garibaldi and His Enemies*, 298. Garibaldi's fateful decision to forgo an elected assembly is discussed in Hibbert and in Gambino, *Blood of My Blood*, 71–72. Garibaldi's trip to England in 1864, for "medical advice and to pay a debt of gratitude . . . to the English people," yielded gracious, warm receptions and on April 11, as he entered London on a special train, five hundred thousand people welcomed him. One observer wrote, "No sovereign from overseas was ever received by them as they received the Italian hero." Gilmour, *The Pursuit of Italy*, 341. His grand reception was occurring at precisely the time repression in the South was reaching its formal, and visible, completion.

13. Hibbert, *Garibaldi and His Enemies*, 288, 341.

14. Gilmour, *The Pursuit of Italy*, chap. 8; Gambino, *Blood of My Blood*, 52–56. My paternal grandfather, Thomas, who arrived in New Haven in 1914 (his family originated

in Ortona, on the Adriatic, and resettled in Basilicata), and his friends told my brother, Richard, and me about the "Northern Problem" and the harm it did in the South the way his father and uncles described it to him. For the American view of the appropriate "Italian" language, see, for example, Henry Wadsworth Longfellow, "A Review of a History of the Italian Language and Dialects (1825)," reprinted in *Dante in America: The First Two Centuries*, ed. A. Bartlett Giamatti (Binghamton, NY: State University of New York at Binghamton, 1983), 35–51.

15. Liberalism in the West was concerned primarily with unification. No analogue appeared within Western circles to the American Revolution, the defeat of the British, and the need for a new, truly national constitution and policies fit for growth and practical forms of ensuring unity. The intellectuals in both nations stood passively once they "discovered" the Renaissance; they believed it could be taught only in the language and appreciative culture of the North—though, actually, "Italian" was still a language in flux, an integration of dialects (including Sicilian) used by Dante, Petrarca, Boccaccio, and Machiavelli, and the language of Tuscany, not the "Italian" of the historically French-speaking Piedmont. As Henry Wadsworth Longfellow put it to broad acclaim, "the crude melody of the Sicilian" would not suffice. Gambino, *Blood of My Blood*, 55; Longfellow, "A Review," 35.

16. Smith, *Modern Italy*, 69–72 (emphasis added); Duggan, *The Force of Destiny*, 215–27, 228.

17. Gambino, *Blood of My Blood*, 52–53. See Duggan, *The Force of Destiny*, 228; also see Count Maffei, *Brigand Life in Italy: A History of Bourbonist Reaction* (London: Hurst and Blackett: London, 1865), 215–16, 257, for a documented description of the 1863 Pica law and Count Maffei's recitation of the government's rationale, based on the "patriotic" imperatives of "old Piedmont," for widespread summary executions throughout the South of what Maffei acknowledged to be "political brigandage." Maffei's account was published in England, part of the effort to revise and color the facts. Also reported, as set forth in Patrick Keyes O'Clery, *The Making of Italy* (London: Kegan Paul, Trench, Trübner, 1892), 305: "According to the Italian Journal *Il Commercio*," published on November 8, 1862, the Piedmontese—then the Italian army—"had sacked and burned the following towns: Guaricia (Molise), 1,322 dead, Campochiara (Molise), 979 dead, Casalduni (Molise), 3,032 dead, Pontelandolfo (Molise), 3,917 dead, Viesti (Capitanata), 5,417 dead, San Marco (Capitanata), 10,612 dead, Rignano (Capitanata), 1,814 dead, Venosa (Basilicata), 5,952 dead, Basil (Basilicata), 3,400 dead, Auletta (Principato Citeriore), 2,023 dead, Eboli (Principato Citeriore), 4,175 dead, Montifalcone (Principato Ulteriore), 2,618 dead, Montiverde (Principato Ulteriore), 1,988 dead, Vico (Terra di Lavoro), 730 dead, Controne (Calabria Ulteriore II), 1,089 dead, Spinello (Calabria Ulteriore II), 298 dead." This listing—forty-nine thousand dead—occurred *before* the imposition of martial law. The areas in parentheses are the regions where the towns were located. See, also, David Halberstam, *The Best and the Brightest* (New York: Random House, 1972) (Rostow was ". . . particularly irritating—this verbose, theoretical man who intended to make all his theories work," 43; McGeorge Bundy could not "resist a put-down . . . and, at times, there seemed to be a certain cruelty about him, the rich, bright kid putting down the inferior," 45; "using power in the private elitist sense," 54; "They are linked to one another rather than to the country; in their minds they become responsible for the country but not responsive to it," 60; William Bundy, "more the snob and more arrogant," 394.)

18. Gambino, *Blood of My Blood*, 52–53; Duggan, *The Force of Destiny*, 228; Riccio, *The Italian American Experience in New Haven*, 2. The 1893 law, which imposed martial law on the South, was titled *Legge Pica*, named after a legislator who represented an area adjacent to Rome.

19. The South, it was determined, should be compelled to pay the cost incurred by the North in executing the war, really the cost of the audacity to engage in insurrection against the Bourbons and, later, the Piedmontese. A lesson must be taught. The men in Garibaldi's army were ignored, treated like rebels, many jailed or worse. It only increased Southern animosity. Members of the Bourbon military were welcomed into the new "Italian" army, with old scores to settle. Gambino, *Blood of My Blood*, 54–57.

20. See, Ouditt, *Impressions of Southern Italy*, "Introduction, The End of Europe," 5nn12–13 (online edition); Desmond Seward and Susan Mountgarret, *Old Puglia: A Portrait of South Eastern Italy* (London: Haus Publishing, 2009), 395–97; *Reactionary Enlightenment* (blog), July 25, 2015, www.reactionary-enlightenment.tumblr.com; "Historical Perspective of a Hidden Genocide," *Neapolitan Independentism* (blog), May 25, 2011, www.neapolitan-independentism.blogspot.com/2011/05/historical-perspective-of-hidden.html; and internal sources. In some settings, including the British and Italian Parliament, the North's conduct was confronted rhetorically to no practical effect, the official record of dissent in Italy—including by Deputy Francesco Proto—apparently erased. In 1863, during debate in the British Parliament, Benjamin Disraeli raised questions concerning the North's invasion to no effect. Another member, Cavendish Bentinck, said the new Italy was in "a civil war, a spontaneous popular movement against foreign occupation." O'Clery, *The Making of Italy*, 294. And see *Official Parliament Debate*, May 8, 1863, 103–104. Deputy Francesco Proto of Naples introduced a motion to require an investigation of the occupying army's repressive conduct; the parliamentary leadership would not allow it and erased the record of its submission. Prior to confiscation of Naples' gold, Piedmont's reserves approximated twenty-seven million lire in gold.

21. Gambino, *Blood of My Blood*, 52–54; Duggan, *The Force of Destiny*, 254–55; Sandra Benjamin, *Sicily: Three Thousand Years of Human History* (Hanover, NH: Steerforth Press, 2006), 323–26.

22. "The peasants . . . were indifferent to the conquest of Abyssinia [by Mussolini in 1935]," Carlo Levi wrote, "and they neither remembered the [Second] World War [, though fought largely on southern soil,] nor spoke of its dead, but one war was close to their hearts and constantly on their tongues: This was the war of the brigands. . . . All of them spoke of it with as much passion as if it were only yesterday. . . . Many places . . . were named for their deeds. And . . . they are not boasting. . . . They have gentle hearts and patient souls . . . and the overbearing power of fate. But when, after infinite endurance, they are shaken to the depths of their being and are driven by an instinct of self-defense or justice, their revolt knows no bounds and no measure." Levi, *Christ Stopped at Eboli*, 139–40. See also Hibbert, *Garibaldi and His Enemies*, 273 (When Garibaldi entered Eboli, "the entire population, so it seemed, was in the streets").

23. Gambino, *Blood of My Blood*, 74–75, 84–86 (Gambino's grandparents' description).

24. Gilmour, *The Pursuit of Italy*, chap. 8.

25. Donna R. Gabaccia, *Italy's Many Diasporas* (New York: Routledge, 2000), 51; Gilmour, *The Pursuit of Italy*, chap. 7, 176, etc., n10.

26. Duggan, *The Force of Destiny*, 293–97.

27. Benjamin, *Sicily*, 326; Riccio, *The Italian American Experience in New Haven*, 1, quoting Booker T. Washington's *The Man Farthest Down: A Record of Observation and Study in Europe* (Garden City, NY: Doubleday, Page, 1912).

28. Javier Lavina and Michael Zeuske, eds., *The Second Slavery: Mass Slaveries and Modernity in the Americas and in the Atlantic Basin* (Berlin: LIT Verlag, 2014), 85–89; Jennifer Guglielmo, *Living the Revolution: Italian Women's Resistance and Radicalism in New York City, 1890–1945* (Chapel Hill: University of North Carolina Press, 2010), 32–35.

CHAPTER 4

THE CHOICE

1. San Lorenzello's dense stone interior, three stories high in places, housed artisans and families, open markets, communal societies, and Saint Lawrence Martyr Church, all connected by walkways ingeniously constructed in stone to ensure easy passage. Working farms surrounded the town. Along the Titerno were the clay pits used to craft tile and pottery that decorated homes in the region and formed one thread of the aesthetic skill its residents brought to America. The mayor of San Lorenzello in 2019 was Antimo Lavorgna; interview with Dolph Santello (born in New Haven).

2. Guglielmo, *Living the Revolution*, 10–43.

3. Gambino, *Blood of My Blood*, 118.

4. "Citizens Plead Necessity for White Supremacy," (New Orleans) *Times Democrat*, July 25, 1899. See also, Jessica Barbata Jackson, "The 'Privileged Dago'?: Race, Citizenship and Sicilians in the Jim Crow Gulf South, 1870–1924" (PhD diss., history, University of California–Santa Cruz, 2017), 117n25.

5. These Italian immigrants, arrested for their looks (the only people arrested were Italian) and their envied success in commerce, were dragged from prison in broad daylight and murdered viciously—hung, shot, bludgeoned while hanging from a scaffold—by a mob (described as New Orleans' "best elements" among its citizenry) discontented after a jury of their peers, following a full trial, refused to find those tried guilty of any crime. The *Register* also editorialized that these "professionals and merchants" had "felt it their duty to stamp out imported customs dangerous to the security of their homes and their families"—which, at the time, included virulent, extralegal (and legal) repression of African Americans through the same assumptions and mentality. Richard Gambino, *Vendetta: A True Story of the Worst Lynching in America, the Mass Murder of Italian-Americans in New Orleans in 1891, the Vicious Motivations behind It, and the Tragic Repercussions That Linger to This Day* (Garden City, NY: Doubleday, 1977). Gambino summarized what was to come: "In July 1901, Italians were attacked by a mob in Mississippi. In 1906, a mob in West Virginia killed several Italians and maimed several others. Italians were attacked in Tampa, Florida, in 1910. In that same year an Italian was pulled from a jail in Willisville, Illinois, and shot to death. Another Italian met the same fate in 1911. . . . Bigoted Americans responded to the incitement of people like [Henry Cabot] Lodge. In August 1920, mobs invaded the Italian neighborhood of West Frankfort, Illinois, dragging people of all ages and both sexes from homes, beating them with weapons and burning whole rows of their homes. The attacks were repeated, and the Italians fought back, turning the small neighborhood into a battleground. It took five hundred state troopers to

end the fighting. At its end, hundreds of Italian-Americans were left homeless." Gambino, *Blood of My Blood*, 120–22.

6. Italian Americans used existing and newly formed community and national groups to protest the wrongdoing. The Italian community of Beaumont, Texas, which was "threaten[ed] with violence," wrote to its citizens through the community newspaper, *L'Italo Americano*: "Countrymen, the moderation which you have displayed upon this occasion shows to the world that to the Italians by right belongs the title of the leaders of civilization. Continuing thus our elevated course, respecting the law which they have trampled upon, our own enemies will at last recognize our own superiority in this respect. . . . Supremacy of the law must be our motto and the only aim of our desire." Peter Vellon, "Black, White, or In Between?," *Ambassador* (NIAF) (Fall 2000): 10; Gambino, *Blood of My Blood*, 118–19; "A Review of the Lynching," *New York Times*, March 22, 1891; *New Haven Register*, "Hennessy Is Avenged," March 14,1891, 1.

7. Riccio, *The Italian American Experience in New Haven*, 10–18. My mother emigrated in 1916, at six years old, with her mother to meet her father and brother, also living in Fair Haven. She described the stench in steerage, how incapacitated my grandmother was from seasickness, and the moments of fresh air she found during the day when playing with others on deck. See also Guglielmo, *Living the Revolution*, 10–43.

8. John Dos Passos, *Facing the Chair: Story of the Americanization of Two Foreign Born Workmen* (Boston: Sacco and Vanzetti Defense Committee, 1927).

9. Gambino, *Blood of My Blood*, 50–51, 85. See also Duggan, *The Force of Destiny*, 267–70. Gambino captured one source: "Reflecting the Pope's hostility to Italian unification, the Papal Nuncio called the [Neapolitan and Sicilian] guerilla 'more abominable than the Arab and barbarian invaders.' It was a double insult, for the people of the [South] are descendants of both indigenous ancestors and the many invaders who were absorbed into the population, including Arabs."

10. Richard Gambino described it: "As it had always been, it was up to them alone to solve their problems. It began with many decisions by many individual families. . . . Each family decided which of its members were to leave, where they were to go, how, and for what aims." Gambino, *Blood of My Blood*, 75–76.

11. The 1900 (Twelfth) Census of the United States, Schedule No. 1, Population (June 6, 1900), New Haven Township. See also the 1920 and 1930 censuses. The men who earned money and returned to Italy have been characterized, pejoratively, as "Birds of Passage." For many of these pioneers (hardly unique to Italian immigrants), their purpose also was to gather and convey intelligence so that families could make solid, intuitive choices. Such a characterization might more aptly apply to, for example, Winston Churchill, who came as a private citizen to make money and to promote his books. My mother's great-uncle came to America in the 1870s, from Ortona, on the Adriatic coast, and returned with what was understood as knowledge of where to go and why. It would be another generation before my grandfather, then living in Basilicata, left with one son to make the journey to New York, then New Haven. Using his skills as a carpenter to find financial stability in New Haven, my grandfather then was joined two years later by his wife and children, including my mother.

12. The 1900 (Twelfth) Census, New Haven Township. See also the 1910, 1920, and 1930 censuses.

13. The stature of parents and grandparents solidified because of their courage and

risk taking. Only over time did their children and grandchildren understand and appreciate that determination to prosper in a new nation despite the roughness of the reception the younger generations did not always have to endure. Interviews with the Hon. Guido Calabresi and Santello; see also A. Bartlett Giamatti, "Commentary" in *The Italian Americans*, ed. Allon Schoener (New York: Macmillan, 1987).

14. Italians from the South—already exposed to the cultures, rule, and architecture of Spain, France, Eastern Africa, Greece, and the Roman Empire; historic trade with the peoples of Africa; and the regular intrusion, sometimes welcomed and sometimes not, of church officials and priests from Rome—migrated to South America, Canada, Africa, elsewhere in Europe, and the United States. See Giamatti, "Commentary," on the expectation of the "inevitability of hard work"; Gambino, *Blood of My Blood*, 87. See also Anthony V. Riccio, *From Italy to the North End* (Albany: State University of New York Press, 2017).

15. Martin Collier, *Italian Unification, 1820–1871* (Oxford, UK: Heinemann Educational Publishers, 2003), 75–78; Gambino, *Blood of My Blood*, 87; Jane Jacobs, "Introduction" in *The Death and Life of Great American Cities* (New York: Random House, 1992, originally published in 1961). For further affirmation and a more detailed analysis of the North End's culture and the imperative for community preservation, see also Anthony V. Riccio, *Boston's North End: Images and Recollections of an Italian American Neighborhood* (Guilford, CT: Globe Pequot Press, 2006). The Southern Italian *la pieta,* "a compelling obligation" to the poor, was made more essential in America. Phyllis H. Williams, "Care of the Aged and Other Dependents," in *South Italian Folkways in Europe and America: A Handbook for Social Workers, Visiting Nurses, School Teachers, and Physicians* (New Haven, CT: Yale Institute of Human Relations, 1938), 183.

16. New Haven Directory (1902); interview with Elria Giamatti Ewing, in which she recollected the fine tools that Angelo used, later owned by her father; author's review of New Haven Clock Company records (New Haven Museum and Historical Society archives); interview with various American-made clock antique dealers; 1910 census; U.S. Registration Card, (April 12, 1918) (according to the 1910 census, Angelo was naturalized as a citizen of the United States. The 1930 census indicates that Maria was naturalized as well). See also comments of Philip Paolella Sr. (b. 1915 in New Haven, CT, d. 2009) in "Conversation for Bart," Yale Manuscripts and Archives, Yale University Library, RV 411, Box 1U (1990). The two- and three-family house with space for renters brought Angelo further financial stability. A family friend seeking a loan to start a new business turned to Angelo, who shared his recognized creditworthiness by guaranteeing the loan repayment with the newly formed Italian American bank. He'd also "find rents and buildings for his fellow compatriots" who sought places for neighborhood business ventures and to settle newly arrived friends and relatives in Wooster Square and Fair Haven.

17. Interview with Santello. Those skills, and others alluded to throughout this work, were widely shared among Southern Italian women. Guglielmo, *Living the Revolution* (women and migration culture).

18. While Angelo was in New Haven, the Giammatteis moved to Telese, an ancient, once-walled city located near the confluence of the Volturno and Calore rivers and well known for its medieval structures, thermal bath works, and crafts. Telese is a few miles southwest of San Lorenzello; it is likely the Giammatteis took Concetta to San Lorenzello for the wedding. See ship manifest, SS *Perugia*, certified on May 5, 1905; interview with Santello (the Giammattei family move to Telese). I visited Telese in 2006.

19. Concetta was married to Raeffaele (Ralph) Giammattei (unrelated). Ralph arrived in New Haven in 1885, at three years old, with his parents from the nearby village of Faicchio. The couple lived on Poplar Street, and then moved to Main Street in Fair Haven. Angelo's brother, Francesco, married Italian-born Concetta Mary Codianne in 1902 and lived on Franklin Street, also in Fair Haven, with the last name Giamatto. Maria Grazia's brother, Antonio, was married in 1910. Interview with Santello.

CHAPTER 5

THE NEW HAVEN THEY ENTERED

Epigraph is from Dr. Anthony Stephen Fauci's acceptance speech, Sons of Italy Foundation Humanitarian Award, May 2016.

1. Rob Gurwitt, "Death of a Neighborhood," *Mother Jones*, September/October 2000 (Oak Street); Riccio, *The Italian American Experience in New Haven*, 349 (life in the Wooster Square neighborhood).

2. See, for example, U.S. Census Bureau (New Haven), 1910, 1920, 1930, and 1940; Riccio, *The Italian American Experience in New Haven*, 19–22, and 19n5.

3. The halls were often constructed and painted (murals as well as exterior) by immigrants, and funds for construction were raised through community events without regard for the religious beliefs or race of those attending. In public schools, where most of the teachers and virtually all of the principals were Anglo-Saxon or Irish, the "Lord's Prayer" was the Protestant rendition, said daily until prayer was no longer recited in public schools. Riccio, *The Italian American Experience in New Haven*, 383 (Fair Haven); interview with Calabresi (public school prayer) affirmed by the author's own experience in New Haven public schools; Jacobs, *The Death and Life of Great American Cities*, 35.

4. Italian immigrants also moved to New Haven's outer limits often to farm, to raise animals, and to perfect entrepreneurial skills they had developed in their region's economy. If a small parcel of land was available in a back or side yard or could be rented even at a distance from their homes, they planted vegetables to provide inexpensive family meals (the so-called Mediterranean Diet) and to distribute to neighbors in need as gifts or as barter for services. Typically, they planted escarole, tomatoes, corn, and beans; cultivated small grape arbors; and grew herbs—basil, garlic, oregano, thyme—to accompany basic staples such as macaroni and sweet potatoes. See Anthony V. Riccio, *Farms, Factories, and Families: Italian American Women of Connecticut* (Albany: State University of New York Press, 2014), 191; Gurwitt, "Death of a Neighborhood" (Oak Street); Riccio, *The Italian American Experience in New Haven*, 369–73 (life in the Hill neighborhood). My grandparents, who lived on Clay Street a few blocks from the Giammatteis in Fair Haven, grew corn, tomatoes, and various herbs in their side yard for medicinal purposes and food preparation. They also rented a parcel of land in the rural, eastern portion of New Haven, easily accessible by trolley, for the same purpose.

5. Informal interview with Roberta Maresca Sansone (born in 1938; her family owned the Maresca & Sons Funeral Home on Chapel Street, founded in 1888, which still stands); informal interview with Rosemarie Foglia Lemley (her father's regular walk from Wooster Square to the Hill neighborhood for pastries). My grandfather was among the founders of the Santa Maria Magdalena Society in Wooster Square. See also, *Plan for New Haven, 1910*, 16 (physical conditions) ("The dependence of the people upon street

railway facilities has already become almost as complete as in the greatest of centers of populations, as shown by the fact that, in the year 1907, the number of street railway passengers in New Haven reached a total of 31,599,453—about 243 rides per capita.") A considerable amount of interaction occurred among people and places in all three neighborhoods and other areas of New Haven and the surrounding countryside.

6. Simone's work moved his son (and dutiful apprentice) to say, "I can imagine Michelangelo doing something like that on the scaffolding." So, too, could his neighbors: the ancient churches, with fine statutes, delicate carvings, Renaissance-inspired ceilings, and glasswork were the social as well as the religious center of the Neapolitan villages, including San Lorenzello, Amalfi, and Atrani. In those villages, as in New Haven, local artists restored or created anew the models of painters from Caravaggio to Michelangelo or, often, their own imaginative characterization of saints especially revered by Southern Italians. Riccio, *The Italian American Experience in New Haven*, 246–57.

7. Riccio, *The Italian American Experience in New Haven*, 22, 249–57; Branford Electric Railway Association, *New Haven Streetcars* (Charleston, SC: Arcadia, 2003) (Grand and Chapel streets, and their geographic range and intersection); interview with Rose Sansone (in Riccio, *The Italian American Experience in New Haven*, 390–91). She is my aunt. As a young girl, she confronted the sign in the entranceway to Saint Francis that singled out her and her brother, Matthew (my father), for exclusion; interview with James and Roberta Sansone (story of our fathers as young boys); interview with Rosemary Foglia Lemley (school usage for performing plays and her father's experience listening to and singing opera, affirmed by James Sansone's father's experience of performing regular opera renditions to neighbors).

8. The midwife was Antonetta Brocale, who signed the birth certificate. Val was baptized on March 4, 1911, at Saint Michael's Church in Wooster Square, likely with family friends and a large and still-growing extended family in attendance, along with his godparents, Paschal Veringia and Michelina Frenza. Baptism Register, Hartford Diocese, 1911, of Valentine Giamatti; Birth Certificate, State of Connecticut, February 9, 1911, Office of the Registrar, New Haven, CT. "Americo" was the spelling used later by Val. My mother, born in Italy, named her children Neil, Richard, and Diana, each name a departure from family antecedents, though we all emerged with family-derived middle names, as did Valentine Giovanni (John) Giamatti. My father was born in June 1912, on Clay Street, only a few blocks from the Giammatteis. As I learned unexpectedly when I introduced Bart to my parents at an informal gathering before a civic event, our parents had played together as children and our grandparents knew each other.

9. The family attended Saint Donato's Church once it was constructed. They did not attend services in Saint Francis Church, despite its proximity on upper Ferry Street. Italian immigrants and Italian-language priests were not allowed upstairs in the Irish Catholic sanctuary.

10. New Haven Public Schools, Teacher's Daily Record of Attendance, 1917 through 1925, Heritage Ethnic Center, Southern Connecticut State University; interview with Dino Giamatti. Val would have recognized easily by then the allegory: the use of the rough maneuver, fraught with hidden meaning—envy, fear, the need for acceptance.

11. The school was named after Horace Strong, a former member of the Board of Education. The school, still standing, was about a six-block walk from Strong's home. Ferry Street and the surrounding neighborhood were mixed ethnically (Irish, Polish,

English, and German names appear on school attendance and nearby residential census records and in the 1910 and 1920 United States Census); interview with Roberta Maresca Sansone (her father's treatment in school); see also Riccio, *Farms, Factories, and Families*, 143 (ridiculed and slapped by Irish teacher). My mother and her friends who attended Hamilton Street School (which was operated under contract with New Haven by Catholic nuns) were subjected to the commonplace use of the ruler to deter the use of Italian or to ridicule dress. My father, who attended Strong and Clinton Avenue Schools, was ridiculed, along with his friends, for occasionally speaking Neapolitan. Both retained their knowledge of various dialects in order to speak with neighbors, friends, and relatives. Sadly, the harshness of their experience was typical and led to a loss of the dialects. See Riccio, *The Italian American Experience in New Haven*, 279 (vanishing dialects). Unlike Maria Giammattei, my maternal grandmother learned English. My grandfather, like Angelo, learned it before and during the first year of his arrival. See also Riccio, *The Italian American Experience in New Haven*, "In Loco Parentis," 48; interview with Calabresi (". . . be like us."). I attended Strong School for three years, walking daily with my brother, Richard, along walkways that Val, Americo, and their sisters would have walked.

12. Joseph DiCerbo, Val's first cousin (and a former seminarian before he emigrated with his parents to live briefly with the Giammatteis), told his daughter that "he admired [Val's] intelligence . . . [He] always had a book in his hand" and when DiCerbo went looking for him, "he would be curled up somewhere reading." Because of Joseph's education, Val had the opportunity to hear and appreciate another language he also heard regularly at church: Latin. In this same context, Val had the benefit of knowing the Italian culture, its history, its literature, varying ways of thinking about words and phrases, the intent of linguistic emphasis, and the related use and vitality of gestures. See Hillhouse High School Yearbook (1928) (Val's description of his interests); excerpt from email by Joseph DiCerbo's daughter, Carol Ann DiCerbo Carbutti, to John Manzi (December 9, 2016), included here with Mr. Manzi's and Mrs. Carbutti's permission.

13. The daylong gathering (the "outing") was usually held in wooded or rural settings. The men were rarely without suits and collared shirts, the women were always in dresses, and everyone contributed simple food or threadbare hand-me-down equipment for bocce, horseshoes, softball, and cards. The gatherings went on with walks, conversation, barbeque, and plates of macaroni, and, in time, the fried dough apizza. Riccio, *The Italian American Experience in New Haven*, 226 (Italian societies); 227, 245 (sports stories); and 221–45 (the industrial leagues and Waterside Park). My father played basketball and softball with the National Folding Box Company, Fair Haven, teams from the late 1920s through the 1940s (see "Close Finishes in D Division Clashes," *New Haven Register*, January 8, 1942, box score). New Haven Clock Company records and photographs (outings and sports teams), New Haven Museum and Historical Society, New Haven, Connecticut. My grandmother, mother, and their neighbors organized a stand at an annual fundraiser for St. Donato's Church, held in a field nearby. A small fire was built to bring the olive oil to a boil in two or three large black vessels and to ensure the tomato sauce was at a constant simmer. My grandparents, whom we lived with for almost seven years (barely a generation later, and only a few blocks distant from the Giammattei home on Ferry Street), and my mother together with other young women gave life to the fried dough apizza with marinara sauce, grated cheese, and fresh oregano at the St. Donato's benefit two blocks from their home, then on Lombard Street.

14. Ponselle's family emigrated from the Volturno Valley, where the South's Garibaldi-led army confronted the Bourbons. Mary Jane Phillips-Matz, *Rosa Ponselle: American Diva* (Boston: Northeastern University Press, 1997), 6–7, 79–80, 167, 280–85. Dr. Verdi and Sylvester Poli were long-time acquaintances of Ms. Ponselle. Two other Italian friends also lent financial and professional encouragement: James Ceriani and Sebastian Conte. Today, a full-body painting of Ponselle hangs in the foyer of the Baltimore Civic Opera House, where she once served as director. In New York's Times Square, on 46th Street, is the recently restored statute of Ponselle, along with Mary Pickford, Marilyn Miller, and Ethel Barrymore.

15. The Circolo del Sannio, organized by former residents of Cerreto Sannita, which is near San Lorenzello, was founded in 1897 in the Hill/Oak Street/Legion Avenue neighborhood. Riccio, *The Italian American Experience in New Haven*, 246–57 (artists and singers), 292 (life in the Legion Avenue neighborhood), 368 (life in the Hill neighborhood), 225–26 (Italian societies); interview with Calabresi; comments by Philip Paolello, "A Conversation for Bart," recording, Yale University archives ("I had the privilege of knowing Angelo . . ."; Angelo's creditworthiness and high standing with the banker in co-signing a mortgage for his father's business venture); interview and note, John Manzi (December 7, 2016). Angelo's grandfather, Nicolas DiCerbo (also from San Lorenzello), who married Maria Giuseppe Lavorgna (Maria Grazia's sister), stayed with his two children (including John's mother, Angella) in the Giammattei home on Ferry Street in 1917 and 1918, until Nicolas settled (he was employed at the New Haven Clock Company) and his wife and other children came to New Haven. Val was seven years old. Eventually they settled in a two-family house on Pearl Street in New Haven, where John's parents moved and he was raised. With respect to Angelo and Maria's communal role: "Newly arrived immigrants learned helpful ways to make the sudden transition . . . to an urban, fast-paced way of life from more experienced compatriots who spoke the same language and understood their needs." Riccio, *The Italian American Experience in New Haven*, 225–26. The Giammatteis had friends from San Lorenzello and nearby Campania towns who lived in Fair Haven and the Hill/Oak Street/Legion Avenue neighborhoods. Angelo, given his arrival in 1896 and range of experience in real estate, employment, and housing in different neighborhoods, and his recognized creditworthiness in borrowing money, would have been among the people who provided guidance, and he and Maria temporarily housed newly arrived family friends who needed stability and guidance until they got settled.

16. See Alexis de Tocqueville, *Democracy in America* (New York: Mentor Books, 1956), 198–202.

17. Riccio, *The Italian American Experience in New Haven*, 254 ("Here in New Haven you couldn't get work unless you were Irish or your name didn't end in a vowel. It was sad. . . . And there were jobs. . . . We all lived together but we couldn't work together"); "You Couldn't Get a Job," 112 ("My sister graduated from Hillhouse [New Haven] High School. The Water Company, the United Illuminating Company, and the New Haven Gas Company used to give three top students in the class a job. When it came to my sister's graduation—she was one of the top three [academic students] in her [Hillhouse] class—she didn't get the job because her name was Barone. Italian people couldn't get jobs. Italian people couldn't go to be a fireman. Italian people couldn't go be a policeman"); "Shining the Shoes," 115 ("We shined shoes in the cold, cold weather on the

corner of Chapel and High Street. Our hands were frozen, me and my brothers. . . . A big Dartmouth student with a cigar in his mouth . . . said, "give me a shine you guinea bastards").

18. Riccio, *The Italian American Experience in New Haven*, 86–87 (including a proverb from my grandfather, Cristoforo Proto, told by my aunt, Rose Sansone).

19. To give more context to Poli's letter: "I have often been pained, as have others of my deserving countrymen, at the persistency with which the reports of offenses against the law committed by men or women of the Italian race are embellished with the announcement that the offender is an Italian . . . How rarely do we read the newspaper description of a crime committed by John Jones, an American, James Blank, an Englishman, or Paul Dash, a Frenchman. . . . Why then this insidious distinction against the Italian?" This discrimination, Poli wrote, "is an unfair reflection of a people, the great overwhelming majority of whom are [an] industrious, peaceful, law abiding element of this and other American communities." It is "a fact . . . that the constant repetition . . . does tend to degrade [Italians] in the eyes of their fellow-citizens." In 1926, when the Augusta Lewis Troup School in New Haven was dedicated, one of the speakers was "Mrs. Sylvester Z. Poli . . . who was a close friend of Mrs. Troup. In presenting a Carrara marble bust of Mrs. Troup, created by the local sculpture, Ferbo Ferrarri," Mrs. Poli said, "No school could have a better patron saint. . . . I feel now that this noble and saintly woman is with us in spirit. I feel her presence pervading this occasion. . . . I am sure that the destiny of the school is to be a noble one in every respect." See Joan Cavanagh, *Augusta Lewis Troup: Worker, Activist, Advocate* (New Haven, CT: Greater New Haven Labor History Association, 2008) (with an introduction by Bill Berndtson); "Augusta Troup Gets Her Due," *New Haven Independent*, November 4, 2013; "S. Z. Poli on the Use of the Word, Italian," *New Haven Evening Register*, July 6, 1910, 1, 10; "New Haven Road to Get Rid of Italian Help," *New Haven Evening Register*, June 6, 1907 (Italian workers seeking a pay increase from the New York, New Haven, and Hartford Railroad, including the threat of a strike to get it); Neil Hogan, with Joan Cavanagh, Debbie Elkin, and Mary Johnson, *Moments in New Haven Labor History* (New Haven, CT: Greater New Haven Labor History Association, 2004), "Sargent Strike Marked Presence of Italians," 36–37 and endnotes. A concern similar to that expressed by Sylvester Poli was expressed in 1903 by Paul Russo in "Italians as American Citizens," *Literary Digest*, September 19, 1903, 346 (interview with New Haven attorney and Italian language daily newspaper founder Paul Russo).

20. Riccio, *The Italian American Experience in New Haven*, 111 ("To Save Ten Cents"); interview with Santello; New Haven Clock Company records, New Haven Colonial and Historical Society, New Haven; interview notes with Sam Perry, antique clock historian (Wales, England, and owner of period clocks from Connecticut, 2016); 1930 New Haven census (identifying Angelo Giammattei's occupation).

21. Interview with Riccio ("It was the women who saved the money. They had the toughness to manage"); Guglielmo, *Living the Revolution*, 1–109. (Women had managed households and earned income in Southern Italy, especially while their husbands endured the daily uncertainties of work on distant farms or were abroad earning money.) New Haven Clock, where Angelo worked, required strict dress codes and special care with hygiene, workspace cleanliness, and management of dust. Angelo wore a dress shirt, collar, and tie daily; his skill improved until in short order he assumed responsibility for

quality control and the technical adjustment of clocks and watches to fit the company's standards. New Haven Clock shipped its merchandise throughout the United States and globally. Its reputation was shared with its employees in regular newsletters and bulletins. Angelo had a responsibility to preserve the company's reputation. One additional virtue of his artisan craft: the family could, and did, avoid the commonplace disability and cost of an industrial accident. Maria also shared skills with Angelo: managing property; renting space; understanding the full meaning and use of a mortgage, including as an investment; and, of necessity and likely through her husband (who spoke and wrote English), dealing with municipal officials and lawyers on the related transactions and compliance with applicable ordinances. The Giammatteis did not accumulate financial comfort and, in time, they confronted serious uncertainties during the Depression, but like many other Italian immigrants in New Haven, the basic, steady rules of living were set and embedded in the lives of their children.

22. Studley published an "Open Letter" in the *New Haven Evening Register* that proposed the appointment of a committee that would "employ experts to prepare a plan for the improvement of New Haven." Rollin Woodruff, Republican governor of Connecticut and a resident of New Haven, chaired the committee. *Plan for New Haven 1910* (facsimile edition), preface by Yale Architectural Historian Vincent Scully, introduction by Alan J. Plattus, afterword by Yale Professor Douglas W. Rae (San Antonio, TX: Trinity University Press, 2012), 3. Yale graduates or affiliates on the committee included Studley, George Seymour (honorary degree, 1913), George Watrous (Yale Law 1897), William Farnam (Yale 1866), Frederick Grave, James Moran (Yale Law 1884), Harry Day (graduate and Corporation member), Anson Phelps Stokes Jr., and Henry H. Townshend (Yale 1897). Max Adler, another member, was a Bavaria-born Jew who was an established member of the community, having arrived in the 1850s and, with Isaac Strouse, formed the Strouse Adler Corset Company in the 1860s. He, too, was a Yale graduate (PhD 1891). Although Governor Woodruff was not a Yale graduate, he bequeathed an ample scholarship to the university upon his death. The substantial magnitude of the wealth among those who contributed a modest "$100" to get the committee started is set out in Douglas Rae, *City: Urbanism and Its End* (New Haven, CT: Yale University Press, 2003), 130–31. Poli, the later-appointed member, was an active entrepreneur who constructed and managed theaters and other entertainment centers in Pennsylvania and throughout New England, including in New Haven. He and his wife, Rosa, also were fervent activists in the New Haven community, especially in selling war bonds and organizing Italian American women to aid the Red Cross during World War I. See Christopher Sterba, *Good Americans: Italian and Jewish Immigrants during the First World War* (New York: Oxford University Press, 2003), 92, 139, 140. When Yale sought support for local students, he aided the university's purpose and especially the Italian American students. See also, for example, his membership on the Citizens Committee to commemorate Yale's historic move to New Haven. George Henry Nettleton, ed., *The Book of the Yale Pageant, October 21, 1916* (New Haven, CT: Yale University Press, 1916), 241. His spirit in contributing to the vitality of urbanism in New Haven and elsewhere was comparable to the private sector attitude that Daniel Burnham sought and captured in Chicago. See also Mark Fenster, "A Remedy on Paper: The Role of Law in the Failure of City Planning in New Haven, 1907–1913," *Yale Law Journal* 107, no. 1093 (1998): 1102n51. Fenster's study only further emphasized

the dilemma that Chicago and Daniel Burnham had confronted and, unlike the old Yankee stock in New Haven, had through persistence and private sector initiative managed successfully to ensure the outcome they sought.

23. Plattus characterized the planning and architecture subtlety as the "City Practical, or City Functional and Scientific." *1910 City Plan*, "Introduction."

24. Plattus also gave their admonition special emphasis in his review. See the Plan's "Present Conditions and Tendencies," *1910 City Plan*, 13–14, and "Introduction," xii, 4.

25. *1910 City Plan*, 15–16 (emphasis added except where indicated otherwise).

26. *1910 City Plan*, xi.

27. *1910 City Plan*, 21, 22, and 56 (changes in and near Yale and related street grid). Aspects of the plan that also required municipal support and funds were completed: the parks—particularly improvements at Edgewood (the neighborhood where Bart Giamatti lived when he was a member of the Yale faculty) and West River—and two of the buildings critical to the urban vision shared by Olmsted Jr. and Gilbert, New Haven Public Library and the New Haven (Union) Railroad Station.

28. See, for example, Thomas S. Hines, *Burnham of Chicago: Architect and Planner* (Chicago: University of Chicago Press, 1979), 319–45. Chicago industrialists and business leaders, over time and with a spirited mentality and willingness to part with substantial sums of money, ensured the success of the Chicago Plan. And as Hines makes clear, architect and planner Daniel Burnham worked methodically with municipal agencies over a decade to slowly aid them in assisting the plan's implementation with, no doubt, little disruption to their daily function. Private sector preparation and commitment led the way in an era when that mattered. Yale's Studley, unfortunately, had neither Burnham's credentials nor persistence nor cachet, locally or nationally.

29. In at least two different sections of his book *City*, 68 and 183, Yale historian Douglas Rae examined the failure of the 1910 Plan primarily to look for scapegoats, other than Yale and the old Yankee stock. First, he picked on Sylvester Poli, though without citing any evidence that Poli opposed or interfered with the committee's work or grand purpose or even attended any of the committee's meetings. Nor did Rae indicate why, other than a disquieting assumption, Poli would view his inclusion on the committee as being with "high company." Instead, Rae dwells on Poli's 25th wedding anniversary party, praised for its tastefulness by the *Evening Register* and attended, as Rae recognized, by a broad range of people of varying religions, ethnicities, and employment (local merchants, laborers, lawyers, doctors) but, alas, not the local, old Yankee and Yale stock. Presumably their absence was evidence of something sinister and blameworthy with respect to the fate of the 1910 Plan. Rae, however, failed to recognize that among those who did attend (including within his gratuitous reference to the "gaggle of physicians with Italian surnames"), 77, were two Yale graduates: internationally known and locally revered surgeon Dr. William Verdi (Yale Medical 1894) and newspaper owner and lawyer Paul Russo (Yale Law 1893). Verdi's and Russo's educational credentials seemed to matter to Rae's argument, though probably not to Poli, who with his wife, Rosa Leverone, had invited the men and women they considered "high company" (which Rae, further undercutting his already indefensible argument, acknowledged might have included the old Yankee stock members he identified). In addition, it's not clear where Poli would have gotten such power or why he would oppose the plan. There was no history yet of consequential Italian immigrant voter registration, organization, and voter turnout. See Morty Miller,

"New Haven: The Italian Community" (senior thesis, Department of History, Yale, 1969), 103–6. Rae's second scapegoat is Mayor Frank Rice. Here, Rae just lacks perspective on how urban plans came to fruition in other cities like Chicago, or precisely the value Rice and city government added to the 1910 Plan's prospect, typical of what many city governments contributed with success elsewhere. Rice's administration also had the distinct advantage of being efficient, admired, and largely corruption free, a benefit Daniel Burnham did not have in Chicago. When Rae then implies (without factual support) that because New Haven had numerous grocery shops, neighborhood banks, and similar small family ventures (many owned by Southern Italians and Jews), city government was somehow constrained to embrace the 1910 Plan (see, for example, *City*, 84–116), he portends, perhaps unwittingly, precisely the critique and mentality embraced, ruinously, not by Olmsted Jr. and Gilbert but by 1950s urban renewal advocates such as Robert Moses, Dick Lee, Edward Logue, and the architect/highway planners Yale employed. See also Rae on "suburban architecture . . . [and] the housing ideal of the New Urbanism," 234. The New Urbanists, many of whom studied under New Haven–born Vince Scully, derived their model of the walkable community and pattern of housing (size, scale, density, and manner) from areas in Wooster Square and West Rock built long before "suburban architecture." In fact, some of the earliest architecture used in creating new communities in the carefully planned "greenbelts" around cities was, indeed, derived from urban design, including prefabricated houses sold in Sears catalogs. However, suburban housing, even that built in the era Rae alludes to (and certainly later), was automobile dependent, often built without sidewalks, and definitely built on spacious plots and in deliberate isolation from retail and racial and ethnic integration. All of those factors are relevant to the New Urbanism evaluation of any style of housing. See, for example, Congress for the New Urbanism, *Charter of the New Urbanism* (New York: McGraw-Hill, 1999), Principles 11, 12, and 15, and Principles 19–27.

30. Gambino, *Blood of My Blood*, 119.

31. One lawyer from New Haven, the *Register* reported, was denied the opportunity to speak with his union clients. In Wisconsin, a judge had taken custody of the five-year-old daughter of an accused, then convicted Italian immigrant demonstrator, even though her family had offered to raise the child. Clarence Darrow interceded and argued, successfully on appeal, that the conviction be reversed. Judge Kenesaw Mountain Landis, perhaps as a premonition of things to come and among the reasons he was chosen Baseball's first commissioner, presided at trials of labor activists arrested for merely exercising free speech. "In times of peace," Landis wrote, "you have a legal right to oppose, by free speech, preparations for war. But when once war is declared, that right ceases." Jeffrey J. White, "Stamping Out the Reds: The Palmer Raids in Connecticut," *Hog River Journal*, Autumn 2005; *Hartford Courant*, November 9, 1919, 1; Angelo Giammattei's draft registration card, signed and filed in New Haven on September 18, 1918; Paul Avrich, *Sacco and Vanzetti: The Anarchist Background* (Princeton, NJ: Princeton University Press, 1991), 94–95, 106. See also *Bianchi et al. v. Wisconsin*, 169 Wis. 75 (1919) (Italians convicted in Milwaukee for demonstrating against the war and conspiracy to commit murder of a policeman killed subsequent to the demonstration, with Mary Nardini's infant son sentenced to twenty-five years in an orphanage), reversed on appeal (Darrow argued).

32. "ALL ALIEN REDS TO BE DEPORTED," "200 RADICALS HELD AFTER WIDE RAID," "Another Arrest Made in Local Clean-Up of Reds," "Does America Face

Industrial Revolution?," *New Haven Evening Register*, November 8, 9, and 12, 1919, 1; All of this news also was reported in New Haven's Italian language daily, *Il Corriere*, which had the largest circulation in Connecticut. It began publication in 1896 and stopped in 1953. It covered international and national news on the first few pages, local and state news in its interior pages; Woodrow Wilson, Third Annual Address to Congress (December 7, 1915).

33. Other Connecticut cities subject to Palmer's raids included Bridgeport, Waterbury, Hartford, and New Britain. On January 25, 1920, the editors of Connecticut's newspapers published their collective view for all of New Haven to read: "State Editors Endorse Reds' Deportation," *New Haven Evening Register*, November 25, 1920, 1; "Hold Banechi for Circulating Red Pamphlets," *New Haven Evening Register*, January 4, 1920, 1; "Greatest Raid Ever Conducted by Government Agents Clears Twenty Cities of Undesirables," *New Haven Evening Register*, January 3, 1920, 1. For estimates of the number of Italian Americans who served in the Armed Forces (some estimates exceed four hundred thousand), see Major Peter Belmonte, USAF, "Italian Americans in World War One," in *Italian Americans: A Retrospective on the Twentieth Century*, ed. Paola Alessandra Sensi-Isolani and Anthony Julian Tamburri (New York: American Italian Historical Association, 2001), 29 (service was well in excess of the community's percentage of eligible citizens).

34. In short order, A. Mitchell Palmer was incisively criticized by prominent lawyers and judges, and his reputation irrevocably stained. One federal judge in Massachusetts characterized the government's conduct as "the terroristic methods" of "a mob." Novelist Upton Sinclair called it the "White Terror." Harvard Professor Felix Frankfurter led a nationally recognized panel of lawyers who, with methodical care, factually and legally humiliated Palmer's wholesale disregard of civil liberties and the First Amendment. *Colyer, et al. v. Skeffington*, 265 F.17, 15, 17–21 (D. Mass. 1920); Upton Sinclair, *Boston: A Documentary Novel* (New York: Albert & Charles Boni, 1928), 194–95, 206–208; Gambino, *Blood of My Blood*, 117–20; *Salsedo v. Palmer*, 278 F. 9 (2d Cir. 1921); Curti, *The Growth of American Thought*, 675; Paul Avrich, *Sacco and Vanzetti*, 96–97; Felix Frankfurter et al., *To the American People: Report upon the Illegal Practices of the United States Department of Justice* (Washington, DC: National Popular Government League, May 1920).

35. Architecturally, the two buildings also had related traces of early American, Greek, Roman, and Italian elements (arched windows, recessed entranceways, masonry construction, decorative panels); "History of the New Haven High School, 1917," New Haven High School Class Book; *Freshman Hand Book*, School Customs, Yale, Class of 1926; New Haven Colonial and Historical Society, New Haven, CT (New Haven High School records). Rae, *City*, 170–71 (the number of New Haven High School students attending Yale); informal interview with Judith Schiff (Hillhouse High School).

36. The intention of connecting the two schools was to encourage students to explore special interests, get exposure to the rigor of an excellent faculty, and to retain friendships. The eating commons was located in Hillhouse to ensure daily interaction among students regardless of their course of study. See "History of the New Haven High School, 1917."

37. Commercial also housed a modest-sized gymnasium. "History of the New Haven High School, 1917"; "William Verdi," *Yale Alumni Weekly*, Professional Appointments (March 1919), 684; Report of the Board of Education of the State of Connecticut (1914–1915), 336; William Seabrook, "Italian Americans," in *Americans All: A Human*

Study of America's Citizens from Europe (1938; repr., Redditch, UK: Read Books, 2013) (Verdi and Poli).

38. Friends joined Val at Hillhouse from Strong School, as did others in his immediate neighborhood, including Frank Tortora, who lived on nearby Grand Avenue and entered New Haven High School two years later. Tortora entered Yale in 1930, graduated *cum laude* in 1934, graduated from the University of Rome medical school, became an admired and respected surgeon and urologist in New Haven, and was eventually Yale's oldest living graduate before his death in 2015, at age 102. See *Yale News*, May 2015. Eugene Rostow was later dean of the Yale Law School.

39. Brooks Mather Kelley, *Yale: A History* (New Haven, CT: Yale Press, 1974), 379; George W. Pierson, *Yale: The University College, 1921–1937* (New Haven, CT: Yale University Press, 1955), 67–68, 148–152, 184.

40. Christine Rosen, *Preaching Eugenics: Religious Leaders and the American Eugenics Movement* (New York: Oxford University Press, 2004), 3–4, 5–14; and see generally Adam Cohen, *Imbeciles: The Supreme Court, American Eugenics, and the Sterilization of Carrie Buck* (New York: Penguin Press, 2016). See also Kelley, *Yale*; Pierson, *Yale: The University College, 1921–1937*.

CHAPTER 6
THE DARKEST AURA AND ITS REACH

1. Interview with Calabresi (the neighborhood below Orange Street, the outer limit for university faculty, was considered the "Italian Ghetto"). See also Rae, *The City*, 127–36, 267–70 ("Upscale Localism") and Morty Miller, "New Haven: The Italian Community," 102 ("One of the forces aiding the development of close neighborhoods was residential discrimination by the native population, for example, which prevented the immigrants and their children from living wherever they wished.").

2. The approximately three thousand to thirty-five hundred students included a small number from towns around New Haven who paid a special fee.

3. Dixwell/Newhallville was near the large Winchester Repeating Arms Company, built in 1866 and expanding in solid bursts. Italian and Jewish families remained and thrived near Saint John the Baptist and Saint Anne's Church on Dixwell Avenue and Winchester Repeating Arms. After Val's graduation from Yale in 1932, it was into this neighborhood that the Giammatteis moved. See New Haven Colony Historical Society, "Dixwell Avenue and Newhallville," in *New Haven: Reshaping the City, 1900–1980* (Mount Pleasant, SC: Arcadia, 2002), 79–90. (The Dixwell Community House was built in 1924–1925.) See also Kelley, *Yale*, 128, 278–79n16; Colin M. Caplan, "Dixwell Avenue and Newhallville," in *Then and Now: New Haven* (Mount Pleasant, SC: Arcadia, 2006), 65; Elizabeth Mills Brown, "The Winchester Triangle," in *New Haven: A Guide to Architecture and Urban Design* (New Haven, CT: Yale University Press, 1976), 168. See also *Yale University v. Town of New Haven* (1898).

4. Vincent J. Scully, "Preface," in *Plan for New Haven 1910* (2012 ed.). As Scully described it, like many of the planning and architectural ideas that found life in the early years of America, the nine-square layout derived from British travel and observation throughout Europe. The life of Inigo Jones and the derivative skill of Thomas Jefferson or James Oglethorpe (Savannah, Georgia) reflected the same experience in pattern books

(which reemerged under the New Urbanism) and architectural styles. The best-known example of this travel and copying with imagination (Italy to Jones to the colonists) derived from the Italian Renaissance architect Andrea Palladio (1508–1580). See, for example, Witold Rybczynski, *The Perfect House: A Journey with Renaissance Master Andrea Palladio* (New York: Scribner, 2002). Two notable examples of the Palladio to Jones to Jefferson transfer are Monticello and the White House.

5. From the outset of its founding, Yale exercised its political power with the state legislature to coerce the closure of a rival college, compensate another community with public funds so that Yale could hire its minister, ensure "general infusions of cash" from public monies to defray university expenses for decades, have Connecticut taxpayers pay for the purchase of the first school of medicine, construct what is today called "Connecticut Hall," and pay for the construction of "Union Hall." After all that, Yale "warned [New Haven that] if the city did not support the college, the institution might decline and 'it may go down to such a depth as will sink with it the value of all property of every branch of business, and, what is more, the honor and reputation of our city,'" in order to receive local funds for its own operating expenses. Each time it sought to expand the breath of its tax exemption in Connecticut, including when it added the state governor to its corporate board under its state-granted charter, Yale sought and received yet more public money. Perhaps the quintessentially slick political and financial maneuver was when, in 1890, following the enactment by Congress of the Land Grant Act of 1890 (Morrill Act of 1862, as amended) for the purpose of establishing state colleges and universities to enhance agricultural and husbandry skills throughout the nation using funds derived from the use and sale of publicly owned federal lands, Yale used its influence with the governor and legislature to be designated the state agricultural school. When agricultural societies complained—the funds were used to hire faculty, expand the university, and detach the curriculum from the practical purposes they and the Morrill Act expected—the legislature finally created what, in time, became the University of Connecticut in the township of Storrs. Yale sued Connecticut for funds still to be paid under its agreement and prevailed. Kelley, *Yale*, 11, 26, 35, 59, 103, 153–54, 288–91; Morrill Act (named after Justin Morrill, R-VT), Pub. L. 37-130, 12 Stat. 503, as amended, Pub. L. 51-841, 26 Stat. 417. See also Mark J. Roy, "Land Grant Status Acquired through Struggle," University of Connecticut *Advance* (1998) and Walter Stemmons, *Connecticut Agricultural School, A History* (Storrs, CT: Connecticut Agricultural College, 1931), 54. The "Yale-Storrs Controversy," as it was called, was held in abeyance. Following creation of a special investigatory commission, Yale was awarded $154,604 in 1896. The award is the equivalent of approximately $4,200,000 in 2019 dollars.

6. Kelley, *Yale*, 278 and 278n16, and *Yale University v. Town of New Haven*, 71 Conn. 316, Supreme Court of Errors, Third Judicial District, October Term (1898). The 1834 statute establishing Yale's tax exemption included dormitories and dining halls but did not include property held in the university's name and used by a professor or land purchased for speculative purposes. More litigation followed.

7. Yale students murdered two townspeople, students attacked the High Street Firehouse, and a subsequent brawl with townspeople warranted "two military companies to keep the peace." Furthermore, a rough confrontation with townspeople occurred when "a body removed from the West Haven cemetery" was discovered at the Yale Medical School. A stabbing occurred between two students. With confident impunity from Yale

administrators, the alleged offender skipped bail in the local court. The "great riot" with local townspeople occurred along Chapel Street "whereupon the students . . . pulled out pistols and began to fire." In the subsequent grand jury inquiry, the "students . . . either refused to testify or lied. The college officers confessed their inability to help." Kelley, *Yale*, 215–18.

8. Kelley, *Yale*, 35–36.

9. Grant, *Passing of the Great Race*, 9 ("privilege of birth"), 10 ("Polish Jew"), and see 63 ("south Italians"). Madison Grant, *Conquest of a Continent* (New York: Charles Scribner's Sons, 1933; reprint, Burlington, IA: Ostara, 2011), 145 ("A group not homogeneous").

10. Geoffrey Kabaservice, *The Guardians: Kingman Brewster, His Circle, and the Rise of the Liberal Establishment* (New York: Henry Holt, 2004), 45, 53; Owen Johnson, *Stover at Yale* (1912; repr., New Haven, CT: Yale Book Store, 1997), 83, 108. Johnson's *Stover at Yale* was released amid considerable national expectation and then widespread readership. "From the fall of 1911 into the spring of 1912, Americans avidly following the experiences of *Stover at Yale* serialized in the pages of *McClure's* magazine were captivated by a unique and unforgettable college hero. One of the 'chosen,' Dink Stover dared to assert his individuality and risk all rather than achieve success through conformity." See the introduction to the 1997 edition by Judith Ann Schiff, chief research archivist, Yale University Library; see also the foreword by Kingman Brewster. Johnson was credited with having captured the Yale mentality and culture of his era. See Lewis Lapham, "Quarrels with Providence," *Yale Alumni Magazine*, March 2001) (Stover [Johnson] on Yale).

11. "How many Jews among them? And are there any *Coons? . . . Don't let any colored transfer get rooms* in College." Frederick Jones, dean, Yale College (1922 letter to Yale's Dean of Admissions Robert Corwin, emphasis in the original). See Karabel, *The Chosen*, 112–13, 582nn7–18 (emphasis in the original); see also the late nineteenth- and early twentieth-century influence of one of Yale's most praised scholars and widely acclaimed teachers, Professor William Graham Sumner. Joseph Soares, in *The Power of Privilege* (20, 209n26), described Sumner's writings and teaching: "Survival of the richest social Darwinism had its American spokesperson William Graham Sumner, Yale's first professor of sociology, to explain how welfare was immoral and ineffective, and why the upper class owed the lower class nothing." See William Graham Sumner, *What Social Classes Owe to Each Other* (New York: Harper & Bros.,1883). Numerous students took Sumner's courses, including economist and eugenicist Irving Fisher. As Brooks Mather Kelley noted accurately, albeit with the thrust of calcified indifference to assessing consequence, "There was always some doubt in the minds of the town folk whether the college was an asset or a parasite." Kelley, *Yale*, 278 (quoting historian Henry Seidel Canby), 215–19.

12. Although it was Galton who provided the name "eugenics"—from the Greek meaning the "well-born or "good in birth"—this "science" had disquieting antecedents in America that predated and reemerged immediately after the Civil War. See, for example, Louis Menand, *The Metaphysical Club: A Story of Ideas in America* (New York: Farrar, Straus and Giroux, 2001), 97 (Louis Agassiz); Anne Farrow, Joel Lang, and Jenifer Frank, *Complicity: How the North Promoted, Prolonged, and Profited from Slavery* (New York: Ballantine Books, 2006), xxvii–xxix ("Introduction") and virtually all of the remainder of the book; Cohen, *Imbeciles*, 46–50. Galton's research had emerged much earlier, but for reasons described in this text, his work, once it was embraced and elevated by Grant and others, made him and it seminal reading in America.

13. Established scientists—biologists, zoologists, and embryologists—and historians demonstrated that neither Galton's measurements nor his assumptions about Anglo-Saxon, European immigrant, African American, or Asian behavior were accurate. Historians especially undermined the finality of Galton's conclusions about timing: many people, they explained accurately, had not been able to demonstrate their full potential because of forced labor, slavery, imperialism, and political, educational, and economic repression. The Reverend John Ryan, who had tirelessly led the Catholic Church's efforts to protect immigrants that sought stability and freedom in America, spoke and testified throughout the country against legislation that sought to embody eugenics' "solutions." In 1931, Pope Pius XI issued *Casti Connubii*, an encyclical that challenged the "pernicious practice" of eugenics and reminded, "Those who hold the reigns of government [that they] should not forget that it is the duty of public authority by appropriate laws and sanctions to defend the lives of the innocent." Cohen, *Imbeciles,* 101–3 (judicial decisions in New Jersey—eugenics law signed by Governor Woodrow Wilson—Iowa, New York, Michigan, Indiana, Oregon, and Nevada). See especially the veto message of the Nebraska governor: the enacted sterilization law is "more in keeping with the pagan age than with the teachings of Christianity. . . . Man is more than an animal." Karabel, *The Chosen,* 18–19. Ryan's writings were instrumental in adding practical definition to Franklin Roosevelt's New Deal legislation. Ryan's imperatives, not unlike those of Mother Cabrini and, later, Cardinal Joseph Bernardin emerged from hands-on experience within immigrant communities and the teachings of Pope Leo XIII's 1891 encyclical. See also *Casti Connubii* (1931), paras. 66, 67, 68, and 69; Neil Thomas Proto, "Catholic Social Teaching in America and Those Who Defined It" (prepared for Congresswoman Rosa DeLauro, D–CT, and distributed to her colleagues, June 15, 2005, and reproduced in www.SaccoVanzettiExperience.com, "Author"); Richard Conniff, "God and White Men at Yale," *Yale Alumni Magazine* (May/June 2012). Cardinal Bernardin was awarded an honorary degree by Bart Giamatti in 1983. "Pomp and Humor as Yale Graduates," *Yale Daily News*, May 24, 1983.

14. The three began at what, for them, was the beginning: "The settlers of the thirteen colonies were overwhelmingly Nordic, a very large majority being Anglo-Saxon in the most limited meaning of the term." From this beginning, the three also proceeded with their unimpeachable dogma based, cavalierly, on already discredited science: "We now know, since the elaboration of Mendelian Laws of Inheritance, that certain bodily characters . . . are transmitted in accordance with fixed mathematical laws." Karabel, *The Chosen,* 80, 83–85. Lothrop Stoddard, *The Rising Tide of Color against White World-Supremacy,* with an introduction by Madison Grant (New York: Charles Scribner's Sons, 1922). Stoddard's book title seeps into F. Scott Fitzgerald's *The Great Gatsby* (New York: Charles Scribner's Sons, 1925), 17 (Tom Buchanan).

15. Gregor Johann Mendel (1822–1884), an Austrian scientist and Augustinian friar, gained posthumous recognition as the founder of the science of genetics. His work was largely confined to pea plants yet embraced full bore by eugenicists as the "the laws of Mendelian inheritance"; Rosen, *Preaching Eugenics,* 3–4, 5–14. Rosen also quotes Galton: "Eugenics must be introduced into the national consciousness, like a new religion." Rosen notes that the Reverend Myron W. Reed of Denver embraced the new religion saying, "It is difficult to find in a shipload of Poles or Huns ten men that will make Americans. Like insects under the rotten log, they like darkness and confinement." In 1926, the

Reverend Phillips Endecott Osgood, rector of St. Mark's Church in Minneapolis, took to the podium on Mother's Day: "We see that the less fit members of society seem to breed the fastest and the right types are less prolific."

16. Princeton's Stoddard confidently summarized the heart of this "threat to the United States: the 'invasion of immigrant Alpines and Mediterraneans, not to mention Asiatic elements like Levantines and Jews.'" The melting pot, he declared, was "an absurd fallacy," for "each race-type, founded ages ago, and 'set' by millenniums of isolation and inbreeding, is a stubbornly persistent reality." Grant, *The Passing of the Great Race*, 11; Karabel, *The Chosen*, 83, 103–5; Roosevelt's speech in Washington, DC, to the National Congress of Mothers (1905).

17. The Eugenics Office's regular bulletins contained widely circulated studies that read as if a collective of Frankenstein monsters were given a measuring stick, a stethoscope, and the complete freedom to conjure mathematical formulas and charts of hereditary maladies to force men, women, and children inside and outside their largely coerced "colonies" (institutions) to prepare for sterilization, indefinite confinement, and isolated, lonely, and welcomed death, all under the force of government and law. "Heredity of Feeble-Mindedness" by Henry H. Goddard, PhD; "Preliminary Report of a Study of Heredity in Insanity in Light of the Mendelian Laws" by Gertrude L. Cannon, AM, and A. J. Rosanoff, MD; "The Study of the Inheritage of Epilepsy" by Charles B. Davenport and David F. Weeks, MD, contained in Eugenics Record Office, Cold Spring Harbor, New York (1910, Bulletins 1–5); see also Philip R. Reilly "Involuntary Sterilization in the United States: A Surgical Solution," *Quarterly Review of Biology* 62 (June 1987): 153–70.

18. Indiana enacted sterilization laws for prisoners. Other states did as well. There were judicial challenges that succeeded in overturning almost all of those statutes, but on narrow grounds (for example, that such statutes denied due process under the Fourteenth Amendment to the Constitution because the patient had no right to appeal or to cross examine the doctors who had decided to perform the operation or because the law applied *only* to prisoners). In short order, those statutes were revived and expanded to cover *all* residents in the state and involve more deliberate review, though as a practical matter they still exclusively used doctor-determined decision making. More lawsuits were likely. See, for example, in Indiana: *Williams v. Smith*, 190 Ind. 526, 131 N.E. 2 (1921) and "Eugenic Sterilization in Indiana," *Indiana Law Journal* 38, no. 2 (1963): 275–89. See, generally, E. S. Gosney and Paul Popenoe, *Sterilization for Human Betterment* (New York: Macmillan, 1929); Richard Donnelly and William Ferber, "The Legal and Medical Aspects of Vasectomy," *Journal of Urology* 81, no. 2 (1959): 259–63; and Frank Lindman and Donald McIntyre, eds., *The Mentally Disabled and the Law: The Report of the American Bar Foundation on the Rights of the Mentally Ill* (Chicago: University of Chicago, 1961).

19. Angell is referred to as the president of the Carnegie Corporation and the Carnegie Foundation in W. S. Hunter, *James Rowland Angell, 1869–1949: A Biographical Memoir* (Washington, DC: National Academy of Sciences, 1951). Laughlin would be institutionally connected to Yale and retained by the state of Connecticut to expand its own program. His "legal reasoning" was supported by the attorney general of Connecticut. The AES promoted eugenics through public lectures, journals, conferences, and exhibits at county and state fairs, including a contest for the best sermon on a eugenic theme, a series of competitive "fitter family contests," and exhibits such as Mendel's Theater and the "flashing light exhibit," a large board titled "Some people are born to be a burden

to the rest." Lights were set to blink at periodic intervals to demonstrate how often a "defective" was born in the United States. One such display was shown in Philadelphia during the celebration of the Declaration of Independence. See also Cohen, *Imbeciles*, 4–5 (eugenics display), 139–42 (legal decisions and Laughlin's role).

20. The vote was 69–9 in the United States Senate. Connecticut Senator Frank Brandegee (who graduated from Yale in 1885, two years before Madison Grant) voted for it; Connecticut Senator George McLean (not a Yale, Harvard, or Princeton graduate) voted against it. See www.govtrack.us/congress/votes/68-1/s126. See also Colonel N. G. Osborn, *Men of Mark in Connecticut* (Hartford, CT: William R. Goodspeed, 1906) (Brandegee).

21. Cohen, *Imbeciles*, 133–35; Ewa Barbara Luzcak, *Breeding and Eugenics in the American Literary Imagination: Heredity Rules in the Twentieth Century* (New York: Palgrave Macmillan, 2015), 115; see also the movie *Tomorrow's Children* (1934) (protest against eugenics practice in the early 1900s, titled *The Unborn* in the United Kingdom); *Against Her Will: The Carrie Buck Story* (television, 1994); Mary Jane Ward, *The Snake Pit* (New York: Random House, 1946), as well as the 1948 movie by the same name; Aryeh Neier and David J. Rothman, "Under Lock and Key: How Long?" *New York Review of Books*, December 17, 2015, 70.

22. "Unfit" included newly arrived immigrants (not otherwise returned because of "health tests" at the port of entry); the poor (including Anglo-Saxons, those in the "back country"); women raped or found to be "promiscuous," "bad," physically endowed in appearance, or likely to give birth out of wedlock; alcoholics; and those with epilepsy, contagious disease, mental abnormalities, deafness, blindness, learning or physical disabilities. They also included persons who were suffering from senility or the antecedents of autism and those who, by someone's judgment, were unable to fit into normally accepted societal mores. Cohen, *Imbeciles*, 133–35; Conniff, "God and White Men at Yale." See also Luzcak, *Breeding and Eugenics in the American Literary Imagination*, 115; Mae M. Ngai, "The Architecture of Race in American Immigration Law: A Reexamination of the Immigration Act of 1924," *Journal of American History* 86, no. 1 (June 1999): 67–92. (Ngai recognized that the act "was intended principally to restrict immigration from the nations of southern and eastern Europe and used the notion of national origins to justify discrimination against immigration from those nations." She also observed correctly that other groups of residents already in America—Asians and Mexicans—were so eugenically demonized within Congress that they were placed in a distinct yet further ostracized category or affirmatively excluded.)

23. At the Connecticut Agricultural College (predecessor to the University of Connecticut), genetics professor Leslie Clarence Dunn—who, among others, once supported eugenics—fought, and failed, to deter the embrace of eugenics' solutions in Connecticut. Others, including future Yale botanist Edmund Sinnott, who had once authored genetics publications with Dunn, held tightly to his belief in precisely those solutions. The eugenics forces prevailed. Indiana's statute allowed for the exercise of more independent authority over the "unfit." The Connecticut statutes were enacted in 1909, 1912, and 1919. The "relief" for some families unable to care for "disabled" children was emphasized, not as a societal obligation but as long-term relief of a financial burden on taxpayers. For the Connecticut statutes, see "An Act concerning the prevention of procreation," introduced by Representative Wilbur Tomlinson in February 1909, passed by both houses, and signed by Governor Frank B. Weeks in August 1909. The bill, as approved,

is available in Eugenics Record Office, Bulletin No. 1, Cold Spring Harbor, New York, and was reprinted in *General American Breeders Magazine*, 1910, "Legal, Legislative, and Administrative Acts of Sterilization," 17. See also Statutes of Connecticut, Title 22, chap. 137, sec. 2691 and 2692 (1918). Governor Weeks had been an assistant to the superintendent of the Connecticut Hospital for the Insane. He also served there as a trustee for more than thirty years. See Lutz Kaelber, "Eugenics: Compulsory Sterilization in 50 American States," presentation at the Social Science History Association (2012). See also, "Preliminary Report of the Committee of the Eugenic Section of the American Breeders' Association to Study and to Report on the Best Practical Means for Cutting Off the Defective Germ-Plasm in the Human Population" (1911); "The Feeble Minded," a talk by Dr. George H. Knight (1895), 559–62 (presented at the annual meeting of what became the American Association on Mental Retardation, then called the Association of Medical Officers of American Institutions for Idiotic and Feeble-Minded Persons), cited and available through Lawrence B. Goodheart, "Rethinking Mental Retardation: Education and Eugenics in Connecticut, 1818–1917," *Journal of the History of Medicine and Allied Science* 59, no. 1 (2004): 90–111. See also Susan Parish, "AAMR Leadership at Century's End," in *Embarking on a New Century: Mental Retardation at the End of the 20th Century*, ed. Robert Schalock, Pamela C. Baker, and M. Doreen Croser (Washington, DC: American Association on Mental Retardation—now American Association on Intellectual and Developmental Disabilities—2002), 245. See N. G. Osborn, *Men of Mark in Connecticut: Ideals of American Life Told in Biographies and Autobiographies of Eminent Living Americans* (Hartford, CT: Kiand, 1910); Cohen, *Imbeciles*, 63–71; Anthony Sposato, with Barbara Mellone, ed., "A History of Genetics Research and Education at UConn Storrs," University of Connecticut (2016); Melinda Gormley, "Scientific Discrimination and the Activist Scientist: L. C. Dunn and the Professionalization of Genetics and Human Genetics in the United States," *Journal of the History of Biology* 42, no. 1 (Spring 2009): 33. Some women, it is now clear, were not told of the operation's surgical purpose or effect. Thousands of others were wrenched from families throughout Connecticut and placed in segregated institutional colonies, where, it appears, most died or were let free only after authorities ensured that they were no threat to the social order or, certainly, that they could not have children.

24. See, for example, Darrel Abel, *Democratic Voices and Vistas: American Literature from Emerson to Lanier* (1963; reprint, Lincoln, NE: iUniverse, 2002), 41 (Emerson); and Farrow, Lang, and Frank, *Complicity*, 37 (Emerson). The God-designed imprimatur seeped, then gushed into Yale's contribution to the missionary slave mentality in, for example, Hawaii, beginning in 1820 through the overthrow of the constitutional government in 1893, the annexation in 1898, and the subsequent, fervent effort to eliminate the Hawaiian and Asian culture and language. The imprimatur was central to Hawaii missionary leader Asa Thurston's (Yale 1816) call to convert the heathen to Christianity. In March 1869, the *New York Tribune* found that "contract labor"—Asians and Native Hawaiians—on plantations owned by the sons and grandsons of missionaries (who would lose their subsidy if they engaged in commerce directly), including Thurston's, "has for some time past, taken on a development which leaves little difference between it and the slave trade." See Proto, *The Rights of My People*, 11–13, 39–40, 47, 63–67 (Asa Thurston, Lorrin Thurston, *New York Tribune*), including the role played by Harriet Beecher Stowe in justifying the "good slave owner"; Kelley, *Yale*, 126, 491n32 (Asa Thurston). See also Charles K. Whipple,

Relation of the American Board of Commissioners for Foreign Missions to Slavery (Boston: R. F. Wallcut, 1861; repr., New York: Negro Universities Press, 1969), 1 (Appendix) (missionary tolerance of slavery on Choctaw Nation reservation). That same mentality also was critical to Yale-educated Arthur F. Judd (Class of 1862, Honorary Doctor of Law 1894), who would preclude "Our natives" from voting in Hawaii elections after annexation to the United States was approved. Tennant S. McWilliams, *The New South Faces the World: Foreign Affairs and the Southern Sense of Self, 1877–1950* (Tuscaloosa: University of Alabama Press, 1988), 31. In 1920, Yale Graduate School Dean Wilbur Cross traveled to Hawaii to commemorate Yale's special role in creating that mentality (and to ensure financing for a continued Yale presence in research), including in his speech to the Chamber of Commerce on "Americanization." In it he emphasized the importance of education to eliminate any remnant of speech or culture character not American, and he later praised the language instruction because it ensured that the Asians especially spoke with a good New England accent. He also described the growing availability (which he noted in hand) of the "Professional Americanizers . . . who hope to reduce Americanization to a science, and then they will do the job quickly." Wilbur Lucius Cross Papers, Box 15, Folder 180, Yale University Archives, and related articles, "Yale and Hawaii," *Yale Alumni Weekly*, October 1, 1920, 31, and "The Other Half of the Problem," *Honolulu Star Bulletin*, April 1920. See also Proto, *The Rights of My People*, 119–120, 226nn265–268 (rapid demise of African American voter registration in Louisiana based on the methodology advocated by Senator Henry Cabot Lodge in Massachusetts to thwart Italian immigrant voting, the popularity of the movie *Birth of a Nation* in 1915, the U.S. Supreme Court decision in *Plessy v. Ferguson* [1896], and subsequent decisions over the next five decades).

25. John Doyle, "Measuring 'Problems of Human Behavior': The Eugenic Origins of Yale's Institute of Psychology, 1921–1929," *MSSA Kaplan Prize for Yale History* 3, 2014.

26. Collectively they sought a third eugenicist, Princeton Professor Carl C. Brigham, whose 1923 study showed, with "undeniable" certainty, "the undesirable results which would ensure from a cross between the Nordic in this country with the Alpine Slav, with the degenerated hybrid Mediterranean, or with the negro, or from the promiscuous intermingling of all four types." When Brigham was unable to join the faculty, he was appointed to the AES Council to ensure his availability in New Haven. Doyle, "Measuring 'Problems of Human Behavior.'"

27. Doyle, "Measuring 'Problems of Human Behavior,'" 24–30, 36–38 (concern about racial insensitivity), 54 (one purpose of the Institute); "University Notices," *Yale Daily News* (May 27, 1925); Paul Popenoe and Roswell Hill Johnson, *Applied Eugenics* (New York: Macmillan, 1918). See also "Lucky in Love," *Yale Daily News*, February 13, 1928 (Professor Ellsworth Huntington's argument in favor of eugenics); "Thomson Wins Prize in Ten Eyck Competition," *Yale Daily News*, December 20, 1922. One participant in the Eyck Competition described the "'spawning' of the unintelligent lower classes. . . . The only advantage is offered by the science of eugenics, by which the preponderance of the lower classes may be reduced and the preservation of the intelligent assured."

28. Letter, Angell to Osborn (January 3, 1930), Yale University Archives.

29. To the students at Yale, Angell was almost as candid. He described the Institute's purpose, with the slyness required by public discussion, as concerned with "problems of human nature and the social order [and] the material alleviation of the present ills from which humanity suffers." Unable to constrain himself, at least to those who knew

his plainest intention, he added that, "Obviously the time had come for some form of human engineering, such as had not previously existed." James Rowland Angell, "The Institute of Human Relations," *Yale Banner and Potpourri*, 1932, 16–19. And, generally, Doyle, "Measuring 'Problems of Human Behavior.'"

30. Grant, *The Passing of the Great Race*, 23.

CHAPTER 7
FORMING THE INTELLECTUAL LIFE

Epigraph is from Allon Schoener, *The Italian Americans* (New York: Macmillan, 1987), 12.

1. No one in Val's family has a recollection of which track event he might have participated in. *Hillhouse High School Class Book* (1928), 61, 233, 246; *State of the New Haven Schools* (New Haven Ethnic Heritage Center, 1928).

2. Lev described how the women in the village had turned to her grandmother for guidance to save their children from the expected slaughter inflicted, once again, by the Cossacks. The village's men had left to defend the synagogue. "Even when one reads about a pogrom, it seems impossible that such a thing could really occur among civilized races of people," Lev wrote. Her grandmother led village women and children to a hideaway underground, where they waited amid the horror-filled sounds above. Emerging from "their prison," they saw "the bodies of beloved ones strewn along the road like so many slaughtered animals." *Hillhouse Gleam*, New Haven High School Records, New Haven Colonial and Historical Society, New Haven, CT; Riccio, *The Italian American Experience in New Haven*, 81 and throughout (on the oral tradition); interview with Dino Giamatti; interview with Elria Giamatti Ewing.

3. The saints' role was related to why they'd been canonized. Saint Michael was, as Riccio described it, the knight-warrior, sword in hand, ready to battle, to protect Jews and Catholics alike against Satan in suspected and unsuspected form. "Yet he's venerated as a saint." Purgatory and limbo also were sometimes incorrectly used interchangeably. Riccio, *The Italian American Experience in New Haven*, 207; see also Williams, *South Italian Folkways in Europe and America*, 135; Peter Brown, *The Ransom of the Soul: Afterlife and Wealth in Early Western Christianity* (Cambridge, MA: Harvard University Press, 2015); G. W. Bowersock, "Money and Your Soul," *New York Review of Books*, May 15, 2015), 28 (money, a way of ensuring grace in the afterlife and adulation from the clergy in this one). The Southern Italian irreverence within the Church was directed especially to choices concerning the harsh realities of daily living and decisions about sex and family.

4. Douglas Bush, *Pagan Myth and Christian Tradition in English Poetry: Jayne Lectures for 1967*, (Philadelphia: American Philosophical Society, 1968), 1–2. Bush and his works on Edmund Spenser, the Renaissance, and specific aspects of *The Faerie Queene* are relied upon in Giamatti's first book, *The Earthly Paradise and the Renaissance Epic* (Princeton, NJ: Princeton University Press, 1966), also the subject of his PhD dissertation (1963–64), 247n10, 284n30, 288, 307, 308, 310; interview notes, Riccio (December 28, 2016), and see Riccio, *The Italian American Experience in New Haven*, 209. In his famed lectures on "Pagan Myths and Christianity," Douglas Bush captured the historical and practical transformation from one to the other: "In its beginnings Christianity itself assimilated elements of pagan religion and thought. . . . Then Latin was the language of learning and the

professions, and of the universal church, the heir of the Roman Empire, and all students of classical Latin necessarily absorbed classical [Greek and Roman] mythology." More importantly, as Bush also points out: "One general fact may be stressed at the outset: in ancient as well as later times Greek and Roman myth was not a body of fixed data but was always evolving, often confusedly and contradictorily, acquiring new embellishments and new meanings." Bush, *Pagan Myth and Christian Tradition in English Poetry*, 1–2. One other cultural characteristic, recognized in the immigrant community in New Haven and more the product of practical knowledge of life's connection to nature and to God—perhaps a derivative of Saint Michael's purpose in life—was *il malocchio*, the "evil eye" and how, largely through herbal medicine properly applied or stimulating selective muscles combined with nonliteral appeals to God, ailments inflicted on the body could be relieved, the evil thwarted. It is not merely a predecessor to holistic medicine but the joining of pagan mythology and Christianity with empirically based knowledge of physiology and psychology. It wasn't just a matter of believing it but also an awareness of its elements and the fact that others, including non-Italians, attested to its success.

5. Interviews with Santello. It's not clear why the priest refused, and after a generation the details, though not the basic facts, are no longer remembered. What precisely occurred to make this episode so decisive in Val's view of Catholicism as faith? To his cousin, Dolph Santello, as relayed to Dolph's own son, the episode may have merely confirmed a disposition in progress—the Southern Italian irreverence and skepticism fostered by the clergy—or combined with other, practical episodes he'd witnessed and no longer talked about.

6. See, for example, *Modern Language Journal* 11 (April 1927): 466–67; *Bulletin* (New England Modern Language Association) 8–15 (1918–1925): 91.

7. *Buck v. Bell,* 274 U.S. 200, 207 (1927); Louis Menand attributes Holmes's decision in *Buck v. Bell* to his fundamental belief in eugenics. "Holmes's defense of civil liberties [in some cases] had nothing to do, in other words, with the notion that such liberties were owed to people merely by the fact of their being human—a belief he held in conspicuous contempt. He could defend the right of socialists and pacifists to express their views on grounds that those views represented a legitimate social interest, and at the same time exhibit indifference to the suffering of, for example, Southern blacks victimized by de facto segregation," and, while barely acknowledging her presence in the case or seeking truth about her condition, Holmes showed complete contempt for Carrie Buck's state-sponsored exploitation and those he knew awaited the same fate. Menand, *The Metaphysical Club*, 56, 457n51, 596–99. See also Liva Baker, *The Justice from Beacon Hill: The Life and Times of Oliver Wendell Holmes* (New York: Harper Collins, 1991), 599–604. See especially, Paul A. Lombardo, *Three Generations, No Imbeciles: Eugenics, the Supreme Court, and* Buck v. Bell (Baltimore: Johns Hopkins University Press, 2008), 157–84; Cohen, *Imbeciles*, 267–80.

8. The decision had no equivocation in its principles, no warrant by lower courts to question some lapse in its reasoning. It provided no clear path in unsettled legal precepts for a constrained inmate sentenced to sterilization or his or her family to consider a new lawsuit. The underlying unethical conduct (Buck's lawyer, who had colluded with the state to frame the lawsuit's legal issues and select Buck for trial, did not question the legitimacy of the "science" involved or the methodology of Buck's selection or the fact that none of her siblings, neither of her parents, nor her infant daughter had the

requisite indicia of mental "unfitness") also was affirmed for everyone in the "eugenics community" to know. The inexplicable conduct, which was more than just a vote (one or more drafts of the opinion were circulated, informal discussions were easily available, and at least one judicial conference with the other justices was held), displayed by Justice Louis Brandeis, who joined Holmes's opinion, remains unsettling to many and largely ignored, especially by Brandeis's most thorough and acclaimed biographers. There is no reference to *Bell* in the text of Melvin I. Urofsky's seemingly seminal book on Brandeis, *Louis D. Brandeis: A Life* (New York: Pantheon Books, 2009), 639, except in a morally neutral endnote, 874. Presumably, for Urofsky, Brandeis's support was so inexplicable a departure, it shouldn't cloud Brandeis's reputation for commitment to civil rights and civil liberties, though it does, in part because of the way Urofsky treated it. The case also is not cited in Alpheus Thomas Mason, *Brandeis: A Free Man's Life* (New York: Viking Press, 1946). Professor Jeffrey Rosen, in *Louis D. Brandeis: American Prophet* (New Haven, CT: Yale University Press, 2016), 116, confirmed that Brandeis's decision to join Holmes might not be inexplicable. Rosen cited another affirmation of Brandeis's eugenics view expressed to his daughter after the decision. Justice Butler's dissent, though he wrote no opinion and did not subsequently speak or write about it, is often attributed to his Catholicism. Maybe he recognized, before Pope Pius XI did in 1931, that "Those who hold the reins of government should not forget that it is the duty of public authority by appropriate laws and sanctions to defend the lives of the innocent." See also the thoughtful analysis and research on Brandeis's and Butler's decisions in Cohen, *Imbeciles,* 212–82; William E. Leuchtenburg, "Mr. Justice Holmes and Three Generations of Imbeciles," in *The Supreme Court Reborn: The Constitutional Revolution in the Age of Roosevelt* (New York: Oxford University Press, 1995), 15; Ashley K. Fernandes, "The Power of Dissent: Pierce Butler and *Buck v. Bell*," *Journal for Peace and Justice Studies* 12 (2002): 115–34. And see Cohen, *Imbeciles,* 317 (post *Buck v. Bell* judicial treatment); Lombardo, *Three Generations, No Imbeciles,* 110 (Buck's daughter).

9. The Supreme Court's action was welcomed by *Time* magazine; *Literary Digest*; the Charlottesville, Virginia, and Birmingham, Alabama, newspapers; and the *American Journal of Public Health.* The *Yale Daily News* merely carried on reporting the eugenics views of Professor Ellsworth Huntington and those who agreed with him. The Catholic Jesuit Order, through its magazine *America*, objected. The *Hartford Times* did as well. Lombardo, *Three Generations, No Imbeciles,* 250–54; Cohen, *Imbeciles,* 280–84; "Book on Eugenics Causes Country-Wide Comments," *Yale Daily News*, December 14, 1927; Molly McCully Brown, *The Virginia State Colony for Epileptics and Feebleminded: Poems* (New York: Persea Books, 2017).

10. A Defense Committee was formed immediately after the arrest. Its leaders, mainly Italian immigrants, were supported by Jewish activists at the *Forward*. A majority of the contributors to the Defense Committee were Italian immigrants and Italian Americans throughout the nation, who contributed quarters, dimes, and single dollar bills. Riccio, "Justice Denied: The Execution of Sacco and Vanzetti," in *The Italian American Experience in New Haven*, 61; Michael Angelo Musmanno, *After Twelve Years* (New York: Alfred A. Knopf, 1939), 323–35. It was reported in the *New Haven Evening Register* (Associated Press story), on August 30, 1927, that the Defense Committee raised approximately $350,000 between 1920 and 1927, roughly the equivalent of $4,600,000 in 2019 dollars; A. Bartlett Giamatti, "Commentary," 22.

11. Judge Thayer's prejudicial statements in and out of court and the prosecutor's ridicule of the Italian witnesses who had struggled to speak English were especially egregious. Gardner Jackson in Boston, William Allen White, and Heywood Broun in New York grappled in the trenches with prejudices they despised. Toward the end, Walter Lippmann joined the fray in lofty terms reflected of his late entry and temperament. Prominent lawyers and personalities gave credence to the deeply held beliefs of Italian immigrants and their children—Roger Baldwin (the American Civil Liberties Union supported the defense from almost the outset); Elizabeth Glendower Evans, a friend of Justice Louis and Mrs. Alice Brandeis; Jane Addams; Harvard historian Samuel Eliot Morison; Alfred Landon of Kansas; Louis Pasteur; Anatole France; Albert Einstein; Madame Marie Curie; and the Wisconsin Legislature through resolution. Eventually poets and writers—Edna St. Vincent Millay, Upton Sinclair, John Dos Passos, and Dorothy Parker—added their voices. G. Louis Joughin and Edmund M. Morgan, *The Legacy of Sacco and Vanzetti* (New York: Harcourt, Brace, 1948) (includes the case's literary and cultural effects); Roberta Feuerlicht, *Justice Crucified: The Story of Sacco and Vanzetti* (New York: McGraw-Hill, 1977), 393, 405–6. See also Neil Thomas Proto, "Sacco and Vanzetti: The Literary and Cultural Effects of the Controversy for Their Lives," presented at the conference of the Dante Alighieri Society of Cambridge, Massachusetts, 1997 (reprinted at www.SaccoVanzettiExperience.com). In 1997, with the support of U.S. Representative Rosa DeLauro, Mayor John DeStefano, Judge and former Yale Law School Dean Guido Calabresi, and Dean Anthony Kronman, a daylong symposium was held at Yale Law School followed by an evening dinner that included a musical excerpt from the still-unproduced (in America) Belgian production of *Sacco and Vanzetti*. In 2002, with the support of Representative DeLauro, Mayor DeStefano and city officials, Yale University, Southern Connecticut State University, and nonprofit and individual volunteers, a yearlong commemoration of the seventy-fifth anniversary of the execution of Sacco and Vanzetti was held throughout the city. The musical drama, "American Dream: The Story of Sacco and Vanzetti" was performed at the Shubert Theatre. The Alighieri Conference, the Yale Symposium, and the yearlong commemoration are described in detail, as well as the author's own body of work, at www.SaccoVanzettiExperience.com; see the following in the *New Haven Evening Register*: "Sacco Appeal Placed before Governor Fuller," April 11, 1927; "Sacco and Vanzetti Plea before State Assembly," April 12, 1927; "Sacco-Vanzetti Appeal Rejected—World Strike Called," August 19, 1927. See also citations in subsequent endnotes.

12. On April 29, 1927, Yale Law School Professor Charles Edward Clark (later dean and United States Court of Appeals judge) and Rabbi Stephen Wise of New York (a vocal critic of the trial) spoke at the "Mass Meeting on Sacco and Vanzetti at Sprague [Hall]," sponsored by the Yale Liberal Club. Philosophy Professor Charles A. A. Bennett wrote that students had "only vague ideas concerning" the case, assuming (correctly) that "Italians . . . or members of labor associations . . . would be expected naturally to sympathize with Sacco and Vanzetti." But, he explained, they were not alone. "[Concern] is shared by disinterested persons of every profession and class. The thing has reached a stage where no decent man can evade his responsibility. It is a duty of everyone who cares about fair play, and this country's reputation for justice," to learn the facts and understand the implications. From the letters reprinted in the *Yale Daily News*: "The people of Massachusetts are going to deal with Sacco and Vanzetti as they think best. We believe they are guilty, and have so recorded our conviction. . . . The courts have spoken, so be

it"; another student admonished the student body to write the governor as individuals, not "as a Yale plea. This impression to the public should be avoided." And, from another student: "There has been sufficient froth and vulgar ferment about the Sacco-Vanzetti affair . . . . The case was of no essential concern to the nation at large." The letter was signed "Brahmin." In reply, another student posited that, "It is regrettable that [Brahmin] display such astonishing ignorance of the facts of a case which has been under discussion for seven years and has, besides attracting world wide interest, secured the sincere support of able lawyers and people of prominence all over the country, in an effort to see justice meted out." Finally, another wrote, "If only a little more attention were paid to the true facts of the case, perhaps the eager sentimentalists would be quiet." *Yale Daily News*, April 29, April 30, May 9, and May 12, 1927, Literary Supplement No. 4 (C. P. Grimes).

13. On April 30, 1927, Professor Charles Edward Clark concluded, after reviewing the evidence and conduct of the judge, that both men were innocent. Clark's colleague, Dean Robert Hutchins, and their mutual friend, Columbia Law Professor William O. Douglas, joined Clark. Douglas, some years later, fused together what had come to define the meaning of "law" to immigrant arrivals still intent on defining their own view of citizenship and fairness. "What Mitchell Palmer . . . did to hapless foreigners in New England in the 1920s was a lasting scar, because it flouted constitutional standards. . . . [We now have] a government subject to the will of the politicians in power. A notorious example of this neglect of the Constitution is found in the Sacco-Vanzetti trial." William O. Douglas, *Go East, Young Man* (New York: Random House, 1974), 167, 446; Bruce Watson, "To Save Sacco and Vanzetti," *Smith Alumnae Quarterly* (Spring 2008): 32; *Cincinnati Inquirer*, April 14, 1927, 7; Joughin and Morgan, *The Legacy of Sacco and Vanzetti*, 293 (Mary E. Woolley). On May 19, 1927, Frankfurter's book was favorably reviewed in the *Yale Daily News*.

14. Anti-Fascist Italian immigrants and others challenged Mussolini's surrogates and supporters in America and, by implication and often directly, the support Mussolini received from American bankers and industrialists. Anti-Fascist riots had broken out in New York, New Haven, and elsewhere as early as 1922. Clarence Darrow interceded to represent the Italian immigrants charged with inciting riots. The men were acquitted. Michael Angelo Musmanno became a Navy rear admiral, Nuremberg trial judge, and Pennsylvania Supreme Court justice. He was fluent in Italian and spoke easily to the defendants and their families. Feuerlicht, *Justice Crucified*, 366; Neil Thomas Proto, "An Unfinished American Injustice," *Italian America*, September 1996, 12; Dorothy Gallagher, *All the Right Enemies* (New Brunswick, NJ: Rutgers University Press, 1988), 98–136 (Carlo Tresca and the anti-Fascist riots); William Salomone, "Fascism and the Second World War," in *Images: A Pictorial History of Italian Americans*, ed. Helen Barolini (New York: Center for Migration Studies, 1986), 175.

15. Adam Cohen, "Harvard's Eugenics Era," *Harvard Magazine*, March–April 2016: "As eugenics grew in popularity, it took hold at the highest levels of Harvard. A. Lawrence Lowell . . . was an active supporter. Lowell . . . was particularly concerned about immigration—and he joined the eugenicists in calling for sharp limits. . . . Lowell also supported eugenics research. When the Eugenics Record Office, the nation's leading eugenics research and propaganda organization, asked for access to Harvard records to study the physical and intellectual attributes of alumni fathers and sons, he readily agreed." See also, John Trumpbour, ed., *How Harvard Rules* (Boston: South End Press,

1989), 201 (Lowell's conduct, his deliberate suppression of evidence, and his draft of the final report days before the completion of testimony); Musmanno, *After Twelve Years*, 253 (Lowell Committee); Herbert B. Ehrmann, *The Untried Case: The Sacco-Vanzetti Case and the Morelli Gang* (London: Martin Hopkinson, 1934) (the confession and role of the Morelli gang; Ehrmann was a member of the defense team).

16. Two members of the defense team drove to the Cape Cod home of Justice Holmes to request a stay of the execution until the Supreme Court acted. Holmes declined. They drove to see Justice Brandeis. He convinced the lawyers that he had a conflict that warranted abstention—his wife, Alice, had housed Rosina Sacco in property she owned in Dedham while the trial was in progress nearby. And, unknown for decades, Brandeis had, through correspondence, privately encouraged his friend Felix Frankfurter to support both men. Musmanno then made two attempts almost simultaneously. He petitioned President Calvin Coolidge, then in South Dakota, to request Governor Fuller to stay the execution or even pardon the two men. Coolidge declined to act. And he located Chief Justice William Howard Taft, on holiday in Canada, to seek the same kind of stay Holmes had denied. Musmanno chartered a plane to go in either direction if necessary. The lawyers went back to Holmes. He declined a second time. He would not intrude on a state court matter. Chief Justice Taft said no. Holmes said no a third time. Justice Harlan Fiske Stone, when approached at his summer home, summarily declined to act. Musmanno, *After Twelve Years*, 346–95; Baker, *The Justice from Beacon Hill*, 607–11.

17. Musmanno, *After Twelve Years*, 385–87. See also Adrienne M. Naylor, "Memorializing Sacco and Vanzetti in Boston," *Inquiries Journal* 2 (2010).

18. Historian Richard Gambino described his grandfather's deeply ingrained memory: "The outcome . . . was simply another confirmation of the ancient belief of the Italian immigrants that justice, a very important part of their value system, had little to do with the laws and institutions of the state." Gambino, *Blood of My Blood*, 122; Neil Thomas Proto, "Only Silence is Shame," *Italian America* magazine (March 1997), 12n24. See also, from the *New Haven Evening Register*, "Hope Wanes for Sacco and Vanzetti," August 22, 1927; "Two Justices Reject Appeals to Intervene, August 22, 1927; "United States Is Calm as Riots Rage Abroad over Sacco and Vanzetti, August 23, 1927; "N.H. Woman Aids Kin of Doomed Pair," August 23, 1927; "America Takes Death Very Quietly," August 23, 1927; "Sacco-Vanzetti Die Denying Their Guilt," August 23, 1927. The local woman who aided the "kin" referenced in the *Evening Register* article was Dr. Edith Jackson, journalist Gardner Jackson's sister.

19. Giamatti, "Commentary," 13.

20. John W. Sterling (Yale 1864), founder and partner in the Wall Street law firm of Sherman & Sterling, was born and raised in Stratford, Connecticut. Upon his death in 1918, at seventy-four years old, he bequeathed $15,000,000 to Yale University for a variety of purposes. It was, at the time, "one of the largest, if not the largest, single gift ever made to a university." In time, the bequest served three purposes: the construction of the gothic-inspired and iconic Sterling Memorial Library and other buildings including the Law School, the creation of the highest-ranking endowed chair within the Yale culture, and "to some extent . . . the foundation of scholarships." When Yale finally processed the Sterling bequest, scholarships were created for entering undergraduates. Although the precise number of scholarships awarded is unclear, by 1928 (specified in more detail by 1930), Yale offered "Free tuition for a full four-year undergraduate

course . . . to eight New Haven men in the entering class. . . . These scholarships are restricted to students who have been residents of New Haven for a period of at least five years. Preference is shown, other things being equal, to graduates of New Haven High School." The awards committee included representatives of the city of New Haven, the New Haven High School, the undergraduate schools of the university, and the Bureau of Appointments. Rigorous academic standards had to be met during all four years, and the recipient had to give "concrete evidence of his financial need by earning at least a substantial part of his expenses during term time and vacations." See, "$15,000,000 Sterling Bequest to Yale," *New York Times*, July 17, 1918; see also John A. Garver, *John William Sterling, Class of 1864 Yale College* (New Haven, CT: Yale University Press, 1929), reviewed by Frederick Hicks in *Yale Law Journal* 39, no. 926 (1929–1930); "Yale Receives Bulk of Sterling Estate," *New York Times*, August 23, 1919. Sterling was considered gay in twenty-first century terms.

21. *Catalogue of Yale University, 1928–1929* (New Haven, CT: Yale University, 1928); *Catalogue of Yale University, 1930–1931* (New Haven, CT: Yale University, 1930). The 1930–1931 catalogue specified that fifteen scholarships would be awarded to New Haven High School graduates, and ten more to graduates of other Connecticut high schools.

22. Marcia Graham Synnott, *The Half-Opened Door: Discrimination in Admissions at Harvard, Yale, and Princeton, 1900–1970* (Piscataway, NJ: Transaction Publishers, 2010), 133 (originally published by Westport, CT: Greenwood Press, 1979).

23. Of the 790 students who graduated in 1928, almost all the Italian American women expressed the expectation of additional education at Albertus Magnus, New Haven Normal School, Connecticut College for Women, Arnold College, Columbia, the Yale Music School, and nursing programs at Saint Raphael's Hospital. The same for the Italian American boys: Yale, NYU, Duke, Holy Cross, Brown, and Fordham, among others. Under modest assumptions, close to 90 percent of the Italian American graduates intended to pursue higher education. *Hillhouse High School Class Book* (1928) (author's review).

24. The poem was written in 1875. Henley was recovering from a near-death illness; musical arrangement for the poem was by Franz Carl Bornschein.

25. Yale made certain of its facilities available to New Haven High School students under defined and compensable circumstances, including its library, golf course, and (once constructed) its gymnasium, and for graduation ceremonies, its large auditorium, Woolsey Hall. The York Square campus provided meeting space, recruitment opportunities, and employment for Yale graduates committed to teaching, and an easily reached, highly regarded school for their children. See also "Yale and New Haven: A Study of the Benefits Derived Locally from an Endowed University," Yale University, New Haven, CT, 1937, 32–35; New Haven Colonial and Historical Society, New Haven, CT. The New Haven High School folders contain dozens of photographs and pamphlets, plus newspaper articles of class reunions, to which people traveled great distances and walked only a few blocks (people whose lives tempered the history of New Haven). Notable alumni included Democratic Town Chairman Arthur Barbieri, musician Artie Shaw, U.S. Representative Robert Giaimo, Yale football legend Albie Booth, All-American football player Floyd Little and basketball player Mike DiNapoli, pollster Louis Harris, Mayor John Daniels, Judge Constance Baker Motley, Yale football star Levi Jackson, actor Ernest Borgnine, and basketball teams that won state and New England championships.

CHAPTER 8

THE YALE HE ENTERED

1. Angell to Corwin, January 6, 1933, Yale University Archives; see also Karabel, *The Chosen*, 119; Soares, *The Power of Privilege*, 26.

2. Angell to Corwin, January 6, 1933; see also Karabel, *The Chosen*, 119; Soares, *The Power of Privilege*, 26. See, for example, "The Admissions Requirements as Applied to the Sons of Yale Alumni," cited in Synnott, *The Half-Opened Door*, 154.

3. Karabel, *The Chosen,* 19–20.

4. In *Stover*, the possibility or even relative value of learning, in academic terms, was the subject of debate. "Just what does our type take from here to the nation?" Stover asks [the question itself filled with cultural presumptions and the criteria for admission]. The answer: "First, a pretty fine type of gentleman, with good, clear, honest standards; second, a spirit of ambition and a determination not to be beaten; third, the belief in democracy." The "belief in democracy" is dismissed immediately. "You're wrong on the democracy . . . I mean the feeling of man to man." "All of which means," Stover's friend concludes, "that we are simply schools for character." Johnson, *Stover at Yale*, 247–49.

5. See George W. Pierson, *Yale College: An Educational History, 1871–1921* (New Haven, CT: Yale University Press, 1952), 233–34, and Karabel, *The Chosen*, 19–20; Kelley, *Yale*, 298–314. "Brave Mother Yale," was written by Charles Edmund Merrill (Yale 1898) and Thomas G. Shepard (copyright 1903, held by Shepard).

6. William Beinecke twice failed out of Phillips Academy and, without a high school diploma, was admitted to Yale in 1932. See Pierson, *Yale College: An Educational History, 1871–1921*, 233–34. See also Karabel, *The Chosen*, 19–20; Kelley, *Yale*, 298–314. The emergence of student sports—football more than others—had taken a romantic and "manly" hold in the national psyche (thanks to sports writers like Grantland Rice), but especially at Yale. Walter Camp (Yale 1880), Yale's star player, coach (as that term was then understood), and critical molder of the rules that still define football in America, had taken on the stature of knighted prince, an independent, popular, attractive, successful iteration of Dink Stover. The grand football stadium (Yale Bowl) opened in 1914, and the equally grand entrance to the athletic fields dedicated in Camp's honor in 1926 (which elicited contributions from throughout the nation, including from faculty and students at New Haven High School) gave permanence to a debate about athletics versus scholarship that reemerged regularly. The tension between athletics and academics underpinned, in part, the faculty's frustration. The Fisher Report and a change in academic emphasis, expectation of student performance, and the curriculum (more classical liberal arts, with numerous courses, such as Latin and Rhetoric, were made mandatory) also emerged just prior to and during Angell's presidency. That is, for those who understood or cared about the fullness of the intellectual opportunity it provided. Val Giamatti was among them. See also "New Haven High School Certificate of Contribution," December 31, 1926, Hillhouse Folder, New Haven Colony and Historical Society, New Haven, CT.

7. Thomas Bergin, chapter in *My Harvard, My Yale*, ed. Diana Dubois (New York: Random House, 1982), 161–62; Kelley, *Yale*, 311.

8. Not conduct or a perspective with respect to the outside or post-Yale world, which was the attitude reflected in *Stover at Yale* (many student leaders expected to and did head to Wall Street). Bergin appreciated the "unadulterated rapture [of] Cervantes,

Dante and Shakespeare, followed by Tink's [Chauncey Brewster Tinker] seventeenth-century course [in English literature]." Bergin, *My Harvard, My Yale*, 161–62; see also, Clarence Whittlesey Mendell, "The Subdivision of the College," *Yale Banner and Pot Pourri*, 1930, 10.

9. Two other constraints in Val's life added practical meaning to this essential discipline: like Thomas Bergin, Val worked part time during all four years and full time in the summer and, for his own imperative of vanity and blending in, he used some of that money to buy collegiate-style clothes at, among other places, the quintessential Yale thread, J.[acobi] Press store on York Street. Style mattered to him. His purchases and friendship with former Hillhouse classmate Paul Press were remembered decades later. Bergin, *My Harvard, My Yale*; Mollie Wilson, "Paul Press of J. Press," Kerkari.com; oral history, "A Conversation for Bart," RU 411, October 6, 1989 (Press); Kelley, *Yale*, 347 (Tinker); Paul H. Fry, "History of the English Department," Yale University, Department of English, September 2008, english.yale.edu/about/history-department (Tinker).

10. Judge Guido Calabresi (who knew Lipari and DeVane) believes DeVane's appointments also may have cost him the presidency following Seymour's departure. Interview with Calabresi.

11. Lipari was recruited from the University of Wisconsin, where he'd taught pre-Renaissance and Renaissance literature for the previous four years. Lipari was born in Sicily, Italy; was educated at Columbia University, where he'd been an instructor; and taught at Trinity College in Hartford, Connecticut. His knowledge of Romance languages included French and Spanish (he'd written and lectured about the works of Lope de Vega, a Spanish playwright, poet, and novelist). He was, in short order, embraced throughout the growing foreign language community for his ideas and commitment to teaching at an exciting time in the development of romance language education and for producing academic literature of special usefulness to the same purpose. Lipari's obligation was to develop an Italian language and literature program and enhance Yale's other romance language disciplines, which already had talented, experienced teachers. See, for example, Angelo Lipari, *The "Dolce Stil Novo" According to Lorenzo de' Medici: A Study of His Poetic "Principio" as an Interpretation of the Italian Literature of the Pre-Renaissance Period, Based on His "Comento"* (New Haven, CT: Yale University Press, 1936); Lipari, *The Structure and Real Significance of the Decameron* (New Haven, CT: Yale University Press, 1943); Robert S. Crawford, ed., *Wisconsin Alumni Magazine* 25, no. 9 (July 1924), 361 (Lipari's departure); Robin W. Winks, *Cloak and Gown: Scholars in the Secret War, 1939–1961* (New Haven, CT: Yale University Press, 1996), 29–30 (description of DeVane); interview with Calabresi (on DeVane's promotion of professors and its harm to his prospect of succeeding Seymour).

12. John Chipman Gray, "Review of *La Divina Commedia di Dante Alighieri* (1813)" in *Dante in America: The First Two Centuries*, ed. A. Bartlett Giamatti (Binghamton: State University of New York, 1983), 3–26; informal interview with Professor Robert Hollander.

13. "It would be endless to repeat the many passages" Dante also had "furnished to the most celebrated English writers," Gray wrote. Dante influenced Shakespeare and John Milton in his *Paradise Lost*, though *Paradise Lost*, Gray wrote, "consists altogether in a few general, though beautiful passages, [yet] its effects on the mind and heart are far feebler than those of Dante's narration." Gray, "Review of *La Divina Commedia*"; informal interview with Hollander.

14. See "Italian Society to Present Modern Comedies by Bracco," *Yale Daily News*, April 29, 1930; "Comedies to Be Presented by Cast of Italian Society," *Yale Daily News*, May 1, 1930; interview with Guido Calabresi.

15. Val was active in the *Centro Espanol de Yale* (the Spanish Center), directed by Professor Jorge A. Buendia from Ecuador, who developed, along with his colleagues, new oral and written techniques for teaching the language. It may have been through the Spanish Center that he perfected his skill in Portuguese and met former Hillhouse graduate and Yale day student Thomas Bergin. See Jorge A. Buendia, "Methods of Teaching Spanish at Yale," *Hispania* 27, no. 2 (May 1944): 178–208. Buendia described the evolution of teaching Spanish at Yale since 1929.

16. Val also took honorable mention in the *Figli d'Italia* Prize (for written scholarship) in his junior year (first prize went to his friend Salvatore Joseph Castiglione). "Prizes and Premiums," *Yale Banner and Pot Pourri*, 1931–1932, 44.

17. Performed originally in 1913, the play was a new form of theater, perfected by Italian playwrights from a form that originated before the Renaissance and took on new meaning after the disfiguring effects of trench and mustard gas fighting during World War I. Michael Vena, trans. *Italian Grotesque Theatre* (Madison, NJ: Fairleigh Dickinson University Press, 2001), 49; Marrone, *Encyclopedia of Italian Library Studies,* 438. Two examples in literature include the oddly shaped, yet not frightening, characters in Lewis Carroll's *Through the Looking Glass* and Victor Hugo's *Hunchback of Notre Dame*, or, in architecture, the grotesques (not the gargoyles) that adorned buildings. The play, as translated by W. Somerset Maugham, was produced in the Guild Theatre in New York in 1933. Humphrey Bogart and Shirley Booth starred. Leo G. Carroll played Cirillo Zanotti.

18. The story has complexity for the actors. After Paolo asserts to his friends that "he is required to kill an unfaithful wife to retain his self respect or otherwise commit suicide," he learns of his wife's infidelity. Unable to kill her, he stages her death and sends her abroad under a different name. A decomposed body is then discovered, and Paolo is confronted with accusations and exposure of his lack of principle. Throughout the play, Paolo has a cynical alter ego, the banker, Cirillo Zanotti—the role played by Valentine Giamatti. The play's form, challenging to the writer and performers, is "grotesque," not as the term is commonly defined—ugly, unsightly, distorted—but as it was understood in painting, storytelling, poetry, pottery, and architecture: ironic, unnatural, the distinct and unexpected separation of how a person appears and the actual persona. In Lipari's Italian Society, to perform the play required the nuanced understanding of fashioning the double meaning, the allegory, the unexpected conveyed to the human eye and ear, the skill at melding into one work of art the seeming contradiction—and then, of course, to perform, before an audience, in impeccable Italian. "Italian Play to Be Given," *Yale Daily News*, April 30, 1931; "Italian Society Play," *Yale Daily News Pictorial Supplement*, no. 26, May 2, 1931. In the photograph of the play, published in the *Yale Daily News*, Val sits on stage with dignified poise, a handsome 6 feet, 165 pounds, confident, as if he's mastered more than the precision of the language, that his Italian heritage also had yielded a feeling for how the language and its meaning should be conveyed. There is a contended joy in his face, not merely at succeeding with the play, but at discovering another method of teaching through theater.

19. Only a few years earlier, women workers at Gilbert involved with handling chemicals had insisted, successfully, in having the company provide free medical

check-ups for each of them to ensure there was no risk to their health. The work action was covered in the *New Haven Union*, a local paper. The Lucky Strike advertisement was titled "Do You Inhale? Is this question too revealing for other cigarettes?" Interview with David Ewing and Elria Giamatti Ewing; New Haven Directory (1922), 499 (Rose Giammattei working at A.C. Gilbert). The work action by women employees occurred in 1926. See Neil Hogan, *Moments in New Haven Labor History* (New Haven, CT: Great New Haven Labor History Association), 51 (the labor action was reported in the *New Haven Union*, March 3, 1926).

20. Val never talked about Americo later, other than to say "it had been a hard life, at times," though his son Bart would have learned of the nature of Americo's death from Val's sister, his Aunt Helen, if not from his father directly. Interviews and related notes, Kim Formica, Lavorgna family historian.

21. The International Institute for Foreign Women was designed to provide recently arrived immigrants with language instruction and the elevation of their own cultural traditions for the benefit of local New Haven neighbors. The New Haven Evening High School was formed for adults and young people who could not attend during the day. Yale 1932 Statistical Questions (completed October 23, 1931), Yale University Manuscripts and Archives (student records), and related "Confidential" report (January 1932) concerning "lists of students available for positions"; Benjamin Gorman, "The Community and You: Learning Your Way around Fair Haven," prepared for the Yale–New Haven Teacher's Institute, 1982, 11–12. Alfred Carleton Gilbert (Yale Medical 1909), an Olympic pole vault champion, was a well-liked entrepreneur (my aunt worked in the factory in the evening shift, roughly 3–11 p.m.); and see Alfred Carlton Gilbert, *The Man Who Lives in Paradise: The Autobiography of A. C. Gilbert* (New York: Rinehart, 1954). See also George E. Pozzetta, ed., *Americanization, Social Control, and Philanthropy* (New York: Garland, 1991), 285 (International Institute for Foreign-Born Women, Gary, Indiana, experience); interview with Elria Giamatti Ewing.

22. Di Sorbello was a skilled linguist with a broad knowledge of Italian literature and was active in various Italy and Italian American literary journals. Although he was born into his father's Italian family, di Sorbello's mother was from Philadelphia. Di Sorbello had visited America periodically and decided to remain. Along with farmers in Marches, Campania, and Basilicata, he helped Allied soldiers escape captivity and sure death. Di Sorbello's valor was recognized. See I.S.9. Camp 59 Survivors (Operation Ratberry), testimony of Allied Servicemen who were prisoners of war at Servigliano, Italy (March 1, 2015).

23. Dr. Giuseppe Sergi, who was affiliated with the Universities of Bologna and Rome, was the primary critic. Sergi was born in Messina, Sicily, and was a Garibaldi volunteer at age nineteen. See Grant, *The Passing of the Great Race*, chaps. 4, 5, and 6; Angell Papers, Yale University Archives, Box 113, Folder 1156 (correspondence between Racca and Angell and Racca's attached curriculum vitae; letter from the institute's executive secretary, Mark May, to Angell, September 30, 1930). In September 1930, President Angell was informed that the institute wanted Racca to remain. Once his credentials were confirmed by Fosdick, Racca, with Yale's imprimatur, began his descent onto the Italian immigrant communities—now, of course, into their second generation and distant in time and experience from the culture of their villages—to engage in his "laboratory" research. Though he focused on Wooster Square in his report, he digressed to

describe his experience in the Italian immigrant communities in Hartford, Connecticut. See Angell Papers, Yale, Box 113, Folder 1156 (Raymond Fosdick to Angell, October 24, 1930; Racca's proposal for the New Haven study, October 9, 1930).

24. Racca's *Preliminary Report,* 4, 7. Racca's influence endured at Yale into the twenty-first century. Stephen Lassonde begins his 2005 book *Learning to Forget: Schooling and Family Life in New Haven's Working Class, 1870–1940* (New Haven, CT: Yale University Press), with "In 1932, Vittorio Racca, researcher and interpreter for a child health study sponsored by the Rockefeller Foundation, was dispatched to investigate the role of family life in the welfare of Italian immigrant schoolchildren in New Haven." Lassonde presents Racca's findings with the assumption that they are accurate; in an endnote, Lassonde identified the "Institute of Human Relations" records as the source of Racca's study but not the institute's organic presence in Yale University. In fact, throughout the text of the book and the index there is no mention of President Angell or eugenics or their effect within Yale or on the mentality and prejudice that underpin Racca's (or other) research and findings. See also, Rae, *City,* 173.

25. Angell's reputation and influence as an informed, stanch eugenicist (affirmed by his Yale credential) was global. Leonard Darwin (Charles Darwin's son), who had been an active eugenicist in England and the United States, asked Angell to write the introduction to his book, *What Is Eugenics?*, published in 1932, by the Third International Congress of Eugenics. Angell, after summarizing the younger Darwin's decades of diligent, forceful dedication, wrote that, "More urgently, the problem of selecting the better and suppressing the poorer stocks, must be given exhaustive study." "Introductory Statement," by Angell, dated December 12, 1929, in Leonard Darwin, *What Is Eugenics?* (New York: Third International Congress of Eugenics, 1932).

26. "Science and Literature," lecture presented at Brown University, 23–28 (emphasis added), Wilbur Lucius Cross Papers, MS 155, Series II, Box 19, Folder 240, Yale University Archives. More fully, he said, "But we have a strong government. Recent experience shows that it would not be difficult to add a few more amendments to the Constitution, should they be needed. A President with a backbone we can always find when we want one. The number of our Cabinet Officers has already more than doubled since Washington's time. A Secretary of Eugenics would mean only one more." In subsequent lectures on this same subject, Cross, even more politically canny than Angell about what was necessary or appropriate to say publicly, eliminated the reference to, among other things, "A Secretary of Eugenics." More revealing, when in 1940 a Brown official asked for a copy of his lecture, Cross wrote that, "Owing to the advance in science in the last fifteen years, there are some details now quite out of date." Cross did not mention eugenics as among them. In the period between 1925 and 1938, Cross not only enforced the Connecticut law on sterilization when he became governor, but also supported the 1936 eugenics study in Connecticut led by Harry Laughlin, director of the Eugenics Record Office and, for a period, president of the American Eugenics Society located in New Haven.

27. Cross was, according to the *Daily News,* "a member of the executive committee of the Institute from its inception and, as dean of Yale University Graduate School, took a leading part in its organization." "Distinguished Educators to Speak at Formal Institute of Human Relations Dedication: Addresses to Be Broadcast on NBC Network," "Dean of the Medical School Writes on the Institute," "Institute Is Important to Many Diverse

Studies," *Yale Daily News*, May 9, 1931, 1. See also, *Yale Daily News* on Racca (same date, 6). Wilbur was a member of the advisory board of the American Eugenics Society, now located in New Haven. He also was (apparently at the same time) a member of the Rockefeller Foundation Board of Directors, which had helped fund the institute, and the Rockefeller General Education Board. It was Wilbur who chaired Hoover's White House Conference on Child Health, which included sessions on eugenics. Ray Wilbur and Wilbur Cross also would have confidence in the prominent presence of George Vincent, former president of the Rockefeller board, and in the supportive comments of Milton C. Winternitz, dean of the Yale Medical School and an American Eugenics Society founder. The AES Advisory Board, which included Wilbur, is listed on correspondence in the author's possession directed to various organizations planning state fairs at which the AES hoped to have display booths and advertisements. *People, Eugenical Panorama*, April 1931, 40, in Eugenics Record Office, Cold Spring Harbor, New York.

28. "President Angell to Give Baccalaureate Address at Commencement Exercises," *Yale Daily News*, May 31, 1932, 1, and subsequent photographs.

29. Marshall S. Bidwell (Yale Law 1858) had an eclectic career in the law and politics in the United States and Canada. He ultimately settled in New York. The scholarship in his name was established through the bequest of Benjamin Silliman and awarded to a graduate for "his personal merit and his ability and promise as a scholar." *Yale Endowments: A Description of the Various Gifts and Bequests Establishing Permanent University Funds* (New Haven, CT: Yale University, 1917), 75. Harry W. Foote (Yale 1866) was born in New Haven. He was a professor of chemistry at Yale and among the membership of the 1911 Hiram Bingham III Yale-Peruvian Expedition. *Yale Endowments*, 94. The Bidwell and Foote scholarships were combined in 1920 to ensure a larger grant of funds to meet the increased cost of tuition and fees since the time when both scholarships were established. *Reports Made to the President of Yale University* (New Haven, CT: Yale University, 1919–1920), 277–78.

30. Val had excelled in Latin, French, Spanish, and Italian; had acquired a working knowledge of German and Portuguese; and did well in English and philosophy. "Phi Beta Kappa," *Yale Banner and Pot Pourri*, 1932; "History of the Class of 1932," *Year Book 1932*, 59 (see profiles of Maynard Mack and Valentine Giamatti). Phi Beta Kappa was founded at William and Mary College in 1776, at the dawn of the formation of America in its most revolutionary posture. Val's courses and grades were available in his application to Harvard for its PhD program, acquired with the approval of Elria Giamatti Ewing.

CHAPTER 9

FASCISM AND RACE AT YALE

Epigraph is from Allon Schoener, *The Italian Americans* (New York: Macmillan, 1987), 9.

1. See, for example, the documented depth of anti-Semitism in Karabel, *The Chosen*, and Soares, *The Power of Privilege*, 21–27.

2. Though both men were primarily focused on admission criteria as the method for exclusion (including through I.Q.-type tests, which, to their disappointment, non–Anglo-Saxons passed), Angell and Corwin brought their exclusionary imperative to a darker level. In 1922, within a year of Angell's arrival, they sought from each of the

undergraduate deans data on whether "students of Jewish origin," especially "local origin," had more disciplinary and cheating ("cribbing") infractions than others that might be a basis for exclusion. Following the preparation of elaborate charts on "Hebrew" infractions, and "Hebrew" reliance of university financial support, they decided on restricted percentage goals to limit Jewish acceptance. See, generally, letter to Dean Frederick Jones (May 19, 1922) and related graphs and charts, news articles, and correspondence in Angell's Papers, Box 116, Folder 1193, Yale University Archives; Kelley, *Yale*, 41, 109 (Hebrew).

3. That reality no doubt weighed as a factor on both Castiglione and Giamatti (and likely Bergin) as they assessed their futures and the joy of teaching that each was intent on ensuring would become a way of life. Gerard N. Burrow, *A History of Yale's School of Medicine: Passing Torches to Others* (New Haven, CT: Yale University Press, 2002), 107 (Winternitz); Pierson, *Yale: The University College, 1921–1937*. Pierson noted that in 1937 the highest grade point average in the history of the university was achieved by Paul Pasquariello, the son of Southern Italian immigrants—a straight 98 average in all four years. Pasquariello, from Hartford, Connecticut, died in 2002. His obituary, published in the *Hartford Courant*, noted that Attorney Paul J. Pasquariello, 86, was born in Brooklyn, New York, August 12, 1916, "a son of the late Andrew and Rose Pasquariello. . . . He was a graduate of Yale University in 1937, and the Yale School of Law in 1940. . . . He also broke records at Yale University with a 98, four-year average, the highest ever in the history of the University. He was a member of Phi Beta Kappa and Order of the Coif. He was the recipient of numerous awards and prizes during his years at Yale, one of which was a six-week trip to Italy, for his proficiency in Italian." *Hartford Courant* (September 28, 2002). Interview with Calabresi (in his freshman year at Yale, two of the top ten students by grade average were Italian, including Calabresi, which even then caused special attention).

4. See "The Jewish Problem" designated file in Angell Papers, Box 116, Folder 1193, Yale University Archives; Soares, *The Power of Privilege*, 21–27. The nude photograph with measurements was used when Bart Giamatti entered Yale in 1956 and throughout the entirety of the Griswold era and the Brewster era (ending with the Class of 1971) until women were admitted.

5. The Offspring Act drew from the American state models as a means for eliminating the "unfit." The Restoration Act excluded Jews and the "politically unreliable" from civil service employment, restricted the number of Jewish students at German schools and universities, and largely excluded Jewish participation in the medical, legal, and acting professions. These legal actions in Germany were well known by the Yale-hosted American Eugenics Society, praised as a model by Harry Laughlin, and understood by President Angell and those around him. Angell also was receiving letters from well-known supporters of German anti-Nazi intellectuals who wanted to relocate to America. He demurred, while criticizing the German universities but not their eugenics laws. Foreign-language newspapers, particularly the *Forward*, reported on the emerging systematically imposed threats, exclusions, and deaths of Jews in Germany to, among others, New Haven's intertwined ethnic communities. See Hans-Walter Schmuhl, *The Kaiser Wilhelm Institute for Anthropology, Human Heredity and Eugenics, 1927–1945: Crossing Boundaries* (Boston: Springer, 2008), 87, 90, 144, 147, 274; Lombardo, *Three Generations, No Imbeciles*, 199–203 (Laughlin, Hitler, eugenics laws); Cohen, *Imbeciles*, 124–25 (Laughlin).

6. At that time, Mussolini and the Fascists had begun to exercise subtle and overt forms of anti-Semitism and, in eastern Africa, a form of eugenics cloaked in the rhetoric of colonialism. "His regime was vile," British explorer Denys Finch Hatton wrote, referring to Somalia. "Women and children butchered in cold blood after men had been rounded up and flattened out with machine guns. All decent thinking Italians are disgusted by his regime." Banking and industrial leaders in America, the heart of Yale's donors, were financial and advisory supporters of Mussolini. At the outset of the 1933 United States Senate Committee hearings into the causes of the 1929 stock market crash, Wall Street banker Charles E. Mitchell sought to excuse his presence as a witness because, he asserted with confidence, he was sailing to Italy to advise Benito Mussolini. Ferdinand Pecora, the committee's erudite chief counsel, who was born in Sicily, wasn't impressed and directed Mitchell to appear. Following the highly reported success of the hearings—especially Mitchell's admission of considerable financial manipulation to benefit himself and his friends—Angell and the Yale Corporation's Prudential Committee refused to allow Pecora to speak at the university. See Rockefeller family involvement with Mussolini, in Daniel Okrent, *Great Fortune: The Epic of Rockefeller Center* (New York: Viking, 2003), 279–80; Ron Chernow, *The House of Morgan: An American Banking Dynasty and the Rise of Modern Finance*, (New York: Grove Press, [1990] 2010), 277–78 (especially Morgan partner, Thomas Lamont). Pecora's "Reminisces" (recorded in 1961 and 1962), reviewed with the permission of the Columbia University Oral History Archives, Rare Book and Manuscript Library; Michael Perino, *The Hellhound of Wall Street* (New York: Penguin Press, 2010), 288–89. Professor Jerome Davis (Divinity School), after consultation with Law School Dean Clark and Professor William O. Douglas (who was "certain Woolsey Hall would be well filled"), wrote to Carl Lohman, Secretary's Office, seeking permission from the Corporation's Prudential Committee (June 7, 1933). Lohman responded to Davis informing him that the request was denied (June 12, 1933); Davis proposed to Lohman, at the Law School dean's suggestion, the alternative use of Sprague Hall or the Yale Law School auditorium (June 30, 1933), and Lohman replied that the committee was "not pleased with the suggestion that Mr. Pecora speak from any Yale platform" (July 7, 1933), Yale University Archives. Pecora did participate in a moot court competition six years later, while serving as judge on the New York Supreme Court. See *Yale Daily News*, May 20, 1933, 2.

7. The Fascist vice counsel, whose new office was located near the university, sought to introduce Bottai. "[A] man in the audience jumped upon his chair and, addressing the assemblage, unbraided the work of the Fascisti." Police entered. Shouts were joined by epithets. "The theater for the next 15 minutes," the *New Haven Evening Register* wrote the next day, "represented a pro-British meeting in a Dublin Square." The assistant city attorney, Peter Trenchi, arrived and pleaded for calm, but not before he made clear his belief that "the Fascisti organization has gone beyond the law in its activities." The police remained. Order was restored. "Police Quell Disturbance at Local Meeting, Italian Radicals Object to Address by Deputy, a Fascisti Leader." *New Haven Evening Register* (September 19, 1921), 1; Stanislao G. Pugliese, *Carlo Rosselli: Socialist Heretic and Antifascist Exile* (Cambridge, MA: Harvard University Press, 1999), 174; Smith, *Modern Italy*, 396 (Jewish laws); Laura Kalman, "Some Thoughts on Yale and Guido," *Law and Contemporary Problems* 77 (2014): 15–16; interview with Calabresi. Calabresi, as previously stated, also believes that Dean DeVane's action in elevating a Jew and a Catholic to full professorships

likely cost him the presidency among surprised and disgruntled Yale Corporation members; see also "Renata Calabresi, An Anti-Fascist, 96," *New York Times*, December 20, 1995, B15, and "Massimo Calabresi, 84, Yale Medical Professor," *New York Times*, March 20, 1988, A20; Nunzio Pernicone, *Carlo Tresca: Portrait of a Rebel* (Oakland, CA: AK Press, 2010), 139 (Bottai in New Haven); Liner Ahead of Time: Presidente Wilson Speeded Up So Operation Could Be Performed Here on Passenger," *New York Times*, August 19, 1921), 13 (Bottai's purpose discussed); "Italian Group to Run Rockefeller Unit," *New York Times* (March 3, 1933, 1 (Bottai); Okrent, *Great Fortune*, 280 (*Fortune Magazine*: "democracy . . . is dead." And, as to Lamont, "he must have known that [Mussolini] had declared a police state eight years earlier, [and] abolished parliament two years after that"); "Guido Calabresi: A Foreigner in New Haven, 1940–1945," ed. Norman I. Silber (New Haven, CT: Yale Law School, 2016), an adapted preview selection from *Outside In: The Oral History of Guido Calabresi* (forthcoming). See also Sara Wheeler, *Too Close to the Sun* (New York: Random House, 2007), 186 (Finch Hatton in Somalia in 1923); Riccio, *The Italian American Experience in New Haven*, 161 (Fraternal Hall anti-Fascist rally).

8. Men joined the strikers. The International Ladies' Garment Workers joined with the Amalgamated Clothing Workers of America, which helped organize and garner additional support. See "For a Better Future: The 1933 New Haven Garment Strike," *New England Historical Society* (July 9, 2013): 32.

9. Pugliese, *Carlo Rosselli*, 174. Bianca would earn a PhD in French from Yale and would become chair of the Italian Department at Albertus Magnus College. They later would become friends of the Giamatti family, no doubt in part because both families spoke out against Fascism in similar ways. In the 1930s, however, the Calabresis, like many other anti-Fascists, were *persona non grata*, largely "non-persons" in the eyes of the Fascists. Their fate and the treatment of other anti-Fascists were well known in America. Long before Salvemini actually came to America, his exile to London, for example, was followed closely. See Walter Lippmann, *Public Philosopher: Selected Letters of Walter Lippmann*, ed. John Morton Blum (New York: Ticknor & Fields, 1985), 186–87.

10. See A. M. Sperber, *Murrow: His Life and Times* (New York: Bantam Books, 1987), 45–46, 50–58. Duggan explained to Angell that the Italian government "has offered . . . five fellowships covering tuition, board, and lodging, and a discount on all Italian lines going to Naples or Genoa . . . in exchange for five similar students coming to the United States" to study in the graduate or professional schools. Duggan wanted Yale to accept one, or perhaps all five. Yale and other universities already had exchange programs sponsored by France.

11. Professor Charles Bakewell was educated at Harvard and served in Red Cross units in World War I in Italy. He joined Yale's Department of Philosophy, headed the American Philosophical Society, and ran successfully as a state senator and member of Congress. On his arrival in New Haven, Bakewell was welcomed into the Italian community because of his service, gracious temperament, and command of the Italian language and its dialects. He knew Dr. Verdi, who also had served in the war in France as a surgeon. Angell Papers, Box 116, Folder 1186, Yale University Archives (Duggan to Angell, March 23, 1929, and Angell to Cross, March 25, 1929). Angell passed the Duggan request on to Cross, with the expectation that he would find a credible Yale representative "glad to study literature and art for a year."

12. Richard T. Hull, ed., *The American Philosophical Association Centennial Series: Presidential Addresses, 1901–2000* (Charlottesville, VA: Philosophy Documentation

Center, 2013) (biography and address of Charles Montague Bakewell); Bakewell to Angell (May 15, 1929) and Cross to Angell (January 13, 1930), Box 116, Folder 1186, Yale University Archives.

13. Both Verdi and Poli had a long history of providing similar support and encouragement to Italian immigrants and their children. At this juncture, Verdi had created the infrastructure and practical philosophy of St. Raphael's Hospital, which served New Haven's immigrant community in a manner Yale affiliates and other private hospitals would not, and he had solidified his national reputation as a surgeon. Poli was managing more than two dozen theaters throughout the northeast, creating careers for numerous young actors and musicians, while still living in the Hill/Oak Street/Legion Avenue neighborhood. See Burrow, *A History of Yale's School of Medicine*, 264–66 (Dr. Verdi); William H. Verdi, "Some Principles of Intracranial Surgery," *New England Journal of Medicine* 163 (August 18, 1910). Verdi was born in Naples, Italy, in 1873. An alumnus of Hillhouse High School, he graduated from Yale's Medical School in 1894.

14. In 1934, the fellowship recipient was Salvatore Castiglione. By early 1930, Verdi and Poli had contributed at least $1,500 toward the Italian Fellowship Exchange Program, ignoring Yale's new, self-serving claim that the cost to them would be much higher. Their contribution continued, and Verdi sought to establish a permanent fund of $30,000 to ensure the opportunity for an Italian American from New Haven to experience the fullness of Italy. Though the permanent fund would not come to fruition—Angell eventually took the choice of students away from Lipari, which troubled Dr. Verdi, and the Fascist-appointed vice counsel in New Haven was unable to raise sufficient funds on his own—it didn't matter. Mussolini and Hitler had done enough damage in Africa and Europe that most universities in America had, in 1938 and 1939, stopped their foreign exchange programs to both Italy and Germany.

15. Giamatti, "Commentary," 13. The fortunes of the New Haven Clock Company, deeply harmed by the Depression and the advent of electrical clocks, warranted layoffs. Angelo was not among them, though he likely took a cut in earnings. Although Val continued to earn money as a teacher and tutor, real estate rental income lessened substantially. Angelo's and Maria's skills at managing money, however, allowed them to continue to provide homes for their daughters' families. In 1934, after Val's return from Italy, the Giammatteis moved from Ferry Street to the Dixwell Avenue/Newhallville neighborhood. The move created the option for Angelo, which he exercised later, to work at the closer Winchester's factory, which had maintained decent employment levels. The Giammatteis purchased 65 Lilac Street, a three-family house in an urban residential neighborhood with local stores, easy trolley access to Yale, and proximity to Saint Ann's Church on Dixwell Avenue. St. Ann's was established largely as an Italian American parish, which Angelo and Maria joined. As a practical matter, the Giammatteis, like many other Italian families in New Haven, understood and expected hard times. They adjusted to their new circumstances. "Clock Business Tick-Tocking Way Back to Prosperity," *New Haven Register* (January 6, 1935); New Haven Clock Company Records, New Haven Colony and Historical Society, New Haven, Connecticut; interview with Dolph Santello. Eventually, Angelo purchased a nearby home for his daughter Helen; her husband, George; and their son, George. There is a photograph of Angelo readily accessible through the Ancestry website. He's holding a young child—his grandson, George Urquhart—as they

walk together in the Dixwell Avenue/Newhallville neighborhood. Informal interview with George Urquhart.

16. The Grimké sisters, Angelina and Sarah, once they reached maturity (and long after Silliman's visit) and to the consternation of their family, moved north and became well-known advocates for women's rights and abolition. Gerda Lerner, *The Grimké Sisters from South Carolina: Pioneers for Women's Rights and Education* (Raleigh: University of North Carolina Press, 2004; originally published under a different title in 1967); Kelley, *Yale*, 138 (Silliman's visit).

17. Kelley, *Yale*, 135–38, 153.

18. The electoral deal was struck in the back room of Wormley's, an elegant, politically tempered hotel in Washington, DC. Leaders of both political parties joined, solicited, or ignored Southern racism well into the 1960s, including John Kennedy. Only Harry Truman actually eschewed the South electorally, almost at peril of reelection. See Rayford W. Logan, *The Betrayal of the American Negro: From Rutherford B. Hayes to Woodrow Wilson* (New York: Collier Books, 1965), 3–47, 85–86, 115–118 (Supreme Court), 188. Proto, *The Rights of My People*, 31; In *This Republic of Suffering: Death and the American Civil War* (New York: Knopf, 2008), Drew Gilpin Faust juxtaposed Douglass's despair in 1883 with President William McKinley's 1898 formal announcement "to the South . . . that 'the time has now come in the evolution of sentiment and feeling under the province of God, when the spirit of fraternity we should share with you in the care of the graves of the Confederate soldiers'" (269). Faust failed to mention the far more likely cause of Douglass's lament: the disquieting deal struck at Wormley's and the immediate Southern enactment of laws to ensure that the social, cultural, and political structure and inequities of slavery, and other forms of eugenically rationalized conduct, were formally protected and enforced.

19. "Yale, A National University," in *New Englander and Yale Review, 1890* (New Haven, CT: William L. Kinglsey, 1890), 184–86.

20. See the following articles in *Yale Alumni Weekly* 22, no. 32 (April 25, 1913): "Eighty Five's 'Sentimental Journey' to South Carolina" by James R. Roy, 801; "Yale and the South," 803; "The Yale National Spirit," 804.

21. *Yale Alumni Weekly* 22, no. 31 (April 13, 1913), 773–74. In 1928—when Valentine Giamatti was about to graduate from New Haven High School—Yale established "University Regional Scholarships for outstanding students from three areas—the Far West, the South Atlantic, and the Southwest. All three were places," sociologist Professor Jerome Karabel wrote, "from which Yale drew few students, but all three had small Jewish populations." The scholarship program began in 1932, the year after Calhoun and other human bondage advocate designees were announced as the names of Yale's new residential colleges. See Karabel, *The Chosen*, 215–16. The other colleges were Davenport, Edwards, Berkeley, Trumbull, Dwight (the first Dwight, not his son), Stiles, and Silliman. See Antony Dugdale, J. J. Fueser, and J. Celso de Castro Alves, *Yale, Slavery and Abolition* (New Haven, CT: Amistad Committee, 2001), appendix 1 (Table of Namesakes of Yale Residential Colleges).

22. "350 Students from Italy Due Tomorrow," *New Haven Evening Register*, October 7, 1934, 1–2; letter, Kirby to Angell (August 10, 1934), Angell Papers, Yale University Archives. Committee members included U.S. Ambassador Breckinridge Long, Dr. John Finley, and William E. Stevenson of Princeton, among others. See "Gustavus Kirby,

Leader in Sports," *New York Times*, February 28, 1956 (obituary); Carolyn Marvin, "Avery Brundage and American Participation in the 1936 Olympic Games," *Journal of American Studies* 16, no. 1 (1982): 81–105 (includes discussion of Brundage's anti-Semitism and the proposed boycott of the 1936 Olympics). In *No Ordinary Time: Franklin and Eleanor Roosevelt: The Homefront in World War II* (New York: Simon & Schuster, 2008), 515–16, Doris Kearns Goodwin captures Breckinridge Long's anti-Semitism and his favorable view of Mussolini, both of which would have melded with Angell's view.

23. Angell to Racca (October 2, 1934), Angell Papers, Yale University Archives.

24. Letters, Lohmann to Angell (September 15, 1934) and Angell to Lohmann (September 25, 1934), Angell Papers, Yale University Archives. The Italian vice counsel helped in organizing all of these events.

25. Kaye was direct: "It is appropriate at this time to express our attitude toward Fascism and its relation to the American student body." Pointing to Dean Roscoe Pound, Kaye wrote that "viewed concretely, Dean Pound has accepted a stamp of approval from a University that has not only discarded academic freedom, and become a servile political prop, but which is a pseudo-intellectual symbol of ruthless regimentation and persecution. . . ." Italy, Kaye wrote, "has done the same . . . [and] . . . Yale has become an object of derision to the Italian leaders." The students from Italy "have been most completely . . . inculcated with the spirit of Fascist demagoguery" and should not be welcomed on the Yale campus. Kaye made clear that the National Student League did not oppose them because they were Italians: "Indeed, we feel a deep sympathy for the Italian students of the Mussolini regime," whose purpose, however, is to "whip up a favorable attitude toward their Fascist terrorism." Letter, Kaye to Angell, and typed note on front of Kaye's letter (September 3, 1934), Angell Papers, Yale University Archives. The Harvard episode was not without complexity. See Peter Conradi, "Meanwhile: When Harvard Played Host to Hitler's Right-Hand Man," *New York Times*, November 30, 2004, which was based in part on reportage from the Holocaust Conference held at Boston University, where, with documentation, the role of Harvard and some among its alumni was far more ambivalent toward, and in some cases supportive of, Hanfstaengl than understood in 1934. The National Student League was one of a number of left-thinking student groups that emerged during this time period of much broader social criticism of America's failure to recognize the harm occurring to workers, those trying to form labor unions, and the poor. The league was reported to have sent a delegation to Appalachia (Harlan County, Kentucky) to aid hungry miners and to support the hearings—contentious, highly publicized, and occasionally violent—held there by American intellectuals, who included, among others, John Dos Passos, Sherwood Anderson, and Theodore Dreiser. See *Harlan Miners Speak: Report on Terrorism in the Kentucky Coal Fields Prepared by Members of the National Committee for the Defense of Political Prisoners* (New York: Da Capo Press, 1970, originally printed by Harcourt, Brace in 1932), and, for example, Alessandro Portelli, *They Say in Harlan County: An Oral History* (New York: Oxford University Press, 2011), 200. See also chapter 3, "The Conversation," of Neil Thomas Proto, *To a High Court: The Tumult and Choices That Led to United States of America v. SCRAP* (Lanham, MD: Roman & Littlefield, 2006, now available in iBook and eBook).

26. According to the reply to Angell, Kaye "recorded excellent as a freshman, and again last year he had an average of 80," but he had to leave school for financial reasons. He was, however, from New Haven, that is, "local." The *New Haven Evening Register*

covered only the impending arrival of the students, not the league's letter. Angell did not reply to Kaye. Kaye released his letter to the *Daily News*, which published it in full. The evening before the arrival, the league hosted an "Open Forum and Discussion" on "Aspects of Fascism," at Yale's Pierson College. The students present later informed President Angell that collectively they "deeply regret and object specifically to 1. The official character of the visit and reception of this group as Fascists; and 2. The permission given to them to parade in the Yale Bowl." "Reception of Fascists Protested by Students," *Yale Daily News*, October 5, 1934; "Open Forum Will Be Held on 'Aspects of Fascism,'" *Yale Daily News*, October 11, 1934; David Clendenin (Yale 1928) to Angell, written on behalf of "the forum" (October 8, 1934). See also a letter to Kaye written after the Italian students' departure from New Haven from R. M. Chesterfield, secretary to the university, and Kaye's reply (October 8, 1934), Angell Papers, Yale University Archives.

27. "Italian Honor Students Pay Visit to City and Yale," *New Haven Evening Register*, October 7, 1934; "Visiting Italian Students to Watch Columbia Game and to Parade in Bowl," *Yale Daily News*, October 6, 1934.

28. "Anti-Fascist Society Concludes Statement," *Yale Daily News*, October 11, 1934; "DeCicco Scores Instigators of Demonstrations," *New Haven Evening Register*, October 9, 1934, 8.

29. "300 Students of Italy Get Gala Welcome," *New Haven Evening Register*, October 7, 1934, 1.

30. When, a few months later, the Yale Germanic Club was meeting with "Dr. Richard Sallet of the German Embassy" to "talk informally on 'The New Foundation of the German Commonwealth,'" the National Student League reminded students that Hitler has "brought truculent oppression to religious and working-class groups of Germany." "Nazi Propaganda and the Yale Campus," letter to the Chairman of the *News*, *Yale Daily News*, December 11, 1934.

CHAPTER 10

ROMANCE OF THE HEART AND THE LIBERAL MIND

1. Aeneas, a Trojan, actually had his poetic origin in the Ancient Greek epic the *Iliad*, attributed to Homer. The *Aeneid*, among other works of literature and history, connects Ancient Greece to Rome's Latin and culture, and to both Italy and Dante's work.

2. The Etruscan League of States, a nation of a kind (a monarchy transformed into a republican form of governance), had in some locations the characteristics of urban structure (multistory architecture, roads, bridges, water and sewer systems), especially in modern-day Rome, and an organized spiritual culture that, in important respects, was an antecedent to Christianity, not in its beliefs but in its geography. Rome was its center. The civilization lasted from roughly 700 BC to the fourth century BC, when, after warfare, it was carefully—that is, with the preservation of stone works, dwellings, customs, and artifacts—incorporated into the Roman Empire. See, for example, Larissa Bonfante, ed., *Etruscan Life and Afterlife: A Handbook of Etruscan Studies* (Detroit, MI: Wayne State University Press, 1986); John North Hopkins, *The Genesis of Roman Architecture* (New Haven, CT: Yale University Press, 2016); John F. Hall, ed., *Etruscan Italy* (Provo, UT: Brigham Young University, 1996), 149; Ingrid D. Rowland, "The Long Reach of Rome," *New York Review of Books*, April 20, 2017, 16; Peter Levi, "The Youth of Virgil," in *Virgil:*

His Life and Times, chap. 1 (New York: St. Martin's Press, 1998); informal interview with Linda Gillison, professor of emerita, classics, University of Montana, May 25, 2017. Dante on Virgil: "And are you then that Virgil and that fountain of purest speech? . . . Glory and light of Poets! . . . For you are my true master and first author."

3. Throughout the yearlong trip, learned decorum, the thoughtful presence of other classmates, and obligatory guidance from Smith's mentors provided constant and expected companionship. They were chaperoned. Also aboard ship was Dr. Iago Galdston, a Russian-born psychiatrist and educator trained in Vienna and a spokesperson for the New York Academy of Medicine, and his wife, Dr. Theresa Wolfson, the education director of the International Ladies' Garment Workers' Union. Both befriended Val and Peggy during the voyage across the Atlantic. See Peggy Walton's photo album of Italy trip, accompanying notations, and interviews with David and Elria Giamatti Ewing.

4. He could speak the dialect fluently; had to explain the transformation of Giammattei to Giamatti; had enough of the physical traits of an ancestor to be recognized with a few paces of walking and a profile look (though his height might have baffled his aunts and uncles); probably found cousins who looked like his sisters, cousins, and neighbors; saw an abundance of Catholic churches; met families with familiar names; was lauded with pride as having the seeming prosperity of a successful emigrant from both villages; and was treated to a special meal of good cheeses, local wines, homemade pasta, and succulent grapes or figs.

5. The time in Perugia was constrained by introductions of students from other nations, language classes, a broad introduction to art and architecture, and regular walks and excursions throughout the city, where Peggy photographed Etruscan structures that she recognized immediately. Then into the countryside, to farms and the public laundry, and the meaning of incorporating into daily life the virtue and influence of antiquity, especially urban density and walkability, because, in part, it retained its welcomed definition of civilization and continuity. The common teaching practice at the university was something close to immersion: Italian was spoken as frequently as possible in the classroom and on the road.

6. Harriet Rubin, *Dante in Love* (New York: Simon & Schuster, 2004), 54–61. Peggy's photographic journal and notes indicate that they viewed the town, basilica, and San Damiano's monastery close up, and from the hilltop they viewed the ruins of the Rocca Maggiore, perhaps with lunch basket in hand. The meaning Francis attributed to envy, fire, and charity found a place in the *Commedia* with nuanced and redefined application. And Dante, by deliberate choice, was buried in a Franciscan tunic.

7. Peggy's photograph album and notes show that snow covered the hillside in San Marino, and then they traveled south to Orvieto and to Rome, where Peggy stood with a travel mate in a fitted, full-length tailored coat, arm locked at the elbow held against her waist, looking confident and elegant, the Arch of Constantine the backdrop. In late April 1934, they traveled south by train and boat to Sicily, Palermo first, then the eastern coastline, to the famed town of Taormina to see its ruins, the Greek influence, its Teatro Antico di Taormina. The took long walks into its hillsides and to enjoy a day for conversation and reading in the rocky alcoves of its beaches. They returned north, crossed the Straits of Messina, entered Salerno, and then south to the Temple of Hera II, the vivid remnant of Greek architecture and tribute—strong, majestic, a reflection of the depth in the Southern Italian cultural heritage.

8. The apartments also were located between the famed Cathedral of Saint Mary of the Flower and the Duomo di Firenze, the architectural wonder of Filippo Brunelleschi.

9. FDR seemed intent on demonstrating his newly acquired *bono fides*, or maybe just making a point that no one, including those who had succeeded in the way the Harvard culture held of value, was immune from flattery. Family photograph and interview with Ogden. See also John T. Bethell, "Frank Roosevelt at Harvard," *Harvard Magazine*, November 1, 1996; *Cincinnati Enquirer*, Cincinnati, OH, April 22, 1934, 11.

10. Perfecting his language skill and getting a firsthand appreciation for the culture was his imperative. The Catholic Church, its political machinations unabashedly revealed, had moved to Avignon, France, in the fourteenth century. Val also would be closer to Spain—its language and politics—and the debate in France over the fate of France's own Jewish citizens and those of Germany who sought self-exile in Paris, where Italian anti-Fascists also sought refuge from Mussolini. Val chose to enter a setting that teemed with controversy, historical and current, and that was entangled deeply in his heritage and expanded knowledge of European culture.

11. Research would eventually take him to the Library of Congress to dig through Revolutionary correspondence and records, and deep into Yale's archives and likely those in Philadelphia and New York or locations where Digny had provided valuable service as soldier and engineer, including Digny's documented capture by the British in South Carolina. Val also was taken by the prospect—well received in academic circles that delved aggressively into the full cultural and political influence that had surrounded the romance languages—of exploring the principles of democracy as embraced in the Italian (Philip Mazzei's relationship with Thomas Jefferson among them) and French (Marquis de Lafayette) cultures, with the manner of giving those principles practical meaning (the risk of death) in the aspirations of American independence. Digny, Val suspected, also had left correspondence and perhaps relatives in Italy. Valentine Giamatti, Mount Holyoke College Archives (draft, related notations, and completed PhD dissertation submitted to Harvard and later revised, expanded, translated into Italian, and submitted to the University of Florence).

12. Mary Walton and related college records, Smith College Archives; personal papers of Elria Ewing Giamatti.

13. Giacosa was renowned largely because of the breadth of his skill: He'd written the production of *La Signora di Challant* (The Lady of Challand) especially for French actress Sarah Bernhardt, and it opened in New York in 1891. He also wrote three librettos used by Giacomo Puccini in *La Bohème, Tosca*, and *Madama Butterfly. Come le Foglie*, a comedic drama originally staged in 1900, was described this way in its original production: "The *deus ex machina*, Massimo, who saves all that is worth saving in this family that is breaking up like the season of autumn and falling like leaves (*come le foglie*), has the great merit of being natural and no mere machine." See *Saturday Review of Politics, Literature, Science, and Arts*, June 23, 1900, London, England, 787; photographs and play handbill in author's possession; Smith College Archives; Joanne Bentley, *Hallie Flanagan: A Life in the American Theatre* (New York: Knopf, 1988), 368, 373, 392, 403.

14. There would be no long evenings writing the dissertation, and finally Val would have the opportunity to teach, his credentials recognized, and to do so in Montpelier, home of the state capital. The town also was within the Walton historic milieu, close to ancestral roots, Peggy's home, Smith College, and places she'd vacationed as a child—and,

as Val would have welcomed immediately, it was next door to Barre, a vibrantly diverse community with a long history of Italian American stone mason craftsmanship and political activism by virtually every ethnic and religious group it attracted. New Haven and Yale were reachable within a day, though not easily. On Barre, see, for example, Bernard Sanders, ed., "Vermont Labor Agitator," *Labor History* 15, no. 2 (Spring 1974): 261–70 (interview with Mose Cerasoli of Barre).

CHAPTER 11
MELDING THE PAST INTO THE FUTURE

1. The "junior college originated at the University of Chicago in 1892, when President William Rainey Harper organized the Liberal Arts college into upper and lower divisions. The lower division was given the name 'Junior College' in 1896." The college's purpose was readily agreed to: the high school program was "incomplete and inadequate preparation for life, the junior college [would serve] to round out the general education of students." The movement took a new turn when Professor A. F. Lange of the University of California persuaded the California State Legislature to authorize "the establishment of junior colleges as units in the public school system." Eldon Hubert Martin, "The Birth of the Junior College," in *Vermont College: A Famous Old School* (Nashville, TN: Parthenon Press, 1962), 177–83; Vermont Junior College, *Catalogue, 1937–1938* (1937), 6–18; "Dr. Hewitt Accepts Headmastership," *Montpelier Seminary Bulletin* 25 (May 1936): 1.

2. In 1936, "more than six hundred junior colleges existed in the country"; approximately ninety were independent, and 175 were church related. The existing Montpelier Seminary, a theological center for young clergymen, and the institutionally related "Collegiate Institution for Young Women" were combined and transformed into the two-year college program. It was "a Christian College," but the selection of students was nondenominational from the outset. Dr. Hewitt was a Methodist clergyman, author of poetry, chairman of the Vermont Board of Education, a former state representative, and the preacher at Middlebury College (where he'd been awarded the Doctor of Divinity degree and where Val and Peggy would later add definition to the highly regarded language program). He also was responsible for the Montpelier Seminary. Martin, "The Birth of the Junior College," 177–83; Vermont Junior College, *Catalogue, 1937–1938*, 6–18; "Dr. Hewitt Accepts Headmastership," 1.

3. Collegiality thrived within a small faculty, whose members had teaching experience at schools that included Boston University; Duke; Yale; the state universities of Wisconsin, Maine, and Iowa; and foreign universities in Bulgaria and Austria. Eugenics was challenged directly. Studies in 1932 showed that discrimination, not science or even faux science, was at the heart of "bad heredity," though institutionalization and sterilization continued under various Vermont government agencies. See, for example, Henry Taylor et al., *Rural Vermont: A Program for the Future* (Burlington, VT: Vermont Commission on Country Life, 1931). The history of eugenics in Vermont, derived from formal documents and oral histories, was methodically recovered and told in *Vermont Eugenics: A Documentary History*, a project begun in 1986 and formally expanded through various individuals and the WEB Project. See also Nancy L. Gallagher, *Breeding Better Vermonters: The Eugenics Project in the Green Mountain State* (Lebanon, NH: University Press of New

England, 1999). The 1931 enactment was preceded in similar form by a 1912 Vermont law. The law was vetoed by Governor Allen M. Fletcher on the basis of a thorough opinion written by Attorney General R. E. Brown that demonstrated the proposed law's unconstitutionality and "unwarranted and inexcusable discrimination and classification"; the veto was, nonetheless, overridden by the legislature. *Buck v. Bell* precluded any such constitutional objection to the more expansive 1931 law, which, though "unwarranted and inexcusable," remained available and prevailed in other states. According to one estimate, 253 recorded sterilizations were performed in Vermont, as recorded by University of Vermont researchers and posted in "Eugenics: Compulsory Sterilization in 50 States," under the supervision of Dr. Lutz Kaelber, associate professor of sociology, University of Vermont.

4. *Montpelier Seminary Bulletin* 26 (December 1936): 2–4.

5. Peggy's sister Elizabeth served as maid of honor, and sister Kathryn as bridesmaid. Peggy was described as "a tall slender girl, . . . a graceful attractive figure" in her mother's wedding gown of ivory cream satin, with long train and sleeves, and deep yoke of lace. The veil, which "fell in sweeping slopes beyond the train," was made of Venetian lace, purchased in Italy and worn by her aunt at her own wedding. The alcove at the front of this simple New England church was decorated with small hemlock trees, with a "background . . . of a continuous tiered mass" of white lilies, blue delphiniums, and yellow calendulas. Also present at the wedding were Val's sister Helen and her family; a number of his cousins, including Dolph Santello and his parents; and the Festas, Val's sister's family. Angelo and Maria were unable to attend; Maria had become ill, and Angelo remained at home to care for her. But both called from New Haven to speak to Peggy and Val just before the reception began. Relatives and friends from throughout New England and the Northeast, including the Santellos, arrived via a special train arranged by Peggy's grandfather. Interviews with Dolph Santello, Elria Giamatti Ewing, and David Ewing; "Historic Church Setting for Miss Walton's Bridal," *Portland Evening Express,* July 1, 1937; "Giamatti-Walton Bridal in South Berwick, Saturday," *Portland Sunday Telegram,* July 4, 1937; "Miss Walton Bride in Church Ceremony," *Wakefield Daily,* July 6, 1937.

6. "Historic Church Setting for Miss Walton's Bridal"; "Giamatti-Walton Bridal in South Berwick, Saturday"; "Miss Walton Bride in Church Ceremony."

7. See, for example, Williams, *South Italian Folkways in Europe and America.* Her study was likely undertaken and written during Angell's tenure and certainly Racca's (she acknowledged reliance on his data, xvii), and her frame of reference is limited severely by her own reliance on studies in New York City and in Sicily (the ancestral home of few Italians in New Haven), where her assumptions originate (assuming they have validity or even relevance to, in some cases, people more than two generations removed from family arrival to New Haven). Some conclusions are flat out inaccurate, such as that Italian immigrants believed "Women should not work outside the home" (18). Most women did, including at factory work they brought home (see Riccio, *Farms, Factories, and Families,* 1–138, 191–373). In Sicily, where Williams draws her assumptions, women both worked outside of the home and led labor uprisings over unfair treatment. See Guglielmo, *Living the Revolution.* Stereotypes—pointless ones at that—and ignorant assertions also are rampant throughout the Williams book (72, maladjusted clothing), (53, the poor quality of the Mediterranean diet), (32, despise Jews). Anthony Riccio dispels all of them in his works. Williams, for example, also transformed the saying, "Take it easy," into evidence

of laziness and languor (23), when, in fact, it was used to convey watchfulness, prudence, and awareness of mischief. She makes no reference to the embrace of eugenics by the Institute of Human Relations, which funded her study, or any reference to the harsh working conditions or discrimination that continued to confront Italian Americans. Her study, not unlike others done in New Haven, seems more like a justification for more funding and the legitimacy of eugenics than an aid in helping others deal with what was by then the second or third generation of Italian Americans and not newly arrived immigrants. Her studied analysis of religion, health and hospitals, and care of the aged and children are, as affirmed by Riccio, largely accurate. Professor Maurice R. Davie and Professor James G. Leyburn, both sociologists, were among those who remained critics of eugenics. Each realized, however, that the eugenics influence (the institutional and "non-institutional roots") at Yale—among alumni and students, in and at other academic institutions (teaching and examples of eugenics tempered high school and college text-books for decades), among state governments, and in other parts of the world—warranted constant, if not always successful, vigilance. The United States Supreme Court decision in *Buck v. Bell* only added to the boldness of continued adherence. See, also, the role Davie and Leyburn played, and the strong anti-eugenics writing and advocacy of one-time Connecticut and later Columbia professor L. C. Dunn before, during, and after World War II. Melinda Gormley, "Geneticist L. C. Dunn: Politics, Activism, and Community," (PhD diss., Oregon State University, 2006), 410nn45–47.

8. See *Skinner v. Oklahoma*, 316 U.S. 535 (1942), which, while striking down an Oklahoma statute requiring forced sterilization of certain criminals because it did not apply the law equally, did not overrule *Buck v. Bell* or find the punishment unconstitutional. See also Victoria F. Nourse, *In Reckless Hands* (New York: W. W. Norton, 2008).

9. In May 1936, following Laughlin's and national publications' praise and reportage on Germany's new and broadly implemented eugenic laws and the formal collaboration between various American doctors and German eugenicists (with Rockefeller and Harriman funding), Laughlin "was chosen by the Nazi Administrators [at the University of Heidelberg] to receive the honorary degree of Doctor of Medicine for his work in the 'science of racial cleansing.'" Although Laughlin was unable to attend, the award was widely known and both criticized and applauded. His receipt of the award didn't alter the commission's or Governor Cross's decision to retain him. Lombardo, *Three Generations, No Imbeciles*, 201–14.

10. The Carnegie-Laughlin Report is available, with related correspondence and newspaper articles, at the Truman State University, Pickler Memorial Library, Harry H. Laughlin Papers, Manuscript Archives Collection L1, in Kirksville, Missouri, where Laughlin received his bachelor's degree. Unless additionally noted, the information on the content and process of the report and related documents are derived from the actual documents in the Laughlin Papers. The report, in some form, also is available in the Museum of Natural History in New York, as well as at Yale University Library. See, with respect to this note, *Exhibit of the Human Resources of Connecticut, Their Survey and Conservation. Draft and Final Report Submitted to the Commission and Governor (1937)*, Harry H. Laughlin Papers, Truman University, Pickler Library. See also Heidi M. Rydene, "The Connecticut Human Resources Surveys of 1938 and 1948 Examined as Local Examples of the Eugenics Movement in the United States" (master's thesis, Southern Connecticut State University, 1988). (Rydene located and quoted from Cross's 1925 Brown lecture,

excerpted previously, which provided some, though not all, of the historical context for Cross's attitude toward eugenics in that stage of its public exposure, including his intent to enhance knowledge of its legitimacy.) See also the thorough review of the report's content in Paul Bass, "Cross Era's Dark Secret Resurfaces," *New Haven Independent*, September 24, 2014. Bass sought and included Yale historian Daniel J. Kevles's argument that Cross had no actual intent to implement the report's solutions (though no new legislation was proposed) and "may not even have known of the mimeograph's [report's] existence." Kevles also opined that a copy of the report "does not seem to have been officially circulated, if it was circulated at all." Exempting Cross from any responsibility concerning the Carnegie-Laughlin Report and related documentation seemed to be Professor Kevles's intention, but it's contrary to the facts.

11. The study was largely an in-depth, hands-on field survey, undertaken in all Connecticut towns (some with more detail than others), within eight specific families (given fictional names) through previous and current generations, and in all Connecticut institutions, state and federal, that had responsibility for male and female "inadequates" (hospitals, mental institutions, and prisons). The survey's results were analyzed at the Eugenics Record Office. *Survey of Human Resources in Connecticut*, 50, Truman State University Archives.

12. In one state institution analyzed by Laughlin, there were 1,340 patients considered "feeble-minded." Of those, 407 were "American Yankee," more than 30 percent of the total. Individually, they were the highest by far of any ethnic or racial group on Laughlin's list (Italians, Russian Jews, Irish, American Negroes, Germans, Slovaks, Magyars, and a dozen others were identified). Nonetheless, Laughlin concluded, "The mentally deficient persons . . . are more heavily [drawn] from the more recent immigrant races than from the older pioneer stocks." The primary object of the report's solutions, like those targeted in the 1924 Immigration Act, the studies in New Haven, Yale's admission process, and the eugenics movement from the outset, were largely immigrant families and their children, like those in New Haven's neighborhoods. See, for example, "The Feeble-minded within the Population," chart II, *Survey of Human Resources in Connecticut*, Truman State University Archives.

13. *The Survey of the Human Resources of Connecticut, Report Number One Now Ready*, 1; Cross letter to Laughlin and Commission Resolution (November 14, 1938), Harry H. Laughlin Papers, Truman State University Archives.

14. "Report Urges Saving Sound Racial Stock," *Hartford Daily Courant*, November 27, 1938. The introductory portion of the report possessed by the Eugenics Record Office, as written by Laughlin, appears to be an unedited version (before it was reviewed by state officials—perhaps the commission chairman or others—and imprinted with the Connecticut seal) of what is contained in the introduction to the report actually submitted and distributed publicly under the Connecticut state seal. It also appears that the five volumes, which contain statistical data (men and women already sterilized in Connecticut, for example) and proposed solutions (including euthanasia), were not edited, and the reportage and discomforted reaction of the *Hartford Courant* (which may have included answers to questions directed to Cross) suggest that the *Courant* reviewed the content of the five volumes, the report, and perhaps the unedited report.

15. "Reception Dance at Vt. Junior College," *Burlington Free Press*, September 25, 1938; "Christmas Party at Vermont Junior College and Seminary," article provided by

archivist, Vermont School of Fine Arts, December 21, 1938 (Val served as general chairman, music provided by Billy Benjamin's Bandoliers); "Romance Language Club of VJC Holds Meeting," *Montpelier News*, December 15, 1939, and *Barre Times*, December 15, 1939.

16. Communication with David Ewing, May 30, 2016.

17. Letter from Laughlin to Bush (June 6, 1938), Harry H. Laughlin Papers; Lombardo, *Three Generations, No Imbeciles*, 213–14. Laughlin died in January 1943.

18. Jill Reilly, in "Did Yale University Plan to Create an Intellectually Superior Race of Children after World War Two?," *Daily Mail*, February 13, 2012, reasoned that Yale's offer to house the children of British intellectuals during the early war years was motivated by eugenics. See, for example, "Faculty Committee Houses Children from War-Torn Oxford, Cambridge," *Yale Daily News*, September 23, 1940. Reilly relied, in part, on the assertion by Yale Professor Gaddis Smith that President Angell was a "fanatic eugenicist," information that some of the faculty members who took in children were eugenicists, and interviews with the children, now adults. However, by the time the events in the story occurred (1940), Angell had been replaced. Robin Winks, in *Cloak and Gown*, reviewed the same incident without mention of any eugenics imperative. The first edition of Winks's book was written in 1986, well before the revelations concerning wartime activity and the Yale-required nude photographs.

19. Eugenics "science" in widely used grammar, high school, and college textbooks, including through the New Haven Public Library, were commonplace. Ronald P. Ladouceur, "Ella Thea Smith and the Lost History of American High School Biology Textbooks," *Journal of the History of Biology* 41, no. 3 (2008): 435–71. See, for example, *Civic Biology* (1918); *Civic and Economic Biology* (1922) ("One of the reasons why Greece, Rome, and the other great nations of antiquity perished is that they violated the principles of eugenics. If our nation is to live its people must be of the best, and their blood must not be contaminated by that of the unfit. What is your state doing to improve the next generation?" 337); *Modern Biology: Its Human Aspects* (1926) ("A high class human family can retain its excellence only so long as the marriages of its members are with individuals of the same type. Marriages with lower types can result only in a deterioration in the sum total of desirable family qualities," 347); *New Haven Free Public Library Bulletin, No. 1* (1913), 3; Aaron Gillette, *Eugenics and the Nature-Nurture Debate in the Twentieth Century* (New York: Palgrave Macmillan, 2007), 149.

20. By 1939, that aggression included German occupation of the Rhineland (the French border), the unconstrained bombing and munitions support (also with Mussolini's support) for General Francisco Franco's forces in Spain (by 1939 understood, in part, as preparation for a broader war), the annexation of Austria, and the occupation of Sudetenland (in Czechoslovakia) and major portions of Poland. From 1933, Lindbergh's well-known relationship and advocacy of the German mentality, from Hitler and Hermann Göring through Teutonic superiority, included his embrace of eugenics. That he received (and retained)—despite severe criticism from Jewish organizations, in particular—the Service Cross of the German Eagle in October 1938, awarded to him by Göring on Hitler's behalf, affirmed the discomfort he'd already caused among many of his former admirers, though not all of them. By then, Hitler's eugenics had been unequivocally transformed into law and been given harsh reality without constraint. Any notion that democracy or principles of free expression were extant in Germany, or Italy, was dashed,

except for those men and women who believed it unimportant or not sufficiently valued in their personal calculus, including at Yale. Lindbergh, "Aviation, Geography, and Race," *Reader's Digest* 25 (November 1939): 64–67. See David Gordon, "America First, the Anti-War Movement, Charles Lindbergh and the Second World War, 1940–1941," presented at the New York Military Affairs Symposium, September 26, 2003, 8–9 (discussion of eugenics and Lindbergh's article); A. Scott Berg, *Lindbergh* (New York: Berkley Books, 1999), 413–14, wherein Berg mentions the title of the *Reader's Digest* article. But the term "race" didn't engage him enough to describe the fullness of Lindbergh's writing or even the historic eugenics context in the United States of the article's content. And see, for example, Edgar McInnis, *The War: First Year* (London: Oxford University Press, 1945), 7–80 (the timing and direction of Hitler's aggression). In *The Guardians*, Geoffrey Kabaservice, having established Kingman Brewster's uninterrupted adulation of Lindbergh since childhood, sought to distance Brewster from Lindbergh's overt display of anti-Semitism by claiming, awkwardly, that Lindbergh didn't give voice to it until his speech in Des Moines, Iowa, a year after he spoke at Yale at Brewster's request. Brewster, as Kabaservice implies, apparently made no connection between Lindbergh and the Nazis, or Lindbergh and Hitler, or both Hitler and the Nazis *and* Jewish repression and death, let alone broadly inflicted sterilization on others, all sanctified in law, or the *Reader's Digest* article (which Kabaservice fails to mention), published long before Brewster's invitation, or the subsequent radio address, discussed later in the text, or the full breadth of eugenics, including at Yale. See Kabaservice, *The Guardians*, 19, 74–77, 81–90. Nor does Kabaservice mention that Brewster knew all of it (highly likely) and that it wasn't decisive in his thinking then or later. Kabaservice also makes only one passing reference to James Rowland Angell (46) and no reference to eugenics, which was thriving in, around, and throughout Yale and the culture that Brewster and Lindbergh embraced, albeit in different ways.

21. Kelley, *Yale*, 367.

22. *Phoenix*, Commencement, Vermont Junior College Montpelier Seminary (1938).

CHAPTER 12

FINDING HOME

1. Although the hospital has expanded, the original structure and the views are still preserved.

2. *Phoenix* (June 1939), 34.

3. "Coming as a member of the first staff," the students wrote in the *Phoenix*, "Prof. Giamatti by his superior training and pleasing personality has contributed much to the early life of the college. . . . Our best wishes for his success [and] . . . our thanks for the interest and aid given to us in all of our undertakings." In December 1942, Val returned as the principal speaker at the annual Alumni Day gathering, the size of the crowd tempered only by "gasoline and tire rationing" necessitated by the war. "Enrollment at Vermont Junior College Doubles," *Burlington Free Press*, September 21, 1938; "Junior College Offers New Courses," *Burlington Free Press*, March 28, 1938; "Reception-dance at Vt. Junior College," *Burlington Free Press*, September 25, 1938; *Catalogue, Vermont Junior College*, 1939–1940, 9; *Phoenix*, Commencement (June 1939), 34; "Andreoletti again Heads Alumni Association," *Alumni Bulletin*, vol. 1, Vermont Junior College, December 1942.

4. Val applied for admission to the Harvard Graduate School of Arts and Sciences on February 18, 1939. He cited his Yale degree and his two years in Yale's graduate program (and the diploma for Italian language proficiency he'd received from the University of Perugia). On request, he submitted the complete transcript of his grades and, especially, the details of his language fluency in Latin, Spanish, French, Italian, and Portuguese. Admission to the program required a level of skill in German, which Val had accomplished at Yale, and the university certified he'd passed its reading examination. He was formally admitted on April 21, 1939. Valentine Giamatti Records, Harvard Graduate School Archives. Permission for access to these files required the approval of Elria Giamatti Ewing, which she gave the author and Harvard.

5. There is no through street. Shaler enters directly onto Mt. Auburn Street. Across the street is a park that gently hugs the winding bend in the Charles River. The apartment, intimate yet carefully laid out for comfort and efficiency, is about a six-block walk from the university through leafy streets and residential neighborhoods.

6. Charles Bossi, an Italian poet and diplomat (born in 1758) who supported and spread France's influence in Italy; Vittorio Alfieri (born in 1749), who mastered numerous languages and traveled widely throughout Europe before settling in Italy to establish his reputation as a dramatist and poet; and Almeida Garrett (born in 1799), a Portuguese poet, playwright, novelist, and political leader whose grandfather was the Irish son of an Italian father. Garrett was educated by the storytelling of a Brazilian nanny and provided ideological pamphlets in support of liberal revolutions. Department of Romance Languages and Literature, Harvard University Archives, Pusey Library, examined by the author. Val's dissertation was available to the author at the Mount Holyoke Archives.

7. Adelina died on February 18, 1940. She was thirty-five years old. Maria died on August 28, 1940. "Giammattei," *New Haven Evening Register*, April 29, 1940, and death certificate, New Haven Hospital, August 30, 1940. The wake occurred in the Albert Porto Funeral Home, 128 Washington Avenue, in New Haven. Both Giammatteis were buried in St. Lawrence Cemetery.

8. *Boston Globe*, June 20, 1940, published the list of graduates. See also letter of May 14, from Valentine Giamatti, requesting two tickets, Harvard University Archives; Valentine Giamatti, *Yale Alumni Record*, July 31, 1940, Yale University Archives.

9. "My daughter, Elena Maria, was born June 14. My son, Bart, who is two years four months old has shortened her name to Elria," Valentine John Giamatti (Yale 1932), *Yale Alumni Record*, July 31, 1940, Yale University Archives.

10. Kabaservice, *The Guardians,* 18–19.

11. Brewster's family history and relationships, however emotionally and culturally affecting (divorce, his father's remarriage, and profoundly conservative political orientation), tempered his choices. Kabaservice, *The Guardians,* 23–25 (Brewster's father). Since his youth, Brewster knew about every Yale graduate "that mattered"—including Dean Acheson, A. Whitney Griswold, and Cyrus Vance, among others, each of whom was helpful in his decision to select Yale and in providing choices available to him later in life. See Kabaservice, *The Guardians,* 20, 32 (Dean Acheson), 32 (A. Whitney Griswold), 32, 51 (Cyrus Vance).

12. Yale's most reliable source of racial, ethnic, and religious diversity and of the economically poor during this period was the largely Italian, Irish Catholic, and Jewish student body of New Haven's Hillhouse High School and the surrounding communities (Bridgeport, Stratford, Hartford, the Naugatuck Valley), although according to Brewster's

biographer, these Italian Catholic, Irish, and Jewish students were not even "remotely ethnic" in 1940—at least not to him, perched in 2004. Kabaservice, *The Guardians*, 47, 62–67.

13. There is no indication that Brewster, as a student, spent any meaningful time walking the streets of New Haven beyond a few blocks from the campus, or that he pondered or wrote about its interdependent physical or geopolitical relationship to Yale, or that he had any socially active involvement in the community or its neighborhoods. Marc Wortman, "The Forgotten Antiwar Movement," *Yale Alumni Magazine*, July/August 2016.

14. Kabaservice, *The Guardians*, 284–85.

15. As historian Marc Wortman described Brewster among his classmates, albeit with a generosity and retrospective application of labels reflective of political presumptions from Wortman's era, he was one of the "social liberals *within the limit of their elite sphere*." That is, at base, no actual experience. Put differently, in 1940, "social liberal" was a label with no basis in fact or applicable to Brewster. Wortman, "The Forgotten Antiwar Movement" (emphasis added.) In *The Guardians*, Kabaservice implies (46), perhaps as a foundation for seeking to explain Brewster's conduct much later in life, that Brewster's realization of social disparities, presumably acquired at Yale, began when he observed that (in Kabaservice's words) "undergraduates walked past grown men selling apples in New Haven streets." Kabaservice cites a *Yale Daily News* editorial written while Brewster was its leader. In fact, the editorial was actually a call for charitable giving for a once-a-year drive for a range of purposes, especially to aid in providing "war relief," an effort in which Brewster had no formal role. The responsibility for the editorial was attributed to John Osgood Morris, an editor, not Brewster. "Thy Brother's Keeper," *Yale Daily News*, September 27, 1940.

16. When, in *The Guardians*, Kabaservice characterizes Brewster as "liberal" in 1940, if not beyond, he seemingly relies on two odd comparisons to justify it: Brewster to his ultra-conservative, Republican, and eugenics-driven father (17) (some threads of which Brewster, admittedly, never shed, beginning with his articulated disdain for Franklin Roosevelt and continuing with his lifelong Republican affiliation) and to conservative Republican William F. Buckley's group (12) (which included an incalculable number of people, including many conservative Republicans). Buckley also used the term "Liberal Establishment" as a means of discrediting the men who controlled the fate of discriminatory admission to Yale and similar institutions. It's also unlikely Brewster fairly would have characterized himself as "liberal" in 1940, though he likely would have embraced the term "Establishment" as Kabaservice defines it. See Kabaservice, *The Guardians*, 47, 62–67 ("Shabby").

17. Karabel, *The Chosen*, "Yale's Opposition to Legislation against Discrimination," 210–13; Dan A. Oren, *Joining the Club: A History of Jews and Yale* (New Haven, CT: Yale University Press and the American Jewish Archives, 1985), 177–79.

18. Yale's rationale for opposition was, in part, that through its admissions decisions, Yale selected students who'd provide the "leadership and effective influence and service in the life of the community." Through the lobbying efforts of its New Haven lawyer, Frederick Wiggin of Wiggin and Dana, Yale successfully opposed every effort by the Connecticut legislature to intrude upon its discriminatory practices. That effort continued through the Griswold-Brewster administration. Through 1961 and 1962, "Yale stood alone as the most gentile college in the Ivy League." Karabel, *The Chosen*, 327–37; Soares, *The Power of Privilege*, 25, 42.

19. "Cohort after cohort of Yale men would walk from their freshman dorms on old campus over to Payne-Whitney Gymnasium, stand in line on the fourth floor, and enter one at a time into a room without windows. Inside, two technicians would instruct the youth to disrobe before they would place metal pins against his spine that would both measure and hold each youth in position while three photographs were taken." Karabel, *The Chosen*, 327 (body measurements); Soares, *The Power of Privilege*, 42. Soares draws from Ron Rosenbaum, "The Great Ivy League Nude Posture Photo Scandal," *New York Times Magazine*, January 15, 1995, 26–31, 40, 46, 55–56; Dick Cavett, *Brief Encounters* (New York: Henry Holt, 2014), 109–15.

20. There is documented evidence the practice lasted through the Class of 1971 (photographs taken in 1967), at least among male students—past the time that Yale claimed to have altered its exclusionary admissions policy, when, one might reasonably conclude, the photographs were no longer warranted for any purpose. The nude photograph practice occurred at other Ivy League and elite women's schools and a few outside of those, though in the narrow world of Yale historians, authors tend to look for comparison only to elite schools, sometimes as an explanation, if not a justification, for a practice's existence and continuation. Soares, *The Power of Privilege*, 42 (George May, Dean of Yale College, speaking to the Class of 1967); Rosenbaum, "The Great Ivy League Nude Posture Photo Scandal"; Andrew Letendre, "The Naked Truth about Yale's Posture Program," *Yale Alumni Magazine*, June 22, 2015. The Yale photographer attempted nude photography at the University of Washington, but a female student actually objected, and the photographer and his practice were publicly banished.

Yale's official response to Rosenbaum's questions: "We searched, but there's nobody around who was involved with the decision." Though "the decision" was known when, for example, Kabaservice wrote *The Guardians*; Kelley, *Yale*; and Lassonde, *Learning to Forget*, none of them mentioned this twenty-five-year practice. R. Inslee Clark, whom Kabaservice elevates to the exclusion of others (the first Jewish member of the Yale Corporation, William Horvitz, for example) in the gradual process of change in Yale's admission process, was still alive and may have had access to the photographs. Yale officials no doubt passed over Clark as a source because he was so highly praised at and outside of Yale (*The Guardians*, 259; and, earlier by Kabaservice in "The Birth of a New Institution," *Yale Alumni Magazine*, December 1999) and later at Horace Mann School, where he was headmaster and president from 1970 until 1991. It was almost immediately upon his entrance to Horace Mann in 1970, presumably for the first time in his life, that Headmaster Clark and other faculty members were reported to have engaged in pedophilia, male prostitution, and related forms of sexual abuse. See Amos Kamil, "Prep-School Predators: The Horace Mann School's Secret History of Sexual Abuse," *New York Times Magazine*, June 6, 2012; Amos Kamil and Sean Elder, *Great Is the Truth: Secrecy, Scandal and the Quest for Justice at the Horace Mann School* (New York: Farrar, Straus and Giroux, 2015); *Horace Mann Report*, hmactioncoalition.org.

21. See "Congress Should Designate Categories Granting Deferment, Says President," *Yale Daily News*, February 24, 1941 (Winternitz's remarks); Allen M. Hornblum, Judith L. Newman, and Gregory J. Dober, *Against Their Will: The Secret History of Medical Experimentation on Children in Cold War America* (New York: St. Martin's Press, 2013), 48. The noted source relied upon by Hornblum and his colleagues for the precise words used here ("a Catholic Institution for children in New Haven") is the report transmitted to the War Department, "Annual Report of the Commission on Neurotropic

Virus Diseases, 27 March 1945" (Neurotropic Virus Diseases, Commission on, December 1944–June 1945; Series II; Records of the Armed Forces Epidemiological Board, Gorgas Memorial Library, Walter Reed Army Institute of Research. In the author's possession.) Yale, of course, would have the precise characteristics of the children involved, the informed consent, and the inducement, if any, provided to the society of nuns to volunteer the orphans. So, too, might the Catholic Church. See George Roberts, *Surviving Highland Heights: The Orphanage* (Ocala, FL: Life Circle, 2009). The orphanage, which went through a dramatic transformation in quality and administration, closed in 2012. Testimony and recollections (in various blogs and sites where relatives are seeking information) from some residents make clear they were grateful to have a home. Others had experiences they repressed for years. Mary O'Leary, "Lack of Funding Forces St. Francis Home in New Haven to Close Its Doors after 160 Years," *New Haven Register*, September 12, 2012. See also Saul Krugman, "The Willowbrook Hepatitis Studies Revisited: Ethical Aspects," *Review of Infectious Diseases* I (January–February 1986): 158 (reference to three 1940s hepatitis studies; Dr. Robert Ward, Yale).

22. In 1938, toward the end of Angell's presidency, Butler described in the *Nation* magazine the cruelty of the seven-day work week, the absence of pensions, the low wages (some maids were paid $12 a week), the absence of paid vacation days, the summer layoffs without compensation, and the resulting need for workers to turn to forms of state and local assistance. By 1941, the American Federation of Labor (A.F. of L.) and the Congress of Industrial Organizations (C.I.O.) joined with the New Haven labor council to elevate the worsening neglect of workers at Yale into practical forms of organization and action. Herbert Janick, "Yale Blue: Unionization at Yale University, 1931–1985," *Labor History* 28, no. 3 (1987): 349–69; Neil Hogan et al., "Discontent of Yale Employees Erupted in 1941," in *Moments in New Haven Labor History* (New Haven, CT: Greater New Haven Labor History Association, 2004).

23. Yale maids were "well represented [at the organizational meetings], for the men took special care to point out these employees received no sick leave, no Sundays off, and no vacations." In a city where union organizing was often led by women, the maids had special encouragement and the experience of others to draw upon—sisters, cousins, brothers, sons, and daughters at the three high schools and neighbors, especially among Italian Americans, Jews, and a growing number of African Americans. Moreover, "the critical problem for New Haven," it was acknowledged in the *Yale Daily News*, "is Yale's vast tax exempt property in the center of the city," the services New Haven provided without compensation or even a small amount in lieu of taxes, and Yale's "'inadequate' wage system" that further shifted the burden to ensure minimal levels of sustenance onto local government, neighbors, and families. Labor organizing meetings were held at Falcon Hall, on Franklin Street, in the Wooster Square neighborhood. Yale President Seymour resisted the change. He claimed that Yale's labor policies were comparable with "other universities," especially Harvard. A study showed that Harvard's waitresses were unionized, and Harvard was making a payment to Cambridge in lieu of paying taxes. Yale stood abandoned by its choice of comparison. "PM Says 'New Haven's as It Is Partly Because Yale Is Here," *Yale Daily News*, April 10, 1941; "A.F. of L. to Determine Yale Labor Status," *Yale Daily News*, April 14, 1941; "CIO Organizers Make Second Bid for Yale Union, A.F. of L. Questions Seymour on Wages, Conditions of University Help," *Yale Daily News*, May 2, 1941; "Yale, A.F. of L. Study Labor Problem Here. Personnel Director Goes to

Investigate Policy of Harvard Unions. Harvard Labor Satisfied; Waitresses Unionized. Janitors Non-Union," *Yale Daily News*, April 25, 1941.

24. E. W. Cook, "Strike Imminent If Yale Refuses Union Shop Plea, Hospital Light to Continue Despite College Shutdown Threatened for Monday," *Yale Daily News*, November 6, 1941; "CIO Employees Vote to Strike and Cut Off Lights, Heat, Room Service," *Yale Daily News*, November 8, 1941; "Deadlock Holds—Strike at 9," *Yale Daily News*, November 10, 1941; and see editorial, "The Future of Organized Labor," *Yale Daily News*, November 14, 1941, 4. See also "Yale Confers with Union as Strike Begins," and "Pickets Patrol Yale Powerhouse Area Undisturbed," *New Haven Evening Register*, November 10, 1941, 1; "Yale Normal as Employees Resume Work, 5-Point Agreement Paves Way to Resumption of Labor Parleys," *New Haven Evening Register*, November 11, 1941, 1.

25. John Wilhelm, "The Yale Strike Dossier: "A Short History of Unionization at Yale," *Social Text*, no. 49 (Winter, 1996): 13 [Duke University].

26. The Falls neighborhood was proximate to South Hadley High School and retail and commercial institutions along nearby Main Street, where imaginatively constructed canals were used to generate electricity and ship goods. At the turn of the century, railroad tracks were built to enhance shipping from the five paper and plastic mills that lined the canals.

27. Although the college originally required students to attend a weekly spiritual service, Mount Holyoke was founded on a nondenominational basis. Personal religious beliefs were for students and parents to decide and were not used as a basis for admission, which was approached, like the curriculum and appointment of faculty, with a liberal spirit and purpose. Arthur C. Cole, *A Hundred Years of Mount Holyoke College: The Evolution of an Educational Ideal* (New Haven, CT: Yale University Press, 1940). Mount Holyoke College archivists have compiled a "Selected Bibliography of Publications Relating to Mount Holyoke College," available on MTHoloke.edu, Archives and Special Collections. See also *South Hadley: A Study in Community Life*, by the Students in Economics and Sociology 117, 1946–1947, under the direction of Elizabeth R. Brown, Harriet D. Hudson, John Lobb (South Hadley, MA: Mount Holyoke College, 1948).

28. Irene Cronin and the South Hadley Historical Society, *Images of America: South Hadley* (Mount Pleasant, SC: Arcadia, 1998); author's observation, use of historical maps, interviews with Elria Giamatti Ewing and Bart's childhood friends, identified elsewhere in endnotes or text. Dino Giamatti was born on July 10, 1943.

CHAPTER 13

WITNESS IN WAR

1. Lyon traveled on her own as far as Detroit to raise the money, often in small amounts and frequently in kind—bedding, quilts, and household goods for the family-style residences she envisioned for her students. It was early in the nineteenth century. Horse and buggy, stagecoach, or just horse, all of which her rural upbringing ensured she could handle. There were physical risks. The risk of failure was high: it would be understatement to suggest men of means were discomforted by her proposal. Elizabeth Alden Green, *Mary Lyon and Mount Holyoke: Opening the Gates* (Hanover, NH: University Press of New England, 1979). Mount Holyoke Female Seminary, as it was originally

designated, was renamed Mount Holyoke College in 1893. The seminary notion faded quickly. *The Mount Holyoke* 10 (June 1900–May 1901): 247–51, published by Students of Mount Holyoke College (early architecture).

2. In 1901, a full-time professor of Italian joined the faculty and remained until 1928. French and Spanish courses were stabilized in the yearly curriculum, but the availability of an Italian-language course, let alone culture and history offerings, was more unpredictable. Italian Language and Literature Department Records, 1942–1976, Mount Holyoke College Archives.

3. Woolley was the first woman to graduate from Brown University with a bachelor's (1894), then a master's degree (1895). She joined the faculty at Wellesley College, where she taught biblical history and literature, and became a full professor in 1899. Marks was a member of the National Woman's Party, a strong voice against the execution of Sacco and Vanzetti, and a political supporter of Eugene Debs for president. At Mount Holyoke, she invited notable novelists, playwrights, and poets to lecture and meet with students; started a theater for experimental plays; and continued to research, write, and publish on national social problems. Woolley was an officer in the American Civil Liberties Union, a vocal supporter of women suffrage, the president of the American Association of University Women, an advocate for African American civil and political rights, and a United States delegate to the 1932 Conference on Reduction and Limitation of Armaments in Geneva, Switzerland. See, for example, Jeannette Marks, *Life and Letters of Mary Emma Woolley* (Washington, DC: Public Affairs Press, 1955); Anna Mary Wells, *Miss Marks and Miss Woolley* (Boston: Houghton Mifflin, 1978); and a review of Wells's book by Lee Chambers-Schiller in *Frontiers: A Journal of Women Studies* (Spring 1979): 73.

4. Ham made a formidable impression but was recently widowed and had children. He'd earned his bachelor's degree at the University of California, served in World War I, then came east to Yale, where he received his doctor of philosophy in English, joined the faculty, and continued to act, a skill he developed in England while doing research. He also was a faculty member at Albertus Magnus, an all-women's college in New Haven, a fact that mattered to the trustees. The prospect of a single man leading the college caused discomfort. It was not until Ham married Hilda Sargent, granddaughter of New Haven's industrial leader George Sargent (whose plant, located in the Wooster Square area, was among New Haven's largest employers of Italian immigrants and well known to Valentine Giamatti), that Mount Holyoke offered him the position. My fraternal grandfather, Christopher Proto, was among the employees at Sargent. "Man to Mount Holyoke," *Time*, June 15, 1936; Wolfgang Saxon, "Roswell Ham Dies; Ex-College Chief," *New York Times*, July 24, 1983; *Doctors of Philosophy of Yale University 1861–1927* (New Haven, CT: Yale University Press, 1927), 98; Ann Karus Meeropol, *A Male President for Mount Holyoke: The Failed Fight to Maintain Female Leadership, 1934–1937* (Jefferson, NC: McFarland, 2014) (details of the opposition and support for Ham).

5. Frost to Ham, Amherst, MA, October 10, 1937, Roswell Ham Papers, Mount Holyoke Archives.

6. In 1940, Ham supported the Birth Control Federation of America by serving on its national committee, to the expressed gratification of Margaret Sanger on behalf of the National Committee for Planned Parenthood and "the progress of the movement for planned families in the United States." Ella Tambussi Grasso was governor of Connecticut when Bart Giamatti was president of Yale. She did not have the wealth of

many of her classmates at Mount Holyoke, though she'd emerged as an admired leader in encouraging liberal perspectives in political discussion about the Depression's effects and in academic research in sociology and economics with practical application to the lives and conditions of industrial working families, especially women. With detailed data and close analysis, she wrote that ensuring worker's compensation for accidents and illness should be a state responsibility, not entrusted to the private, often arbitrarily applied insurance industry. Her interests—and her leadership skill, she later acknowledged—had been nurtured by the "enlightened Mount Holyoke emphasis on public service." In a manner welcomed within the college's tradition, she wrote prophetically in the *Mount Holyoke News*, about the "red Raid" in Chicago instigated by the Dies Committee and the way civil liberties were systematically repressed in Europe, and she chastised her classmates for not sharing the depth of her concern. "All the knowledge we so avidly pursue is knowledge—for what?—if we do not intend to make practical application of what we learn to everyday problems." Jon E. Purmont, *Ella Grasso: Connecticut's Pioneering Governor* (Middletown, CT: Wesleyan University Press, 2012), 2, 31–35, 39–50. During Ella's undergraduate years, Eleanor Roosevelt had visited campus and spoke informally to Ella and others about providing workers, especially women, with easy access to education. Frances Perkins, before and after becoming the first woman cabinet officer, secretary of labor, did the same, adding her own concern about industrial safety. The faculty, almost exclusively women, was experienced and forceful about dealing with real-world problems; many among them had been in the workplace, endured and witnessed discrimination, believed strongly in fairness and duty. The "Dies Committee"—the United States House of Representative's Special Committee on Un-American Activities—was about to investigate Roswell Ham. Purmont, *Ella Grasso*, 33–34.

7. Ham had supported the Republican forces in the Spanish Civil War and, into the early 1940s, aided families that sought protection in France and the United States from Franco's success. In early 1941, he also invited and welcomed Eleanor Roosevelt to the Mount Holyoke campus. Letter and Investigative Report from D. M. Ladd to various officials in the Federal Bureau of Investigation (March 12, 1943), Roswell Ham Papers, Mount Holyoke College Archives; Gerhard Sonnert and Gerald Holton, *What Happened to Children Who Fled Nazi Persecution* (New York: Palgrave Macmillan, 2006), 213; letter from Sanger to Ham (February 28, 1940) and letter from Roosevelt to Ham (January 24, 1941), Roswell Ham Papers, Mount Holyoke Archives. When war's inevitability added clarity and obligation, Ham directed the college's reorganization of its campus facilities and grounds for an Industrial War Training Program, and the United States Navy and women Marine Corps educational programs. From the outset of the war, students' fathers, brothers, and neighbors, at home and in South Hadley, enlisted or were drafted. Sisters, mothers, and student volunteers helped in Red Cross and nursing efforts. South Hadley also felt the war's effects. Its rural character slowly began to diminish; as South Hadley's industrial workers grew in number, the area was designated "a critical area for labor" by the United States, Westover's military facilities were expanded, and land was used for new housing. Purmont, *Ella Grasso*, 31–35; Brown et al., *South Hadley: A Study in Community Life*, 2–3.

8. Purmont, *Ella Grasso:* 2, 39–50; interview with Rose Criscitiello Longo (September 3, 2006).

9. Interview with Rose Criscitiello Longo (September 3, 2006) 5; Mount Holyoke News Release (May 5, 1950), Giamatti Records, Mount Holyoke Archives.

10. "Fay Bennett Watts, 88; Helped Rural Poor," *New York Times*, December 29, 2002; Fay Bennett, "Farm Workers, 1955," *Crisis*, June–July 1955; "Fay Bennett," Natural Sharecroppers Fund, *Roots and Branches* (2002) (tribute); and see discussion of her leadership role in Robert Cohen, *When the Old Left Was Young: Student Radicals and America's First Mass Student Movement, 1929–1941* (New York: Oxford University Press, 1993), particularly "Activist Impulses: Campus Radicals in the 1930s."

11. Jewish students, including Joseph Lash and Budd Schulberg, helped establish chapters and provided forcefully crafted imperatives to action. Lash and Schulberg, like Bennett, were concerned about the rise of Mussolini, the Spanish Civil War, and the eugenics oppression directed against Jewish and non-Teutonic students and faculty within German and Italian universities. See Cohen, *When the Old Left Was Young*, particularly "Activist Impulses: Campus Radicals in the 1930s"; Melissa Kravetz, "Giving Youth a Voice: U.S. Student Perceptions of Adolf Hitler, 1933–1939" (thesis, history department, University of California–Santa Barbara, May 2003); "Joseph P. Lash Is Dead: Reporter and Biographer," *New York Times*, August 30, 1987. See also, for example, Lash, *The Campus Strikes against War* (New York: Student League for Industrial Democracy, 1935); Nicholas Beck, *Budd Schulberg* (Lanham, MD: Scarecrow Press, 2001); "Budd Schulberg, 'On the Waterfront' Writer, Dies at 95," *New York Times*, August 5, 2009.

12. Nothing in America's formal "neutrality" among the belligerents in Europe, or in Asia, impeded the flow of decisive private American industrial and financial support for Spain's Franco, for Mussolini, for Japan, and, in the case of Germany, eugenics research support for Hitler's treatment of the "unfit." The national debate, already fierce, evolved in intensity as Franco ousted the Republican forces in Spain with German, Italian, and American industrial aid; Italy occupied areas in Eastern Africa; Japan expanded its presence in China and the Pacific; and German forces marched into Austria, eastern Czechoslovakia, Poland, and then France. Wortman, "The Forgotten Antiwar Movement." See also Kabaservice, *The Guardians*, 70–81, and other sources cited in the notes that follow.

13. Compared to World War I, Norris wrote, "It seemed to me there was no similarity in the challenge which confronted the American people." George Norris, *Fighting Liberal: The Autobiography of George W. Norris* (New York: Macmillan, 1945) ("Lend-Lease," 392); Thomas N. Guinsburg, "The George W. Norris 'Conversion' to Internationalism, 1939–1941," *Nebraska History* 53 (1972): 477–90 (especially n1).

14. Geopolitical realist Nicholas Spykman, Latin American historian A. Whitney Griswold, and Yale President Charles Seymour recognized the legitimacy of the need to prepare for war, including the imperative set out by President Roosevelt that, "The principles of morality will never permit us to acquiesce in a peace dictated by aggressor nations and brought at the price of other people's freedom." "Professors Concur in Comments on Roosevelt Address to Congress," *Yale Daily News*, January 7, 1941; "Nicholas Spykman Decries Defense for Hemisphere, *Yale Daily News*, February 26, 1941; cf. Kabaservice, *The Guardians*, 79.

15. Stimson and Roosevelt were in New Haven at the same time. On June 18, 1940, Stimson boldly and with precise clarity supported both conscription and the lend-lease proposal, broadly defined to include aid in harboring and repairing British ships.

He also confronted what he knew was the growing elevation of Lindbergh: "We should, every one of us, combat the defeatist arguments made in this country as to the unconquerable power of Germany. I believe that if we use our brains, instead of our prejudices we can . . . beat her again as we did in 1918." Henry L. Stimson and McGeorge Bundy, *On Active Service in Peace and War* (New York: Harper & Brothers, 1947), 318–20; Wortman, "The Forgotten Antiwar Movement"; Arnold Whitridge, "Where Do You Stand?" *Atlantic*, August 1940 (Whitridge was especially critical of the anti-allied critiques by Yale students with nothing comparable directed against Germany, despite its well-known atrocities and aggression, and the contradictory petitions for and against intervention, signed by the same students and sent to the president); Charles Seymour, "War's Impact on the Campus," *New York Times Magazine*, September 29, 1940. Though Seymour backed Wendell Willkie, he also supported American aid to England, which Willkie eventually did as well.

16. Contrary to the presumption, and their motivation for action, held by Brewster and his classmates that young people had entered World War I uncritically and naïvely (though the parents of Brewster's classmates likely did), working-class youths had rallied strongly against intervention in World War I and the draft, often at peril of being arrested, beaten, and imprisoned, as many were by government troops and police. The same dissent occurred among women such as Jane Addams. Compare Kabaservice, *The Guardians,* 72–73, with, for example, Samuel Eliot Morison, *The Oxford History of the American People* (New York: Oxford University Press, 1965), 849; C. Roland Marchand, *The American Peace Movement and Social Reform: 1898–1918* (Princeton, NJ: Princeton University Press, 1973); Jeffrey A. Johnson, *"They Are All Red Out Here": Socialist Politics in the Pacific Northwest, 1895–1925* (Norman: University of Oklahoma Press, 2008); Pacific Northwest Labor and Civil Rights Projects, University of Washington, "Antiwar and Radical History Project–Pacific Northwest," World War I (Rutger Ceballos), www.depts.washington.edu; Geoffrey R. Stone, "Judge Learned Hand and the Espionage Act of 1917: A Mystery Unraveled," *University of Chicago Law School Journal* (2003): 337–41.

17. Kingman Brewster and Spencer Klaw, "We Stand Here: Two Yale Students Defend Their Isolationism," *Atlantic*, September 1940; Kabaservice, *The Guardians*, 72, 78, 79.

18. Although three other men of later accomplishment—Gerald Ford, Potter Stewart, and Sargent Shriver—lent their names to forming the group, a fact invariably relied upon to demonstrate something about Brewster or this late phase of the anti-interventionist movement, none among them sought the public prominence or the continued role that Stuart and especially Brewster did. Ford dropped out quickly. Stewart remained to lend his name to the Yale chapter, though few biographical essays, when describing his time at Yale, even mention his involvement, as if it were incidental or inconsequential to his more important, deep-seated Republican–Wendell Willkie cultural imperative. When Stewart was nominated to the Supreme Court in 1958, not even the *Yale Daily News* mentioned his "America First" involvement, though it discussed at length his other political and foreign policy activities. Monroe Price, "Unsilent Undergraduate, Potter Stewart Joins the Court," *Yale Daily News*, October 9, 1958. Both Ford and Stewart saw naval combat in World War II and received commendations. Shriver, however, took a subtle pathway distinct from the others. In *Sarge: The Life and Times of Sargent Shriver*, Scott Stossel described Shriver's deep commitment to Catholic Social Teaching and his

enlistment in the Navy, through combat and the bravery that warranted a Purple Heart, that emerged more powerfully as his undergraduate choices evolved and he made them. His earlier response to what he saw in Germany, however, is worthy of note, at least the way Stossel described it. In his second trip to Germany, in 1936, he came to appreciate, through attending a local Catholic Church with his host, that the number of parishioners had dwindled as they were taken away, imprisoned, or killed by the Nazis for disagreeing with Hitler's policies. Persecution was widespread and deadly. Shriver then was driven by Buchenwald, which even in 1936 was a visibly brutal concentration camp. In an account not written by Shriver, but that Stossel believed accurate, "as they neared the gate, a group of perhaps fifty men in denim work clothes, their shaved heads bare to the sun, marched four abreast, guarded by soldiers." Stossel concluded, "The image of those men seared itself into Shriver's consciousness. He would never forget their shaved heads, how they marched four abreast, not permitted to look left or right, only straight ahead. . . . As Buchenwald faded into the distance behind him, Shriver lapsed into silence. There was nothing to say. This was thousands of miles away from his happy-go-lucky life at Yale, but it felt a lot farther away than that. . . . He was of the growing conviction that the United States, if it knew what was good for it, would keep a prudent distance from the affairs of Europe." Scott Stossel, *Sarge: The Life and Times of Sargent Shriver* (Washington, DC: Smithsonian Books, 2004), 39, 53. It was a response not obviously congruent with other values that informed his character. In time, he decided on a pathway: before the formation of "America First" and before Lindbergh made his appearance at Yale, Shriver went into downtown New Haven in the spring of 1940 and enlisted in a Naval Reserve program that required he begin forms of actual sea-duty training immediately, while still completing his final year at Yale Law School. He wanted the debate that he believed important, yet committed himself as a personal thread in that debate to the defense of the nation's values as he understood them, not just its geography. Later he recognized his misjudgment: "History proved that my judgment was wrong, neither for the first time nor the last. I wanted to spare American lives," Shriver wrote in 1964. "If that's an ignoble motive then I'm perfectly willing to be convicted." Stossel, *Sarge*, 58. Shriver, although living a lifetime decidedly liberal in deed, is not included by Kabaservice among Brewster's "Establishment" cohorts, presumably because he was Catholic and did not share Brewster's elitist view of decision making.

19. Brewster and Spencer Klaw replied to Whitridge's *Atlantic* article, "Where Do You Stand?" with "We Stand Here," as if in a family dispute worthy of national attention. *Atlantic*, September 1940. "Before the young Elis returned to campus in the fall, 'America First'" (as it was now called), was a national organization "embracing all comers 'who want to keep out of the European war.'" Kabaservice, *The Guardians*, 74–75 ("Brewster took care to ensure that the noninterventionist movement on campus was not led by social outcasts or malcontents but by 'students who had attained relative respect and prominence during their undergraduate years.'") It's unclear who precisely Brewster intended to exclude, and why he wanted to keep the group small in number, except that he wanted to transform it with greater ease, which he and Stuart did. Many nonsocial outcast students who opposed American involvement in Europe formed their own groups under different leaders. And Brewster's attitude also may explain why Gerald Ford, who'd not gone to Yale as an undergraduate, chose, albeit for a differently stated reason, to withdraw from participation.

20. Lindbergh thought Brewster was "honest, and able . . . and theatrical." David Gordon, "America First: The Anti-war Movement, Charles Lindbergh and the Second World War, 1940–1941," presented at the New York Military Affairs Symposium, September 26, 2003, 8; Wortman, "The Forgotten Antiwar Movement"; Kabaservice, *The Guardians*, 74, 76–77. Kabaservice alludes to the presence of Jews (relying on Scott Berg's biography of Lindbergh) in the formation of "America First," again, like the use of Ford, Stewart, and Shriver, as if their presence acted to legitimate the organization's purpose or Brewster's role. The few prominent Jewish leaders cajoled to join America First departed once it became clear the organization's membership included well-known anti-Semitic personalities and bigoted displays of temperament. Gordon, "America First," 12, and see n74. See also, "Lindbergh Sees U.S. Unprepared to Change Course of War Abroad," *Yale Daily News*, October 31, 1940.

21. In addition to his opposition to the war, modified as the election grew nearer, Willkie criticized the New Deal as an intrusion on business and industry. He'd captured the Republicans, especially the business culture that tempered the Yale mentality. He was a former utility executive and lawyer. He'd fought, unsuccessfully, to stop the formation of the Tennessee Valley Authority, the Roosevelt and Progressive proposal to bring electricity to a region of the nation long neglected by the utility industry. "Where Unity Counts," *Yale Daily News*, November 6, 1940; and, see, for example, *Ashwander v. TVA*, 297 U.S. 288 (1936) (upholding the United States' authority to create the TVA).

22. "We are by popular conception," a *Yale Daily News* editorial acknowledged, "and to a lesser degree by fact a stronghold of privilege. We are in large degree products of the business class." "Where Unity Counts," *Yale Daily News*. In October 1940, Yale student and faculty support for Roosevelt (and affiliation with the "national 'Roosevelt College Clubs of America'") and, in December, support for American aid to the allied governments emerged with clarity, including from President Seymour, who'd backed Wendell Willkie (apparently out of concern for Roosevelt seeking a third term) but had endorsed such aid from the outset. "Roosevelt Backers Plan Rally Tonight," *Yale Daily News*, October 1, 1940; "Students, Faculty State Reasons for Backing 'Aid to Allies' Group," *Yale Daily News*, December 9, 1940. "Roosevelt Landslide Sweeps Nation to Smash Third Term Tradition," *Yale Daily News*, November 6, 1940.

23. Roosevelt won the electoral college 449 to 82, the popular vote 27 million to 22 million, and New Haven 45,555 to Willkie's 29,809. "Roosevelt Landslide Sweeps Nation to Smash Third Term Tradition," *Yale Daily News*, November 6, 1940; interview with Calabresi; "Guido Calabresi: A Foreigner in New Haven," 17; and see Riccio, "Women in Italy during WW II," in *Farms, Factories, and Families*, 303–14 (the rise of Fascism and anti-Semitism in Italy).

24. DeVane and other faculty members of long standing—Spykman, Griswold, and President Seymour among them—sought from the outset of the debate to create an atmosphere of fairness and seriousness of purpose within the four corners of the university, how best to ensure that those students who were there would remember these moments as tempered by a liberal acceptance and respectful encouragement of differing views. DeVane and his colleagues wanted every voice to be heard without frown or derision by others, and all students thrived under his wisdom. "Faculty, Students, Unite in Urging Renouncement of Party Differences," *Yale Daily News*, November 6, 1940.

25. U.S. Senate Hearings, Committee on Foreign Relations, To Promote the Defense of the United States (February 7, 1941), 612–20 (Brewster), 632–34 (Bennett). "Senate Calls Brewster to Hearing," *Yale Daily News*, February 8, 1941. Senator Robert Taft (R-Ohio) also called Edwin Borchard of New Haven, Connecticut, who submitted written testimony opposed to the bill, though primarily on the grounds that individual nations, especially the United States, were slowly discarding the unanimity principle of the League of Nations Charter in determining if a nation was an aggressor, by, as the bill would allow, one nation (by its president) to decide. U.S. Senate Hearings, 653–54.

26. U. S. Senate Hearings, 612. Only a select portion of the testimony was reprinted in the *Yale Daily News*. See "Senate Calls Brewster to Hearing," *Yale Daily News*, February 8, 1941.

27. Brewster accused Roosevelt of engaging in "wishful thinking" about the value of American aid and, under questioning, said that Roosevelt, by waiting until after the election to outline anew the growing gravity of the European War, had "breach[ed] the faith with the American people." "We are resentful," Brewster continued in his testimony, "of the deceit and subterfuge which have characterized the politics of foreign policy. We have not been moved by, rather we have been impatient with, the name-calling and ac-cusation technique. Perhaps that is why we have listened to Colonel Lindbergh whether we agree with him or not, and have admired his courage and straightforwardness. We resent the unwillingness of certain people to be honest and square with the public." U.S. Senate Hearings, 612–13.

28. Senator Thomas Connally (D-Texas), through a series of questions forced Brewster to acknowledge that the Yale chapter was affiliated with the national orga-nization. Despite his personal role in the formation and expansion of "America First," especially his known admiration of Lindbergh, he came to this acknowledgment with seeming discomfort, only after multiple questions. U.S. Senate Hearings, 617.

29. Brewster said, "Never before has it been proposed that one man should have the power to forfeit the armed forces of the nation as he sees fit, even without certificate from the Chief of Staff or Chief of Naval Operations and without regard to any exist-ing laws." Brewster's lack of precision mattered. He may have meant to say the *Army* Chief of Staff, and the "certificate" may have meant that the sale or lease of a ship, for example, would not harm America's military capability, though that's not at all clear from the context he created or the way he wrote it. He also added that the bill gave the president power "without limit." Senator Connally: "What you mean is that by the exercise of these powers the President could get us into war. That is what you mean, isn't it?" Brewster: "Yes." Senator Connally: "Under the Constitution he could get us into war now, couldn't he? Do you realize that he is the Commander in Chief of the Army and the Navy?" Brewster: "Yes." Senator Connally: "And without this bill." Brewster: "I real-ize that." Senator Connally: "Without this bill he could send the fleet to Europe now." Brewster: "I believe he can." Senator Connally: "And thereby he could probably get us into war?" Brewster: "I believe he can." U. S. Senate Hearings, 617.

30. Senator Connally had challenged Brewster: "Are you engaged in name call-ing? . . . Who are you talking about, and when was that?" Senator Barkley posited, "In other words, the exercise of freedom of speech . . . that we boast about in this country as American citizens, that is deceit and subterfuge? Is that true?" Brewster: "They have said one thing when they went a lot further in their own minds. . . ." Barkley also posited:

"Whom did you have in mind in that statement?" Brewster equivocated, his precise tone and manner unknown, until Senator Barkley asked Brewster whether his "rather strong language . . . amounts to an accusation of deliberate misrepresentation and deliberate deceiving the people of the United States." Brewster, referring to Roosevelt, believed Roosevelt had engaged in a "breach of faith with the American people." Senator Barkley declared, in question form: "And many equally patriotic men and women differ about these matters?" Brewster: "I agree." Barkley: "You would not want to leave that impression, would you, that everybody who disagrees with you, even about this bill, are dishonest and not square with the public?" Brewster: "Certainly not." Barkley: "That is all." U.S. Senate Hearings, 618–20.

31. U.S. Senate Hearings, 632–35; Bennett was not mentioned in the *Yale Daily News* article that described Brewster's testimony or in Kabaservice's recitation of Brewster's testimony. See also her letter to the editor, Fay Bennett, "Youth War Stand," *New York Times*, August 4, 1940. Bennett, since at least 1938 and for the remainder of her life, was a dedicated spokesperson for sharecroppers, labor, and civil rights in the United States and abroad.

32. Henry Wells (Yale 1936, Law School 1939) formed the "All-University Peace Committee," which organized letter writing, lobbying, and "meetings open to the public." The Peace Committee was joined by the "Fellowship of Reconciliation of the [Yale] Divinity School," the "Graduate School Peace Committee," the "American Student Union," and "Dwight Hall." The Peace Committee received the endorsement of Senator Burton K. Wheeler of Montana. The broader-based "College Men for Defense First," led by Richard A. Moore (Yale 1936), was composed of young alumni from sixty colleges. When, on February 14, 1941, Governor Philip F. La Follette of Wisconsin came to Yale to speak at Woolsey Hall, Brewster *and* Moore shared the podium as additional speakers. Perhaps these students believed the message of "America First" was wrongly parsed, or its narrow winnowing of student adherents or its anti-Semitic national affiliations too discomforting. "LaFollette to Lead Attack on Lend-Lease Bill Tonight," *Yale Daily News*, February 14, 1941 (College Men for Defense First). See also "Congress Should Designate Categories Granting Deferments, Says President," *Yale Daily News*, February 24, 1941.

33. See, for example, Kabaservice, *The Guardians*, 77, 81 (1991 interview by Kabaservice).

34. Yale University, under remunerative contracts with various military departments, agreed to extensive use of its campus and alterations in its teaching programs and course requirements to ensure men were properly trained and prepared in linguistics and science. One temporary effect (discarded, in time) of having non-Yale-selected students on campus during and immediately after the war: "They were . . . often unwilling to tolerate at Yale the discrimination that they had fought against abroad." One permanent effect (slowly evolving, in time) was that they opposed the obvious discriminatory membership criteria in the student societies (not undemocratic because the vote was secret, as Brewster believed, but because it was wrong to exclude anyone on the basis of race or religion). Their affirmative dislike was described in a history written by then-student A. Bartlett Giamatti, who, as Daniel Oren described it in *Joining the Club*, "recorded one observer's . . . comments": "It was the skepticism of these veterans which first permitted the early, organized mockery of the senior societies to reassess themselves." Also among those institutional arrangements Yale and the military agreed to was the continuation of

the Reserve Officer Training School, its precise name and format evolving over time since World War I, its presence at Yale seemingly permanent until the Vietnam War. Oren, *Joining the Club*, 161–62.

35. See, for example, Jim Proser with Jerry Cutler, *I'm Staying with My Boys: The Heroic Life of Sgt. John Basilone, USMC* (New York: St. Martin's Press, 2010), 270–71. He was awarded the Navy Cross and the Purple Heart postmortem and was buried in Arlington National Cemetery.

36. See, for example, "DeLauro Presents Raymond Ciarlelli Overdue WW II Medals," press release, March 21, 2009; Rachel Chinapen, "New Haven's Triangle Park: WW II Monument Dedication Is Thursday," *New Haven Register*, November 6, 2013; Esteban Hernandez, "World War II Veteran Seeks Donations to Frame Painting," *New Haven Register*, May 6, 2017; Pamela McLoughlin, "African American World War II Veterans Share Stories of War amidst Segregation," *Journal Register* (Connecticut), November 7, 2010 (George Street, New Haven); Ukrainian American Veterans (1945 and 1991 tributes); Mary M. Donohue, "Al Marder: A Life of Conviction," *Connecticut Explored* (April 14, 2016); Riccio, *Farms, Factories, and Families*, "While the Boys Were Gone," 319. The author had five cousins and three uncles serve in World War II; all but one saw action in Africa or Europe. One is buried in the National Memorial Cemetery in Hawaii (Punchbowl Crater): Frank A. Proto (awarded Purple Heart, D-Day invasion), *New Haven Register*, November 1, 2010; Salvatore Prisco (U.S. Army, Africa campaign, POW), *New Haven Register*, October 19, 2014; George Proto (U.S. Army), *New Haven Register*, October 26, 2012; Donato Storlazzi (enlisted on December 19, 1941, buried in Punchbowl, National Cemetery, Hawaii), *New Haven Register*, December 9, 1989. See also Jennifer Kaylin, "Lindbergh Lands in New Haven," *Yale Alumni Magazine*, May 2002; Jonathan Horn, "Yale: An Arsenal of Democracy in World War II," *Yale Daily News*, February 21, 2001; informal discussion with John Wilkinson (Yale 1960) about Memorial Hall Plaza during walk through the Yale campus.

37. Given the state of medication and the uncertainty of Angelo's form of care, other causes may have contributed to his death. Informal interview with George Urquhart; author's visit to burial site.

38. In a subsequent encounter between Helen Walton and Max Ascoli, a vehement anti-Fascist involved with the Mazzini Society (broadly active throughout New England, including in New Haven, under various iterations), Ascoli confirmed he knew Val and admired his speeches during and immediately after the war. Interview with David and Elria Giamatti Ewing and author's notes; see also "Guido Calabresi: A Foreigner in New Haven," 58 (the Calabresi family relationship with Ascoli).

39. "Italian Teacher Discusses Reactions to War," *Holyoke Transcript-Telegram* (hereinafter, *Holyoke Telegram*), September 24, 1943.

40. Dr. Calabresi was fearful that the United States would not make the distinction between the people of Italy and the Fascist leaders when the Allied invasion occurred, the same fear Val spoke about in Massachusetts. Calabresi warned: "When the time comes . . . the armies of the United States should not invade Italy as an enemy power. . . . They should come to the shores of Italy as friends fighting for liberty from a Nazi domination and its Fascist puppets." Laura Kalman, "Some Thoughts on Yale and Guido," *Law and Contemporary Problems* 77 (November 2, 2014): 16n8 (quoted from the *New York Times*).

41. When, in 1942, 1943, and 1945, the United States Congress's Special Committee on Un-American Activities, chaired by Congressman Martin Dies Jr. (D-Texas), continued its investigation of alleged Communist influence throughout the United States, with the aid, often at the initiative of, the Federal Bureau of Investigation, the FBI focused on Mount Holyoke's president, Roswell Gray Ham. The Bureau went back to 1938 and traced Ham's activities through 1943. If Ham knew about the 1943 investigation, it didn't deter his conduct. Eventually, President Ham joined seven other college presidents who publicly "protested the abuse of power by the Un-American Activities Committee. . . . 'as a glaring example of disgraceful procedure.'" The FBI chronicled each of his sponsorships of radical causes he'd endorsed between 1938 and 1940, and added his public support for the National Federation of Constitutional Liberties and for freeing or pardoning two men who, he believed, were jailed for exercising their constitutional rights: Sam Adams Darcy for organizing longshoremen into labor unions in San Francisco and Morris Schappes (Moishe Shapshilevich, a Ukrainian Jew, whose family fled Tsarist Russia) for declining to name names of other members of the Communist Party to a New York legislative investigative committee. Letter and Investigative Report from D. M. Ladd to various officials in the Federal Bureau of Investigation, (March 12, 1943). At a later date, in 1952, the FBI would, once again, turn its attention to President Ham as part of a broader investigation into colleges and universities in the Northeast. Memorandum from Belmont to Ladd (FBI) (December 16, 1952), 1, and attachment, 1, 3–5 (the FBI investigation was undertaken with the approval of the director, J. Edgar Hoover). Roswell Ham Papers, Mount Holyoke College Archives; Douglas Martin, "Morris Schappes Dies at 97: Marxist and Jewish Scholar," *New York Times*, June 9, 2004; Tony Michels, ed., *Jewish Radicals: A Documentary History* (New York: New York University Press, 2012), 126.

42. Val and Peggy and Professor Bianca Maria Finzi-Contini Calabresi, Massimo's wife, met as teachers at Middlebury's Language School in Vermont. The assessment of both men was prophetic. The Allied invasion and the ensuing political strategy of division and unnecessary mayhem had lasting effects. Val witnessed it still unfolding when, a few years later, he returned to Italy on his first sabbatical. He would retain these themes and speak of them directly, publicly, and through action for the remainder of his life. "Italian Teacher Discusses Reactions to War," *Holyoke Telegram*, September 24, 1943; see also (discussed later in the text), "About the City," *Holyoke Telegram*, September 18, 1943 (Giamatti described the "Italian People in the War"); "Says Italians Want Peace in Coming Parley," *Waterbury* (Connecticut) *Republican*, April 15, 1945 (speaking to the American Association of University Women); "Holyoke Faculty Member to Address Jewish Center Group," *Holyoke Telegram*, November 16, 1945; "College Club Books Talk by Professor," *Knickerbocker News*, May 12, 1947 (Mount Holyoke Club). These articles are preserved in the Valentine Giamatti Papers, Mount Holyoke College Archives, and in his family's archives.

CHAPTER 14

FAMILY LIFE IN SOUTH HADLEY

1. Longo also said, "He was very well liked. . . . It was the appointment of the president that brought Val to Mount Holyoke. . . . That he had been on the faculty at Yale, and Val knew him. And so when he got appointed president of Mount Holyoke, he asked Val to come and teach." Interview with Rose Criscitiello Longo.

2. Anthony Valerio, *Bart: A Life of A. Bartlett Giamatti by Him and about Him* (New York: Harcourt, 1991), 13–15 (quoting from Cynthia Mann, "Insight").

3. Valerio, *Bart*, 12 (quoting from William Henry III, "Yale's Renaissance Man").

4. In time, the number of students enrolled in Italian courses rose from eighteen to "more than 150." The play was written by Italian playwright, Dario Niccodemi. Rose Longo was in it. "We all thought it was great," she said. "All in Italian." Val was "good, good. . . . It was his play." Interview with Longo; linguist Anthony Riccio's translation of Niccodemi's work (July 4, 2017).

5. "The Study of Italian at Mount Holyoke College" (1946). Valentine Giamatti Papers, Mount Holyoke College Archives; interview with Frank White.

6. *Italian Grammar* excluded "all obsolete forms, superfluous rules, and highly idiomatic constructions" to ensure that, with classroom instruction, students could focus on the essential rules to establish a solid foundation. Valentine Giamatti, *Minimum of Italian Grammar* (New York: S. F. Vanni, 1947, 1957, 1964).

7. Val's goal was "to help guide the reader pictorially and to allow for quick reference and review." Val credited two scholars and artists, Henry Rox and Lincoln Scott, with giving practical life to his intention. Val melded excerpts from Dante's work, his own annotations of locations and canto numbers, and new drawings by Rox especially. See Dava Sobel, *Galileo's Daughter* (New York: Walker, 1999), 18; *Panoramic Views of Dante's Inferno, Purgatory, and Paradise* is available in the Valentine Giamatti Papers, Mount Holyoke College Archives; Giamatti, *Minimum of Italian Grammar;* see also Mount Holyoke News Bureau, special to the *Springfield Daily News*, April 22, 1949, Valentine Giamatti Papers, Mount Holyoke Archives.

8. "About the City," *Holyoke Telegram*, September 18, 1943 (Giamatti described the "Italian People in the War"); "Says Italians Want Peace in Coming Parley," *Waterbury* (Connecticut) *Republican*, April 15, 1945 (speaking to the American Association of University Women); "Holyoke Faculty Member to Address Jewish Center Group," *Holyoke Telegram*, November 16, 1945. Each of these articles is in the Valentine Giamatti Papers, Mount Holyoke College Archives.

9. "Center PTA Executive Group Meets Tonight," *Holyoke Telegram*, October 7, 1952.

10. Various of Bart's grammar and high school friends, as well as others who knew the family during this period, included Andrew Vitali, Bill Mazeine, Frank White, Martha Johnson, George Nash, Ingrid Apgar, Norma Stiles Monat, Sally Benson, Cecile Rondeau, and Jean MacLeod Keatley, each of whom offered valuable recollections. Their tone and excerpts from those recollections (as well as existing documentation) also informed this section. Interview and related email, Jean MacLeod Keatley (grammar and high school friend) through Dr. Peggy Ann Brown (June 14, 2017); Sally Benson (various communications and meeting in June and July 2017); interview with Bill Mazeine (neighbor, close friend in grammar and high school, and through adulthood); interview with Andrew Vitali (neighbor, close friend in grammar and high school, and through adulthood); and interview with Frank White (neighbor, close friend in grammar and high school, and through adulthood).

11. Written comments by Jean MacLeod Keatley to Dr. Peggy Ann Brown and author (numerous in 2017).

12. Ogden interview.

13. Mazeine interview; Vitali interview.

14. Vitali interview; Mazeine interview; White interview; "Guido Calabresi: A Foreigner in New Haven," 13.

15. Mazeine interview. The author walked through the old Center School, now used as a community center. The school building remains almost wholly intact from the era when the Giamattis lived there. The furniture, electrical outlets, plumbing fixtures, auditorium (which served as the stage for recitals and school gatherings), and gymnasium—its one basket still standing, the echo of players running and shooting easily imagined. Outdoor is the field, the place were students played—where Bart and his friends played football, where he stood tall as the quarterback.

16. David Bakish, *Jimmy Durante: His Show Business Career* (Jefferson, NC: McFarland, 1995), 7, 16–17. Durante appears in Ken Burns's multipart series *Jazz*, and his recording of "Make Someone Happy," from the movie *Sleepless in Seattle* (1993), remains legendary. "Female-Fables" was made available to the author, with written permission to use it, by its editor, Martha Johnson; interviews with Vitali and Elria Giamatti Ewing.

17. Interview with Dino Giamatti; interview with Mazeine.

18. Charles Dickens, *A Christmas Carol* (London: J. B. Lippincott, [1853] 1915 and multiple times thereafter). Writers have also suggested that Dante's influence is likely reflected in Dickens's novel, *Hard Times*. See, for example, Stephen Bertman, "Dante's Role in the Genesis of Dickens's A Christmas Carol," *Dickens Quarterly* 24, no. 3 (September 2007): 167–75, and Rubin, *Dante in Love*, 20–21.

19. The common parlance in New Haven, at Frank Pepe's Pizzeria Napoletana on Wooster Street, which Val knew and frequented, probably with parents and later as a student, through adulthood.

20. Interview with Lennie Ogden.

21. "Enthusiasm for Italian Makes 'Sala Italiana' Necessity, Trustees and Mr. Ham Back Italian Department Members," *Holyoke Telegram*, May 2, 1947; photograph, "Luciana Ribet and Valentine Giamatti, head of Italian dept. (assistant in Italian) Sept. 1946," Valentine Giamatti Papers, Mount Holyoke College Archives.

22. Longo added that there actually were not that many Italian American students. "There was one black girl in our class. . . . They made a point of having students of various colors and background," an intent that began with Mary Lyon and continued as the composition of the Northeast changed. By the time Ham became president, Mount Holyoke had a student body from dozens of states, multiple ethnicities and religions, and a few foreign countries. The "disparities" that did exist had largely to do with wealth (clothing and travel experience). Longo interview; Vitali interview.

CHAPTER 15

MATURITY FROM EXPERIENCE

1. Photograph, *Holyoke Telegram*, April 1948, Valentine Giamatti Papers, Mount Holyoke Archives; interview with Frank White.

2. By the fall of 1947, the wives of American and British diplomats had convinced the British Royal Air Force (which was about to relocate) to allow the use of a small portion of the sprawling Villa Torlonia, which had served as its headquarters, as a children's school. The large estate—described as "actually a collection of some four or five villas set down in the midst of a lovely great park of tall trees, green lawns, and long shaded

walks"—had been rented to Benito Mussolini and his family from 1925 to 1943, when, after his demise and death, the British command occupied the main building. Joseph Harrison, "This World, Mussolini 'Footprints' Fade in Italy," *Christian Science Monitor*, November 29, 1948.

3. "Political Situation Tense in Italy, Giamatti Writes," *Holyoke Telegram*, April 7, 1948; "Mount Holyoke Press Release, for Special Issue, Giamatti v. Cramer," (September 1948),Valentine Giamatti Papers, Mount Holyoke Archives; interview with Elria Giamatti Ewing.

4. Foreign relations and military conditions were among the matters he discussed, plainly indicative of his insistence on staying informed and his continued correspondence with friends in Italy. He once shared the podium with the representative from the Westover Air Force Base. In each instance, he'd focus particularly on the "spirit of the Italian people, who want only family security in a peaceful Europe." In February 1949,Val and the Italian Department were presented with an oversized silk banner used at the 1887 Il Palio di Siena, the famed international horse race festival held in Siena's central piazza. In the photograph are Val; Signor Enrico Somaré, an Italian art critic who'd met Val during the sabbatical; and two students, identified as Ursula Honegger, Class of 1952, from Sandy Hook, Connecticut, and Joyce McLean, also Class of 1952, from Garden City, New Jersey. "Italians Want Peace, Security, Lions Club Told," *Holyoke Telegram*, September 17, 1948; Mount Holyoke Press Release, for Special Issue, Giamatti v. Cramer"; "Prof. Giamatti Meets Junior League" (newspaper not identified), 1948; "An Award Winner" (newspaper not identified), February 1949, Valentine Giamatti Papers, Mount Holyoke Archives.

5. Castiglione, an eminent linguist then teaching at Georgetown University's School of Foreign Service, had been selected director in 1947. Middlebury was not the first intensive *modern* (that is, European) language study program in America, but it took on a unique character: "The Middlebury Language Schools were the first in the country which gave only advanced courses concentrated upon a single language, and which required exclusive use of that language in the entire life of the school." In time, secondary schools and colleges found the Middlebury methodology without parallel. Middlebury's national stature increased as the summer program expanded its offerings to French in 1916 and Spanish in 1917. In 1927, Middlebury offered gradations of certificates, degree credits, and the degree of "Doctor of Modern Languages." The program was rigorous intellectually, the curriculum remarkably varied, the grading carefully done. In 1932, the Language School offered Italian. From the outset, the school was open to high school, college, and graduate students and to individuals from private companies and nonprofit institutions seeking a new or renewed level of skill. The intention to teach was critical to admission. Students came from throughout the nation. The Italian School, like the schools in French, Spanish, German, and Russian, had its own residence hall, food service facility, meeting rooms, and stage setting. The program was total immersion, the abandonment of any other language except Italian. Middlebury also began a comparable program in English, located in a remote country setting, beneath the hillsides of Bread Loaf, Vermont. Stephen Albert Freeman, *Middlebury College Foreign Language Schools, 1915–1970: The Story of a Unique Idea* (Middlebury, VT: Middlebury College, 1975), 1–24. I also was able to review the files from this era and later periods through the 1970s and to discuss the nuances of the program's history and location with the special collection director, Rebekah Irwin, and postgraduate fellow Mikaela Taylor.

6. Middlebury College Summer Language Schools brochures (1947, 1948, 1951, 1952, 1953), Middlebury College Archives; the college's reply to an inquiry, apparently from the FBI, seeking an explanation for a departed teacher's status, Middlebury College Archives.

7. "Buckley Slams Atheism, Collectivism at Yale," *Yale Daily News*, October 15, 1951; William F. Buckley Jr., *God and Man at Yale: The Superstitions of "Academic Freedom"* (New York: Regency Publishing, 50th anniversary ed., 2002).

8. Buckley entered Yale in 1946 and graduated in June 1950. As a student, he'd been an outspoken critic of aspects of Yale's administration, including during his tenure as co-editor of the *Daily News*. Sam Tanenhaus, "William F. Buckley: The Founder," *Yale Alumni Magazine*, May/June 2008.

9. At the 250th anniversary, Buckley's criticism received a response. (Wilmarth S. Lewis: "It would be a pity if we [alumni] nullified so much generosity by imposing our wills upon the universities. . . .") Griswold and ex-president Seymour, followed by the leaders of Cambridge, Oxford, and Harvard, led the anniversary celebration processional. Invitees also included the presidents of colleges and universities throughout the nation that were led by Yale graduates. "Leaders Hail Yale on the 250th Birthday," *New York Times*, October 19, 1951; "Old Eli Stepsons Acclaim 250th Year," *Life* magazine, October 29, 1951, 44.

10. "Publisher's Notes," *Springfield* (Massachusetts) *Republican*, September 30, 1951; "Former News Chairman Says Yale 'Atheistic,'" *New Haven Evening Register*, October 15, 1951, though, here, too, the vitriol contained in the "Buckley is a fascist" comment likely provoked the editor's interest and began local awareness of the nature of Yale's distress, including financial, which was revealed two days later. "Yale Reveals Plans for New Fund Campaign," *New Haven Evening Register*, October 17, 1951; Bruce Barton, "The Professors," *Washington Evening Star*, December 9, 1951; Mary McGrory, "Yale Graduate Says Faculty Is Atheistic," book review, *Sunday Star* (Washington, DC), November 18, 1951.

11. A substantive, respectful response to Buckley's critique occurred from at least one faculty member, Economics Professor John Perry Miller, and from students who also thoughtfully argued against Buckley's "authoritarian" approach (alumni-driven determination of educational content) as the foundation for an informed instructional debate in an academic institution. The Economics Department had been criticized nationally ("scorned," according to the *Yale Daily News*) for its inadequacy, and warranted new faculty and approaches to research. Yale's Department of Religion, already the subject of criticism for the mediocrity of its program, was ripe, students claimed, for external and internal review. In an insightful editorial in the *Yale Daily News*, Buckley was characterized as "steeped in stifling orthodoxy . . . a child of the Middle Ages," who still, for "four tempestuous years . . . successfully battled [for] education . . . [including] from his position as chairman of this newspaper." Although the book, the *Daily News* continued, "is characterized by naïveté, misinformation, quotations out of context, and the crassest dogmatism . . . we urge every Yale undergraduate to read it." By 1951, Yale's imposition of a strict F "Christian" or religious discipline (for example, mandatory Chapel and biblical instruction) had dramatically diminished or disappeared altogether, a fact easily acknowledged without debate. Yale also prided itself on being a "liberal arts college"—though the term "liberal" shouldn't be confused with an ideological imperative. Yale's reputation, deliberately established, was decidedly "conservative." The rough ideological, unconstrained

hyperbole of faculty and Corporation members reflected, in short order, Yale's insecurity and cultural hypocrisy on matters of race and religion. John Perry Miller, "The Economist Speaks," *Yale Daily News*, October 15, 1951; Ray B. Westerfield, "A Professor Indicts," *Yale Daily News*, December 5, 1951; "Economics at Yale: I, Department Furor," *Yale Daily News*, December 5, 1951; "Economics at Yale: II, A Murky Past," *Yale Daily News*, December 6, 1951; Theodore Green, "The Christian Speaks, A Critic's Forum," *Yale Daily News*, October 15, 1951 (introduced or at least affirmed the accusation that Buckley's proscription was "the fascist alternative to liberalism"); "Bill's Book," *Yale Daily News*, October 24, 1951.

12. See Kelley, *Yale*, 411 and 411n52 for details. See also similar Treasurer's Reports in 1951–1952 through 1955–1956 (Box 7, Folders 31–36, and others, Yale University Archives), which Kelley relied upon. See Larry Newman, "Yale President Reports Grave Finance Status, Griswold Cites Costs, Declares University 'Needs New Capital,'" *Yale Daily News*, November 19, 1951; "Yale Reveals Plans for New Fund Campaign," *New Haven Evening Register*, October 17, 1951.

13. An unattributed chart exists in Griswold's papers that examined, comparatively, the number of Hebrews and Roman Catholics among Yale students in each class from 1949 through 1952. Griswold Presidential Papers, Yale University Archives (RU 22, "Religious Affiliations," comparative compilation of Hebrews, Roman Catholics, and Protestants in the Classes of 1940–1950, 1950–1951, 1951–1952 by number and percentage). See also Oren, *Joining the Club*, 266–98; Karabel, *The Chosen*, 327–33; "Religion at Yale, a Department Moribund," *Yale Daily News*, April 22, 1953. In one almost macabre reflection of this mentality, the *Yale Daily News* announced that "Anthropologists Earnest A. Hooton and Frederick Stagg have . . . just completed a project studying Crimson [Harvard] bodies in the 1890's in the light of their present day positions in the world." The researchers had "access to 2631 photographs of nude Harvard men. . . ." It may be forever unclear to whom Harvard and Yale gave access to their nude photographs. "Harvard Nudes Compare Well with Norm; Muscles Are Better Than Those of Army," *Yale Daily News*, November 29, 1951.

14. McGeorge Bundy, "The Attack on Yale," *Atlantic*, November 1, 1951. The article, after a severe critique—wherein Buckley is compared unfavorably (to the right) to conservative Republicans Mark Hanna and Robert Taft, and favorably to Herbert Hoover, and a few thousand words are devoted to the "ignorance" of Buckley's effort to engage the alumni—concluded that "neither of these things [an effect on the alumni or the Corporation] is likely to happen—and least of all in response to the crusade of William Buckley, Jr." Bundy consulted with Griswold and others at Yale before publication. Alvin S. Felzenberg, *A Man and His Presidents: The Political Odyssey of William F. Buckley Jr.* (New Haven, CT: Yale University Press, 2017), 48–52 ("God and Bill at Yale"). See also Kabaservice, *The Guardians*, 132–33 (Bundy's anger). Kabaservice, like Kelley, *Yale* (434), lists all the positions Buckley took *after* (some *long* after) the book was published, presumably to give comfort to Yale's reliance on its anti-Catholic fervor in 1951.

15. William F. Buckley Jr., "The Man Himself Speaks Up," *Yale Daily News*, December 3, 1951 (Griswold's letter to an alumnus quoted in its entirety). See previous note and Felzenberg, *A Man and His Presidents*, 48–52.

16. Felzenberg, *A Man and His Presidents*, 48–52 ("God and Bill at Yale,"); James Green, "God and Man at Yale and Beyond: The Thoughts of William F. Buckley, Jr. on

Higher Education, 1949–1955," *American Educational History Journal* 39, no. 1 (2012): 208–10.

17. Coffin's letter was written to an alumnus and made public. Max Eastman, "Buckley v. Yale," *New York Times*, November 15, 1951; Peter Viereck, "Conservatism under the Elms," *New York Times*, November 4, 1952; Milton Bracker, "Yale Survey Finds No Real Influence or Threats to Academic Freedom," *New York Times*, February 18, 1952. See also "Buckley, Warne Debate Freedom and Education," *Springfield Union*, May 5, 1952 (Amherst debate); "College Teachings Broadside Target," *Springfield Republican*, January 1, 1952; George M. Marsden, *The Soul of the American University* (New York: Oxford University Press, 1994), 19.

18. See, for example, "Bozell in for Buckley, Religion, Error, and Straw Men," *Yale Daily News*, October 24, 1951. Buckley's forum was held with "every practicing minister (of every faith) associated with Yale, and a half dozen Yale Divinity School students who act as 'denominational counsellors' to Yale undergraduates. Every person present affirmed that nothing in the section was traceable to Catholic thought." See also the thoughtful response by the *Daily News* editors, which identified factual errors ("A Few More Instances"). See also "Undergraduate Backing for Buckley," *Yale Daily News*, October 18, 1951 ("inexcusable dragging in of Mr. Buckley's Catholicism"); "This Buckley Business," *Yale Daily News*, October 19, 1951; "Bill's Logic," editorial, *Yale Daily News*, December 3, 1951.

19. In a matter of unique consequence to Yale, the Buckley-Bundy dialogue slipped into Skull and Bones in "one of the bitterest controversies ever to split an Eli organization." It apparently was not the first time that society membership would matter at that level. George B. Watson III, "Dispute over 'God and Man at Yale' Causes 'Struggle for Power' within Secret Society," *Yale Daily News*, November 24, 1951; Kabaservice, *The Guardians*, 34–35, 132–33, 167 (Bundy).

20. To the extent the book bore a relationship to Buckley's Catholic upbringing, most Catholics, especially Italian immigrants, believed in their social duty to others, affirmed since at least Pope Leo XIII's encyclical on Catholic social teaching in 1891 and essential to the revered work of Mother Cabrini.

21. There were numerous lodges and tents, tennis courts, baseball fields, a swimming pond, and a horse stable. Entrance requirements were simple: "well-bred boys [and girls] who will be interested to carry out its purposes. The life is simple, the fare is plain; the beds are hard, the orderly duties are homely. The boys [and girls] who come must be ready to contribute their share of help and good-fellowship." Age of admission ranged from nine to fifteen years old; campers came from throughout New England, New York, and as far west as Illinois. The camp was established to provide not only physical activities, but mental and intellectual ones as well. Courses were available to supplement school-year subjects or to prepare for new ones. Raphael J. Shortlidge, *A Summer Camp for Boys* (established by Dr. C. Hanford Henderson in 1896, headmaster, from 1912) (1941 ed.).

22. Note to Dr. Peggy Brown and author from Jean MacLeod Keatley (June 14 and various others, 2017).

23. Most editions of the *Marienfeld Monitor* focused on activities the boys engaged in, such as descriptions of efforts to improve the library by contributing books; fish caught by whom in the camp lake; capturing live animals—woodchucks, for example—for observation and "to learn how to care for them"; learning proper food preparation—peeling

potatoes; and helping reseed and improve the camp's forest reserve. See especially Bart on baseball: Bart Giamatti, "Harrisville," *Marienfeld Monitor*, July 18, 1952, provided by David Ewing. Interview with David Ewing; author review of newspapers at Ewing home and those donated by Ewing for inclusion in the Giamatti Papers located at the Baseball Hall of Fame.

CHAPTER 16

THE DUTY OF CITIZENSHIP: MOUNT HOLYOKE AS PRISM

1. Victor Navasky, *Naming Names* (New York: Viking Press, 1980), 335 (state universities); Kelley, *Yale*, 355; "A. Whitney Griswold, 1906–1963," *Yale Alumni Magazine*, May 1963; "Yale Honors Educator Dismissed by California Loyalty Oath," *New York Times*, June 11, 1951; "Yale Head Upholds Individual's Worth," *New York Times*, June 12, 1951; "Liberal Arts in Peril," *Yale Daily News*, April 25, 1953; Diane Johnson, *Dashiell Hammett: A Life* (New York: Random House, 1983), 161–62, 257, 265–71 (Hollywood, libraries, and books). Richard Nixon was on the House Committee from 1947 through 1950.

2. Commencement address, "Liberty Means Responsibility," June 1951, Roswell Ham Papers, Mount Holyoke College Archive.

3. Interview with Elria Ewing Giamatti.

4. Sally Benson to Dr. Peggy Ann Brown and author (June 23 and July 1, 2017).

5. Interview with Ewing Giamatti; *Mount Holyoke Alumnae Quarterly* (Winter 2006), 4–5; "South Hadley Plans for Big Celebration, Town Will Observe 200th Anniversary, *Holyoke Telegram*, September 2, 1953 (Val on committee); "South Hadley, Annual Dinner to Be January 28," *Holyoke Telegram*, January 18, 1957 (The "Know Your Town Group" held in South Hadley Falls, Peggy Giamatti on planning committee).

6. Sigmund Diamond, "Archival Adventure along the Freedom of Information Trail: Universities and the FBI in the McCarthy Period," *Midwestern Archivist* 12, no. 1 (1987): 31 (quoting from an internal FBI memorandum, and correspondence between J. Edgar Hoover and Attorney General Herbert Brownell); "McCarran Group Lists M.I.T., Harvard and Wellesley," *Boston Sunday Post*, November 11, 1952. Ham is in "his most untenable position, I think we ought to get up a very good summary of Ham and furnish it to the McCarran Committee. Ham certainly is the type of individual who ought to be considered in any investigation of Communist Infiltration into Education." Letter, Ladd to Belmont, FBI (December 16, 1952), Roswell Ham Papers, Mount Holyoke Archives; letter, Nichols to Tolson (December 5, 1952), Roswell Ham Papers, Mount Holyoke Archives.

7. "Candidates Meet the Voters," *Holyoke Telegram*, February 26, 1957; "Candidates Speak at Session Tonight," *Holyoke Telegram*, February 19, 1954; both available in Valentine Giamatti Papers, Mount Holyoke Archives. Furcolo had become a successful lawyer, practiced in Springfield, and lived in Longmeadow. He'd first sought local public office in 1942, unsuccessfully. He enlisted in the Navy and saw action in Japan. In 1946, he ran as a liberal Democrat for Congress but lost in a close election when the Republican Party won Massachusetts by wide margins.

8. Garrison Nelson, *John William McCormack: A Political Biography* (New York: Bloomsbury, 2017); Alonzo Hamby, "Reds under the Bed," book review, *New York Times*, December 12, 1999.

9. Harry S. Truman, "Rear Platform and Other Informal Remarks in Massachusetts and Connecticut," October 27, 1948, online in Harry S. Truman Presidential Library and Museum, www.trumanlibrary.org/publicpapers/index.php?pid=2010&st=&st1=. President Harry Truman came to Springfield during the election and told the crowd: "I understand that Foster Furcolo is your candidate for Congress here. Send him down there so he can cooperate with the President in doing the right thing." Kennedy reportedly responded by notoriously failing to vote on important bills, and, erroneously, blamed Furcolo for not attending a meeting with Truman over patronage in Massachusetts. Nelson, *John William McCormack*. (Both Truman's schedule and a post-meeting photograph verified Furcolo's attendance.)

10. Interview with U.S. Representative Rosa DeLauro (D-Connecticut). Furcolo also received national attention because of the thoroughness he brought to the special congressional committee created to investigate the mass killing in the Katyn Forest in eastern Poland during World War II.

11. During the election, Kennedy aide Ted Sorensen secretly provided support and information to Saltonstall. Theodore Sorensen, *Kennedy* (New York: Harper & Row, 1965), 73–75. (Kennedy directed Sorensen to "help Republican Saltonstall.") Kennedy, to the consternation of liberals, also did not criticize Senator McCarthy during the Senate debate on his censure and missed the actual vote because of surgery that could occur only in New York. Arthur Herman, *Joseph McCarthy: Reexamining the Life and Legacy of America's Most Hated Senator* (New York: Free Press, 2000); "Sen. McCarthy Begins Defense in Censure Case," *Springfield Union*, November 5, 1954.

12. "Kennedy, Furcolo Split Shocks: Both Democrats, Labor, Are Reluctant to Believe Rift Has Developed," *Springfield Union*, October 12, 1954. It was called the "Kennedy Snub," and after the election, which Furcolo lost by less than 30,000 votes, Furcolo said, "We analyzed the election returns and we were knifed." "The Kennedy Snub," *Springfield Union*, November 5, 1954. The press and the state's political leaders considered it the Irish effort to stall the Italian American rise in the Democratic Party. Robert Dallek, *An Unfinished Life: John F. Kennedy, 1917–1963* (New York: Little, Brown, 2003), 200 (JFK: "That goddamn guinea"); Giamatti Ewing interview. See also Michael Connolly, "Showing More Profile Than Courage," *Historical Journal of Massachusetts* (Winter 2002): 51, 51n52 (Kennedy-Furcolo split); Michael O'Brien, *John F. Kennedy: A Biography* (New York: Thomas Dunne Books, 2005), 304–7. In New Haven there exist a dozen or so outdoor wall hangings of prominent New Haven–born people who achieved success, defined in a number of ways. One is John Foster Furcolo. Another is actor Paul Edward Valentine Giamatti, Bart Giamatti's son.

13. Kabaservice, *The Guardians*, 167 (Bundy); "Pusey Will Be Acting Dean until Naming Bundy's Permanent Successor," *Harvard Crimson*, January 5, 1961. Kennedy friend and Harvard Dean McGeorge Bundy, who, as Furcolo and others knew well was "tone deaf" to discrimination, went out of his way to criticize Furcolo's candidacy for governor in 1956. It didn't work. ("Of course, Furcolo is not a wicked man," a political advertisement quoted Dean Bundy as saying. "He is something more dangerous than that. He is a bad governor.") "Nominations Submitted," *Springfield Republican*, March 20, 1959 (Giamatti appointment).

14. Kelley, *Yale*, 427, 428 (Italian American accent), 429–30.

15. Lee to Griswold (July 2, 1960), Griswold Papers, Yale University Archives. It's unclear what role Lee played as director of public relations in attacks on Buckley's Catholicism.

16. Lee had worked closely with Griswold, or certainly believed he had, though, in fact, Griswold was only president for two years of Lee's fourteen-year tenure at Yale. He had written for the New Haven newspapers and worked in public relations for the Chamber of Commerce, composed largely of middle- and upper-income men who lived and worked in the suburbs and who held or controlled large industrial and commercial interests located in New Haven.

17. In 1958 or 1959, Lee told this story to Yale political science professor Robert Dahl, who was then researching his book, *Who Governs? Democracy and Power in an American City* (New Haven, CT: Yale University Press, 1961; 2nd ed., 2005), 118–19 (Lee as Scottish, English, and Irish). By then, the wholesale destruction of far more than inadequate residential structures already had occurred, with little to replace what had been destroyed other than a massive state-built, New Haven–approved highway and more highway construction planned. Dahl, *Who Governs?*, 120. Other authors who subsequently used this same quote relied wholly on Dahl. See, for example, Fred Powledge, *Model City: A Test of American Liberalism* (New York: Simon & Schuster, 1970), 28–29, 29n10. Lee was asked by Douglas Rae in 2002 or so—fifty-one years after it supposedly happened—and, as Rae properly pointed out, the experience had been recounted so frequently in Lee's lifetime that it had "literary echoes." This time Lee had yet a different version. Rae, *City*, 302–3. Earl Yohance Lin, from Wesleyan University, is not certain it happened at all. "Mayors, Slums, and Universities: Urban Renewal, Civic Leadership, and Community Response in Two Connecticut Cities" (honors thesis, Wesleyan University, 2015), 80. Lee's public relations skill, in 1958 and 1959, likely was in play, and, as Lee easily would have discerned, Dahl was looking to measure the reasons for Lee's presumed success, not to question it. And, as was evident by 1959 (when Dahl made his inquiry), and as discussed later in this book, architecturally attractive, structurally solid office buildings and retail establishments, religious institutions, and homes where these "slum" conditions did *not* exist or could have been repaired easily were torn down as well, and the street grid eliminated. Whatever Lee might have been talking about in 1958 or 1959 bore no relationship to the facts on the ground, if Dahl had paid attention to the obvious.

18. The Housing Act provided funding for new public housing (Title III), mortgage insurance for individual home buyers (Title II), and the elimination of "slums" (Title I). Housing Act of 1949, Pub. L. 81-171; G. William Domhoff, *Who Really Rules? New Haven and Community Power Reexamined* (Piscataway, NJ: Transaction Publishers, [1978] 2010), 63–86; Rae, *City*, 28, 216, 302–4.

19. The 1951 election was followed closely by the *Yale Daily News* because, in part, of Lee's relationship to Yale. "Local Democrats Name Lee as Candidate for Mayoralty, Seeks Return Bout," *Yale Daily News*, September 27, 1951; "Lee Charges Celentano with Violating Charter," *Yale Daily News*, October 30, 1951; "Lee Hurls Charges at Local Newsman," *Yale Daily News*, November 6, 1951; "Lee Loses in Court Battle: Fay Must Certify Returns," *Yale Daily News*, November 14, 1951; "Lee Refuses to Accredit Vote Count," *Yale Daily News*, November 15, 1951.

20. Barbarito, the popular president of the Italian American Columbian Democratic Club located in the Fair Haven neighborhood, was elected tax collector. Arthur Barbieri,

whose family lived in the Fair Haven and Dixwell/Newhallville neighborhoods and who withdrew from Yale and a Sterling Scholarship in order to help support his parents and siblings, was elected town clerk. *New Haven Register* articles include, among others, "Major Rivals Press Claim," November 1, 1951; "Fireworks Cut as Candidates Air Platforms," November 2, 1951; "The City Election," editorial, November 2, 1951 (supports Celentano for, among other reasons, "an increasing ability to handle the City's affairs efficiently"; "Mayor and Lee Rest Up for Final 2 Days," November 3, 1951; "Candidates to Stage Many Rallies Today," November 4, 1951; "Mayor Pledges Strides Ahead if Reelected," November 4, 1951; "Lee Reviews Aims of Party at Hill Rally," November 4, 1951; "The Real Issue in Tomorrow's Election," editorial, November 5, 1951; "Early Voting Light in City Election," November 6, 1952; "Usually Dull Vote Tabulation Job Turns into Drama Packed Evening," November 7, 1951; "Election Results," editorial, November 7, 1951; "Democrats Plan Election Protest," November 7, 1951.

21. Barbieri, who later battled Lee frequently over the elevation of Yale appointees, often to the exclusion of everyone else, and who would later become the Democratic town chair, had demonstrated that an Italian American Democrat could do what FDR had done among Italian American and other city voters: win. In *Who Governs?*, Yale's Dahl attributed this transformation largely to Lee (see, for example, 61), but like other inaccurate aspects of his pioneer study, he missed the reality of ward elections and the popularity of local aldermen and FDR-leaning organizers, like Barbarito, Barbieri, and Alderman Bart Guida, to bring out Democratic voters. "Columbian Club Endorses Lee for Mayoralty," *New Haven Evening Register*, September 1, 1951. (Barbarito was president; the club was considered tantamount to the Ward Committee.) Democrat Guida, who would later be a bane to Lee and who would eventually be elected mayor, had provoked opposition from the Irish-controlled Democratic city leadership because of his independence; he won his ward by one hundred votes more than Lee garnered. "Guida Set to Open Ward Battle Tonight," *New Haven Evening Register*, September 21, 1951 ("I was elected to represent the people and not the bosses."). See also "Guida Wins Primary by 18 Vote Margin," *New Haven Evening Register*, September 25, 1951; "Guida Opposes Party on 1952 City Budget," *New Haven Evening Register*, October 21, 1951. Perhaps Dahl, perched at Yale (and solicitous of President Griswold, with whom he shared an early draft of his work), was smitten in 1958, 1959, and 1960 by the adulation Lee was receiving and Yale's role in it. Portion of Dahl's draft and noted solicitation of comments from Griswold, Griswold Papers RU-22, Box 76, Yale University Archives.

22. In the 1939 mayoral election, Mayor John Murphy (D) successfully defeated Celentano (R). Guido Calabresi recalled that there was "so much anti-Semitism and anti-Italianism. Remember, this was just after the campaign that Celentano was beaten by Murphy in one of the most . . . racist campaigns going in which 'Celentano, the Italians, and the anarchists and that' and so on. And that was still in the air and we knew it." Calabresi interview. Professor Richard Gambino, relying on Professors Daniel Moynihan and Nathan Glazer's famed studies on, among other things, ethnic discrimination, referenced the continued acceptable nature of the Italian American slur reflected in the comment by a "world famous Yale professor" on the announcement of an Italian American candidate for mayor of New York: "If Italians aren't actually an inferior race, they do the best imitation of one I've seen." Gambino, *Blood of My Blood*, 107–8.

23. The broadcast, over WAVZ radio, was led by sportscasters Dick Petty and Tiny Markle. The Harvest Festival theme was carried through in contests for essays, poetry, and drawings for the game booklet. Almost three thousand students, parents, faculty, and local residents participated in a joint rally throughout the York Square campus, followed by a parade to the Bowl led by each school's elected King and Queen (Cross: Mark DeNegre and Beverly Shaw; Hillhouse: Robert Lassen and Fannie Lou Hubbell). After the game, the Harvest Festival Ball was held at the New Haven Armory under the sponsorship of the local business community. The victorious team received an engraved silver cup, and each player from both teams a gold football pendant donated by local craftsman and jeweler Bob Savitt. The *New Haven Evening Register* covered the entire pageant for three days, beginning with the full-page headlines: "Hillhouse Favored over Cross in Expected High Scoring Tilt Tomorrow." The coaches, Sam Bender of Hillhouse and Ray Tellier of Wilbur Cross, revealed the expected performance of their best backfield players: for Cross, "speedster" Charles DeMartin, "high scoring" Garry Wald, end Bob Finnegan, running back Arnold Amore, quarterback Haywood Meyers, and co-captain Edward Marrone; for Hillhouse, "breakaway runner" Russell Hamilton, "shifty" Frankie Williams, quarterback Santo Listro, running backs Lorey Zernitz and Ed Huggins. "Hillhouse Nips Wilbur Cross 14–13," "Zernitz and Badger Score on Passes for Acs in Second Quarter—Wall, Amore Tally for Governors," *New Haven Evening Register*, November 11, 1951.

24. Norman Roy Grutman, "Town and Frown," *Yale Daily News*, November 15, 1951.

25. The criticism came from a few students and from New Haven educators and organizations. "Communication Clean-up," *Yale Daily News*, November 21, 1951; "A Statement of Policy," *Yale Daily News*, November 21, 1951; Giamatti, "Commentary," in *The Italian Americans*, 16, 20.

26. Griswold said, perhaps with Lee's cooperation: "I am deeply distressed at the public nuisance for which the undergraduates of Yale were responsible today, and on behalf of the University I wish to extend my sincere apologies to the community. No matter how the affair started, the undergraduates who formed a mob, impeded traffic, and otherwise trespassed upon the city, were responsible for their actions. . . . They took these actions in disregard of repeated appeals from both University and City officials." "The Riot: Mobs, Hoses, and Billy Clubs," *Yale Daily News*, May 14, 1952 ("President Griswold's Statement"). The following articles are from the *New Haven Evening Register*. "Griswold Orders Full Probe of Riot," May 14, 1952 (front-page photograph, College Street, and internal pages of photographs); "Riot at Yale," editorial, May 14, 1952; "Young Defends Action against Yale Rioters," May 15, 1952; "Yale's Responsibility," editorial, May 15, 1952.

27. Office of the Mayor, press release, May 14, 1952, William Celentano Papers, New Haven Colonial Historical Society. In a letter to Griswold, New Haven City Employees Association President Martin Griffin also was direct: "We witnessed the sickening spectacle of a mob of Yale students rioting in College Street. . . . Unabashed hoodlums . . . [who] resisted firemen and policemen who were endeavoring to restore order." Griffin wanted the responsible students expelled. Griffin to Griswold (May 14, 1952), William Celentano Papers, New Haven Colonial Historical Society.

28. Violation of city ordinance. See articles referenced in notes 26 and 27 in this chapter.

29. "Good Humor Starts Riot of 1,500 at Yale," *Chicago Tribune*, May 14, 1952.

30. The committee was concerned about student sexual mores and "excesses" and ways for administrators to contain the rambunctiousness of undergraduates. Their failure to date, which the riot only emphasized, was blamed on, among other influences, "being a male college in a city with 'mechanical and often sordid urban amusements,' [and] the proximity of . . . women's colleges . . . coupled with those of adolescent growth: ignorance, temperamental qualities, [and the] influence of friends." Minutes of the meeting of the President's Committee on Manners and Morals (January 13, received January 17, 1951), Griswold Papers, Yale University Archives.

31. "The *Register's* Poison," *Yale Daily News*, May 15, 1952.

32. "Police Quell Yale Riot, Jail 4 Undergraduates, 8 treated for Injuries," *Yale Daily News*, May 14, 1952; "Ice Cream Sellers' Argument First Attracts Student," *Yale Daily News*, May 14, 1952; "The *Register's* Poison," *Yale Daily News*, May 15, 1952. David B. Harned, "University Inaugurates General Probe of Riots, Will Ask into City Methods, Student Acts," *Yale Daily News*, May 15, 1952; "The Riot in Retrospect: Of Childishness and Bloodshed," *Yale Daily News*, May 15, 1952. The editorials from the *Daily News* condemned the student conduct but focused as well on the conduct of the police and the importance of a balanced inquiry into the propriety of police conduct. In "The *Register's* Poison," the *Daily News* drew special attention to the unfair harshness of an editorial in the *New Haven Evening Register*. To the *Daily News*, the *Register* had failed to capture, objectively, the fault and different kind of public duty required to measure police conduct. Instead, the *Register* editorial was filled with a "remarkable polemic grounded on ignorance and half-truths" when "maturity" was called for to deal with "a staggering community problem posed by city-University relations." What likely resonated locally from the *Register's* editorial, though New Haven's residents didn't need the editorial to do so, was the *Register's* assertion that "this mob was not made up of playful boys." "Riot at Yale," editorial, *New Haven Evening Register*, May 14, 1952.

CHAPTER 17
THE CONNECTIONS FORM

1. At the time, admission into Mount Holyoke required that an applicant had successfully completed foreign language study. On the effect of Latin, Greek, and Italian on subsequent knowledge, see Denis Feeney, *Beyond Greek: The Beginnings of Latin Literature* (Cambridge, MA: Harvard University Press, 2016). See also "Found in Translation," Professor Gregory Hays's review Feeney's book in *New York Review of Books*, June 22, 2017; communication with Sally Benson (July 4, 2017); correspondence and notes from Jean MacLeod Keatley.

2. Communication with Jean MacLeod Keatley (June 14 and various others, 2017).

3. "Giamatti Wins Oratorical Event," *Holyoke Telegram*, February 16, 1954; "Giamatti and Miss MacLeod Winners of Oratorical Contest," *Holyoke Telegram*, May 7, 1954.

4. Sally Benson to Dr. Peggy Ann Brown and author.

5. Communications with Jean MacLeod Keatley.

6. Bill Mazeine interview. The local garage and gas station on Silver and College streets, and the tone of the atmosphere, were captured poignantly by Anthony Valerio in *Bart: A Life of A. Bartlett Giamatti by Him and about Him*, 4.

7. David Halberstam, *Summer of '49* (New York: Avon Books, 1990), 115–17. See also White interview.

8. The Red Sox apparently did not have a formally designated captain from 1943 to 1965. Glenn Stout and Richard A. Johnson, *Red Sox Century: One Hundred Years of Red Sox Baseball* (Boston: Houghton Mifflin, 2000).

9. Halberstam, *Summer of '49*, 115–17 (also mentioned is Bart's friend Frank White); and see David Halberstam, *Teammates: A Portrait of a Friendship* (New York: Hyperion, 2003) (Willams, Pesky, DiMaggio, and Doerr); A. Bartlett Giamatti, "Yale and Athletics," in *The University and the Public Interest* (New York: Atheneum, 1981), 77 (Plato).

10. Tens of thousands of Italian immigrants were forced out of their homes and relocated, property confiscated or left unattended, some interned, many, including Metropolitan opera and musical star Ezio Pinza, jailed without cause and just plain humiliated in public. In Pinza's case, it was the anti-Fascist leader in New York, Carlo Tresca, who verified Pinza's loyalty and contributed to his release. Interview with Elria Ewing Giamatti; Sarah Goodyear, "When Being Italian Was a Crime," *Village Voice*, April 11, 2000; "Former Red Sox Star Dom DiMaggio Dies at 92," *Boston Globe*, May 8, 2009; Steve Chawkins, "State Apologizes for Mistreatment of Italian Residents during WW II," *Los Angeles Times*, August 23, 2010; Allon Schoener, *The Italian Americans* (New York: Macmillan, 1987) (Giamatti's "Commentary" and 188–92).

11. "A. Bartlett Giamatti . . . and in with the New Commissioner," *Trentonian* (New Jersey), April 6, 1989.

12. "A. Bartlett Giamatti," *Trentonian*; A. Bartlett Giamatti, *Take Time for Paradise: Americans and Their Games* (New York: Summit, 1989), 82; Giamatti interview with Cynthia Mann, "Insight," *Holyoke Telegram* (1985) (reproduced in Valerio, *Bart: A Life*, 14–15).

13. Interview with Frank White.

14. Interviews with Frank White, Andrew Vitali, and Dino Walton Giamatti.

15. Interview with Frank White; interview with Dino Walton Giamatti; Valerio, *Bart: A Life*, 23, excerpt from Judy Van Handle, "Hometown Stunned, Saddened," *Boston Globe*, 1989. Excerpts from Giamatti's "Green Fields of the Mind" were read frequently during Boston Red Sox games, and his words to the Massachusetts Historical Society in 1985 were reprinted outside the Red Sox front office. Exchange of notes among Dr. Peggy Brown, Sara Coffin, archivist and curator, Boston Red Sox, and Cassidy Lent, librarian, Giamatti Research Center, Hall of Fame, Cooperstown, New York. See also A. Bartlett Giamatti, "Baseball and the American Character," delivered to the Massachusetts Historical Society (1985) and reprinted in A. Bartlett Giamatti, *A Great and Glorious Game: Baseball Writings of A. Bartlett Giamatti* (Chapel Hill, NC: Algonquin Books, 1998), 57 (edited by Kenneth S. Robinson, foreword by David Halberstam).

16. The description of the fair makes clear that the Giamattis and the club's members reached far, eclectically and deeply, into the broad community to ensure both success and fun. The parade was "open to local residents and students" at South Hadley High School and all the public schools. Faculty and townspeople acted as judges of the best costume, the theme based on Dante and the Renaissance era. The parade culminated at the Giamatti home, arranged with lights around the back-yard's periphery, and booths set throughout with a "fortune teller, a spike-driving contest, sideshow, and turtle races." A resident of South Hadley Falls "offered to be a human target for a game of skill," and another resident

provided "horses for children's rides." And, to not miss an opportunity for further educa-tion, the film *A Chance to Live*"—an Academy Award–winning documentary dealing with the Boys'Town in Italy run by Monsignor John Patrick Carroll-Abbing—was played at the college chapel. Kay Rendenbaugh, news release, Mount Holyoke News Bureau, May 5, 1950; and related correspondence and article referring to the fair, its timing, and purpose, Valentine Giamatti Papers, Mount Holyoke College Archives.

17. Norma prefaced her recollection: "One of my memories of the Giamatti family is the Dante Fair, which they hosted at their house on Silver Street. This was for the chil-dren of the town and consisted of a parade through the town to their house. As I remem-ber, we wore costumes and marched behind a fire engine. At their house, college students who were dressed in costumes managed games and booths of activities." Interview notes from Norma Stiles Monat to Dr. Peggy Ann Brown and author.

18. Mount Holyoke Press Bureau, news release, March 10, 1953, Valentine Giamatti Papers, Mount Holyoke Archives.

19. See Joan Davidson, Mount Holyoke News Bureau, 1954; Mount Holyoke News Bureau, July 1, 1954; Valentine Giamatti Papers, Mount Holyoke College Archives.

20. Andrew Vitali interview.

21. The feeder schools to Yale included, among others, Phillips Academy (Andover, northeastern Massachusetts), Hotchkiss (Berkshire Mountains, northwestern Connecticut), Exeter (southeastern New Hampshire), Taft (central Connecticut), Choate (southern Connecticut), Kent (Episcopal Church, northwestern Connecticut), Belmont Hill (near Cambridge, Massachusetts), Saint Paul's (Episcopal Church, Concord, New Hampshire), and Groton (northeastern Massachusetts). Karabel, *The Chosen*, 204–6.

22. DeVane's observation, captured by Kelley in *Yale: A History* (432), based on a report demonstrating a "deplorable ignorance of the extraordinary intellectual resources at Yale."

23. The related challenge for Peggy was that Bart be admitted for only one year, his senior year. There existed at Phillips, at that time, a slight change of attitude about the composition of its student body. The school was looking for applicants from what it called the "Newspaper Boy Program," not related to any diminishment in academic credentials but the acceptance of "non-legacy" students, maybe from rural towns, who demonstrated the discipline to "get up early" and do well in the rigors of Phillips's intense daily expectations. Perhaps a deficiency was recognized among Phillips students that Bart, then and certainly after admission, didn't suffer. Bart was not considered within that program's parameters, but the attitude underpinning the program may have affected the headmaster's openness to the one-year admission, along with Bart's creden-tials, his "legacy" status, and the fact that the Giamattis were going to pay. Notes from discussion, Andover Academy Archivist staff and historian.

CHAPTER 18

THE FATEFUL VISIT

1. During this visit, Val left the family's station wagon in Helen's care for the dura-tion of his sabbatical (and, on his return, he gave it to Helen).

2. "Democrats Regain Control of City," *New Haven Evening Register*, November 4, 1953; "Both Parties Seek Victory in the Election," *New Haven Evening Register*, November 1,

1953 (The New Haven Plan and the Citizen Action Committee); "Lee Stresses Six Steps in Slum Clearance," *New Haven Evening Register*, November 1, 1953; "The Voter's Day," *New Haven Evening Register*, November 2, 1953; "Early Vote Heavy in City Election," *New Haven Evening Register*, November 3, 1953; "20,000 Votes Recorded Here up to 10 A.M.," *New Haven Evening Register*, November 3, 1953; "Republicans Elect Only 9 Aldermen," *New Haven Evening Register*, November 4, 1953.

3. The new Democratic town chairman, Arthur Barbieri, favored Barbarito for mayor. Barbarito and other popular vote getters, and the new town chairman, had delivered the Democrats, especially among Italian Americans. In the Yale-dominated wards, where the Old Yankee Republicans once voted for a socialist rather than an Italian American Republican, the prejudicial element of the strategy also was effective. Lee won their fear-induced tolerance—and their vote. Dahl, *Who Governs?*, 46–49, 55; Rae, *City*, 308–9. See also, "Republicans Elect Only 9 Aldermen," *New Haven Evening Register*, November 4, 1953 ("He expects Yale to grant him a two-year leave of absence").

4. The plan was revised periodically through 1944. Rotival's plan had been available to the City Plan Commission and was embraced by the Greater New Haven Chamber of Commerce. Lee had worked with and for the chamber earlier in his life. Rotival had been hired by the chamber as an advisor and then was offered an advisory position with the newly formed New Haven Redevelopment Agency in 1951, though the terms of the agreement were not finalized or work begun until 1953 and 1954, pursuant to the contract entered into between Lee and Rotival.

5. In the 1944 city plan, "Tomorrow Is Here," Murphy "request[ed] opinion" from the public on the plan, which included making block-by-block residential improvements, cleaning yards, taking down old fences, "widen[ing] main streets, and retaining good existing structures," and locating new retail outlets and a farmers' and wholesale market nearby. Rotival Papers, Box 202 B, Yale University Archives.

6. This fictional "Quinnipiac Valley Region" was expressly included by Rotival (after Lee's election) in all subsequent correspondence, reports, and contracts during his formal relationship with the Lee administration from his first meeting with Lee, in 1953, through 1965. Design and implementation of the plan also was based on the equally fictional political and legal assumption that Rotival would design plans for the surrounding suburbs as well, which never happened (though to be paid exclusively by New Haven, if done). See letter, Rotival to Logue (December 23, 1953); memorandum, Rotival to Logue (January 15, 1954); letter, Rotival to Logue (May 26, 1954); Western Union telegram (August 25, 1954); and final Rotival and Lee signed contract (January 1, 1955, negotiations begun in 1953, work performed in 1954), wherein Rotival expected to design a new plan "for the Metropolitan Area and the City . . . and adopted by the City and the *suburban towns*" (emphasis added), and "Whereas, the development of the Harbor and the *Quinnipiac Valley* are essential in order to provide the economic base for an effective urban renewal program" (emphasis added), and "1) Preparation of Comprehensive Plans . . . 2) c) *Quinnipiac Valley Development Plan*. . . ." (emphasis added). See also, for example, letter, Rotival to Logue (January 15, 1954), Rotival Papers, Box 37, Yale University Archives; "Selection of Urban Development Areas," and "Definitions of Objectives" (May 17, 1951) (Rotival: "go straight to the core of the diseased organism"), Rotival Papers, Boxes 35, 37, 38, 39, Yale University Archives.

7. Letter, Rotival to Logue (December 23, 1953), Rotival Papers, Box 37, Yale University Archives.

8. The advice came from Political Science Professor Henry Wells. Allan R. Talbot, *The Mayor's Game* (New York: Praeger, 1970), 9; "Recommendation to New Haven Redevelopment Agency" (May 17, 1951) "Rotival Recommendations," Rotival Papers, Box 37, Yale University Archives.

9. "The Rebirth of a City: New Haven," M. E. H. Rotival & Associates, Rotival Papers, Box 202 B and Box 37, Yale University Archives. "Relocation of the existing housing units in other locations, with or without the assistance of the housing Agency of New Haven." Memorandum, Rotival to Carroll (February 1, 1955), Rotival Papers, Box 37, Yale University Archives.

10. The Supreme Court decision confirmed the legitimacy of the model zoning code as constitutional (not a taking of private property) and within the local government's police power in *Village of Euclid, Ohio v. Ambler Realty Company*, 272 U.S. 365 (1926). Euclid contended that, by enacting its zoning code, it was engaged in the improvement of the health and safety of its residents by regulating the uses of property, including forbidding "all industrial, manufacturing, trade, and . . . wholesale and retail stores" on property owned by Amber Realty, which Euclid considered residential. The Supreme Court, through one of its most conservative members, Chief Justice George Sutherland, who had been a United States senator from Utah, found that this form of government regulation and proscription of private property use was proper. At the District Court (Northern District of Ohio), Judge David Westenhaver, had probed for Euclid's real intention. In reviewing the original lawsuit filed by Ambler Realty, he found that the "health and safety" rationale use by Euclid was mere pretext. Jewish, Italian, Polish, Hungarian, and African American working families occupied Euclid Avenue, which traversed the industrial section of Cleveland before entering Euclid. Once entering Euclid, the avenue contained the residences of John D. Rockefeller, Euclid's lawyer (and the 1924 model zoning code's national advocate), and a group of houses referred to as "Millionaire's Row." Euclid Avenue, in Euclid, had become a likely place for new housing for Cleveland's workers. Looking at previous Supreme Court cases that had stopped housing restrictions intended to exclude African Americans, Judge Westenhaver concluded that "it is equally apparent that the next step in the exercise of this police power would be to apply similar restrictions for the purpose of segregating in like manner various groups of newly arrived immigrants. The blighting of property values and the congestion of population, whenever the colored or certain foreign races invade a residential section, are so well known as to be within the judicial cognizance. . . . The plain truth is that the true object of the ordinance . . . is to classify the population and segregate them according to their income or situation in life." *Amber Realty Co. v. Village of Euclid*, Ohio 297 F. 307 (1924) 313–16. The District Court concluded that it was precisely this discrimination that Euclid intended. In the Supreme Court, after the oral argument was heard, Chief Justice Sutherland agreed to allow new briefing by *amicus curiae*, friends of the court, who were advocates of the model code. Sutherland made no explicit reference to race or ethnicity in his decision or the District Court's reliance on them.

11. *Village of Euclid, Ohio v. Ambler Realty Company* was decided in the same era the Court affirmed eugenic sterilization in *Buck v. Bell* and the execution of Sacco and Vanzetti. Whichever small retail or commercial stores might retain political or commercial

value in the Oak Street/Hill/Legion Avenue neighborhood Rotival wanted consolidated in one location (comparable to the suburban shopping plaza), out of the way, to make more space for large projects that would serve the mythical "Region's" benefit and to implant the physical character of suburban values into New Haven. The Hill section, Wooster Square, and other neighborhoods would, according to Rotival, "continue to deteriorate, eaten away by the cancerous action of mixed land-uses." "Rebirth of a City: New Haven," Rotival Papers.

12. Rotival had relied on "the citizen committee" in previous projects. In New Haven, the Greater New Haven Chamber of Commerce already had a relationship with him, and with Dick Lee. His plan fit into their vision and interest, which was the region, not New Haven. The composition of the citizen committee was suburban. It would be more than twenty years before New Haven, under Mayor Ben DiLieto, elevated the newly formed New Haven Downtown Council as a counterweight to the chamber. The council's executive director and driving force, Aldrich Edwards, along with New Haven Development Administrator John Sawyer, lived in New Haven.

13. At no time did Celentano (or Murphy before him) abandon the idea of New Haven–focused planning or preclude the implementation or continued discussion of the 1910 plan. See, the 1952 City Plan, New Haven Colony Historical Society, New Haven, Connecticut. Rae and Dahl believed that because the Redevelopment Agency was initiated by Celentano, he was somehow implicated in what Lee later did, which was to operate the agency with his assistant, Edward Logue, as a government largely of its own, detached from typical forms of public accountability. The new federal law required a redevelopment agency, and its original legal structure and Celentano's temperament in operating it were modest, not removed from other processes of city government and public accountability.

14. "Lee promised to take six specific steps," the *New Haven Evening Register* reported, which included "Wide citizen participation in 'a civic crusade to eradicate all blighted sections of the city.'" Further, "he had in mind the formulation of a 'Baltimore Plan,'" which, he said, "is known from coast-to-coast as the closest approach to a fully effective program of housing and rehabilitation in the country." In fact, the Baltimore Plan, in neighborhoods of substantially larger dimension and more dangerous conditions than New Haven's, was focused on community cleanup of back yards and alleyways, public and private financing of the installation of new electrical wiring and public bathroom facilities, repainting, and the installation of gardens and small parks. The Baltimore Plan, at that time, was about neighborhood preservation, not wholesale demolition and relocation. *The Baltimore Plan*, Encyclopedia Britannica Films (1953, available on YouTube); "Lee Stresses Six Steps in Slum Clearance," *New Haven Evening Register*, November 1, 1953. See also "Where Do We Go Now? Home Loving Wooster Square Refugees Want to Know," *New Haven Evening Register*, June 12, 1955 (self-help).

15. Edward Logue (Yale 1942, Law 1947) was Lee's neighbor, "assistant," and eventual director of the urban renewal agency. His experience in labor and state government was hardly formative for this new position. His experience with urban planning and neighborhood revitalization was less than Lee's. He had Yale relationships and an imprimatur that Lee did not. He also had the Yale "leadership" and cultural mentality writ large. A "bloodless administrator," the *New York Times* wrote. He "always horrified me," Jane Jacobs would later say. "Edward Logue, Visionary City Planner, Is Remembered,"

New York Times, April 23, 2000. And see Samuel Zipp and Nathan Storring, eds., *Vital Little Plans: The Short Works of Jane Jacobs* (New York: Random House, 2016), 278 (footnote); letter, Lee to Rotival ("Roty") (November 17, 1953), Rotival Papers, Box 37, Yale University Archives.

16. Lin, "Mayors, Slums, and Universities, 103 and 103nn 225–26 (Yale's role); memorandum, Lee to Rotival, "Follow-up Commissioner Hill's Decision on Oak Street Connector and Agreement with State Highway Department" (October 27, 1954), Rotival Papers, Box 36, Yale University Archives (Lee and Rotival's role as advocates and in the connector's location. Lee assured Rotival we got "everything we asked for"). Rotival's plan (already advocated and designed for state officials), included new variations concerning the proposed state-interstate highways around New Haven's periphery (from New London and Hartford to New York), with multiple entrance and exit ramps for New Haven proper, a major roadway around New Haven's central core ("Ring Road"), and a "connector" from the state-interstate highway into and through the Oak Street area. By 1953 and 1954, with the debate and expected enactment of the National Interstate and Defense Highways Act by Congress, this "connector" became a four-lane to six-lane highway proposal with expansive rights of way, as if built in the suburbs. Its actual layout, however, also extended geographically well beyond the Oak Street area. See also Conor Bagley (Yale 2016), "Landlocked Blues on the Coast: How New Haven Disconnected Itself from the Sea" (senior thesis, environmental history, Yale University, 2014), in author's possession ("the placement of New Haven's highways was shaped by individual decision making and could have turned out very differently"). The National Interstate and Defense Highways Act, Pub. L 84-627, signed by President Eisenhower on June 29, 1956, was actually an amendment to the existing Federal-Aid Highway Act of 1944 and various other statutory antecedents, certainly going as far back as 1919. The measure passed after Eisenhower demonstrated that a military convoy couldn't easily and speedily reach California from Washington, DC. The secretary of defense in 1956—as massive defense highway construction was being built and planned—was Charles E. Wilson, former president and chief executive officer of General Motors. Jean Edward Smith, *Eisenhower in War and Peace* (New York: Random House, 2012), 553–55, 650, 651–54.

17. The connector and right-of-way property were primarily privately owned and became subject to condemnation by Connecticut as a stand-in for New Haven. The proposed connector's construction—in fact the construction of even the proposed major highway along New Haven's periphery (largely on city-owned property, what then constituted its waterfront and major portions of Waterside Park)—could only be done with Lee's approval. He gave it, once assured of the route he wanted and that state and federal funding would be available. He followed the same reasoning and decision path in the Wooster Square neighborhood with the same connector. Lin, "Mayors, Slums, and Universities," 103 and 103nn225–26 (Yale's role); memorandum, Lee to Rotival, "Follow-up Commissioner Hill's Decision on Oak Street Connector and Agreement with State Highway Department." See also Bagley, "Landlocked Blues on the Coast."

18. The Yale School of Planning shared in the responsibility for the "New Haven Experiment" and legitimized the Rotival Plan and perspective. See, for example, "Yale Gets $67,000 Grant for City Planning Study," *New Haven Evening Register*, April 29, 1957 (School of Architecture and Design, "on the eve of a full-scale conference at Yale . . . on Interurbia—the huge regional cities of 'urban stripes' which are rapidly emerging. . . .

promoted by Yale program . . . in city and regional planning"); Architectural Supplement, "From Weir to Rudolph," "Contemporary Design Gradually Accepted as Colleges Abandon Traditional Style," "New Forestry Lab Will Continue Trend to Modern Architecture," *Yale Daily News*, November 21, 1957; letter from Secretary to Rudolph (January 14, 1958), Griswold Papers, RU 22, Box 200, Yale University Archives (Saarinen on the Corporation's Planning Committee; Rudolph added as well); letter to Buck (July 30, 1957) and to Griswold, Griswold Papers, RU 22 Box 200, Yale University Archives (June 11, 1957), 6, 18 (meetings began in 1954, property disposition and availability to Yale in Oak Street/Hill/ Legion Avenue neighborhood and Dixwell/Newhallville neigbor-hood); letters, Saarinen to Buck (March 9, 1960) and Buck to Saarinen (March 14, 1960), Griswold Papers, RU 22, Box 213, Yale University Archives (Saarinen involved with city officials, defined the purpose of Dixwell Avenue Redevelopment Project, provided guid-ance, which New Haven always considered, and usually accepted); memorandum (March 12, 1958), Griswold Papers, RU 22, Yale University Archives (The ring road, boundary of Dixwell Project to include Yale required roadway changes to ensure Yale would not pay). Yale and Logue agreed Yale would know of city plans so it could decide to buy property. Lee and Griswold agreed Yale would receive all "future plans." New Haven identified property along highway routes and elsewhere where Yale should acquire prop-erty, especially in the Dixwell Avenue project area (March 7, 1958); and see also notes of Oak Street meeting with Yale, Rotival, Lee, and Logue, Griswold Papers, RU 22, Yale University Archives ("Logue also stated that personally he would be willing to sell the University the land [in Oak Street]. At twenty-five cents a square foot if only we could be induced to embark on this venture!"); letter, Buck to Griswold on meeting of Building Committee (June 11,1957), 18; Saarinen to Logue (March 17, 1958), Logue to Griswold (March 10, 1958), "Yale and City" (Rudolph and Saarinen as municipal "plan-ners"), Griswold Papers, RU 22, Yale University Archives (AWG 2/6).

19. Lee and Logue also expected Rotival to manage any disputes with the New Haven City Plan Department, where they expected, and got, disagreement. The com-mission's publicly described purpose was to supplant government accountability; its duty was "to arrest the decline of the central business district and to coordinate the efforts of all citizen boards and agencies with those of city departments," Rotival Papers, Box 292B, Yale University Archives (17, "The New Haven Experiment. . . ."); Rotival retained Nicholas deB. Katzenbach, then on the Yale Law School faculty, to be his agent in New Haven in dealing with the Redevelopment Agency and the citizens commission that Lee proposed to create. See exchange of correspondence and agreement on fees and duties, with Lee's support. Lee to Katzenbach (August 26, 1954); Katzenbach to Rotival (and Carroll) (September 4, 1954); Rotival to Katzenbach (October 8, 1954), Rotival Papers, Boxes 36, 37, and 38, Yale University Archives. Rotival opened an office in New Haven and hired a staff, including a former architectural student and a faculty member from the Yale Department of Architecture. Stephen Carroll to Logue (August 12, 1953), Rotival Papers, Yale University Archives; "Group Formed by Mayor at Luncheon Here," *New Haven Journal Courier*, September 28, 1954; letter, Lee to Carl Freese (copy to Griswold with cover note from Lee) (August 24, 1954), Griswold Papers, RU 22, Yale University Archives; letter, Lee to Griswold (November 9, 1955), Griswold Papers, RU 22, Yale University Archives. Throughout the next decade, at Logue's frequent request, Rotival, headquartered on Wall Street in New York City, and his New Haven office staff, housed in city-owned offices, remained essential to the day-to-day guidance and the correction

of failures of the Redevelopment Agency and City Plan Department through personal intervention and written guidance or directives. Sometimes, to Rotival's consternation, actions he believed could and should be handled by City Plan officials were immediately passed on to him. He was compensated $52,000 for the first six months of his contract, signed on January 1, 1955, roughly the equivalent of $490,000 in 2019 dollars. Those amounts remained fairly constant for the next decade. At the time, the mayor's salary was $10,000 a year (the equivalent of $93,000 in 2019).

20. See previous note. See also Professor Vincent Scully on Orr's "Saarinen Era" architecture within the University and New Haven, in *Yale in New Haven: Architecture and Urbanism*, ed. Vincent Scully et al. (New Haven, CT: Yale University Press, 2004), 301–2 ("banal," "destructive," "skinned and vacant look").

21. Rotival congratulated Lee on his victory on November 4 and 10. Rotival Papers, Box 37, Yale University Archives (Lee to Rotival November 17, 1953). Also, see note 6 of this chapter.

22. Inside Futurama was the large-scale display model of the grand expressway, the steady moving automobile, the vastly dispersed suburban communities amid green pastures, the city in the distance, the absence of the "neighborhood," and the absence of transit, no trains to be found. Five million visitors experienced it. To Rotival, the vertical building, for office, retail, and residential use, was central to his plan for New Haven. "The Birth of a City: New Haven," Rotival Papers, Box 202 B, Yale University Archives; Norman Bel Geddes, *Magic Motorways* (New York: Random House, 1940); Paul Mason Fotsch, "The Building of a Superhighway Future at the New York World's Fair," *Cultural Critique* (2001): 65–97. See, generally, Le Corbusier, *Towards a New Architecture* (1931, repr., New York: Dover, 1986).

23. Robert Kanigel, *Eyes on the Street: The Life of Jane Jacobs* (New York: Knopf, 2016), 142–56, and "Ten Minutes at Harvard," 169–70; "Philadelphia's Redevelopment: A Progress Report," *Architectural Forum*, July 1955, reprinted with annotations in Zipp and Storring, *Vital Little Plans*, 55 (Part Two, City Building, 1952–1965); "Pavement Ponders and Olympians," *Architectural Forum*, May 1956, reprinted in Zipp and Storring, *Vital Little Plans*, 66; "The Missing Link in City Redevelopment," *Architectural Forum*, June 1956, reprinted in Zipp and Storring, *Vital Little Plans*, 70.

CHAPTER 19

THE CITY

The epigraph is from A. Bartlett Giamatti, *Play of Double Senses: Spenser's* Faerie Queene (New York: Prentice Hall, 1975), 17–18.

1. R. W. B. Lewis, *Dante* (New York: Penguin Group, 2001), 2, 48–49.

2. Dante's *De Vulgari Eloquentia*, "a tract on the superiority of the vernacular over Latin for the writing of poetry," and the *Convivio* ("Banquet"), "a celebration of the mode of the long poem called a *canzone* (song)," were among the ways Dante explored language before he began the *Commedia*. R. W. B. Lewis, *Dante*, 12, 53 (model citizens). See also Rubin, *Dante in Love*, 102–4 (new language), 16, 23 (love for Beatrice), 59 (love as creativity).

3. William Manchester, *A World Lit Only by Fire: The Medieval Mind and the Renaissance—Portrait of an Age* (Boston: Little, Brown, 1992), 25–26, 104–7.

4. R. W. B. Lewis, *Dante,* 10–11, 128.

5. Virgil, *The Aeneid*, trans. Robert Fagles (New York: Viking, 2006), 2–6.

6. The original of the article is in the Giamatti family album, shared with the author in July 2016 by David and Elria Giamatti Ewing.

7. Nicolas S. Witschi, "Roman Holidays: American Writers and Artists in Nineteenth Century Italy," review, *Henry James Review* 24, no. 2 (2003): 193–95.

8. *Holyoke Telegram*, August 24, 1955.

9. "Priest Thanks Mt. Holyokers and Others for Assisting Italian Boys Project," *Holyoke Telegram*, November 11, 1954.

10. Salvatore J. LaGumina et al., eds., *The Italian American Experience: An Encyclopedia* (New York: Routledge, 2000), 263–64; Giamatti, "Commentary," in Schoener, ed., *The Italian Americans*, 9.

11. Giamatti, *The Earthly Paradise and the Renaissance Epic*, originally his Yale PhD dissertation; "The Green Fields of the Mind," *Yale Alumni Magazine,* November 1977; Giamatti, "Commentary," in Schoener, ed., *The Italian Americans*, 13.

12. *Holyoke Telegram* (August 24, 1954); "Impressive Post-War Progress in Italy Told at Jewish Center," *Holyoke Telegram* (December 6, 1955). Valentine Giamatti Papers, Mount Holyoke Archives.

Chapter 20

An Education

1. The African American student was from Washington, DC; one of the Asians was from Korea. Sorota had excellent academic accomplishments. Fordham's reputation, in academics melded into athletics, was solid. Sorota taught them both to his teams. Dino Giamatti interview; *Pot Pourri* (Phillips Academy yearbook, 1956), 15; David Maraniss, *When Pride Still Mattered: A Life of Vince Lombardi* (New York: Simon & Schuster, 1999), 31–47.

2. Exeter was a rival school to Phillips, though only of a kind. The composition of the student body was close to identical: boys only, white Anglo-Saxon Protestant, wealthy, and instead of being assured entrance to Yale, they were assured entrance to Harvard.

3. Susan McIntosh Lloyd, *A Singular School: Abbot Academy, 1828–1973* (Andover, MA: Phillips Academy/University Press of New England, 1979); Francesca Balboni, "Andover Stories: Abbot a Leader in Its Own Right for 150 Years," *Andover Townsman*, Andover Historical Society, March 17, 2011.

4. *Pot Pourri* (1956), 94–95.

5. Tuition cost $1,400. Extras—books, etc.—were estimated at $250 a year. The remainder to properly educate and house a student, approximately $1,300, was financed by the school. *Phillips Academy Catalogue* (1956), 44.

6. Kemper was a graduate of the United States Military Academy, Columbia, and Williams, with a doctor of literature from Tufts. "Andover Remembers," *Andover Bulletin* (Spring 1989).

7. The purpose of Sunday Morning Chapel was explained in the school catalog: "Phillips is an inter-denominational school whose origin and tradition rests firmly upon a liberal Protestant faith and system of values." Faculty members, the headmaster, and the school's various ministers gave sermons. Students who were Jewish or Catholic could attend services elsewhere on campus or in Andover. "This arrangement recognizes two sets of values: a close connection of each boy with his own chosen denomination, and a

program of worship within the life of the school that emphasizes the common elements in our religious faith." The goal: to "help develop the boy's confidence in religion as a source of strength" and as a means by which Phillips Academy "endeavors to achieve harmony and unity in diversity." *Phillips Academy Catalogue* (1956), 30.

8. "Every boy takes part. . . ." There were two objectives: "to train boys to do useful work well and to reduce the operating costs of the Academy." Work assignments were considered "an essential part of the democratic life of the Academy." *Phillips Academy Catalogue* (1956), 37–41.

9. Bagnoli was from Englewood, New Jersey. Harrison had a BA from Yale and an MA from Trinity College in Connecticut.

10. *Phillipian*, "New Congress to Revise Procedure" (February 16, 1956); *Pot Pourri* (1956), 155–56.

11. *Pot Pourri* (1956), 156–57. See also "Philo's Forrest, Knipe, McCall, Giamatti Drop Roxbury Latin," *Phillipian*, February 23, 1956; "Philo Drops Dual Debate to Exeter," *Phillipian*, May 3, 1956.

12. *Pot Pourri* (1956), 96–99.

13. "Forrest, Hegeman, and Giamatti Victors in Ninetieth Draper Speaking Competition," *Phillipian*, February 11, 1956.

14. William Smith Jr., "Bob Bohorad Awarded Means Essay Prize, Giamatti, Forrest Capture Second, Third," *Phillipian*, April 26, 1956.

15. *Pot Pourri* (1956), 147; Tom Bagnoli, "Andover Remembers," 25; *Pot Pourri* (1956), 96–98.

16. Men could visit an Abbot residence hall on particular days, card in hand; sit quietly in the foyer while the card was delivered; then sit in quiet conversation, no more than thirty minutes, while being watched to ensure neither touching nor notes were exchanged. There was, however, the dance. It appears that "couples" met only through "blind dates," though, at least according to some photographs in the Phillips yearbook, intimacy managed to find expression.

17. *Phillips Academy Catalogue* (1956), 43. Other graduates entered, among other schools, Harvard, Princeton, Brown, Stanford, Dartmouth, Cornell, Columbia, Williams, Holy Cross, Lehigh, University of Miami, North Carolina State, and University of Kansas.

Chapter 21

Yale

Epigraph is from A. Bartlett Giamatti, *Play of Double Senses: Spenser's* Faerie Queene, 25.

1. William Henry Vanderbilt, son of Cornelius Vanderbilt, attended Yale in the early 1890s. After his son's death during his junior year, the elder Vanderbilt paid for the construction of the Hall as a memorial tribute. "Legendary Vanderbilt Suite Is the Sweetest of Campus Abodes," *Yale Daily News*, February 4, 2005.

2. Interview with Guido Calabresi.

3. "Obituary: Maynard Mack, Distinguished Yale Scholar and Literature Teacher," *Yale Daily News*, March 19, 2001; Giamatti, *The Earthly Paradise and the Renaissance Epic.*

4. Tinker had written about, among other writers, James Boswell and the early English poets. He'd been on the faculty when Val was a student, and he was a good friend of Mount Holyoke President Roswell Ham. DeVane appointed the first Jewish and first

Catholic professors in the humanities. His appointments were discussed previously, and see "Guido Calabresi: A Foreigner in New Haven," 35–37; Alvin Kernan, *In Plato's Cave* (New Haven, CT: Yale University Press, 1999), 61.

5. Rachel Donadio, "1958: The War of the Intellectuals," *New York Review of Books*, May 11, 2008.

6. Ella Scantlebury was of West Indian and Irish descent and married to Barbados-born Burt Scantlebury. More of her life is discussed later, when she and Bart meet. "'In the Still of the Night,' the Five Satins Recorded Biggest Hit in Church Basement," *New Haven Register*, March 3, 2014. Saint Bernadette's Church School had impeccable acoustics. It was made available through the request of altar boy and saxophone player Vincent Mazzetta, who played during the recording. The Morris Cove neighborhood, in the eastern part of the city, was in transformation from a semi-rural old Yankee enclave into a largely Italian America neighborhood, strongly stimulated by the threat and reality of urban renewal. Interview and exchange with Cliff and Patricia Hurley Chieffo, May 9, 2017. "Court Sustains Rock and Roll Ban, Freed to Bring Suit against Mayor," *Yale Daily News*, May 8, 1958; "Rock and Roll Pied Piper," *New York Times*, May 20, 1960. Freed's concert was banned in May 1958. Lee also stopped a concert in progress in March 1955. The Five Satins, like Paul Giamatti and Foster Furcolo, are honored on an outdoor billboard in downtown New Haven.

7. Frank Pepe began with a cart, then opened his apizzeria in 1925 on Wooster Street. He used coal-burning ovens. He knew Angelo and Maria from St. Michael's Church and Val from his regular visits from childhood on. Sal Montagna, who had worked at Pepe's since 1939, knew Bart. "Though the days tend to blend together, Sal has fondest memories of A. Bartlett Giamatti, the late former president of Yale University and former commissioner of Major League Baseball. 'I knew Bart when he was a student at Yale, and over the years got very friendly with him . . . a perfect gentleman,' he says." "Pepe's Is a Tribute to Tradition and Precision," *Yale Daily News*, October 5, 1995.

CHAPTER 22

THE LOSS OF CIVIC DUTY

1. Internal Yale memorandum, Griswold Papers, RU 22, Box 165 (March 31, 1955); Oak Street involvement would intensify "after Connector" is built, and then "all fringe properties within these boundaries should be acquired." "Long Range Planning," Griswold Papers, RU 22, Yale University Archives (November 14, 1957).

2. The following sources are partially reflective of previously cited ones. They warrant inclusion again in a more expanded form at the outset of this chapter. The Yale School of Planning shared in the responsibility for the "New Haven Experiment" and for legitimizing the Rotival Plan and perspective. See, for example, "Yale Gets $67,000 Grant for City Planning Study," *New Haven Evening Register*, April 29, 1957 (School of Architecture and Design, "on the eve of a full-scale conference at Yale . . . on Interurbia—the huge regional cities of 'urban stripes' which are rapidly emerging. . . ." Yale city planning program "in city and regional planning," and role of Saarinen and Rudolph); "From Weir to Rudolph," "Contemporary Design Gradually Accepted as Colleges Abandon Traditionally Style," "New Forestry Lab Will Continue Trend to Modern Architecture," *Yale Daily News*, Architectural Supplement, November 21, 1957 (Saarinen on the

Corporation's Planning Committee; Rudolph added as well); letter from Secretary to Rudolph (January 14, 1958), Griswold Papers, RU 22, Box 200; letter to Buck (July 30, 1957). See also letter to Griswold, Griswold Papers, RU 22, Box 200, (June 11 1957) (meetings began in 1954, property disposition and availability to Yale in Oak Street/Hill/ Legion Avenue neighborhood and Dixwell/Newhallville neighborhood) 6, 18. Saarinen, involved with city officials, defined the purpose of the Dixwell Avenue Redevelopment Project and provided guidance, which New Haven always considered and usually accepted. Griswold Papers, RU 22 Box 213, Saarinen to Buck (March 9, 1960), and Buck to Saarinen (March 14, 1960) (The Ring Road). Boundary of Dixwell project to include Yale required roadway changes to ensure Yale would not pay. In a memorandum, Yale and Logue agreed Yale would know of city plans so it could decide to buy property. Griswold Papers, RU 22, Yale University Archives (March 12, 1958). Lee and Griswold agreed Yale would receive all "future plans." New Haven identified property along highway routes and elsewhere where Yale should acquire property, especially in the Dixwell Avenue project area (March 7, 1958); and see also Griswold Papers, RU 22, Oak Street meeting with Yale, Rotival, Lee, and Logue. ("Logue also stated that personally he would be willing to sell the University the land [in Oak Street]. At twenty-five cents a square foot if only we could be induced to embark on this venture!") Buck to Griswold on meeting of Building Committee (June 11, 1957), 18. Saarineen to Logue (March 17, 1958), Logue to Griswold (March 10, 1958), "Yale and City." Rudolph and Saarinen as "planners." Griswold Papers, RU 22, Yale University Archives (AWG 2/6).

    3. Lee's relationship to Rotival and admiration for Griswold's architects yielded two personal trophies: the Oak Street Connector was renamed "the Richard C. Lee Connector" and, in the remnants of the Hill neighborhood, where in 1967 New Haven's civil disturbance erupted, Eero Saarinen designed the Richard C. Lee High School, which opened in 1962. The high school resembled a giant, concrete World War II military bunker, close to windowless and located in precisely the kind of urban setting void of all the amenities (athletic facilities especially) Lee and others claimed required the relocation and the demolition of Hillhouse and Wilbur Cross. The building no longer serves as a high school. Lee's failed intention to destroy the Federal Court House also yielded a grand insider's irony: in 1999, Mayor John DeStefano, who, like his predecessors, had to devote considerable effort and resources to manage and seek to undo all the harm Lee had caused, got the United States to agree that the Court House would be named in Lee's honor. *New Haven Register*, November 18, 1999; see Lee's invitation to Griswold, Griswold Papers, RU 22 Box 166 (November 30, 1962). See also "The Maturing Modern," *Time* magazine, July 2, 1956), 50, 57 (Saarinen's home). For details about other people's homes, including poor workmanship, materials, and locations, see, for example, New Haven Colony Historical Society, *New Haven: Reshaping the City, 1900–1980*, 87 (Dixwell Community House); Brown, *New Haven: Guide to Architecture and Urban Design*. Rudolph's Oriental Mason Gardens (blocks of prefabricated housing—trailer-sized units trucked to the site, described as "stark," and "more of a ghetto than a vibrant neighborhood"—were demolished within a decade). And see Gail Collins, "A 'Vision,'" *New York Times*, April 29, 1979, and Rudolph, in "99% Invisible" podcast by SkepticLab: "People hated it. . . . The good folks who inhabited these dwellings thought that they were beneath them" (December 15, 2016). Also see Ryan E. Smith, *Prefab Architecture: A Guide to Modular Design and Construction*, foreword by James Timberlake (Hoboken, NJ: John

Wiley & Sons, 2010), 35; Caroline Winn, "Small Houses, Big Ideas," (honors thesis, art history, Wofford College, Spartanburg, SC, 2016), 29, 39; Rudolph was reported to have said, "I thought, and I suppose the mayor thought, they were perfectly good enough for them." *Paul Rudolph & His Architecture*, University of Massachusetts–Dartmouth, prudolph.lib.umassd.edu (available to the author; the url is now disabled). Other projects were built in the same modernist character or suburban imperative: New Haven Coliseum (torn down); Dixwell Plaza; Public Library and Shopping Arcade, Dixwell Community Center; United Church of Christ in the Dixwell neighborhood; Church Street South housing (torn down), and see Jonathan Hopkins, "Raze? Preserve? Or Renew?," *New Haven Independent*, October 30, 2015. For Professor Vincent Scully on Orr's "Saarineen Era" architecture within the university and New Haven, see *Yale in New Haven*, 301–2 ("banal," "destructive," "skinned and vacant look"). Saarinen lived in an elegant, conventional nine-room Victorian-style home made of brick.

4. Rae, *City*, 315–22; Scully, *Yale in New Haven*, 297.

5. Scully, *Yale in New Haven*, 297; Rae, *City*, 316–20. In May 1958, Logue called Rotival to task for his failure to define and complete the "Quinnipiac Valley Study" paid for by New Haven. Letter, Logue to Rotival (May 2, 1958), Rotival Papers, Box 35, Yale University Archives. Rotival's response was that he was too occupied by resolving disputes with the City Plan Department, at Logue's request. In November 1961— long after the demolition of two communities and plans for the demolition of much of downtown and the alteration of the Dixwell neighborhood—the Quinnipiac Valley Development Corporation was artificially "created" in the Connecticut Legislature by New Haven's initiative for a few months, composed of four towns along a narrow and fluctuating-in-size strip of the Quinnipiac River. With $30,000 from the Connecticut Legislature, the corporation did a study related to industrialization (when water power and river commerce were close to being replaced) and then ended its existence. Rotival to Andrews (contract for additional work) (November 9, 1961), Rotival Papers, Yale University Archives; "Valley Unit Backs Area Plan Agency," *New Haven Journal Courier*, November 30, 1961.

6. "New High School Plan Follows 1947 Survey," *New Haven Journal Courier*, July 7, 1955; "Bids Invited on New School," *New Haven Evening Register*, December 23, 1955 ("follows the recommendation of the Butterworth Report"). See also "CAC Unit Urges New Building for Hillhouse," *New Haven Evening Register*, February 7, 1953; letter, Norris Andrews, city planner, to Lee (March 29, 1955), Griswold Papers, RU 22, Yale University Archives. The 1947–1948 Butterworth Plan, an investigation of New Haven's future educational needs established by Mayor Celentano and relied upon by some Board of Education members in 1955 for their support of the sale, provided little, if any support for the offer Lee made. The report did not recommend that *any* of the buildings be demolished (Wilbur Cross was only thirty-five years old, fireproof, and in "good condition," according to Andrews and the city's external valuation; Hillhouse was about the same age as other public schools in New Haven, which continued to operate for educational purposes). Hillhouse and Boardman Trade were to be "abandoned" as *high schools*. No one suggested that the property—the original York Square—be sold. Nor did anyone suggest that one or more of the buildings could not be converted to another educational or municipal purpose (a choice not within the authority of the Butterworth investigators to recommend, but a choice available to Lee). The two new high schools the Butterworth

Report recommended, built when circumstances allowed, were to be located on opposite sides of the city, east and west. Assuming one was built first (on the eastern side of the city), Cross was to be retained as a high school until a second new high school could be built near Edgewood Park, on the western side of the city. A new vocational school to replace the *purpose* of Boardman Trade was to be built *inside* New Haven. *Only* Cross, if necessary and when it stopped serving any other purpose, was to be sold to Yale because it could continue to be used. None of this happened, and New Haven was left without a trade school. The Butterworth Report made no effort to consider the economic or social effects of any of its recommendations, other than important educational effects. In 1955, broader effects were considered, by Yale. The *Register* hoped (thinking, incorrectly, that the sale terms were really open to negotiation and change) that such an assessment would be made by the city or the Board of Aldermen, though it was not. When one Education Department official, William Iovanne, suggested Wilbur Cross should be retained as a junior high school, he was immediately contradicted. "A New Look at Cross High School," *New Haven Evening Register*, August 1, 1955 (retained as junior high school; "How little official or public debate has been given to them."). The deal had already been struck privately, though Iovanne may have known that and been trying to alter the Lee-Griswold deal. The full Butterworth Report is available at the New Haven Public Library.

7. The program offered a PhD and master's degree. Letter, Engleman to Griswold (May 21, 1954), Griswold to Engleman (May 25, 1954), Griswold Papers, RU 22, Box 146. A few years later, in 1958, Yale created a master's program in Teaching in its Graduate School based largely on the liberal arts, limited to Yale undergraduates and women from Smith and Vassar, with "teacher training" ancillary. To Engleman, who was very popular among educators, teaching aspirants, and faculty in the local schools, the Yale program bore little relationship to what teachers needed, and, though producing excellent graduates, was not highly regarded locally and more likely resented. In the mid-1960s, the program waned. Although unsuccessful, it had considerable meaning in another context, discussed later: the admission of women. See "Yale College to Admit Co-eds from Smith and Vassar in Fall," *New York Times* (March 24, 1958) and related internal description. "The Master of Arts in Teaching Degree," Griswold Papers, RU 22, Yale University Archives; interview with Patricia Chieffo (March 28, 2017); and see Thomas Farnham, *Southern Connecticut State University: A Centennial History 1893–1993*, Southern Connecticut State University: New Haven, CT (1993), 114–68 (Finis Engleman); and Finis Engleman, *The Pleasure was Mine: 70 Years in Education,* Danville, IL: Interstate Printers and Publishers (1971), 58.

8. Yale had recommended the external New Haven appraiser. Logue shared the Andrews recommendation and the valuation with Griswold. Letter, Andrews to Lee (March 11, 1955), Griswold Papers, RU 22 Box 229, Yale University Archives. Internally, in March, New Haven city planner Norris Andrews suggested to Lee a market-driven analysis for the sale of the three schools and land based, in part, on comparable, local property values ($2.59 per square foot) and noted the fact that the acreage that Hillhouse and Boardman Trade were built on (4.48 acres) was more than sufficient to build two new colleges the size of Yale's other residential colleges. This valuation approach was different from the conservative basis of the city's external evaluation done in accordance with "insurance purposes" standards ($1.25 per square foot and replacement cost), though it also concluded that Cross was in "good" condition, less than thirty-five years old, and

fireproof. "This figure [$1.25 per square foot]," Andrews wrote Lee, "appears very favorable [to Yale] and is much lower than existing values in any block adjacent to the Yale Campus. A good measuring stick at this time is a square foot value of the land acquired by the Telephone Company at Howe, George and Dwight, which value is $2.59 per square foot." In fact, Yale's own internal per square valuation was the same or higher. One implication of Andrews's analysis was that the Wilbur Cross School and land (1.76 acres) did not have to be sold or could be sold at a premium. More importantly, New Haven had leverage. Andrews recognized that: "There is no question in my own mind that it would be very difficult for Yale to assemble acreage at this low value per square foot anywhere less close in the present Campus." After private meetings between Yale and Lee, the valuation approach beneficial to Yale, however, became the publicly known appraised valuation, $3.2 million, put forth by New Haven (although even under this conservative approach, the valuation actually was $3.36 million). Yale's valuation was put at $2.8 million when finally it was made public. Lee also wanted "to transfer this land to Yale and at the same time receive from Yale one high school designed to the City's specifications to be located on the corner of Boulevard and Edgewood on land now a City park [estimated at] $3,200,000." That approach was abandoned as well.

9. Letter, Yale treasurer to Samuel Park Jr., copy to Griswold (April 11, 1955), Griswold Papers, RU 22, Box 229; and see Minutes (January 27, 1955) ("perfectly obvious that because of the complete occupancy of all available space"), Yale University Archives.

10. Terms of agreement were fixed on June 10, 1955, in "Confidential Memorandum" from Lee to Griswold, signed by Lee. All three buildings and the six-acre campus were committed to Yale for a $3,000,000 purchase price. "To the end of avoiding premature disclosures and the unfavorable effects of the same . . . ," the terms shall be "held strictly in confidence."

11. The *New Haven Evening Register* and members of the Republican Party objected to any further dealings with Yale, the former thinking the land should be (and that it could be) open to bidding by private entities in order to keep it on the tax roll, the latter thinking $3 million was a sweetheart deal, probably knowing that it was. The *New Haven Evening Register* editors also wanted negotiation with Yale to begin and for the Board of Aldermen to hold hearings and solicit bids. The "weak spot," the *Register*'s editor contended, "is whether the sites might bring more money . . . a hotel, retail center, an office building." All that was made public were the appraisal totals, not the different methodologies, and not Norris Andrews's market approach or the retention of Wilbur Cross. "Selling the High Schools," "Yale Bid $3 Million for City High Schools," *New Haven Evening Register*, July 8, 1955. "Board Favors Yale Offer for High Schools," *New Haven Evening Register*, July 7, 1955. However, the sites Lee wanted for one of the schools, especially the public park area on Edgewood Avenue, required approval by the Board of Park Commissioners.

12. Philip Mancini, the Republican candidate for mayor in 1955, sought to expose the underlying negotiations. He "accused the Mayor of dirty dealings with Yale" on Oak Street and the three schools, and contended that federal money will subsidize Yale projects. *New Haven Journal Courier*, November 7, 1955; "Mancini Says Lee Answers Are Too Vague," *New Haven Evening Register*, November 6, 1955; "Mancini Says City Lost in Sale to Yale," *New Haven Evening Register*, November 8, 1955. Lee readily won the election.

13. "Aldermen Approve Sale of 3 Schools to Yale," *New Haven Journal Courier*, August 7, 1955. A proposal to submit the sale to public referendum was defeated, at Lee's insistence. Alderman Henry DeVita also questioned the effect of Lee's employment relationship with Yale: "It's pretty hard to fight City Hall and to fight Yale," he said, "but you don't know whether you're fighting one or the other because they are all tied up."

14. For many students, New Haven's urbanity became merely a possible bus stop pass-through on the way to school. Architecturally, the two new high schools were bland metal and glass, square and rectangular boxes, one blue, the other red (each school's "colors"), the interior white and inspired by frugality. They would cost in excess of $7.5 million, well above the estimated cost even with reductions in quality and the elimination or postponement of some functions. "More Trouble from 'Hurry-Up High Schools,'" *New Haven Evening Register*, December 7, 1956. The *Register* found the entire process suspect and ill considered. The two high schools were completely renovated and the exterior redone in brick during the mayoral administration of John DeStefano.

15. Once the so-called relocation process began to play out, and the bulldozers and cranes began to operate nonstop for the next four years, the human suffering and disappointment and the economic harm to New Haven was voiced, albeit heard only in quarters unable or unwilling to stop either the suffering or the harm. "Hill Notifies Landowners of Highway Plans," *New Haven Evening Register*, June 3, 1954; Bush would later turn on Lee in 1961 when it appeared Lee might have senatorial aspirations. Bush was a member of the Senate committee that oversaw the disbursal of federal highway money; he exercised his influence frequently as Logue and Lee learned how to isolate the Redevelopment Agency and the federal money he ensured from public accountability. G. William Domhoff, "Who Really Ruled in Dahl's New Haven?," University of Southern California (monograph ed., first posted in 2005), www.whorulesamerica.net/local/new_haven.html, 9–10, 28–31. See also, G. William Domhoff, *Who Really Rules? New Haven and Community Power Reexamined*, 45, 46, 47, 48, 81, 105.

16. Teresa Gabucci in Riccio, *The Italian American Experience in New Haven*, 413.

17. See generally, Paul Bass and Douglas W. Rae, *Murder in the Model City: The Black Panthers, Yale, and the Redemption of a Killer* (New York: Basic Books, 2006) (Warren Kimbro).

18. Rob Gurwitt, "Death of a Neighborhood," *Mother Jones*, September/October 2000.

19. Gurwitt, "Death of a Neighborhood."

20. Lou and Rose Marie Guarino in Riccio, *The Italian American Experience*, 423.

21. Argento's mother was never able to adjust to their new home, distant from her friends and her daily routine in Wooster Square, itself the next cultural victim of urban renewal. Theresa Argento in Riccio, *The Italian American Experience*, 414.

22. The Oriental Masonic Gardens. Smith, *Prefab Architecture*, 35.

23. Riccio, *The Italian American Experience*, 414–16 (Argento), 418 (Rossi); "State Buys Waterside Park for $1.2 million," *New Haven Journal Courier*, February 18, 1956. The sale included the City Supply House, Engine House 7, and fire training grounds.

24. Rae, *City*, 338–40 (residential and racial impact).

25. The buildings included the eight-story Kilfeather Building, only thirty-five years old, with a working fountain and park nearby, occupied by numerous national companies, including Otis Elevator, Electrolux Corporation, M.G.M. Distribution, Republic Pictures

Corporation, and I. Neuman & Sons, Inc., which contained the Columbia Printing Company and Warner Brothers Picture Distribution Corporation. The area was once referred to as New Haven's "Film City." Gone. (New Haven's major downtown movie theaters would be demolished in a different phase of urban renewal.) The 184 buildings also included Gilbert's Bakery, Isadore Skolnick's stores, and numerous family-owned businesses whose owners lived in New Haven, in the neighborhood, or on the buildings' second and third floors. Demolished as well were the Congregation Sha'arei Torah synagogue, four small churches, and the Oak Street Parish House. "Oak St. Connector to Cut Big Swath in City Building," *New Haven Journal Courier*, January 18, 1956; "Connector Dooms 184 City Buildings," *New Haven Evening Register*, January 17, 1956; *New Haven Evening Register*, January 16, 1956 (individual housing, businesses, Italian, Jewish institutions, Russian Mutual Aid Society demolished).

26. Bart's cousins, the Santellos, also were displaced to make way for the interstate coming from the north that merged into I-95 and the Oak Street Connector. In short order, the birthplace of his father's friend, former classmate, and director of the Middlebury language program, Salvatore Castiglione, would be lost to the same highway's politically directed sway inward. A June 12, 1955, article in the *New Haven Evening Register* quoted Mrs. Gallina: "We've lived here all our lives and to us it's the nearest place to heaven on earth." "I'm broken-hearted," said Mrs. Vece. "Practically my whole family was born here." Mrs. Ferrigno added, in "halting troubled English," "We're a family of five. . . . We're very poor people. . . . Those flowers were like a life to me. I took care of them as if they were children. Just because the cars have got to live, my roses will have to die."

27. "They had brownstone houses on the street, they had all kinds of beautiful houses, all they needed was a little bit of hot water, heat in them." Tom Consiglio in Riccio, *The Italian American Experience*, 425.

28. Ralph Marcarelli in Riccio, *The Italian American Experience*, 408–9.

29. DeLauro: "The doctors were here, the midwives were here, the grocery stores, the butcher, the shoemakers, the chicken man, the dry goods store, the baker, everything was down there." Luisa would soon enter elective politics and carry with her the cries and sadness and wrong-headedness of what her neighbors and community endured. Luisa DeLauro in Riccio, *The Italian American Experience*, 422; "State Buys Waterside Park for $1.2 Million," *New Haven Journal Courier*, February 18, 1956.

30. Eugene and Frances Calzetta, Riccio, *The Italian American Experience*, 406.

31. Riccio, *The Italian American Experience*, 406 (Calzettas), 408–9 (Marcarelli), 416 (Argento), 418 (DeLauro), 420 (Pat Barone), 425 (Nappi), 426 (Frank DiLieto).

32. Many of the Italian and Irish families who had moved with others to Fair Haven, the Annex, and Morris Cove, once the domain of old Yankee families like the Townshends (Henry Townshend Jr. would be the 1961 candidate for mayor), were welcomed into those neighborhoods. The Jews and Irish who remained moved largely to Westville, and Polish families closer to Saint Stanislaus Church in the State Street neighborhood. African American families moved into homes, apartments, and, along with other refugees, housing projects in Fair Haven, Dixwell, Wooster Square, or Dwight (west of Yale) and to the periphery of the city. Collectively, their politicization was completed, their intuitive knowledge of their interest honed further by urban renewal. Many among them—though, as we'll see, they voted for Townshend in 1961 in order to disable

Lee—immediately returned to an active role in neighborhood Democratic Party politics in their wards. Others struggled to remain in New Haven near friends or relatives, as the highway's route continued to cut neighborhoods in halves or thirds or obliterated them completely, and the redlining sometimes caused families to accept anything that was seemingly stable and hope for a decent second move.

33. As quoted in Soares, *The Power of Privilege*, 26.

34. Frank Teodosio was the first to call. He knew them all; they ate at his restaurant every day. Priests from the nearby churches arrived as quickly as the firefighters. Thomas Dobroski and his three cousins rushed toward the locked fire escape, women trapped above it. It wouldn't open. One yelled "please don't leave me, I have four children." The four men created a human ladder as best they could. Others, caught in the backup, were burned immediately as the fire blasted through windows and engulfed their feet and legs. The fire escape snapped open quickly, throwing women a dozen feet against the frozen ground. Thomas's cousin, Walter Myjak, had sledge hammered out the pin that locked the metal stairs in place. The Red Cross appeared next. Dobroski received "extreme burns to his hands." His cousins were Stanley, Walter, and Frank Myjak. Carmine Prete, "who sustained burns and a fractured ankle after he jumped from the fourth floor, refused to be taken to the hospital until all those who had escaped were taken away by ambulance and continued helping in the rescue work. Peter Aiello . . . ran to the scene, where he helped women on the fire escape to safety." "Mrs. Josephine Nastri saw her husband Joseph Nastri, a foreman . . . wrapped in flames after helping her and another woman escape to safety." Morris Baer, the owner, kept going in and out of the blaze to rescue women until he never returned. Mrs. Therese Sullo stayed behind to help Mr. Baer. Both died. Riccio, *The Italian American Experience*, 321.

35. Matthew Proto, my father, was standing among them. One phone call and we were in the car. I was eleven. My father had friends who worked there. My mother, a tailor, knew them as well. We stood on the corner of Franklin and Chapel. The fire smoldered, hoses slithered through and around cars and trucks, firemen in black boots and gear, water everywhere, frozen, then shattered by ambulance after ambulance that arrived. They sped off with sirens blaring. The colors were dark, blurred by movement and tails of smoke and flames still rising. My father held my shoulder as we watched. He had tears in his eyes. I didn't recall seeing that before. I learned later in life, when I entered Southern Connecticut State University, that one of our neighbors, Louise DiRuccio, who had been instrumental in forming the Alumni Association and welcoming new students to higher education, lost her mother to that fire in 1957.

36. "Four Dead in Franklin St. Fire, Five Missing Believed Trapped, Plant Ruined in One of City's Worst Disasters," "Mass of Flames on Ramp, Screams 'Don't Leave Me.'" (Angelina Di Rienzo, Jessie Mongillo, Alma Bradley, and Grace Pitman were dead. Thirty-three others were taken to the hospital, seventeen too serious to release.) "Mayor Orders Factory Razed Before Search," "17 Admitted to Hospitals for Treatment," *New Haven Journal Courier*, January 25, 1957, fire news and photos on 2, 4, 8, and 16; "Fatal Factory Blaze Shocks City, Death Toll of Nine Now Probable, Officials Launch Probe," "Renewal Plan Was to Claim Site of Blaze, Lee Says City Ready to Buy Building Where Five Lost Their Lives," "4 Men Hailed for Releasing Fire Escape," "City and State Launch Probes of Fatal Fire," "Fire Toll in Wooster Area Is 35 Dead in Past 15 Years," *New Haven Evening Register*, January 25, 1957; "Firemen Search Ruins for Last Victims of Factory

Fire," *New Haven Evening Register*, January 27, 1957; "2 Fire Victims Found" (Morris Baer and Josephine Marotta; within a day the bodies of Thelma Lynn and Joseph Nastri were discovered), "Collins Gives Warnings on Fire Escape Routes," "Firemen Search Factory Ruins for Bodies of Four Victims," "Fire-Swept Factory Met Safety Code, State Says," "None Blamed in Blaze on Franklin Street," *New Haven Evening Register*, January 28, 1957 (all the "minimal standards" were met; and "most" but *not all* of the shops in the building were inspected. The spokesman acknowledged that "the disaster could have been eliminated by a little education and instruction," namely, a fire drill. It never happened.); "Death Claims Tenth Victim of Loft Fire," (Therese Sullo), *New Haven Evening Register*, January 31, 1957; "Woman, 66, Dies, 15th Victim of Factory Fire Blaze," *New Haven Evening Register*, February 3, 1957 (Matilda DiRuccio); "Escape Used in Fatal Fire to Be Tested," *New Haven Evening Register*, May 9, 1957; "Failure to Push Escape Bar Held Clue in Factory Deaths," "Awards Made to Two More Victims," "Tests Show Fire Escapes Were in Good Working Conditions," *New Haven Evening Register*, May 10, 1957 (The tests were held in May, conducted by trained firemen, no fire or risk to their lives at stake, on a mechanism they knew how to operate, which, the fire chief and coroner concluded, meant the fire escape "was in working order at the time of the blaze"); "Coroner Urges New Fire Code," *New Haven Evening Register*, May 29, 1957. And see "25 Years Don't Dim Tragedy of Killer Fire," *New Haven Register*, January 24, 1982 ("I still get nightmares from it," Edward Prete said, and he "was unable to cover his expenses. . . . He asked the bank holding his mortgage to reduce his payments for a while, but the bank refused." Johanna Bradley, a paralegal in New Haven, now doing the same work in Florida, compiled these and other articles at the author's request. See, especially, Riccio, *The Italian American Experience*, "Franklin Street Fire," 320–34.

37. Exit doors were not plainly marked, all doors opened inward rather than outward, the fire escape didn't work in the cold and was never subjected to anything resembling practice or even employee instruction, the wooden floors were oil soaked from daily maintenance on machines, no sprinkler system existed, and rags and cloth dust accumulated wherever the employer directed—in corners, in the basement, as stuffing in broken windows. "No [state] inspection report record was seen for the Thomas Machinery Sales Company, first floor occupants of the building," where the "fire is believed to have started." Under what historian Anthony Riccio described as "an eerie photograph of the Franklin Street Fire's aftermath, showing a fireman walking away from the smoldering burned-out hulk," was the following: "A tragic fire is not the way to clear-out the blighted parts of our city." It came from Dick Lee's Citizens Action Commission. Riccio, *The Italian American Experience*, 322. Mayor John DeStefano, two decades later, sought to mute the starkness of the new school's appearance and blend it into the neighborhood.

38. Fifteen were killed and thirty-six injured in the fire. The dead: Morris Baer, Alma Bradley, Sophie Christodoulides, Angelina Di Rienzo, Matilda DiRuccio, Winifred Freeman, Herbert Horowitz, Anna Jones, Thelma Grillo Lynn, Josephine Marotta, Jessie Mongillo, Joseph Nastri, Grace Pitman, Angelina Romano, and Therese Sullo. Riccio, *The Italian American Experience*, 321–22. The highest workmen's compensation (for a woman) awarded to her husband (as long as he didn't remarry) was calculated at $21.45 a week for six years. Fifty-four claims were made, for a total of $5 million. With everyone exonerated, the families settled for a total of $400,000. Some of those injured were

unable to cover essential expenses. "Awards Made to Two More in Fire Here," *New Haven Evening Register*, May 10, 1957. And see "25 Years Don't Dim Tragedy of Killer Fire," *New Haven Register*, January 24, 1982.

39. Dino was fourteen years old; Elria, a senior at Northampton School for Girls, was on a school tour in the northern Cape Cod region of Massachusetts.

40. Denver, to "the Pueblo Indian town of Taos," New Mexico, Hoover Dam, Las Vegas, through the Mojave Desert, a stay at Lake Tahoe, into California to Monterey and Carmel. In San Francisco, they visited friends they'd made during Val and Peggy's sabbaticals to Italy. On the return, they drove through Reno and Cody, and then Salt Lake City, where they saw their first "real rodeo." They drove north to Mount Rushmore, through the Black Hills, then east to Chautauqua, New York, where they visited friends. Marion O'Connell, "South Hadley Professor Tours West with Family," *Holyoke Telegram*, August 7, 1957; interview with Dino Giamatti (September 15, 2015).

41. Interview with Andrew Vitali (March 3, 2017); *Neptunia* ship manifest (August 28, 1957).

CHAPTER 23

UNDERSTANDING YALE

Epigraph is from J. B. Priestly, from the playwright's introduction to Charles Dickens, *Scenes of London* (New York: Macmillan Collectors Library, 2018), xi (originally published in 1947 by Pan Books). Priestly also selected works from *Sketches by Boz* (Dickens), first published in 1839.

1. Lord Saye and Sele and Lord Brooke are commemorated yearly by Saybrook students. The college's banner, its colors, insignia, and coat of arms reflect the founding of Old Saybrook and the two men, and are visible in ceremonies, football games, commencement exercises, and the college's dining hall. Because the college and its neighbor, Branford College, were financed with the generosity of members of the Harkness family (who also funded much of the 1930-era expansion under President Angell), the family's coat of arms and various family portraits and memorabilia appear in the college's interior. The Fellows also intended "to single out accomplishments of unusual enterprise and imagination in various fields of study that might remain unrecognized by the regular University awards for high scholarship. . . . The names of the recipients were to be inscribed on the south wall of the . . . Common Room." No more than two or three would be given yearly.

2. Mann, "Insight," *Holyoke Telegram*, excerpt in Valerio, *Bart*, 13–15.

3. Lewis's work on Dante was cited earlier. Kernan, *In Plato's Cave*, 85 (1954 appointments; see also Kernan's recollection of Giamatti's appreciation for Kernan's early critique of Giamatti's writing, 167).

4. Fry, "History of the Department." Robert Penn Warren, *All the King's Men* (New York: Harcourt, 1946); Kernan, *In Plato's Cave*, 87; R. W. B. Lewis, *The American Adam: Innocence, Tragedy, and Tradition in the Nineteenth Century* (Chicago: University of Chicago Press, 1955); R. W. B. Lewis, *Edith Wharton: A Biography* (New York: Harper & Row, 1975); Maynard Mack, *King Lear in Our Time* (Abingdon, UK: Routledge); and see "Robert Penn Warren, Albers, Poyre See Need for New Literary Forms," *Yale Daily News*, March 1, 1959.

5. "Comparative literature" is defined, in part by Webster with more variation in various university catalogs, as the interrelationship of literature of two or more countries often of different languages and the influence of one upon the other—for example, Dante upon Spenser. English writers such as John Milton, William Blake, Alexander Pope, William Wordsworth, Lord Byron, and Alfred Lord Tennyson were influenced by Dante.

6. Yale University, *Undergraduate Course of Study, Fall and Spring Terms*, 1956–1957, 1957–1958, 1958–1959, 1959–1960, and English Major, 1956–1957 catalog, 89–95.

7. "Professor Giamatti to Speak Twice in New Haven," *Holyoke Telegram*, December 4, 1957. Peggy considered Janet Murrow a role model and friend. Murrow remained a trustee until 1959 and maintained a residence in South Hadley. In 1970, she became a teacher and curator of the college's art museum. "Janet Brewster Murrow, 88, Radio Broadcaster," *New York Times*, December 22, 1998; interview with Elria Giamatti Ewing and David Ewing (relationship between Janet Murrow and Peggy Giamatti); Sperber, *Murrow: His Life and Times*, 50–51; "Mount Holyoke Trustees on Inspection," *Holyoke Telegram*, 1956. Val addressed "The *Circulo Italiano*, a New Haven Literary Society," actually established during his time at Hillhouse High School, which in the 1930s rarely included Italian American members. He frequently sought (and likely did here) to ensure that the origin of the Dante translations and Etruscan artifacts came from the villages of those Italian immigrant families who came to America. He also addressed "The Associates of the Yale Library" on "A Bibliophile, Dante, and Lady Fortune." He put "on display 30 volumes of his Dante Collection of Illustrated Dante works," including a 1555 edition "famous for being the first to include the word "Divina' in 'La Divina Commedia.'" The display may have included his highly valued instructive compendium of the works he'd collected, which provided a description of each edition, year published, language used (Arabic, Japanese, Polish, Welsh, English, Italian), where published, unique characteristics (prefatory comments, illustrations), method of printing or form of creation, and their content that, in his view as a linguist, reflected variations in translation worthy of special attention.

8. One critical comparative thread was whether the edition had illustrations, a factor that determines its value and explains how the edition was actually created and the collaborative connection among the artist, translator, and publisher. There also was merit in the artist and the illustrations standing alone: Salvador Dali, William Blake, and Sandro Botticelli, for example. Some illustrations are fantastical images, each illustrator seeking to capture a place or moment in Dante's journey. Others include intricate woodcuts, many filled with fine craftsmanship, which contain information unique to a time period or the illustrator's perspective that Giamatti discerned, sometimes just enough to move scholars to find new subtleties in that period's knowledge or the illustrator's unique intention. The author has examined the Giamatti compilation and the collection. "Valentine Giamatti Dante Collection," Mount Holyoke Archives and Special Collections; "Mr. Giamatti at Alumnae Weekend" (October 1953), Giamatti Papers, Mount Holyoke Archives; Valentine John Giamatti, *Directory of American Scholars*, 6th, 7th, and 8th editions (New York: R.R. Bowker, 1974, 1978, and 1982) (languages, linguistics, and philology). It's unclear on what factual basis James Reston Jr. concluded that Valentine Giamatti's academic credentials were "modest" because he "did not write . . . the 'book'" about Dante or that Val had "insecurity" about his writing skills, which, ultimately, ensured that, for his son, Bart, "there

was a strong drive to realize what [his father] had been so close to achieving but never had." James Reston Jr., *Collision at Home Plate: The Lives of Pete Rose and Bart Giamatti* (New York: Harper Collins, 1991), 16–17. Valentine Giamatti had a remarkably credentialed (two Ivy League degrees and two PhDs, and numerous awards) and highly praised life as a splendid teacher of international scholarly renown and as a public intellectual who spoke and acted with clarity and principle about matters of his day within his community, at Mount Holyoke, in Italy, and in the nation. Bart Giamatti, in every public and private expression about his father, had the exact opposite belief Reston posited: his father was a model, an expression of the full, wonderful life led productively that he could only hope to emulate no matter how many books he wrote. And the Valentine Giamatti Dante Collection, including his analysis of each volume and its continued use by scholars globally, is an accomplishment that Dante scholars cherish and admire. In a rush to force a contrast or similarity to Pete Rose, Reston, not infrequently, made a mistake in fact or judgment. This endnote is here in the text because in the mid-1950s, Val Giamatti was barely halfway through his career.

There would be more than two hundred editions of the *Commedia* in the collection by the time Val donated it to Mount Holyoke. The earliest is 1481; many editions are in different languages and in various interpretations of dialects. Translations into English include one by Yale's Thomas Bergin and a contemporary one (on the "Inferno") by Poet Laureate Robert Pinsky. Scholars worldwide have availed themselves of it, and Mount Holyoke hosts the Annual Valentine Giamatti Lecture on the "Renaissance Era, Dante and His Works." The title page of his compendium is simple and appropriate. In the center, in calligraphy, is "Giamatti," encircled by *Vagliami il lungo studio e il grande amore, che m'ha fatto cercar lo tuo volume.* Taken from *Commedia,* the "Inferno," it reads, in context: "May the long study and the great love that have made me search your volume avail me. You are my master and my author." Virgil, who became Dante's guide through his journey down to Inferno and upward toward Paradise is "my master and my author." The "long study" refers to Dante's study of Virgil, undertaken during Dante's exile from Florence. "Your volume" refers to Virgil's work, *The Aeneid.*

The collection, along with other artifacts of Etruscan art and coinage (also collected by Peggy), remained in their home, available for teaching and perusal by students and invited groups. Val also became a member of the Massachusetts chapters of American Archeological and Numismatic societies. The collection was made periodically available for public display and lectures, including Val's especially comprehensive talks on the history of foreign language education in America. See, for example, "Mount Holyoke Professor to Be Oct. 12 Speaker," *Springfield Republican,* October 1957; "Dr. Giamatti Exhibits Rare Dante Collection," *Holyoke Telegram,* February 8, 1957.

9. Advertisement, *Yale Daily News,* February 12, 1958; informal interview with John Merriman (origin of Giamatti's view of the residential colleges); Robert Moncreiff, *Bart Giamatti: A Profile* (New Haven, CT: Yale University Press, 2007), 24–26 (Dan Catlin). The "Master" at a Yale residential college is now referred to as the "Head of College."

10. Yale *Yearbook* (1960), 16, 17, 18, 22, 23.

11. Yale *Yearbook* (1960), 35.

12. "Yale Film Society," *Yale Daily News,* September 8, 1958.

13. "Allen Ginsberg Reads Poetry," *Yale Daily News,* November 25, 1956; *Yale Yearbook* (1960), 35, 36, 45.

14. "Academic Indifference at Yale, Some Proposals toward the Solution of the Problem," Aurelian Society, Box 1, Folder 4, Yale University Archives; "Chauncey Appointed Ass. Dean; Aid Carroll in Yale College Duties," *Yale Daily News*, April 16, 1958.

15. In 1910, students came together "to encourage and promote high character, gentlemanly conduct and the molding of one's career to a life to the community." Among other activities, the society had promoted the creation of the university's honor system and, through its members, established Book Prizes and travel grants for undergraduates. The Aurelian Society was the first society to accept women once the university allowed for their admission. See, generally, *Guide to the Aurelian Honor Society* and *Guide to the Loomis Havemeyer Papers*, MS 632 and RU 220, Yale University Archives.

16. "Lightfoot Voted Head of Charities Drive; Tobin Vice-Chairman," *Yale Daily News*, November 5, 1957.

17. "Giamatti, Price, Bose Chosen to Lead 1959 Yale Charities Drive," *Yale Daily News*, December 10, 1958.

18. *Danton's Death* (which premiered in 1835, and was set during the French Revolution); *The Inspector General* (a satire about corruption in city government during the time of the czars, by Russian-Ukrainian dramatist Nikolai Gogol); the Undergraduate Festival of the Dramatic Arts (three days of college theater, which included women performers); *Grand Tour* (an original musical); and, Shakespeare's *Julius Caesar*. The Dramat concluded with Samuel Beckett's *Waiting for Godot*. Yale Yearbook (1960), 292–94.

19. "Inspector General Names for Dramatic Production," *Yale Daily News*, February 2, 1959, and reviews (excerpts from the *New Haven Evening Register* and the *New Haven Journal Courier*) in the *Yale Daily News*, March 2, 1959; "Dramat Plays; Forceful, Farcical," *Yale Daily News*, January 14, 1957.

20. In this fulsome embrace of stage in all of its forms, Bart also would have joined local family members to attend the performance at Sprague Memorial Hall given by his second cousin Leopoldo Joseph Camera. Leo, as he was known among friends and former army buddies (he'd served in World War II), was an accomplished composer of wind and brass instruments, and the first student to graduate from Yale's School of Music with that skill. That was a proud moment for his parents: Valentine Giamatti's cousin Leonora Giammattei, born in Italy, and her husband, Ferdinand Camera. Formal bulletin poster, "Yale University School of Music, Percussion Recital, by Leo Camera assisted by Wind and Brass assembles, Chamber Orchestra, Thursday, May 8, 1958"; "Bulldog Ban Excels in Woolsey Hall," *Yale Daily News*, February 25, 1957. Genealogical confirmation, Kim Formica.

21. Abram Smith was a graduate of Rutgers with a master's degree from Columbia. He had a reputation for innovative plays and for encouraging excellent academic performance among his players. On multiple occasions, he was selected New Jersey Coach of the Year, and at the end of his career he was elected into the state's Football Coaches Hall of Fame. He also had an aesthetic thread and was known locally as a portrait painter. Captain Brown was the first man to swim through accessible portions of the Panama Canal and inspired others to follow, including the first woman. Because of his reputation and skill, Brown was retained by famous escape artist Harry Houdini to ensure his rescue if, in his escape performances, he failed to surface timely. "Higgins Funeral Home Announcement," September 2004; "Panama Canal Stunts Began Early," *Panama Canal Review*, August 1966; *Documents of the Assembly of the State of New York, 1914* (Albany, NY:

J.B. Lyon, 1914), 9 (Brown as distance swimmer); Lisa Bier, *Fighting the Current: The Rise of Women's Swimming, 1890–1926* (Jefferson, NC: McFarland, 2011), 72. Plainfield had, and in many respects still has, a robust, mixed residential and retail core, with multifamily and individual homes, churches of various denominations, and a conventional street grid, dotted with small parks, a YMCA, and 1920s-era municipal buildings (author's review of photographs and walking visit).

22. "Dramat Names Cast Selections for Spring Play," read the *Yale Daily News,* April 1, 1958. *Cyrano* had a newly created musical score and other innovative variations that enticed Drama School students, who (especially for women's roles) auditioned along with others. Dick Cavett (Yale 1958) got the part of Ragueneau, a poet and pastry chef who is a friend of Cyrano. Toni Smith, the *News* announced "will play the role of Roxanne," a difficult character role, a woman of superficial intellect but complex physical drives with whom two men, including the deeply woven personality of Cyrano, are in love. Performances were scheduled in the University Theatre, at Connecticut's American Shakespeare Theatre Musical Festival in Stratford, Connecticut, and one performance in New York's off-Broadway Phoenix Theater.

23. Toni had a minor part in the Drama School production of the 1950 Broadway comedy *Happy as Larry*, a glamorous one (Marilyn Monroe) in a late-night performance that the *Daily News* characterized as "Festival Activities" (though seeking to "run forever," the "Festival" was shut down by "the campus cops [who] closed the gates at three"), and a major one in Thornton Wilder's *The Skin of Our Teeth* (she played Sabina, who performed two distinct roles in the play, a maid and a temptress). The reviewer thought she gave "a laudable performance in a difficult and challenging role." In the musical *Cyrano*—Bart in the wings—the student reviewer thought her performance "while vocally more than simply competent did not seem to invest her role with sufficient warmth." "Drama School Produces Comic 'Happy as Larry,'" *Yale Daily News*, November 7, 1957, "Yale Drama to Present 'Skin of Our Teeth,'" *Yale Daily News*, February 27, 1958; "Success Out of Chaos," *Yale Daily News*, February 28, 1958; "Festival Activities Show Kaleidoscopic Range," *Yale Daily News*, March 31, 1958; "Dramat's 'Cyrano,'" *Yale Daily News*, May 5, 1958.

24. William F. Buckley sought support from Skull and Bones during his public battle with Yale over his book, and society membership apparently was a factor when the Yale Corporation selected Griswold, not an obvious first choice, for president, a fact that Giamatti likely knew as a student and certainly knew later. There were only fifteen students elected—"tapped"—in their junior year by their predecessors, who prepared to graduate into the status of welcomed and active guests until death. Interview with Calabresi on Griswold's selection as president and how Skull and Bones members used their influence to oppose William DeVane's nomination (because of his elevation of the first Catholic and Jewish professors), allowing Corporation Board member Dean Acheson and others to bring their own influence to bear in order to nominate the less-known and uncontroversial Griswold.

25. "The novelist's [Dickens's] recent American tour, 'the adulation with which he was everywhere fawned upon,' and 'the base ingratitude displayed in his letters to the London papers, just published in this country,' were made subject to grave comment, some wondering if they were not forgeries." Mack also drew considerable attention to the fact that the early members were the most intellectually gifted in their class, and that

the society's high quality "did not escape the attention of contemporary newswriters, one of whom alleged that the foundation of the new society commended a new era in everything exalted and noble." These early members, Mack concluded, had "to build better than they know." And they did. Maynard Mack, *The Society as an Ideal: The Pains of Vigilance, 1871–1942*, 1–12 (unpublished, except for six copies) is available in the Yale Archives.

26. "Heroes: A Look at Black History in Connecticut," SNET, 1989; "Alumni Association Dixwell Community House, Fifth Annual Awards Dinner-Dance," *New Haven Register*, April 3, 1982; "A Woman Well Worth Remembering," *New Haven Register*, October 25, 1995; "A Salute to Ella B. Scantlebury," New Haven Lawn Club, April 29, 1977; "You Could Feel Her Warmth," *New Haven Register*, September 11, 1996, provided by the Greater New Haven African American Historical Society of the Ethnic Historical Archives Center, New Haven, CT (Southern Connecticut State University); Moncreiff, *Giamatti: A Profile*, 199.

CHAPTER 24
LEARNING GRISWOLD AND BREWSTER

1. Griswold to Lee (May 6, 1958), Howe Jr. to Griswold (May 9, 1958), Lee to Griswold (May 9, 1958), Griswold to Lee (May 9, 1958), Griswold Papers, RU 22, Box 166, Yale University Archives.

2. Scully, *Yale in New Haven*, 341–42. See, for example, Dan Kaferele, "Yale Plans Resumption of Aid to Area Pupils," *New Haven Evening Register*, January 6, 1979 (Giamatti's public announcement).

3. The Hillhouse (York Square) Papers at the New Haven Historical Society are filled with photographs of Hillhouse High School alumni gatherings, men and women coming from all over the nation as well as locally to celebrate a unique urban academic experience. See also "School Days Recalled by Boardman Class of 1904," *New Haven Evening Register*, May 23, 1954. See generally, Neil Thomas Proto, "The 'Crimson Horde' Captured the Soul of New Haven," *New Haven Register*, March 23, 2008; *Crossroads*, Wilbur Cross Yearbook (1958) (basketball team and schedule of wins). My parents and I were present at the game to watch my brother, Richard, play for Cross.

4. "Seventeen Freshmen Reported to the Dean for Riot Activity," *Yale Daily News*, February 11, 1958.

5. The 1953 "undergraduate disturbance" was, to Griswold, "an outburst of childishness," handled, he wrote to the police chief, "highly efficiently." Griswold to New Haven police chief (May 12, 1953), Griswold Papers, RU 22, Yale University Archives. "Quick Police Action Quells 2,500 Elm Street Rioters," *Yale Daily News*, May 12, 1953. Another disturbance occurred in 1954. "Snowballs . . . and a Hero," *Yale Daily News*, January 16, 1954. Lee attributed it to students "without parental supervision." Lee to Griswold (January 21, 1954), Griswold Papers, RU 22, Yale University Archives.

6. Forty undergraduates were arrested on and near York Street for disturbing the peace, for alcoholism, and, for one visiting student, punching a policeman. Six patrol cars and ten police officers were necessary to quell the disturbance. The student who punched the policeman was "countered with a nightstick blow" to the head. "Two Arrested in Early Morning Fracas; Police Beat Resisting Ohio State Student," *Yale Daily News*, April 10, 1958.

7. The first parade was held in 1842, and parades continued until at least the 1890s. In 1949, during the administration of William Celentano, the Hibernian Ball was held, a black-tie affair, which, like many of the ethnic and religiously tempered celebrations in the city, welcomed friends and organizations of all backgrounds. By then, the neighborhoods' Catholic schools and churches, though still dominated by Irish hierarchy, were decidedly mixed in ethnic and racial composition. Joan Moynihan and Neil Hogan, *New Haven's St. Patrick's Day Parade* (Charleston, SC: Arcadia Publishing, 2006), 13, 21.

8. "Yale Snowball Fight Ends in 25 Arrests," *New Haven Evening Register*, March 13, 1959; "Police Arrest 16 Yale Students as Flare-up Mars Parade Windup," "Regret Voiced to Community by Griswold," *New Haven Evening Register*, April 15, 1959.

9. Griswold to Rostow (March 23, 1959), Griswold Papers, RU 22, Yale University Archives (When Lee called Griswold, "He [Lee] was sobbing."). See also Schimer to Griswold (January 20, 1960), Griswold Papers, RU 22, Yale University Archives; Nagle to Griswold (November 20, 1959), Griswold Papers, RU 22, Yale University Archives; "42 Students to Face Court on April 11," *New Haven Evening Register*, April 18, 1959. (One student "was arrested for abusing an officer two days after the St. Patrick's Day disturbance." Yale's chaplain for Catholic students was the Reverend Edmund O'Brien.)

10. "A Challenge for Yale's Undergraduates," *New Haven Evening Register*, April 16, 1959.

11. Three faculty members created a fund to provide financial support for the lawyers who represented the arrested students. The response was tepid. "Snowballs, Riots, Police Tactics," *Yale Daily News*, March 15, 1959.

12. "Snowballs, Riots, Police Tactics," *Yale Daily News*, March 15, 1959.

13. The commission, in an attached report, concluded that, "College authorities [Harvard, MIT, and Radcliffe] and students have made a real effort to cooperate with the police." Harvard had an identification card system that effectively ensured individual accountability for wrongdoing (university police asked students for their cards when there was an infraction). Report of the Commission to Study Yale—New Haven Community Relations (September 1959); Commission to Lee and Griswold (September 14, 1959), Griswold Papers, RU 22, Yale University Archives. The implicit suggestions in the Harvard "attachment" to the commission's report didn't seem to resonate with Lee or Griswold. Yale, confronted with a dispute over whether the new Saarinen-designed hockey rink was tax exempt, wasn't about to embrace any civic-based change to its local obligation and earned tax exemption.

14. Within weeks, Griswold—as vice chairman of the Citizens Action Commission, acting like a government official—also formed a Committee on Juvenile Delinquency in New Haven. One member, newly appointed Police Sergeant Biagio DiLieto, would become mayor during Bart Giamatti's presidency; Henry Chauncey Jr., who served as the committee's director, would later become secretary of Yale under Brewster (and, for a period, under Giamatti). The committee produced a Yale-sponsored Study of the Welfare of New Haven Youth and held meetings, yet little of enduring consequence came from either. "Promotions Given Two in Police Department," *New Haven Evening Register*, March 3, 1959; DiLieto to Griswold accepting offer (October 27, 1959), Griswold Papers, RU 22, Yale University Archives; "City, Yale Map Action on Student Riot," *New Haven Evening Register*, April 13, 1959.

15. "Nisi Decisions Granted in Yale Snowball Fight," *New Haven Evening Register*, April 11, 1959.

16. "Yale Plans Study to End Incidents," *New Haven Evening Register*, April 17, 1959; "Mayor Appoints 3-Man Commission to Study Student-Police Friction," *Yale Daily News*, April 1, 1959; "Snowballs, Riots, Police Tactics," *Yale Daily News*, March 15, 1959; "Police Charge, View of Elm Street Skirmishing," *Yale Daily News*, March 15, 1959; "Students, Police Clash in Riot," *Yale Daily News*, March 15, 1959; "Three Members of Faculty Ask Yale Community to Pay Student's Legal Expenses," *Yale Daily News*, March 20, 1959; "Fund for Arrested Students," *Yale Daily News*, March 20, 1959; "Badge Number 100," *Yale Daily News*, March 20, 1959; "Politics and Police," *Yale Daily News*, March 20, 1959; "Yale Suspends 4 for Roles in Riot; Legal Aid Mounts," *Yale Daily News*, April 1, 1959 (swastika hanging from Calhoun window); "Unfinished Business," *Yale Daily News*, April 14, 1959; "The Unpaid Heroes," *Yale Daily News*, April 13, 1959 (appeal to students not contributing to fund).

17. Daniel Oren concluded, with some reserve: "In the manner in which it removed racial, religious, and sexual barriers from its admissions process, Yale was to prove consistent in its character with TIME's description." Oren, *Joining the Club*, 188; "The Steady Hand," *Time*, June 11, 1951, 57.

18. Alexander M. Bickel, *The Least Dangerous Branch: The Supreme Court at the Bar of Politics* (Indianapolis, IN: Bobbs-Merrill, 1962).

19. Guido Calabresi attributes the changes in hiring at the Law School, in part, to Dean Acheson, then a Corporation member and good friend of Felix Frankfurter and Griswold. Those changes led, in time, to further changes in the Law School's admission policy. Interview, Guido Calabresi.

20. Karabel, *The Chosen*, 330, and see critically supportive role played by the Reverend William Sloane Coffin Jr.

21. See Karabel, *The Chosen*, 327–37 (conflicting faculty expectations; the Doob Report of the President's Committee on Freshman Year; alumni committees), 342.

22. See also Nancy Weiss Malkiel, *"Keep the Damned Women Out": The Struggle for Coeducation* (Princeton, NJ: Princeton University Press, 2016), 54–57, which reflects Griswold's and Howe's efforts to elevate the admission of women into the colloquy, though her argument would have benefited from an appreciation of the effect of the riots and anti-intellectualism on the foundational success of Griswold's approach, the delay and contentiousness caused by Brewster's embrace of his own and the alumni's historically retrogressive notion of "leadership," and the still uncollaborated claim of Inslee Clark (see note 29 in this chapter).

23. "Yale College to Admit Co-eds from Smith and Vassar in Fall," *New York Times*, March 24, 1958.

24. "Yale-Smith-Vasar [*sic*] Program Planned to Recruit, Train Future Teachers," *Yale Daily News*, March 31, 1958 (emphasis added).

25. "Women at Yale," *Yale Daily News*, April 2, 1958; "On the MAT," *Yale Daily News*, March 31, 1958.

26. Though the *Daily News* editorial was skeptical, if not condescending and dismissive, concerning the admission of women, one professor noted, "The fellows seem to be intrigued with the idea of women in the classroom." Or, as another person observed, Yale men seemed sort of apathetic about it. Two years earlier, when Dean Arthur Howe had

provoked a harsh student response to a similar suggestion about the admission of women (and Griswold had to issue a reassurance to discomforted undergraduates, probably those who had had only private school education), the *Daily News* response allowed the *Crimson* to evoke the accepted understanding of the Yale mentality: "Thus traditional conservatism responded to the 'dangers' of co-education!" By 1958, that mentality showed signs of cracking until Brewster, unable to recognize its purpose and power, sought to deny its value and patch it over. Michael Churchill, "Female Yale: Plainly Attractive," *Harvard Crimson*, November 22, 1958. See also "Yale Ends 250 Year Celibacy; Coeds to Enter in September," *Columbia Spectator*, March 25, 1958; "Women at Yale," *Yale Daily News*, April 2, 1958; "On the MAT," *Yale Daily News*, March 31, 1958; author's exchange of notes with Wilkinson, March 10–12, 2018. John Wilkinson and Virginia Tansey were married on August 10, 1963, in St. Rose of Lima Church in Short Hills, New Jersey.

27. Griswold's internally created faculty committee had done the same, though in order to increase intellectual requirements for admission and something resembling normality in daily student life. Griswold could have written the *Crimson* article (he likely would have explicitly included "riots" as one manifestation of the effect on undergraduate "health"), though, in reality, he may have been pleased with its contribution to the colloquy. "Did Mass 'Lust' Cause 'Raw Antics?'" *Yale Daily News*, October 11, 1963; Soares, *The Power of Privilege*, 61–70.

28. Brewster was succeeded, albeit briefly, by Hanna Holborn Gray, who had been his provost. She had accepted the presidency of the University of Chicago. Her designation by the Corporation reflected a formal reality and a respectful gesture.

29. Most of Brewster's academic, cultural, and practical experience had been in Boston and at Harvard Law School, as student and teacher. In *The Power of Privilege*, Joseph Soares examined with care Brewster's rhetoric and conduct from the moment he assumed the presidency in 1963 to this pronouncement, quoted above, in the *Yale Alumni Magazine* in 1966 and identified the difference between the rhetoric (including how it has been characterized in retrospect) and the unexceptional reality of admission results, including once Brewster was in complete control of the admission process and personnel after 1966 (66–96, 87). Soares also found Kabaservice's hagiography on Brewster implausible (lacking in factual support) on the matter of admissions and was especially skeptical of the claim, not verified or even verifiable until 2052, made by Inslee Clark, the admissions dean, that an unidentified Yale Corporation member said to him at a Corporation meeting, "These are America's leaders. There are no Jews here. There are no public school graduates here." Daniel Oren was the first author to quote Clark in his 1985 book, based on a 1981 interview. Oren, *Joining the Club*, 272, 398. Given the consequential meaning of the quote, Oren tried but couldn't verify its accuracy or even its existence in any available records, but for reasons not specified, he accepted it and asserted that the Corporation meeting, which included a presumably acquiescent Brewster, took place in 1965, before William Horowitz was elected to the Corporation on June 20, 1965, effective July 1, 1965. However, Kabaservice, who interviewed Clark again in May 1993, has certainty about the date as "spring of 1966." In the room, therefore, when this anti-Semitic (actually anti–about everyone not a White Anglo-Saxon Protestant from a private school) comment was allegedly made were not only the liberals John Lindsay and Reverend Paul Moore (who also, presumably, sat in silence) but the newly elected William Horowitz. *The Guardians*, 260–61, 512. The stretch by both authors to

search for convenient dates and a basis to include the quote is understandable in the case of Kabaservice. He doesn't mention Horowitz anywhere in his book, let alone the long effort by Jews and others to change the admission policy before Brewster or Clark showed up. See also Kabaservice, "The Birth of a New Institution," *Yale Alumni Magazine*, December 1999; Kingman Brewster, "Admission to Yale: Objectives and Myths," *Yale Alumni Magazine*, October 1966.

CHAPTER 25

NEITHER GRISWOLD NOR BREWSTER

First quotation: "Complete Text of Statement by President," *Yale Daily News*, May 8, 1953.

Second quotation: Kingman Brewster, "Admission to Yale: Objectives and Myths," *Yale Alumni Magazine*, October 1966.

1. Herbert Janick, "Yale Blue: Unionization at Yale University, 1931–1985," *Labor History* 28, no. 3 (1987): 355 (quoting from the Seymour Papers, Committee on Labor Relations at Yale University [The Tuttle Report]).

2. Nyman had considerable industrial and university experience with employee health and working conditions. "Our employment relations difficulties," Nyman explained, "stem largely from our past and present lack of reliable management engineering data," which also had had other "unfavorable consequences." Nyman to Griswold (July 26, 1950), Griswold Papers, Box 177, Folder 1617, Yale University Archives. Nyman was primarily an efficiency expert and generally supported the value of labor unions and "humane" relationships with workers in ensuring that end. See Deborah Sue Elkin, "Labor and the Left: The Limits of Acceptable Dissent at Yale University, 1920s to 1960," (PhD diss., Yale University, November 1995), especially chapters 3 and 4.

3. Nyman identified for Griswold what was necessary financially to ensure that employment conditions and relations were consistent with "the best modern standards," including social security payments, heath and life insurance, accident prevention programs, an employee clinic and "free consultations about their health problems," pension plans, wages "to a level more favorable with the rates of local business and better paying eastern universities," improved work room conditions that met "modern standards of illumination, ventilation, working space," introductions to Yale physical plant and mission, athletic and cultural programs (very common in New Haven industry well into the early 1960s), training courses toward higher-paying positions, and the establishment of joint management-employee committees. Nyman to Griswold (July 26, 1950) and attachments, Griswold Papers, Box 177, Folder 1617, Yale University Archives.

4. Nothing happened without his approval or direction. See, for example, Sanford to Griswold (April 7, 1953), Griswold Papers, RU 22, Yale University Archives (personnel). He reiterated Griswold's position: "the Union's demands can't be met." The Corporation also "announced support of President Griswold's stand against Union demands." "Corporation Backs Griswold Statement," *Yale Daily News*, May 11, 1953. Separating himself from Union officials and negotiations was his choice; Griswold certainly didn't separate himself from the public or private responsibility for the treatment of Yale's employees.

5. "Complete Text of Statement by President," *Yale Daily News*, May 8, 1953; see also, "University Employees May Strike," *Yale Daily News*, April 14, 1953; "Negotiations

Set Final Parley before Thursday's Walkout," *Yale Daily News*, May 5, 1953; "Hopes Fade for Early Strike End: Griswold Refuses Union Demand," *Yale Daily News*, May 8, 1953; "Strike Still Far from Settlement," *Yale Daily News*, May 14, 1953 (split in unions; Teamsters deliver to power plant).

6. Gaddis Smith joined the Yale faculty and became, under Brewster, a professor of history, where he remained during Giamatti's presidency. His original, perhaps authentic, views on labor relations at Yale were certainly known to Bart Giamatti before and during his presidency.

7. The university, Smith wrote, had done "everything within its power to keep the wages of its employees in line with the cost of living." The *Daily News* opposed a ten-cents-an-hour raise for all employees; the five-cents-an-hour Yale proposal "shows the University is willing to do all within its power to cooperate." On the Union shop, Smith opposed it: "A Union should obtain and hold its members because of the benefits it offers, not through coercion. Workers deserve the right to seek jobs without having to join a union. This is the University's position and we think it right." In the same context, Smith also supported the use of students to replace striking workers. As the administration has emphasized, Smith concluded in perfect and threatening harmony, "Yale is today battling against tremendous financial odds. . . . Before they suffer a substantial loss in pay [the employees] would be wise to realize this fact and return to work." "University in the Right," *Yale Daily News*, May 8, 1953.

8. On one occasion, the Union sought to clarify its position over a dispute about Yale's use of someone at the power plant who, the Union contended, was a "strike breaker." The Union president submitted to the *Daily News*, "A Letter: The Union Answer." University officials did not have to respond to the Union position. Smith interceded. "We do not ordinarily comment in direct answer to a communication," he wrote, "but the letter above from the president of the Yale employees Union so flagrantly misrepresents the University's position that we feel we must break with precedent." The editorial characterized the merits of the Union's explanation as "laughably foolish." "Strike Still Far from Settlement," *Yale Daily News*, May 14, 1953.

9. Griswold's statement and Smith's narrative were understood to suggest that Yale would offer academic credit to students who replaced the laborers. "Residential college masters imported brooms, mops, and other pertinent appliances"; and maintenance work "for students has already been made compulsory in Berkeley and Silliman colleges." "The Strike: Pro and Con" was published in the *Yale Daily News* on May 9. And the strikers got "occasional good-natured encouragement from students—coffee and cake or even an occasional offer to carry posters." In addition, "Several Law School professors canceled classes or held them at the Jewish Community Center rather than cross the picket lines. Philosophy Professor Paul Weiss plan[ned] to hold his classes in the Board Room of the [*Yale Daily*] *News*." "Union Refuses to Man Hospital's Power Plant," *Yale Daily News*, May 12, 1953; "Varied Student Reaction Attacks Yale, Defends Union," *Yale Daily News*, May 12, 1953; letter to Griswold and Whiteman, Yale Law School dean, from Alexander Hoffmann (a law student) (May 14, 1953), Griswold Papers, RU 22, Box 177, Yale University Archives; "Hopes Fade for Early Strike End; Griswold Refuses Union Demand," *Yale Daily News*, May 8, 1953.

10. Letter, Paul Weiss to Griswold (May 6, 1953), Griswold to Weiss (May 8, 1953), Weiss to Griswold (May 9, 1953), Griswold Papers, RU 22, Yale University Archives (personnel). (Emphasis added.)

11. See, for example, Gladys Lack to Griswold (A. Whitney) (May 8, 1953, May 13, 1953, and May 15, 1953), who also hoped A. Whitney would ensure "every man and woman who works for Yale a decent living wage in decent working conditions"; "Year-End Communications," *Yale Daily News*, May 14, 1953; "Flagrant Misrepresentation" (critical of Griswold's "fantastical advertisement") *Yale Daily News*; and Weiss's comments, already described.

12. In May 1954, the legitimacy of that criticism, albeit only suspected within the Union, was affirmed. A threatened strike was avoided by a modest pay increase, though the university had budgeted substantially more financial resources to pay higher wages than it claimed it could afford. Letter, Buck to Griswold (May 13, 1954), Griswold Papers, RU22, Yale University Archives (personnel, more money budgeted).

13. The Union combated Griswold foremost by using the *Yale Daily News* as a publicity organ: "Facts on Yale's Wage Question," *Yale Daily News*, May 6, 1953. The Union posed the question "Are These Decent, Living Wages?" and challenged Griswold's contention that wages should be "frozen . . . because of an operating deficit in budget" through the use of anecdotal evidence that Yale was spending money on construction improvements and repairs. The Union tried again soon after: "Members of the Yale Community, Let Us Look at the Record," *Yale Daily News*, May 14, 1953. Griswold's position was affirmed by university spokespersons with generalized declarations: "Yale's present operating deficit; and the cutback already made in scholarship funds, 'frozen' faculty salaries, and other 'rigid economies to help meet the deficit.'" A "Union shop . . . would not only be unfair, it would restrict the individual's personal liberties." "Yale Workers Strike Today, To Picket Entire University," *Yale Daily News*, May 7, 1953.

14. The Anglo-Saxon physical expression of power through silence or subtlety of condescension, here also control of the money and, with Smith, comfort with the *Daily News* was met with few overt acts of physical retort by Union members or students. When one departure from civility occurred—really, personal criticisms of Griswold—the Union president apologized to Griswold and he accepted it. See, for example, letter, Ivey to Griswold (October 23, 1953), Griswold to Ivey (October 30, 1951), Griswold Papers, RU 22, Yale University Archives.

15. In 1953, the Union was composed of power plant operators, college guards, general maintenance crews, maids, and janitors. Importantly, during the strike dining hall workers were not members of any union and reported for work. And the Teamsters Union, which controlled delivery of fuel oil to the power plant, declined to support the Federation of University Employees. Fuel was delivered, and the plant operated. It would be more than a decade before the Union, which would change leadership (Vincent Sirabella) and its name (Local 35) and find a new, sophisticated institutional umbrella that valued the preservation and use of historical experience, began to properly organize the numerical gains it had made during Griswold. "Yale Workers Strike Today, To Picket Entire University," *Yale Daily News*, May 7, 1953; "Dining Hall Employees Vote to Join the Union: Negotiations on Contract Set for May 9," *Yale Daily News*, May 11, 1955.

16. "Carpenters Begin Strike in City Area," *New Haven Evening Register*, April 1, 1958; "Union Pickets to Halt Area Construction," *New Haven Evening Register*, April 10, 1958; "Carpenters Await Word on Contract," *New Haven Evening Register*, April 15, 1958; Hogan, *Moments in New Haven Labor History*, 61.

17. Frederick Cowles (Yale 1959), "On Right to Work," *Yale Daily News*, November

8, 1958 (support for Union shop); "The Growing Threat of Unionism," *Yale Daily News*, May 13, 1958 (union power "evokes all too familiar memories of the robber barons of the turn of the century who could also dictate terms to the laboring force").

18. "All future employees" hired by Yale in those job classifications otherwise eligible for union membership would be obligated to pay dues to the union. "Employee Local, University Reach Contract Agreement," and "Working for Yale: Local 35 Watches Members Rights," *Yale Daily News*, May 3, 1962.

19. "Yale Social Scientists Study Uses of Alcohol; Probe Psycho-Physical Effects Group," *Yale Daily News*, October 7, 1953; "Freshman Class Plan to Produce Blackface Show," *Yale Daily News*, October 7, 1953.

20. Janick, "Yale Blue," 349.

21. Statement by Griswold (September 2, 1961), Griswold Papers, RU 22, Yale University Archives (the Stevens New Haven Development Corporation, $4,500,000, mortgages on real estate).

22. Merchants letter (July 24, 1957), and accompanying news article, "Sound Redeveloping—But No 'Railroading,'" *New Haven Evening Register*, July 21, 1957; brochure (undated) to Griswold, Griswold Papers, RU 22 (Series 1), Box 165, Yale University Archives (quote in the text is from the brochure and reiterated in the *Register* article). Small business apprehension intensified: see next endnote). See also "Connecticut Life," (November 4, 1962), 26–27, Griswold Papers, RU 22, Box 167, Yale University Archives (it was in "Connecticut Life," a news insert, that Lee's assertion that his housing destruction and Diaspora in the Oak Street neighborhood was for the poor and the rich was transformed into "The City isn't just for the poor," with reference to the University Towers).

23. The Central Civic Association received a pro forma reply. One of New Haven's oldest, most prominent merchants also filed suit to retain his place downtown. His victory in the Connecticut Supreme Court elevated the choice confronting New Haven—the court's discomfort with the city's taking of land in excellent condition from one private owner to resell it to another private owner for demolition and a new project (the one Yale supported). *Bahr Corporation v. O'Brion, New Haven Redevelopment Agency*, 146 Conn. 237 (1959), objection to the taking of private land for private use (Savitt Jewelry Store, located on Church Street, taken by New Haven for sale to private developer of downtown retail project). The store eventually agreed to a price and was relocated. Many small retail stores simply either closed or moved to the suburbs.

24. One major proponent of urban renewal, a Yale graduate, had come to New Haven from Pittsburgh (in Pittsburgh, the forced Diaspora was largely Italian and African American) and justified the decimation of such neighborhoods as "cancers where communism can grow, or the future of democracy is uncertain." Lee tried a similar theme shortly after that, certainly appreciating that the grander the enemy, the more power he could wield. In the late 1950s and into the 1960s, ACTION found its primary vehicle: Dick Lee and New Haven. Domhoff, "Who Really Ruled Dahl's New Haven?," 32; Domhoff, *Who Really Rules?*, 41, 82–83 (the Pittsburgh experience); "City 'Rebirth' Forecast at Chamber of Commerce Dinner," *New Haven Evening Register*, February 11, 1954 (Arthur Van Buskirk, Yale 1918); "Throngs View Parade, Hear Lee on Green," *New Haven Evening Register*, June 1, 1954 (Communism's threat "must be met with political . . . strength.").

25. Dahl's work, submitted in draft form for Griswold's approval, was faulty factually and conceptually and ultimately harmful in misleading the nation. Dahl paid homage to Lee bordering on adulation and wholly failed to recognize Yale's prominent role, perhaps out of fear of Griswold or of disrupting his stature within the university, perhaps from weak scholarship or simple naïveté. The obvious was all around him. By the late 1950s Yale was, in all its forms and relationships in New Haven and in DC, visibly orchestrating a self-centered major expansion at the expense of neighborhoods and taxpayers. Dahl, *Who Governs?*, 124, 129, 138, 205, 264. In September 1961, Saarinen died. "Eero Saarinen Will Leave Lasting Influence on Yale," *New Haven Journal Courier*, September 1, 1961. An active, vibrant New Haven Chamber of Commerce long predated Dick Lee's arrival (see Rae, *City*, 188; Domhoff, *Who Really Rules?*, 23–25, 44); see, for example, letter, Johnson (chamber president) to Rotival (December 4, 1951), Rotival Papers, Box 37, 38, 39, Yale University Archives. In fact, the chamber actually hired Rotival as a consultant, published its own ten-point program during the Celentano mayoralty, had regular, well-attended meetings and its own office, worked closely with the more industrial-centered business organizations, and, for a period, hired Dick Lee in one of his pre-mayoral vocational iterations. Lee did a lot of things; that he "nearly *invented* a business community" by creating the Citizens Action Commission is not historiography. At best, it's a hollow tribute, though contradicted by fact (including Rae's own in *City*), that merely added to Dahl's misleading contribution to the Lee and Yale mythology. Douglas Rae, "Foreword," in Dahl, *Who Governs?*, vii. The Citizen Action Commission was, from the outset (as already shown) nothing more than a public relations advocacy tool for Lee and Griswold, not a business association (or even composed exclusively of business members or members from New Haven) independent of Lee. And by physical design urban renewal had the exact opposite effect. It both destroyed hundreds of small businesses throughout New Haven and, in its fictional "Quinnipiac Valley Region" orientation, neglected the meaning of their local and especially neighborhood location and purpose.

26. Jacobs, *The Death and Life of Great American Cities*; Edward Logue, "Urban Ruin—or Urban Renewal? The Time for Decision Is Now, if We Are to Save Our Blighted Cities from Themselves," *New York Times*, November 9, 1958.

27. Zipp and Storring, *Vital Little Plans*, 278 footnote, and see Kanigel, *Eyes on the Street*, 166–67, 210–11.

28. Ironically, the trust found its initial impetus from the librarian of the Yale School of Art and Architecture, John D. Hoag. Secure, persistent, and knowledgeable, he was able to identify with documentary history, buildings on and off the Yale campus that Griswold could not destroy without an informed fight.

29. Peggy Flint, *New Haven Preservation Trust: A Ten Years War, 1962–1972* (New Haven, CT: New Haven Preservation Trust, 1972).

CHAPTER 26

THE PURPOSEFUL MAN

1. "Toni M. Smith Engaged to Wed Senior at Yale, Student at Columbia Will Be Married to A. Bartlett Giamatti," *New York Times*, September 26, 1959. The Aurelian Society required the fifteen juniors selected by Bart and his classmates to be in attendance. A spirited evening followed, filled with one last debate and discussion of why

Aurelius—whose bust stood in one corner of the room—was worthy of such attention and admiration. Bart introduced the guest speaker and a thirty-minute piano recital of Chopin's works. The Chopin recital was by Robert Browne (Yale 1956); the guest speaker, Sterling Professor of Philosophy Brand Blanshard. "15 Members Initiated at 50th Anniversary of American [sic] Society," Yale Daily News, May 18, 1960.

2. Yale Class Book (1960), 347–48; "Class Day, Steam and Corinthians," Yale Daily News, June 13, 1960.

3. Yale Class Book (1960), 347–48; "Class Day, Steam and Corinthians," Yale Daily News.

4. Yale Class Book (1960), 350; "Renewal Program Basis for Success of Lee's 10 years," Yale Daily News, November 5, 1963 (faculty).

5. The poem was published in the yearbook in English. "252nd Commencement Held," Yale Daily News, June 8, 1953.

6. Yale University yearbook (1960), 253.

7. "Morse, Ezra Stiles to Be College Names, Pollard, Sewall Appointed New Masters," Yale Daily News, April 7, 1959; Samuel F. B. Morse, Foreign Conspiracy against the Liberties of the United States (New York: Leavitt, Lord, 1835); Samuel I. Prime, Life of Samuel F. B. Morse (New York: D. Appleton, 1875); Antony Dugdale, J. J. Fueser, and J. Celso de Castro Alves, Yale, Slavery and Abolition (New Haven, CT: Amistad Committee, 2001), 25 (Morse). Morse ran for mayor of New York City on the "Nativist" ticket— anti-Catholic, anti-immigrant, and pro-slavery. Slavery, he later wrote, was "carried out according to Divine direction," and, he argued forcefully during the Civil War that it should be preserved.

8. See, for example, in the Yale Daily News, "A Postscript on Faubus," September 27, 1957; "Integration Inevitable," September 25, 1958; "More Bayonets in Dixie," September 30, 1957; "Pro-South," October 2, 1957; "King Accepts Speaking Invitation to Lecture on Integration Issue," December 9, 1958.

9. In 2008, an effort was made to explain the decisions in 1959, including that the Morse family lived in New Haven and Yale needed its money. During Griswold's tenure, beginning long before 1959, Yale built twenty-six new projects, including the two new colleges (and the purchase price of the land). Contrary to the assertion made by Professor Gaddis Smith, Griswold also, albeit reluctantly, accepted federal money to the extent of 20 percent of the university's budget. Kelley, Yale, 439. Raising "money" from the Morse family was not an imperative or, it appears, the subject of discussion in 1959. And, as is clear from the very public context concerning immigrants, race, and Catholicism within which the names were selected that the "inflammatory aspects of Morse's personality" (by which the writer of the 2008 article must have meant Morse's political views as candidate and public advocate, not his stogie disposition) were not merely "overlooked." They just were not important to those making the decision, or, as Professor Gaddis Smith put it, the decision was indeed "a reasonable choice." "Morse, Stiles Beat Out Taft and Webster," Yale Daily News, April 1, 2008.

10. "Martin Luther King Will Arrive Today; To Speak in Woolsey," Yale Daily News, January 14, 1959; "King Appeals for Passive Resistance to Promote Good of Full Integration," Yale Daily News, January 15, 1959.

11. See Scully, Yale in New Haven, 309–11 (Scully on the two colleges); Donald Albrecht and Eeva-Liisa Pelkonen, eds., Eero Saarinen: Shaping the Future (New Haven, CT:

Yale University Press, 2010), 243–45; Dugdale et al., *Yale, Slavery and Abolition*, 7 (Stiles), 25 (Morse); "Morse, Stiles Beat Out Taft and Webster," *Yale Daily News*; "Yale Lets Contract for New Colleges," *New Haven Journal Courier*, June 24, 1960.

12. Griswold authored five books on foreign and domestic affairs and on education. His speeches often included references to foreign affairs and international policy. The five books were *The Far Eastern Policy of the United States* (New York: Harcourt, Brace, 1938); *Farming and Democracy* (New York: Harcourt, Brace, 1948); *Essays on Education* (New Haven, CT: Yale University Press, 1954); *In the University Tradition* (New Haven, CT: Yale University Press, 1957); and *Liberal Education and the Democratic Ideal* (New Haven, CT: Yale University Press, 1959). And see Karabel, *The Chosen*, 222 (biographical description of Griswold).

13. See Kelley, *Yale*, 433–35 (Griswold on liberal education and freedom of expression; and, at Yale's 250th commencement, Griswold honored Edward C. Tolman, who had refused to take a loyalty oath in California).

14. Griswold Papers, RU 22, Yale University Archives; "Yale Address," *Hartford Courant*, June 27, 1959.

15. Inaugural Address (1951), Griswold Papers, RU 22, Yale University Archives; "252nd Commencement Held," *Yale Daily News*, June 8, 1953 (The Chittenden Prize for the "highest rank in scholarship" in the Class of 1953 was achieved by Guido Calabresi); Griswold's declaration of Rights and Responsibilities was understood by the *Yale Daily News* to mean "once and for all, that a Communist, by his very nature, is unfit for any post on a university faculty." "Problems in Focus," *Yale Daily News*, June 6, 1953; "Senator McCarthy on Good Track," *Yale Daily News*, October 21, 1953.

16. "Yale Makes Cole Porter Doctor of Humane Letters at Special Ceremony," "2000 Students—900 Seniors Receive Diplomas Amidst Rain, Speeches, Prizes, Black Robes," *Yale Daily News*, June 13, 1960.

17. "Yale Makes Cole Porter Doctor of Humane Letters at Special Ceremony," "2000 Students—900 Seniors Receive Diplomas Amidst Rain, Speeches, Prizes, Black Robes," *Yale Daily News*. In 1985, Giamatti awarded an honorary degree to "Smoky Joe" Wood (former Yale baseball coach), who had pitched for the Boston Red Sox, at a brief ceremony in Wood's home. John Wilkinson also was present.

18. *Yale University Bulletin, Graduate School, 1961–1962*, 89–90; *Yale University Bulletin, Graduate School, 1963–1964*, 18. Giamatti wrote in his yearbook profile that he might attend Harvard. Harvard has no record of his application.

CHAPTER 27
REFINEMENT, EXPANSION, AND PERSPECTIVE

The epigraph is from A. Bartlett Giamatti, *The Earthly Paradise and the Renaissance Epic* (Princeton, NJ: Princeton University Press, 1966).

1. "A. Bartlett Giamatti Marries Toni Smith," *New York Times*, June 19, 1960; correspondence with David Ewing; author's view of the wedding-party photograph.

2. Day Prospect Hill School was the product of a merger of two prominent private girls schools, Day and Prospect Hill, in 1960, just prior to the Giamattis' return to New Haven. Aspects of the merger are discussed on the Hopkins Grammar website (and its merger with Day Prospect Hill). Day Prospect Hill graduates still retain their distinct identity through Facebook.

3. Few milestones in the history of Middlebury's Language School were as important to its mission as the decision made after the end of World War II to establish a presence abroad. The Language School had done so in France, Spain, and Germany. Its director looked to Val and Peggy Giamatti to ensure the credible establishment of Middlebury's graduate school in Florence, Italy. The appointment was effective from the fall of 1961 to June 1962. Elria already was in Florence studying Italian. Peggy and Val's knowledge of Middlebury's expectations, Florence, and their existing friendships and credibility in Italy's academic and cultural community made them an obvious and valuable choice. The entire venture—students, travel, hospitality, mentoring, and their awareness of Italy's history and politics—created a special opportunity for the pursuit of scholarship in expanding Val's Dante collection and their collective and increasingly sophisticated interest in Etruscan artifacts. Thirteen American students enrolled in the Middlebury program at the University of Florence, where Val had received his second doctorate degree. "Actually, I was planning to take a Sabbatical leave anyway," the *Holyoke Telegram* reporter quoted Val as saying. His intent was "to bring himself up to date on all facets of Italian culture. When the chance to direct the Middlebury School turned up, he accepted it." Val also delved deeper into Dante's *Divine Comedy*, as he and Italian scholars explored "its interpretation in the light of modern dynamic psychology," a new field of interest to him and others, yet another vehicle for his teaching and public speaking. Middlebury laid out the Giamattis' duties: help students define their program, aid in their study, oversee their final examinations, and, for Val, determine their grades and write personal development reports. The most important of his duties, however, was to ensure that students met outstanding writers and artists in Italy, an obligation he welcomed. Florence would be the base for the widely anticipated seven hundredth anniversary of Dante's *Divine Comedy*, still being planned, including in Ravenna and Verona. As a renowned scholar and teacher, Val would be involved in that as well. "Post in Italy for Professor, On Sabbatical," *Holyoke Telegram*, November 28, 1960; "Bound for Italy," *Holyoke Telegram*, September 20, 1960. This family experience, and the earlier ones at Middlebury, later resonated for their son when, in the early 1970s, the director of Middlebury's equally famed Bread Loaf English Summer Program reached out to the highly prized professor of English at Yale, A. Bartlett Giamatti, to join the summer program faculty.

Val and Peggy had created a schedule that ensured enough time for Val to give two lectures on Dante—one in Florence, the other in Rome—and for themselves to explore Spain, Greece, and France in pursuit of Dante, Etrusca, and moments of relaxed joy with each other. "Bound for Italy," *Holyoke Telegram*, September 20, 1961; Frank Merrick, "Mt. Holyoke's Prof. Giamatti Home after Year-Long Sojourn in Italy," *Holyoke Telegram*, August 23, 1962. Consistent with Italian law, they were able to bring out of the country "several Etruscan artifacts which date from 2300 B.C." and a known forgery of a fourteenth-century triptych (three-paneled picture) to study as part of Val's growing interest in recognizing differences in artifacts. He was occasionally asked to provide guidance on the legitimacy of area and national museum collections and possible purchases. Merrick, "Mt. Holyoke's Prof. Giamatti Home after Year-Long Sojourn in Italy"; Jenette Weatherhead, *Mount Holyoke* (January 1961) in Giamatti Papers, Mount Holyoke Archives (Val's lecture in Florence); *Cronache Culturali, Il Pianeta Terra* (United States Information Agency Program Booklet, 1962) in Giamatti Papers, Mount Holyoke Archives (Val's lecture). "Giamatti Visit [to New Haven]," *Holyoke Telegram*, August 11, 1960.

4. University Towers brochure (May 21, 1959), Griswold Papers, RU 22, Box 167, Yale University Archives; "Discussion of the Relocation Process" (September 19, 1962), Griswold Papers, RU 22, Box 166, Yale University Archives.

5. "Lee Likely Winner in Re-Election Bid," *New Haven Journal Courier*, November 7, 1961; "Mayor's Vote Lowest Since First Election, Setback May Hurt Senate Aspirations," *New Haven Journal Courier*, November 8, 1961; "Lee Wins Re-election by 4,000 Votes; Townshend Sees GOP Victory in 1963," *New Haven Journal Courier*, November 8, 1961; "May Says Lee Experienced a Spectacular Fall," *New Haven Journal Courier*, November 8, 1961.

6. Townshend had personal knowledge through family heritage of the original 1910 City Plan. He and his wife, Doris, were ardent preservationists; Townshend sought to stop redevelopment for an in-depth survey of its purpose and effects.

7. Political power and a means of insisting on it, lessons learned from the local as well as national experience of others, was massing in skill and numbers on Yale's flank. Lee proposed affordable housing in the Newhallville neighborhood and housing rehabilitation in the Dixwell neighborhood. "New Project Planned Here, Lee Declares, Negotiations Under Way for 200 Units in Dixwell Area," *New Haven Evening Register*, October 26, 1961; "Townshend Bids That Mayor Lee Make Promise to Serve Term," *New Haven Evening Register*, October 22, 1961.

8. "Townshend Reveals New Renewal Plan, Bush Joins Criticism of Delays in Midtown Work," *New Haven Evening Register*, October 20, 1961; "Lee Assails Bush's Stand, Says Senator Contradicts Past Praise of City Redevelopment," *New Haven Evening Register*, October 20, 1961; "CORE Pickets Stage March at City Hall," *New Haven Evening Register*, October 9, 1961; "One Sign Read: 'No University Towers on Dixwell,'" *New Haven Evening Register*, October 17, 1961; "Optimistic Picture Presented on City Redevelopment Program, Yale Intention Is Lauded," *New Haven Evening Register*, October 17, 1961.

9. "Lee to Give Major Talk at Parade," *New Haven Journal Courier*, September 4, 1961. See also "Lee, Barbieri Rally Party for Election," *New Haven Journal Courier*, September 15, 1961; "Lee Raps Townshend on Assessment Issue," *New Haven Journal Courier*, September 21, 1961; "Townshend Hits Smear by Lee," *New Haven Journal Courier*, September 22, 1961; "Top Democrats Urge Push for New Voters," *New Haven Journal Courier*, October 6, 1961; "Townshend Charges Administration with Destroying Business Climate," *New Haven Journal Courier*, October 11, 1961; "Candidates Clash over Renewal as Campaign Nears Final Hours," *New Haven Journal Courier*, November 6, 1961; "Negroes Hail Gains in Election, Look to Further Advances by '63," *New Haven Journal Courier*, November 9, 1961. On Bart Guida, see "Guida to Oppose Geeland for Finance Board Post," *New Haven Evening Register*, December 28, 1954 ("Guida outspoken. . . ."). Those harmed by redevelopment, largely Italian and Jewish voters, led the change, though the *Journal Courier* noted that the defections were more widespread. They could take comfort, nonetheless, in disrobing Lee's pretense and thwarting his ambition. Lee's margin of victory came primarily from the Dixwell Avenue neighborhood wards, where African Americans turned out to ensure the victory of local aspirants, not merely Lee. "Lee Disappointed in Plurality," *New Haven Journal Courier*, November 8, 1961.

10. In the praise repeated in Battell Chapel and in Griswold's burial in the Grove Street Cemetery was the way Yale paid tribute to its presidents. The *New Haven Evening*

Register covered his death respectfully. Also see "President Griswold Is Dead," *Yale Daily News*, April 19, 1963, extra edition; "Griswold Dead at 56," *Harvard Crimson*, April 20, 1963; "Services for President Griswold in Battell Chapel This Afternoon," *Yale Daily News*, April 27, 1963.

11. Interview with Calabresi; Giamatti's deeply held belief about intellectual responsibility; and see Epilogue.

12. "President Griswold Is Dead," *Yale Daily News*; "Griswold Dead at 56," *Harvard Crimson*; "Services for President Griswold in Battell Chapel This Afternoon," *Yale Daily News*; "Griswold Points Out Goal of Liberal Arts in Hartford Address," *Yale Daily News*, December 17, 1956.

13. In 1970, during the Black Panther trials held in New Haven's state courthouse, there was some semblance of social purpose demonstrated by students; nowhere near the risk to citizens or property (most local citizens, including in the African American community, stayed away, and local retail establishments boarded their windows, by then a generally accepted practice learned not from student demonstrations but from urban riots); and far more methodical and knowledgeable use of the presence of force by Yale and the local and state government (well learned from decades of local and national experience, including in Washington, DC). See Neil Proto, *To a High Court: The Tumult and Choices That Led to United States of America v. SCRAP* (Lanham, MD: Rowman and Littlefield, 2006), 1–22 (and sources cited therein), and see www.ToAHighCourt.com (photojournal). The Yale student body was comparatively cooperative (roaming outside the campus or the New Haven Green was constrained, and the large number of demonstrators and violent confrontation projected rhetorically, with the exception of a single, confined incidence of tear gas use near the courthouse), if not borderline docile in attitude, not about the legal and cultural issues but about conduct. Within the courtroom, virtually every request for the admission of evidence by both sides was granted by the judge, and, at the end of the trial, neither side complained about unfairness in the trial or sought to appeal formally any rulings or, following a hung jury, the judge's admonition and final ruling that no new jury was going to be empanelled. The case was over. In an otherwise thorough presentation of facts and use of interviews, and by ignoring their own facts, Yale professor Doug Rae and Yale graduate Paul Bass concluded that because Judge Harold Mulvey believed, among his other reasons, that the enormous publicity surrounding the trial would make it difficult to find new jurors who hadn't formed views in support of innocence or guilt or made a determination about some aspect of the evidence or some factor unrelated to the evidence, the defendants hadn't received a fair trial. Douglas Rae and Paul Bass, *Murder in the Model City*, chapter 22, "Days of Decision" (the oddly strained effort to lend credence to Kingman Brewster's claim about injustice in the trial when Rae and Bass had demonstrated the exact opposite: the defendants, including Bobby Seale, received a fair trial in New Haven, and Judge Mulvey ensured it. Whatever his claim meant elsewhere—Chicago, for instance—in New Haven, Brewster was wrong.) See also Sam Roberts, "Michael Koskoff, Litigator Who Aided Black Panthers and Gun Victims, Dies at 77," *New York Times*, April 28, 2019 ("My father and I set out to prove that a black radical could receive a fair trial," he said, "and we did.").

14. Peter Axthelm and Paul Steiger, "Police Wielding Nightsticks Subdue 1,500 Rioting Students," *Yale Daily News*, May 10, 1963; Phil Coombs, "Arrested Students

to Face Court This Friday," *Yale Daily News*, May 13, 1963; "Yale Faces Aftermath of Thursday's Riot," *Yale Daily News*, May 13, 1963 (photograph with caption, "Students Lift, Carry Car"); "Riot Sweeps Princeton; State Police Called as 1,400 Storm Town," *Yale Daily News*, May 8, 1963. Princeton students had burned benches, unsettled trash cans, overturned a Volkswagen, and interrupted rail service. Fourteen students were arrested. See also "Did Mass 'Lust' Cause 'Raw Antics?'" *Yale Daily News*, October 11, 1963.

15. Axthelm and Steiger, "Police Wielding Nightsticks Subdue 1,500 Rioting Students."

16. "Communications," *Yale Daily News*, May 14, 1963; "Yale Faces Aftermath of Thursday's Riot," *Yale Daily News*; Phil Coombs, "Yale Students to Face Court This Friday," *Yale Daily News*, May 13, 1963; "Arrested Students Face Trial Today," *Yale Daily News*, May 29, 1963.

17. "Yale Presidency to Be Studied by Corporation," *Yale Daily News*, May 13, 1963; "Snooping Around," *Yale Daily News*, September 20, 1963 (the delay in Brewster's appointment). Coffin had been the chaplain at Andover, but he arrived after Giamatti graduated.

18. "An Isolated Riot?," *Yale Daily News*, May 14, 1963.

19. "Yale Student Arrested in Dixwell Housing Riot," *Yale Daily News*, November 5, 1963.

20. "CORE Pickets Stage March at City Hall," *New Haven Evening Register*, November 9, 1961.

21. Wallis Finger, "From the 'Bland Leading the Bland' to the Mississippi Freedom Vote: William Sloane Coffin Jr. and the Civil Rights Movement, at Yale University, 1958–1963," *MSSA Kaplan Prize for Yale History* 4, 2004 (Coffin's recollection of his conversation with Giamatti).

22. Coffin, before entering the Yale Divinity School and joining the clergy, had a ruptured family life and troubled experiences involving himself and others who died at his directive while at the Central Intelligence Agency. "Coffin Heads Student Group in Africa," *Yale Daily News*, September 20, 1960; "Coffin to Speak on Civil Rights Activities, Conservatives Charge," *Yale Daily News*, November 27, 1961; "Chaplain Political?," *Yale Daily News*, October 30, 1961. Coffin began his career at Yale by supporting the participation of Yale students and others in housing and community building efforts in Africa, in important respects his own form of the Peace Corps.

23. Raymond Arsenault, *Freedom Riders: 1961 and the Struggle for Racial Justice* (New York: Oxford University Press, 2006), 269–76. The others who left New Haven that day included professors Gaylord Noyce of Yale, David Swift and John Maguire of Wesleyan University, and George Smith, an African American Yale law student. Clyde Carter and Charles Jones, both African American students from Johnson C. Smith University in Charlotte, North Carolina, joined them en route.

24. Members of the Yale Law School faculty challenged arrests and previously accepted interpretations of the law, once largely the daily battle of only the NAACP's legal defense effort; faculty from other schools, particularly Howard University; and private practitioners and jurists mostly in the South. "A Summer of Civil Rights," *Yale Daily News*, September 25, 1963 (arrest in Baltimore). Also arrested with Coffin and Wilkinson were Coffin's wife, Eva Rubinstein, Yale Professor Richard Sewall and his son, David Sewall, and historian Jesse Lemisch. "Coffin, Pollak Crusade for Negroes in Alabama," *Yale Daily News*, May 9, 1963; "Coffin, Pollak Cite National Hypocrisy,"

May 13, 1963; "Students Right to Visit Cuba Defended by Yale Law Faculty," *Yale Daily News*, September 20, 1963; Wilkinson to author (April 5, 2015).

25. "Mayor's Statement (telegram to Wallace)," *Yale Daily News*, September 20, 1963.

26. "Political Union Withdraws Speaking Invitation to Alabama Segregationist Governor Wallace at Request of Provost Kingman Brewster," *Yale Daily News*, September 20, 1963.

27. "Political Union Withdraws Speaking Invitation to Alabama Segregationist Governor Wallace at Request of Kingman Provost Brewster," *Yale Daily News*, September 20, 1963; "Yale Issues Official Release," *Yale Daily News*, September 27, 1963 (Brewster affirmed that "he asked the officers of the Political Union to consider rescinding their invitation.").

28. Subsequent interviews along Dixwell Avenue affirmed that view; "many of them were insulted by the thought of physical disruption" stating, "there would be no violence." "Interviewed on Wallace Issue," *Yale Daily News*, September 27, 1963.

29. The students were convinced the motivation to preclude Wallace from speaking was Lee's fear that Paige would take African American votes in the mayoral election. Victor Chen, "Students Picket City Hall," *Yale Daily News*, September 25, 1963.

30. Harvard and Radcliffe's Young Democrats extended an invitation, which Wallace accepted. So, too, did the University of Pennsylvania, where Wallace was scheduled to speak on November 6. Princeton had invited Mississippi Governor Ross Barnett; Brown instituted a Civil Rights Series and invited Wallace followed by James Farmer, national director of the Congress of Racial Equality; and Harvard affirmed its commitment to free speech. "The Great Tradition," *Yale Daily News*, September 27, 1963. No matter how Brewster's conduct was characterized, the chilling effect on the exercise of the First Amendment was a precedent of ambivalence that he retained. To the credit of the law school and others, once again in defiance of Brewster's ambivalence, Wallace was reinvited, but he declined. "Bulletin," *Yale Daily News*, October 1, 1963. The Yale radio station, with the aid of precisely the local African American political and legal representatives Brewster feared, and Professor Louis Pollak of the law school, collectively interviewed Wallace while he was in Cambridge. And see notes below.

31. "Wallace Harvard Speech Aired Today by WYBC," *Yale Daily News*, November 4, 1963 (involvement of Professor Pollak; Douglas Schraeder, Yale Law School student; Earl Williams, lawyer and vice president of the New Haven Chapter of the NAACP; and the Reverend Edmund Edwards, a civil rights leader and clergyman); "Wallace Attacks Court as Political, Incompetent," *Yale Daily News*, November 5, 1963 (speech for Harvard and Radcliffe Young Democrats).

32. In *The Guardians*, Kabaservice is, ultimately, seeking to undermine the 1974 C. Vann Woodward Report, which was critical of Brewster's failure to give preeminent meaning to the First Amendment, beginning with the Wallace affair. In doing so, Kabaservice incorrectly dated the Montgomery explosion and murder, the scheduled Wallace speech, Brewster's request to the Political Union to rescind it, and the date of the mayoral election (*The Guardians*, 178). He relied on Tom Cavanagh, "George Wallace in '63: Disinvited or Postponed?," *Yale Daily News*, February 5, 1975, written from twelve-year-old recollections, as the basis for his attempted effort to discredit the Woodward Committee Report. The report was flawed because, Cavanagh wrote, the committee had relied only on the *Yale Daily News* reportage for its facts and, despite the committee's composition of historians and lawyers, its factual research was "superficial." In fact, as the

report stated at the outset, the committee (1) "reviewed the record of the past decade"; (2) "sought . . . the opinions of all members of the University community who wished to make their views known"; (3) issued "repeated invitations in the press [which] brought in numerous written statements"; and (4) "held advertised public hearings and recorded hours of testimony and advice." See also the subsequent refutation of the Cavanagh assertions in the *Daily News*. Paul A. Rahe Jr., "O Tempora, O Mores," *Yale Daily News*, April 3, 1975; Tom Spahn, "Letter to the News," *Yale Daily News*, February 17, 1975 (Brewster's public affirmation of his original request to "rescind" the invitation). Moreover, the Political Union's internal minutes state that Brewster's request was understood as a request for "rescission." Also, Brewster was informed fully of the Woodward Committee Report's *proposed* content and sought to have a member, lawyer Lloyd Cutler, modify the report to deflect blame. Foremost, no matter how characterized, Brewster's conduct was in intent and effect to chill the exercise of the First Amendment; whether he sought to rescind the invitation or have it rescinded for November 4 (unchallenged by anyone) doesn't save it from First Amendment scrutiny or criticism, especially in an academic setting. Brewster's underlying purpose, as confirmed by Cavanagh's article, was to satisfy Dick Lee's fear and direct or implicit threat to withhold police protection. To elevate the alleged legitimacy of that fear of uncontrollable African American violence, Kabaservice cites a *New Haven Evening Register* article (*The Guardians*, 178, 501n169) that he contends included a threat from the local NAACP chapter that inviting Wallace was like "having Eichmann or Goering parade before a gauntlet of survivors." Neither the article cited ("Aid Says Wallace Considering News Parley Instead of Speech," *New Haven Evening Register*, October 1, 1963) nor an earlier one that immediately followed the cancellation ("Wallace 'Officially Unwelcome' Here," *New Haven Evening Register*, September 20, 1963) contains any closely comparable language. In fact, in the September 20, 1963, article, no one took the position that Wallace should not come to Yale. The Reverend Edwards, pastor of the Dixwell Avenue Congregational Church, said, "It would be unpleasant and it should be. But I would like to see him come. It would be a chance for us to say to him what we really feel. . . . Our forces of law and order would be equal to such a task as protecting the right of an individual to speak. If they couldn't, it would be the same thing Wallace is guilty of in Alabama." Letter, Brewster to Jones (December 23, 1969), cited by Kabaservice in the same paragraph in the text (*The Guardians*, 178, 501n168), also does not include the quoted language. Kingman Brewster Jr. Papers, Box 124, Folder 15 (January 1969), Yale University Archives.

33. Economics Professor (now emeritus) William Brainard (MA 1959, PhD 1963) was Giamatti's provost for the last five years of Giamatti's presidency. Brainard returned to teaching and research when Giamatti left the presidency, and remained a close friend and confidant until Bart's death. Giamatti paid special tribute to his friendship and professional relationship with Brainard by dedicating to him *A Free and Ordered Space: The Real World of the University* (New York: W. W. Norton, 1988). Informal interview with Brainard.

CHAPTER 28
FATE

1. The website of the National Institutes of Health defines CMT as "one of the most common inherited neurological disorders, affecting approximately 1 in 2,500 people in

the United States. The disease is named for the three physicians who first identified it in 1888—Jean-Martin Charcot and Pierre Marie in Paris, France, and Howard Tooth in Cambridge, England. CMT . . . comprises a group of disorders that affects the peripheral nerves. The peripheral nerves lie outside the brain and spinal cord and supply the muscles and sensory organs in the limbs."

2. Elria (Elena Maria) married David Parry Ewing, who had been a friend of the Giamattis since childhood. The wedding was held on August 3, 1963. David had just graduated from Yale (Class of 1963) and accepted a teaching position in Sierra Leone, where Elria, a recent graduate of Columbia University, also planned to teach English. Toni ("Mrs. A. Bartlett Giamatti") was the matron of honor. In a simple ceremony, Bart and his brother, Dino, served as ushers. A series of events before and after the ceremony were held at the home of Mrs. Graham Mazeine, the mother of Bart's friend Bill. Mrs. Mazeine also offered the use of their guest bedroom for Elria's friends who needed a place to stay. "As luck would have it," Bill Mazeine recalled fondly, "two Wells graduates who were attending the wedding stayed at our house. . . . Marcia was one, and we have been married for 53 years." Note from Bill Mazeine to the author; "David Ewing Weds Elena M. Giamatti," *New York Times*, August 3, 1963; "Miss Giamatti Names Wedding Attendants," *Holyoke Telegram*, August 2, 1963; "David Ewing Weds Elena M. Giamatti," *Holyoke Telegram*, August 3, 1963.

3. Dino Giamatti's Atlantic House Hotel in Scarborough, Maine, is depicted in Valerio, *Bart*, 18; see also "American Legion Baseball: Libby-Mitchell Announces Awards," *Keep Me Current, News from Where You Live.com* (Falmouth, Maine), August 25, 2012. ("Dino Giamatti was a longtime Scarborough businessman who ran the Atlantic Hotel at Kirkwood Road for two decades. The brother of the late MLB Commissioner, A. Bartlett Giamatti, Dino has been a generous supporter of legion baseball and Scarborough youth sports for more than 25 years.") Although he had a second heart attack, Val remained chair of his department and continued teaching. In 1964 and 1965, Val and Peggy returned to Italy for the 700th Dante Anniversary. "Mr. Giamatti was one of 600 Dante Scholars from 25 different countries and six continents attending the Dante celebration in Italy." They visited "Verona where Dante was in exile and Ravenna where Dante died." He added to his collection "a Salvador Dali; a Rauschenberg, of which there are only 250 copies in existence; an edition illustrated by 50 contemporary Italian artists; a collection of medieval miniatures published by the Italian state department and a Botticelli edition." He had received a "rare Armenian edition" from a Mount Holyoke student, Sally M. Renjilian, in 1959. "Mount Holyoke's Dante Scholar Plans Program," *Springfield Daily News*, December 7, 1968. A precious gap also had been filled by a former student: an Arabic edition was found in a bookstore in Cairo. "Gap Filled," *Holyoke Telegram*, May 21, 1964 (Miss Jeanette Pond, Class of 1935); "A Rare Edition," *Holyoke Telegram* (1959) (Miss Renjilian was aided by her fiancé, 1st Lt. Cleveland Peeke). "In 1966, shortly after floods destroyed many of the building and art treasures of Florence, he ran an art auction to raise money for disaster relief and the restoration of many of the art treasures. He donated many of his own pieces to this effort." See "Valentine Giamatti, 71; Scholar, Mount Holyoke Professor Emeritus," *Boston Globe*, March 21, 1982. "Thirteen foreign students will recite the immortal words of Dante's "Divine Comedy' next week in Mount Holyoke College's new multi-language dormitory." Students were from China, Japan, Sweden, Finland, Norway, Mexico, Denmark, England, Germany, France, Netherlands, and Italy. "Mount Holyoke's

Dante Scholar Plans Program," *Springfield Daily News*. Collection "exhibited at Trinity College, Wilbraham Academy, Middlebury College and Mount Holyoke," next at Smith and Amherst. See also Joan Lauritzen Miano, "A Visit with Mr. Giamatti, Dante and the Etruscans," *Mount Holyoke Alumnae Quarterly* (Spring 1963). The depth of Val's physical limitation was readily apparent within the Giamatti family and, in part, outside of it. Bart's close friends, Bill, Andy, and Frank, came to learn about its fuller meaning through the alteration in the family's living patterns and over time.

4. Giamatti, *Play of Double Senses*, quoted with purpose in Valerio, *Bart*, 17.

5. In *Collision at Home Plate*, James Reston contends that the effects of Charcot may have emerged during Bart Giamatti's time at Princeton, in 1964 or 1965. Giamatti's severe ankle injury in adolescence was more likely the cause of his reservation about engaging in activities that might reinjure it. Similar symptoms of gout, which he complained about later in life, also may have been in play. His normal agility seemed largely undiminished during his time at Yale, even through his first few years as Yale's president and, even then, the constraint on his walking was only marginally noticeable to good friends and not until, under the demands of travel and fundraising, he put on weight.

6. "After some reflection," he told Cynthia Mann, "he supposed his choice of scholarship in English and Italian literature was 'some sort of ethnic confluence.'" Cynthia Mann, "Insight," *Holyoke Telegram* (1985), excerpt in Valerio, *Bart: A Life*, 13.

7. Chaucer was Controller of Customs and Justice of Peace, and Clerk of the King's Works during the period he wrote *The Canterbury Tales*; that is, he had a position in government and knew something of politics and civic duty.

8. See, generally, Edmund Spenser, *Spenser's The Faerie Queene, Book I*, ed. George Armstrong Wauchope (London: Macmillan, 1903; Project Gutenberg ed., 2005). Spenser's pre– and post–*Faerie Queene* works reflected how he thought about Renaissance writers: *The Shephearde's Calendar* (1579), written as dialogue; *Amoretti* (1595) and *Epithalamion* (1595) written as poetry about his love, courtship, and marriage to his second wife, Elizabeth Boyle. Spenser also wrote *A Veue of the Present State of Ireland* (1596), which prescribed a harsh program for the reform of Ireland into an English-speaking colony by eradicating about every thread in its culture and livelihood. Whether through prudence or preoccupation with other matters, *A Veue of the Present State of Ireland* was not published or widely known until after Spenser's death.

9. Raleigh was spelled "Ralegh" in Spenser's era, a spelling Giamatti used in later writing.

10. Within a few years, Raleigh, having secretly married one of Elizabeth's ladies in waiting, was jailed for precisely that reason and was decidedly out of favor. Prior to that sobering event, Raleigh had brought *The Faerie Queene* to Elizabeth's attention. When Elizabeth's treasurer objected to the large amount she sought to bestow on Spenser, she replied: "Then give him what is reason." When even that amount didn't arrive, Spenser wrote the Queen directly, in the manner of the day: "I was promis'd on a time, To have a reason for my rhyme: From that time unto this season, I receiv'd nor rhyme nor reason."

11. The fullness of Giamatti's description is "The epic alone had the size and scope to encompass what poets felt about life. . . . The great epics of the Renaissance are tales of journeys, crusades, wandering, pilgrimages, explorations—all leave-takings in search of a home, or something permanent, final, and fixed. Whether paladins left their sword king and pursued elusive feminine beauty (to their disgrace, madness, or death); or sailors left

Portugal to find India; or crusaders left Europe to recapture Jerusalem; or knights left the Queen's court in search of honor and glory; the search was out across the world and the mind to find tranquility, Truth or heroic glory." *The Earthly Paradise*, 123–24; Giamatti described the English and Renaissance poets that influenced Spenser's work. *The Faerie Queene* "was written by a poet who was, like so many of the Renaissance men of letters, first a public official, whose interests were far broader than his scholarship. . . . He was not finicky about where his material came from, any more than Shakespeare was. . . . [Spenser] used everything he touched, and he changed everything he used." *The Earthly Paradise*, 232–90, especially 235–37.

12. Virgil, *The Aeneid*, trans. Robert Fagles, 177.

13. Giamatti, *The Earthly Paradise and the Renaissance Epic*, 124; Valerio, *Bart*, 6 (quoting from Kevin Paul Dupont, "Giamatti, A Simple Lover of Baseball," who also quotes from the *Hartford Courant*).

14. Giamatti, *The Earthly Paradise*, 3–4.

15. Giamatti, *The Earthly Paradise*, 123, 283.

16. Giamatti, *The Earthly Paradise*, 95–96, 98 (the journey away and to God), 102, 114 ("and with me everlastingly shall be a citizen of that Rome whereof Christ is a Roman"), 116, 151, 183 (duty), 184 (the City).

17. Bergin was a mentor to Bart and the product of the same Hillhouse High School culture as his father. Bergin's scholarly contributions to Renaissance literature, especially regarding Dante, Boccaccio, and Petrarch, were unparalleled, even then, in their intellectual and practical value. The "Master Pieces," however, are a tribute to Bergin's poetry, erudition, and wit in speeches made and notes posted during his years as Master of Timothy Dwight College. Seung was a PhD candidate in philosophy at the time (he graduated in 1965). He had crossed safely into South Korea at the outbreak of the Korean War and, with encouragement to pursue his studies, entered Yale on scholarship. "Master Pieces: From the Files of T.G.B.," selected and edited by T. K. Seung and A. Bartlett Giamatti (New Haven, CT: Timothy Dwight College Press, 1964). The pamphlet is contained in Bergin's Papers, Yale University Library, MS 1629 (it incorrectly spells Seung's name).

18. Ventadorn lived and traveled in southern France (Provence), northern Italy, and England in the twelfth century. His work, his approach, and use of poetry had substantial influence on the development of other musical traditions. The challenge to the editors was in the language, local French dialects and Latin derivatives, and in finding, editing, and correcting English translations. Stephen G. Nichols (Yale 1963), John A. Galm, and A. Bartlett Giamatti, eds., *The Songs of Bernart de Ventadorn* (Chapel Hill: University of North Carolina Press, 1962, a subsequent, unaltered edition). The book contains forty-one poems. The BBC television movie, *The Devil's Crown* (1978) includes Ventadorn as a character.

19. Informal interview with Robert Hollander.

20. "Thousands View 263rd Commencement," *Yale Daily News*, June 15, 1964.

CHAPTER 29

FEARLESS

Epigraph is from A. Bartlett Giamatti, *Exile and Change in Renaissance Literature* (New Haven, CT: Yale University Press, 1971), 4.

1. Interview with Hollander; Moncreiff, *Bart Giamatti: A Profile*, 28; Reston, *Collision at Home Plate*, 55–56.

2. See earlier discussion and Talya Nevins, "Eugenics at Princeton," *Nassau Week*, April 12, 2015; Thomas C. Leonard, *Illiberal Reformers: Race, Eugenics, and American Economics in the Progressive Era* (Princeton, NJ: Princeton University Press, 2016), 73, 111, 163; Harriet McBryde Johnson, "Unspeakable Conversations," *New York Times*, February 16, 2003.

3. Daniel James Brown, *The Boys in the Boat* (New York: Viking, 2013), 283–84.

4. When selected president of Yale, Bart described Toni's continued professional work as a commonplace expectation. Question: "What were the considerations [in your decision]?" Answer: "Oh, the considerations are familial? I have a wife who's got a job; she's good at it. I don't decide what she does; she's a woman with a job—she's a first-rate teacher—I say that because she teaches English and I can make that judgment. She, I'm not going to sit here and talk about what she's going to do vis-à-vis her job. She'll do that; that's the way it is and that's the way it ought to be." "Election as 19th President," press conference (December 20, 1977), Giamatti Speeches and Articles, Box 1, Folder 16, Yale University Archives. That expectation also implied a reality: unlike her predecessors, Toni was not a "faculty wife," a circumstance that did not impede or deter her husband's selection as Yale's president.

5. Hollander interview; Reston, *Collision at Home Plate*, 57. And see "Class Notes," *Princeton Alumni Weekly* 48 (September 26, 1947): 16 (Andy's Diner).

6. See, generally, Charles Singleton, "The Irreducible Dove," *Comparative Literature* 9, no. 2 (Spring 1957): 129–35; Harry Berger Jr., *Figures of a Changing World: Metaphor and a Changing Culture* (New York: Fordham University Press, 2015), 76. The debate, again in simple terms, was about the difference between traditional epic fiction from medieval works through the Renaissance poets, versus history blended with storytelling. In twentieth-century terms, the argument is whether Dante wrote historical fiction or something more akin to biblical parables. In an important respect, however, it is not a difference resolved then or now but a clash of perspectives about a poem that mattered to about every serious literary figure that followed, including in America. Henry Wadsworth Longfellow, Charles Eliot Norton, Charles Dickens, James Russell Lowell, Ezra Pound, and T. S. Eliot, among others, each considered it allegory. One resulting and resounding question relates to the meaning of the *Comedy* as an antecedent, its form of influence on others—for example, Dante's influence on Spenser.

7. Giamatti also acknowledged Singleton's relevance to Dante literature in his own writing. *The Earthly Paradise*, 120. ("E. Auerbach and C. Singleton are represented in all three anthologies, and their writings though very different, have been probably the most influential of recent times.") And, years later, when editing, with Hollander's help, an anthology of works commemorating Dante's place in America after two hundred years, Giamatti included one of Singleton's works, albeit as a contribution to inquiry, not as a revelatory new school of thought. Giamatti, *Dante in America*, 244. Singleton was later discovered to have committed either appropriation or plagiarism in his Dante translation. See Hollander's critique in "Charles Singleton's Hidden Debts to Thomas Okey and John Sinclair," *Electronic Bulletin of the Dante Society of America*, February 12, 2006.

8. Giamatti, *Earthly Paradise and the Renaissance Epic*, 350.

9. Informal interview with Hollander; interview with Dino Giamatti.

10. Hollander told this story to author James Reston Jr., who recounted it in *Collision at Home Plate*, 57–58. He told it to this author so that we could explore its meaning. In July 1966, he drove with Bart to Yankee Stadium to see the Red Sox and Yankees play in a doubleheader. Giamatti had already returned to New Haven, though he spent that summer teaching at NYU. This was the way Reston described it: "The professors found themselves seated next to two thick-armed teamsters who did not share Giamatti's enthusiasm for the Red Sox and who, with every succeeding beer, became menacingly intolerant of Giamatti's shrill boosting of the visitors. . . . Giamatti seemed oblivious to the fact that his burly neighbors were becoming increasingly sore. He insisted on competing for elbowroom on the thin metal armrest between them until, during the tight second game, nasty remarks began to be exchanged. Hollander suggested a hotdog. Giamatti refused. More hostile exchanges. Hollander suggested a hotdog. Bart declined. Joe Pepitone was on deck in the sixth inning, and Bart despised the Yankee first baseman as only one Italian can despise another [*sic*]. In the nick of time, Hollander grabbed his friend by the collar, pulled him out of his seat, and dragged him out to the concession stand. 'Look Bart, that guy is about to throw a punch at you. . . . When he does, his even bigger friend is going to hit *me!*'" In addition to reflecting something about Giamatti's commitment to engagement or the friendship between the two men, Reston's hyperbolic characterization of the two other fans as "teamsters" suggests they actually declared their profession, and that, in a manner wholly unnecessary to Hollander's story, Reston couldn't suppress his own disquieting stereotyping ("as only one Italian can despise another"), intent on characterizing an entire ethnicity or, in the eugenics culture, an entire "race," not merely a Red Sox enthusiast and Italian American/English-descended Giamatti enjoying a game.

11. Interviews with Elria Giamatti Ewing and Dino Giamatti; Reston, *Collision at Home Plate*, 56.

12. Reston, *Collision at Home Plate*, 55; Giamatti, *Earthly Paradise*. See also "University Press Publications," *Princeton University Weekly Bulletin*, October 1, 1966.

13. There were other "gardens" of special beauty that, however harmoniously depicted, warranted close, even skeptical attention. Some are false, misleading, or duplicitous in purpose (Milton's *Paradise Lost*, for example, inhabited by a deadly mischievous Satan) and filled with veiled enticement or deceptively presented fraud, or, in fact, were mere preludes or way stations to the earthly paradise, most without criteria or standards of conduct for entering and enjoying their pleasures. You needed to know that differences existed and to discern and act accordingly. The false garden wasn't the end; you were still on the journey, acquiring knowledge from being tested mattered if you expected to "to do true justice." Giamatti, *Earthly Paradise*, 16, 18–20 ("a desirable way of life").

14. Giamatti, *Exile and Change in Renaissance Literature*, 4.

15. Giamatti, *Earthly Paradise*, 15, 26–27 ("We remember that Hesiod and Pindar identified the Golden Age with the Islands of the Blessed. Now, Virgil does not deal with these islands, but he does treat at length a place which after him was identified with the islands and which exhibits standard Golden Age characteristics. This is, of course, Elysium. . . . Inhabited by those who are blessed . . . and [Virgil] describes how the inhabitants vie in . . . dance and song. . . . Behind the landscape and its moral significance we sense the presence of all the ancient places. . . . Because of the blessed quality of Elysium, buttressed by suggestions of the Golden Age . . . Virgil's opening lines on Elysium became such a great source for later Christian Latin accounts of the earthly paradise.").

See also "To have a sacred grove so high that it almost reaches heaven is an interesting classical precursor of what was to become Christian belief: that the earthly paradise was on a mountain top, often so high that it touched the moon." Giamatti, *Earthly Paradise*, 44–45, 45n46 footnote. Or, as he describes Horace's "respect . . . for the virtues of a small, private landscape whose rugged and noble simplicity reflects the ideals of the inhabitant or beholder." Giamatti, *Earthly Paradise*, 45. And see generally, Valerio, *Bart: A Life*, "Introduction," and so on.

16. Giamatti, *Earthly Paradise*, 25–26.

17. Giamatti, *Earthly Paradise*, 15.

18. Giamatti, *Earthly Paradise*, 94 (emphasis added).

19. Giamatti, *Earthly Paradise*, 114–18 (emphasis added).

20. The "City" imagery, in some respects more consequential and personal than the imagery of the garden, emerged later as well, in his writings, speeches, and especially his civic conduct before and after becoming president of Yale and in his subtler reflections on baseball. Foremost, it's where he spent a majority of his life. See, for example, Giamatti, *Take Time for Paradise* (1989), 47 ("Community").

21. Giamatti, *Earthly Paradise*, 83.

22. Giamatti, *Earthly Paradise*, 118–19 (emphasis added).

23. Giamatti, *Earthly Paradise*, 348–50.

24. Giamatti, *Earthly Paradise*, 349.

25. Giamatti, *Earthly Paradise*, 127, 299 (emphasis in original).

26. Bob Hollander did not think Giamatti politically conservative. He knew Bart as committed to personal obligation, responsibility, reason and reasoning, the value of memory and history, and the way that understanding and using words were the dutiful vehicle for ensuring freedom and fairness. Hollander, informal interview. In *Collision at Home Plate*, 76–78, Reston, in an oddly parsed, strained attempt to make Giamatti "conservative," described and relied upon, among other things, Bart's principled vote in support of the First Amendment and those students who protested against Yale's "institutional racism" whom Brewster sought to punish. A majority of the faculty also opposed Brewster. Reston also attributed to Giamatti, with no factual or even rhetorical connection, the conduct of *Brewster's appointee*, who, at Brewster's direction, threatened protesters through a bullhorn—threats the faculty (including Giamatti) refused to uphold. Reston relied upon the account and interpretation of Robert Brustein, former dean of the Yale Drama School, who had been fired by Giamatti. See Robert Brustein, *Making Scenes: A Personal History of the Turbulent Years at Yale, 1966–1979* (New York: Random House, 1981); and see Robert Kagan, "Getting Even," review, *Commentary*, June 1, 1981. Reston also asserts that the students being chastised were "Giamatti's students" from Stiles College, when, in an earlier sentence, Reston acknowledged that Giamatti wouldn't become Master of Stiles until the following year. Reston, *Collision at Home Plate*, 79. When after being named president, Giamatti was asked about his political perspective, he said, "I am an independent voter and always have been. I don't know whether I ever voted a straight ticket in my life . . . I don't find an easy way to characterize myself. What looks pretty conservative in an academic community like Yale does not necessarily look very conservative somewhere else." "Italian American Professor Is New President of Yale," *Italian Tribune News*, January 27, 1978, Giamatti Public Papers, Yale University Archives, Box 1, Folder 16.

27. Reston, *Collision at Home Plate*, 75.

28. Reston described an incident at Princeton to support his characterization of Giamatti that, in fact, does the exact opposite: it shows Giamatti as the nonconformist, the irreverent activist singularly challenging the Princeton faculty after only one year, in part, by challenging their skill as teachers. The incident involved a proposal to eliminate Latin as a requirement for admission to romance languages graduate study. Giamatti voted against it, his experience telling him that the discipline required to master Latin opened not merely the classics (which Reston diminished as not a sufficient reason to warrant Giamatti's vote), but the history of most modern languages and cultures; the political, mathematical, and architectural history of a vast swath of the world from Great Britain to Northern Africa to Asia Minor; and fundamental elements of major religious writings of contemporary meaning, not the least of which is Christianity. In addition, Giamatti would have presumed that the challenge to engage students in Latin and the current value of its derivatives in postgraduate study was *in the teaching*. Only a few paragraphs earlier in *Collision at the Plate*, Reston posits—then ignores—exactly the same point. Giamatti, he writes, made "Dante and Edmund Spenser fun and amusing as well as profound and relevant . . . [and made] connections between the seemingly esoteric concerns of the Renaissance poets and the concerns of modern America." In every context, including this one, Giamatti displayed his high expectations of teachers, affirmed by what he'd witnessed in his father, which correlated good teaching to ensuring the public duty of responsible citizenship, including the duty to challenge the threat to liberty. Put differently, Giamatti's action was as much a challenge to the faculty and its duty as it was in support of Latin as a prerequisite to graduate study.

29. Moncreiff was uniquely able to gain access to Giamatti's personal evaluations, which were helpful and revealing. *Bart Giamatti: A Profile*, 28. When Giamatti was selected president of Yale, his Princeton colleagues added, in retrospect, that he was "witty and well-read," and had "a real capacity as a scholar and teacher with a fine sense of play and humor." "Bart Giamatti, New Yale President, Was Faculty Member Here," *Princeton University Weekly Bulletin*, January 9, 1978.

30. See, for example, *Daily Princetonian*, June 4, 1965 (appointed to Board of Advisors for AB candidates); "Faculty Promotions," *Daily Princetonian*, April 12, 1965 (associate professor).

31. Moncreiff, *Bart Giamatti: A Profile*, 29; Reston, *Collision at Home Plate*, 56–57.

32. Moncreiff, *Bart Giamatti: A Profile*, 29.

33. "At faculty teas, he could amuse his colleagues with such high jinks as improvising 'Giamatti's list of academic afflictions,' starting with 'dissertation dysfunction' and 'tenure tremens.' A few supercilious members of senior faculty were not amused by his ribbing about academic life and interpreted Giamatti's attitude as a lack of seriousness." Reston, *Collision at Home Plate*, 57.

34. Giamatti, *Earthly Paradise*, 123.

35. In *Collision at Home Plate*, 56, Reston, presumably drawing from interviews, wrote that "the first symptoms of a menacing degenerative disease were beginning to show [at Princeton]. Giamatti dismissed the condition as gout, and his friends did not pry further, even as his limp became more pronounced." Although Giamatti had inherited Charcot-Marie-Tooth, and symptoms (the awkward walk or deliberate hand stretching) appeared later in his presidency, he also suffered periodic and problematic effects from the

serious anklebone injury he sustained in childhood. Personal observation (beginning in 1979) and informal interview with Wilkinson. Throughout Bart's life, other than his family and childhood friends, the only Yale friend he told about the Charcot-Marie-Tooth disorder was Wilkinson, whom he'd confided in after John had met his parents and seen his father during a trip to Florida to raise money early in his presidency. He wanted neither sympathy nor a change in expectation and, to his delight, he got neither.

36. Moncreiff, *Bart Giamatti: A Profile*, 29. Moncreiff had a close personal relationship with Mack, who'd encouraged him to write the Giamatti biographical profile.

37. Her mother, Peggy, Elria said, had the best skill at Italian grammar and pronunciation in the family, and her own skill exceeded her brother's. However skilled he was compared with others and capable of teaching the course with excellent proficiency, Bart was aware of his limitations, and his deeper interest was in using Italian in pursuit of other literary and friend-driven interests. Elria Giamatti Ewing interview.

38. Moncreiff, *Bart Giamatti: A Profile*, 30; see "Faculty Changes for '66," *Daily Princetonian*, May 4, 1966 (announcement of departure).

39. When asked about his Princeton departure following his appointment as Yale's president, he said, "'I had to have the sense,' he joked with the press, 'that if I said yes, everyone wouldn't leave for Princeton the next morning.'" *Princeton University Weekly Bulletin*, January 9, 1978.

40. Moncreiff's modestly measured *Profile* of Giamatti was published in 2007 to warm reviews. He also graciously consented to an interview. Hollander confirmed the story's accuracy with the same saddened animation he'd earlier described his friendship with Giamatti. Moncreiff, *Bart Giamatti: A Profile*, 30.

41. Among them was Professor Gaddis Smith, one personification of the conservative mentality of the *ancien régime*, who Giamatti knew had sided forcefully when an undergraduate, as head of the *Yale Daily News*, with Griswold's indefensible arguments against formation of Labor's closed shop and a small ten-cent-an-hour pay increase. Smith was also in favor of the creation of a powerfully constraining framework for university–Labor relations, later exacerbated by Brewster—a framework that Giamatti was confronted with when the responsibility to deal with it was his. Smith's "jealousy" at Giamatti's selection was the term Robert Moncreiff used in describing to me, and implicitly in his book, Smith's attitude displayed during Giamatti's tenure and what it may have encouraged, however unwittingly. Informal interview with Moncreiff and *Bart Giamatti: A Profile*, 134 (Smith's aspiration for being named president, certainly a continuation of the Griswold, Brewster cultural mentality), 148 (Smith's resident college student who allegedly knocked Giamatti down). In lectures Smith gave years after Giamatti's death on the history of Yale and in its relationship to New Haven, he deliberately excluded any readings from Giamatti's years as president, even though they marked a dramatic alteration in the university's relationship with New Haven. His teaching assistant, Judith Schiff, on loan from the University Archives on special assignment related to the subject matter, was sufficiently offended by Smith's conduct that she distributed copies of various Giamatti speeches and other materials to the students. Informal interview with Schiff and review of Smith's course readings.

42. Jeremy Waldron, "How Politics Are Haunted by the Past," review, *Of Politics*, and *The Making of Modern Liberalism* by Alan Ryan, *New York Review of Books* (February 21, 2013), 40–41 ("An institution . . . has a genealogy—layers of significance that represent

what it or something like it has meant to a hundred generations before our own. And those meanings continue to resonate or, to change the metaphor, they are continually unearthed in the archeology of our thinking").

EPILOGUE
YALE—IN EPIC BATTLE

Quotation is from Frank Deford, "A Gentleman and a Scholar," *Sports Illustrated,* April 17, 1989.

1. Clements produced his commentary at a time when the fate of both men was revisited in Sidney Lumet's two-part *Sacco and Vanzetti Story* on NBC television. Robert J. Clements, "Letters from Rome: The Triumph of Sacco and Vanzetti," *Columbia University Forum* 4, no. 4 (Fall 1961). See also, Robert J. Clements, *The Poetry of Michelangelo* (New York: New York University Press, 1965).

2. *New York University Bulletin*, Graduate Summer Session, Day and Evening Courses, Announcement (1966), 33.

3. *Education* was designated for removal and storage in LC's basement in order to protect it during Yale's May Day protest in 1970. Despite proper labeling, the George Park Fisher Memorial Windows were removed, stored, and lost or mislaid. No harm having come to the exposed *Education*, it was relocated to its current location. See "A Tale of Two Windows," *Yale Alumni Magazine*, January/February 2010; "Through a Glass, Still Darkly," *Yale Alumni Magazine*, January/February 2008.

4. One of his earliest Yale-period works was "Proteus Unbound: Some Versions of the Sea God in the Renaissance," published in a compilation of studies as part of a sophisticated exchange of thoughts between scholars in "Linguistics and Literary Criticism" and in honor of René Wellek and edited by, among others, Lowry Nelson Jr., both of whom helped in Bart's formal and informal education. Peter Demetz, Thomas Greene, and Lowry Nelson Jr., eds., *The Disciplines of Criticism: Essays in Literary Theory, Interpretation, and History* (New Haven, CT: Yale University Press: New Haven, 1968), 437–75.

5. Associate professor of English in 1968, associate professor of English and comparative literature in 1970, tenured professor at thirty-one, full professor in 1970 at thirty-three, the Frederick Clifford Ford Professorship in 1976, and the John Hay Whitney Professorship in the Humanities in November 1977. Yale University news release, November 2, 1977 (announcement by provost and Acting President Hanna Gray). Informal interviews with Professor Paul Fry and Sterling Professor David Quint.

6. Calabresi interview.

7. Charles T. Davis, *Black Is the Color of the Cosmos*, ed. Henry Louis Gates Jr. (Washington, DC: Howard University Press, 1989), "Foreword" by A. Bartlett Giamatti.

8. Giamatti also had a growing interest in detective mysteries, one in particular that he turned to during the summers for its setting, characters, and the form love took— Robert Parker's private detective, Spenser. It was in the first episode in 1985, when the books were refashioned into a television series, that Spenser, when engaged by a client, publicly crossed paths with Giamatti's poet: "Spenser with an 's' instead of a 'c.' You know, like the poet?" "Poet?" "Yeah. Edmund Spenser. He wrote the Fairie Queene." "Fairie Queene? I don't think I read that." "Ah, it's adventures about chivalry. Knights, honor, truth. You know? Moral code." *Spenser: For Hire*, "Promised Land" (Pilot, 1985), based

on book by Robert B. Parker. Giamatti's interest in Parker's books was known by only a few people outside his immediate family. They included John Wilkinson and, through an exchange in correspondence, Robert Parker. I first learned of the correspondence from Giamatti's executive assistant and friend, Regina Starolis. Parker's formal papers, donated to Boston University, include at least one of Giamatti's letters. Parker reported that Giamatti told him that, "I write better about love and sweat than anyone else. I think he was right." "Robert B. Parker Interview," *Yankee Magazine*, October 2003.

9. Giamatti's articles on baseball were easily the most popular of his works. But with a thread to empathy he witnessed through his own family experience, in New Haven, and at Yale, Giamatti wrote his most poignant cultural work, while still a professor, about Muhammad Ali. "Ali's outlandish acting conceals the fear of being marginal," Giamatti wrote in "Hyperbole's Child," *Harper's Magazine*, December 1977 ("To act out completely what is, in his view, it means to be black in America, to be always living on the margin, on the edge, in a position where, despite the pain of your work and the beauty of your play, a man may announce with superb casualness any given moment that you have been counted out.").

10. This battle is a deeply moving, hard-fought, engaging, and important thread in Yale's history, with roughly displayed antecedents in eugenics (and see Buckley's comment and related correspondence in *Yale Daily News* and the *Yale Alumni Magazine*) only partially set forth here, expressed before and during Giamatti's tenure when he broke with the conservative Corporation to ensure clarity about his position as president on the rights of gay students or anyone else's sexual preference or orientation. See, for example, Giamatti, Freshman Address, September 1983 ("sexual preference") and Freshmen Address, September 1984 ("sexual preference"), President's Speeches, Yale University Archives (Giamatti's writings, speeches, and media articles, talks, and film are generally available though his formal papers are not); "Why They Call Yale the 'Gay Ivy,'" *Yale Daily News*, July/August 2009 ("President Giamatti had provided very subtle but effective leadership in this. The whole thing could have been very different if someone else was in Woodbridge Hall"); *Yale Alumni Magazine and Journal*, February 1984 and March 1985 (formation and response to GALA, which originally stood for the Gay and Lesbian Association); James Brooke, "Homosexual Yale Alumni Returned to a Mixed Greeting," *New York Times*, June 3, 1985; Shanelle Roman, "A Divided Bench," *Yale Daily News*, September 26, 2016.

11. Giamatti, along with other university presidents, was invited to tour the Central Intelligence Agency during the Reagan presidency. In a meeting with then-Director William Casey, Giamatti criticized the agency's discriminatory policy against gay individuals and the meaning of their life choices, telling Casey "his policy on gays, homosexuals, has got to stop." David Ewing interview.

12. Moncreiff, *Bart Giamatti: A Profile*, 48.

13. Moncreiff, *Bart Giamatti: A Profile* (back cover).

14. Giamatti, A Free and Ordered Space, 303.

15. Labor strikes occurred under Brewster's administration in 1968, 1971, 1974, and 1977 (each was one to twelve weeks in duration). John Wilhelm said that, under Brewster, Yale had a "snobby, dictatorial attitude.' . . . Brewster had 'upper class written all over him, and he always appeared to be completely uninterested in their problems. Bart is more down-to-earth.'" "Giamatti Is Given Top Marks at Yale," *New York Times*, May 22, 1980.

16. "An Italian American Professor Is New President of Yale University," *Italian Tribune News*, January 27, 1978. Giamatti expressed unease and skepticism with the process Brewster used, namely a merger with Vassar and its relocation to New Haven, and Brewster's underlying discomfort with women as intellects, academics, and equals. The Vassar plan was received with discomfort among the faculty of both institutions at a cost of time, public criticism, and embarrassment. Finally, the obvious path was followed. "But I think," Giamatti said, "it's been a great thing for Yale." Kabaservice, *The Guardians*, 293–99. Yet Brewster couldn't restrain himself from his fundamental belief in the unyielding discrimination of the *ancien régime*. His speech in 1969 to the incoming class that, for the first time, included women, called for the making of "1,000 male leaders." See, for example Malkiel, *Keep the Damned Women Out*, 156–57; Henry Louis Gates Jr. and Cornel West, *The Future of the Race* (New York: Vintage, 2011) (ebook).

17. His observation of Brewster was generous, yet tempered by the underlying reality of what he'd learned, disliked, and would bring to an end. "I envy his superb capacities to engage the world. But I am not conscious of competing with his image, of having to confront and destroy the predecessor, as Harold Bloom writes of poets. I knew my predecessors as persons and perhaps that's why they aren't public figures to me." In William Henry III, "Yale's Renaissance Man," reprinted, in part, in Valerio, *Bart: A Life*, 12. See also, Giamatti, "Address at the Freshman Assembly," September 5, 1978 ("Nothing is more antithetical to the collaborative structure or mutually respectful nature of the university than coercion in any form. Coercion strangles the civic spirit. Whether coercion is subtly of the self . . . [in] the denial of the right of free speech or the imposition of racist attitudes . . . or is coercion [through] impressing their desires on others with no regard for the rights and dignity of others—coercion of any kind is anathema to the university and to humane individuals everywhere, and we condemn it.")

18. Route 34, a continuation of the not-yet-completed Ring Road, was related to the Oak Street Connector in the Rotival/Yale/Lee Plan. African Americans "in the path of [the] Route 34 extension have been moving to Bridgeport, Waterbury, and Ansonia." *Yale Daily News*, Summer Issue, 1967. Ironically—and likely deliberately—the summer issue of the *Daily News* was devoted to touting the accomplishments of Dick Lee: "Mayor Lee's Politics of Progress," "Innovation, Initiative in New Haven," and a reprint of a *New York Times* article that included a photograph of brownstones, which were among the few that Lee left standing, and the nicely clean Oak Street Connector. Professor Vince Scully described his reasons for objection to yet more roadways and dislocation midway through one *Daily News* article, but his facts and argument were dismissed by Lee's spokesperson, Melvin Adams. In an interview, John Wilkinson describes Giamatti's dislike of Lee.

19. Letter to Brewster concerning Yale's antiquated fair employment programs (July 18, 1967). Brewster Presidential Papers, Box 156, Yale University Archives.

20. "Yale Rapped Again, Counsel Succeeding Harris as Hill Parent Assn. Head," *New Haven Evening Register*, August 30, 1968. Brewster to Willie Counsel, Hill Parents Association (August 31, 1968) and "5 City Blacks Assail 'Malignant' Society," *New Haven Register*. Brewster Presidential Papers, Box 113, Folder 6, Yale University Archives.

21. In the School of Art and Architecture and Department of Planning, Brewster was confronted by the legitimate reevaluation by new students and some faculty of the school's disquieting institutional role in New Haven. The activists reconstituted the school's charter and ensured a larger student role in school decisions, including decisions concerning

the admission of more local African Americans. They had witnessed, in the constrained historical manner typical of Yale students, what was occurring in the Hill neighborhood when they arrived and examined it, and the ultimate effect of "top-down" urban renewal (neighborhood destruction and, by the mid to late 1960s, the forced relocation of African Americans and others) with deep apprehension. Neither their attitude nor their focus on what, by then, were Yale-owned property and expansion plans was allowable by Brewster. The institutional conflagration within Yale—once students and faculty offered admittance to a group of students they had selected—was rough and decisive and resulted in the dismissal or reprimand of students and faculty, Brewster's letter to those students admitted to encourage their withdrawal, and the end of the Department of Planning as then known. See, for example, correspondence among Brewster, Chauncey, other Yale officials, Ford Foundation, School and Planning students, and the Black Workshop, and Brewster's letters to admitted students and to those students and faculty who organized the institutional and perspective changes. And especially cf. the "Position Paper" from the Faculty-Student Forum of the City Planning Department (May 30, 1969), the letter from the Black Workshop to Brewster (April 29, 1969), and "The Recent Destruction of the City Planning Department by the Yale Administration Shows That Yale Intends to Continue Serving the Rich," with Brewster's "Memorandum to School Faculty and Students" (May 26, 1969) and "Memorandum to All Members of the Faculty (May 28, 1969). Brewster wanted a department that would be more benign and certainly not focus on Yale's history and his own in New Haven. Brewster Presidential Papers (May 1968 through June 1969), RU 11, Series I, Box 26, Folder 9, Yale University Archives. See also Brian Goldstein, "Planning's End? Urban Renewal in New Haven, the Yale School of Art and Architecture, and the Fall of the New Deal Spatial Order," *Journal of Urban Renewal* 37, no. 3 (2011): 400–22, and documents cited therein.

22. Brewster Presidential Papers, Box 179, Folder 21, Yale University Archives. See, for example, Ecklund to Brewster (December 22, 1966), Hummel to Chauncey (October 3, 1967), Brewster to Ives (July 18, 1967) (street closings, High, Wall, Tower Parkway, York Place, Hillhouse).

23. See "How We Stopped the Ring Road," *New Haven Independent*, February 4, 2014 (role played by Alderman William Rees, local citizens, and State Representative Robert Oliver), and Oliver's related testimony in Hartford, General Assembly, Committee on Roads and Bridges (April 11, 1967), 572. Also see *Yale Daily News* articles below about the opposition of Alderman Michael DiRienzo (chair of the Transportation Committee) and State Representative Bruce Morris.

24. "$15 Million Highway through City Proposed," *New Haven Register*, December 21, 1965 ("Legion Avenue is home." "We don't want to leave the Hill. We like it here." We "don't want to live in a project or a skyscraper." "This will be the third time we will be moved," from a Scranton Street resident. "Our entire Dixwell Avenue will be cut off from both the University and downtown.") See "Long-Range Plans: Highway to Grid Yale," *Yale Daily News*, May 2, 1967; "More 'Urban Removal'?," *Yale Daily News*, May 4, 1967; "Loop to Go Underground," *Yale Daily News*, May 3, 1967; see also "Lee Asks State to Delineate Rt. 34 Path," *New Haven Register*, January 27, 1966; "City Ring Road Study Is Ordered," *New Haven Register*, April 2, 1967. Informal interview with labor historian Bill Berndtson.

25. Lee to Scully (July 22, 1966), Scully to Lee (July 25, 1966), Lee Papers, Series I, Box 76, Folder 1434, Yale University Archives, and see Vincent Scully, "The Threat and

Promise of Urban Redevelopment in New Haven," in *Building the Nation*, ed. Steven Conn and Max Page (Philadelphia: University of Pennsylvania Press, 2003) (reprint of Scully article published in 1966).

26. General Assembly, Committee on Roads and Bridges (April 11, 1967), 572–81 (Brewster: "I wish to record as emphatically as possible, my urgent plea for the passage of H.B. No. 3194 [Griswold's bill]." And see Griswold bill, Diagram of "Proposed Crosstown Highway," from the *New Haven Register*, September 22, 1965. See also Brewster to Lee on Dempsey meeting ("the City and the University speak with one voice"); exchange within Yale about a "feeler" request from Lee's director of redevelopment for a Lee professorship at Yale, which was unanimously rejected but lingered in subsequent correspondence, Appleby to Kaufman (June 8, 1965); Kaufman to Chauncey (June 15, 1965); Pollock and Row to Kaufman (June 16, 1965), Brewster Presidential Papers, Box 50, Folder 3, Yale University Archives.

27. See "Potential Summer Unrest," Commission on Equal Opportunities (May 12, 1967), memorandum to Lee and Redevelopment Agency officials from, among others, John Daniels, the Reverend Sidney Lovett (Chairman), and Richard Belford, which described the warning signs of possible violence and discontent, and solutions for lessening them. Lee Papers, Series III, Box 114, Yale University Archives. In introductory remarks to a "Housing Seminar, New Haven's Urban Renewal Another Cause of Unrest," Henry Parker, Black Coalition president, focused on what Hill and Dixwell leaders expected and had not received: "clean up slums," "better housing," "more playgrounds," better shopping opportunities, and no more "relocation [which] has the effect of rendering black people more powerless because people who are uprooted and moved from one neighborhood to another, *do not vote*"(June 1, 1968) (emphasis in original). Lee Papers, Series I, Box 93, Yale University Archives.

28. The statistical data showed that 25 percent of the approximately 550 people arrested for assaulting the police, looting, and carrying firearms were "whites" from Fair Haven, the Hill, and Morris Cove. "New Haven Disturbance Arrest Study," New Haven Police Department (September 20, 1967), document marked "Confidential." ("It is immediately apparent that this was not an exclusively Negro [and non-white] disturbance" or one confined to the Hill neighborhood. Discontent, the department stated, existed throughout New Haven and spread quickly, though the effects were concentrated in the Hill. In the study's conclusion, the department informed Lee, "It can be said, at least as far as the inner-city participants were concerned, that this was an outpouring of the dispossessed and the frustrated, by inner city standards.") See also "Police to Beef Up Force," "Economic Loss in the Millions," "Lee Vows to Restore Order," "Harris Says City Needs a 'Commitment,'" "Aid for Fleeing Families: While Some Raise Havoc, Some Help" (led by Mary Harris), *New Haven Register*, August 22, 1967; "Show of Force Halts Outbreak," "And Now, Where Do We Go from Here?," *New Haven Register*, August 23, 1967. And see also *Report of the National Advisory Commission on Civil Disorder* (New York: Bantam Books, March 1968, advance copy), 308, 310, 325–26, 391 (charts, "New Haven," "Levels of Violence"). In the summer of 1967, before leaving for graduate school in Washington, DC, I worked as a summer school counselor at Prince Street School, within a few blocks or so of the disturbance in the Hill neighborhood. The summer school program was directed by (later, and now-retired) Connecticut Supreme Court Justice Lubbie Harper and coordinated with other programs by educator John Esposito, who, like Harper, had been

a renowned athlete at Wilbur Cross High School. (See Harper listed in "Wilbur Cross Hall of Fame," *New Haven Register*, March 27, 2005, as a three-letter athlete.) Esposito was an All-State and All-American football player in 1953, when the school was located on the York Square campus. We were encouraged to remain on Prince Street as much as possible to keep the adjacent playgrounds and school open, which we did. Harper worked closely with neighborhood residents to restore calm and ensure fairness.

29. See letter from Mrs. Joan T. Thornhill to Kingman Brewster (September 6, 1967). Thornhill, who lived near both the university and the Hill, wrote Brewster of her "deep disenchantment with the university" following her conversation with Sam Chauncey, Brewster's assistant, shortly after the Hill area had exploded, seeking, at the request of the Hill Parents Association, "one of [Yale's] residential colleges for the overnight housing of a group of children and mothers." She knew that "churches and families throughout New Haven and surrounding areas were calling in to volunteer their homes and churches for the housing and feeding of from two to 200 people." She learned that the NAACP had made a similar request earlier that day and had been refused. Chauncey, personally sympathetic, said that "Yale could not give the appearance of providing physical protection for anyone when . . . the city would not guarantee it a force in large enough numbers to secure it." Thornhill called Lee's office. His assistant demurred and never confirmed Chauncey explanation. "I then began thinking, from whom would the university need 'adequate police protection' should Yale house dependents from the Hill: rioting arsonists . . . whose families were sheltered inside? Insurrectionists who wanted to burn Yale to the ground? Irate Yale alumni? Faculty? Masters? Fellows? The press? Politicians? Who?" She wrote to Brewster, "No one" who had accepted children and women "asked for 'adequate police protection.'" Yale, "on whose president the mantle of 'nobless oblige' drapes with grace, refused to help, put forth a faint-hearted excuse. . . . Or perhaps Yale was involved in what it perceives to be its *true* community: the community of those who hold power." On September 11, Brewster replied. He made it "quite clear that the University's action and inactions during the August upheavals were either decided by me or immediately ratified by me." Thornhill to Brewster (September 6, 1967) and Brewster (draft and final) to Thornhill (September 11, 1967). See Brewster Presidential Papers, Box 161, Folder 6, Yale University Archives.

30. In Lee's press conference during the enormous display of state and local police, fully armed, "All the questions centered around 'New Haven's image nationally as a model city.'" *New Haven Register*, August 22, 1967.

31. Lee, without a hint of conflict or public disclosure, had maintained, during his mayoralty, a private "consulting arrangement with the Ford Foundation," through August 31, 1967, managed by Ford President McGeorge Bundy, a former Vietnam War advocate under Lyndon Johnson and close friend of Kingman Brewster. Ford also had been financing New Haven and Yale programs, while paying Lee. When it appeared that Ford was not going to renew the arrangement, Lee turned to Brewster "to give Bundy a budge." One message was relayed to Brewster with elementary clarity before, during, and after the civil disturbance: no matter what Yale did or said, Lee wanted Yale's adulation and Brewster's help. Lee to Brewster (September 7, 1967), Brewster Presidential Papers, Box 160, Folder 13, Yale University Archives. And see the 1965 "feeler" for Yale to offer Lee a professorship, which Brewster also knew about.

32. Lee actually raised the problem with Brewster privately in 1965 ("We are going to have to face up to a problem we have all been putting off. . . . I'm not getting into

the merits of the question at this time but . . . my staff is feeling the heat.") Lee to Brewster (January 20, 1965); Einhorn to Brewster (August 6, 1967) (based, in part, on Harvard's documented contributions to Cambridge and Boston), Brewster Presidential Papers, Series I, Box 88 and Box 160, Folder 13, Yale University Archives. See also "Yale Failing Obligations, Einhorn Says," *New Haven Evening Register*, September 5, 1967; "Yale Stands on Argument University Is Tax-Exempt," *New Haven Evening Register*, August 2, 1967; "City Shifts Attitude on Yale Role," *New Haven Journal Courier*, March 24, 1969 (the Guida Amendment "would require tax-free schools to get aldermanic approval before removing any land from the grand list"); "New Haven Puts Tax Issue to Yale," *New Haven Register*, March 29, 1969; "Yale Alumni Fund to Brewster" (April 11, 1969) (Fund should not pay New Haven), Brewster Presidential Papers, Box 160, Folder 16, Yale University Archives. Brewster declined Lee's request concerning payments or taxes in a letter, dated April 13, 1969, published in the *Yale Daily News*, and see "City Not Surprised," *Yale Daily News*, April 7, 1969.

33. Reasons the state dropped the Ring Road included "political and public controversy." Meeting memo (September 16, 1968), Brewster Presidential Papers, Box 179, Folder 22, Yale University Archives.

34. Powledge, *Model City*, "Hail and Farewell," 296–306 (the 1969 Democratic Party Convention in New Haven). Urbanists wanted to talk about "lead poisoning. Kids are dying in the Hill [in] the so-called Model City." That and similar dangers existed throughout the city in old and in "new" urban renewal housing, and residents and party members wanted help. Among those seeking to be considered for mayor in 1969 was Alderman John Daniels, first elected in the fateful 1961 election, from the Dixwell/Newhallville neighborhood. Daniels was elected mayor twenty years later after a distinguished public service career as state senator, during which he defended and protected the city's interests, including in the five-year-long North Haven Mall battle (the harmful effect of the proposed regional mall on minority business and employment in New Haven), the DiLieto administration's effort (with President Bart Giamatti's support and Secretary John Wilkinson's intervention) to challenge the harm Lee had done in creating the presumption that New Haven's purpose was to serve suburban interests. Daniels also was selected to the All-State Football Team in 1954, when Hillhouse was located in the York Square campus. "John Daniels, City's First Black Mayor, Passes," *New Haven Independent*, March 15, 2015. Henry Parker was elected Connecticut state treasurer in 1975 and "led the movement under the late Gov. Ella Grasso to have Martin Luther King's birthday made a holiday in Connecticut." See "Parker Honored for Lifetime of Service," *New Haven Register*, May 3, 2010. He also was a candidate for mayor in 1979. On the North Haven Mall controversy, see "Black, Hispanic Caucus Plans Legislative Fight against Malls," *Hartford Courant*, December 12, 1983 (Representative Walter Brooks and Senator John Daniels); "In Capitol Hearing, New Haven Attacks Shopping Mall Plan," *Hartford Courant*, December 15, 1983 (testimony by Mayor Biagio DiLieto, Senator John Daniels, and Mayor Thirman Milner of Hartford); "Mall Subcommittee Will Study Entire State," *New Haven Register*, December 15, 1983; Hearing, U.S. House Subcommittee on Government Operations, 97th Cong. 2nd sess. (September 9, 1982) (especially testimony of Mayor Biagio DiLieto, accompanied by John Sawyer, development administrator, and Neil Proto, special counsel, 3, and Gerald S. Clark, board member of Dixwell Merchants Association, Science Park, and as a "member of New Haven's minority business community, that the impact of the proposed North Haven Mall will harshly and disproportionately affect New Haven's

minority businesspersons, workers and their families," 204–217); Dick Polman, "City, Suburb Wage Battle of the Mall," *Philadelphia Inquirer*, August 12, 1985; "In City Mall Fight, Proto Led Pack," *New Haven Register*, September 1, 1985. On the inauguration held at Woolsey Hall, see Shelia Rubin, "DiLieto: Let's Find a 'Better Way,'" *New Haven Journal Courier*, January 2, 1980, 1, 14; Stanley Venoit, "Ceremonies Inaugurate DiLieto Administration," and "Mayor Claims Streets 'for People,'" *New Haven Register*, January 2, 1980, 51; "DiLieto Swamps Logue," and "Parker Vote Hurt Logue, DiLieto Equally," *New Haven Journal Courier*, September 12, 1979. Although Yale was founded in 1701, its charter to establish a college in New Haven was granted in 1716. The subsequent reference to Yale's "264-year history" is calculated from that starting date in New Haven.

35. See Hank Levine, "Images, Not Issues," *Yale Daily News*, September 22, 1971. And see, Hank Levine, "Images, Not Issues . . . Again," *Yale Daily News*, September 27, 1971 (Levine's reply to criticism, which did not come internally), and two letters to the editor concerning the general election (October 7, 1971): "Guida is the candidate of orthodox, spendthrift liberalism in this election" (from a Capra supporter, who opposed such liberal conduct), and, as if history began in 1969 or was taught that way, Guida, another Yale student claimed, is building Route 34 (this segment actually was begun in 1957, and Lee continued it through his departure) "that will cut the Hill in half and displace Blacks and Puerto Ricans." Unmentioned by either Capra supporter was that Guida had led the revolt against Yale's buying small apartment buildings and converting them into "student housing" so as to remove them from the tax rolls. And see Hank Levine, "Numbers Never Lie," *Yale Daily News*, November 5, 1971 (analysis of Guida's ability to win handily in the African American wards, even in the primary with Henry Parker in the race). In the 1972 presidential election, Town Chairman Arthur Barbieri and Mayor Guida ("Barbieri . . . had been an early and ardent booster of the McGovern candidacy") supported George McGovern and Sargent Shriver, who won in New Haven, taking twenty-four of the thirty-one wards, with a 76 percent turn-out (close to Barbieri's projection). Nixon won in Connecticut. "State GOP Broom Can't Sweep City," *New Haven Register*, November 11, 1972; informal interview with Joseph Carbone, who organized Students for Guida and later served as Mayor DiLieto's chief of staff. We both retained a copy of the Levine, "Images, Not Issues" article, now slightly tattered.

36. Middlebury College, Commencement Address (August 11, 1973). Edmund Spenser, *The Faerie Queene*, Book 1, Canto VIII.

37. Interview with Calabresi.

38. Mary Griswold's comment was made to different people with slight variations, her intent understood precisely the same in every case. John Wilkinson put it succinctly: "the meaning was that she did not think a Catholic should be president of the university." Interviews with John Wilkinson (April 8, 2016; October 19, 2015, and informal interviews), who heard it from two colleagues and witnessed Giamatti's reaction. Earlier informal interview with Wilkinson (April 25, 2014) and notes ("Relieved he wasn't Catholic"); interview with Guido Calabresi (June 7, 2016), who recalled sharing with Wilkinson what Mary Griswold had said, a report that was independent of how her comment to others had reached Wilkinson. (Guido Calabresi: "[She asked,] 'Is Bart Catholic?' And I said, 'No. . . .' And she said, 'Oh wonderful!' Of course, [Bart] was angry. It would make anyone furious.") Wilkinson recalled that Giamatti believed it was Italian "profiling" and was "offended by it."

39. Kernan, *In Plato's Cave*, 268. The incident, described by Giamatti to Kernan, occurred during the evening celebration of Giamatti's inauguration as president.

40. See, for example, "Achieving Financial Equilibrium at Yale: A Report on the Budget," Yale University, December 1977, 7; Emma Edwards, "Balancing Those Books at Yale," *Atlanta Constitution*, May 26, 1981; "Giamatti Is Given Top Marks at Yale," *New York Times*, May 22, 1980; "For Giamatti, the Road Show Is Important," *New Haven Register*, September 28, 1980 (fundraising).

41. The Reverend Theodore M. Hesburgh, C.S.C.: "Opposing the forces of darkness and coercion, he raises a fearless voice in defense of the tradition and values of liberal education. To promote the order essential to sustain excellence, he has boldly initiated academic and fiscal reform and has insisted on quality, fairness and humanity in university affairs. With incisive wit and deep seriousness of purpose, he has extended his influence beyond the university to the city and the commonwealth. On an energetic patron of civility in our society." Notre Dame, 137th Commencement, May 1982, conferring the doctor of laws degree on Angelo Bartlett Giamatti.

42. In a central reflection of his consistent exercise of his duty and belief, Giamatti did battle, when necessary and without indirection or subtly, against interference with the tenets of liberal education or the misguided action of government, especially by and under conservatives, particularly Republicans. "Budget Cuts Spur Lobbying Efforts, Yale Fights Reagan," *Yale Daily News*, April 16, 1981. His eloquent, deeply admired, and severely criticized attack on the "savagery of spirit" and "arrogance" of the "Moral Majority," by name, struck deeply into the Reagan-Bush political and cultural coalition. See, for example, Baccalaureate Address, May 23, 1981; Robert D. McFadden, "Head of Yale Calls Moral Majority 'Peddlers of Coercion' on 'Values,'" *New York Times*, September 1, 1981; Randall Beach, "Giamatti Cheered," *New Haven Register*, May 24, 1981.

43. "Yale's history has not in this century always been marked by such a meritocratic ideal; we all know there were times when individuals were excluded from Yale because of quotas, absolutely unacceptable rules based on race or religion. Those days are gone and must never return." Giamatti, "A Free and Ordered Space," delivered to the senior class as the baccalaureate address, May 1985. Reprinted in Giamatti, *A Free and Ordered Space*, 278, 281. "The heterogeneity of talent and origin, experience and interest [among students], is not achievable by simple formulae or by institutionalizing special privilege." Inaugural Address of President A. Bartlett Giamatti, October 14, 1978.

44. See, for example, his resumption of the Sterling Scholarships in 1979, mentioned previously, and his establishment, with Mayor Frank Logue and Gerald Tirozzi, superintendent of schools, of the Yale–New Haven Teachers Institute, "whereby colleagues from the school system and the University collaborate in summer seminars on teaching methods and on designing curricula for use in the high schools." Dinner for President A. Bartlett Giamatti, January 6, 1979. See also Inaugural Address, October 1978: ("We must be mindful of the community in which we live. No college or university in a city can regard its fortunes as separate from that city. . . . The University must do all it can to assist the City in its development, and in those ways that it legitimately can, it will." And "A university cannot expound those goals and expect a larger society to find them compelling. It cannot become a repository of national hope and a source of national leadership, unless it strives to practice what it preaches"). Giamatti's affirmative encouragement and conduct in New Haven had the effect he wanted. See *Hartford Courant*, December 8, 1978, and *Courant* interview transcript, 46–47, Giamatti

Speeches, Yale University, RU 65, Boxes 1 and 2, Yale University Archives ("Protests don't strike them as the only way to move it. You have a much greater number of kids tutoring in the New Haven community than you did ten years ago. . . . These kids are much more interested in going out and tutoring, working through the Scouts, work-ing in urban situations; they're not collecting in huge masses, talking about it all the time. Because you're not going to see them on that as an activity that's going to do anything for the people out in the city"). And see his own formal civic involvement as model before becoming president (board member of the Connecticut Ballet, the Foote School, and the Arts Council of Greater New Haven). Although Giamatti remained a registered Independent, he expressed a desire to register as a Democrat to his sister, Elria, likely in the campaign of 1979, when he would have understood the fervent enthusiasm for Biagio DiLieto in the Democratic primary. In fact, in a manner not shared with others, he arranged a private meeting with DiLieto a year before the 1979 primary through Yale's long-time chief of police, Louis Cappiello. When DiLieto won the primary, Giamatti arrived at the campaign's headquarters at a former car dealership on Whalley Avenue to offer congratulations, amid street-choking traffic and raucous public enthusiasm. Informal interview with Joseph Carbone, who served as DiLieto's campaign director and eventually chief of staff, and is now president and CEO of The WorkPlace, a nonprofit agency that supports retraining and employment; personal ob-servation. See Paul Schott, "Business Council Recognizes WorkPlace's Carbone with Top Award," *Stamford Advocate*, November 28, 2016. And see "Hamden Man Spared No Effort for Kids," *New Haven Register*, September 29, 2010 (Cappiello obituary); interview with Elria Giamatti Ewing. Giamatti offered, and DiLieto accepted, the use of Woolsey Hall for the mayoral inauguration held on January 1, 1980. Giamatti found in DiLieto a congenial, determined personality and practical intellect, a civic doer without Lee's insecurity and obsequiousness (DiLieto had an almost photographic memory of the definition of words that the two would often argue about, and wide-ranging historical knowledge of his own, New Haven's, and Bart's cultural heritage). Of serendipitous im-portance, the two shared a love of "the city," its urbanity and need for revitalization in its core and values that were antithetical to the Lee and Yale mentality of separating New Haven from its culture and history. DiLieto campaigned on this sensibility to victory in 1979 and governed with it through Giamatti's tenure as Yale president. Interview with Carbone. And see endnote 34 of this chapter.

45. Giamatti, *The University and the Public Interest*, 7–8 (the book is a compilation of articles and his addresses given in various settings to students and alumni). "The process by which those values and others are learned is the educational process, and that process has a deep and abiding purpose . . . namely, the shaping of citizens. . . . How, in short, we choose a civic role for ourselves—is the basic purpose of an education in a democracy." In a theme that evolved from his 1960 oration as a Yale senior, he added: "[I] would argue that without an ethically-based civic sense, nourished in an individual through education, larger social claims issue merely into programs for action with no controlling perspective about what the action is for. . . . Historically, education has been the best stay against such confusion, by fostering the civilizing ability to make choices and to act responsibly for others on the basis of those choices." Giamatti, Address to Yale Law School Alumni, October 20, 1979: "The purpose of an education in a great private institution is to pre-pare people for the full claim of citizenship, for the proposition that one's life and the values embodied in one being be of some use, or value, to other people."

Works Cited

Books

Abel, Darrel. *Democratic Voices and Vistas: American Literature from Emerson to Lanier.* 1963. Lincoln, NE: iUniverse, 2002.

Albrecht, Donald, and Eeva-Liisa Pelkonen, eds. *Eero Saarinen: Shaping the Future.* New Haven, CT: Yale University Press, 2010.

Arsenault, Raymond. *Freedom Riders: 1961 and the Struggle for Racial Justice.* New York: Oxford University Press, 2006.

Avrich, Paul. *Sacco and Vanzetti: The Anarchist Background.* Princeton, NJ: Princeton University Press, 1991.

Baker, Liva. *The Justice from Beacon Hill: The Life and Times of Oliver Wendell Holmes.* New York: HarperCollins, 1991.

Bakish, David. *Jimmy Durante: His Show Business Career.* Jefferson, NC: McFarland, 1995.

Bass, Paul, and Douglas W. Rae. *Murder in the Model City: The Black Panthers, Yale, and the Redemption of a Killer.* New York: Basic Books, 2006.

Beck, Nicholas. *Budd Schulberg.* Lanham, MD: Scarecrow Press, 2001.

Bel Geddes, Norman. *Magic Motorways.* New York: Random House, 1940.

Benjamin, Sandra. *Sicily: Three Thousand Years of Human History.* Hanover, NH: Steerforth Press, 2006.

Bentley, Joanne. *Hallie Flanagan: A Life in the American Theatre.* New York: Knopf, 1988.

Berg, A. Scott. *Lindbergh.* New York: Berkeley Books, 1999.

Berger, Harry Jr. *Figures of a Changing World: Metaphor and the Emergence of Modern Culture.* New York: Fordham University Press, 2015.

Bergin, Thomas. "My Native Country." In *My Harvard, My Yale,* edited by Diana Dubois. New York: Random House, 1982.

Bickel, Alexander M. *The Least Dangerous Branch: The Supreme Court at the Bar of Politics.* Indianapolis, IN: Bobbs-Merrill, 1962.

Bier, Lisa. *Fighting the Current: The Rise of American Women's Swimming, 1890–1926.* Jefferson, NC: McFarland, 2011

Bonfante, Larissa, ed. *Etruscan Life and Afterlife.* Detroit: Wayne State University Press, 1986.

Bosworth, R. J. B. *Mussolini's Italy: Life under the Fascist Dictatorship, 1915–1945.* New York: Penguin, 2006.

Brown, Daniel James. *The Boys in the Boat*. New York: Viking, 2013.

Brown, Elizabeth Mills. *New Haven: A Guide to Architecture and Urban Design*. New Haven, CT: Yale University Press, 1976.

Brown, Molly McCully. *The Virginia State Colony for Epileptics and Feebleminded: Poems*. New York: Persea, 2017.

Brown, Peter. *The Ransom of the Soul: Afterlife and Wealth in Early Western Christianity*. Cambridge, MA: Harvard University Press, 2015.

Brustein, Robert. *Making Scenes: A Personal History of the Turbulent Years at Yale, 1966–1979*. New York: Random House, 1981.

Buckley, William F. Jr. *God and Man at Yale: The Superstitions of "Academic Freedom."* 1951. 50th anniversary edition, New York: Regency, 2002.

Burrow, Gerard N. *A History of Yale's School of Medicine: Passing Torches to Others*. New Haven, CT: Yale University Press, 2002.

Bush, Douglas. *Pagan Myth and Christian Tradition in English Poetry*. Jayne Lectures for 1967, Philadelphia: American Philosophical Society, 1968.

Calabresi, Guido. "Guido Calabresi: A Foreigner in New Haven, 1940–1945." Oral history memoir edited by Norman I. Silber. New Haven, CT: Yale Law School, 2016. (Adapted preview of forthcoming publication *Outside In: The Oral History of Guido Calabresi*.)

Caplan, Colin M. *Then and Now: New Haven*. Charleston, SC: Arcadia, 2006.

Cavett, Dick. *Brief Encounters*. New York: Henry Holt, 2014.

Chernow, Ron. *The House of Morgan: An American Banking Dynasty and the Rise of Modern Finance*. 1990. New York: Grove Press, 2010.

Churchill, Winston. *A History of the English-Speaking Peoples*, vol. 1. New York: Dodd, Mead, 1956.

Clarke, Margaret Harriman. *Chelsea in the 20th Century*. Portsmouth, NH: Arcadia, 2004.

Clements, Robert J. *The Poetry of Michelangelo*. New York: New York University Press, 1965.

Cohen, Adam. *Imbeciles: The Supreme Court, American Eugenics, and the Sterilization of Carrie Buck*. New York: Penguin, 2016.

Cohen, Robert. *When the Old Left Was Young: Student Radicals and America's First Mass Student Movement, 1929–1941*. New York: Oxford University Press, 1993.

Cole, Arthur C. *A Hundred Years of Mount Holyoke College: The Evolution of an Educational Ideal*. New Haven, CT: Yale University Press, 1940.

Collier, Martin. *Italian Unification, 1820–1871*. Oxford, UK: Heinemann Educational Publishers, 2003.

Congress for the New Urbanism. *Charter of the New Urbanism*. New York: McGraw-Hill, 1999.

Cronin, Irene, and the South Hadley Historical Society. *Images of America: South Hadley*. Charleston, SC: Arcadia, 1998.

Curti, Merle. *The Growth of American Thought*. 3rd ed. New York: Harper & Row, 1964.

Dahl, Robert A. *Who Governs? Democracy and Power in an American City*. 2nd ed. New Haven: Yale University Press, 2005.

Dallek, Robert. *An Unfinished Life: John F. Kennedy, 1917–1963*. New York: Little, Brown, 2003.

Doctors of Philosophy of Yale University, 1861–1927. New Haven, CT: Yale University Press, 1927.

Domhoff, G. William. *Who Really Rules? New Haven and Community Power Reexamined*. Piscataway, NJ: Transaction Publishers, [1978] 2010.

Douglas, William O. *Go East, Young Man: The Early Years*. New York: Random House, 1974.

Dugdale, Antony, J. J. Fueser, and J. Celso de Castro Alves. *Yale, Slavery and Abolition*. New Haven, CT: The Amistad Committee, 2001.

Duggan, Christopher. *The Force of Destiny: A History of Italy since 1796*. London: Allen Lane, 2007.

Ehrmann, Herbert B. *The Untried Case: The Sacco-Vanzetti Case and the Morelli Gang*. London: Martin Hopkinson, 1934.

Engleman, Finis. *The Pleasure Was Mine: 70 Years in Education*. Danville, IL: Interstate Printers and Publishers, 1971.

Farnham, Thomas. *Southern Connecticut State University: A Centennial History, 1893–1993*. New Haven, CT: Southern Connecticut State University, 1993.

Farrow, Anne, Joel Lang, and Jenifer Frank. *Complicity: How the North Promoted, Prolonged, and Profited from Slavery*. New York: Ballantine Books, 2006.

Feeney, Denis. *Beyond Greek: The Beginnings of Latin Literature*. Cambridge, MA: Harvard University Press, 2016.

Felzenberg, Alvin S. *A Man and His Presidents: The Political Odyssey of William F. Buckley Jr.* New Haven, CT: Yale University Press, 2017.

Feuerlicht, Roberta. *Justice Crucified: The Story of Sacco and Vanzetti*. New York: McGraw-Hill, 1977.

Flint, Peggy. *New Haven Preservation Trust: A Ten Years' War, 1962–1972*. New Haven, CT: New Haven Preservation Trust, 1972.

Frankfurter, Felix, et al. *To the American People: Report upon the Illegal Practices of the United States Department of Justice*. Washington, DC: National Popular Government League, May 1920.

Freeman, Stephen Albert. *The Middlebury College Foreign Language Schools, 1915–1970: The Story of a Unique Idea*. Middlebury, VT: Middlebury College, 1975.

Gabaccia, Donna R. *Italy's Many Diasporas*. New York: Routledge, 2000.

Gallagher, Dorothy. *All the Right Enemies*. New Brunswick, NJ: Rutgers University Press, 1988.

Gallagher, Nancy L. *Breeding Better Vermonters: The Eugenics Project in the Green Mountain State*. Lebanon, NH: University Press of New England, 1999.

Gambino, Richard. *Blood of My Blood: The Dilemma of the Italian-Americans*. Garden City, NY: Anchor Books, 1974.

———. *Vendetta: A True Story of the Worst Lynching in America, the Mass Murder of Italian-Americans in New Orleans in 1891, the Vicious Motivations behind It, and the Tragic Repercussions That Linger to This Day*. Garden City, NY: Doubleday, 1977.

Garver, John A. *John William Sterling: Class of 1864 Yale College*. New Haven, CT: Yale University Press, 1929.

Gates, Henry Louis Jr., and Cornel West. *The Future of the Race*. New York: Vintage, 2011. ebook.

Giamatti, A. Bartlett. "Commentary." In *The Italian Americans*, by Allon Schoener. New York: Macmillan, 1987.

———. *The Earthy Paradise and the Renaissance Epic*. Princeton, NJ: Princeton University Press, 1966.

———. *Exile and Change in Renaissance Literature*. New Haven, CT: Yale University Press, 1971.

———. "Foreword." In *Black Is the Color of the Cosmos*, by Charles T. Davis, edited by Henry Louis Gates Jr. Washington, DC: Howard University Press, 1989.

———. *A Free and Ordered Space: The Real World of the University*. New York: W. W. Norton, 1988.

———. *Play of Double Senses: Spenser's* Faerie Queene. New York: Prentice Hall, 1975.

———. "Proteus Unbound: Some Versions of the Sea God in the Renaissance." In *The Disciplines of Criticism: Essays in Literary Theory, Interpretation, and History*, edited by Peter Demetz, Thomas Greene, and Lowry Nelson Jr. New Haven, CT: Yale University Press, 1968.

———. *Take Time for Paradise: Americans and Their Games*. New York: Summit, 1989.

———. "Yale and Athletics." In *The University and the Public Interest*. New York: Atheneum, 1981.

———, ed. *Dante in America: The First Two Centuries*. Binghamton, NY: Center for Medieval and Early Renaissance Studies, 1983.

Giamatti, Valentine. *Minimum of Italian Grammar*. New York: S. F. Vanni, 1947, 1957, 1964.

Gilbert, Alfred Carlton. *The Man Who Lives in Paradise: The Autobiography of A. C. Gilbert*. New York: Rinehart, 1954.

Gillette, Aaron. *Eugenics and the Nature–Nurture Debate in the Twentieth Century*. New York: Palgrave Macmillan, 2007.

Gilmour, David. *The Pursuit of Italy: A History of a Land, Its Regions, and Their People*. New York: Farrar, Straus and Giroux, 2011.

Grant, Madison. *Conquest of a Continent*. New York: Charles Scribner's Sons, 1933.

———. *The Passing of the Great Race: Or, The Racial Basis of European History*. New York: Charles Scribner's Sons, 1916.

Gray, John Chipman. "Review of *La Divina Commedia di Dante Alighieri* (1813)." In *Dante in America: The First Two Centuries*, edited by A. Bartlett Giamatti. Binghamton: Center for Medieval and Early Renaissance Studies, State University of New York, 1983.

Green, Elizabeth Alden. *Mary Lyon and Mount Holyoke: Opening the Gates*. Hanover, NH: University Press of New England, 1979.

Grippo, Theodore. *With Malice Aforethought: The Execution of Nicola Sacco and Bartolomeo Vanzetti*. Bloomington, IN: iUniverse, 2011.

Guglielmo, Jennifer. *Living the Revolution: Italian Women's Resistance and Radicalism in New York City, 1890–1945*. Chapel Hill: University of North Carolina Press, 2010.

Halberstam, David. *The Best and the Brightest*. New York: Random House, 1972.

———. *Summer of '49*. New York: Avon Books, 1990.

———. *Teammates: A Portrait of a Friendship*. New York: Hyperion, 2003.

Hall, John F., ed. *Etruscan Italy*. Provo, UT: Brigham Young University, 1996.

Herman, Arthur. *Joseph McCarthy: Reexamining the Life and Legacy of America's Most Hated Senator*. New York: Free Press, 2000.

Hibbert, Christopher. *Garibaldi and His Enemies: The Clash of Arms and Personalities in the Making of Italy*. Boston: Little, Brown, 1966.

Hines, Thomas S. *Burnham of Chicago: Architect and Planner*. Chicago: University of Chicago Press, 1979.

Hogan, Neil, with Joan Cavanagh, Debbie Elkin, and Mary Johnson. *Moments in New Haven Labor History*. New Haven, CT: Greater New Haven Labor History Association, 2004.

Hopkins, John North. *The Genesis of Roman Architecture*. New Haven, CT: Yale University Press, 2016.

Hornblum, Allen M., Judith L. Newman, and Gregory J. Dober. *Against Their Will: The Secret History of Medical Experimentation on Children in Cold War America*. New York: St. Martin's Press, 2013.

Hull, Richard T., ed. *The American Philosophical Association Centennial Series: Presidential, 1901–2000*. Charlottesville, VA: Philosophy Documentation Center, 2013.

Hunter, W. S. *James Rowland Angell, 1869–1949: A Biographical Memoir*. Washington, DC: National Academy of Sciences, 1951.

Jacobs, Jane. *The Death and Life of Great American Cities*. New York: Random House, 1961.

Johnson, Diane. *Dashiell Hammett: A Life*. New York: Random House, 1983.

Johnson, Jeffrey A. *"They Are All Red Out Here": Socialist Politics in the Pacific Northwest, 1895–1925*. Norman: University of Oklahoma Press, 2008.

Johnson, Owen. *Stover at Yale*. New Haven, CT: Yale Book Store, 1997.

Joughin, G. Louis, and Edmund M. Morgan. *The Legacy of Sacco and Vanzetti*. New York: Harcourt, Brace, 1948.

Kabaservice, Geoffrey. *The Guardians: Kingman Brewster, His Circle, and the Rise of the Liberal Establishment*. New York: Henry Holt, 2004.

Kamil, Amos, and Sean Elder. *Great Is the Truth: Secrecy, Scandal, and the Quest for Justice at the Horace Mann School*. New York: Farrar, Straus and Giroux, 2015.

Kanigel, Robert. *Eyes on the Street: The Life of Jane Jacobs*. New York: Knopf, 2016.

Karabel, Jerome. *The Chosen: The Hidden History of Admission and Exclusion at Harvard, Yale, and Princeton*. Boston: Houghton Mifflin, 2005.

Kelley, Brooks Mather. *Yale: A History*. New Haven, CT: Yale University Press, 1974.

Kennedy, John F. *A Nation of Immigrants*. London: Hamish Hamilton, 1964.

Kernan, Alvin. *In Plato's Cave*. New Haven, CT: Yale University Press, 1999.

Lasch, Christopher. *The True and Only Heaven*. New York: W. W. Norton, 1991.

Lash, Joseph. *The Campus Strikes against War*. New York: Student League for Industrial Democracy, 1935.

Lassonde, Stephen. *Learning to Forget: Schooling and Family Life in New Haven's Working Class, 1870–1940*. New Haven, CT: Yale University Press, 2005.

Lavina, Javier, and Michael Zeuske, eds. *The Second Slavery: Mass Slaveries and Modernity in the Americas and in the Atlantic Basin*. Berlin: LIT Verlag, 2014.

Le Corbusier. *Towards a New Architecture*. New York: Dover, 1986. Reprint.

Lehmann, Chris. *The Money Cult: Capitalism, Christianity, and the Unmaking of the American Dream*. Brooklyn, NY: Melville House, 2016.

Leonard, Thomas C. *Illiberal Reformers*. Princeton, NJ: Princeton University Press, 2016.

Leuchtenburg, William E. "Mr. Justice Holmes and Three Generations of Imbeciles." In *The Supreme Court Reborn: The Constitutional Revolution in the Age of Roosevelt*. New York: Oxford University Press, 1995.

Levi, Carlo. *Christ Stopped at Eboli*. Translated by Frances Frenaye. New York: Farrar, Straus, 1963.

Levi, Peter. *Virgil: His Life and Times*. New York: St. Martin's Press, 1998.

Lewis, R. W. B. *Dante*. New York: Viking Penguin, 2001.

Lipari, Angelo. *The "Dolce Stil Novo" According to Lorenzo de' Medici: A Study of His Poetic "Principio" as an Interpretation of the Italian Literature of the Pre-Renaissance Period, Based on His "Comento."* New Haven, CT: Yale University Press, 1936.

———. *The Structure and Real Significance of the Decameron*. New Haven, CT: Yale University Press, 1943.

Lippmann, Walter. *Public Philosopher: Selected Letters of Walter Lippmann*. Edited by John Morton Blum. New York: Ticknor & Fields, 1985.

Lloyd, Susan McIntosh. *A Singular School: Abbot Academy, 1828–1973*. Andover, MA: Phillips Academy/University Press of New England, 1979.

Lombardo, Paul A. *Three Generations, No Imbeciles: Eugenics, the Supreme Court, and* Buck v. Bell. Baltimore: Johns Hopkins University Press, 2008.

Longfellow, Henry Wadsworth. "A Review of a History of the Italian Language and Dialects (1825)." Reprinted in *Dante in America: The First Two Centuries*. Edited by A. Bartlett Giamatti. Binghamton: State University of New York, 1983.

Luzcak, Ewa Barbara. *Breeding and Eugenics in the American Literary Imagination: Heredity Rules in the Twentieth Century*. New York: Palgrave Macmillan, 2015.

Mack, Maynard. *The Society as an Ideal, 1871–1942*. Unpublished manuscript (except for six copies), available in the Yale Archives.

Maffei, Count. *Brigand Life in Italy: A History of Bourbonist Reaction*. London: Hurst and Blackett, 1865.

Malkiel, Nancy Weiss. *"Keep the Damned Women Out": The Struggle for Coeducation*, Princeton, NJ: Princeton University Press, 2016.

Manchester, William. *A World Lit Only by Fire: The Medieval Mind and the Renaissance—Portrait of An Age*. Boston: Little Brown, 1992.

Maraniss, David. *When Pride Still Mattered: A Life of Vince Lombardi*. New York: Simon & Schuster, 1999.

Marchand, C. Roland. *The American Peace Movement and Social Reform: 1898–1918*. Princeton, NJ: Princeton University Press, 1973.

Marks, Jeannette. *Life and Letters of Mary Emma Woolley.* Washington, DC: Public Affairs Press, 1955.

Marrone, Gaetana, ed. *Encyclopedia of Italian Literary Studies,* vol. 1. New York: Routledge, 2007.

Marsden, George M. *The Soul of the American University.* New York: Oxford University Press, 1994.

Martin, Eldon Hubert. *Vermont College: A Famous Old School.* Nashville, TN: Parthenon Press, 1962.

Mason, Alpheus Thomas. *Brandeis: A Free Man's Life.* New York: Viking Press, 1946.

McInnis, Edgar. *The War: First Year.* London: Oxford University Press, 1945.

McWilliams, Tennant S. *The New South Faces the World: Foreign Affairs and the Southern Sense of Self, 1877–1950.* Tuscaloosa: University of Alabama Press, 1988.

Meeropol, Ann Karus. *A Male President for Mount Holyoke College: The Failed Fight to Maintain Female Leadership, 1934–1937.* Jefferson, NC: McFarland, 2014.

Menand, Louis. *The Metaphysical Club: A Story of Ideas in America.* New York: Farrar, Straus and Giroux, 2001.

Michels, Tony, ed. *Jewish Radicals: A Documentary History.* New York: New York University Press, 2012.

Morrison, Samuel Eliot. *The Oxford History of the American People.* New York: Oxford University Press, 1965.

Morse, Samuel F. B. *Foreign Conspiracy against the Liberties of the United States.* New York: Leavitt, Lord, 1835.

Moynihan, Joan, and Neil Hogan. *New Haven's St. Patrick's Day Parade.* Charleston, SC: Arcadia, 2006.

Musmanno, Michael Angelo. *After Twelve Years.* New York: Alfred A. Knopf, 1939.

Neilson, William Allan. *Smith College: The First Seventy Years* (unpublished manuscript), ca. 1946.

Nelson, Garrison. *John William McCormack: A Political Biography.* New York: Bloomsbury, 2017.

New Haven Colony Historical Society. *New Haven: Reshaping the City, 1900–1980.* Mount Pleasant, SC: Arcadia, 2002.

Nichols, Stephen G., John A. Galm, and A. Bartlett Giamatti, eds. *The Songs of Bernart de Ventadorn.* Chapel Hill: University of North Carolina Press, 1962.

Norris, George. *Fighting Liberal: The Autobiography of George W. Norris.* New York: Macmillan, 1945.

Nourse, Victoria F. *In Reckless Hands.* New York: W. W. Norton, 2008.

O'Brien, Michael. *John F. Kennedy: A Biography.* New York: Thomas Dunne Books, 2005.

O'Clery, Patrick Keyes. *The Making of Italy.* London: Kegan Paul, Trench, Trübner, 1892.

Okrent, Daniel. *Great Fortune: The Epic of Rockefeller Center.* New York: Viking, 2003.

Oren, Dan A. *Joining the Club: A History of Jews and Yale.* New Haven, CT: Yale University Press, 1985.

Osborn, Colonel N. G. *Men of Mark in Connecticut.* Hartford, CT: Goodspeed, 1906.

Ouditt, Sharon. *Impressions of Southern Italy: British Travel Writing from Henry Swinburne to Norman Douglas*. New York: Routledge, 2014.

Parish, Susan. "AAMR Leadership at Century's End." In *Embarking on a New Century: Mental Retardation at the End of the 20th Century*, edited by Robert L. Schalock, Pamela C. Baker, and M. Doreen Croser. Washington, DC: American Association on Mental Retardation (now American Association on Intellectual and Developmental Disabilities), 2002.

Parrington, Vernon Louis. *The Colonial Mind, 1620–1800*. Volume 1 of *Main Currents in American Thought*. New York: Harcourt Brace Jovanovich, 1927.

Perino, Michael. *The Hellhound of Wall Street*. New York: Penguin, 2010.

Pernicone, Nunzio. *Carlo Tresca: Portrait of a Rebel*. Oakland, CA: AK Press, 2010.

Phillips-Matz, Mary Jane. *Rosa Ponselle: American Diva*. Boston: Northeastern University Press, 1997.

Pierson, George Wilson. *Yale College: An Educational History, 1871–1921*. Volume 1 of *Yale: College and University, 1871–1937*. New Haven, CT: Yale University Press, 1952.

———. *Yale: The University College, 1921–1937*. Volume 2 of *Yale: College and University, 1871–1937*. New Haven, CT: Yale University Press, 1955.

Powledge, Fred. *Model City: A Test of American Liberalism*. New York: Simon & Schuster, 1970.

Pozzetta, George E., ed. *Americanization, Social Control, and Philanthropy*. New York: Garland, 1991.

Priestley, J. B. "Introduction." In *Scenes of London Life: From "Sketches by Boz"* by Charles Dickens, xi. London: Macmillan Collectors Library, 2018. First published in 1947 by Pan Books (London).

Prime, Samuel I. *Life of Samuel F. B. Morse*. New York: D. Appleton, 1875.

Proser, Jim, with Jerry Cutter. *I'm Staying with My Boys: The Heroic Life of Sgt. John Basilone, USMC*. New York: St. Martin's Press, 2010.

Proto, Neil Thomas. *The Rights of My People: Liliuokalani's Enduring Battle with the United States, 1893–1917*. New York: Algora, 2009.

———. "Sacco and Vanzetti: The Literary and Cultural Effects of the Controversy for Their Lives." Presented at the conference of the Dante Alighieri Society of Cambridge, Massachusetts, 1997. www.SaccoVanzettiExperience.com.

———. *To a High Court: The Tumult and Choices That Led to United States of America v. SCRAP*. Lanham, MD: Rowman & Littlefield, 2006.

Pugliese, Stanislao G. *Carlo Rosselli: Socialist Heretic and Antifascist Exile*. Cambridge, MA: Harvard University Press, 1999.

Purmont, Jon E. *Ella Grasso: Connecticut's Pioneering Governor*. Middletown, CT: Wesleyan University Press, 2012.

Rae, Douglas. *City: Urbanism and Its End*. New Haven, CT: Yale University Press, 2003.

Report of the National Advisory Commission on Civil Disorder. New York: Bantam Books, March 1968 (advance copy).

Reston, James Jr. *Collision at Home Plate: The Lives of Pete Rose and Bart Giamatti*. New York: HarperCollins, 1991.

Riccio, Anthony V. *Boston's North End: Images and Recollections of an Italian American Neighborhood*. Guilford, CT: Globe Pequot Press, 2006.

———. *Farms, Factories, and Families, Italian American Women of Connecticut*, Albany: State University of New York Press, 2014.

———. *From Italy to the North End*. Albany: State University of New York Press, 2017.

———. *The Italian American Experience in New Haven*. Albany: State University of New York Press, 2006.

Roberts, George. *Surviving Highland Heights: The Orphanage*. Ocala, FL: Life Circle, 2009.

Rosen, Christine. *Preaching Eugenics: Religious Leaders and the American Eugenics Movement*. New York: Oxford University Press, 2004.

Rosen, Jeffrey. *Louis D. Brandeis: American Prophet*. New Haven, CT: Yale University Press, 2016.

Rosenberg, Chaim M. *The Great Workshop: Boston's Victorian Age*. Portsmouth, NH: Arcadia, 2004.

Rubin, Harriet. *Dante in Love*. New York: Simon & Schuster, 2004.

Rybczynski, Witold. *A Clearing in the Distance: Frederick Law Olmsted and America in the Nineteenth Century*. New York: Scribner, 1999.

———. *The Perfect House: A Journey with Renaissance Master Andrea Palladio*. New York: Scribner, 2002.

Salvemini, Gaetano. *Italian Fascist Activities in the United States*. New York: Center for Immigration Studies, 1977.

Schmuhl, Hans-Walter. *The Kaiser Wilhelm Institute for Anthropology, Human Heredity, and Eugenics, 1927–1945: Crossing Boundaries*. Boston: Springer, 2008.

Schoener, Allon. *The Italian Americans*. New York: Macmillan, 1987.

Scully, Vincent J. Preface to *Plan for New Haven, 1910*. San Antonio, TX: Trinity University Press, 2012. Reprint.

———. "The Threat and Promise of Urban Redevelopment in New Haven." In *Building the Nation*, edited by Steven Conn and Max Page. Philadelphia: University of Pennsylvania Press, 2003.

Scully, Vincent J., Catherine Lynn, Erik Vogt, and Paul Goldberger, eds. *Yale in New Haven: Architecture and Urbanism*. New Haven, CT: Yale University Press, 2004.

Seabrook, William. "Italian Americans." In *Americans All: A Human Study of America's Citizens from Europe*. Redditch, UK: Read Books, 2013. Reprint.

Sensi-Isolani, Paola Alessandra, and Anthony Julian Tamburri, eds. *Italian Americans: A Retrospective on the Twentieth Century*. New York: American Italian Historical Association, 2001.

Seward, Desmond, and Susan Mountgarret. *Old Puglia: A Portrait of South Eastern Italy*. London: Haus Publishing, 2009.

Sinclair, Upton. *Boston: A Documentary Novel*. New York: Albert & Charles Boni, 1928.

Smith, Denis Mack. *Modern Italy: A Political History*. Ann Arbor: University of Michigan Press, 1997.

Smith, Jean Edward. *Eisenhower in War and Peace*. New York: Random House, 2012.

Soares, Joseph A. *The Power of Privilege: Yale and America's Elite Colleges*. Stanford, CA: Stanford University Press, 2007.

Sobel, Dava. *Galileo's Daughter*. New York: Walker, 1999.

Sonnert, Gerhard, and Gerald Holton. *What Happened to Children Who Fled Nazi Persecution*. New York: Palgrave Macmillan, 2006.

Sorensen, Theodore. *Kennedy*. New York: Harper & Row, 1965.

Spenser, Edmund. *The Faerie Queene, Book I*. Edited by George Armstrong Wauchope. New York: Macmillan, 1903. Project Gutenberg edition, 2005.

Sperber, A. M. *Murrow: His Life and Times*. New York: Bantam, 1987.

Stemmons, Walter. *Connecticut Agricultural School: A History*. Storrs: Connecticut Agricultural School, 1931.

Sterba, Christopher M. *Good Americans: Italian and Jewish Immigrants during the First World War*. New York: Oxford University Press, 2003.

Stimson Henry L., and McGeorge Bundy. *On Active Service in Peace and War*. New York: Harper and Brothers, 1947.

Stossel, Scott. *Sarge*. Washington, DC: Smithsonian Books, 2004.

Stout, Glenn, and Richard A. Johnson. *Red Sox Century: One Hundred Years of Red Sox Baseball*. Boston: Houghton Mifflin, 2000.

Sumner, William Graham. *What Social Classes Owe to Each Other*. New York: Harper and Brothers, 1883.

Synnott, Marcia Graham. *The Half-Opened Door: Discrimination in Admissions at Harvard, Yale, and Princeton, 1900–1970*. Piscataway, NJ: Transaction Publishers, 2010. Reprint.

Talbot, Allan R. *The Mayor's Game*. New York: Praeger, 1970.

Tocqueville, Alexis de. *Democracy in America*. New York: Mentor Books, 1956. Reprint.

Trumpbour, John, ed. *How Harvard Rules*. Boston: South End Press, 1989.

Urofsky, Melvin I. *Louis D. Brandeis: A Life*. New York: Pantheon Books, 2009.

Valerio, Anthony. *Bart: A Life of A. Bartlett Giamatti by Him and about Him*. New York: Harcourt, 1991.

Vena, Michael, trans. *Italian Grotesque Theatre*. Madison, NJ: Fairleigh Dickinson University Press, 2001.

Virgil, *The Aeneid*. Translated by Robert Fagles. New York: Viking, 2006.

Warren, Wendy. *New England Bound: Slavery and Colonization in Early America*. New York: Liveright, 2016.

Wells, Anna Mary. *Miss Marks and Miss Woolley*. Boston: Houghton Mifflin, 1978.

Wheeler, Sara. *Too Close to the Sun*. New York: Random House, 2007.

Whipple, Charles K. *Relation of the American Board of Commissioners for Foreign Missions to Slavery*. New York: Negro Universities Press, 1969. Reprint.

Williams, Phyllis H. *South Italian Folkways in Europe and America: A Handbook for Social Workers, Visiting Nurses, School Teachers, and Physicians*. New Haven, CT: Yale Institute of Human Relations, 1938.

Winks, Robin W. *Cloak and Gown*. 2nd ed. New Haven, CT: Yale University Press, 1996.

Zipp, Samuel, and Nathan Storring, eds. *Vital Little Plans: The Short Works of Jane Jacobs.* New York: Random House, 2016.

JOURNAL AND MAGAZINE ARTICLES

Bennett, Fay. "Farm Workers, 1955." *Crisis* 63, no. 2 (1955): 331–32, 379–80.

Bertman, Stephen. "Dante's Role in the Genesis of Dickens's A Christmas Carol." *Dickens Quarterly* 24, no. 3 (2007): 165–75.

Bethell, John T. "Frank Roosevelt at Harvard." *Harvard Magazine*, November 1, 1996.

Buendia, Jorge A. "Methods of Teaching Spanish at Yale." *Hispania* 27, no. 2 (1944): 178–208.

Chambers-Schiller, Lee. Review of *Miss Marks and Miss Woolley* by Anna Mary Wells. *Frontiers: A Journal of Women Studies* 4, no. 1 (1979): 73–75.

Cohen, Adam. "Harvard's Eugenics Era." *Harvard Magazine*, March–April 2016.

Connolly, Michael. "Show More Profile Than Courage." *Historical Journal of Massachusetts*, Winter 2002.

Diamond, Sigmund. "Archival Adventure along the Freedom of Information Trail: What Archival Records Reveal about the FBI and Universities in the McCarthy Period." *Midwestern Archivist* 12, no. 1 (1987): 29–42.

Donnelly, Richard, and William Ferber. "The Legal and Medical Aspects of Vasectomy." *Journal of Urology* 81, no. 2 (1959): 259–63.

"Eugenic Sterilization in Indiana," *Indiana Law Journal* 38, no. 2 (1963): 275–89.

Fenster, Mark. "A Remedy on Paper: The Role of Law in the Failure of City Planning in New Haven, 1907–1913." *Yale Law Journal* 107, no. 4 (1998): 1093–123.

Fernandes, Ashley K. "The Power of Dissent: Pierce Butler and *Buck v. Bell.*" *Journal for Peace and Justice Studies* 12, no. 1 (2002): 115–34.

Fotsch, Paul M. "The Building of a Superhighway Future at the New York World's Fair." *Cultural Critique* 48, no. 1 (2001): 65–97.

Giamatti, A. Bartlett. "Hyperbole's Child." *Harper's Magazine*, December 1977.

Goldstein, Brian. "Planning's End? Urban Renewal in New Haven, the Yale School of Art and Architecture, and the Fall of the New Deal Spatial Order." *Journal of Urban History* 37, no. 3 (2011): 400–22.

Goodheart, Lawrence B. "Rethinking Mental Retardation: Education and Eugenics in Connecticut, 1818–1917." *Journal of the History of Medicine and Allied Science* 59, no. 1 (2004): 90–111.

Gormley, Melinda. "Scientific Discrimination and the Activist Scientist: L. C. Dunn and the Professionalization of Genetics and Human Genetics in the United States." *Journal of the History of Biology* 42, no. 1 (2009): 33–72.

Green, James. "God and Man at Yale and Beyond: The Thoughts of William F. Buckley, Jr. on Higher Education, 1949–1955." *American Educational History Journal* 39, no. 1 (2012): 201–16.

Guinsburg, Thomas N. "The George W. Norris 'Conversion' to Internationalism, 1939–1941." *Nebraska History* 53 (1972): 477–90.

Gurwitt, Rob. "Death of a Neighborhood." *Mother Jones*, September–October 2000.

Hollander, Robert. "Charles Singleton's Hidden Debt to Thomas Okey and John Sinclair." *Electronic Bulletin of the Dante Society of America*, February 2006.

Janick, Herbert. "Yale Blue: Unionization at Yale University 1931–1985," *Labor History* 28, no. 3 (1987): 349–69.

Kalman, Laura. "Some Thoughts on Yale and Guido." *Law and Contemporary Problems* 77, no. 2 (2014): 15–43.

Krugman, Saul. "The Willowbrook Hepatitis Studies Revisited: Ethical Aspects." *Reviews of Infectious Diseases* 8, no. 1 (1986): 157–62.

Ladouceur, Ronald P. "Ella Thea Smith and the Lost History of American High School Biology Textbooks." *Journal of the History of Biology* 41, no. 3 (2008): 435–71.

Lindbergh, Charles. "Aviation, Geography, and Race." *Reader's Digest* 25, November 1939.

Marvin, Caroline. "Avery Brundage and American Participation in the 1936 Olympic Games." *Journal of American Studies* 16, no. 1 (1982): 81–105.

Naylor, Adrienne M. "Memorializing Sacco and Vanzetti in Boston." *Inquiries Journal* 2, no. 1 (2010).

Ngai, Mae M. "The Architecture of Race in American Immigration Law: A Reexamination of the Immigration Act of 1924," *Journal of American History* 86, no. 1 (1999): 67–92.

Proto, Neil Thomas. "Only Silence Is Shame: The 70th Anniversary of the Execution of Sacco and Vanzetti." *Italian America*, April 1997.

———. "Sacco and Vanzetti: An Unfinished American Injustice." *Italian America*, September 1996.

Reilly, Philip R. "Involuntary Sterilization in the United States: A Surgical Solution." *Quarterly Review of Biology* 62, no. 2 (1987): 153–70.

Roberts, Gary Boyd. "Notable Kin, Yale, Its Presidents, and Kings, Part Three." *New England Ancestors*, Winter 2001.

Sanders, Bernard, ed. "Vermont Labor Agitator." *Labor History* 15, no. 2 (261–70): 1974.

Singleton, Charles. "The Irreducible Dove." *Comparative Literature* 9, no. 2 (1957): 129–35.

Stone, Geoffrey R. "Judge Learned Hand and the Espionage Act of 1917: A Mystery Unraveled." *University of Chicago Law School Journal* 70, no. 1 (2003): 335–58.

Vellon, Peter. "Black, White, or In Between?" *Ambassador* (National Italian American Foundation), Fall 2000.

Verdi, William H. "Some Principles of Intracranial Surgery." *New England Journal of Medicine* 163 (1910).

Watson, Bruce. "To Save Sacco and Vanzetti," *Smith Alumnae Quarterly*, Spring 2008.

White, Jeffrey J. "Stamping Out the Reds: The Palmer Raids in Connecticut." *Hog River Journal*, Autumn 2005.

Witschi, Nicolas S. "Roman Holidays: American Writers and Artists in Nineteenth Century Italy." *Henry James Review* 24, no. 2 (2003): 193–95.

"The Yale Strike Dossier: A Short History of Unionization at Yale." *Social Text* 49, Winter 1996.

NEWS SOURCES

(Details about individual news articles are given in the endnotes.)

Andover Bulletin

Andover Townsman

Atlanta Constitution

The Atlantic

Boston Globe

Boston Sunday Post

Brooklyn Daily Eagle

Burlington Free Press

Chelsea (Massachusetts) *Record*

Chicago Tribune

Christian Science Monitor

Church History

Cincinnati Enquirer

Columbia Spectator

Columbia University Forum

Commentary

Il Commercio

Connecticut Explored

Il Corriere (New Haven)

Cumberland News (British Columbia)

Daily Mail (UK)

Daily Princetonian

General American Breeders Magazine

The Goodrich, A Monthly Magazine (B. F. Goodrich, Akron, Ohio)

Hartford Courant

Harvard Crimson

Holyoke Transcript-Telegram

Honolulu Star Bulletin

Independent (New Hampshire)

Italian Tribune News

Journal Register (Connecticut)

Knickerbocker News

Life

Literary Digest

Los Angeles Times

Modern Language Journal

Montpelier News

Montpelier Seminary Bulletin

The Mount Holyoke

Mount Holyoke Alumnae Quarterly

Nassau Week

New England Historical Society

New England Modern Language Association Bulletin

New Englander and Yale Review

New Haven Evening Register

New Haven Free Public Library Bulletin

New Haven Independent

New Haven Journal Courier

New Haven Register

New York Review of Books

New York Times

New York Times Magazine

New York Times Sunday Book Review

Panama Canal Review

Philadelphia Inquirer

Phillipian

Phoenix (Vermont Junior College Montpelier Seminary)

Portland Evening Express

Portland Sunday Telegram

Princeton Alumni Weekly

Princeton University Weekly Bulletin

Richmond Planet (Virginia).

Roots and Branches (Natural Sharecroppers Fund)

Saturday Review of Politics, Literature, Science, and Arts (London)

Sports Illustrated

Springfield (Massachusetts) *Daily News*

Springfield (Massachusetts) *Republican*

Springfield (Massachusetts) *Union*

Stamford Advocate

Time

Trentonian (New Jersey)

University of Connecticut Advance

Vermont Junior College Alumni Bulletin

Village Voice

Wakefield Daily
Washington Evening Star
Washington Post
Waterbury (Connecticut) *Republican*
Wisconsin Alumni Magazine
Yale Alumni Magazine
Yale Alumni Weekly
Yale Banner and Potpourri
Yale Daily News
Yankee Magazine

INTERVIEWS (FORMAL AND INFORMAL)

Andover Academy archive staff and historian
William Brainard, former Yale provost
Hon. Guido Calabresi, U.S. Court of Appeals Judge
Joseph Carbone, former Mayor DiLieto chief of staff
Cliff and Patricia Hurley Chieffo
U.S. Rep. Rosa DeLauro, D-CT
Elria (Elena Maria) Giamatti Ewing and David Ewing
Paul Fry, Yale professor
Dino Giamatti
Linda Gillison, professor emerita of classics, University of Montana
Robert Hollander, professor emeritus, Princeton University
Rosemarie Foglia Lemley
Rose Criscitiello Longo
John Manzi
William Mazeine
John Merriman
Helen ("Lennie") Moss Ogden
Sam Perry, antique clock historian
Celeste Proto
David Quint, Yale professor
Anthony Vincent Riccio
James Sansone
Roberta Maresca Sansone
Dolph Santello
Judith Schiff, Yale University archives
George Urquhart

Andrew Vitali

Frank White

John Wilkinson, former university secretary of Yale

Friends of the Giamatti family in Holyoke: Martha Johnson, George Nash, Ingrid Apgar, Norma Stiles Monat, Sally Benson, Cecile Rondeau, and Jean MacLeod Keatley

ARCHIVES

(Mayor) William Celentano papers, New Haven Colonial Historical Society

Columbia University, Oral History Archives, Rare Book & Manuscript Library, Ferdinand Pecora

Eugenics Record Office, Cold Spring Harbor, New York (1910, Bulletins 1–5; *People*, *Eugenical Panorama*, April 1931)

(Elena Maria) Elria Giamatti Ewing, personal papers

A. Bartlett Giamatti papers, National Baseball Hall of Fame

Mary Walton Giamatti papers (private collection)

Valentine Giamatti records, Harvard Graduate School Archives

Valentine Giamatti Lecture and Dante Collection, Mount Holyoke College Archives

Roswell Ham papers, Mount Holyoke Archives

Middlebury College Archives

Mount Holyoke College Archives, Italian Language and Literature Department Records, 1942–1976

New Haven Census records

New Haven Clock Company records and photographs, New Haven Museum and Historical Society, New Haven, CT

New Haven High School records, including *Hillhouse Gleam* issues and the report, "Yale and New Haven: A Study of the Benefits Derived Locally from an Endowed University," Yale University (1937), New Haven Colonial and Historical Society, New Haven, CT

New Haven Public Schools records, Heritage Ethnic Center, Southern Connecticut State University

Robert Parker's papers, Boston University, letter from A. Bartlett Giamatti

Smith College Archives

Strong School (Fair Haven), attendance records

Yale University Archives

James Angell papers

Kingman Brewster papers

Wilbur Lucius Cross papers

A. Bartlett Giamatti presidential papers (currently only speeches and public documents are available)

Valentine John Giamatti, Alumni Record, July 31, 1940

A. Whitney Griswold papers

Dick Lee papers

Philip Paolella Sr., "Conversation for Bart," Yale Manuscripts and Archives, Yale University Library

Maurice Rotival papers

Yale 1932 Statistical Questions

OTHER SCHOLARLY, LEGAL, AND HISTORICAL WORKS

"Achieving Financial Equilibrium at Yale: A Report on the Budget." Yale University, December 1977.

Angell, James. Introductory Statement (December 12, 1929) to the Third International Congress of Eugenics: New York (1932 ed.).

Annual Report of the Commission on Neurotropic Virus Diseases, 27 March 1945. Commission on Neurotropic Virus Diseases, Commission, December 1944–June 1945, Series II. Records of the Armed Forces Epidemiological Board, Gorgas Memorial Library, Walter Reed Army Institute of Research.

Annual Report of the State Board of Conciliation and Arbitration for the Commonwealth of Massachusetts, 1912, 1916, 1917.

Ashwander v. TVA, 297 U.S. 288 (1936).

Bagley, Conor. "Landlocked Blues on the Coast: How New Haven Disconnected Itself from the Sea." Senior thesis, environmental history, Yale University, 2014.

Bahr Corporation v. O'Brion, New Haven Redevelopment Agency, 146 Conn. 237 (1959).

Buck v. Bell, 274 U.S. 200, 207 (1927).

Colyer et al. v. Skeffington, 265 F.17, 15, 17–21 (D. Mass. 1920).

Crossroads, Wilbur Cross Yearbook (1958).

"DeLauro Presents Raymond Ciarlelli Overdue WW II Medals." Press release, March 21, 2009.

Documents of the Assembly of the State of New York, 1914. Albany: J.B. Lyon, 1914.

Doyle, John (Jack). "The Eugenic Origins of Yale's Institute of Psychology, 1921–1929." Senior essay, history of science, history of medicine, Yale University, 2014.

Elkin, Deborah Sue. "Labor and the Left: The Limits of Acceptable Dissent at Yale University, 1920s to 1960." PhD diss., Yale University, November 1995.

"Eugenics: Compulsory Sterilization in 50 States," under the supervision of Dr. Lutz Kaelber, associate professor of sociology, University of Vermont.

Fernald, Rebecca. "From Sea to the South." Winter study project, Williams College, 1973.

Finger, Wallis. "From the 'Bland Leading the Bland' to the Mississippi Freedom Vote: William Sloane Coffin Jr. and the Civil Rights Movement, at Yale University, 1958–1963." *MSSA Kaplan Prize for Yale History* 4 (April 5, 2004).

Fry, Paul H. "History of the English Department." Yale University, Department of English, September 2008.

Giamatti, A. Bartlett. Address at the Freshman Assembly, September 5, 1978; Freshman Address, September 1983; and Freshmen Address, September 1984. President's Speeches, Yale University Archives.

———. Address to Yale Law School Alumni, October 20, 1979.

———. Baccalaureate Address, May 23, 1981.

———. Commencement Address, Middlebury College, August 11, 1973.

———. Eulogy for Valentine John Giamatti, April 15, 1982.

———. Inaugural Address of President A. Bartlett Giamatti, October 14, 1978.

Giamatti, Valentine John. In *Directory of American Scholars*, 6th, 7th, and 8th editions. New York: R.R. Bowker, 1974, 1978, and 1982.

Gordon, David. "America First, the Anti-War Movement, Charles Lindbergh and the Second World War, 1940–1941." Paper presented at the New York Military Affairs Symposium, September 26, 2003.

Gormley, Melinda. "Geneticist L. C. Dunn: Politics, Activism, and Community." PhD diss., Oregon State University, 2006.

House Joint Resolution 175. Designating October 1993 and October 1994 as "Italian American Heritage and Culture Month." 103rd Cong., 2nd sess., August 5, 1994.

Hearing, U.S. House Subcommittee on Government Operations. 97th Cong. 2nd sess., September 9, 1982.

Housing Act of 1949, Pub. L. 81-171.

Kaelber, Lutz. "Eugenics: Compulsory Sterilization in 50 American States." Presentation at the Social Science History Association, 2012.

Kravetz, Melissa. "Giving Youth a Voice: U.S. Student Perceptions of Adolf Hitler, 1933–1939." Senior honors thesis, history department, University of California-Santa Barbara, May 2003.

Lake, Concetta. "Chelsea under Fire: Urban Industrial Life, Crisis, and the Trajectory of Jewish and Latino Chelsea." Honors thesis, Boston College, 2011.

Laughlin, Harry H. Papers, Manuscript Archives Collection L1, Truman State University, Pickler Memorial Library, Kirksville, MO. Carnegie/Laughlin Report (eugenics) and related correspondence and newspaper articles; *Survey of Human Resources in Connecticut.*

Lin, Earl Y. "Mayors, Slums, and Universities: Urban Renewal, Civic Leadership, and Community Response in Two Connecticut Cities." Thesis, history and American studies, Wesleyan University, 2015.

"Master Pieces: From the Files of T. G. B.," selected and edited by T. K. Seung and A. Bartlett Giamatti, Timothy Dwight College Press (1964). The pamphlet is contained in Thomas Goddard Bergin's Papers, Yale University Library.

Miller, Morty. "New Haven: The Italian Community." Senior thesis, Department of History, Yale University, 1969.

Morrill Act, Pub. L. 37-130, 12 Stat. 503, as amended, Pub. L. 51-841, 26 Stat. 417.

National Interstate and Defense Highways Act, Pub. L 84-627, 1956.

Neptunia ship manifest, August 28, 1957.

New York University Bulletin, 1966.

Pacific Northwest Labor and Civil Rights Projects, University of Washington. "Antiwar and Radical History Project–Pacific Northwest," World War I.

Phillips Academy Catalogue, 1956.

Pope Pius XI. *Casti Connubii*. 1931.

Pot Pourri, Phillips Academy yearbook, 1956.

"Preliminary Report of the Committee of the Eugenic Section of the American Breeder's Association to Study and to Report on the Best Practical Means for Cutting Off the Defective Germ-Plasm in the Human Population," 1911.

Report of the Board of Education of the State of Connecticut, 1914–1915

"Report on the Formation of Children's Aid Society." Maine Senate, 67th Legislature, No. 110 (1893).

Reports Made to the President of Yale University. New Haven, CT: Yale University, 1919–1920.

Rydene, Heidi M. "The Connecticut Human Resources Surveys of 1938 and 1948 Examined as Local Examples of the Eugenics Movement in the United States." Master's thesis, Southern Connecticut State University, 1988.

Salsedo v. Palmer, 278 F. 9 (2d Cir. 1921).

"A Salute to Ella B. Scantlebury." New Haven Lawn Club, April 29, 1977.

Sardella, Mark. "The Walton Family of Wakefield, Massachusetts." Blog, August 29, 2013. www.marksardella.wordpress.com.

"Selected Bibliography of Publications Relating to Mount Holyoke College."

Skinner v. Oklahoma, 316 U.S. 535 (1942).

South Hadley: A Study in Community Life. By the students in Economics and Sociology 117, 1946–1947, under the direction of Elizabeth R. Brown, Harriet D. Hudson, and John Lobb. South Hadley, MA: Mount Holyoke College, 1948.

Spenser: For Hire. "Promised Land" (Pilot, 1985). Based on book by Robert B. Parker.

Taylor, Henry. *Rural Vermont: A Program for the Future*. University of Vermont, Special Collections, 1931.

Truman, Harry S. "Rear Platform and Other Informal Remarks in Massachusetts and Connecticut." October 27, 1948. Online in Gerhard Peters and John T. Woolley, The American Presidency Project. www.presidency.ucsb.edu.

U.S. Senate Hearing, Committee on Foreign Relations. To Promote the Defense of the United States, February 7, 1941.

Vermont Eugenics: A Documentary History.

Vermont Junior College catalogues, 1937–1938, 1939–1940.

Village of Euclid, Ohio v. Ambler Realty Company, 272 U.S. 365 (1926).

Williams v. Smith, 190 Ind. 526, 131 N.E. 2 (1921).

Wilson, Woodrow. Third Annual Address to Congress, December 7, 1915.

Winn, Caroline. "Small Houses, Big Ideas." Honors thesis, art history, Wofford College, 2016, 29, 39.

Woolley, Mary Emma. "The Relation of Educated Women to the Peace Movement." Speech, Carnegie Hall, New York, April 1907.

Yale *Class Book*, 1960.

Yale Endowments: A Description of the Various Gifts and Bequests Establishing Permanent University Funds, New Haven, CT: Yale University, 1917.

Yale University Bulletin, Graduate School, 1961–1962, 1963–1964.

Yale University catalogues, 1956–1960.

Yale University v. Town of New Haven, 71 Conn. 316, Supreme Court of Errors, Third Judicial District, October Term (1898).

Yale University yearbook, 1960.

INDEX

Note: Illustrations are indicated by page numbers in *italics*. Information in notes is indicated by *n* between page number and note number.